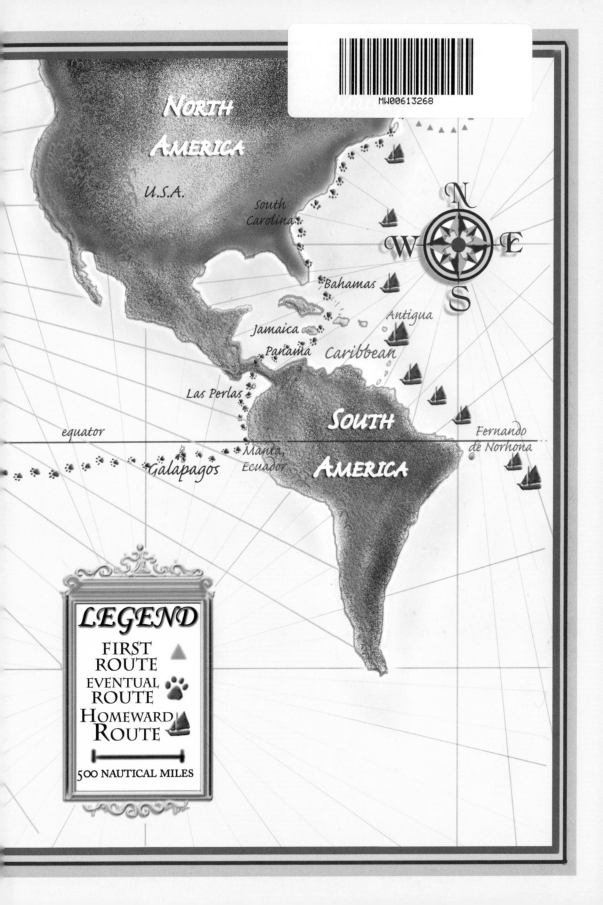

World Voyagers

Amy P. Wood, Philip J. Shelton and Stewart P. Wood

*To Ann Pater
Great fruits come from great
trees !
Sail with paws!
Amy + Phil*

This book is dedicated to all the furred, feathered and
finned creatures that nourish our souls and enrich
our lives.
To our parents, for teaching us how to appreciate all
that is good in the world, and to always look at the
dessert menu first.
And especially to Ben and Than, who suffered the
most, while gaining the least, during the three years
we sailed over the far horizon.

Book Orchard Press Inc.

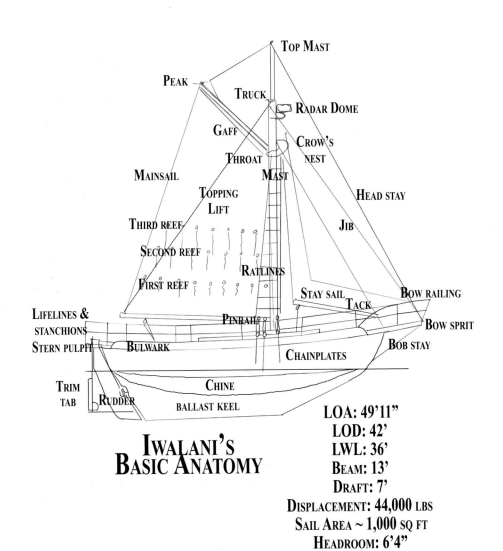

TOP MAST

PEAK

TRUCK

RADAR DOME

GAFF

CROW'S
NEST

THROAT

MAINSAIL

MAST

HEAD STAY

TOPPING
LIFT

JIB

THIRD REEF

SECOND REEF

RATLINES

FIRST REEF

STAY SAIL

TACK

BOW RAILING

LIFELINES &
STANCHIONS

PINRAIL

BOW SPRIT

STERN PULPIT

BULWARK

CHAINPLATES

BOB STAY

TRIM
TAB

RUDDER

CHINE

BALLAST KEEL

IWALANI'S
BASIC ANATOMY

LOA: 49'11"
LOD: 42'
LWL: 36'
BEAM: 13'
DRAFT: 7'
DISPLACEMENT: 44,000 LBS
SAIL AREA ~ 1,000 SQ FT
HEADROOM: 6'4"

Introduction

The Boat, the Plan, the Dream
with a Lot of Dirt in Between

We built a boat at the end of the earth and sailed it around the world. We did this because it was a desire that burned in our hearts like the glowing embers at the end of a forest fire. Smoldering and smoking, the red-hot coals of circumnavigation retained their heat long after the woods had been destroyed, the wildlife displaced and the landscape permanently altered. It was a goal we could not abandon despite divorce, death threats, scant money and extreme seasickness. While en route following our dream, we were chased by pirates and cyclones, saw huge waves that towered over our boat blocking out the moon, and buried our most valuable crewmember at sea.

Our boat was named "Iwalani", which means "Heavenly Seabird" in Hawaiian. My husband Phil's eldest son gave her a name long before she ever had a backbone. She was the realization of a lifelong dream for my husband and the end of a tempestuous nightmare for both of us. Phil used to lie on the beaches of Long Island, New York watching yachts sail by and would say "Someday that will be me out there, sailing next to a beach with some kid lying in the sand wishing he were me."

But as a wooden boat builder, he knew his trade was becoming a dying art, not a get rich quick scheme. Phil had over twenty-five years of boat building experience behind him after apprenticing with his grandfather in Long Island and teaching his skill to others. One after another, he built schooners, dinghies, duck boats, or yachts, only to see them sail off to fulfill their ambitions and specifications, sometimes making their owners very rich. But, coming from meager finances, he had not yet built a boat for himself.

Me, I wanted to sail around the world in a catamaran. Fast. Beating the records for circumnavigating held by women. My childhood best friend had already set sailing records. Why couldn't I? But, I was a veterinarian working for someone else. I barely could afford one hull, let alone two, and I didn't have the necessary racing experience.

"Why go fast, when you can go slow?" Phil asked me one time when I still knew him as Mr. Shelton. It was fate and a reality check on my part that brought us together. I owned my own boat and supported a boyfriend to maintain it. The maintenance on the boyfriend was becoming increasingly more expensive-especially after he fell off a ladder and shattered his arm, resulting in long trips to Portland for rehabilitation. I enlisted him in the boat building apprenticeship program at the Maine Maritime Museum where Phil was his instructor. At first I paid no attention to the daily stories coming from across the dinner table about the "incredible Phil," who could scarf a joint with a chainsaw, steam bend and fit a plank by eye, or drill a four-foot hole straight and true for a prop shaft, whatever that all meant.

Whoa. Stop a minute. My mother says all the rest of this is unnecessary. The Publishing Manager says to leave it in. Whom to believe? Mother? Boss? Skip ahead to Chapter 1, if you are one of those who listens to your mother.

On one of my days off I decided to bake some cookies and drop them off at the Apprenticeshop. I was curious about this "Phil" who could do all these amazing feats with wood, bake a pizza and do all the household chores, with a baby strapped to his back, while his wife was away earning her doctorate.

Phil, standing to the far right holding
Nathaniel, with his merry band of apprentices.

I will never forget the afternoon I first saw him in the fall of 1992. He was standing at the far end of the Apprenticeshop. The light from the long stretch of windows on the south side was pouring through thick and yellow, illuminating each speck of saw dust suspended in the air like tiny fireflies. Phil, alone, was illuminated by the Vermeer-like lighting.

"Oh god no!" I said to myself when I saw him. Twelve years earlier while I was still an undergraduate student I had had a dream about a man. Not just about any man, but the dream, about the man. In the dream I had been looking up a boat's companionway at a man holding onto a long tiller. The intense devotion I felt in the dream stayed with me for long after I woke up. The man was wearing a heavy wool sweater, had a beard and the most incredible blue eyes I had ever seen. As with some dreams that twist, roll and end up plunging into macabre Freudian territory, this too, ended with the man in the boat being replaced by a man in my chemistry class, the "cretin of chemistry" the others called him. If I squinted hard enough and with the right stretch of imagination, the man in my chemistry class could be converted into the man in the dream. One day when the chemistry cretin sat at my laboratory table, I asked him if he knew how to sail. "Sure" he replied. "I love it." We were married much to everyone's confusion several months later. After I discovered that he had a sixties notion of fidelity, didn't know a toe rail from a taffrail, and posessed a violent temper punctuated with punches, I cut my losses as soon as I graduated from veterinary school and moved to Maine,

I wanted a partner with the devotion of a Labrador retriever, minus the drool, and found it with my next beau. However, I soon discovered a successful relationship requires a true partnership.

In my spare time I stayed on my sailboat "Petrel" alone, trying to think up a unified field theory or an equation to test for prime numbers. I began painting landscapes and caring for orphaned baby birds and rodents. I was a practitioner of the tweezer method of global salvation, plucking one animal at a time out of the cauldron of chaos. I felt like the clock was ticking and I was racing for an unknown destination. It wasn't babies my body craved for, but some other quest for life,seeing, knowing or experiencing all there was to offer. The Labrador was content in coming home and watching TV. I thought television was a varied menu tempting the palate but offering cardboard fare. There were too many things to eat, flowers to smell, and bird calls to hear.

After the first few moments of seeing Phil at the Apprenticeshop, I knew trouble lay ahead. Falling in love with a man while caring for a boyfriend provides fodder for soap operas. Falling in love with a married man is the stuff of tragedies. Our lives became no different.

4

A few months after our meeting, the Labrador invited Phil over for dinner. Phil's wife was in Russia and their kids were staying with the grandparents. Phil arrived carrying a loaf of his own freshly baked bread in one hand and a letter in the other. Wordlessly, Phil handed the letter to the Labrador and the bread to me.

"That is the most outrageous thing I have read!" panted the Lab as he handed the letter over to me a few minutes later. "I know a really good lawyer."

The letter was addressed to Phil's wife and was a love letter from a man she had been secretly meeting for the past twenty years in New Hampshire. Phil had found it while putting his wife's laundry away.

"Do you know this Chris?" I asked Phil.

He shook his head. "I have no idea who he is."

Perhaps the most disturbing thing about the letter was the familiarity with which the paramour wrote about Phil, like he was an old sailing buddy.

"And how is Iwalani coming?" he wrote. "Has Phil been able to do much work on it? I shall miss you when you are on the high seas but will have to content myself with the many years of love we have shared together…"

"You don't need a lawyer," I said. "You need a marriage counselor. A divorce is just too drastic and doesn't solve anything."

"It is too late," Phil replied, "I always told her, I would give her three strikes and then she was out. Strike one was a long time ago, strike two was with one of my students, not too long ago. And now this. This is her third strike. I just can't trust her anymore. How can I? I should have caught on to the fact that it doesn't take most people twenty years to get their doctorate. All these years of marriage have been a complete lie. I cannot sail around the world with someone I can't trust."

For most of my life I have kept a journal, an unlined book where the confusing assortment of thoughts, paintings, poems, inventions or mathematical equations of day to day life gets sorted out from the neuronal heap in my brain and organized into black and white. For that day, I wrote one line- "I have now found out who the man in the dream is, and it is very bad." I kept the journal hidden inside the cushion of a couch rarely used by humans.

One night several months later, the Labrador appeared at my office with tears in his eyes and my journal in his paws. I felt like a person who had kicked a puppy. I tried explaining to him that nothing had changed, my feelings toward him were still the same; they would never change. The man in the dream meant nothing. It was a dream. This was reality.

He felt he could no longer live with me if I was in love with someone else. He said he needed to talk to Phil. I told him that if Phil knew of my feelings, none of our lives would ever be the same again.

Amy and Phil tie the knot.

The Labrador drove down to Phil's house, located at the end of a dirt road, at the tip of a peninsula, on the furthest island of an archipelago twenty miles south of Bath, Maine. Dripping tears onto Iwalani's keel, the Labrador changed the course of all of our lives forever, revealing to Phil what I never would have.

For the next five years Iwalani remained in suspended animation while the four of us fought over the future of Phil's children. Phil lost his sons, and gained a new wife. I kept my boat, sold my house, gave away my inheritance and gained a new husband, one with a beard and eyes bluer than the sea. Phil's ex-wife finally got her doctorate and moved their children to upstate New York, against the court order. The despair over losing his children and not being able to do a thing about it, was replaced by the belief that at least they were attending a great school system. All of us became half as rich, but twice as wise.

In the meantime, Phil built the world's largest rotating globe for Delorme mapping company in Yarmouth, Maine. I started making money selling my paintings and became a part time veterinarian. Planks began appearing on Iwalani's bottom. Lists were started for all the things we needed for a long distance cruise. Tears became nothing more than water stains on concrete.

Phil's ideal boat for a circumnavigation was a traditional Colin Archer pilot cutter. Just pouring the lead keel would have exceeded the budget for the entire project.

One day, years before I knew him, Phil happened to find his students at the Apprenticeshop furtively gathered around something. On closer inspection, he saw they were reverently fingering the pages of a paperback book. Expecting something of a lascivious nature, he, too, joined in on the page turning. That was when he saw her, Olga. In profile, she was remarkably similar to his ideal Norwegian: big up front, narrow to almost a point in the rear. She had a straight deep keel and looked rugged enough to take any punishment that Neptune and the other gods of the sea could dish out. The book was George Buehler's <u>Guide to Backyard Boat Building</u>. What was exceptional about Buehler's design was that instead of the complicated process of traditional carvel construction, George had modified the design to a simpler V-bottom plan. Instead of being round and curvy under the waterline, Olga was slab-sided. What difference would that make? The fish were the only ones who would know of her unconventional underside. The main advantage of this type of construction was that she could be made of short, thick planks of clear Southern yellow pine. The advantage for Phil was that he could build the boat on weekends and evenings after work by himself. He didn't need an assistant to help him steam bend long planks.

Iwalani's ribs taking shape

After Phil secured a copy of the book for himself, Iwalani soon began to take shape. Phil raised the middle of the boat a foot from Olga's design, erasing the banana sheer. Over and over he worked George's figures for the displacement, not coming up with the same numbers at all. George's weight seemed off by ten thousand pounds. Finally, Phil gave up and and called him in Washington State.

"Yes," George said while clearing his throat. "She was a little high on the waterline.

We just backed up a concrete truck and poured cement in the bilge until she floated like a duck." Another secret to Buehler's unconventional success is to use concrete and scrap iron for ballast. Phil had a friend, an expert in underwater concrete, who helped devise the formula. Iwalani's ballast keel has lots of large stone aggregate concrete surrounding full-length interwoven bars of heavy gauge railroad track.

*   *   *

A boat is much more than a rudder, a hull and some sails. It represents freedom and the physical manifestation of the dreams that can lie deep in a person's imagination. Iwalani grew from the ground up, frame-by-frame, bolt-by-bolt, quietly sprouting in the dark of our barn, from the deep pools of Phil's imagination. First, in 1990, he built the barn to house the dream, and then with the help of heavy machinery and curious friends, he poured the keel. In 1998, he began building again in earnest. Illuminated only by cantankerous fluorescent lights, which in winter hummed and flickered, he barely had enough light to see a plank, let alone the screw to fasten it by.

Towards the end of the twentieth century, while most people were worried about Y2 compliance, we began to worry about sail rigs. Buehler's book mentioned a marconi rig but didn't include a sail plan. Phil made another phone call to George. "What do you want to build that design for?" he asked when Phil mentioned what he was building. "That was one of my worst designs. She's too heavy…"

"Uh, George," Phil interrupted, "I'm almost done and am working on the rig."

"Where are you?"

Unsure if he meant location or stage of construction, Phil answered "In Maine."

"I used to live there. Worked at Holden's boatyard. I hate Maine. Too many bugs and the people will drive you crazy."

Phil obviously hadn't caught George on a good day.

After weeks of going over George's sail plans, days of head scratching and a constant feeling that something wasn't right, Phil took a day off and went to visit his friends at North End Shipyard in Rockland, where gaff rigs rule. His list for equipment to complete a Marconi plan was getting longer by the day and more expensive by the hour. When he returned from Rockland, he asked me, "What about a gaff rig for Iwalani?"

"Uh, well," I stammered, "it sure would be pretty."

My own boat is a thirty three-foot Rhodes Swiftsure centerboard sloop. She is Marconi rigged with roller furling and a shoal draft, a quintessential old ladies boat. "Petrel" is designed for sailing during the day, anchoring just before teatime, having a gourmet dinner and then settling back next to the woodstove against fluffy chintz pillows with a glass of sherry, a cigar and a good book. She is easy for me to handle alone. It will only be a matter of time before more women discover the joys of owning their own sailboat.

A sailboat is a moveable cottage where time can stand still and responsibility for your own destiny is held in the hand like a teacup. Despite all my precautions with navigation, anchoring, fog, engine maintenance, and a cantankerous alcohol stove, my worst experiences on Petrel always involved the roller furling. It would jam at the most inopportune moments. I decided that no matter what, Iwalani would have no roller furling, just old fashioned hanked on jibs. But a gaff rig?

"My own experience," Phil went on, "is with dead eyes and lanyards, rope stropped blocks, lace lines and pinrails, not this complicated thing," he said picking up the marconi sail plan and tossing it to the end of his drafting table. "Besides, the mast will be shorter. It will be easier to build, stronger. If, heaven forbid, we roll over in a storm, it would be less likely to snap off. We might lose the topmast, but we would still be able to sail. If something fatigues or breaks, I'd be able to repair it. This thing is just too complicated and expensive, too."

He had me there. I wasn't looking forward to buying thousands of dollars worth of stainless steel fittings that would be destined to fatigue and break after two years of hard use. But my knowledge of gaff rigs was limited to just two words- "peak" and "throat." Everything else was a mystery. I did know they sailed to windward about as well as a cardboard box.

"We aren't going to windward," Phil placated me. "And, if we do, we have an engine to assist."

With renewed vigor Phil started tackling the gaff sail plan for Iwalani. For days he punched numbers into the calculator and went through several pencil erasers. On the fourth day, I saw that he had several paper cutouts of Iwalani's underwater profile folded lengthwise and balanced on a pin.

"What the heck are you doing?" I asked.

"I am determining the center of lateral resistance."

"The what?"

"It's a single point on the hull, which, if pushed on while the boat is in the water, the boat would move evenly sideways."

"Oh." I went over to his drafting table and saw that he had made cross hairs through each sail in the sail plan.

"Is that for target practice?" I asked.

"No. I have to determine the center of effort for each sail."

"What good is that?"

"The difference between the center of lateral resistance and the center of effort is called the lead. This will determine where the mast will go."

I looked at his technical drawing. "I think it should go here," I offered, pointing to a spot a few inches ahead of where he had drawn the mast.

"Why?" he asked, showing no sign of the usual irritation he has whenever I am contrary.

"Because it looks right. And besides I don't want the mast in the middle of the salon table."

"I've been working on this for days! Right there? Hmmmm. Well, I am a boat builder. It's not like I can't move it. Besides, I've never known a boat with lee helm. OK, maybe." That was how we decided where the mast would be.

*   *   *

Iwalani is ruggedly built of two-inch southern yellow pine and Douglas fir. Her cabin top and decks are double sheets of three-quarter inch thick MDO board. Denser than plywood and used for road signs, it is more expensive than regular plywood but better adapted to handling moisture. The entire deck is covered with sheets of dynel and epoxy, ensuring no leaks below decks. Sandwiched between the MDO sheets we laid copper foil to form the mysterious ground plane, which helped to turn Iwalani into a giant antenna so we could speak by radio to virtually anywhere on the planet.

I made a list of all the electronics I wanted to bring: microwave, Cuisinart food processor, ice cream maker, blender, microscope, electric clippers (for shaving animals and Phil sometimes too,) single side band radio, vacuum cleaner, VHF radio, Inmarsat, mixer, computers, scanner, CD writer, stereo, autopilot, radar, depth sounder, navigational lights, ten interior lights, a twelve volt TV and VCR (which we used once, before it died and then we turned to the computers for watching DVD's), and countless power tools. Phil designed and installed the electrical system to handle it all. An inverter handled the 110 side of the electronics, but the main storage system were two Lifeline AGM battery banks, yielding us a total of 1200 amp hours of electricity. These could be charged from running the engine, by a 160-amp alternator on a sixty-three horsepower Westerbeke diesel, or the Wind Baron wind generator designed for land use.

Coming from a Northern climate, we opted not to include solar panels, a decision I regretted later as they would have been great for the top of the hard dodger we installed in Australia.

I told Phil I would not go without a toilet. He reluctantly acquiesced, saying a bucket would be easier. A toilet needed a holding tank, as well as a direct overboard discharge line. Phil hates having unnecessary thru-hulls. So the entire head was plumbed with two seacocks, using a complicated system of y-valves and diverters. He also hates plumbing, so I consented to having all the hoses visible instead of hidden behind some compartment. As a result Iwalani's head looks like the final fray between an octopus and a plastic pipe salesman.

For health reasons, I decided it would be safer to desalinate our own water, rather than relying on water from foreign ports or drinking water with chlorine in it. This necessitated buying an expensive watermaker system, which could work off the batteries. In hindsight, an engine drive system would have been cheaper and just as reliable, as we rarely used the watermaker when the engine wasn't running. We had not figured on the boisterous conditions preventing the seawater water pick-up tube from working while at sea. Due to the movements of a boat at sea, the seawater pick-up tube spent half of its time out of water, unable to suck water into the watermaker. When it was calm, it was usually from no wind, so the engine would be on anyways; but, it was true freedom being able to make drinking water from wind power, which we did at many unspoiled anchorages.

The watermaker gave a virtual unlimited supply of water, which meant we could have a real shower. This necessitated pressurized water with back-up hand pumps at each sink. While we were in luxury mode, we installed a hot water tank, which could run off engine heat or excess electricity from the wind generator. I never regretted hot showers on cold days.

Instead of a windvane self-steering system we opted for an electric autopilot attached to a trim tab of Phil's design. After an aborted attempt using my father's antique Tillermaster, we switched to the most robust Raytheon Autohelm. The Autohelm was attached to the railing surrounding the boomkin and the retractable arm fit on a stainless steel bolt shaped by a grinder. This "nubbin" as I called it, was threaded through a six inch bronze rudder steering which slipped over a steel pole, locked in place with a bolt for a key, and welded to the trim tab. The trim tab was bolted to the rudder above and below the waterline, using locust blocks and angle iron. The trim tab itself is a rudder of sorts, only instead of steering a boat, it steers Iwalani's main rudder. The main rudder of Iwalani is massive. Four inches thick, it weighs close to three hundred pounds. Thus it is, with each "arm" steering the rudder in front of it, that all forty four thousand pounds of Iwalani can be steered with just two fingertips, by steering with the "nubbin" (or, more conveniently, pushing the buttons on the remote control.) This is what the autopilot did, day after day, year after year, while drawing only one amp of power. This, by far, was the single most important piece of equipment on our voyage. It would have been impossible to hand steer Iwalani by the enormous tiller which dominates her cockpit.

Because of my fears of hitting a partially submerged container fallen from a ship, I had a piece of plywood, a large stone, hammer, nails and snorkeling gear ready for instant deployment, stored in the galley near the pizza pans. If we were holed, I would be overboard in less than two minutes ready to nail on a patch. I wasn't sure a hammer would work underwater, hence the stone. Phil laughed and made fun of my "holing kit," but he realized it allowed me to sleep at night, so he never disturbed it nor borrowed the orange-handled hammer.

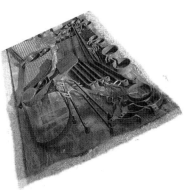

Iwalani's hardware

Together we laminated Iwalani's spars from two-inch thick fir and gallons of epoxy. The mast lay curing for days, taking up the full length of the boat shop with eight hundred and forty two clamps sandwiching it together. I could not see how this mangled block of laminated wood could ever become a highly varnished round spar, but it did so, by Phil removing the edges with an electric planer. Four sides became eight sides, which soon became sixteen sides, and so on, until finally the wooden beam became a round, tapered, smooth sided, beautifully varnished mast.

The hardware was designed by Phil and built by a local blacksmith named Jerry Galuza. We had one hundred and ten individual pieces of ironwork-goosenecks, chainplates, deadeye strops, gudgeons, pintles and crows nest hardware, all of which were totally alien to me. As I wasn't sure what their purpose in life was, until much later, nor their correct names, they became the eyeball thingies, the strap doohickey, the loopy bits, the hinges, the cage. I was responsible for getting them galvanized in Massachusetts and making sure none of the pieces were lost in the process, since we had no spares.

Every night Phil worked building Iwalani until nine p.m., then came in for supper and worked on the web page. He got the URL, worldvoyagers.com, and began in earnest writing and researching the information contained in its pages.

"What on earth are you doing that for?" I would keep asking him as he worked some nights until two a.m.

"You'll see," he'd reply.

I thought it was a huge waste of time. It wasn't until much later that I began to appreciate how writing a weekly log made us take longer glances at scenery and people; how a weekly chore kept us from becoming too bored.

I was in charge of the interior painting on Iwalani, which I did the week Phil was away in Long Island studying for his Captain's license. How it happened to coincide with the coldest time of year in Maine was anyone's guess. At six a.m. I went out to the shop and stoked the woodstove, then went inside Iwalani and turned on the two electric space heaters. By three in the afternoon I would have the inside of the boat to forty-five degrees Fahrenheit, the minimum temperature needed for the house paint we used. I painted until three in the morning when the paint fumes forced me to quit.

Rose painting on settee

I didn't want anchor decorations, illustrations of knots, sailing ships, blue cushions with white piping, or any of the other nautical motifs used on yachts. I knew we were on a boat and didn't need the décor to remind me. Instead, I wanted Iwalani to look like the interior of an English cottage. I painted the bead board walls a faint yellow and did rose flower designs on the settee backs. A few years later these were replaced with scenes of Iwalani sailing around the world. Our cushions were dark green velvet and we had twenty-four chintz flowered pillows of varying sizes to stuff into holes in the hull if the need ever arose.

The bilges and anchor locker were painted with red lead. The former was soon repainted with bottom paint when I thought about the possibility of marine worms eating a wooden boat from the inside out.

We were among the first Americans guilty of Chinese offshoring; our sails were made in China. It was too bad we couldn't have used one of the local Maine sail makers, but we were on a strict budget. The Maine quotes varied from seven thousand to fourteen thousand dollars; the Chinese sails cost us three thousand dollars and were exceptionally well made, with very fine hand stitching and needlework. I did have to swallow hard when we removed the tightly packaged sails and saw dirty bare foot prints on the mainsail, but at least they were adult sized. The mainsail lasted the entire trip with no problems. It and the Foruno radar were the only things on board that worked full time and needed virtually no maintenance for the three years we were gone.

On April 27, 2000, Iwalani was launched not far from our house. Phil's

photo courtesy of Robinhood Marina

superstitious beliefs prevent the movement of any boat on a Friday. As a result, Iwalani was moved by truck on Thursday, so she could sit at the Robinhood boat yard ready for the Saturday launch. We spent our nights and days working, feverishly painting the bottom, installing bilge pumps and through hulls, all the things we would not be able to do once she was in the water.

I had been forewarned by Phil of the bad luck that would befall us should I not shatter the bottle of champagne on the first swing. Every boat we knew whose christening had gone awry had either sunk, burned in a fire, or was lost at sea. Hours before the launch, I passed the job onto Phil's eldest son, Ben, who had been responsible for naming her Iwalani in the first place. "Sure, I'll do it," he said. "How hard can it be? Just whale on it."

At the time of the launch, I almost thought the job would come back to me. Ben looked around at the large crowd, a little nervous at first, tapping the champagne bottle in the palm of his hand. Wordlessly and with a mighty swing, he sent bits of green bottle and bubbles of champagne toward every point of the compass. Iwalani was christened on the first blow.

Slowly she was lowered by travel lift into the water. Phil said later he felt the cold April water on his back as Iwalani's keel touched the water for the first time. She floated high and proud, looking a bit strange to us. We had built her in the boat shop where we continuously knocked our heads on the overhead rafters; at fifteen feet above ground level they were still not high enough. We had always seen every part of her up close, never being able to stand back and see the whole picture.

At first she looked a little like a headless duck floating on a small pond. She seemed outrageously big for just two people to sail. Her waterline was high, she had no mast, no spars of any kind, no lifelines, a temporary bowsprit, no boomkin. We had the next two months to install all this before our departure date (as well as load and store hundreds of boxes of equipment and supplies). We lived by lists, which only seemed to get longer, while our own fuses became shorter, and shorter....

WORLD VOYAGERS

He prayeth well, who loveth well
Both man and bird and beast.
He prayeth best, who loveth best
All things both great and small ;
For the dear God who loveth us,
He made and loveth all.

-Samuel Taylor Coleridge
The Rime of the Ancient Mariner

Chapter 1

Azores Aborted

July 2000
Gulf of Maine

What on earth am I doing out here? It's three a.m., cold, foggy. I have been on my watch for three hours, one more to go. What day is it? I can't remember. We left Georgetown around eight p.m. I'm pretty sure it was Monday. What day is it now? Tuesday. We've only been gone seven hours. Already I am confused. We should be about thirty miles off midcoast Maine. We are motoring into a southeast wind, right on the nose, heading for the Azores. I am wearing a heavy sweater underneath my foul weather gear. I'm still cold. It's July but it feels like January. I check the compass. We're still heading 135°.

The radar screen casts an eerie green light around the cockpit. Un-stowed gear lies strewn about. Some of it is tied down, some not. Milk crates full of tools slide back and forth with each upward and downward pitch she makes as she pounds into the head seas. Slide, slam. Slide, slam. I look about in the dark for a piece of line to make some of this junk more secure. The only line I can find is the end of the main sheet.

Oh well, it will surely piss Phil off if I tie some of this stuff down with the main sheet line, the bitter end, as he would call it. But what the hell? Bitter, you bet. I am pissed that we are out here in the first place. We were not ready to leave for our circumnavigation and at the last minute began suffering from cold feet, wondering whether we were doing the right thing at all.

I finished the cloth dodger on Saturday. I made all of the soft stuff on board: the cushions, sheets, pillows, dodger, after I got a quote from a professional for way too much money. As a veterinarian, I was trained to sew flesh, not fabric. Overnight I became a seamstress. It didn't bother me that everything looked like it had been sutured, not stitched. The dodger looked like Frankenstein's umbrella. But at least it was doing its job now. I was relatively dry. So what, if it was puckered and threads hung down like icicles on a Christmas tree? Visible incisions and suture lines showed where I had gotten pissed off and decided to take a little tuck here and there. It was functional and very ugly. Weird. Usually, I am the one more worried about how something looks.

We had left Georgetown despite my cries to the contrary. "The boat isn't finished!" I whaled.

"Zip it" was my husband's catchy new phrase. "We need to beat the hurricanes."

My clients at work had been saying either one of two things to me- "It must be nice," or, "You must be nuts."

"I don't want to be eighty years old and sitting in a rocking chair wondering what its like off the coast of Madagascar," Phil would say when asked why on earth we were leaving our lives behind. The life we had built together on land had finally come close to being idyllic. And yet, when Iwalani was out in the barn, tied like a horse to stanchions, quietly waiting for us to climb on her back and take off, we could not ignore her, no matter what our families or friends said to us.

Over the garden and down the stream, to exotic places we go. ...

We live on a saltwater farm in Maine. Our land, bordered on three sides by fields, trees, rocks and marsh, is shared with no other humans. Our neighbors vary, depending on the season, from nesting songbirds, eagles, and osprey to moose, deer, or the occasional porcupine as the days become short and the grass long. At other times, when the land scratches lean and the light hangs low, more aggressive predators move in as they scour our barns and outbuildings looking for a quick scurrying lunch.

The nature of a saltwater farm is such that from the front door one can cross over the vegetable garden, where tomatoes and cabbages outdo each other to produce the most explosive and colorful heads, to the calm shores of any one of hundreds of small rivers and tributaries which perforate the Maine coast. From our river and front door, we can throw out a line and catch striped bass, bluefish or even sturgeon. Further downstream, mussels, clams, lobsters and cod can be found by anyone possessing the time or the boat.

And, where river meets sea, sits the lighthouse. As the last lookout, it perches high on a tawny humped up island, warning neophytes with a flash and a moan, like a tired grandmother knitting on a porch rocker, that should you pass beyond her, you will be on your own and out of the reach of her protective gaze.

Beyond the lighthouses, blue acre after blue acre of sea can be furrowed away until one day, a person wakes from a constantly moving pillow and sees that the fog shrouded granite ledges and balsam fir have been replaced with sandstone parapets and spice scented trade winds. This is the nature of a saltwater farm and from where we built Iwalani.

*   *   *

Three fifteen am. I check the radar screen. It is set to check for a radius of three nautical miles. I push the buttons for six miles. Bingo. There is a small blip five miles to the east of us. I check the engine gauges. Oil pressure, temperature all OK. I zoom the radar out to eight miles, twelve miles, twenty miles. The blip and I are the only things that seem to exist.

It is time to write down our position on the chart and in the logbook. I struggle down the companionway ladder after wrapping the now un-clipped end of my safety harness around me. It is awkward maneuvering with so many clothes and a five-foot nylon umbilical line. The chart is nowhere to be seen. Boxes of screws, cables for the computer peripherals, pens, pencils, spare batteries, sunglasses, all litter the surface of the navigation table. The chart is somewhere underneath. I scrape a small square area away. Pencils go rolling. Some tumble off to the left under the electrical panel where they will travel downward into the unreachable corners of the bilge.

Stewart jumps off a settee, comes over to my feet and meows. I pick him up and press his purring motor to my chest and rub his cheek with mine. Early on I thought I would be bringing my entire menagerie on the trip. Phil convinced me otherwise when he told me each pet would cost roughly one thousand dollars to go through Australian quarantine. Stewart would be coming no matter what; he is too much a part of my life, and neither of us can stand to be separated from one another. My sister took Sydney, my old Labrador cross, and we got housesitters to take care of my dachshund Polly, and Emily, my older three-legged cat.

Already I miss the other animals, but, Stewart has a gift for making me feel better, no matter what I am going through. I kiss him on the lips and put him down on the floor where he staggers like a drunken sailor over to his dry food dish to see if anything is left in it. It's empty. He looks over beseeching me for food.

"Breakfast, lunch and dinner, Stew. You know the rules. No snacks, even if our schedule seems screwed up to you."

He yawns and jumps back up on the settee.

We are using a GPS "road map" program to navigate. Using paper charts, which we both still insist on having, we plug in the latitude and longitudes of buoys and get a graphic picture on the computer of where we are in relation to where we are heading.

I am not completely familiar with the use of the program. On the computer screen I see a dotted line indicating the position of the course we are following and a green arrow with a green box-like tail trailing behind. The green arrow is right on the dotted line. It appears we are right on course. But the program has no navigational features; the sea, as indicated on the computer screen is just one big blue expanse.

At the bottom of the computer screen I read off the latitude and longitude and record it in the log book, along with our course, speed, wind direction and current position. I had failed to notice I was reading off the latitude and longitude of the cursor for the mouse, located somewhere off screen, not our current position. I go back up and re-check the position of the small target on the radar. It has moved one mile toward us. Hoping to see this other boat's lights, I peer futilely into the foggy mist. Nothing reveals itself through the green and red running light reflections on the damp cloud surrounding our own boat. The visibility is about ten feet. Judging from the size of the return on the radar screen, I can see that it is not a large ship, most likely a fishing vessel of some sort. I am not happy that it is coming toward us.

I watch on the radar as the larger target, now two miles off our stern, starts heading north. Instead of one target it has now split in two. A smaller weak target remains in its original position. Did they leave something behind? Another faster boat closes in on the small target. I am getting a bad feeling about what is going on out here and want to put as much distance as possible between all of us. I have heard rumors that the Gulf of Maine is the ideal spot for drug running. I feel like we may be caught in the middle of a large transaction.

The clock chimes eight bells. It's midnight, and my watch is over. I go back up to the cockpit for a look around. Drops of moisture splatter down on my head from the boom. It is wet everywhere. Reluctantly, I go back down below to wake Justin for his watch.

My husband Phil, had daydreams of his two sons sailing around the world with us. While this might have been a great experience for them, I also saw that it wasn't going to be a reality, as neither boy showed much interest in any stage of Iwalani's ten-year construction. Neither Phil nor I were in any position to say they had to go. They lived with their mother, and she, according to the courts, provided primary residency. We had always hoped they would join us for the first leg, the trip to the Azores, and maybe to other parts further along, depending on school vacations and interest. Nathaniel was the first to bail out. "Too boring," he said, when we asked him why.

Justin

We signed Justin up as Nathaniel's replacement. A friend of Phil's older son, Ben, Justin is a talkative, bright fellow anxious to travel beyond the woods of Maine. He is equipped with numerous novels, several prepackaged US army meals, and an enviable assortment of long underwear.

Ben and Justin were going to help us get the boat to the Azores and then fly home. Justin arrived two weeks before departure and helped Phil with many small details. He built our ratlines and whipped the ends of every line on the boat, earning the name "Whipping Boy," whereas Ben lay supine in his bunk down below, sometimes for hours doing nothing but staring at the ceiling. We called him "Bunk Boy."

Two days before we were due to leave, I went down below and talked to Ben. "You don't want to go, do you?"

"Not really" was the somewhat reluctant reply coming from behind the curtain that gave each pilot berth a modicum of privacy.

"Why not?"

"I don't want to leave my friends behind. I don't have my computer, and it's going to be boring."

"Maybe at times it will be boring, but think of all you will be missing if you don't go! You'll only be gone for five weeks, three of those at sea. Justin will be with you so at least you'll have one friend. It will be hard on your father if you don't come."

"I know. That's why I haven't said anything."

"Well, you can't live life just to make other people happy. I think your father will be very disappointed, but I am sure he will understand."

Phil understood but wasn't pleased about it. Rejection hurts in whatever form it takes. So neither of Phil's sons were with us–only Justin, Ben's best friend. Little did we realize then that this casting off the lines which tied Phil to his sons would weigh all three of them down every day for next three years.

I reach my hand between the curtains of Justin's bunk and gently shake him. I feel sorry he has to get out of a warm dry bunk for a dripping cold watch. But he gets up without complaint. I head forward carrying Stewart and join Phil in the fo'c'sle berth.

One watch down, two thousand, one hundred and ninety more to go.

*　　*　　*

The next day we are still punching into four-foot seas. I am beginning to feel seasick and throw up a roast beef sandwich from lunch. We have an entire icebox filled with sandwich meats and the very idea of having to eat it all, makes me feel even sicker.

At three thirty every afternoon one of us has to check in with Herb Hilgenberg on the single side band radio. Every day Herb volunteers his time from his home in Canada to give weather forecasts to yachts on passage in the Atlantic. However, if a yacht fails to check in, or can't conform to Herb's strict protocols, they must suffer the consequences of a "Herbal" lashing. I have heard erudite people become so nervous and tongue-tied that they can barely stammer which hemisphere they are in. For this reason most yachts just listen in and get entertainment from the embarrassment of others.

After talking to Herb, Phil reports to us that a cold front is due to pass at midnight just about the time I will be getting off my watch. The fog has cleared off, but it is still cold and gray. We are finally sailing with a twelve-knot breeze from the southwest. I am still not feeling great but manage to open some cans for supper, chili for Phil and myself, Spagetti—O's for Justin, as he says the chili is too spicy, and for Stewart, canned cat food. Battling the can opener is about as much effort as I want to put into dinner.

While on land daydreaming about life at sea and falling to sleep on a bed that didn't buck, I had visions of creating stir-fries, curries and sushi. But the reality of chopping and containing all those little bits when the cutting board itself was moving about hadn't been part of the fantasy.

After dinner, I sit out in the cockpit reading. I periodically scan the gray horizon for ships and errant containers, while wishing for a new stomach. Justin comes up from down below adjusting his harness.

"Hey what's up?" he says as he places a cushion behind his head on the windward cockpit settee.

"Not much" I reply. "Your watch isn't for awhile."

"Yeah well I can't sleep. Are you feeling any better?" he asks.

"A little. But I'll tell you, that's the last time I want to see a cow at sea. I don't know what I was thinking." I put the book down on my stomach.

"Yah, it's not hard to see why the old sailors ate hardtack. I have a craving for salted crackers."

"Me, too. And I don't even like them. I'm going down to see if Phil left us any," I say, putting my book onto the floor of the cockpit.

"Get me some, too," Justin adds.

"Get me some, too, what?" I ask.

"What?"

"You are supposed to finish the sentence with please and/or thank you," I say using my best voice of authority.

"I don't bother with those pleasantries. They are implied."

"Well, you still need to use them out here, unless it's a life or death situation, no need for saying, 'get the jib down quickly, please,' but other wise, please say 'please'."

"I am untrainable. My parents tried for years to get me to say those words. They don't bother anymore."

"No animal is untrainable," I respond.

I pass him the package and then pull it away– until I hear "thank you." None is forthcoming.

"I am not going to say it," he answers.

"Fine. Suit yourself," I go back down the companionway to put them back in the cupboard.

"I'd just as soon get them myself anyhow."

I resume reading my book with the remaining gray light of the day.

"What's up with Phil?" Justin asks me, his mouth full of dry crackers.

"You mean Mr. Zip-it?"

"Yes. That's all he says lately. He seems kind of quiet." Justin stuffs more crackers into his mouth.

"I guess it's because his sons aren't with him. Sailing around the world has been his life's ambition and you and I aren't supposed to be here. It was always meant to be Ben, Nathaniel and Phil's ex wife."

"I can't imagine her out here. She once drove her car over my mother's lawn because she didn't know where the driveway was."

"Oh, I don't know," I reply, "It's pretty much a straight shot from here to the Azores. Anyone can do it. And everyone is doing it. Or at least that's what the newspapers tell me. "

"That would have been cool if you could have gotten some money writing for them." Justin's teenage eyes light up with the thought of easy cash.

"Tell me about it," I reply. "Or at least reimbursement for getting the web page uploaded. I'm not sure how we are going to pay for everything. I have no idea how much everything is going to cost. I have a fully stocked small animal hospital on board. Hopefully I can make a little money doing vet work. Phil hopes to do repairs on people's boats."

"There's always Beulah, your sewing machine. I am sure people will rush right over for sewing jobs once they see your beautiful dodger," Justin says twirling a hanging thread between his fingers.

"I wonder if we can make money selling teenage boys to slave traders in the Azores?"

"No, please don't. I was only kidding," Justin feigns a high-pitched voice.

"Ha ha! You said it!" I exclaim.

"What?" he asks innocently.

"Please!"

"Darn it. It was a complete accident. I'm going down below to listen to Nick Danger."

"Please, don't wake Phil."

"Do you think he is pissed off at me?"

"No, not yet. I don't think so. You've been a big help. I just wish that Ben could have pitched in more."

"What do you supposed was bothering him. He certainly was acting peculiar." Justin's parents had recently gone through a divorce too, but with a lot less nuclear fallout than Phil's. He pulls his knees up to his chin.

"I don't know," I say scanning the horizon for ships.

"Ben didn't say much to me either. It could have been girlfriend problems too. There's plenty of her to worry about," he says snickering.

It is now too dark to read my book.

"I thought you were going down below to listen to CD's?"

"I'm having too much fun annoying you," he replies.

Clouds approach from the northwest and the wind starts to pick up. We now have a four-foot following sea. I notice that the jib sheet tied to the belaying pin is trying to pull the pinrail out of its lashed position between the stays.

"Before you go back down below- I need to get the jib down," I say to Justin. "Then maybe we can get the pinrail back in its correct position."

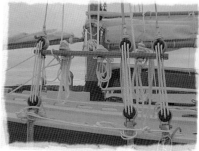

Pinrail with dead eyes (round blocks) and lanyards (rope wound through them)

We both make our way to the bow and begin unfastening and checking lines to the pinrail, with the hope that one of us will eventually find the jib downhaul. Phil had been nagging both of us to memorize the lines but neither of us had gotten around to it.

"God damn it," I scream at myself for not knowing which line is the correct one. Lines heading aloft are everywhere, some at the pinrail some tied to stanchions, as Phil had not yet put in cleats, hoping to wait a few weeks to find out where they would be needed. Finally, I find the right rope. Justin unfastens the halyard while I pull on the downhaul. We both furl the sail, then I put on the sail ties, while Justin sits astride the jib boom riding it like a bar room bull while throwing an imaginary lasso into the air.

"This is more fun than roping hogs!" he hollers as Iwalani bucks.

I start to laugh, but the new motion of the boat is uncomfortable with the reduced sail. I run over to the leeward rail just in time to throw up crackers and candy coated popcorn.

"Yahoo!" he yells while lassoing the air.

Laughter and seasickness are not great companions. I end up with candy-coated popcorn in my eyes while trying to stifle my chortling.

Phil comes on deck after hearing all the hog calling and spousal spewing. "What the hell is going on up here? Can't a guy off watch get some rest? Justin that could be dangerous- what if you fell? Jesus- what are you two doing?"

"Not much at the moment," Justin says sheepishly.

I point to the pinrail and wipe my face.

The three of us work the wooden board back between the shrouds.

"Here is a job for Whipping Boy. Both of these will have to be lashed in place better. Better yet, we both should take care of it," Phil says matter-of-factly.

I regain control of my stomach and go below to turn on our running lights and retrieve the ditty box. Phil lashes the port pinrail while Justin re-lashes the starboard side. It is completely dark when they are done.

"Tilly is trying to steal the boat!" Phil yells at us.

Justin and I turn to look at the stern. Iwalani begins riding erratically down the waves. Wind and rain splatter the decks.

"I don't know about you guys, but I'm freezing," Justin says as he disappears down below.

"Tilly has come off the trim tab and we're off course," Phil yells to me. "I'll go aft and re-attach it. You hand steer. Just keep us from jibing!"

The wind starts whistling through the rigging. My stomach is beginning to churn like the seas around us.

Phil dons his foul weather gear and harness and heads aft while I use all the strength in my arms and brace both legs to steer the boat. I feel like I am in a washing machine. The darkness of the night and the movement of Iwalani over the waves makes me feel like I am weightless and don't know which way is up.

'Just focus on the compass heading and steer the boat,' I tell myself. I don't notice that the wind has clocked and is now more northerly. I realize it too late.

There is a simultaneous "THWACK" and stream of blue language coming from the stern of the boat.

"Jesus Christ! I told you not to jibe the boat!" Phil yells at me.

The boom and mainsail are now pinned against the running back stay. Iwalani heels deeply trying to spill the wind. Miraculously nothing breaks. The rain stops, but my heart is pounding and the wind is still whistling.

"What do I do?" I scream to Phil.

"Get us on course!" he yells back.

"We are on course!"

"Didn't you notice the wind has changed direction?"

"Not until now!" I swing the tiller in the opposite direction so the boom can get back on its correct side.

"Hey, do we still have three humans on board?" Justin yells out to us while standing on the ladder in the companionway. "What was that ungodly sound?"

"You mean Phil and me yelling at each other or the sound of the boom almost snapping in half from the back stay?"

"Um, well, the yelling I'm used to..."

The three of us work together to get the rest of the sails down, and then Justin retreats to his bunk.

We lie a hull-no sails up, no motor, just rolling and drifting with the push of the following sea. Phil quietly lies on the port side of the cockpit staring up at the sky, while I try to get comfortable opposite him.

"I am really sorry," he speaks softly to me. "I have been a complete ass for the last few weeks. I don't like being this way."

The moon comes out from behind black clouds. How symbolic I think to myself. The storms clouds are disappearing.

"I think we need to turn back," I say as I watch the clouds scud past. "We just aren't ready. I had to sheet in the jib today, and, since there are no cleats, I had a hard time re-tying it to the stanchion. Boxes are crashing around on the deck; gear on the nav station is falling in the bilge. This is no way to sail across the Atlantic. Besides I didn't bring enough crackers and we are almost out of juice."

"Who'd have thought crackers would be high on my list of food at sea?"

"And grapefruit juice," I add.

"I thought I'd be able to finish the boat while we were underway," Phil says.

"And I thought I'd be able to learn the ropes while we were underway."

He reaches over and holds my hand while Iwalani drifts with the seas. When it starts to get light, we raise sail and head for Swans Island, one day away. I am so exhausted I fall into the cockpit well and use a piece of plywood for a blanket, various tools for a pillow. We arrive at four in the morning and cook up a huge breakfast of scrambled eggs and bacon, which in short order becomes our traditional meal each time we arrive in port.

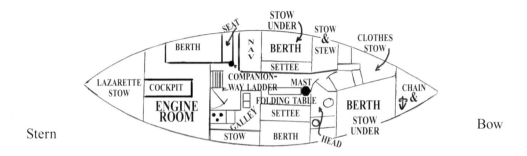

Iwalani's Layout

Chapter 2

Full Circle

August 2000
Gulf of Maine

Our second attempt for the Azores is much less hurried. I get Scopolamine patches for my seasickness and start off wearing a whole patch behind my ear. Phil and Justin decide to use the drug too. We work for a week finishing the most important things in the boat and buying a more reliable autopilot. "Tilly" moves into the closet as a back up. She is just too slow and unreliable for intense downwind conditions. Our new autopilot is controlled from the cockpit, so we don't have to dance around the swinging tiller to change course.

I feel better about the condition of the boat, but Phil is even more grumbly, complaining that we have wasted a valuable week. The weather forecasts now issue warnings of a hurricane bouncing around to our south. Phil is right, we are leaving too late; Hurricane Alberto sits and spins, waiting for our arrival in the Atlantic.

Our third night out dark clouds cloak Iwalani like a hood on a falcon. We are sailing over the submerged landmass that connects Cape Cod to Nova Scotia, the rich fishing grounds of the Georges Banks, leaving the relatively protected waters of the Gulf of Maine in our wake. During Justin's watch he nervously calls down to us through the companionway, "Hey guys, there's lightening out here!"

We quickly unplug all the electronics and watch as angry bolts flash overhead like an electronic sword fight. It isn't a comforting feeling knowing that our mast is the tallest thing around for hundreds of miles.

I leave the boys to fend off the electrical storm and try to get some sleep in the forward berth with Stewart. Each time I doze off I awake to the sound of a woman screaming or a child crying. The voices sound like they are outside the hull, not actually in the boat. Stewart hears them, too, as he sits upright without purring, staring at the floorboards. I finally give up on sleep and go up to see how Justin is doing on his watch.

"Boy, am I glad to see you," Justin says, wiping his hands through his damp hair. "Can you do something about the old woman in the rocking chair?"

"Uh, Justin, what woman exactly are you referring to?"

"That old hag there," he says pointing to the stern of the boat, "She's knitting in the rocking chair, on the wave just following the boat."

With my own experience of hearing voices in the bow, I actually get up and peer off in the darkness to take a look for myself.

"I think it's time we remove the Scopolamine," I tell him. "One of the side effects are hallucinations. Hopefully the screaming women and the old bag in the rocking chair are just products of a wild imagination pumped up by drugs."

24

For the last four days I have been seasick, despite the Scopolamine, but I haven't told anyone. I keep a small plastic sandwich bag in my pocket, and when I have to throw up, I do it in the bag. Then, when no one is watching, I throw the baggie overboard.

I peel off our Scopolamine patches. Justin goes to bed early complaining that he doesn't feel well. He is unusually quiet. Other than the nuisance of vomiting, I haven't felt sick up to this point. I'm not hungry either but am thirsty beyond compare.

I sit out in the cockpit wishing I had brought warmer clothes. I have sweaters, socks and wool hats, but wish for mittens, long underwear and a parka. It is freezing. We still have periodic bursts of lightening far off in the distance and some annoying downpours.

Phil had installed a lightning rod at the top of the mast before we left. A three foot bronze spike that he sharpened to a weapon like point, it is attached at its base to a metal plate and wire that go all the way down the starboard shroud and into the water. During some of the lightning flashes, I swear that it looks like it is coming loose. I start to feel sick.

I get the spotlight and shine it at the top of the mast. There is no doubt about it, the three foot long, stiletto sharp, human shish kebab spike, is swinging in wide circular arcs with each roll Iwalani makes.

I watch it swing round and round, imagining all the different ways it could come and skewer one of us. I figure no place is safe on the boat. With sixty feet of height the bronze spear would have time to gather enough speed and momentum to pierce the two-inch cabin top like a sewing needle through a negligee. I throw up into a baggie and toss it off into the darkness.

The next morning Justin is still in his bunk. I hate to wake him, but I am getting very tired.

"I don't feel very good," he moans to me when I try to rouse him.

"Better stay right in your bunk," I reply. For the next four hours I cover his watch, trying not to fall asleep myself.

Hurricane Alberto is still to our south, but the swell is making it particularly uncomfortable. Phil has all he can do to monitor the radio schedule with Herb. Justin starts to feel better and practices his knots with small pieces of string.

"I just can't do it," Phil screams. He quickly comes out on deck and vomits over the leeward rail.

"Cool!" Justin says holding up his string, "He's like a salad shooter- only he's ejecting perfectly sliced pieces of banana!"

"See if I ever eat a banana again," Phil groans.

That night, Justin is 100% back to normal, but I can't get Phil out of his bunk.

"I don't feel very good." Phil whispers. It's rare that Phil gets sick. Seasickness is not in his vocabulary. I take his temperature. It is 103° F.

"Do you have any stomach pains?" I ask him.

"Humph," he says pointing to his lower right abdominal quadrant. I palpate his belly and find a hard mass that feels like a frozen bratwurst sausage—right where his appendix would be. Phil hits my arm when I palpate it.

My mind starts spinning. He's got appendicitis. I go into the medicine cabinet and search for my two favorite antibiotics. I can't remember if you can use them together in humans, but at this point I don't care. Along with some ibuprofen, I make Phil swallow a handful of pills.

"You've got to go to the bathroom and get your bowels moving," I tell him.

"Yah, whatever. Just leave me alone."

I go up to the cockpit and watch the lightning rod spin round and round. By now it is making forty-five degree arcs. It is definitely getting worse. My thoughts drift back to Phil. Here we are four days from anywhere. Do I call on the radio and get him airlifted off? Is he seasick? Or does he have a virus. Is he just constipated? Maybe we all have a virus. Do I call a ship and risk all of our lives, as we try to come near a two hundred foot steel tanker with less than ideal conditions?

I run through the scenario of having to remove Phil's appendix at sea. I have everything on board to do it. The anesthesia will be a little tricky, but as long as I think of Phil as nothing more than a big ape, we'd be OK. I can duct tape him to the table so he won't roll around.

While contemplating how best to handle an appendectomy at sea, I run through the full gamut of medical emergencies. Electrocution. Jesus. What if one of us was struck by lightning? Or we were electrocuted doing some electronic repair? I had no diuretic on board to handle pulmonary edema. What else am I missing? Are we really prepared? I thought I was, but now I am not so sure. I work myself into a nauseous froth and fill up a sandwich bag. Over it sails, its bright yellow contents looking black in the darkness.

What if Phil got obstructed like a male cat? I have urinary catheters for both humans and animals. But can I put an IV catheter in myself? Phil has needle paranoia. I can not count on him for my medical needs. I know I am getting dehydrated from all my vomiting. The skin turgor on my forearm is looking like a Chinese Sharpei. I pinch my wrist skin and the pleats stay folded like stacks of miniature towels. It is mildly entertaining.

The only thing I can keep down is cranberry or grapefruit juice. Water comes right back up. We don't have enough juice to get to the Azores, despite my recalculating our juice needs after the first attempt at a crossing. The three of us are drinking four liters of juice a day, even without the Scopolamine patches. We have three days supply at our present intake level, then we have powdered juice crystals and after that, plain water. Is it the water that is making us sick? Larry the canary isn't singing anymore. We brought him a long as a backup for the carbon monoxide detector. Something isn't right.

Yet Stewart is fine. He is eating, has no vomiting and is drinking the same water with no ill effects. I lean down the companionway to check on him just to be sure. He is stretched out sleeping in Justin's bunk.

The only good thing about being dehydrated is that it means I don't have to pee. What a nightmare that is at sea! I have to go into a stinky confined space of the head, remove layer upon layer of heavy clothes, pee without having the contents of the bowl slosh over the side and spritz my all ready foul smelling pants, then reach down under the sink cabinet to open the intake and outflow seacocks, without getting sprayed by the still sloshing contents of the toilet bowl. Then I have to stand up, pump out the bowl, and reach down to close the seacocks.

It is a workout and invariable leads to me filling the toilet with vomit, which necessitates reaching down opening the seacocks, and repeating the whole process. It is a never-ending cycle.

I haven't peed in over forty-eight hours, but now I have to go. I am half way through Phil's watch and still have my four-hour watch after that. I go down below and check on Phil, who is still sleeping, and then stumble into the head.

While in the process of opening the seacock I get an up close and personal look at my urine. Is it brown? I turn the light on. Not only is it brown, but it has a tinge of mahogany red to it. Jesus, that's not good. The thought that maybe I am sicker than I feel, and will have to do an appendectomy on my husband make me nauseous. Out comes the baggie.

Jesus! I hold the baggie up to the light and look closely at the contents. I am now throwing up coffee grounds, which can only mean one thing; I am bleeding into my stomach. I am so stressed I am giving myself an ulcer.

Things are going from bad to worse. I am so tired the thought of climbing up the companionway stairs seems like launching an expedition to the moon. I turn the radar on, set the watchman and guard zone for fifteen miles and sit down onto the folding galley seat. Before too long I fall off that and onto the floor of the galley, partially covered with a raincoat.

"Well that's some way to spend a watch." Phil nudges me with his foot. "Are you alive? Would you like some French toast if I made it?"

I am happy to see he is feeling better. It is now daylight and from the looks of the sky through the hatches, it is another gray and rainy day. I don't know how long I have been asleep, and I don't care. I drag myself over to the settee. I am not hungry. After they have a big breakfast, Phil comes over and sits by me.

"I guess it's your turn for this bug," he says while rubbing my back.

"I'm not so sure it's a bug. I've been throwing up since the second day out."

"What? How can you hide that from me?"

I produce my latest baggie from my pants pocket. "Easy."

"Jesus! Honey, that doesn't look good at all. What have you been doing with the baggies?"

"I chuck them overboard."

"This won't do. Think of the turtles, they'll mistake those for jelly fish," he says while walking over to the nav station. He pulls out the small-scale chart that shows our progress inch-by-inch, day-by-day. "This is where we are now," he points to a small x just six inches away from the Maine Coast. "This is where we are going." He unfolds the chart the rest of the way and points to a spot almost two feet away from our present position. "You will be dead by then."

"Not to mention causing the extinction of the entire population of North

Atlantic sea turtles," I add. "I didn't want you to know I was sick. I don't really feel seasick, just incredibly tired. I don't want to be the reason we have to turn back. Again."

"Hurricane Alberto is getting closer to us. That's why there is this swell from the South. Halifax is just three days away, I think we need to turn north," Phil says.

Stewart looks up at me almost nodding his head in agreement. No matter how tired or sick I feel, I still manage the daily ritual of cleaning his litter box, feeding him breakfast and dinner, cleaning Larry's cage and putting food and fresh water into his cage, which sometimes is no easy feat in pitching seas. This is the first morning everyone is going without attention.

"I am sorry, guys. I guess you are right."

"It should be you that turns the boat," Phil says.

I reluctantly stagger up the companionway, using what is left of my strength to hang on to the ladder. The seas seem steeper than last night and just standing requires effort. I sit in the cockpit for a second looking around at the dismal gray sea and sky, and then push the button for the autopilot onto "standby." I take one look at Phil, check the running back stays to make sure we would still be on the correct tack, then push the tiller to starboard. Eagerly Iwalani swings off the wind and faces north.

"What's our course going to be?" I ask Phil.

"Stand by one, I'll plot it out. We may need to jibe. You go down below and get some sleep, Justin and I can handle it."

I feed Stewart then take a nap. I wake up later feeling confused. Stewart is trying to suck on my earlobe. I realize we are hearing birds singing outside the boat. How long have I been asleep?

"Oh good you're awake," Phil greets me. "I sent Stewart up to wake you. Come on out on deck."

I start to grab my raincoat. "You won't need that." Phil yells down to me.

I come out on deck. Turning the boat around has produced a dramatic change. The sun is shining. The air is warm. The seas are calm. Birds are singing. Only it isn't birds.

"Are we near the Gulf Stream?" I ask.

"Maybe an eddy, but not the main stream. Look at the dolphins."

I go up to the bow. The "birdsong" I have been hearing is dolphins. There is a whole family of them riding in our bow wave. Two babies only a few feet long are staying very close to their mothers. Off on the horizon we see spouts from much larger whales.

The seas are now behind us, and Iwalani is moving along at a much quicker pace.

"This is a vast improvement!" I cry. "I'm starving."

"Nothing like blue skies to improve one's appetite," Justin mutters.

"I am sure the vast majority of my seasickness is psychological. I was scared to death of Hurricane Alberto, not to mention one of us getting impaled by the lightning rod, " I point to the still swinging bronze spear high on top of the mast.

"There's no way it would come down," Phil assures me.

"But it's loose, though. Surely with that much movement up there the bolt or whatever is holding it in place will fatigue and break."

"It's impossible. But, if it will make you feel better I can climb up and saw it off."

"Not out here. It was bad enough I was worrying about operating on you for appendicitis. I don't need to worry about you falling from the mast."

"I won't fall. Why would I want to let go? The halyard would be completely in your hands."

"Exactly my point. I don't trust myself hauling you up and down."

"You could use the windlass…"

"You know me and mechanical things; I could get a rope override. Then what would I do?"

"OK, fine, I'll wait until we're in Halifax," Phil says.

*　　*　　*

We arrive in Canada two days later. After a quick phone call to Canadian customs announcing our arrival we take down our "Q" flag and head off to "The Pressgang Restaurant" where we have the most spectacular meal imaginable.

The following day I haul Phil up the mast so he can saw off the bronze lightning rod. Justin is anxious to have some time on his own, so he takes our fiberglass dinghy, the Grape, out for a sail.

"See you can do it. That wasn't so bad," Phil says as I lower him to the deck and he hands me the lightning rod. "It really wouldn't have come down."

"Thank you for taking it down. It wasn't helping me at all."

"Yes, but now we have no protection from a lightning strike."

"We'll just have to unplug all the electronics anytime there is an electrical storm."

We stand and watch Justin maneuvering the Grape around a fleet of small racing dinghies.

"What do we do now?" I ask Phil.

"Well, I can think of a few things," Phil says to me while grabbing my waist.

"No, I mean, in the long term. We told our housesitters we'd be gone for three years. My replacement at work has already started. I don't have the courage to admit failure."

"We'll just have to play it by ear and head south for the winter, through the inland waterway, bucking into head winds, just what I didn't want to do."

"What do we do with Justin?" I ask.

"Well, he really has been a big help for me."

"Yes, I know, but sometimes too much of a help. I try to do something, and he is right next to me, nudging me out of the way, doing it for me. I will never learn how to sail this boat. I enjoy his company, but sometimes I wish he had an on/off switch."

"Or was prepackaged as a dehydrated mix, just add water when needed! I can sail Iwalani without your help, but I can't let you get that sick again. It's spousal abuse."

"I don't want to abandon the circumnavigation," I say picking the dead leaves off my potted rosemary plant. "We have worked so hard to get to this point in our lives. I know I can do it. Just us, with Stewart and Larry the canary. It will be easier, I am sure. It is more stressful for me to have an extra person along. I have to cook for Justin as well as us. I have become a galley slave; he has no desire to help with dishes, or cooking."

"You know that plant has to go."

"What?" I ask.

"That rosemary. The smell of it at sea is enough to make anyone sick," Phil says.

"It is pretty bad. Who'd have guessed?"

"Justin came close to throwing it overboard while you were sleeping, but I stopped him."

I throw the dead leaves overboard. "Thanks for saving it's life." I pause for a moment and pick up the lightning rod lying on the cabin top. "Last night, Justin and I were talking about what would happen in a really bad storm and Iwalani was sinking. He said he'd radio the coast guard and ask to be picked up. I asked him, 'You mean you would risk someone else's life to save your own?' 'Sure,' he said, that's what they get paid for.' Well, I don't share that philosophy. We chose to do this. We must be responsible for ourselves every step of the way. He sounded surprised when I told him how I feel." I play with the sharp point, glad it is no longer on top of the mast.

"Tell you what, if you can make it around the Jersey coast without getting seasick, I will reconsider a circumnavigation."

"And Justin?" I ask.

"Well, he said to me the other night he wanted to go back to Maine and find a job. I think he's sick of us old farts anyway."

"Somehow, I need to get self confidence. I need to know all that you know, or at least a small fraction of what you know. I am sure I won't get sick if I know I can sail Iwalani by myself."

"Excuses, excuses," Phil mutters.

"No, I mean it. Fear is a powerful GI stimulant. I have to learn not to be afraid."

"OK, we'll go back to Maine. Then for a month, I'll do all the cooking and shopping and you do everything else, " Phil says while unhooking the bosun's chair from the peak halyard.

"It's a deal. And the world? Are we still going to sail around the world?"

"That depends on you and the New Jersey coast– and there will be no sandwich bags allowed."

Chapter 3

Too Much Land Under Our Keel

August-December 2000
Georgetown, Maine to Florida and beyond.

We are in the heart of hurricane season and decide to wait until the last possible moment before making our way south through America's big ditch, the Intracoastal Waterway. Our plans of following the trade winds around to the Azores and Canary Islands, and then across the Atlantic to the Caribbean, have to be forgotten. After dropping Justin off with his mother in Bar Harbor, Phil and I take a leisurely month sailing back to Georgetown.

Justin had been good about going on "clunk patrol," ferreting out almost every squeak and pacifying it with line, padding or one of Stewart's beds. But with Justin gone and even more gear on board, Iwalani starts to sound like a gypsy caravan rolling down a rutted road. She is a cacophony of plates jarring, pans crashing, glasses swinging, bottles banging, anchors clanging, sheet blocks clacking and doors jiggling. Rattles and squeaks are not only annoying at sea, but signify movement of some sort, which can eventually lead to chafe or metal fatigue. It is important to cease the din in order to avoid wearing something out to the point of its breaking.

Despite having owned my own boat for years and spending all of my childhood messing about in boats, I still have no blue water experience. I mistakenly thought that an offshore passage I made a few years earlier on my boat Petrel, with my father and nephew to Canada, counted as blue water sailing. Phil scoffed and said I have no idea what the ocean is really like. I soon found out the truth of his apprehensions, as well as the fact I also have never learned the finer aspects of sailing. Up until this point I always thought that the sails on a boat were for propulsion. After beginning Phil's Deck Ape Training 101, I learn that the sails are also important for steering. Tight spots, especially, need careful sail trim. Backing the jib becomes just as important for steering, as using the tiller.

Phil will stand in front of the mast so he can observe everything, yet not get in the way. He will not say a word unless I am in danger of doing something really stupid. Then he goes through a short throat clearing routine. If I still fail to catch on, he politely says, "Ahem, aren't you forgetting something?"

He has me do everything by myself, raise all the sails, navigate, check, repair, and run the engine, anchor under sail, leave anchor under sail. The final lesson comes in Southwest Harbor maneuvering Iwalani amongst the entire fleet of brand new glistening Hinckley yachts. These sleek cruising debutantes bob and twinkle their shiny black hulls like heavily mascara'ed teenagers at a dance, waiting for some clumsy oaf to hit on them or, in my case, *hit* them. Raising the main and backing the staysail at just the right moment, then bringing up most, but not all, of the anchor, I manage to sail all forty-four thousand pounds of Iwalani around the potential lawsuits. The maneuver is made all the more exciting because we don't carry insurance, as no insurance company would come near us when they discovered we are sailing around the world in a boat we built ourselves.

"You see, you can do it!" Phil exclaims. "You only forgot one thing."

I look around trying to see what I have forgotten, simultaneously going through the mental checklist: I checked the oil and antifreeze level in the engine, (in case we needed to turn the engine on at the last minute if a collision with a Hinkley was imminent–we were bold, but not stupid) autopilot on, mainsail sheet free of the tiller, jib ready to haul, computer on, GPS on, depth sounder on, chart ready, windlass on, the mainsail up–agh, there it is–the running back stays. I freed both of them earlier for ease of maneuvering the boom, but I forgot to tighten the windward one now that the mainsail is filled.

"I'll get it this time," Phil says. "It's probably not essential with this small amount of wind, but someday these are going to save the mast."

With all my worry over hitting obstacles in our direct path, I am not paying attention to what is going on in the periphery. Suddenly I see movement out of the corner of my eye.

"Look at this crazy lobsterman!" I yell to Phil. Just aft of the beam, a lobster boat is heading right for us, going about thirty knots.

"Do you think he sees us? Who has the right of way?" I ask anxiously.

"Technically a fishing boat has the right of way when they are fishing, but he's not fishing. We're under sail, so we do, but all this doesn't matter. He's trying to ruin our paint job! Get her headed up."

I grab the tiller and simultaneously push the standby button to the autopilot. Iwalani swings up into the wind while the lobster boat passes ten feet under our leeward rail.

"The world is seven eighths covered in water, and you've got to be in my teaspoon!" the stern man barks at us.

"I don't think he's exactly right about that," I quaver, getting us back on course despite my arms shaking like a leaf. "I don't think there's that much water on the planet."

"Well, maybe if you add in all the fresh water, too," Phil says.

"Then you'd have to add all the animals and people that are sixty-four percent water. Maybe then you could get it up to seven-eighths water. Damn lobsterman, they're always right. "

"It will be nice when we are out on the ocean and don't have to worry so much about getting run over."

"What do you mean? I think it will be way worse out there." Little do I know how prophetic my words would become.

*   *   *

We had been waiting for a cold front to pass through, so we could follow the associated Northerly winds south. Our route was a straight line from the tip of Georgetown across the Gulf of Maine, through the Cape Cod Canal, to Marion, Massachusetts. We were becoming overwhelmed by our goal of a circumnavigation and needed encouragement from people more experienced than us. We visited Herb and Doris Smith, a couple from Boothbay Harbor who had built several boats on their own and had completed three circumnavigations. Their words of advice were to stop focusing on the big picture, and just concentrate on getting from one port to the next.

The winds are light and out of the southwest when we finally leave but are expected to veer to the northwest overnight. I am reluctant to depart because the weathermen are predicting showers when the cold front passes through. By my figuring, the showers will arrive as we are crossing the Boston shipping lanes at three a.m. Showers show up on radar as big ugly blotches and can sometimes obscure any signs of boats or other shipping traffic. There are settings that can be adjusted to filter out rain, but in doing so we could miss small, important things like buoys or boats.

"You worry too much," Phil says shaking his head. "We are as ready as we are ever going to be. There's not enough room on board for another bag of groceries. It's time to head south."

We decide on a system where I will be captain on the odd days and he will be captain on the even days. Our watches are divided up according to the ship's clock–four hours on and four hours off, starting at 8 a.m., with Phil getting the first watch. (We tried dogwatches, but they did not work for us; our schedules remain fixed and easy to adjust to. It always means, though, that Phil gets the graveyard shift from midnight to four a.m., but he says he doesn't mind.)

Around 4:30 in the afternoon, just as Phil comes on watch, I go below to make some tea. Phil yells down that we have our first visitors, three song sparrows and a myrtle warbler. They look exhausted as they circle the boat, eventually landing on the lifelines.

As soon as I am back down below, I hear Phil cursing. "Oh no! You stupid B*#&!#Fng* bird!" When I come back up the companionway, Phil is in the process of turning Iwalani around.

"What's the matter?" I cry.

"One of the sparrows fell in the water."

Sure enough, a brown blob, looking like an old glove, floats on the surface, about fifteen yards upwind of us. Phil is doing his best to maneuver Iwalani around in a tight circle, to a point where I can rescue the spread-eagled sparrow. We have no scoop net on board, (hopefully, the only piece of equipment we have forgotten). I try to scoop the sparrow up with a bucket, without drowning him in the process. When we are about ten feet from him, he raises his head up, looks directly at me and then plunges his face deliberately into the water. Phil becomes frantic trying to get Iwalani close enough for me to reach him. The wind and the waves are working against a successful rescue.

"Forget it!" I whimper. "He's committed sparrow suicide."

"I hope you can do CPR on him because I'm not giving up." The sparrow is quite dead when we finally got him on board. I try breathing into his tiny beak coupled with some chest compressions, but I know this case is hopeless; he is already quite stiff. Our first man overboard drill is a failure.

A few minutes later we get a chance to practice a new method that works only when motoring, backing up to the victim. Within thirty seconds we back Iwalani up to the second sparrow. I lower the bucket, but this time the sparrow rises up off the waves, like the phoenix out of the ashes and lands on the bow railing, looking tired and hungry.

I provide our guests with a fresh water bird bath and some of Larry's canary seed. The meat eaters in the crowd clean the decks of the Georgetown mosquito carcasses. Phil had come very close to scrubbing the decks before we left; all on board are grateful he hadn't. By dusk, we have close to thirty different songbirds eating, drinking and pooping on Iwalani: song sparrows, white-throated sparrows, warblers and juncos. They are all older birds, quite tame, very exhausted, and some even land on my hand.

"He's dead," Phil gulps as he comes up the companionway for his watch.

"Who?" I choke, fear closing my airways.

"Larry."

Relieved it is not Stewart, I go down below and take the lifeless little canary out of the cage. He was not a young bird and had not been singing for some time. He had a preen gland abscess while we were near Halifax and went downhill when Justin left the boat.

One of Iwalani's guests

I perform an autopsy on the kitchen cutting board and am shocked to see a large ulcer in his gizzard.

"What did he die from Doc?" Phil asks while looking over my shoulder.

"Me."

"How so?"

"Stress killed him. I should never have brought him with us. I suppose this could also be some sort of cancer, too." I wrap Larry's remains in a tidy paper towel package, and then throw him overboard. I say no prayer, or parting words. I am mad at myself for being so selfish.

At dusk the sky turns gray and cold. The wind starts to blow from the northwest. We work around the other resting feathered passengers and raise the sails, then shut off the engine. A calm settles over the boat as Iwalani is caught up in the forward wave of her own propulsion, no longer relying on the noisy clatter of the diesel engine.

Off in the distance Phil and I are aware of a flock of sea birds swarming around something in the gray colored water. We think it is a whale. Then the water under the birds becomes awash with white caps, and these white caps come toward us. It is a huge pod of white-sided dolphins.

A strange thing happens to me. I don't know if it is the Scopolamine patch, the death of Larry, or the Japanese book I am reading, which is a story about a maiden who falls in love with a male dolphin, but a melancholy fills my heart like the notes from a sad violin. I feel like human life, and mine in particular, is completely insignificant in the grand scheme of things.

One big male dolphin swims right under Iwalani's railing. Alone, he glides on his side, looking up at me; I kneel down and lean over the bulwark, my fingers outstretched towards him. He raises his flipper up to reach my hand. Rhythmically, he swims alongside, barely undulating, yet effortlessly keeping pace with Iwalani. We spend a minute staring at one another, neither of us blinking. I have the weirdest desire to jump in and swim off with him. Our reverie is interrupted when a small female swims angrily over to him clicking and bobbing her head; Phil, too, comes up to the bow to see why I have become so quiet.

It is at this point I decide to cut my Scopolamine anti-seasickness patch from halves into quarters. Hallucinations or not, I don't need Phil having to explain to people that his wife didn't run off with another man but swam off with a handsome dolphin!

That night we have supper down below at the table, eating stir-fry that has been chopped, sliced and cooked without a single carrot rolling off the former canary autopsy cutting board. It is completely civilized: placemats, silverware and pieces of paper towel for napkins. No rocking, no rolling. No trying to hold a bowl near your mouth and shovel food in with a spoon without spilling it all over one's self. This is cruising in the Gulf of Maine!

At the end of my 8-12 p.m. watch, the sky starts to get light in the north. It looks like the pastel colors that appear before sunrise. Northern Lights! Phil gets up and has a spectacular show during his watch from midnight to four. I actually miss most of it as I sleep from midnight to the eight bells that signal the start of my next watch.

At four a.m., I come on deck after putting on long underwear, two sweaters and foul weather gear. We have crossed over both sets of shipping lanes off Portland, the northern and southern in-bound and outbound approaches, but we are still north of the Boston shipping lanes. Phil says there are a couple of fishing boats on the radar to the west of us but nothing to worry about. I settle in the cockpit for my watch while Phil goes below to mark our current position and crawl into his bunk. I look at the radar and then check the lights on the horizon trying to account for all the blips on the radar screen. I make the mistake of not using the binoculars, an error I never again repeat. At night, an ordinary pair of binoculars not only make little things bigger but can also accentuate the available light of darkness. A black horizon becomes two bands of purple their lenses.

Shore lights, ship lights, jets going into Logan Airport, it all seems a bit confusing. There are some scattered showers to the south of us blocking out part of the radar screen. Too many blips. The airplanes at least move fast across the radar screen and are easy to account for. But the others? Who is who? What is what?

All of a sudden I realize I am looking up at a set of lights that are to the west of us. "Jesus Christ!" I shout. "I didn't realize he was so close!"

I can now see a green light, two white lights and a red light heading right for us. They are getting higher as they approach. It is a fishing dragger, two long metallic arms are out stretched like a bird of prey ready to tear into Iwalani, barreling full steam toward us.

I turn on the spotlight and shine it at our sails. Then I aim the light onto the bridge of the dragger, an illegal thing to do, but who cares at this point. Phil bolts up from down below and stands next to me, quickly taking it all in.

"Forget the spotlight! Turn the engine on, full blast!" he screams.

I don't believe there has been a time in my life when I have moved so fast. I turn the engine on, throw Iwalani in gear, and we lurch out of harm's way within three seconds. That is actually all the time we had before we would have been killed. No time to don lifejackets, no time to launch a life raft, no time to call for help! Iwalani would have been sliced in two, with us crushed among the debris.

There is no one on the bridge of the dragger. We can smell fish and diesel as the bird of prey whooshes behind our stern, never slowing, never altering course. The starboard flopper stopper just barely misses our wind generator. A little after four a.m. on a Monday morning, and not one person is standing on the bridge! We realize later that the crew was all probably dead drunk and in their bunks as they steamed out to their fishing grounds from Gloucester. The captain probably stepped off the bridge for a moment to grab a cup of coffee, not seeing our tricolor masthead light through a haze of fatigue.

*   *   *

"Can we still go on with the circumnavigation?" I ask Phil, as he is just about to climb up the ratlines. "I swear I didn't get sick at all off the Jersey shore." This is the truth, but the passage was less than three days long, I only start to get seasick on my third night out.

"I don't know. How are the gauges?" he asks me in an attempt to bring me back to reality.

I am beginning to enjoy the Intracoastal Waterway. The most exertion needed is to pick up the binoculars from time to time to admire a nice house along the water's edge or to get a better glimpse at a hawk flying overhead. It is civilized, a new view at every turn. Navigating is pretty easy since we are in a long procession of boats and birds heading south. Red and green beacons mark the channel. You just have to connect the dots.

And therein lies the main problem. Me. Ever since I was a kid I had a tendency to draw outside the lines. None of my friends would let me go near their coloring books in grade school once they saw my propensity for crayon experimentation. I actually had one friend burst into tears after I had colored just one picture in her coloring book. Lines? Who needs 'em.

'Stay focused. Stay between the lines. Watch where we are going,' I have to keep repeating to myself. Other than the sound of the engine it is quiet enough for normal conversations, no wind howling, no waves roaring under the keel. Phil is baking bread and taking care of some chafing gear aloft. The water is so calm that jobs ordinarily saved for anchorages can be done underway.

Boink. I feel a shudder in the rigging. I look up at Phil to see if he is shaking the shrouds. Nope. Boink again.

"Have you been paying attention to the depth sounder?" Phil yells down to me. I look at the fathometer. The numbers blink from 9 to 4. Since it is aimed forward of the keel, and the keel itself draws seven feet of water, we have virtually no water in front of us.

"Uh, oh," I say. "We are running aground!"

Instinctively, I shut off the self steering so I can get control of the tiller and use our forward momentum to swing Iwalani to the right toward the red beacon and channel I have strayed from. I was heading for the next green buoy, taking the shortest distance, which meant cutting the corner slightly. My crayon was straying out of the lines.

"WHAT?" Phil shrieks. Running a boat aground was completely foreign to him. "WHAT? STOP THE BOAT! WHAT ARE YOU CRAZY! STOP THE

BOAT!" His normally bright blue eyes have taken on an emergency cerulean blue color as he slides down the ratlines like a fireman heading to a burning school. "WHAT ARE YOU DOING? THE BOUYS ARE THERE FOR A REASON. DO NOT CUT CORNERS. HEAD TO EACH BOUY!!!" Phil yells.

For the first time in a long time, I feel sort of seasick. Iwalani isn't moving anywhere. Since running aground is my fault, I am elected by a single vote, to row the anchor out in order to kedge Iwalani into deeper water. Using a boat hook, I first row around Iwalani poking down through muddy water in order to sound out the bottom. My instincts and the chart are correct; the deeper water lies to the right.

I take a six foot piece of clothesline and tie a small bowline through the trip line eye of the smaller forty five pound anchor, then tie the clothesline to the thwart of the dinghy. The anchor hangs about two feet off the stern of the dinghy, dragging underwater. The theory is I will cut the sacrificial clothesline once I have rowed the anchor out to deeper water. I begin rowing. And rowing. And rowing some more. After fifteen minutes I am still rowing and have achieved a distance of only ten feet from Iwalani's bow.

Suddenly I can hear puffing sounds behind me. Is it the cavalry exhaling? I turn around to look. A school of bottle nosed dolphins heads right for us, their dorsal fins cut the water like dancing butter knives.

"Don't get too excited," Phil says. "They are only here because you stirred up the bottom with Iwalani's keel."

But how can you not admire them? They swim in pairs or in triplets, breaking the water in staggered formation or simultaneously, like Olympic ice dancers. Some of them jump straight out of the water and then land with a loud smack while others lie still on the surface, using their powerful tails to wallop the water with a resounding slap. If only I could lure them to line up on the shallow side of Iwalani and use their melons (heads) to push us to deeper water.

I watch them while I keep rowing in place like a crazed fanatic in an exercise boat at the gym. Then all of a sudden, one of the dolphins jumps out of the water like he is going through a hoop at Sea World. I stop rowing at that point, my two oars poised in midair like exclamation points. "Wow! Did you see that?' I ask Phil.

"Keep rowing."

A few minutes later, Phil looks up from staring at the fixed numbers on the depth sounder and turns to watch the dolphins. "Oh, brother! I can't stand this anymore. I think you've paid enough penance. Come back in, and I'll swap places with you."

I climb up onto Iwalani and exchange places with Phil, as he sits in the bow of the dinghy and purposefully begins rowing. In between strokes of the oars I can hear him muttering under his breath, "I've never been so embarrassed. I've never been so embarrassed."

Other boats pass us, politely averting their eyes like they have stumbled upon a person with his pants down. Iwalani is in no real danger, but this will not be the case a few weeks later.

Phil realizes that this method isn't going to work, as he only manages to get a few feet further than I had. We load all the chain into the stern of the dinghy, turn

Iwalani's engine on, put her in slow forward, so she can't drift into more shallow water and tell Stewart he is in charge while we both climb into the dinghy.

Phil rows while I sit in the stern and pay out chain like a cable layer in the Atlantic. Once we get to the end of the chain, we cut the sacrificial clothesline to the anchor and it drops out of sight in the middle of the channel. We climb back on Iwalani, step on the windlass button and pull her to freedom. All told, we waste about an hour, but have been treated to a better dolphin show than you could have seen at any marine park.

We arrive at Beaufort, North Carolina, after dark, thanks to my grounding delay. We now have the nerve-wracking experience of coming into a tricky unknown city without the benefit of daylight. Phil steers while I turn the spotlight toward the red beacons as we pick our way up the channel. BOINK. We ran aground again. Right in between two red beacons. Phil has gone up to them in a straight line. This might have worked in Maine but not in shifting sand shoals.

Iwalani has enough of this land stuff. Fortunately for Phil, the outgoing tide catches her by the bow and swings her back into deeper water. She is heading back to sea. "That's it!" Phil screams into the night. "I've had enough of this ditch stuff. Tomorrow we are going out into the Atlantic!"

*   *   *

After an easy offshore sail, we re-enter the ICW at Charleston, South Carolina, to pick up my father. He is very fond of cruising the ditch and wanted to escort us to his winter home in Beaufort South Carolina. My parent's house is a few minutes walk and row from the anchorage. Down the street is the very best chocolate store in the world. For the next few weeks we keep busy with computer repairs and small jobs, while feasting on chocolates at night.

Phil has a recurrence of his "appendicitis" pains and we spend a few days at the hospital while they run tests and try to figure out what the problem is. Nothing is found, so I attribute it to too much chocolate. We scale back on the daily intake, and he improves.

My father has a small fiberglass boat with an enormous diesel engine that needs repairs. Phil offers to get Creeker up and running before we leave for points south. None of us can figure out why my father has such a small boat with such a big engine. Creeker idles at Iwalani's top motoring speed.

Before my mother heads up north for Christmas, she vainly tries to convince us to spend the next three years cruising the Caribbean. I take one look at Iwalani, then look at the chart of the Caribbean Sea, and the Caribbean sea just seems too cramped. We built Iwalani to cross oceans, not puddles.

For the month of December 2000, the South experiences the coldest weather in years. Every morning we wake up to ice on the decks and below freezing temperatures. We keep our small woodstove stoked night and day with charcoal briquettes and driftwood collected from the beaches. It might be cold outside, but

Iwalani is snug down below. (Maybe too snug; as one night the carbon monoxide detector goes off while we are sleeping. Through oxygen-deprived muddle-headedness I wonder who is making that infernal racket! Luckily I figure it out and get fresh air into the boat just in time.)

Once a week Phil and I borrow my parent's car to go out to the barrier beach and collect driftwood. We walk bundled up from the cold and carry our hatchets and bow saw in gloved hands. Well-dressed people steer clear of us, as we look like a couple of crazed homeless people. We always have our own section of the beach to ourselves while we cut up firewood.

*   *   *

"I could get pretty used to this lifestyle, even if it is freezing and even if I am sick," Phil sniffles as he blows his nose into his handkerchief. We are carrying our bags of wood back to the boat.

"No kidding. A fantastic chocolate store down the street, art galleries that are selling prints of my paintings, internet access and cable TV at my parents' house, nice people in town, what more could we want?" I say as we take different directions around a frozen puddle.

"Don't forget the Key lime pie they sell at the grocery store. I'm addicted to that. It's about the only thing I can taste with my nose so stuffed up."

"But it is still kind of incongruous to be walking under palm trees in winter clothes carrying canvas bags filled with fire wood. This isn't exactly what I had pictured for a tropical paradise. Plus the whole TV thing is getting boring."

"I know. We should think about leaving in a few days. I have just a few little wiring jobs left to do on Creeker. Hey, did you take the oars out of the dinghy?" Phil asks while shoving one of the canvas bags of firewood under the seat thwart.

"No. Where the heck are they?" I look around, hoping someone had just borrowed them for a few minutes.

No such luck. The oars have been stolen right out from under our noses. I try to stifle back tears as I wander around the waterfront hoping to find someone who had seen two extra-long varnished oars pass by. No one has seen anything.

A disreputable yacht had anchored in the river a few days earlier with a band of scallywags on board, complete with a parrot that perched on one of the young men's shoulders. A group of the scoundrels lean up against the parking lot fence while the parrot screams and throws peanut shells on the ground.

"Hey, you wouldn't by any chance have seen a nice pair of varnished oars walk by?" I ask the man with the parrot.

"Give it up," the parrot screeches at me. "Give it up!"

"No, can't say as I have. Definitely not. Nope. No oars have walked by."

One of the boys laughs. The parrot squawks.

I am tired and coming down with Phil's cold, too. I am pissed off and start crying for no really good reason other than I really liked those oars.

"Quit your blubbering," the parrot-man says. "They were only a pair of oars."

He laughs, the parrot shrieks, and they all hop into a van with blackened side windows and take off down the street. As they speed away, I can see through the rear door window, two varnished oars leaning up against the back seat, like two giant fingers giving the peace sign. It is our first, but not our last, experience with pirates.

"Did you find anything out?" Phil asks me when I meet up with him back at the dinghy. He had gone back to my parent's house to order a new pair of oars.

"No one saw anything, but I am sure it was someone off the junky pirate boat. I thought I saw the oars in the back of the van as they sped away."

"Maybe. But we'll never know, and there is nothing we can do about it now. We should file a police report just in case they screw up and the officials recover them. I just hope whoever has them appreciates them as much as we did."

"I'm freezing," I shudder as we motor the dinghy back to Iwalani.

"I am beginning to feel a bit better. This looks like it is going to be a one bag night," Phil says. He is referring to the boat bag we use for firewood. "It's supposed to get even colder. A cold front is coming through later tonight."

We feed Stewart, stoke the stove, and then head back to shore for a dinner party some friends are having for us. When we return to the boat later that night the wind has picked up and we motor the dinghy slowly over a small chop to get back to Iwalani.

For the last few weeks I have been kept awake by strange sounds outside the hull. Crunching and nibbling, which the dinner hosts assured me, are shrimp munching growth on Iwalani's bottom, not toredos eating through the planks. Two weeks after we initially launched Iwalani in Maine our bottom paint flaked off in big sheets. I am nervous that we are once again having trouble with the bottom paint. I pull my stethoscope out and listen to Iwalani's sides like she is an over sized patient; it only accentuates the crunching, the munching, the clanging, and the banging.

The latter sounds are a more sinister noise heard only from our bunk; a scraping, grating, metallic sound, like a phantom rattling his chains far beneath our pillows in an underwater prison. Our dinner party hosts assured me that the noise was just the anchor chain scraping on the hardpan phosphate bottom of the river. A few days earlier, another younger couple anchored near us told me about an uncharted shipwreck near where we were anchored. No one else could confirm it, so we quickly put it out of our minds and the stethoscope back in the medical kit.

"Where is she?'" I ask Phil. It is so dark and windy that I can't make out Iwalani's anchor light. We finally find her where we had left her, healing over from the force of the wind and the opposing force of the tide. "She's fine," Phil says. "The anchor light just blew out. I guess it's time I build a more reliable electric one."

We climb on board, and, before retiring for bed I take a good look around the salon to make sure everything is properly stowed. At anchor, a person can get very lazy and not put things away after they've been used. With me, it is a continuous battle with entropy. My computer is put away in its pelican box and all dishes are stowed. The only thing on the counter is a bottle of vinaigrette salad dressing that normally hangs over the sink on a brass hook. I leave it. I have been decorating for Christmas, and these things are also not well secured, but I leave them alone. I lay my clothes out on the port settee, instead of stuffing them in the laundry bag, in case I need them in an emergency. I don't have a good feeling about this wind.

For a few minutes we entertain ourselves watching the digital readout for the wind generator. "We're making forty amps of electricity!" we both cry in unison. "That's a new Iwalani record!" But like wind speed indicators, the wind generator only measures peak output. The average electricity we are making is closer to twenty-five amps; which is still an impressive amount.

That night the town closes the bridge to car traffic because of high winds. Just before dawn the wind really picks up. Iwalani heals far over, but when the gust subsides, she doesn't right herself. I shoot out of bed.

"We are aground!" I scream.

Sure enough, I hear the things left on the counter crash to the floor- the soap dish, the brand new bottle of dishwashing soap, the bottle of salad dressing, the small Christmas tree.

Even with his head cold Phil mobilizes faster than any person can humanly do. I follow him out on deck throwing on my clothes as I go. Creeker is still tied along the starboard side of Iwalani. The tide is going out. Darkness blurs the chaos.

Iwalani is stuck on the riverbank, her bow facing down into the river like a dying walrus reaching for a last sip of water. Her stern is in the air like a frozen tail flipper. "Remember what I told you about careening?" Phil yells to me over the wind. I shake my head. "This is the worst case scenario. All of our bilge pumps are in the stern. Water can start flooding in through the bow, once the tide starts coming in."

How had I not run through this disaster in my brain? My imagination had created "catastrophe matinee" for my daytime perusal: seas, winds, pirates, sinking, and floating in a raft adrift for months at a time, receiving top cataclysmic billing. But, despite possessing a fully decorated imagination, I never pictured Iwalani hanging nose down like an icicle. All of our bilge pumps are near the engine, in the stern, or in the middle of the boat. We have no portable bilge pumps to clear the water in the bow. If the forward hatch and port lights aren't completely watertight, the river will seep in before she can float herself off. The boat would be half full of water before the bilge pumps begin working. Phil starts Iwalani's engine, but the prop is already out of the water. The tide is draining out fast. "The engine's not pumping water!" I shout. "Shut it off!"

Iwalani starts to lean over on her port side; Creeker is hanging like a woman's shoulder bag on the starboard side. Iwalani's underwater parts face the wind, which is trying its best to push her over more. Phil grabs the spare three-quarter-inch line, two hundred feet of it, out of the bag on deck, fastens it to Iwalani's bow cleat and leaps into Creeker. "Untie me!" he shouts.

I unfasten the taught lines holding Creeker onto Iwalani. I am thankful that one of us had fastened both lines to the cleat properly. Too often I see people securing a boat to a cleat without making a complete turn around the base of the cleat first.

I get Creeker free while Phil starts her engine. I pay out line while Phil takes off for mid river. Early shafts of daylight allow me to see that several boats have dragged anchor. We had been anchored away from the main fleet, but now over ten boats take up our spot. How the boats managed to stay free of one another is a mystery.

I stand on the high side of Iwalani's decks watching Phil maneuver Creeker into position so he can try to pull Iwalani off the riverbank. He pushes her throttle full forward and Creeker's oversized engine begins pulling and pulling and pulling, but to no avail. Iwalani is stuck. The tide has gone out, and the marsh grass is exposed all around. She doesn't like the feeling of settling onto dry land and gives her rigging a shudder. I can see the underwater parts of her starboard side, but I am too distracted to check for worm damage. The wind is too loud for me to shout to Phil.

I feel as if I should be doing something. I go down below to close the portholes on the downfallen side. It is like entering a fun house at a carnival. Our world is literally on its side. No water is coming in to the boat yet, but the tide is still going out. Stewart is crying for his breakfast. The bottle of salad dressing has fallen off the counter, but has not broken. The cork has fallen out and the floor is covered with a slippery slick wash of balsamic vinaigrette. With the floor at an angle it is more slippery than a ski slope. Stewart is not amused when I tell him he has to wait for his cat food. He starts to lick up the salad dressing.

I go back up topsides and watch Phil move upriver with Creeker. I am ready to give up. "This isn't going to work!" I scream into the wind. Just as the last words head downwind with the gale, I feel Iwalani shudder. Is she trying to move?

Yes! Creeker gives it all she has. Smoke belches out of the tiny motorboat in a thick haze. Inch by inch, I can tell we are moving forward. Creeker is pulling all of Iwalani's forty four thousand pounds. The towline is so tight it is humming like a guitar string in the wind. 'One of us could get killed if something breaks,' I think to myself.

We start to gain momentum. Suddenly, Iwalani slides off the riverbank like a baby out the birth canal. With a massive splash we land back in the river. We are off the land, but are not out of danger. I run back and start the engine. It isn't pumping water! I shut it down and try again. By this time Phil has maneuvered Creeker within earshot.

"The engine isn't pumping water!" I yell over to him. Just as I say that, I hear the coughing sputter of the engine exhaust. I throw the throttle forward to regain steerage control, so Iwalani won't crash into another anchored boat or get blown back up into the river bank. Meanwhile, we are still dragging a sixty-five pound anchor and one hundred feet of chain.

VRRRRREEEEET! I hear a totally unfamiliar sound. "What is that?"

"You just cut the three-quarter line with the propeller shaft razor," Phil yells. "What's the depth sounder say?"

What an idiot! I never turned it on. I go below to turn on the instruments, slipping on the salad dressing. It is now fairly light out, but there are no signs of life from any of the other boats. Phil ties Creeker alongside, and we motor out into the river to re-anchor. We ease up on the throttle. The anchor seems to be holding where we are. I go below to clean up the salad dressing, make coffee and feed Stewart, who by this time is totally upset because his breakfast is the first thing we take care of when we get up and salad dressing is not among his favorite foods.

Iwalani starts drifting near an anchored boat. No one is on board, so I try to raise our anchor while Phil maneuvers our two boats away from the tiny sloop. I get the anchor part way up, only to find that a wire cable is totally wrapped around our flukes, along with the anchor line to the small sailboat. I can't pull the whole mess up without running the risk of breaking the other boat's anchor free. I get in the dinghy and start to cut away the plastic coated wire ensnaring us in its tendrils. Oysters and years of muck coat the trawler line. I don't have gloves. Rusty pieces of fine wire stick into my hands making them look like miniature porcupines. I am glad I am current on my tetanus shot, even though I doubt that the bacterium, which causes tetanus can live in salt water but I don't know.

"Hurry up!" Phil bellows. "I am losing control of the boats."

I cut the last wrap of wire from the small sloop's anchor line. Both of us are free of the cable mess. I realize that the clanking and clanging I had been hearing far down the anchor chain was in fact, the ghostly remains of a wrecked fishing boat. For weeks we had not really been anchored at all, but had our anchor flukes clipped to the wheel drum of trawl cable from the submerged wreck. The strong winds had finally put too much strain on the rusted metal, releasing Iwalani from its tenuous hold.

We re-anchor ahead of all the yachts that had dragged anchor. A few souls are starting to stir and are coming up on deck rubbing their eyes, looking around with a puzzled expression.

You can hear the collective thought emanating from all the boats. "Hey, this isn't where I was anchored!'

*   *   *

We enjoy Christmas vacation with Phil's boys, (who flew to Beaufort from New York) and then after they leave, we slowly head south. We spend one week painting Iwalani in the only place that will haul a wooden boat, St. Augustine, Florida. We start checking in with Herb Hilgenberg for his version of the weather, which our experience has proven to be more accurate than any other forecaster.

I have not mastered the offshore part of living on a sailboat, but I am committed to finishing what we have begun. On the night we plan to cross the Gulf Stream, Herb tells Phil we would be better off hugging the coast and getting to Panama via the western side of the Caribbean.

We leave for the Bahamas against Herb's advice, hoping to make the crossing overnight. "Coast-huggers! Herb has now branded us as coast hugging, cocktail drinking losers," Phil says as I appear for my watch at eight p.m.

"Well, I don't exactly have a lot of off-shore experience," I mumble.

"Now is the time to get it! It's an ideal time to cross the Gulf Stream. The winds are out of the southeast, five knots. We won't have the wind against the current. I've got the engine on, the staysail up and two reefs in the main. She seems to cover the most ground going to windward with this setup. You should expect some drift from the current," he adds before heading down below.

We are leaving the Florida coast near West Palm Beach. The sun has set, but there is still an orange glow over the western horizon. I look at the radar and see a target two miles away. It isn't making a very big blip on the screen but is moving in a fast circle around us. "Strange," I think to myself. Our experience with the fishing boat off Gloucester taught me to be more vigilant. I pick up the binoculars, but still don't see anything. I figure I should wake Phil. He probably is still tossing and turning anyway, as it has been just ten minutes since he went off watch.

I go down below but Phil is already putting his shirt back on.

"I forgot to tell you about the weird boat on radar," he says to me.

"That's why I am down here. I can't see its lights," I add.

"Neither could I. How far away is it now?"

"It's about two miles in front of us. But it seems to be maintaining that distance." We both look at the radar screen. There are no ships on radar within eight miles. "Weird," I comment. "It was right there." I make a mad dash up the companionway ladder with Phil right behind me. "Holy Pattooties!" I scream.

Fifty feet away from us, silhouetted by the western glow of the Florida coast, is a large ship. It breathes down on us like the grim reaper. It's keeping pace with us just off our starboard quarter.

Phil shines the spotlight on it. There are no lights, no markings, no name, no registration, and no hailing port. The hull is painted a flat black, which seems to absorb the light from the spotlight, no light reflects back; even the windows are painted a flat black. It continues to keep pace with us, but maintains a fifty-foot distance.

"What the hell is this?" Phil asks. "How far off the coast are we?"

"Twelve miles," I reply.

"Great. Indian territory. Get on the radio and see if you can hail them."

"You don't suppose they are pirates, do you?" I wonder. I am terrified of the stories I have been reading in popular sailing magazines of modern day pirates. Contrary to popular thinking, there are more pirates nowadays on the seas than at any other point in history. Some of them are poor and hungry fisherman, but a growing number are well armed terrorists who board a ship or yacht, kill everyone on board with their semi-automatic weapons, steal whatever appeals to them, then light the ship on fire or pump it full of bullet holes so it will sink to the bottom without a trace.

"Large ship with no lights, name, or hailing port, at 26° 42' N, 79° 43' W, this is sailing vessel Iwalani, fifty feet to the east of you. It is against US coast guard regulations to pass through American waters with no navigation lights! I will report you to the US Coast Guard."

'Brother, that sounds lame,' I think to myself. What else can I say? 'Please don't kill us. We are just leaving the US to sail around the world. We have a cat on board. We have no weapons. We are just poor woodchucks from Maine, not a fancy drug running motorboat. Leave us alone!'

Within seconds the Coast Guard group at Jupiter Inlet, Florida responds to my radio hails and tells me not to worry. "The situation is under control."

"They're leaving!" Phil yells down to me. Within minutes the mysterious black ship is out of sight.

"Under control? Under whose control?" I gasp. "Do you suppose it was a good guy–one of ours?"

"Probably. We are near enough to the coast and close enough to the Bahamas that they must be nervous about drug smuggling."

"Why didn't they show up on radar?" I ask.

"They were so close they just merged with us on the screen. I'm going back to bed. That's enough excitement for one evening. Remember what I told you about drift."

A few hours later we are in the thick of the Gulf Stream. I have the moving map program up and the little green arrow representing Iwalani on the computer screen has been drifting ever so slightly to the northeast. Now we are heading almost due north. Phil told me to expect drift, but this is ridiculous. Our speed is now down to 2.5 knots, and in the wrong direction! At this rate, we will finally make our way to the Azores.

I go up on deck and take the staysail down, then push Iwalani a bit more into the wind. I come back down below to check the computer. It did little to improve our speed or performance over the bottom. I go back up on deck to put more sail back up.

"What the hell is going on?" Phil asks wiping his eyes. "What are you doing? Have you gone completely mad?"

"I didn't mean to wake you. I am just trying different things to see if I can make our heading better," I explain.

"Make our heading better? You're doing it all wrong. Didn't you ever learn what to do if you are caught in a riptide?"

"Well, sure. Swim across it," I reply.

"Well then, why are you pushing us into the current even more? That's going to slow us down. We need to go across fast, even if it means we don't aim for the direction we want to go. We'll correct our heading when we are out of the stream." He storms over to the pin rail and raises the staysail. Then he stomps over to the throttle and increases the rpm's on the engine. Iwalani is now doing 6 knots but we are still heading north-north-east.

"We're going to miss the Bahamas entirely," I say to him.

"We'll just make landfall further to the North."

"But there isn't anything there–just six-foot spots, reefs and nothing else."

"How long have we been going only two knots?"

"I don't know. A half hour, I guess," I admit.

"Jesus! Didn't I tell you to watch out for drift? You'll never make it flying an airplane." We head back down below in silence to look at the chart.

"Here. We'll be lucky if we can make West Bahama. That's where we'll head for now." Phil says pointing to the northernmost landfall for the Bahamas. He shakes his head and goes back to his bunk.

For the rest of my watch I obsess over the computer screen until the green curser trail and course arrow point in the same direction, indicating our course over ground and heading are the same. There is no more drift; we have crossed the Gulf Stream.

We arrive the following morning in an entirely new climate. With each mile forward, layer upon layer of cold weather clothes are thrown into lockers, not to be worn again for three years. Within hours, we are in the bright turquoise colored water the Bahamas are famous for. Flying fish skim along the sea's surface in front of Iwalani's shadow.

"Holy shit! Stop the boat! We're going to run aground!" Phil yells to me. "Look at the color of that water! What does the depth sounder say?"

"It says we are in forty feet of water," I say.

"We can't be. The depth sounder has to be broken."

"Calm down. It's not broken. This is just the way it is. Welcome to the tropics. You better get used to this color."

"I can't believe we are sailing in water that is forty feet deep and is the color of a seven-foot swimming pool!" Phil screams as we speed eastward. He tosses his shorts down below with the rest of his clothes. "It's hot! I'm hot. To hell with clothes! This is what I dreamed about my whole life!"

I silently watch the excitement of my husband as he runs along the length of the boat completely naked, pausing occasionally to peer over the side. Finally he stands at the pin rail, his long torso leaning against the aft shroud; boat, creator and dream have become one.

Iwalani emerges from the barn Phil built to create her

GLUEING AND PLANING IWALANI'S MAST

Ben christens Iwalani on the first swing. If he had missed, we would have cancelled the circumnavigation!

The Players

Philip J. Shelton
boatbuilder, engineer, author, pizza chef

Nathaniel Shelton
chose to stay home

Amy Peters Wood
artist, veterinarian, author and ships medical officer

Ben Shelton
Also stayed home- "it will be too boring" to go to sea..."

Stewart
ship's cat and chief morale officer

Justin Mecham
"The Whipping Boy" a good kid, really, but sometimes in need of a rheostat. He stayed with us for over two months early on.

Iwalani

Down below
looking forward

Down below looking
aft through engine room
door

Aloft
looking
down

The call of the sea

From the start,
we all kept
written logs

Some of us hunted
for trouble,
while others
hunted for fish.

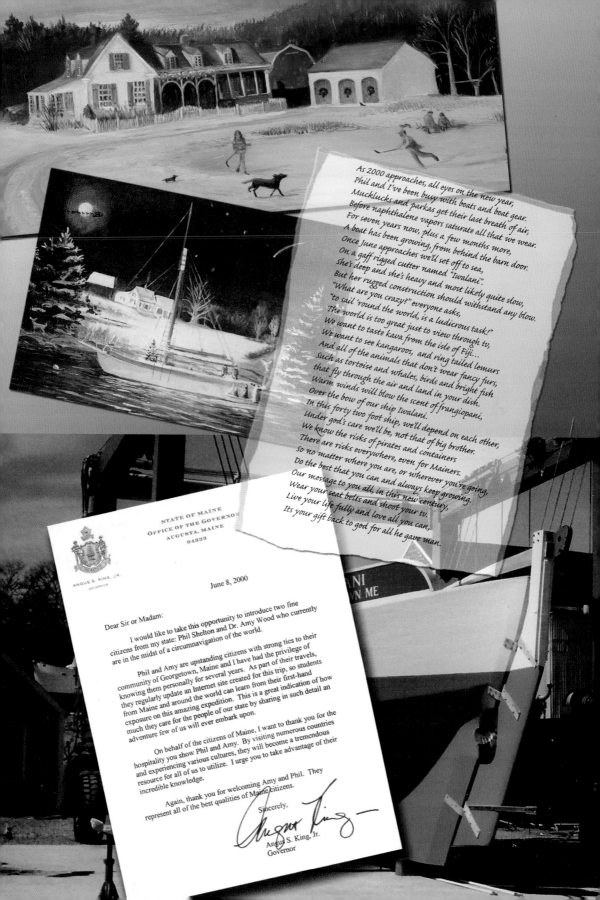

As 2000 approaches, all eyes on the new year,
Phil and I've been busy with boats and boat gear.
Mucklucks and parkas get their last breath of air,
Before naphthalene vapors saturate all that we wear.
For seven years now, plus a few months more,
A boat has been growing, from behind the barn door.
Once June approaches we'll set off to sea,
On a gaff rigged cutter named "Iwalani".
She's deep and she's heavy and most likely quite slow,
But her rugged construction should withstand any blow.
"What are you crazy?" everyone asks,
"to sail 'round the world, is a ludicrous task!"
The world is too great just to view through tv,
We want to taste kava from the isle of Fiji...
We want to see kangaroos, and ring tailed lemurs
And all of the animals that don't wear fancy furs,
Such as tortoise and whales, birds and bright fish
that fly through the air and land in your dish.
Warm winds will blow the scent of frangiopani,
Over the bow of our ship Iwalani.
In this forty two foot ship, we'll depend on each other,
Under god's care we'll be, not that of big brother.
We know the risks of pirates and containers
There are risks everywhere, even for Mainers.
So no matter where you are, or wherever you're going,
Do the best that you can and always keep growing.
Our message to you all, in this new century,
Wear your seat belts and shoot your tv,
Live your life fully and love all you can,
Its your gift back to god for all he gave man.

STATE OF MAINE
OFFICE OF THE GOVERNOR
AUGUSTA, MAINE
04333

ANGUS S. KING, JR.
GOVERNOR

June 8, 2000

Dear Sir or Madam:

I would like to take this opportunity to introduce two fine citizens from my state: Phil Shelton and Dr. Amy Wood who currently are in the midst of a circumnavigation of the world.

Phil and Amy are upstanding citizens with strong ties to their community of Georgetown, Maine and I have had the privilege of knowing them personally for several years. As part of their travels, they regularly update an Internet site created for this trip, so students from Maine and around the world can learn from their first-hand exposure on this amazing expedition. This is a great indication of how much they care for the people of our state by sharing in such detail an adventure few of us will ever embark upon.

On behalf of the citizens of Maine, I want to thank you for the hospitality you show Phil and Amy. By visiting numerous countries and experiencing various cultures, they will become a tremendous resource for all of us to utilize. I urge you to take advantage of their incredible knowledge.

Again, thank you for welcoming Amy and Phil. They represent all of the best qualities of Maine citizens.

Sincerely,

Angus S. King, Jr.
Governor

Iwalani was blessed with good luck from the start

Nova Scotia

Motoring past New York City

Port Antonio Jamaica

While those at home had less luck—note the ghostly cloud over one of the Twin Towers on the far left

CLOCKWISE FROM RIGHT
Fishing fleet Manta Ecuador,
sharing the Panama canal with
one of the big boys, Amy's father
looking nervous in the canal,
Valentine frigate birds,
Jamaican kids

Above then Clockwise:
The "Duke" Leslie Ellington,
sunset over Panama,
Amy, A Kuna Indian mola,
Phil

Chapter 4

Drug Deals and Blow Hards

January 2001
Jamaica to the Pacific

We stay two nights in the Bahamas then push off when the winds are from the Northeast. "Expect storm force winds from the west tomorrow!" Herb says over the radio. "I repeat, storm force winds! I would not leave if I were you." He gives his customary throat clearing punctuation when part of his flock is going against orders.

"I don't care," Phil answers. "They will be fair winds, and we'll go down to bare poles if we have to." And we do. But the sun is shining and our passage through the Bahama channel is fast, free of other yachts and is one hundred shades of Caribbean blue. Psychologically it would have been a different story if it had been raining and the skies were gray, or if it had been at night.

We had one close encounter with a reef on my watch. I looked over and saw it breaking less than a mile away. With trembling hands I thanked whoever was watching over us. Despite the advances with GPS, navigating still requires a person to be paying attention. I hadn't been.

Three days into our eight-day passage (around the east end of Cuba to Panama), both of us are getting tired and are starting to snap at each other. Stewart is doing fine, especially when we catch our first mahi-mahi.

"It's your fish," Phil says with resignation. "You have to kill it."

"How?" I ask as I watch its vibrant colors fading like water spilled on a brightly painted watercolor.

"Bludgeon it," he hands me a wooden belaying pin. I tap it on the head. The fish looks up at me with a glistening eye.

"I can't do this!"

"Don't let it suffer!" Phil says. .

I tap it again.

"Hit it like you mean business. Don't give it little love taps. You've got to really whack it."

"Here!" I say thrusting the belaying pin back to him. "If you're so good at it, you do it!"

"No way! If you're going to catch fish, you have to kill them."

"If you're going to eat what I'm going to catch and cook, you have to kill it!" I say.

"No way! If you're going to buy hooks and gear to fish what you're going to cook and I'm going to eat off the dishes I have to clean, you have to kill it. Besides you're the vet."

"Yes, but you're the great white hunter. You shoot and eat black ducks. That makes you an expert at killing and eating. You kill our chickens too. You can kill this mahi-mahi," I say finally. We are faced with a growing dilemma. Neither of us is going to kill this fish. He begins to flip about as its body becomes starved for oxygen and his beautiful colors fade to gray.

"Just hit it!"

"No. I can't. I'd rather see it flipping around then bash it on the head."

Stewart meows at the bottom of the companionway.

"Fine suit yourself." Phil leaves me on deck with the flipping fish.

"Get me some gin!" I yell down to him.

"No way. You know the rules: no alcohol while we're at sea."

"It's not for me, retard. I'm going to pour it in his gills," I growl.

"Don't call me retard. Dinkface. And you can't waste my gin. Just smack it on the head."

"Your gin? It's our gin, Peckerwart." I kneel down on the deck and watch the fish slowly die. It makes me feel sort of sick that a creature while alive can be such a rainbow of yellow, greens, blues and when dead becomes a cold steel gray. When it is stiff and looking like a supermarket fish, I begin gutting and filleting it. The boat rolls, the knife slips, and I cut a huge gash in the palm of my hand. "Fucking asshole!" I scream at no one in particular. I am pissed off, so I stay on deck and finish cleaning the fish, smearing his slime deep into the knife wound. If I am going to suffer, I might as well get my cut good and infected. Finally, I head down below with the fish fillets and my knife to wash up.

"Look at this!" I say to Phil as I try to separate the edges of my cut. I am hoping for a really big show of blood streaming down my arm, or at least spurting outward in fountain-like arc, but nothing happens. The wound is very nearly healed.

He ignores me. "Look, I'm sorry I called you a retard," I say apologetically, still trying to pry apart my wound. If I can get it to bleed again Phil might feel sorry for me, but I can't entice a single drop of blood from what is now looking like a mild scratch.

"No you're not. You said what you really think," Phil says.

"I don't think you're a retard. You are the smartest person in the world."

"Well, in that case, I think we need to stop for awhile," Phil says tapping his pencil on the chart. "Port Antonio, Jamaica is sort of on the way."

"Um. Fine with me. But you really have to look at my cut. The mahi mahi slime has healed in five minutes what would have taken days."

"No way. You're crazy. Fish slime doesn't heal cuts," Phil says while sharpening the point on his pencil. "This could be a tricky stop, but I think we need it. We are exhausted. We have no charts for Jamaica, but we do have a quarter page diagram in Reed's Almanac. That's more than the schooners two hundred years ago had. But still, we should probably wait for daylight to go into the harbor."

"You are just trying to change the subject. I make the medical discovery of a lifetime, and you blow me off," I grumble.

*   *   *

We arrive in the middle of the night, outside Port Antonio harbor, where we try to lay a hull and wait for daylight. Despite having no sails up, we are still careening toward the island at six knots, from a favorable current and reinforced trade winds. I have to keep the engine on with the gear in reverse half throttle to slow us down so we don't sail by it completely. As soon as it starts to get light, we motor toward the harbor.

"This is crazy! Where is the lighthouse?" I scream to Phil. "It's supposed to be fifty-two feet high and I sure don't see anything."

"See that plume of spray. That's it, hidden by the breaking surf."

"Great! No charts, and if we make a mistake, broken up bits and pieces of our boat will be showered over to the other side of the island."

I spent much of my childhood traveling with my family to many different places: Mexico, the Bahamas, parts of the Caribbean, but Port Antonio, Jamaica, is Phil's first introduction to a third world city. As soon as we round the bend into the harbor, we are surrounded by a fleet of small boats and rafts, paddling, motoring, or barely staying a float, each containing a single man, waving, smiling and attempting to cajole us into buying "whatever, mon."

A small group of people takes our lines as we come alongside the dock for check-in with customs. One couple stands out from the rest, a blonde haired, grizzly Canadian man who looks like he keeps wild animals for pets, and his beautiful, dark haired girlfriend.

"We're John and Carol," the bearded man welcomes us extending his hand. "We heard you on Herb's net and just wanted to see what you and Iwalani looked like. We're in the steel schooner at the end of the dock."

"So? How do we look? Are we what you thought?"

"Anyone with a gaff rig is ok in our books," John says laughing.

We are given the lowdown on how to check in and tips on what to do when the agricultural inspector comes on board. He has been a source of frustration for many of the cruisers. "He'll just sit there. Eventually, you have to pay him to get him off your boat," Carol explains.

"But he's a veterinarian!" I cry. "He can't be dishonest. How much did you guys have to pay him?"

"We paid him ten dollars," she responds. "One boat had to pay twenty, plus give him a couple of steaks."

Later that afternoon the agricultural inspector slowly lumbers onto our boat. "I am pleased to meet you." I say extending my hand. "I am also a veterinarian, from the US." He nods, ignores my outstretched hand and then plops his rather corpulent frame down in the cockpit under our dodger, blocking the companionway. "Would you like to inspect Stewart, the ship's cat?" I politely ask.

He shakes his head. "No, I don't trust cats."

"Stew is very docile. He has bad arthritis and can't climb the companionway ladder. He lives down below unless we bring him out on deck. Here is his paperwork." I pass him Stewart's rather large file.

"I need to take with me any fresh meat," he mutters as he passes back the file unopened.

"Fresh meat? We just have a mahi-mahi we caught. We've eaten everything else."

"I don't need the fish."

"Would you mind if I ask you some questions about what being a vet is like in Jamaica?"

"I haven't practiced in years. You would need to talk to the Vet up the road."

"What sorts of diseases do you have here?"

"Most of the same as you have in the US."

"Heartworm?"

"Yes."

"Rabies?" I ask.

"Yes."

"Hoof and Mouth?"

"No."

"Scrapie?"

"Never heard of it," he admits.

We carry on like this for almost a half hour. I am determined to drive him so crazy he will be begging us to get off the boat, forgoing his "payoff." Two hours later he still sits in our cockpit, blocking the companionway, while the sun starts to set behind the hills on the west side of the harbor.

"Would you like something cold to drink?" I ask. I am starting to run out of questions to plague him with, and my mouth is beyond dry. The agricultural inspector is beginning to wear me down. I can hear Stewart down below crying for his supper.

"That would be nice," he remarks.

"Excuse me, but I need to get down below."

"Not a problem," he answers unmoving. He is prepared to have me walk over him.

"I mean, I will have to walk over you."

"Not a problem," he grunts.

I gingerly step over him, grateful that I am wearing shorts and not a skirt. Phil is down below with Stewart, both of them reading, Phil a book, Stewart his dish. "What are you doing?" Phil whispers to me. "We're starving."

"We are having grilled mahi mahi for supper. Want to set up the barbeque?" I suggest softly.

"How do I get through the companionway?"

"It appears you have to step over the inspector," I reply.

"I'm not doing that!" Phil hisses at me. "Just give him some money and get rid of him."

"No! I will not. It's the principle of the thing. People shouldn't have to pay a bribe just to get rid of him."

"What are you doing?" Phil asks me in a loud whisper.

"Giving him some water," I reply quietly.

"Then he'll never leave! You've got to starve him off."

"That's just plain mean. We can't sit and eat while he's flopped there like a sack of potatoes."

"Well I'm not setting up the grill with him there," Phil grumbles.

"OK fine," I snap. I step up the first two steps of the companionway ladder and tap the inspector on the shoulder. "Excuse me. Would you like some mahi mahi for supper?"

"No thank you."

"Uh, I take it, in order to get you to leave, we must pay you money?"

"That would be nice," he replies.

"Um, how does five dollars sound?" I offer.

"That will be fine," he grunts.

I guess we make out better than most.

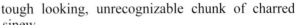

*   *   *

Port Antonio is not among Jamaica's top three tourist spots, which suits us just fine. Markets line the streets selling fresh produce, real oranges, not the brightly colored artificial looking fruit found in the US, but green tough skinned fruit with sweet, juicy, flavorful insides. And pineapples, fresh and delicious, better than any in the world, are sold by young vendors along the side of the road, ready to eat in Ziploc bags for fifty cents. Signs advertising Red Stripe Beer, are plastered to buildings or located in small goat-chewed fields decorated with trash. Shoes are everywhere for sale. Vendors sell barbecued meat that has been reduced to some tough looking, unrecognizable chunk of charred sinew.

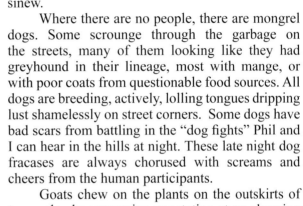

Where there are no people, there are mongrel dogs. Some scrounge through the garbage on the streets, many of them looking like they had greyhound in their lineage, most with mange, or with poor coats from questionable food sources. All dogs are breeding, actively, lolling tongues dripping lust shamelessly on street corners. Some dogs have bad scars from battling in the "dog fights" Phil and I can hear in the hills at night. These late night dog fracases are always chorused with screams and cheers from the human participants.

Goats chew on the plants on the outskirts of town, slowly consuming vegetation at an alarming rate. Children are dressed in school uniforms, clean, cheerful, smiling and singing as they wait in lines for buses. Cars drive fast on the "wrong" side of the road most unafraid to use their horn which competes with the omnipresent boom-piti-boom of the bass from a passing car, street vendor, personal boom box or the reverberation through the hills of someone's very loud stereo. Old Rastafarian pan handlers sit on the side walk, too weak to lift a cup, smelling strongly of cannabis and decay, their skinny black legs and knobby knees like turned ebony balusters from a grand staircase, splayed out for passers-by to step over.

"Hey mon, can I have a twenny?" aggressive teenagers ask us.

"Ven florgen drisken?" we respond in pseudo-Norwegian, a puzzled look on our faces, pretending not to understand the question. Eventually we are left alone.

Gange. The smell of marijuana is everywhere. But we never actually see anyone smoking it. I decide as I walk along with the throngs of people on the street, that I need to try some of this Jamaican pot. Now I do know that it is illegal in the USA, and to be honest, I have no interest in smoking it back home, but I've always felt that, when in Rome, do as the Romans do. Phil, on the other hand, will have nothing to do with this undertaking. But how do I make a deal? I have no idea how a person goes about buying drugs.

A few days later we decide the nonstop Johnny Cash blasting from four-foot speakers at the yacht club, is too much to take. I expected reggae music in Jamaica, not American country and western. We leave the dock and anchor nearer to Navy Island, on the far side of the harbor. That afternoon while I am painting in the cockpit and Phil is below writing the log for the web page, I hear a knock on the hull. I put my canvas to one side, stand up, and look over the bulwark.

"Hey mon, you want some gange?" A handsome young man is sitting astride a small raft comprised of four thick bamboo trunks lashed together.

"Uh. Maybe." I look furtively around hoping no one is filming this. I especially don't want Phil to know what is going on. "I just want to buy one joint," I whisper down to him. Before I can say anything else, the young fellow scrambles up the aft end of Iwalani like it is only inches above the surface. A thin line is tied to his wrist so his raft won't drift away.

"How did you do that?" I ask incredulously. I had always perceived our boat to be free from assault because, relative to other yachts, we have over five feet of freeboard.

"This is good stuff," he says rubbing his chest. I am not sure if he is referring to his genetic makeup or the THC he is very clearly under the influence of. "My name is Lance," he extends his hand to me.

"Hi, I'm Amy. My husband Phil is down below," '*Cleaning his assault rifle.*'

"How much will one joint cost?" I ask quietly.

"What do you have for trade?"

I put together a trade box before I left home of assorted things I thought people could use. Reading glasses, dark glasses, sewing supplies, fish hooks, fishing line, crayons and colored pencils, small notebooks and perfume. Before I open the box, I know none of this is going to appeal to him.

"Any knives? Videos? Whiskey? Books?" he asks.

I keep shaking my head. Books we have, but we have not read them and are saving them for the long Pacific passages. "No, we've got nothing. Rope?" I suggest.

"Maybe. What's it look like?"

I recently found a large coil of polypropylene pot warp used for lobstering in Maine, which I thought given the name, might be suitable for this transaction.

Lance looks it over, then shakes his head. "I need something stronger."

"Oh, well. That's it for my trade goods. How about money? How much would one joint cost?"

"U.S. fifty," he says.

I am rather taken aback at the price. "Wow, I had no idea marijuana is so expensive!"

"An ounce," he adds. "I can't sell you just a joint. But we can smoke one if you want to try it."

I think better of this proposal, since one of the side effects of marijuana on me is an increase in all kinds of appetites, not just eating. This is the main reason for my wanting to buy some pot to begin with, as Phil says he is bored with the more private aspects of our marital life.

"I guess you've got a deal." I hand him all the money I have in my wallet.

He reaches into the folds of his swim trunks and pulls out a ziplock baggie and begins picking through it removing what is left of the seeds. I think he has a notion I might try to plant the seeds when he spies all the herbs I have growing around Iwalani in flower boxes.

"You don't by any chance have some way to smoke this stuff?" I ask him as he hands me the baggie.

"Sure hang on a second," he hands me the string to his raft. "I'll be right back."

He does a perfect dive over the side of Iwalani and swims to the eastern shore of the harbor.

"What's going on up there?" Phil yells up to me.

"Nothing you need to worry your pretty blue eyes over."

"Jesus, honey, what are you doing now?"

"Nothing you need to know about."

"As the captain, I am ultimately responsible for what goes on this ship."

"Then stay down below. Besides it's the 31st. I'm the captain today," I yell back down to him.

I can see Lance's dark figure wading into the water from the far shore. Ten minutes later he swims back to Iwalani using only his right arm, smoking papers raised far out of the water and bone dry in his left hand. I take them from him, thank him profusely and hand him a towel.

"No, mon. I don't need that. You're in Jamaica now. No need for towels."

"Are you hungry?" I figure he must be starving.

"No just thirsty. Have you got any Coca-Cola?"

"No this is a Pepsi ship. Hang on while I get you a cold one."

When I return, he is rolling a joint from his own stash.

"How do you like Jamaica?" he asks me while licking the seal shut on a very tight joint.

"Well, considering we've only been in Port Antonio a few days, and this is the only place we've been in Jamaica, I guess I like it. It's really very pretty here. But there is kind of a trash problem."

"Kind of? There's no money to clean it up. We are a very poor country. All the money leaves by ship and the profits go to a select few. See that cargo ship over there?" he asks me, pointing to a small orange colored container ship tied to the western shore. "That ship is half full of marijuana. Illegally, of course. It is the main export of Jamaica, but none of the profits come back to the people." He reaches further into the folds of his swimsuit and pulls out another baggie with a lighter in it. He lights his joint inhaling deeply. "Where are you from?" he asks handing the joint to me.

"A small island off the coast of Maine."

"Where is Maine?"

"It's the state that's tucked into the Northeast corner of the U.S."

"You must be fairly close to New York. I've never been to the U.S." Lance says, taking the joint back. "Someday I'd like to go to New York City. I've been to London and backpacked through France and Germany."

"Wow. You've been farther than me. How was Germany?"

"OK., I guess. Until I got beaten up by some skin heads."

"That must have been scary," I say before inhaling.

"Especially since I was set up. I didn't know any better. They pretended to be friendly and helpful, and then beat me up and robbed me. I was lucky to be alive and lucky to make it back home. They are a bit prejudiced there."

"I guess there's prejudice everywhere. People are just leery of anything that's different. I'm sure we'll be in places where people will be leery of us just for the color of our skin too," I realize that I am losing the feeling in my legs.

"Where are you heading?" he asks passing the joint back.

I wave the joint away. "That's enough for me. We're going to sail around the world."

"No! Really?"

"Yup. We built this boat and took three years off so we could sail it."

"Wow. Incredible. It's a great boat. People don't realize how little a person really needs in life. What is she? Twelve meters?" he asks.

"Pretty good guess. Even that still seems big. Sometimes I feel like we are a giant turtle with a forty four thousand pound shell on our backs."

"But think of the freedom you have! You can go anywhere!"

"Yes and no. A backpack would be simpler. We can't really travel too far inland because we worry about the boat," I respond.

"Has it been a big adjustment living on a boat?"

"Not really. It's not too different from living where we were. Our island was connected to the mainland by a series of bridges; my friends who live on "real" islands say that doesn't count. We can drive off any time we want, but it's still a long haul to the grocery store. We have neighbors, but they don't live close by. Our life before we moved onto the boat was more isolated. Like tonight, we're supposed to go to a potluck dinner with a bunch of yachties. We rarely socialize at home. Want to come?"

"No, that's OK. I'm supposed to take my girlfriend shopping."

"That sounds like it might be less boring. We're supposed to make something Jamaican for dinner. I bought three lobsters and was going to make them into a salad. What else should I add?" I ask.

"Put a little pinch of gange, add some ground cloves, shred some cabbage and add lots of lime juice. That's Jamaican lobster," Lance responds.

"Sounds great. How did you know all that?" I ask.

"I am a cook. I would love to be a cook in New York."

"Well Lance, if you get there after 2003 look me up. My sister has a restaurant in Massachusetts. I'm sure we could find you a job somewhere. Ethnic restaurants are all the rage in the US." I hand him our boat card and he climbs back down to his raft.

"Good luck with your trip," he calls to me as he paddles off. "And watch out for German skinheads."

*   *   *

We arrive at the potluck dinner and have the round of introductions from John and Carol. Most of the other yachts are career cruisers. Some write for sailing magazines, some have circumnavigated. All but John and Carol are completely infatuated with their cruising life.

One of the writers, Bill, is doing an article for a cruising magazine on cuisine of the region, so he has the local delicacy "Goat's Head Soup," made for the dinner. The dish is an aphrodisiac and is typically served at Jamaican weddings. It is usually made days in advance, but time constraints turn it into a fast food dish that afternoon. His wife Lisa makes Aki, a kind of mush made from a fruit, which tastes like pulverized creamed corn.

Bill watched "Hulk" a local Jamaican, make the Goat's Head Soup and photographed the entire process. Apparently, a real head was removed from a real goat, smashed up with a lead pipe and then all the parts were put in a big pot along with some other choice tid-bits, including the cloven hooves and intestines. Carol is normally a vegetarian. Phil, John, and I, each become one too that night. But we have to hand it to the other cruisers; they are a much braver bunch than the rest of us. They eat politely out of heaping bowls and with each spoonful ask me to identify the various body parts. Once the body part is identified and properly named, they gobble it down without a second thought, while trying to maintain a look of gustatory pleasure.

"How 'bout this?" Bill asks holding up a white piece of cartilage.

"Cricoid cartilage. Part of the larynx."

He swallows it whole. "Have any of you heard of a disease called Scrapie?" I ask.

"No," they respond in unison.

"Bovine spongiformencepahalopathy, Creutzfeldt-Jakob, Kuru?"

"Ya right" Bill teases. "God bless you."

"Mad cow disease?"

"Now you're talking English."

"Let me tell you a little about mad cow disease since it is one of my favorites, but, all of those diseases I mentioned may be variations of the same thing. They are caused by an infectious piece of protein. This is an infection caused by something smaller than a virus. The protein in question is called a prion. Imagine a lawn chair, folded into various positions. This is what mad cow disease is. It's not the protein itself that is the problem, but its twisted shape. The infectious prion protein causes all normal prion proteins to twist up, too, to fold up like uncomfortable lawn chairs. Isn't that cool?" I ask looking around at a lot blank stares.

"Scrapie, the sheep and goat disease, is like mad cow disease. Its caused by a prion, too, and is found in sheep brains. Cows probably got the disease when some countries used diseased animal body parts in livestock feed. The chief veterinary inspector for Jamaica had never heard of scrapie, which may or may not be a good thing, depending on how you look at it."

"Talk about being the informed consumer," Phil whispers to me. "I think you just put the kybosh on a hot time in the old town tonight."

Later we all return to Iwalani where I tell John and Carol about my drug dealings.

"You did what?" John asks in disbelief. "For a while there I thought you were a semi-intelligent person. Haven't you heard about the swipes some of the countries use when you arrive?"

"Swipes?" I ask innocently.

"Sure. They come on board and wipe a test cloth all over your boat to see if you've got any drugs on board."

"Great!" Phil exclaims.

"I'll only smoke my pot outside then," I suggest.

"You should just get rid of it," Carol responds.

"It's not worth the risk," Phil adds.

"And sailing around the world, is there no risk there?" I ask.

"No it's just stupid. This whole sailing thing is stupid and a waste of time, especially the passages," John says.

"Why do you suppose none of the cruising books tell how it really is?" Phil asks.

John and Carol

"The Hitchcocks are really the only ones who mention they get seasick," Carol answers. "The thing I hate most is the loss of personal hygiene."

"I know what you mean. It just seems ridiculous to take a shower and get clean because five minutes later you're all covered with salt again," I add.

"But it sure beats sitting in traffic two hours a day," John says.

"I'm not so sure," Phil speculates scratching his beard. "When you are stuck in traffic, you know that at the end of the day you'll be in a bed with your wife and the bed won't be rolling around trying to throw you out. Even out here you still have to watch out for other humans trying to kill you, but this time they're in large ships."

"Did you know that our brains have a neurotransmitter called anandamide which acts to blunt the blows of day to day life?" I ask. "It is probably there so women will forget how awful childbirth is. Not only that, but the main chemical of marijuana is virtually identical to anandamide. I think I've discovered why so many cruisers all seem like huge pot heads. Life at sea makes us have higher levels of anandamide, so we can forget about the horrors of passage making."

"Speak for yourself," John says throwing a cushion at me. "You should just throw your pot overboard and spend more time at sea!"

"Why don't you guys just come with us to the west side of Jamaica?" Carol asks.

"We can't. We've got my Dad and Phil's sons flying into Panama in two weeks. They are going to be our line handlers through the Panama Canal. It's all arranged, and the plane tickets have been bought."

"Uh oh. Sounds like a case of get-there'itis, the main reason why cruisers and sailors disappear at sea. Having to stick to a schedule and not following the weather and Mother Nature only invites trouble," John says. "Haven't you read the books about crossing the Caribbean Sea in February?"

"Yes, we know. Gale force winds. At least we won't be becalmed."

A few days later we clear out of Jamaica and head for Panama knowing full well it will be an uncomfortable ride. But John was right, we do have get-there'itis.

Chapter 5

Through the Drain Hole like a Bar of Soap, Sort of...

February 2001
Jamaica to Panama

We are very quickly thrown into the "heavy trade winds," with average wind speeds of thirty to thirty five knots. Up until this point my sailing experience with these kinds of wind had been in short bursts. There is really no analogy for what it is like in a boat, stuck in heavy seas for a long period of time. Our life became an elevator that goes to the second floor and back down, never stopping, over and over again. The elevator swings from side to side, forward and backward, and then suddenly lurches off on an unexpected angle. It never stops. You cannot get off.

On Iwalani, our day is divided into four-hour shifts. Four hours of trying to stay awake to watch that big ships aren't running you over, and four hours of trying to sleep. In heavy seas your muscles never relax. If you are not throwing up, you feel like you are going to. Cooking? You've got to be kidding. Finding, then opening, a can of chili, requires thought, ambition and perseverance. It's a noteworthy achievement akin to climbing a high mountain peak.

Cleaning dishes and putting things away are an important and horrible task. The world cruiser, Don Street, once said, "In heavy seas even a cottage cheese container can become a deadly weapon." Our "demise" almost came from a small pat of butter that fell on the floor and subsequently melted into a nearly lethal slick spot despite several cleanings with boiling water and dishwashing liquid.

For five days we had heavy winds and high seas. The screaming in the rigging and roaring waves were taking their toll on our nerves. Iwalani flew along with the wind, but unfortunately strong winds make big waves and they became enemy number one. Waves? I used to like them. Lying on a beach, hearing the surf crashing against the shore used to be a great way to relax. But at sea in rough weather, when a wave crashes, all muscles tense, hands grip the nearest handhold, and a person gets an automatic dive reflex.

Wave heights are determined by taking the average height of the top two-thirds of the waves. According to the weather faxes, we are in fifteen-foot seas, but that leaves the highest of the waves unaccounted for. The faxes tell you nothing about the three witches, the trio of waves that come every twenty minutes, twice as high as the average wave height. The first is big, much bigger than any before; you can hear her roaring greeting sixty feet away. She pushes the boat over hard on its side. Water washes over the leeward bulwark. The wave passes underneath the boat. This water must drain quickly out the leeward side, before her sister, Wave Two hits. She is bigger than Wave One. She crashes hard on the windward side, sending green water over the cabin top, spraying down below if any portholes are left open. If it were Hollywood, it would look like the stagehand had thrown a bucket of water over the stern. But these two, are nothing in comparison to Wave Three, the strongest of the trio. She is the reason many boats get lost at sea. If the boat has not cleared away the water from the first two waves, Wave Three will founder the boat. Wave Three is the biggest of all: barrels of water come over the side, flooding the cockpit and drenching the poor soul tied in out there. Wave Three is sometimes thirty feet high; when we are riding on her crest, the hole left beneath looks like we are peering down from the turret of a Victorian mansion.

One of those waves steals my fishing box, taking all my hooks and lures right over the top of the bulwark and selfishly curling them in her wet wave lips. I sat for two days in the cockpit, knowing full well this was going to happen, but I was pulverized into inert apathy. Countless times in my mind I could see the tackle box floating away. I just had to crawl over to the leeward side and pick it up. But then what was I going to do with it? Tie it somewhere? Secure it? But where? I am furious with myself when my mental images become reality, and the box really does get swallowed by the sea.

It doesn't take long for me to realize the benefits of a "hard" dodger. Our flimsy cloth dodger is totally inadequate for offshore. Forget the dodger idea entirely. A well built pilothouse with bullet proof Lexan is much more practical.

So, here you are wet to the core; it is not cold, just sticky, and unpleasant. Soon the whole boat gets sticky, damp and unpleasant. Damp stinky dishtowels and dirty laundry perfume the air. Sponges become the worst offenders with that rank odor only they can give off. There are no other smells. Far out at sea the ocean has no smell.

Peace and quiet? Hardly! Even in light airs there is still a cacophonous symphony of sounds. Iwalani has her own mix of squeaks, clunks and hums. Together they croon a small repeating song phrase, over and over again. These are the good sounds, the sounds that remind us we are moving forward. But when the wind goes over twenty knots, the whistling begins in the rigging. First to chime in are the running back stays, like a psychotic string section. When the wind is over thirty knots, the rest of the rigging sings forth in a lugubrious soprano chorus. All together it is deafening and nerve wracking.

Why bother brushing your hair? It will only get soaked and knotted from the wind. Marital relations? Yea, right! This is perhaps the hardest part for Phil and me. We have a very hard time sleeping alone. We peck each other on the cheek at the change of each shift. Despite living in a confined space, we rarely see one another.

*   *   *

On the afternoon of day three I look up from the book I am trying to read and see ten feet away a brown object lying in the water streamlined, looking up at me with wide brown eyes showing intense fear. It is so close I can see the "whites" of its eyes. At first I think it is a manatee, but I know that is impossible three hundred miles out to sea. As the next wave passes under it, it hangs in the wave head down, looking like a brown beluga whale. No, that isn't right either. I see it better when the third wave passes under it. I've only seen pictures of that strange shaped head before.

"Oh god, no," I cry, when I realize it is a sperm whale calf, left on the surface by its mother who is, I hope, fishing deep below the surface. I have just read a book about the whaling ship Essex that got sunk by a vengeful sperm whale. That boat had four-inch planks. Iwalani's planks are only two inches thick. All I can think of is that the mother will arrive and find Iwalani between her and the calf. We will be toast. Thankfully, Iwalani sails out of harm's way before the mother resurfaces.

By day four we still haven't eaten much. I make Phil some macaroni and cheese and get sick just looking at it. We are now in some "convection" activity as Herb calls it.–squalls, rain that pours down with such force that everything is gray. I really can't tell if the wind picks up. It's possible, but the deluge of water buffers any increase in sound.

When the rain lets up for a brief moment, I go forward, take the staysail down, and stand transfixed clinging to the mast feeling Iwalani work. I hold onto her stout spar like an electrician climbing a telephone pole. I can feel the energy of the wind pulsing through the fabric of the sails and circuiting down through the wood of the spars, through the cabin top and down to the keel of our boat. Iwalani is like a synapse of nerve to muscle– wind meeting sea.

We put a lazy man's reef in the mainsail the night before, not tying the reef points. This leaves big ballooning bags drooping down from the boom, which quickly fill with water from the squalls. The belly of the reefed mainsail is trapping too much water. I have to bale it out.

With each wave and each trio of witches, Iwalani handles herself with as much difficulty as a cat shaking its paw of water. I start losing my fear. This boat can handle far worse. It is the fear of the unknown that scares me the most. Iwalani can handle quite a bit of wind easily; it is just her humans that have their limits.

I have to get Phil up to help. Filled with trapped water, the sail is too heavy for me to stand under and push up with my back, and impossible for me to reach safely with a bucket. There are more than fifty gallons of water contained in the "bags". We have to get the water out and put in a proper reef. I am worried that carrying that much weight in the sail is unsafe and at the very least, will stretch the fabric. I put the forward jib up after taking the staysail down. We are now carrying more sail than we had previously done, which seems to prevent a lot of the resonance rolling without making Iwalani careen or lose control.

Iwalani's behavior in storm conditions was something we couldn't have entirely predicted when we were designing and building her. We worried about the scuppers, big enough to drain water fast, but not so big that a cat could get flushed over board like a small pea in a slotted spoon. So far, they are just the right size.

I leave the staysail boom on the deck instead of tying it up at the mast. I am lazy, exhausted, and really don't care. Later, when we get to Panama, the movement of the staysail boom on the deck sands a flat spot on the boom and a bare spot on the deck, a permanent reminder for me to finish what I start.

I just want one moment of silence, one hour of not being tossed or rolled around. After baling and re-reefing the sail, Phil and I have a heart to heart talk. We both want to go home. We can find no redeeming features of what we are trying to do. We were not doing anything that hasn't been done by countless others. The people who enjoy this life are seeking something we thought we had found in Maine. This ocean passage is nothing short of torture. Getting to port will be nice, but will we be able to relax? Or would we still worry about dragging anchor, getting robbed, or having a fire on the boat? I decide that people that enjoy this cruising life have nerves of steel and brains of turnip.

A few months ago, I used to look at the cruise ships we passed at night, thinking "what losers!" Now I see those ships all lit up like a Las Vegas Gambling Casino and get totally envious. Those people are having fun! They get into nice crisp cotton sheets at night, mints and orchid blooms on the pillows, scrambled eggs and orange juice for breakfast from a glass that you don't need two hands to hold on to and which will stay where you left it. Phil said the whole problem is that the ocean is pissed off at man for leaving the sea; we chose to become land creatures, and Neptune just hasn't gotten over it.

The afternoon SSB conversation with Herb doesn't sound any better: continued gale force winds and high seas off the Columbian coast. We are ready to throw in the towel. Yet, I still want to go to the Galapagos or at the very least let Iwalani's keel touch the Pacific. The very word "Pacific" means peace; it has to be nicer than the Atlantic. Herb has us go far to the west before we cut south for Panama, avoiding the worst of the blow off the Columbian coast. He seems impressed with our time so far. We had counted on arriving in Panama on Saturday. It is now starting to look like Friday.

Late Thursday night, the waves and wind reach their peak. We are fully under the influence of the Columbian coast. Once every hour or so, we start to see ships heading North from the Panama Canal, eighty miles away.

One motor yacht comes very close to ramming us. Finally, at the last minute I get the Captain on the radio. He says he cannot see us on radar. No kidding, I can't see him either. We are too close and both of our vessels are lost in the wave clutter.

"Can you see our masthead light?" I ask him.

"No," he replies, "I can't see you at all!

I turn on our motoring lights as well as the tricolor masthead light. Finally he can see us, we are less than an eighth of a mile from each other. I tell him we should pass starboard to starboard. "Well, it's a little rough out here for me to do that," is his hesitant reply. He is trying to keep the bow of the motor yacht into the wind, so he won't get rolled over by the waves. Reluctantly, he turns his yacht, while I nudge Iwalani a little more into the wind and we pass each other safely. His boat is over eighty feet long. What is he complaining about? Probably spilling too many martinis. I am the pushy woman of the high seas, and I am very near my breaking point. After we pass, he comes back to me asking if we have a radar reflector up. I tell him we have the most expensive and best radar reflector available. I don't tell him that he doesn't show up on radar either.

I am very nervous after that. Every ship I see on radar I try to reach on the VHF radio, making sure they can see us. I try first in English, and if there is no reply, I try my rusty Spanish, not used since high school. I have a funny conversation with a fellow who sounds like an actor on Saturday Night Live. His English is a little better than my Spanish. He is in total disbelief that we are out sailing, just the two of us, and our cat.

The wind generator is putting out more than enough electricity. Its high pitched hum when the wind really picks up is a little unsettling and makes it difficult for the man off watch to sleep, but its steady flow of free electricity is important for keeping all our electronics running.

Suddenly I hear a plink-plunk, a sound I have not heard before. Our second spotlight died the day before, so I turn on the cabin light in the companionway ladder to see what has broken. I swing its long gooseneck out into the cockpit. The self-steering looks ok, but the wind generator has an eight-inch spring hanging down, wagging in the breeze like a terrier's tail. I quickly scramble down the ladder to try and turn the wind generator off, a real trick when it is blowing hard, as the brake uses magnets. I am fortunate in switching it off quickly. My biggest fear is that the boat will lurch in the wrong direction and swing the spring right into the blades. Fortunately that never happens, but we will now have to use the engine to charge the batteries.

On my four a.m. watch, Phil reports there are lots of ships around and we are now too far to the east. He wants to go right down 79° 55' longitude. We were at 79° 44'. I am still tired. It is hot and stuffy down below with all the portholes and hatches closed. I haven't used the electric fan because I don't want to waste electricity and as a result I get little sleep. I ask Phil to leave the Inmarsat running because the handheld GPS is known to give wrong positions.

"Lucky you, you get to see the sun rise," Phil mutters.

"Yah, right. Very funny."

I watch the tall silver backed waves lit by the full moon, turn into a dull battle ship gray. Dawn in the Caribbean Sea. So much for the sunrise, it is still cloudy. I check our position with the handheld GPS. It says we are still to the east, running down 79° 49 longitude. I click in some more west into the autopilot. I look down the companionway.

'I really should check our position, with the Inmarsat,' I think to myself.

Seven swaying steps downward, I don't have the energy to step over the radar swung into the cockpit and go down the slippery ladder. The radar shows land sixteen miles ahead. Lots of ships are coming at us, like baseballs shooting out of a batting machine. It is seven a.m. Friday morning, but something doesn't feel right. It is still very windy and I am very tired.

Stewart, too, has reached his limit. I feed him a handful of his dry cat food which, unfortunately, is formed into tiny round balls. The veterinarians who designed this food never figured cats would be eating it at sea. Stew has to eat them fast, otherwise they roll right out of his dish. He takes a few quick bites and then goes forward and barfs all over the white rug. He seems depressed, perhaps because I am no longer hugging him. With all the flying fish he has been eating and a cat's nasty habit of cleaning himself after he eats, he manages to coat his fur with a greasy, slimy fishy smelling residue. Hugging him is a little like loving a half full sardine can.

The rest of his cat food balls roll out of the dish and begin skittering around the floor. A bag of whole-wheat flour, has come loose in the pantry and is now shooting out plumes of flour dust between the slats in the louvered door. Iwalani is now a full-fledged garbage scow.

I wake Phil up early. I just want help.

"We are way off course! We are ten miles to the east," Phil snaps at me. "What were you doing on your watch?"

We have to jibe to get back on course. We furl the main, leave the jib up, turn the engine on to charge the batteries, and begin surfing toward the Panama Canal, dead down wind. I try cleaning up down below and give some comfort to poor Stewart who wants to go back to Maine.

Five miles out I begin calling the Cristobal signal station on the radio. They do a very good job guiding us to the canal breakwater. Phil and I are amazed at the design of one of the most important breakwaters in the world. It has a small open mouth facing directly into the howling trades. Fortunately, the depths shoal up fairly far off shore, so the brunt of the large seas stays well away from the canal. Yet, it is a little like running an inlet. The water just outside the mouth takes on a Gatorade green color; Phil mans the tiller, and we shoot through the opening on ten foot breaking seas, like a raft shooting the rapids, just a head of a huge car carrier going the other way. We have made it to Panama.

Calmer Waters

We are directed to the yacht anchorage in the "flats" and motor beyond all the other sorry looking sailboats flying wind worn flags from many foreign countries. Most look as if they have been anchored for a while. A few U.S. boats are scattered around. We anchor, hang the "Q" flag and Panamanian flag I made in Florida and begin to clean the sticky, smelly boat that is our home.

I give Stewart some subcutaneous fluids, as he is dehydrated; I wish I could do the same to Phil and myself. Instead we settle for a cold Jamaican Red Stripe beer out of the icebox and tuna fish sandwiches, my first real food in days. After Phil and I take hot showers, I give Stewart a bath in the sink, an undertaking he really resents until it is over. I think he feels better afterwards. At least, all of us, including the boat, smell better.

The books say quarantine inspectors, drug enforcement agents and all sorts of other officials will come out to the boat. We wait, relatively cleaned up, but no one arrives. After finishing some repairs, we head to bed for a nap, but sleep right through to Saturday afternoon.

The next day we pack the brief case containing all the ship's papers, put on some fancy clothes and head off in the dinghy for the Yacht Club. We become totally soaked by the stiff chop in the process. We land at a rickety wooden dock and walk around looking for guidance.

One would think with the Panama Canal and all the boats that go through it, that there would be an influx of money in the surrounding region. If money is being made in the canal, it is not filtering down to the people of Cristobal or Colon. Buildings seem forlorn and run-down. Cement highrises surround the yacht club, each one exactly six stories tall. Television antennas stick out of open windows like twisted feelers on some huge cement insect. Despite being slightly overcast, the day is still hot. Strong northeast trade winds continue to blow night and day, providing the only relief from the heat.

The locals do not hound us as soon as we touch shore; in fact, we sort of feel invisible. We find the Yacht Club office and begin asking questions about the whole process of getting through the canal: customs, quarantine, immigration, cruising permits, admeasurements for canal transit, transit fees, etc. While we are there, the customs official happens to walk in. We go to his office, and with a wave of his wand-like pen "practique" is granted. No money is exchanged. We walk to immigration, and, after luring the official's attention away from the TV for a few moments and with two loud thumps of his stamp in our passports, (during the commercial break) we are in. The cruising permit place is closed and will have to wait for Monday.

We buy a phone card and begin the calls for getting the boat through the canal. A woman is to meet us on Monday to measure Iwalani and make sure we have four lines, 125 feet long and 7/8 inch in diameter, as well as six large fenders. Besides someone to steer the boat, we are also required to have four line handlers, a job soon to be fulfilled by my father and Phil's two sons, due to arrive in a few days. The canal authorities will provide the pilot, but we are told we must provide him/her with food, sodas and a toilet.

Surprised at how easy everything is going, where we had heard horror stories of all the red tape, we decide to go to the bar and have a beer and some French fries, in honor of John and Carol who introduced us to this bad habit.

Activities on a boat are dictated by waiting for weather or waiting for spare parts. We are now waiting for our scheduled time to go through the canal. We sit at a table and listen into the conversation of some cruisers sitting at the table next to us. A pretty Californian girl talks in an awed voice to two older sun shriveled men from Down Under about their experiences with heavy weather, the topic on everyone's lips since it has been so horribly windy.

The Australian begins talking about the storm he had been in near New Zealand. "We had forty knots of wind for four days, right on the nose- and seas of thirty feet…"

"Weren't you scared and seasick?" she asks.

"No," he replies and then adds, "Lots of cruisers spend six years in a circumnavigation taking anti-seasickness drugs, but not me, I never get seasick."

I furtively, reach up behind my ear to make sure I removed my quartered piece of Scopolamine patch. "Can you imagine," he adds, in between puffs of his cigarette, "going around the world like that on drugs? Imagine what it is doing to your liver and kidneys!"

"He obviously isn't giving much thought to his own lungs," I whisper to Phil.

On our way back to the boat we pass by a somewhat rundown sloop flying a British flag. A naked, shriveled man walks to the stern of the boat and pisses in the water. He waves at us as we motor by.

After three days in Colon it, too, starts to wear me down. I am either soggy or soaked from our dinghy rides to shore. While we are at anchor, Iwalani pitches and heaves like a hobbyhorse. Leaving a glass on the counter is not possible. The air is hard to breathe, heavily laced with smoke from burning on shore and exhaust from the huge ships at anchor upwind from us waiting to go through the canal. The windward side of our white rigging soon becomes black with dirt and grime carried by the trade winds passing over the industries on shore. Our decks are covered in a black film we have to hose off every day.

Colon is dangerous and depressing. With a name sounding like "cologne," it really should be pronounced as it is spelled. There are parts of the city we are told not to walk in, even in broad daylight. People have not figured out what to do with trash. It is dumped along the road and smoothed around with bulldozers to fill low spots. I, too, reach a low spot after eating fried wantons at the Yacht Club which make me sick for days.

We overhear some boats talking about the morning VHF net. I decide the following day to take to the airwaves and announce my services as a veterinarian. There are plenty of boats anchored on the flats and many of them have pets. Little do I realize I will be besieged for the next few days with patients, both two-and four-legged. Phil spends his time refueling Iwalani, a few gallons at a time, while I neuter, excise and then give shots to haired and non-haired rear ends. I did not realize how much I missed working on animals, and am instantly more cheerful. Working on people is a new but not entirely different experience. People can buy medicines and vaccines at the local pharmacy for just a few cents. Human tetanus shots are easy to come by but not easy for the purchaser to administer, so I have people bending over, literally, for Iwalani's services.

Nathaniel, Phil, and Ben at the internet cafe.

My father and Phil's sons arrive midweek. We are scheduled to transit the canal Monday at 5 a.m., which leaves the weekend free to spend with Phil's sons and my father, sightseeing and hanging out. We hire a taxi driver, "The Duke" Leslie Ellington, a wiry local who speaks fluent English, to drive us to a boat trip and tour on Baro Colorado Island, part of the Smithsonian Institute Research Center in the middle of the canal. The ferry is scheduled to leave at eight a.m. We need to leave Iwalani at 5:30. At 5:00 a.m. I have trouble rousing Phil's boys from their bunks. My father chickened out the night before when I told him we would be hiking in a rain forest. He decides to spend the day on the boat. We finally get on the road at seven a.m. with the tires on the Duke's small car barely touching the ground.

We come to a screeching halt at a roadblock set up by a small army of Panamanian policemen carrying machine guns. The Duke speaks in rapid Spanish to the gendarme, and I am only able to follow half the conversation. One policeman looks at Phil and myself, brown and sun worn, then at Ben and Nathaniel, doughy white and sleepy from the states. He shakes his head but waves us on.

"Why did you tell him we are from Panama?" I ask The Duke.

"Because, if they think you are a tourist, they want to hustle you, get $5 each, from you if they can," the Duke says, eyeing me in his rear view mirror.

"But telling him we are your cousins? We look like a car load of mixed nuts, not relatives."

"Don't worry. The Duke takes good care of you," he says as the little car speeds along in the shade of tall overhanging trees. And he does.

By the time we get to the ferry dock the boat has already left. I am close to tears. The Duke asks the guard at the gate about renting a boat, and we are directed to a local marina about ten minutes away. We arrive at the resort and charter a fast pontoon boat, arriving at B.C.I. while the passengers are still getting off the ferry. It cost us eighty dollars, but I have already spent $350.00 for the Smithsonian tour. This is becoming a very expensive day trip.

We have a three-mile hike around the small island which was formed when

The French started the Panama Canal in 1879, after they had entered into an exclusive contract with the government of Columbia, the original owners of the land where the canal was constructed. The French tried making a canal that was completely at sea level. They were running into trouble with the mighty Chagres River that carries a tremendous flow of water.

Their plans called for an aqueduct over the river. The French sold shares of stock (to finance the canal), which became extremely valuable and then, like the dotcom stocks of the 1990's, plummeted to worthless strips of paper when word got out of the tremendous cost overruns and large numbers of workers dying from yellow fever and malaria. One French engineer had drawn up plans for using the Chagres as a source of water to fill locks, a strategy overlooked by the French officials at the time, but which later became the accepted model.

In 1902 a bill in the U.S. Congress was introduced to buy up the bankrupt French company, provided a treaty could be made with the Colombians and provided the plans for an American/Nicaraguan canal were abandoned. The bill passed by eight votes. The French sold their rights to the Panama Canal for

the whole area was flooded for the canal. I was hoping we would see capybaras, the largest rodents in the world. Like their smaller counter parts the guinea pig, they are crepuscular, meaning they are most active at dawn and dusk. We see none but instead find large buttressed trees, iguanas, anteaters, army ants that form a nest with their bodies, leaf cutter ants, tons of butterflies, agouti (large guinea pigs) and white-faced monkeys. It is winter in the rain forest, and it reminds me of early fall in a Northern Hemisphere deciduous forest. The smells, the crackle of fallen leaf litter, erase my preconceived notion of a rainforest as being dripping, damp and dark.

Before we leave, we are shown the original research station, complete with a cot, desk, and some scientific instruments. You could easily imagine a researcher poised over the microscope, sweat dripping from his or her brow in the tropical heat, scrawling thoughts onto a damp notebook. A far cry from the dorms of today with showers, air conditioning, and satellite Internet.

Our Smithsonian guide states that Panamanians are scared of the rain forest, so most people live clustered in cities and villages. There are 236 mammalian species and half of those are bats, including vampire bats. Those are usually found near cattle and fields, not forests. So the fear of the rainforest is really unjustified, but it has resulted in a lot of land that is uninhabited. Panama has more rainforest turned over to the National Park than Costa Rica.

*   *   *

Our canal pilot, "advisor" Rubin, arrives in the dark, at exactly 5:15 a.m. Monday morning. They are called advisors because they don't actually do any of the line handling or steering. They are included in the five hundred-dollar transit fee, and, if you get a good one, they can be a tremendous help. Rubin is a native Colombian, trained with the Colombian Navy and ordinarily a tug boat pilot; the last place in the world he wants to be that early in the morning is onboard an American "yatshit" as he refers to us. Actually, in all fairness, that is how everyone in Panama pronounces yachts, making it into a two-syllable word; Rubin just seems to have a little more emphasis on the last syllable.

There are a lot of yachts going through in February, so every available person gets called in to duty. We are scheduled to transit the canal at first light rafted to two other sailboats: a catamaran from California called Pacific Bliss and a sloop from France called Mon Ami. Pacific Bliss hired two professional line handlers, locals who greet you at the dinghy dock and give you their card. For about sixty dollars, plus a five-dollar fee for the bus trip home, they will help boats with the line handling. They aren't too bad an investment. Pacific Bliss also lucks out with a senior pilot of the canal for their advisor; with twenty years experience, he becomes the pilot in control.

Iwalani takes the starboard most position, with Pacific Bliss sandwiched in the middle. The rafting together goes fine; despite doing it in a cove that is not very protected from the still howling northerly winds and in complete darkness. We are now a single flotilla, fifty feet long and forty-five feet wide, with a total of four engines, one each on Iwalani and Mon Ami, two on Pacific Bliss. The senior advisor goes against regulations and takes the helm of Pacific Bliss, steering us into the first of three locks. He sends two of the professional line handlers over to Iwalani, so we really don't have to do anything. My father, despite failing eyesight, is anxious to help, but is replaced by one of the professionals. Ben and Nathaniel are still in their bunks both of them suffering from head colds.

The line handlers up on the lock throw down a messenger line, a grubby oil soaked piece of manila with a monkey's fist at the end, to each of the four corners of the flotilla. The messenger line is tied on to the loop at the end of our seven eights inch 125 foot long nylon dock lines. The lock line handler walks to the end of the lock holding the end of the messenger line.

forty million dollars. The Colombians saw none of this money. A treaty was made between the Americans and Colombians, which the Colombians did not ratify. The Americans offered to pay $250,000 per year to the Colombians, but they rejected it, saying it was not enough money to lease the land they owned. The Colombians already owned a railroad across the isthmus, which was making that much per year. They figured the canal should make more money than their railroad.

The residents in the Canal Zone wanted to secede from Columbia; if the Colombians didn't sign the treaty, they would become their own Republic of Panama. The Americans agreed to support these new Panamanians if war broke out with the Colombians. A revolution started in 1903; American warships were sent to the area and stood offshore at Colon and Panama City, while the Panamanians and Columbians fought it out.

The Colombians lost, everything: their successful railroad across the isthmus, the annual lump sum for the canal from the Americans, their land and any further rights to the canal. To say that they and some of the other Latin American countries mistrust the Americans, is an understatement. Construction of the canal was finally completed in 1914 by the United States.[1]

1.McCullough, David, The Path Between the Seas , Simon &Schuster 1977.

When the word is given, the line handler on the yacht throws the nylon rope into the water where the lock line handler pulls it up the side of the lock. The loop is placed over a bollard at the top of the lock. The line handler on the boat must adjust his or her lines as necessary. The raft of boats is thus kept in the center of the lock by four lines at the bow and stern of each of the two outside boats. The inside boat doesn't have to do any line handling, but they do have to steer and power the flotilla out of the locks.

Up we go through the first two locks then into the third, eighty feet above sea level. The gates open, we un-raft and off we go into Gatun Lake. We dodge our way through lots of small islands, the tops of hills that became islands with the damming of the Chagres River and creation of the canal locks. Iwalani charges along with mainsail, staysail, jib and motor. She takes the lead and until the final moments beats out the other two boats to the last set of locks at Pedro Miguel and Miraflores.

At Gamboa we feel a change in the air. It becomes less humid; the howling Caribbean northerly winds ease off. We are getting near the Pacific. It is hot but drier. It is only ten thirty in the morning and we are halfway through the canal. It looks like we will do the whole thing in one day. Ben and Nathaniel remain in their bunks.

The experienced advisor leaves Pacific Bliss in Gamboa, and a younger Tom Cruise wanna-be, wearing mirrored sunglasses and Top Gun baseball cap, climbs aboard. He is also Colombian and went to school with our advisor Rubin. It is a joyful reunion. At Pedro Miguel Locks we again have to raft up. It goes well only because Phil can maneuver the entire raft with Iwalani. Rubin and the second advisor, Tommo Cruiso, are still speaking rapidly to each other in Spanish, catching up on long lost classmates, talking about wives and new families, and not paying attention to getting us through the remainder of the canal. It immediately becomes apparent we have a problem. We fly down the length of the thousand-foot lock at eight knots rafted together, with Rubin and Cruiso laughing and gibbering away.

"Excuse me," I say to Rubin, "Don't you think we are going too fast?"

He looks forward and realizes we have less than seventy-five feet left before we crash into the gates at the end. "Full Stop! Full stop!" Rubin and Cruiso order simultaneously.

We have already passed our nylon lines to the lock line handlers, despite having gotten no word to do so. Mon Ami is now into their fourth bottle of wine and have completely forgotten about their lines. They are only tenuously attached to the lock by the manila messenger line. The small messenger line can't hold on to one hundred thousand pounds of raft. Over we drift to the right hand side of the lock. Iwalani rubs up against the wall, gently, no damage done, while Mon Ami scrambles to pass over their nylon lines. Amazingly they don't have seven-eighths inch nylon line.

"What's up with that?" I ask Rubin, "How come they got to use what looks like braided running rigging?"

He turns and gives me a scowl, but doesn't answer.

After Phil and I tell Rubin that conversing with his buddy is becoming dangerous for all of us, they split up and begin to pay more attention to getting

The lock doors close behind us.

us through the remaining locks. The three of us have to motor, tied as one, through Miraflores Lake to the last two locks. We are told that the last lock has a tremendous outflowing current once the doors open to the Pacific. The professional line handlers from Pacific Bliss will be manning the lines at the stern, which requires a bit more strength, while I man Iwalani's bowline, with my father as back-up.

The lock line handler throws down the messenger line, and I tie it to my loop and watch the lock line handler walk down the canal, holding his end of the messenger line.

Suddenly I see it, a three-foot splinter of wood at the top of the lock, peeling away from the uppermost wooden beam.

"Watch out! Large splinter," I yell up to him while pointing at the potential snag. The lock line handler eighty feet above us smiles down at me and waves. "Jesus, Dad, do you see that up there? The line is going to get caught on three foot splinter coming off the top of lock wall."

"I'm sure they must know about it, " my Dad says, shielding his eyes from the sun while trying to see what I am worried about. It is too late, the large splinter grabs hold of the messenger line.

"Stop!" I yell, "It's stuck!" I turn to look at Phil manning Iwalani's tiller.

Phil isn't taking orders from me because I am not in charge. He looks at me and then shakes his head. He is only going to do what the advisor tells him to do. I have two choices at that point. Make my end fast and hope the messenger line will break, or start paying out nylon line until someone in charge makes a decision. I start paying out line. Tommo Cruiso catches on to what is happening and yells, "Slack the line! Slack the line!"

Now of course there are three other lines working the lines besides me, and, because Cruiso is the advisor for the middle boat, the other three line handlers don't know he is yelling, "slack the line," just to me, so everyone pays out line. Sure enough, the messenger line to the stern of Iwalani also gets snagged by the same splinter. Our raft of boats is now completely out of control. The lock workers scramble over the steep side to free the stuck messenger lines. Water has already begun to drain rapidly from the lock as we begin our descent to the Pacific, creating a lot of turbulence inside the lock. Iwalani swings rapidly toward the side of the canal. She hits without a bang or crash, just a big fart sound, as the mooring balls we are using as fenders squish against the side. Our round mooring balls morph into lozenge shapes and protect her from serious damage. Seam compound squeezes out from between the planks like heavy toothpaste and remains on the hull until we finally sand it smooth in Australia, but that is it for damage. The other boats are fine from Iwalani taking the brunt of the crash.

I then have to rapidly un-foul the old messenger line from our nylon line. A requirement for anyone transiting the canal should be for all line handlers to carry knives. Everyday I usually carry a knife, but I am wearing a bathing suit and they don't have pockets.

"Hurry, Doc," my Dad urges.

"I know. I am trying, I need a knife."

"The life raft," Phil yells to me from the stern, fully aware of what's happening in the bow. Water is still cascading out of the lock, and we are rapidly going to sea level, no one in control of our raft. I quickly understand what Phil is yelling and remember the cheap, sheathed knife we have tied to the back of life raft canister. I grab it and despite its rusty state, quickly cut off the old messenger line. The lock line handler throws me a new messenger line. I reach for it and miss.

"Oh dear," my Dad groans. "Come on, Doc, you can do it!"

"I'm a bit nervous," I stammer.

We descend even further. The lock man throws again, and I reach far out and grab onto the messenger line. I tie a fast bowline knot and our nylon rope is pulled aloft and secured. We churn down the final feet rapidly, all four lines working hard to hold us in place.

The skipper of Pacific Bliss is appointed by the advisors to be in control of steering the flotilla out of the chamber. He is not used to the added width of two additional hulls, coupled with the weight of Iwalani on his starboard side, and has a hard time steering us straight.

The big steel doors swing open, and we are thrown out into the Pacific like miscreants from a bar room brawl. Iwalani once again heads for the canal side at a tremendous speed, this time bowsprit first. Our very first taste of the Pacific, and I see that in just a few seconds it is going to come to an abrupt end. I run aft to escape the imminent crash, but Phil quickly puts Iwalani's throttle forward, then slams the tiller to starboard and with our rather large rudder assists Pacific Bliss in steering the flotilla back to center and out the lock doors unscathed.

We are in the Pacific! We disband the raft, wipe our brows, and make our way over to the Balboa Yacht Club.

*　　*　　*

We take many walks along the causeway that follows the canal ending at Flamenco Island. Part of the road is now closed off and is used for walking, jogging, bike riding, and is very safe, clean and a nice place to stretch one's legs. It was once part of the U.S. military base. The United States left a lot of pretty nice property in Balboa, most of which has been turned into colleges, universities, or police academies. When the walkway along the canal was built, curved walled patios were put in under big Panamanian trees. Designed with thick heavy turned balusters and massive railings, the European design looks as if it should be decorating mansions in Vienna, not a military base. With nice benches facing the setting sun, overlooking the canal and volcanic islands to the west, it is all rather romantic.

I have known a few men who have left their wives for Panamanian women. It is easy to see why this happens. The women are quite pretty and dress in provocative short tight skirts and high heels. They pay little attention to Women's Lib. Why bother? With a wink and a crook of the finger they can get a man to do anything for them. They rarely garden, hardly ever row a boat, change a tire, paint the house, rewire a lamp, or build a boat.

With the exception of the Kuna Indians who make beautiful hand sewn molas, which are fabric appliquéd cloths, the Panamanian woman's creativity goes into presenting herself. This became apparent to me in the ladies room at the airport, where we said goodbye to the boys and my Dad. I found myself at the end of a long line extending out the door. As I got closer to the front of the line, I realized we weren't waiting for the toilets but the mirrors in front of which beautiful women were tweaking their make-up to glistening perfection.

So what will become of the canal? It is in tough shape. A lot needs to be done with maintenance and construction. It is old, after all. The boats that go through are not huge; they are limited to less than a thousand feet in length and 110 feet in width. Most of the ships transiting are cruise ships, smallish containerships, car carriers, small oil tankers, grain ships, U.S. destroyers, or yachts.

The day after we transited the canal another yacht didn't fair as well as Iwalani. A tug, also in the lock, came loose and smashed into the yacht, somehow pushing the mast through the bottom of the sailboat. The yacht was sunk, and several on board were injured. When I hear the news, I realize luck is still following in our wake.

photo by John Wood

Nathaniel, feeling slightly better, and Stewart, the master of begging.

Chapter 6

Seaspicion, Sea Lions and Sea Queens

March 2001
Ecuador

We leave Balboa, Panama with very light winds and glassy calm seas, and motor to Las Perlas Islands, ten hours away. We pass a marlin as it swims along the surface, it's dorsal fin partially out of the water. He slowly waves his swordbill like a tired buccaneer. We circle around him, but he has no interest in attaching himself to the cheap lure we drag behind Iwalani. This fish is too well fed.

A little further we see an area in the water alive with white caps. Before we can turn the boat, the white caps start coming for us. This is no tiderip, but thousands of porpoise- swimming, leaping and flying through the air. One half of our ocean is churning and frothing like someone is stirring it with an invisible whisk. Just as quickly as they appear, the dolphins vanish over the opposite horizon.

We thread our way around the southernmost island through rock formations looking like the lower mandible and incisors of a huge dinosaur fossil. I am apprehensive about our course; it looks as if there are breaking waves in front off our bow. I glance behind and see four outboards loaded with men heading straight for us.

'Where the heck did they come from? They know we can't make it through these incisor rocks and are going to plunder our boat once it is wrecked,' I think to myself.

"Can you come up here for a moment?" I yell down to Phil.

"What's the problem?"

"I'm not sure we are heading in the right direction. Our course goes right through a bunch of weird rocks, and we have four outboards rapidly approaching from behind."

"What?" Phil comes up and looks behind us. "Where did they come from? I don't have a good feeling about this."

"Neither do I. Look at where we are heading," I say.

"No, you are right on course. That's the way through to the anchorage," he reassures me.

"Through breaking waves?"

"It only looks like breaking waves. It will be fine when we get there. I'm more worried about pirates. Las Perlas was known for its pirates in the past. All the early cruisers wrote about them," Phil says.

"You don't think we are being overly paranoid, ethnocentric, Americans?" I ask.

"Maybe, but I'd still like to know where they came from."

We both stand helpless in the cockpit as the outboards continue charging right for us and are now a half mile from our stern.

"Should I e-mail my parents before things get messy and we don't have a chance to send out a distress?"

"Good idea. Just write out the text and stand by. Don't push send until I tell you to. Then if I say 'now', push the little red button on the Inmarsat," Phil replies.

The little red button on the Inmarsat is a distress button for an emergency. The Inmarsat office in England would contact our families in the event of a disaster. It was a button I hoped I would never have to push. I remove the piece of tape Phil had plastered over it so it wouldn't get accidentally activated.

I type out a quick message to my parents telling them of our situation and if they got this email it is already too late, and we love everyone and are sorry they have to go through this. Through Iwalani's hull I can hear the outboards now only yards away.

Phil was adamant about not having a gun on board. He felt that a weapon only added to an already charged situation and brought a conflict to a higher level from which a successful outcome was doubtful. I, on the other hand, wanted a canon. At the very least, it would look nautical on the deck and would fit in with Iwalani's traditional style. It would make a good sound when fired at sunset and wouldn't raise as many red flags with foreign countries, or so I thought. I hold my breath. The outboards are now just a few feet from Iwalani's side. They do not cut back on the throttles. I exhale. They would have to slow down to board us.

"¡Hola seniores!" Phil waves smiling to them as they pass just inches away. "What does 'Vaya con dios' mean?" he yells down to me.

"Go with god," I say inhaling the gasoline fumes from the outboards. "Why?"

"It's the name of one of their boats. We are paranoid. But they don't need to be in our teaspoon of water."

"Where have I heard that one before?"

The passage through the dentate rocks turns out to be easier than flossing teeth. We round the corner and see a beautiful stretch of sandy beach with six other yachts at anchor, all nestling together like ducks in a pond.

"I don't think I've ever been so glad to see other cruisers."

"Me too. Usually my heart drops when I see we have to share an anchorage with other yachts, but not this time."

We anchor apart from the other yachts and keep an eye on the outboards anchored on the far side of the beach. The following morning all six cruising boats take off like a flock of starlings, leaving us at anchor alone, bobbing in their wake. The outboards disappeared sometime during the night. We launch the dinghy and row to shore completely alone. The swells are breaking on the beach and this is going to be my first experience getting a dinghy to shore through surf. With Phil coaching, I quickly spin the dinghy around just outside the line of breakers. We head into the beach stern first, leaving the bow to meet the oncoming waves. Our gear is wrapped in a waterproof kayak bag just in case of mishap. I row as fast as I can backwards and land the dinghy during one of the lulls.

We walk up a tiny fresh water stream wading through the water as far as we can until the brush becomes so thick we can't go any further. Even up this stream, far from civilization, we find trash: plastic bottles, shoes and flip-flops. It is depressing. Lots of little coconut palms are struggling to grow amid the rubbish. We return to the beach and find a sandy path that threads inland. Under the shade of overhanging palm trees, several green iguanas are busy laying eggs in the warm soil. They bolt before we get a good look. I have never seen reptiles move so fast. "What's up with that? Why are they so scared of us?" Phil wonders.

"Dinner," I tell him. "Iguanas are hunted for food around here."

On the edge of the path, some inconsiderate cruising boat has left their green trash bag full of cans and more plastic. Some of the bags have been torn open and trash is scattered over the sand and into the underbrush. "Nice," Phil says eyeing the mess.

"What do people think? The local trash union is going to come by and pick this up? What should we do with it?" I ask.

"Leave it. It's not our problem."

"But in away it is. Humans did this and as we are members of that unfortunate race, we are kind of responsible too."

"If you want to row back to the boat and get four large trash bags, then row back out through the surf, pick this all up, row back to Iwalani again through the surf, with four large trash bags trying to blow out of the dinghy, and then transport this stinking pile six hundred miles to the Galapagos, while it drips god knows what onto our decks, be my guest," Phil says.

"What about burning it?" I ask.

"Got any matches?"

"Ok then, burying it?"

"And your shovel?"

Turning my back on the trash, I walk inland behind my husband, trying to pretend it's not there.

March is still the dry season for the Panama region. The rainy season doesn't begin until late April. This time of year the tropical rainforest is very much like any other forest toward the end of its growing period: crackling brown leaves fallen on the ground, the buzz of bees and flies, hummingbirds foraging for nectar, a peregrine falcon or two flying overhead, herons along the dried trickling streambeds, boa constrictors sunning themselves on the side of the path. Stop. Rewind. Boa constrictors? It is our first introduction to tropical snakes, and the snake is more scared of us than we of him. He is well over four feet long, yet his coloring very nearly makes him invisible. We wonder how many other species we fail to notice because of their excellent camouflage.

*   *   *

For the next few days, Iwalani flies through the seas averaging over 140 miles a day. We expect to sail headfirst into the legendary Humboldt Current, the cold water that flows from Antarctica and should slow our progress, but the seas remain smooth and calm, our speed steady contrary to Herb's forecasts, increasing consternation, and fading broadcasts. Soon we hear nothing but static during the Herb-hour.

At seven a.m. I decide to listen in on the radio before the Pacific cruising nets come on the air. I have a hard time staying awake for the last hour of my watch, no matter what time of day it is. Flipping through the hundreds of frequencies on the single side band until a conversation in English comes in is an easy way to try and stay awake. Lurker radio, we call it, and it is our form of reality entertainment.

"We are heading for Salinas. Manta is just too full of fishing boats."

"I heard they are having some kind of fishing fleet convention. Salinas should be much better. They have shops near the marina and we won't have to worry about our outboard getting stolen. Solar Express had their outboard stolen in Manta."

I pull out the atlas to see where Manta Ecuador is. Not exactly on the way to the Galapagos, but not too far out of the way either. A side trip looks interesting.

"Have any of the other boats reached the Galapagos?"

"Break. Break. This is Checkers. We got here two days ago. We came to Santa Cruz because of the oil spill in Wreck Bay. It's very lovely here but totally corrupt. The port captain told us we had to pay the $100.00 park fee. I told him I would go to jail before paying anything of the sort. I told him yachts were exempt from the park fee. He took me in his office and looked it up in the regulation book. He was surprised and even more angry when he found out I was right."

When Phil gets up I tell him about the conversation I overheard. Despite not having any charts, he is up for a trip to Manta.

On our fourth night out, we pick up a couple of hitchhikers, a cormorant that spends his time at the end of the gaff swinging back and forth spraying cormorant poop about the foredeck, as well as a sooty noddy. The first time I saw the noddy, I was just getting off my midnight watch and was unclipping my harness. I looked up and saw a blackbird just inches away, sitting on the life sling. I let out an involuntary "Eek!" which sounded more like a dog barking than a freaked woman. It startled the noddy into flying off.

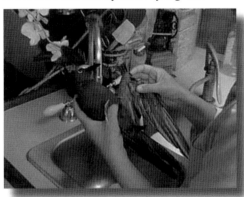

Sooty noddy with wing injury

At 4 a.m., the beginning of my watch, Phil says the noddy is on the bow pulpit and is puffed up and bleeding, it appears he can no longer fly. We catch him and sure enough, he has scraped the equivalent of his wrist, but has no fractures that I can palpate. I bandage his wing, grind up some sardines in the food processor, add water and antibiotics and tube feed him. I feel guilty that I startled him in the middle of the night. He probably injured himself trying to land back on the boat in the dark.

At daylight I try to catch fresh fish for him. I put out one hundred feet of four hundred pound test line with a brand new Panamanian pink feather lure and hook. Some fellow cruisers told me, when a fish strikes, drag it through the water until it drowns, thus, no bludgeoning is needed. Just minutes after I put our new rig out, a school of mahi-mahi come swimming through the water. They leap into the air with such fluid motion, bright yellow, turquoise and cobalt blue colors shimmering in the sunlight around Iwalani as they briefly remain suspended in the air like a child's mobile. They head straight for the lure. One grabs on, and I leave him to drown.

A half hour later I yell down to Phil (who is trying to take a nap), "This isn't going to work! We aren't going fast enough. I'm turning on the engine."

"Why?" Phil yells up to me sounding tired and exasperated.

"He's just swimming behind us in big swooping arcs."

"Who?"

"Gee whiz, an Ecuadorian long distance swimmer," I say sarcastically.

I turn on the engine adding two more knots to Iwalani's speed. We are now dragging the fish at seven knots through the water. He bounces behind the boat like a flattened water skier on top of the waves.

An hour later I turn off the engine. 'Surely he must be dead,' I think to myself. As the boat slows, I reel him in. Another mahi mahi swims along side the one on the lure. "They must be cannibals," I think to myself. "This gruesome scavenger is just waiting for this fish to die, as are we. Buzz off, this fish is mine."

His colors have lost some of their brilliance, but he is far from dead. He flips and flops, struggling to be released from the metal hook in his mouth. I let the line out and again turn the engine on. This time he swims off to the side, out of the prop wash like a dog following on his leash, the other fish at his side.

"This isn't working," I say calling down the companionway. Phil has given up on a nap and is now busy hand sewing an Ecuadorian flag. Stewart is at his side and looks up at me licking his lips.

"This is your fish," Phil says.

"Great. I've heard that one before."

I go down below and get the syringe and feeding tube I've been using on the noddy and fill the syringe up with 20 cc's of Mount Gay rum. I return to the deck and pull the fish up out of the water. He hangs by his mouth limply, tired of fighting, looking up at me with big fishy eyes begging for mercy. I aim the syringe to squirt in his gills when "plop," the hook lets go and he falls back into the sea. The other fish swims rapid circles around him. "Fine, you can have him," I say.

I feel sad, yet relieved. I was hoping for some food that didn't come out of a can. But more importantly, I wanted to put some fish mucous on the noddy's wing injury, to see if my thoughts are correct on the healing properties of mahi-mahi slime.

We seem so alone; any living creature becomes an ally, not an hors d'oeuvre. Mahi-mahi are like the living essence of the ocean, shaped like waves, and colored with every imaginable shade of blue and yellow. Killing and eating them seems so unnecessary while we are so well provisioned. Having the other fish act so frantically attentive is also a bit unnerving.

The next morning, at five a.m., we get ready to cross the equator and have our King Neptune celebration. The winds dropped off over the night and we are motoring. Phil turns the engine off while I wrap Stewart in gold ribbon and appoint him grand master of the ceremonies.

"I don't think I've ever had champagne at five a.m. before," I say putting the bottle to my lips.

"Don't get too used to it. Where did you find the bottle?"

I hand the bottle to Phil. "I almost forgot we had it. Someone brought it to Iwalani's launching. It's been in our bilge for almost a year."

"It's not bad. What else should we do at the King Neptune celebration?" Phil asks, putting his arm around my shoulders.

"You're asking me? You're the old salt. We could watch the GPS display switch from N to S."

"Sounds like about as much fun as watching an odometer flip over to one hundred thousand miles. I was having other things in mind. Hey—don't forget to share some of that with Neptune," Phil says as I take a large swig of champagne.

"You mean pour it over board?"

"Exactly. You'll piss him off if you don't, and then we'll never make it home." I pour some champagne into the sea. "I think you are supposed to be naked when you do that."

I look sideways at Phil, who already has his clothes off. "Yeah right," I respond.

"It's part of the ceremony."

"Whose ceremony?" I remove my clothes anyway and pour more champagne into the sea. A few dolphins join the party, and the only sounds we hear are the soothing puff-puff of their exhalation as we cross the magic line separating north from south.

*   *   *

We sail toward Manta, close hauled, with a rising southwest breeze. When land is sighted, the noddy takes off shakily from the railing perch and lands in the water twenty feet from the boat. He looks up at me then plunges his head under water. He is dead within seconds.

Lurker radio wasn't exaggerating. There are over five hundred fishing boats anchored and tied in long sinuous rafts. The poor fisherman tied up at the end of the raft has to cross over at least fifty other boats to get to his own. All of the boats are wood and are painted in bright colors. Every one of them with a bit of "Manta blue," a color in between turquoise and cerulean blue, painted somewhere on the hull or cabin top for good luck. The Ecuadorians work on their boats with chainsaws and sledgehammers. This is Phil's kind of boat building, no fancy trim or bright woodwork.

Once anchored, we take the dinghy out for a sail, maneuvering around the fishing boats in the harbor. It is just as entertaining for the people and pets on the fishing boats, watching two gringos in a ten foot dinghy, as it is for us, dodging and avoiding entanglement in the web-like weavings of lines and moorings holding this floating city together.

Communication between fishermen is accomplished by signaling with a shrill whistle, involving teeth, lips and tongue. The sound produced would make any New Yorker envious for hailing a cab from the far side of town. The Ecuadorians whistle at us and wave, as we sail the "Grape" down the winding channels separating the boats like suburban streets.

On Monday we head off to get checked in. It is a bit disconcerting walking out of the marina gates nodding at the sentry guards wearing bulletproof vests and armed with machine guns. Yet, on our walk to the city to get checked in, no one accosts us. There is quite a bit of poverty, a lot of trash, problems with sewage, one or two dead dogs decaying on the sidewalk, but the people, overall, seem happy and content.

As we walk over a bridge I hear girlish laughter coming out of a window to our right. Inside a roomful of girls are all giggling and pointing at us. Lying in the center of the room on top of a table is a young woman with both buttocks high in the air waiting to get a tattoo.

"And they think we are amusing?" Phil comments as we walk by.

We finally make it to the immigration office located in the downtown police department. Inside the square courtyard, the police are preparing for an award ceremony. The band pipes up, and most of the Manta police force wanders around with uniforms pressed, shoes, gloves and hats clean and polished. We are ushered into an upstairs room overlooking the courtyard. A large man with lots of gold epaulets is seated behind a desk devoid of any papers. He asks us questions in rapid Spanish, which I cannot understand despite taking four years of high school and college Spanish. Based on the man's body language and anticipation of what he would be asking us, Phil, with little Spanish under his belt, does a far better job interpreting what he is asking. Questions and answers sometimes have to be repeated three or four times before an understanding is reached.

"Trabaje?'

"Yo soy una veterinaria," I tell him thumping my chest with pride. 'El hace barcos," I say pointing to Phil.

The port Captain shakes his head. "Trabaje?"

Again. I repeat what I had said the first time. We have reached a definite barrier. He just doesn't understand what I am trying to say, and I am not entirely sure I understand what he is asking. He gives up and writes something on the line of his form, then reaches into a cabinet and brings out a miniature version of a coat rack, from which a dozen wooden stamps are suspended. He brings a rusty stamp pad out of the drawer. Carefully eyeing each stamp, he selects one from the tree, pounds it into the inkpad, then pummels the stamp onto our paperwork.

A good-looking fellow bursts in carrying thirteen British passports. He is the agent for Lord Portal, a British training vessel that had arrived a few hours before us. He speaks some English and helps get us through the last of the paperwork. Once we pay thirty dollars for the entrance and exit fees, we get our passports back. On the line for "occupacion" they have written "jubilado" for me and "marinara" for Phil. These both sound like Italian foods to me, and I am not entirely sure of their meaning, though I think I am supposed to be retired and Phil is a marine worker of sorts, so I tell them again I am "Un medico para los animals."

"Oh si" the man at the desk says, "una veterinaria!"

Ay caramba! What did they think I was telling them before? Ordinarily, this wouldn't have been important to me, but I was hoping that when we got to the Galapagos I would be able to volunteer my services treating any animals suffering from the oil spill we had heard about on lurker radio. It would make things easier if they thought I was still an active veterinarian and not a "jubilado."

Our route back to the boat goes through an open-air market selling lots of fruit and vegetables, unidentifiable meat, and live chickens. We come to a booth where lots of children are crowded around a tiny little green parrot, a species I don't recognize. The children are trying to hold the bird. He refuses and is biting them right and left. I can't resist. Using my best bird voice, I coax the little bird onto my finger where he won't get off. The owner tries her best to sell him to me, but I am vehemently opposed to owning birds that aren't captive bred. He sure is cute though. We stop at the bank to get change for our American money. It is the last day for Ecuadorian money as they make the switch over to American currency. The entire country will not know the difference between Minnesota or Missouri but will be jingling the U.S. millennium quarters in their pockets, as they lose a bit of their own identity in the process of stabilizing their economy.

We stock up on plenty of Dawn dishwashing liquid, which is one of very few soaps that suds up in salt water. (Dawn is also very good for cleaning oil soaked birds as well as oil spills on sailboat decks.) Our next mission is to try and get an "exit zarpe," as it is called, for the Galapagos, even though the island archipelago is still part of Ecuador. In years passed, most yachts bypassed the Galapagos rather than deal with the paperwork needed for entry. The present administration governing the Galapagos loosened up the requirements considerably for arriving yachts. Since we are technically in Ecuador heading for another port in Ecuador, we decide to leave rather than to wait for the port captain to return from vacation.

We leave Manta and motor west toward the Galapagos, traveling in a narrow band just south of the equator. One of the advantages of traveling in between the five degrees above or below the equator is that there are no cyclones or hurricanes in this region. A disadvantage is the I.T.C.Z., or intra tropical convergence zone, a band of squally weather that travels just above or below the equator depending on the time of year. Another disadvantage is the lack of trade winds. If you are not in squalls, you often have no wind at all—the typical doldrums scenario, and the situation we were now faced with.

I sit in the cockpit with one of the electric fans blowing on me. Despite motoring through perfectly flat seas at about four knots, we aren't even generating enough head wind to blow out a candle. Stewart's preferred method for staying cool down below is to lie on the floorboards with all four legs in the air enjoying a small breeze which is funneled through the boat by the forward hatch and a canvas wind scoop.

Ecuador has some of the least expensive diesel fuel of anywhere in the world, which we are now taking full advantage of. With the engine running non-stop, we are making too much electricity. We run the refrigeration system and make plenty of ice. I make yogurt by boiling UHT milk and letting it cool, adding a tablespoon of old yogurt and then letting this sit in the hot engine room for twenty-four hours. At noontime we make fruit smoothies in the blender with canned or fresh fruit, ice, sugar and home made yogurt. Everything on Iwalani is working. Phil has little to repair. Life couldn't be better, and yet, we are both homesick. We have not gotten any e-mail from Phil's sons for weeks. Both of us feel frustrated and are blaming it on a lack of mental stimulation.

"I can't stand it! I think I am going to throw up. You've got to listen to this," Phil moans. It is 8 p.m. and he has just started the dishes. The banging and clanging of pots usually herald the start of my eight to midnight watch. He and Stewart are listening to two American women on lurker radio. I stagger aft wiping sleep from my eyes while trying to wake up. I grab Stewart and hold him on my lap.

"Have you swum in the deep blue sea yet?"

"Yes! Isn't it fantastic! We have no wind, and we both just swam around the boat."

"I could sail on forever. There are so many stars in the sky. It looks like a giant nonpareil. I feel like I could grab hold and eat each one."

"Yes, and the reflection of the stars in the water is fantastic. It is just so

peaceful."

I pick the sleep snots from the corner of my eyes. "Are we missing something out here?" I ask Phil. "After reading all the books about cruisers and passage making, I was kind of looking forward to this transcendental experience, but it isn't doing anything for me." I put Stewart down on the settee and climb up the companionway. Phil shuts off the radio and follows me up.

"Are you heading up to eat some nonpareil stars?" he asks.

"Yeah, right. "

"Do you know where we are right now?"

"One day from the Galapagos." I look around at the blackness peppered with flaming stars. The drone of the engine is the only sound for thousands of miles. "Well, it looks just like the rest of the ocean to me."

"That's what I mean. Our world is just three miles in any direction of blue, black and white, or any shades of the three. The depths lose their significance. Distance, too, is irrelevant; we could be in twenty feet of water or twenty thousand feet of water. We could be six miles from land or six thousand miles," Phil says.

"It's just like driving your car down a really boring highway, only there are no stops. Time is the only thing that matters," I say.

"I can't wait to get to the Galapagos so we can sleep together."

"Ugh! No offence, but Phil-the-furnace and this heat?" I stand up and look around. "Hey what's that over there?" I ask.

"Over where?"

"It looks like a glowing flare."

"Better go over and take a look," Phil says. " It is so calm out here, it is showing up weakly on radar. Whatever it is, it's almost a mile away." We motor over to the glowing flame like desperate moths.

"It's not a flare. It's a candle on a board," Phil says as he passes me the binoculars. "It probably marks someone's fishing gear. There must be fishermen out here. I'm going to bed. Don't run them over."

It is amazing that such a fragile beacon can be used in these waters to mark fishing gear. I stay out in the cockpit and watch the flame from the candle slowly get extinguished by the darkness of the night.

*   *   *

The following day we arrive at Wreck Bay, San Cristobal, the oldest island in the chain, the second largest town in the Galapagos and the closest island to mainland Ecuador. As such, it has far more vegetation than tourist photos of the Galapagos typically show. Trees and bushes carpet the extinct volcanoes all the way to the mist shrouded peaks. Seeds of vegetation arrive from the mainland via currents, bird feces or more recently, tucked into the tiny treads of tourist shoes. Raspberries are a recent introduction to the islands, and the park officials consider them a blight and are countering the scourge armed with machetes, herbicides and fire. They are not winning the battle.

White sandy beaches and turquoise blue water surround the small harbor in front of the town. The buildings are typically modern Ecuadorian: two story cubist style stucco, with square windows and some scattered arch forms. Mosaic tiles, depicting primitive pictures of sea lions and killer whales are used as a decorative element on some of the buildings. The roads are covered with cement paving stones. Small shops line the roadway, each small store roughly ten feet by five feet, loaded with anything from fishing lures to canned corn–Maria's Tienda, Padre's Tienda, only the owner's name differentiates one from the other. From the back of the stores, behind a lifeless cotton curtain, ubiquitous salsa music gurgles forth in tinny effusiveness.

The Galapagos are the biological equivalent of Mecca for anyone possessing a science background. Here Darwin sailed on the Beagle and noticed subtle variations within species, a phenomenon also noticed by Wallace in Indonesia, and anyone really who would have had enough leisure time and money to just sit and observe nature, without having to worry about feeding a family or being tied to a nine-to-five career. We, too, can detect subtle variations in the sounds that the ubiquitous mynah birds are singing. From Jamaica, to Panama, to Ecuador, an entire species has the bird equivalent of a regional accent.

What Darwin noticed were subtle variations in sizes of beaks and, with the tortoises, in the shapes of their shells. He reasoned that isolation led to these variations. Separated by just enough distance to prevent interbreeding, each island species had only its inhabitants to use as a gene pool. Minor genetic mutations over the millennia led to permanent changes in outward appearances. If a mutation provided a benefit, that animal carrying the genetic modification survived.

The Ecuadorians keep the islands pristine clean; there is no trash floating in the water or heaped up into rotting piles on land. Most of the land in the Galapagos has been turned into a national park. To the eastern side of Wreck Bay a very nice modern Interpretive Center has been built to detail the history of the Galapagos and some of the ecology. Only on the reef can we see any evidence of the recent oil spill. The wrecked ship lies on the reef, belly up, bleeding rust colored liquid into the sea.

Sea lions spread out jelly-like on the beach, on the rocks, and on the bows of small skiffs. Some swim in the water, chasing the big fish that feed on the small fry shimmering in a kaleidoscope of colors under the boats at anchor. Children swim off the rocks, off the docks, off the beaches. Sea lions watch the children with curiosity a few feet away, appearing to be jealous of the children's movements on land, as they kick soccer balls back and forth to one another, but the sea lions are quick to demonstrate their superiority in the breaking waves when they chase the errant ball that slips past a human foot.

There are a few abandoned catamarans and monohulls anchored in the harbor. The sea lions have taken over these broken dreams for their own residence. They climb up the swim platforms or steps on the transom of catamarans and reside mostly in the cockpit. On some of the boats the sea lions have managed to make their way down below. It is a bit unnerving to wave at a head looking out the companionway of an anchored yacht, only to realize that the returned salute comes from a flipper.

In fact, the sea lions have even adopted the human practice of sundowners in the cockpit. Sea lions will gather together on an abandoned boat and party in the cockpit while watching the sunset. The only real difference in a yacht "manned" by sea lions is the pungent aroma wafting from the vessel and their somewhat lackadaisical interpretation of the nautical expression "Shipshape and Bristol

Fashion."

Sea lions, like their external-earless cousins, the seals, are members of the pinniped family. They are believed to be canine-like creatures that returned to the sea. All pinnipeds are prone to the same diseases that our canine companions get: heartworm, distemper and parvovirus. Our arrival coincided with an outbreak of canine distemper. Most of the dogs on the islands had succumbed to the infection and in many places carcasses were rotting in the sun. I start to realize the dead dogs all over the sidewalks in Manta were probably similarly affected and might have served as the source for this infection.

Over the next few days we swim and snorkel with sea lions, hike through the hills of San Cristobal, and take an official tour on park land to a fresh water-filled crater on top of an extinct volcano. This is the only source of fresh water for the dry volcanic island. February and March is also the time of year for the male frigate bird's characteristic breeding display, the bright red gular pouch on their necks, which gets inflated to the size of a soccer ball. We don't see any frigate birds on the ground but watch as they fly around, the gular pouch deflated and flopping in the breeze like the other typical male appendage. Frigate birds also have poor preen glands, so lack the waterproofing characteristics of other ocean going birds; as a result they cannot land on the water. To obtain food, they are masters at bullying a recent catch from another bird or scooping fish or squid from the ocean surface. They are truly amazing fliers, having the lowest weight to wing span ratio of any bird species. Several males at the height of their sexual attractiveness fly around the crater with their flopping bright red pouch visible, a red hot, valentine turn-on for females of their species. Young birds practice their retrieval of foods on the surface of the water, while the elders eye one another. The males try their best to display their swinging scarlet appendage to best advantage. Sometimes there just isn't much to distinguish us from the "animal" world.

One afternoon while seated at a restaurant and swatting flies for entertainment, Phil asks me how I am coming with the log for the web page.

"I'm almost done, but I am hung up on anthropomorphism," I reply.

"Oh, god. Don't go off on tangents. Just write the facts," Phil states.

"But it's part of being here. Remember that sea lion that was swimming around the boat last night making all the racket like it was looking for someone?" I ask.

"How could you miss it? He kept the entire harbor awake."

"But that's just it. I don't think it was a he. It sounded like a she, and I think she was looking for a lost child," I say.

"I'll admit there was that level of anxiety associated with the cries. So what's anthropo-whatever?" Phil asks.

"Anthropomorphism. As a scientist I was trained to be unbiased. Anytime you ascribe human traits to something non human it's being anthropomorphic."

"Ah," Phil chuckles. "With your tendency to give human names to everything in your life, including computers, cameras, cars, I can go on and on. You must be the queen of that."

"No kidding. I had serious trouble in college with it. But, after being here, I think the word itself needs to go to another level. To think humans alone have human traits is obsolete and in itself-anthropocentic."

"And your point?"

"I think evolution encompasses everything—not just beak size, or outward characteristics, but emotions, feelings, desires, fears, greed, love, revenge, hatred, remorse, appreciation of beauty, the whole gamut of what people typically think are only human traits. I think they evolved through other species, perhaps reaching a pinnacle in us. But, we share all these traits with animals. Humans didn't corner the market on them, and it's wrong to think we are above animals supposedly because we have these things and they don't," I say tapping my straw in time to the background music. "What's left for entertainment in Wreck Bay?"

"You have but one choice left—a photo-op with Pepe, the world's oldest tortoise."

"No, thanks," I reply. "I want to find the radio station."

"The what?"

"The radio station. I like this song and I want to find out who sings it."

We pay our bill and head up to the only spire that looks remotely like a radio tower. As we get closer, the salsa gets louder.

"I think we are heading to the right spot," I say to Phil. I pass through a stucco archway in the building and follow the music upstairs. "Aren't you coming?"

"No thanks. This is one Amy tour I'll wait out."

A disc jockey stands behind a desk rummaging through CD's lining shelves. When he sees me he inserts another CD into the player and removes his headphones. He asks in rapid Spanish if he can help me. I begin my faltering Spanish and he shakes his head and leads me into the station manager's office.

"Hello" the man behind the desk says to me.

"Hello," I answer back. "I was hoping you could tell me who sings the song they just played on the radio, something like 'buella buella'."

The man continues to smile, and the corners of his mustache begin to twitch. He opens up his drawer and pulls out a piece of paper and pencil. Then pushes them across his desk toward me. "Please," he says.

I write the question down.

"Ah," he nods, then writes back. "Vuella, Vuella- Magneto."

"Bueno." I reply. "Me gusto mucho."

He retrieves the piece of paper and writes, "Where are you from?"

I read the words in English out loud and then write back in Spanish, "Soy Americana. Nosotros hacer un barco de vuela para voler el mundo."

He makes many corrections on my piece of paper, then writes, "How many years take you?"

I correct his English and answer again in Spanish. Soon we have run out of room on the piece of paper and start working on a new sheet. I tell him about our trip while he writes about his three years living in the Galapagos; then I remember Phil still standing outside in the hot sun. "Mi esposo es," and I point outside.

"Me, too." he scribbles, winking. He shakes his head sadly and smiles up at me. I shake his hand and thank him for the name Magneto, then head out to find Phil who is by this time leaning up against the wall in the shade.

"What took you so long?" he asks.

"I met a very nice man. He has taught himself English from reading old *Time* magazines. He can only read and write it though. He's a little twitchy on the pronunciation, but he knows English better than I know Spanish."

"I thought you were abducted. So who sings the song?"

Just then "Vuella,Vuella" begins to play loudly from the upstairs windows and from all the houses, shops and restaurants in town. I realize the station manager had told the DJ to say something over the airwaves to get everyone in town to crank it up for the American sailors!

*   *   *

We decide to sail overnight to Santa Cruz, the next island to the west. This is the most populated of the Galapagos Islands and the home base for the Darwin Research Center. I am confounded about the lack of quarantine and hope to find out about the distemper outbreak, thinking that either a yacht or a mainland cargo ship has carried the virus to the island.

Porto Ayoro, Santa Cruz, serves as the main base of tourist operations for the Galapagos. Its tourist traps, internet cafés, shops, and small hotels cater to thousands of visitors each year. Almost a hundred yachts crowd the small harbor. All are white fiberglass with a blue stripe and blue sail covers. Because of the crowded conditions, everyone is anchored fore and aft with bow and stern anchors.

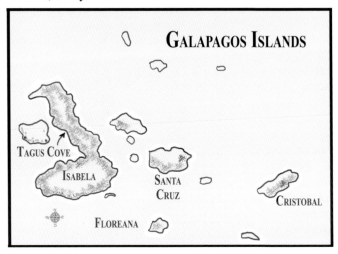

As soon as we are anchored, we are invited to dinner on board our first yacht since eating on Carol and John's schooner back in Jamaica. Medusa is a fast American J boat, built for speed, not looks.

Jason and Lisa had sailed from California via the Cocos Islands. Phil and I have been toying with the idea of returning back to Panama via this island group, and we are curious for more information. The Cocos Islands are known to have some spectacular diving.

After trailing our dinghy off their stern we climb on board Medusa.

"How do you like the Galapagos so far?" Phil asks our hosts.

"Incredibly corrupt," Lisa answers. "We've solved the problem of the fumigation certificate though." I look quizzically at her. "Sure. I made our own certificates on the computer and printed them out. Want to see?"

I follow her down below and marvel at the lack of personal effects in their boat. No pictures, plants, photos, caged animals, charts, books, shells—absolutely nothing in sight. Medusa is a racing boat first, cruising boat second.

"Wow!" I exclaim looking around me. "This boat looks just like it came out of the factory. How long have you been living on it?" I ask with envy.

"Two years. Jason can't stand clutter. I can't stand dirt. I spent all morning cleaning the head with a toothbrush, and then the valves got clogged in the toilet. Jason had to disassemble it. I had to clean the whole bathroom all over again." She reaches into a locker and pulls out a small notebook marked "ships papers", opens it and hands me a sheet with an official looking seal and paragraph written in Spanish detailing the date, time and place of fumigation.

"That's pretty good Spanish," I say somewhat incredulous. "You really made this?"

"Yup. I saved us twenty-five dollars. It really bothers me to pay for something that doesn't get done, and only lines someone's already corrupt pockets."

"That's not true," another yachtie chimes in while poking his head down the companionway. "The fumigators came on board my boat. A man squirted something from a home made spray bottle under the sink."

"That's only because you look like you need fumigating! That's Bill." Lisa says pointing to the man leaning into the companionway. "He's an ex-cop, now single-hander."

"Well we all can't live as sterile as you and Jason. Christ, Lisa, an ant would starve on this boat," Bill jokes back.

"If we carry a lot of stuff, it adds weight and just slows us down."

"Well, someday you might need to eat," Bill says eyeing a package of hot dog rolls.

"What's the matter, Bill? You hungry? Would you all like a hot dog?"

"Sure, sounds great. I could have had a cold cat last night. I had a cat climb up my ladder in the middle of the night," Bill goes on. "You know that boat Roger Henry? Fellow that froze himself into the arctic then wrote a book about it? His cat fell over board. She nearly drowned. I heard her scratching around trying to get up my swim platform. I rescued her and returned her this morning. It can get real lonely at times at sea, I thought about keeping her for myself."

"That would be Halifax." I say. "I've been anxious to meet her."

"Well, I am sure they will want to know there is a vet around," Lisa says.

Once word gets out that there is veterinarian in the harbor, I am back at work again. We spend the next few days touring the islands, repairing boat parts, working on the web page, and removing various growths and tumors on pets, which I package up and send off to a pathologist in the U.S. for analysis. I meet with the director of the Darwin Research station and volunteer my services.

We get invited over to Roger Henry to meet the cat that accompanied her human through an arctic winter. Alvah and Diana Simon were worried that Halifax had aspirated seawater the night she had spent frantically swimming around the harbor.

"Are you sure she sounds alright?" Diana asks me as I remove the stethoscope from my ears.

"She's fine. She'll outlive us all." I scratch Halifax under the chin.

"I don't know what we would do without her, " Alvah says from behind his rather large nav station, where he sits in the bright sunlight with his tanned legs resting on top of a chart. I can tell Phil is starting to get nav station envy. In Iwalani we have room for one chart to be laid out flat, twice as much room as most cruising boats, but "Roger Henry" has enough room for three full sized charts to be laid out. "She is quite a cat. If it were not for her, I would have gone completely insane in the arctic."

"I know what you mean," Phil chimes in. "We feel the same way about our cat Stewart."

"Do you suppose there is any way to stop her from trying to get off the boat?" Alvah asks. "We can't leave her alone. If we are on shore she feels she should to be with us. She has jumped off the boat many times to try and be with us on shore."

"Well you can try operant conditioning," I suggest. I can feel Halifax bristle at the thought. "Reward her for positive behavior and use negative reinforcement for bad behavior."

"Like how?"

"Well, for instance, if she jumps into the skiff as you are leaving, that would be unacceptable behavior, so you would need to squirt her with a water bottle, blow a fog horn or do something equally unpleasant. When she is lying on the boat sleeping, not anxiously scrambling to get off, then you would reward her with a pat, a treat, or some other type of positive reinforcement. It's all a matter of the people taking charge and training the cat, not vice versa."

Alvah and Diana look at one another for a long time not saying a word. I can see the unspoken exchange going between them, *"This woman must be completely mad."*

"Well it's just a suggestion, but it does work," I remark. "Besides you really must be careful about not letting her get to shore here."

I tell them about the distemper outbreak. "Not that she can get canine distemper, it just shows a rather lax attitude about disease here. There are probably plenty of cat diseases she could get on shore," I add, "not to mention the potential diseases she could bring to shore."

"It is rather amazing really that things are so incredibly corrupt in such a fragile pristine place on the planet," Alvah says.

"No more corrupt really than what we yachties are doing to get around the system." I tell them of the fake fumigation certificates circulating amongst some of the yachts.

"There are just too many dotcom yachts out here," Alvah says shaking his head. "Everyone has extra money, so they all bought a boat. What with GPS, anyone can sail around the world. It's no longer the risky venture it used to be."

I look at Phil uncomfortably. We, too, are dotcom profiteers. Most of the money we are using to finance our trip and to build Iwalani came from investments in dotcom stocks which I had sold off the winter before we left.

"Did you go to Wreck Bay?" Alvah asks.

"Yes," we answer simultaneously.

"The ship that ran aground there was carrying bunker fuel," Alvah explains, while adjusting the reading glasses on his nose, "supposedly illegal for this archipelago. The ship belonged to one of the officers in the Ecuadorian navy. He just got a slap on the wrist; no fines, no disciplinary action was taken whatsoever.

And yet, as close to a true disaster as this could possibly be, there is not one ounce of oil spill clean up equipment out here, no oil absorbing booms, nothing. Even paper towels are hard to find. The only thing which prevented a true environmental disaster was cooperative weather."

"I am a little upset at the lack of quarantine laws, too," I say. "Not that we would take our cat to shore, anyway, but it seems a free-for-all, with Ecuadorian dogs on freighters and pets on yachts coming and going. It's not like New Zealand and Australia from what I understand."

Despite Diana's ethereal Nordic looks, she is originally from New Zealand, which is where they are heading. "Where are you going from here?" she asks us.

"We are staying here for a few weeks while Amy helps the Darwin research scientists collect blood samples from the sea lions. They are trying to see what effect the distemper outbreak has had on them," Phil answers. "After that we haven't decided."

"We are thinking about going home. Phil misses his kids and I miss work," I add.

"We'll be here, too, for a few weeks, while Alvah does research for an article. But you really should keep on. You've gotten this far," Diana urges.

"Yes, but heading west from here is like jumping off a cliff; you can't turn around and go back," Phil says.

"Yes, that's true. But you really should join the rest of us lemmings. You will regret it if you don't complete a circumnavigation at least," Alvah says.

"We'll see. Have you got everything you need to get Halifax cleared for New Zealand? Microchip, rabies titer, vaccinations? We have everything on Iwalani to help you get her cleared for New Zealand and can help if you want," I offer.

"No that's ok," Alvah responds. "We don't want to bother you. We'll just get it all done in Papeete."

"It's no bother really," I admit. " If you change your minds you know where to find us. Just remember, training Halifax not to get in your inflatable is going to require some discipline on your own parts first."

The following morning, as I am hanging dishtowels on the lifelines to dry, an inflatable passes along our port side. It is Alvah and Diana wearing hats and dark glasses protecting them from the intense Equatorial sun. They wave a bit sheepishly at me as they get close. Sitting on the middle thwart of the dinghy in all her glory, is Miss Halifax, the queen calico of the northern seas. I can swear she winks at me as they motor by.

I go down below to pour myself another cup of coffee. Phil and Stewart are sitting at the table working on the computer. "Who was that?" Phil asks.

"Alvah, Diana and you-know-who, in the dinghy."

"Boy, they sure took your advice," Phil jokes while hiding something under a pillow.

"What are you two up to?" I ask suspiciously.

"Us? Nothing."

"Oh really? What was that you just hid under the pillow?"

"Um, well," Phil pulls out a can of potato chips.

"Potato chips? At this hour? You're not feeding them to Stew are you?"

"He likes them."

"Maybe so, but they aren't good for him, or you for that matter."

"Here take them. Put them away. I'm through with them anyhow."

I take the can and start to put it up in the catchall basket we have hanging over the sink. Stewart jumps off the settee following the can. He looks up at me and meows for just one more chip.

"Ok, fine. But, don't think you can look at me with those big green eyes and get another," I open the can and give him half a chip, which he greedily devours, then looks up at me for more. "Fine, here's the other half," I relent.

"What were you telling Alvah and Diana about taking control of their cat?" Phil teases. "It's pretty obvious who's in control on this boat."

Only Admirals, Assholes and Kitty Kings can hang out in the companionway!

Chapter 7

Ghosts, Grumps and becoming a Lemming

March 2001,
Galapagos

The following day the wind blows twenty knots from the east.

"This would be a good time to explore Floreanna," Phil suggests.

Floreanna, or Santa Maria Island, lies forty miles south of Santa Cruz. Nomenclature in the Galapagos has been controversial for several hundred years. Each nation frequenting the archipelago during the whaling days gave the islands different names.

"The first thing we will need to do is raise the stern anchor," Phil says as Iwalani lurches up and down from the swell pouring directly into the harbor. "I'll give the bow anchor more slack, so we can drift down on top of it." We use the backstay winch and start to slowly haul the Fortress anchor up.

"My god," I say to Phil as I wipe the sweat from my forehead. "Why is it going so hard?" The anchor line is straight up and down, and Iwalani is slightly healed over as both of us strain on the winch.

"Stop. Something is wrong. We should never have to use this much force. It must be caught on something," Phil says.

"OK. I'll go get my bathing suit on." We have an understanding between us. Phil has an underwater phobia, and I have a fear of heights. As a result I go down and Phil goes up.

I dive into the creamy turquoise water, painfully aware that none of boats anchored in the harbor are using their holding tanks. Fortunately the wind is bringing in fresh ocean water, which is also doing its part in stirring up the sandy bottom. After spitting into my mask and donning it, I yell to Phil, "How deep is it here?"

"Forty feet."

"I'll need my flippers then. They will get me faster to the bottom than going hand-over-hand down the anchor line." Phil throws the flippers into the water, and I grab them before they sink.

"You sure you feel OK with this?" Phil nervously asks down to me.

"Sure. Just don't ever ask me to go aloft."

I take several small breaths to clear my lungs, then dive underwater, using a powerful dolphin kick; I streamline my body, keeping both arms along my sides and one hand loosely holding onto the anchor rode near my thigh. Head first I dive down counting 'One one thousand, two one thousand...' as I go. I figure I travel three feet a second; I should be near the bottom after thirteen seconds. 'seven one thousand, eight one thousand...

BONK. I drive my head into the soft silty bottom. *'Boy, that was close. I could have broken my neck. I guess I am going faster than I thought.'*

I quickly follow the anchor rode around a rather large hard object. Groping, I try to figure what the rope is hung up on. The water is a murky turquoise blue with about a two-foot visibility. Five feet across and round. A wheel? It is a giant tractor wheel. I try to unwind the rope, but it is too taut. My lungs are beginning to pulse with the urgent desire to breath in. I shoot up from the bottom like a cork from a champagne bottle, my lungs and larynx spasming and making strange oinking sounds. Gulping huge amounts of air at the surface, I see Phil pale with fear, leaning far over Iwalani's side.

"Jesus, Honey, you scared the shit out of me. I thought for sure you were caught on something underwater. You were gone an awfully long time."

"We are caught on a giant tractor wheel," I finally yell up to Phil. "We should be able to motor ourselves free. We have enough room to the west to motor Iwalani around the tractor tire. She should be able to free herself if we just point her in the right directions."

I come back on board and draw a sketch of the configuration of rope and tractor wheel relative to Iwalani. Phil lets out more slack on the bow anchor and motors Iwalani around in the necessary directions. After a few minutes we free the stern anchor and get it neatly stowed.

I am already at the windlass button for the bow anchor as Phil powers ahead. *'This sure beats the good old days,'* I think to myself. My own boat, Petrel, has a manual windlass which is so back-breakingly slow that we invariably just give in and haul up the anchor hand-over-hand. Iwalani's windlass is electric and powerful enough to haul a pair of hundred pound anchors and six hundred feet of chain simultaneously. I stand at the bow with my foot on the button and one hand on the salt-water washdown hose, rinsing the anchor chain as it comes up. I am painfully aware that of the hundred or so yachts at anchor in the harbor, at least fifty eyeballs are pointed in my direction, as most cruisers are on deck drinking coffee at that hour. I try sucking in my fat rolls, wishing I were wearing something besides a wet bathing suit.

Finally the anchor hangs just inches above the water while I clean the silt from its flukes with the hose. I turn to place the hose down on the deck and have to make a grab for the lifeline instead. We are now heading into three-foot seas and it is a bit rough. I feel sorry for the poor tourists who are anchored out this far. And then I immediately curse myself for not securing the anchor quickly. The chain jumps out of the windlass gypsy, and all the chain and anchor head for the murky bottom.

"Stop," I yell to Phil. "The anchor has come un-stowed."

I watch in horror as all three hundred feet of uncontrollable chain shoot out of the hawsehole like a never-ending snake from a joke shop peanut butter jar. I am completely powerless to stop it.

"Great!" Phil yells back. "I'll have a hard time holding Iwalani in position with all this wind."

I have seen Phil wear clothes which a homeless person would pass by, splotched with cement, ripped knees, his hair sprouting out like a physics class demonstration on electrical charge, and a beard that looks like it had been gone over by a Mach 3 squirrel. Appearances mean absolutely nothing to him, with the exception of anchoring or docking a boat. Heaven help the person that cannot do this in a seamless and smooth fashion. Fortunately, with the powerful windlass I am able to get all the anchor chain back on board before I look like a complete moron. Still, I am loath to turn around and face my husband.

"Hey, don't worry about it," I hear him call from the cockpit. "It wasn't your fault and nothing bad came of it. Besides you've caught a fish."

"No, it's probably just another booby." I have almost given up on fishing. Our lure only attracts boobies, those well-named seabirds that continuously catapult out of the sky, hook onto the lure and have to be reeled in and unhooked before they drown. Sometimes the same bird will try it all over again.

"No, it's really a fish."

I hurry back to the aft end of the boat and haul in our first Pacific fish, a small bonito. My up-anchoring fiasco is soon forgotten.

The Galapagos have been called the "Enchanted Islands" for their ability to appear and disappear suddenly out of nowhere. In the time it takes me to clean the fish and wash down the decks we have lost sight of Santa Cruz.

A large pod of dolphins appear and swim alongside. They are larger than the species I have seen up to this point and each of them is decorated in fantastic spirals and circular patterns. It looks as if someone had taken a garden rake and tattooed Japanese designs on them.

"What do you suppose made those marks?" I ask Phil.

"Probably sharks."

I can't imagine how a shark could have gouged out a perfect circle, let alone some of the swirls, but it is the only feasible reason for such serrations. After the dolphins leave, clouds arrive and with them rain showers.

"Let's do the cruiser thing and take showers!" I yell to Phil.

I run below and come up with a bottle of dishwashing liquid. Phil has already lathered and rinsed himself by the time I get my bathing suit off.

"Better hurry up," he urges me, "These showers don't last forever."

"Tell me about it." I stand on the deck completely undressed and fully lathered. The rain has stopped.

"Now what do I do?" I run around the deck trying to catch the last few drops dripping from the boom. "Thank god for modern plumbing," I say to Phil as I head down below to rinse off in our shower.

When I come back on deck, I look up and there in front of us is Floreanna, full-sized, towering blue, not hidden by any haze or clouds. It has appeared as suddenly as Santa Cruz had disappeared.

We travel along the western shore and anchor off Black Beach. Several shark fins circle as I set the anchor. I silently pray that there are no hidden obstacles underwater to foul the anchor when it is time to leave. We have the whole place to ourselves, not another boat is in sight.

The sun sets and a full moon rises over the volcanic peaks far to the east. It seems so stark and desolate; just shades of gray as far as the eye can see.

Phil and I watch as a European looking woman suddenly appears on the beach wearing a sequined black cocktail dress which glitters in the fading light. With shoulder-length, light brown hair, she nervously paces back and forth along the shoreline, anxiously looking past us toward the sea and the setting sun. We wave to her, but she never waves back.

"Are you sure we are anchored in an OK spot?" I ask Phil.

"Take a look at the chart for yourself."

"That woman is making me nervous. She's acting peculiar. I feel like she is looking right through us."

"She's probably a tourist who has had a fight with her boyfriend."

"Maybe she is one of the Wittmers trying to get us to come in for a great feast on shore."

"No thanks, she seems too weird for me. I think I'll stay out here for saki and sushi."

Floreanna lacks both tortoises and unique animal species. It does possess a unique human history with a true story of twisted love triangles, hatred, jealousy and perhaps murder.

In the 1930's a German dentist named Ritter arrived on Floreanna with his girlfriend named Dore. Both were married to other people, but they wanted to escape society and find a simpler lifestyle. Ritter and Dore were devoted followers of the philosopher, Nietzsche, who believed that women were on this planet for the sole pleasure of the "warrior man." Ritter wrote about his "paradise Galapagos Island" for a German magazine and attracted the interests of another German family, the Wittmers.

The Wittmers arrived a few years later also seeking the simpler life. Then along came the "baroness," a German peroxide blonde (until her dye ran out), with her two male lovers, Lorenz and Philipson, in tow. Upon arriving, the baroness announced she was in charge of the island. Wearing jodhpurs, riding boots and sporting a whip (with a pistol in her belt for back-up) she believed everyone must bow to her needs. She was going to open a hotel for millionaires. A more polar opposite to Ritter or even the Wittmers could not be found anywhere. Needless to say, much tension arose, with the end result being a tangled web of disappearances, poisonings and differing stories.

The first lover, Lorenz, began to hate the baroness and Philipson and was worried that they were plotting to kill him. The baroness told Margaret Wittmer that a ship had arrived, and she was leaving the island with her second lover, Philipson. They were never seen again. When questioned later, Dr. Ritter said there had been no ships, as his house afforded a view of the beach. Lorenz, decided to sell off the contents of the baroness's house to the Wittmers and the Ritters. The Wittmers were reluctant to buy anything, but the Ritters assured the Wittmers, that the baroness was "never coming back." The money from the sale allowed Lorenz to leave the island, but he was soon found dead on another island, along with the Norwegian fisherman who had taken him from Floreanna.

The alleged vegetarian dentist, Dr Ritter, died of botulism shortly thereafter, supposedly from contaminated meat, in a dish prepared by his girlfriend, Dore!

Yet despite this ancient tabloid history, the Wittmers lived on, eventually building a small hotel on the north side of Black Beach. We first read of this twisted tale in some of the books by circumnavigators from the 1930's who had visited this island and met the people first hand. Everyone has his or her own theories on what really happened, but the people who know the truth have long since died.

The next morning we easily find the port captain's office, as there are only thirty or so buildings on Floreanna, mostly small houses for Ecuadorians who have moved to the island in the last fifty years from the mainland. Tourism has not yet grabbed a foothold here like the rest of the archipelago, and its inhabitants scratch a living with small backyard farms or fishing. The port captain's office is colored the usual blue and white on the outside, with snapping flags civilizing the landscape and painted white stones marching military fashion, outlining the small yard.

We are ushered into the office by a young shirtless teenager, fresh off the volleyball court. A mixed breed dog sprawls on her side on the floor, hot and tired, obviously taking a break from the puppies she is still nursing. Chickens strut in, take a look at us, ruffle their feathers, and then march back outside into the bright sunshine. Soon the port captain strides in, a paunchy older man, wearing a wilted white uniform with gold epaulets. He seems a little confused or is, perhaps, new to the job. The shirtless teenager guides him through the paperwork and fees to be computed on the hand-held calculator. He is having trouble calculating ten percent of 42, the amount we have to pay based on Iwalani's length. The two of them, each manned with their own calculators, arrives at different amounts. Phil and I do our best to stay out of this higher math. Finally, Phil can't stand it any longer and passes our calculator over, which has a percentage key on it. The port captain's face lights up, and, after more button pushing, head scratching and pencil scribbling, the calculator is passed over to me, with the figure $13.20 displayed. Not wanting to argue or go through the math all over again, as I have mentally calculated a figure of $8.40 for the entrance and exit fees, I quietly pay up.

We head over to the Wittmer's pensione, a Bavarian-looking building overlooking Black Beach, where we introduce ourselves to Erica, Margaret Wittmer's granddaughter. She brings us fruit juice, fresh papaya and albums of yachts that have called upon the island since the fifties. We make our own entry in the most recent album and then decide to go on a walking tour.

"Where are we going?" Phil asks me as I head out the door ahead of him.

"I read in one of the books about the pirate caves that the Wittmers lived in when they first arrived. They sound sort of interesting."

"How are we going to find them?"

"There was a map in the book. I committed it to memory."

"Oh, great! Another Amy tour."

"Just a short one. It shouldn't take too long. When the Wittmers arrived, they carried all their worldly belongings from Black Beach up to the caves. They can't be too far."

We head out of town along a dusty track, the only road, in fact, and are joined by a black dog that looks to have had German shepherd somewhere in his ancestry.

Near town the soil is the color of rust and is soft and dusty. As we gradually climbed to higher elevations, the dusty track is soon replaced by coarser, darker, volcanic gravel.

"The dog wants to head up that path. It might actually be a short cut as it heads in the direction we want to go," I say to Phil.

"Fine with me. This gravel is getting in my shoes and is starting to act like sand paper."

"I thought as we got higher up it would get cooler. It's only getting hotter. It feels like a blast furnace," I pant.

"I hope you brought water in the backpack."

"Speaking of that, want to carry it for awhile?" I ask.

"Sure. How rude of me. Let me be donkey-boy. Maybe we should stop and have a little water break?"

We stop and I hand Phil the water bottle and the backpack.

"A pint of water? This is all we have? This won't last long in this heat."

"I know. At least I thought to bring it! Aren't you having any?" I ask.

"No I'll wait."

I look at the small water bottle longing for a sip. If he isn't going to have any, I won't either. I put it back in the backpack. I look uphill at the conical peak of the extinct volcano, which is still a ways off. I had hoped it was actually closer than it looked. The Wittmer place, according to the small map in the book I had read, lay to the south behind the volcano, but I actually hadn't told Phil that. The path curves to the north away from where we want to go.

"I thought this is supposed to be the rainy season," Phil says as we press on, small dirt clouds rising with each footfall.

"It's probably an El Nino year. That's why we never found the Humboldt Current either." We cross over small dried-up streamlets following our dog guide who is taking us in the right general direction.

We pause at the bleached white skeletal remains of a goat. The bleak landscape seeming more and more cartoon-like. "I have to stop for a minute. It's too hot," I gasp.

"Wait here under this bush; the twigs will give you a little shade. I'll scout ahead." Phil removes the backpack and trots off, leaving me with the dog. We both fall back onto the hot ground, panting hard. Some finches fly over to investigate and don't seem to mind that I am there. I can get within a few fingers reach of them before they fly off.

Phil returns ten minutes later. "Where exactly do we have to go?" he asks.

"I'll draw you a picture." Phil takes my pad out of the backpack and I draw a small map. "Here is the volcano. The Ritters lived here, in front of the volcano. The Wittmer's lived here behind the volcano."

"Behind the volcano! Are you nuts? We've gone about four miles already through the desert and the volcano is still two miles away. It's over one hundred degrees out here-we have a pint of water for the three of us, and we still have to get back to the boat before the sun sets, which at this latitude is exactly six o'clock."

"Less than a pint of water," I say to Phil handing him the plastic bottle. "I drank some."

"What about the dog?"

We look at the poor black dog who is now trying to dig for water in a dried streambed. I walk over to him and pour a small amount from the plastic bottle into my cupped hand. He turns his head away. Not wishing to waste a drop I open his mouth and pour the water onto his tongue.

"We're on a goat path," Phil explains. "Goats don't care about going in a straight line; we've zigged and zagged back and forth. Ahead, it zigs and zags more. If you had told me back at the boat that we had to get to the volcano, I would never have gone."

"I know. That's why I kind of omitted that part."

"Well, if you want to keep going, I'll follow."

A cool gust of wind blows on us, providing relief from the unrelenting heat.

We eventually come to a dirt road that snakes off to the right, marked with a sign saying Casa de Somebody or other, 1950. Our shaggy tour guide wants to go down this road so we reluctantly follow. We eventually arrive at a modest house, surrounded by palm trees and lush vegetation. This should have been the Ritter house. A sign in Spanish says, "Keep out, private property".

Our four-legged tour guide takes us up some more paths, which turn out to be nothing more than burro trails that meander and go nowhere in particular. Along the way we pass more bony remains of goats, dogs and burros, all bleached out and parched in the sun. Eventually the goat trails lead back to the road. We realize if we had just kept on straight up the road, we would have arrived at the same spot hours earlier.

"That's what we get for following a dog," Phil laughs.

We continue on, this time with Phil leading. The higher climates smell like the inside of a small chest you might find in your grandmother's attic, somewhat spicy, with a hint of must. There aren't many flower smells in the Galapagos, as there are few flowers. Most flowering plants are white and are pollinated at night. The Galapagos lack the necessary pollinating insects for lots of showy colorful flowers, it is just too hot and dry. There are many species of moth, which do most of the night pollinating, as it is cooler, so perhaps that's why the overall scent is somewhat like a giant attic.

Soon we come to a group of small farms. Tall orange trees overhang the road, and Phil and I pluck several from the branches. The oranges are not ripe, but the tartness and juice revive us. Our tour guide make a side trip under a barbed wire fence, and while standing on his hind legs, drinks from a rain barrel next to an abandoned shack.

"I think we should start heading back," Phil says. "We only have a couple of hours of sunlight left, and it took us three hours to get here, even if we did criss-cross the entire island in the process."

We head back to the boat following the panting dog. My feet are bleeding from the blisters that are now on the top and bottom of both feet. The granular lava dust had sanded down our yacht tender feet into something resembling canned luncheon meat. I am mad at myself for not wearing socks, but I had been so long without them.

"Abe. Abraham. Aloicious. Alberto. Arnold…"

"What are you doing?" Phil asks.

"Trying to figure out the dog's name." The dog is now trotting ahead of us, head erect, nose locked into the small village at the base of the slope; the endless blue of the Pacific spreading out beyond.

"I didn't realize we were so high up. I have a great appreciation for what the Wittmers had to go through when moving their possessions up from the shore," Phil says while pausing to take a photograph.

"Bambino, Bertie, Bennie, Bob, Bill, …"

"Are you ready to head off into that vast blue expanse?" Phil asks looking to the west.

We are still very homesick. We have gotten no e-mail from Phil's kids, which worries him, but makes me think no news is good news. We seem to have every reason to turn back- both of us are missing work and missing our families. Phil feels his brain is becoming stagnant. There are only a handful of cruisers we can relate to, societal cast-offs like ourselves, who want to taste, smell and see as much of the planet first hand as possible.

"I didn't know how much socializing this trip would involve. But, I really want to see a kangaroo hopping through the bush in Australia. Bunny, Bwana, Caleb, Cappy, Cassie..."

By the time I had gotten to all the "R" names we are back at the Wittmers.

"Whisky!" Erica cries as she comes out of a side door wiping her hands on a dishtowel. "Where have you been?"

"Whisky?" I ask. "We never got that far."

"How far did you get?" Erica responds not completely understanding my English.

I tell her.

"He has never walked that far in his life! Tomorrow I will take you up to the caves in my truck."

"That would be great," I exclaim. "One more thing before we go back to the boat. How many tourists are here on the island?"

"None. No. Two. You both," Erica says smiling. "That's it. Next week we have a Swedish family staying with us."

"That's weird," I mutter.

"Why? Don't you like Swedes?" she asks.

"No. I mean yes, I do. It's just that last night while we were still on the boat, we saw a woman with shoulder length, light brown hair, pacing the beach, wearing a fancy black cocktail dress. She looked European. Maybe it was your mother? Or someone staying with another family here?"

The ever-present smile on Erica's face vanishes. "No, there is no one here on the island of that description. You must have seen a ghost."

The following day we meet Erica's mother, Inga Floreanna Wittmer, the second baby born to the original Wittmer settlers on Floreanna Island. She too had suffered a loss, as her husband had succumbed to the infamous Galapagos currents and disappeared at sea while fishing many years ago.

In the book <u>Floreanna</u> Margret Wittmer wrote of baby Inga's second Christmas. The Wittmers had spent weeks making a doll and doll bed to be given to Inga by St. Nick. When Inga unwrapped the present Christmas morning, she was terribly disappointed. "Father Christmas gave me a doll instead of a machete."

Here stands Inga Floreana sixty or so years later, wearing pants and a "CAT" (for Caterpillar) baseball cap, under which curly gray hair sprouts like tightly bound roots from a cracked flower pot. Empty buckets, (that by the end of the morning were filled with yucca and other fruits and vegetables) completely surround her.

I reach to shake her hand but withdraw when I realize she is clenching the machete she had longed for as a child. In fact, the machete never leaves her right hand. It has become a very long digit which she wields with great grace—prying up yucca roots from the parched soil, slicing oranges, guillotining introduced insect pests, and scratching her forehead. I realize this was definitely not the woman pacing the beach and staring out to sea from the night before. Inga Floreanna is as much a part of the island as it is of her. This is not a woman to pine for things over the far horizon. I am sure Phil and I saw the ghost of the Baroness pacing the shores of Black Beach, anxiously waiting for the ship that would never come to take her away.

Piled into the back of Erica's truck, we finally arrive at the Wittmer's first home. Situated behind the volcano and miles from Black beach, they had no view of

Erica and Phil in one of the caves.

the ships that anchored at any of the beaches. For years the family lived in the pirate caves while they built their house. The pirate caves are more like empty eye socket—single room depressions into which inhabitants from long ago carved bunks, chairs and shelves into the soft lava rock. Connected by a narrow path around the perimeter of the hill, the caves are reached by following a narrow circuitous route, sculpted between fifteen-foot rocks.

At the base of the hill, from natural spigots of varying heights, a spring gurgles out fresh cool water onto flat rocks. Even during the present drought, the water is clear and steady, the natural faucets always "on." Large trees, once indigenous to mainland Ecuador and Peru, create great splotches of shade and their leaves, (actual leaf–like leaves, not the cactus variety so prevalent at lower elevations in the Galapagos) rustle in the wind, making the sounds one would hear in a deciduous forest of the northern climes. It is easy to see how the Wittmers had made this their home. It is exotic, bountiful, and yet strangely familiar.

We leave Floreanna after exchanging foods: canned Maine blueberries, sauerkraut, and chocolate for fresh coffee, bananas, papaya, and yucca. Our next stop is Villamil, the town on the south side of Isabella Island. We are told to arrive before sunset, as the pass into the harbor is tricky with breaking waves to either side of the narrow entrance. With little wind to propel us, we arrive well after sunset; the bright moon lights up the area like an enormous overhead street light.

"I see the breakers easily," I call down to Phil who is steering us from the nav station with Stewart by his side. He has the remote control for the autopilot in one hand and is using a chart scanned into the computer with a moving map program from Delorme. Occasionally he glances up at the radar.

"Look at this! We can stay down below and run the boat," he yells up to me.

"That's pretty cool. But what about the small little wooden fishing boats that don't show up on radar?"

"Do you see any?"

"Not yet. But there are lots of cruisers here. In fact, the harbor is full."

We anchor in a gentle swell beyond the protective arm of the southern point. "This is a little like being at sea," I remark to Phil as I grab a glass of water skiing down the sloping counter and heading for imminent destruction.

"Nice catch!" Phil praises while turning on the VHF radio. "And they call this an anchorage?"

"Sea Glass, Sea Glass, this is Yardarm."

"Yardarm, Sea Glass. Switch to seventeen."

Phil and the rest of the anchorage dutifully switch up to listen in.

"I've been looking at the weather patterns for the Marquesas. It looks like it might be a good time to go in two days."

"I agree. If we head south to 8 degrees, then follow the rumline, we should arrive in eighteen days, with favorable conditions there."

"Do we have to listen to that squawk box?" I plead.

"Fine. I'll switch back to sixteen."

"Iwalani, Iwalani, this is Sunbow."

"Wow!" I shriek. "Someone is actually calling us on the radio!"

We met Ken and Judy from Sunbow while anchored in Wreck Bay. They have a very pretty catamaran that was designed by Chris White and built in Maine. When they saw our hailing port, they instantly became intrigued. We had gone on several park tourist trips with them to the other outlying islands and enjoyed their company very much. They invite us over for dinner the following night.

The next day we make water, wash laundry, and clean the boat. Phil grabs a scrub brush and spends the better part of the afternoon attacking Iwalani's waterline which is starting to sport a green fringe. I unpack our ice cream maker and make some fresh vanilla ice cream to take over to Sunbow, which is only possible because of UHT cream (a real cream which requires no refrigeration and is available everywhere but the USA). I spend a wonderful afternoon writing, painting, and playing with Stewart, despite the constant rolling while at anchor. Phil returns from Iwalani's waterline scrubbing and takes a shower. Afterwards, he sits down at the nav station with a rather strange expression on his face.

"What's the matter?" I ask.

"I think I've got shrimp in my ear."

Phil's ears have always been a problem. When he was younger he was in a very bad car accident, which essentially wiped out the inside of his left ear. A surgeon tried to reconstruct an eardrum and canal with various grafts and flaps, which seemed to work well enough, but it was always a constant source of examining, flushing and helplessness for me, pain, itch and deafness for him.

"I'll get the otoscope," I volunteer, thinking to myself, *'Ya right, here we go again.'*

We dutifully stand in our customary position, wedged between the sink and nav station, which allows for the least amount of sudden movements. It always makes me nervous poking the otoscope into a moving target, when I am moving myself.

And then I see it. Waving a tiny little claw at me, while bouncing up and down on Phil's reconstructed eardrum, is a miniature crab.

"You've got crabs!"

"What?"

"A baby crab is bouncing up and down on your eardrum."

"Get rid of it."

"Hang on a minute. Let me try to grab onto him with the alligator forceps." I insert the three-inch long forceps down the shaft of the otoscope. The crab backs up as I open the pincers to nab him. Iwalani rolls. I am scared that I will inadvertently rupture Phil's eardrum. "This won't work. I can use some drops for ear mites, which probably kill him, or we can trying flushing him out."

"*Probably* kill him? I opt for flushing him out."

"Don't move."

I set up the flush and bulb syringe and within a few tries we have the tiny crab swimming laps in the stainless steel bowl.

"Cool," I say as I watch the tiny little crustacean paddle around. "I will never give you grief again when you ask me to look inside your ears."

We pack up the ice cream which by the time we arrive at Sunbow is already starting to melt.

"Sorry we're late," I say to Ken as Judy takes the ice cream and runs to put it in their freezer. "We had a case of crabs."

She returns and they both smile at us. I nearly fall overboard. They are both wearing a set of fake dentures resembling hillbilly teeth. Ken turns his back on me and pulls something out of his pocket. When he swings around he is wearing glasses with very thick lenses held together by a piece of tape on the bridge.

"This is why I like you two," I say to Ken. "You don't take yourselves too seriously."

"I ain't so sure we should let you on board with yer varmints though." Ken says in a hillbilly accent, spit flying out through the gaps in his brown crooked teeth.

"Don't worry. It was only one crab and he's back in the ocean." Then I tell them the whole story.

Because of Sunbow's shallow draft they can tuck themselves up into the mangrove swamps at the head of the harbor, well away from the rest of the cruising yachts. With a steady breeze blowing and a bow oriented cockpit and door, they aren't bothered by mosquitoes, yet they have a steady cool breeze aerating the boat.

Phil with Judy and Ken sporting their "BillyBob" teeth

On shore, not far from the boat, sprawling all over the rocks, are hundreds of marine iguanas, their charcoal gray bodies blending into the dark gray lava rocks. Some abandoned fishing boats are anchored off the other side of Sunbow, and sea lions have taken them over, but, instead of the usual sea lion banter, I can hear a lot of coughing.

"That doesn't sound good," I comment.

"We figure that the really old sea lions retire here and that's why they don't look so hot," Judy says removing her fake teeth.

"More likely they have distemper," I say.

We sit in Sunbow's main salon, which has 360-degree views. The turquoise water surrounding the boat reflects off the bright white walls of the interior.

"This is lovely," I say. "No rolling."

Judy passes each of us a glass of wine, which we place on the table, where it doesn't try to roll off and smash on the floor. The best part about visiting Sunbow is that only one person speaks at a time. "OK. It's my turn," Judy says waving her arms in the air. She makes an imaginary box, "This is my box and I am going to fill it."

She then tells us how she and Ken had met. Both of them had been married before. Her first husband had left her to marry a younger woman, which she took in stride.

"You mean you didn't try to kill her and your ex-husband? Run them off the road? Ruin her financially? Write letters to every person on the planet saying what a horrible person she was and what a horrible man your ex was?" I ask.

"Why should I?" Judy responds. "My children liked her. Making things unpleasant would only have made it hard on them in the long run. Did all of those things happen to you?"

"That and more," I say

"I was not making my ex-wife happy," Phil adds. "She started by having affairs, one of whom was a student of mine. Then it was others, while she was going to school to get her doctorate. I forgave her for the first two, but not the third. She was seeing this man for most of our twenty years together."

"The worst part of it was not one person asked us our version of the story," I say. "I was viewed as a villain and Phil a mad-man. Gradually one by one, people realized they had taken sides with a habitual liar, and some of our friends started to apologize to us before we left Maine, but by then it was too late. The courts gave primary residency of Phil's kids to his ex-wife."

"Is that why they aren't with you now?" Judy asks.

"Partly," Phil says. "They are old enough to decide for themselves what direction they want to take in life. They said sailing around the world was going to be too boring,. I was in no position to force them to come with us."

"Being this far away from his sons is eating away at Phil," I remark. "We have been thinking about turning around and going home."

"And miss Tahiti, the crown jewel of the Pacific?" Ken asks.

"And Australia, too, where I really want to see a kangaroo hopping through the bush," I reply. "But I miss work, and my dogs and my family. I asked the big cheese on the way here to the Galapagos to give me a sign on which way we should go. And, all of a sudden, a shooting star shot out of the west and headed northeast, right in the direction home. 'OK'. I said. 'Maybe that was just coincidental. Where are we most needed?' I asked again. And sure enough another shooting star shot out of the west and headed to the northeast, right in the same direction as the first. Then right after that I got email from my sister that my dog had died."

"Oh that's awful, I am so sorry to hear that," Judy says while pouring more wine.

"It was inevitable, she had cancer in her spleen and in her liver. I just hope it wasn't too hard on my sister."

"Can't you leave the boat and fly home once in a while?" Ken asks.

"Phil is thinking about flying back from Tahiti for Ben's graduation in June."

"Judy is leaving from the Marquesas and flying back to California for the birth of her first granddaughter," Ken says. "Flying back home helps to break the trip up and keeps you from getting stale."

Later that evening, back on Iwalani, Phil and I discuss flying home for a short break.

"Everyone does it," I suggest.

"Yes. And everyone "buddy boats" too. It seems to change the nature of the whole trip. You're no longer on one big voyage but several small adventures," Phil says. "Periodically flying home somehow seems like cheating."

"I don't get the whole buddy boating thing either. The last thing I want to do is make a passage with a bunch of other boats. Not only are you responsible for yourselves, but now you have other people to worry about."

Stewart jumps up on our bunk and tries to muscle in between us.

"We'll leave it up to you Stew, to tell us what we should do. Should we continue sailing west or go home?" Phil asks. Stewart purrs, but doesn't answer.

*   *   *

For the next week we do touristy things: horseback riding to volcanoes, snorkeling, hiking, shopping, while also working on the boat, writing and painting.

"I think we need to explore Tagus Cove," Phil suggests while bracing his leg so he doesn't fall off the settee.

"It's off limits to yachts."

"Yes, but look at how protected it is," Phil points at the chart. "It's a real anchorage. This rolling about is getting old. And besides I want to find Director's name painted on the rocks."

Director was the name of a boat that sailed from New York to Manila in the 1930's. On board was Philip's life-long mentor and friend, Dennis Puleston, author of Blue Water Vagabond and founder of the Environmental Defense Fund, the organization responsible for banning DDT in America.

"I'm game. What are they going to do? Throw us in jail. We can play dumb. Or at least I can. It's not as hard for me," I joke.

We arrive in Tagus Cove, on the easternmost side of Isabella Island, two days later with only a few hours of daylight left. Surrounded by steep stone sides, and completely protected from the seas, we anchor and are the only humans for miles. We launch the dinghy and slowly row around the well-protected harbor. We don't speak, as neither of us wants to destroy the profound silence. Penguins scramble up the rocks and slide back down into the water like children at a country club pool.

The rocks tower up in some places almost vertically. Most cruisers painted their names in steep, but still accessible places. High at the top on a vertical slab of stone are painted names of U.S. military visitors, possessing more guts than the yachting community graffiti artists.

The stone is gray and crumbly, which gives the ship names a ghost-like air of non-permanence. Some of the rocks peel off the hillside like bark from a tree, leaving one or two letters behind. In some places there is an embossing effect as the surrounding unpainted rock has been etched away by rain and elements, leaving the remaining letters to stand out. We scan the cliffs with binoculars, telephoto lenses and Dennis's book, but we cannot find Director's name. Here is Yankee, there are Svaap, Orion and Cimba, fading ghost-like reminders of once famous

Iwalani illegally anchored in Tagus Cove

yachts. The cathedral like stillness is interrupted only by the occasional cough of a sea lion from the far side of the glassy still grotto.

"Now this is an anchorage," Phil whispers to me. "Uh, oh. We aren't going to be alone."

A small cruise ship enters the harbor just ahead of a fog bank.

"Lets row back to Iwalani," I whisper.

When we get back to the boat, we raise our dinghy with the throat halyard and lash it on deck. Phil goes down below to start supper, just as a large inflatable dinghy shoots past us, with its oversized outboard shattering the silence and leaving us rolling in its wake. I watch in amazement as they zoom around the periphery of the harbor going at least thirty knots. After a complete circumnavigation of the harbor, they make their way over to us. A large man stands at the stern of the dinghy, with his hand on the outboard throttle.

"You on board," he yells at me in English with a heavy German accent, "Where is your guide?"

"My what?" I ask, nodding and waving to the American-looking tourists in his care. "Say, all of you wouldn't by any chance have noticed the name "Director" painted on these rocks? My husband and I are cataloging the boats."

"Lady! You are in violation. Where is your guide?"

"We don't have one. We are just staying here one night and are not going to shore."

"You don't have a guide? You must leave at once!"

"We are here photographing a part of history. These names are from yachts that sailed here long ago. We are trying to make a record of their names before they disappear forever."

"I don't care. You must leave at once!"

"Why do you want us to leave at once?" I ask trying to stare him down.

"Because you are in violation! You do not have a guide." With this remark some of the tourists begin to roll their eyes.

"Let me get this straight. You want us to leave on the verge of darkness motoring into a fog bank, running the risk of going aground and polluting these pristine waters because we don't have a guide?"

"You are in vio-"

"Oh, come on..." This is from one of the American tourists seated on the port side. "Let them stay. They don't look like they are doing any harm."

I smile at the woman.

"We will leave for Villamil first thing in the morning," I say, "and, if any of you ladies see the name "Director" and can get a photo, I'll pay a finder's fee-" Before I can finish my sentence, the German revs the throttle on the outboard and speeds away, a large rooster tail wake rising up behind him.

Later that night, while eating dinner, I feel a pulsing hum coming up through the floorboards onto my bare feet. Stewart, too, walks around staring at the floor, looking as if large mice are partying in the bilge.

"What's going on?" I ask Phil.

"The generators for the cruise ship."

We leave the table and go out on deck to have a look around. The German commandant's ship is on the small side, roughly ninety feet, but it is lit up like a Las Vegas casino. Generators are reverberating; loud American rock music is thumping from several outside speakers; kids are jumping off the higher parts of the ship into the water screaming and laughing while their nervous parents flash the ship's spotlights everywhere but at their children.

"Sure was nice until they arrived," I moan.

"Oh, you're just jealous we weren't invited over for cocktails."

"Maybe, but I am a little pissy, too. I think we make far less of an impact on the environment than they do."

As if to acknowledge my statement, a group of sea lions in the corner of the cove start barking and voicing their complaints about the evening's disturbance.

"Yeah. But, lady, you are in violation," Phil teases.

"Oh, great. How much of that conversation did you hear?"

"All of it. It was pretty entertaining actually."

"Thanks for coming up and helping out."

"You were the one that said you could play dumb. You did a pretty good job, I might add."

Despite the noise from our neighbors, we have the best night's sleep in a long time. Iwalani finally stops moving. On the return trip our course takes us between Isabella and Fernandina islands. Uninhabited mountains, dormant volcanoes actually, rise out of the totally calm sea. Dolphins swim alongside us in small schools; twelve-foot manta rays leap from the water and do flips, returning to the water without even a ripple. Not a house, cruise ship or other sailboat is in sight in any direction for the rest of the day.

"I sure hope the Ecuadorians can keep it like this," I say to Phil. " I feel guilty though for coming up here illegally."

"Not me. I wouldn't have missed this for the world."

"You're right. It's incredible; this is what I thought the Galapagos were all about. I would have been really depressed if we had stayed in the "yachts only" areas, but we are no different than the people making the fake documents."

"Aha," Phil announces. "We are now experiencing the other thing the Galapagos are famous for."

"What?" I ask.

"The infamous currents. Our speed is down to two knots."

"At this rate we won't be back to Villamil until early tomorrow morning."

I make supper, and we resume our usual watch schedule—four hours on, four hours off. Despite the cool waters of the Galapagos, the sun had been shining all day and the constant use of the engine has made Iwalani too warm for Phil's tastes and he has stripped down to his customary cruising costume—nothing.

Phil has the midnight to four a.m. watch while I sleep comfortably in our forward berth with Stewart. I wake suddenly, thinking I hear something but I am not sure. A whistle. It wakes me fully this time. Not just any whistle, but the famous Ecuadorian whistle, a sound so shrill and sharp it can peel the enamel off your teeth.

"Amy, get up here!" I can hear Phil yell from the stern.

I turn on the light and see I have an hour to go before my watch.

I throw a shirt and some shorts on over my underwear and climb up the companionway, leaving Stewart to sleep.

"What are you doing?" I ask Phil, who is crouching down in an awkward position in the cockpit.

Over the starboard side of Iwalani I hear all sorts of shouts in rapid Spanish. Poor Phil is embarrassed to stand up for fear of exposing his privates.

"What's going on?" I ask. "Are we being boarded by pirates?"

"No. Not this time. They are fishermen. I think we cut their nets or something."

I come out on deck and lean over the side of Iwalani.

"Buenes noches," I yell down to ten or so fishermen all crowded into a small open launch.

They all begin yelling at me and pointing out to sea.

"Despacio," I yell back.

Half of them stop yelling.

"Mas despacio." I yell again.

Finally the calmest member of the bunch begins explaining to me in slow Spanish what is happening.

I turn to Phil, "You haven't seen any other fishing boats have you?"

"Nothing. Not even a cruise ship."

"A fishing boat is missing."

"I haven't seen anyone, but I didn't even see these guys. They have no lights on board except their cigarettes, and their boat doesn't show up well on radar."

I tell the men we will keep the radar on, and I wish them good luck. They disappear off into the darkness faintly lit by ten orange burning dots, all ship's cigarettes aglow.

"I should have given them a compass or a flashlight at least," Phil says. "If I only had my wits about me."

"Or at least a towel about you," I laugh.

We arrive back at Villamil before light, confident of making the pass with a waning moon and no sunlight. At dawn a small airplane flies overhead, just as we go to bed.

"They must be searching for the fisherman," Phil says.

"I think it would be pretty awful to be in a boat trying to get the engine started and all the while drifting farther and farther from land," I whisper.

"No, what would be worse is to fall overboard and see your boat sail off while shark fins begin to circle," Phil says.

"I have a fear of that every day, waking up from my watch and coming out on deck and not finding you. At least with Iwalani it is almost impossible to fall overboard, with her high bulwarks topped by heavy-duty lifelines. I can't imagine sailing in some of the conditions we have seen with a production sailboat," I add.

We check out of Isabella and are told by the port captain that the missing fisherman has been found alive and well. We head back to Santa Cruz, where I am to meet with the Director of the Darwin Research station.

Despite the ecological importance to the globe, the Galapagos receive little worldwide funding. The Darwin Research Center is trying to change that. They have significantly increased the native tortoise population which was decimated one hundred and fifty years ago when whaling ships stopped for easy provisioning. The foundation gathered the few remaining tortoises and put them into a captive breeding and egg-hatching program.

Because they are approaching the conservation of the Galapagos from a scientific standpoint, they have had to fine-tune their charter to include tourism to provide a sustainable income for the ever-increasing Ecuadorian population. And yet, despite their scientific savvy and highly educated scientists, things are still measured in Galapagos time, where minutes become hours, and days, turn into weeks. We won't be able to help with the distemper outbreak in the sea lion population for weeks, if at all.

Still, by the end of the meeting I am all fired up to save the flightless cormorants from extinction and write out a big check to the Darwin Research Station, with the promise of more money to come. I guess I am still feeling guilty for visiting park property without a guide.

I walk back to the center of town and hop into one of the water taxis at the end of the dock. Yachts are required to use the taxis; landing a dinghy isn't permitted. A boat must signal the taxi with an air horn if they want to come ashore. Consequently at certain times of the day the cruising yachts in the harbor all sound like a flock of honking geese. The launches, painted yellow, sport a cloth canopy to keep the hot equatorial sun off the passengers. One hands the launch driver the fee of fifty cents, and, in exchange, the driver hands the passenger a lifejacket of dubious integrity, which must be worn about the neck while in the boat. If we were to sink, it would be the first thing I would remove.

We are beginning to know the taxi drivers by name. None of them speak English, but my favorite, Guillermo, speaks slow enough Spanish that we have boring but intelligible conversations.

I am a bit sad when I see Guillermo has just left the dock and the only taxi remaining is the rickety old man, who looks like he is in imminent need of CPR, and his equally questionable launch. He lacks teeth as well as eyesight, as he never seems to be able to land the launch correctly. In his fits of exasperation, he usually showers the passengers with Spanish profanity and sprays of saliva through the water cannon sized gap in his upper dental arcade. His preferred method of arriving at Iwalani is to ram the launch straight into Iwalani's side and hope we have enough agility to scramble aboard quickly.

Phil is in the cockpit of Iwalani hanging freshly washed laundry and comes over to the port side to help me aboard.

The driver guns it and rams right into Iwalani's side at full speed. I have already tossed my life jacket back to him, thrown my backpack on the boat, and then reach out to grab Iwalani with my left hand. I hold on to Iwalani's rail while Phil reaches to grab me under the armpit. Suddenly the driver throws the throttle full speed in reverse. I mistakenly try to hold on to Iwalani but am too far away to jump.

In my right ear I hear, "Let go! Let go!" from Phil, and in my left ear I hear a sickening sound like a grizzly bear ripping into a fabric tent, followed by a fire-like pain in my shoulder. The driver realizes if he keeps going backwards I will soon be in the water, so he reverses direction again and rams Iwalani a second time. I scramble on board and never look back.

"Jesus, Honey, why didn't you let go?" Phil asks with concern.

"I don't know. I think I ripped my rotator cuff."

"Your what?"

"The ligaments and tendons that make up the fibrous part of the shoulder joint."

"Great. Now what do we do?"

"Nothing. I'm not having surgery to repair it. I'll just have to live with it. It'll have to heal on its own." I brush past Phil and go down below to put the checkbook in the drawer, pissed off at myself for being so stupid. I am holding my breath trying to ignore the pain I am in. I start to strip off my hot and sweaty clothes, while Stewart sits at my feet staring up at me with concern.

"Here. I brought you some ice, put this on your shoulder. Tell me what happened," Phil says sitting next to me on our forward bunk.

"I wasn't paying attention. I should have let go. I know. It was stupid."

"No, not with your shoulder, with Darwin."

"Well, it looks like things are going to improve for the Galapagos, but not for yachts. They are going to use Australia and New Zealand for examples. There are plans in the future, not to allow animals or plants here. Period. Stewart will be one of the last American cats to visit." When he hears his name Stewart taps me on my leg and meows. "There isn't much you and I can do to help, other than make a handout that the officials can give to the visiting yachts," I say, putting the ice on my shoulder. "Thanks for this."

"That's a start."

"And then what?" I ask.

"What do you mean?" Phil asks.

"Then what do we do? Most everyone has already made the plunge off the edge of the saucer for the Marquesas."

"We are not everyone."

"But do we go west or head back east?"

"I don't know. After I left you at the research station, I called the boys."

"No kidding? How did that go?"

"I asked them would they want to come and spend the summer with us if we came back to Maine?"

"And?" I prod.

"Ben said he was kind of busy, and Nathaniel was even more non-committal."

"Hmm. Sorry to hear that. What do you think we should do, Stew?"

He looks up at Phil, then me, and then over to the corner of the floor where a copper penny has fallen out of my pocket when I threw off my skirt.

I reach down and pick it up with my good arm. "Hey- an Ecuadorian penny. Perfect Stew."

"What are you talking about?" Phil asks.

"Look at this–one side has a picture of the world, the other has the number one. We'll flip the penny. Best two out of three. If it comes up with the number one, we head back to the number one spot in the world—Maine; if it comes up with the picture of the world—we go on. Are you both game?"

"Sure. We each get one flip. You go first, then me. If there's a tie Stew has to flip." Phil says.

I give the penny a toss, catch it and slap it on the back of my hand.

"World," I say. "Your turn," and hand the penny to Phil.

He repeats the process, looks at the penny and then quickly covers it, so I can't see it.

"How 'bout three out of five?" he asks.

"No way. We all agreed."

"Ok. Fine. Fair is fair. It's the world. West we go. And lucky you, Stew. You never had to cast a vote."

Chapter 8

Blue Water Blues

April/May 2001
The Pacific Ocean

Clearing out of the Galapagos is uneventful. Most cruisers have already left in small groups, like high school students after the final bell. We are trailing behind the pack; the Galapagos janitors are already picking up after the cruising flotilla—restocking store shelves and dealing with mountains of trash. The weather window for points to the west is wide open. We have to be out of French Polynesia by cyclone season, which unofficially begins in November. Safe havens from hurricane force winds are six thousand miles away. Our goal is to get to Australia in just six short months.

Once a boat is in the trade winds heading west, it isn't easy to sail back. We agonized over our decision for a long time. The passage from the Galapagos to the next landfall, the Marquesas, is over three thousand miles, making it our longest time at sea. We figure it will take us a month. Before we left Maine, I stood beneath Phil's globe at Delorme and watched the long expanse of South Pacific spin slowly by. Blue, more blue and still more blue. I got seasick back then just thinking about how much ocean we'd have to cross. A month at sea! I could remember in grade school shuddering at the mere thought of Columbus crossing the Atlantic or the Africans shackled in the hold of slave ship's for weeks at a time, it seemed so impossible. And here we are about to do it ourselves, covering a much greater distance and an even longer time at sea.

We couldn't have been more ready mentally or physically. Four weeks at sea would give my shoulder a chance to heal. Pulling on ropes seems to be good physical therapy. My shoulder throbs but no longer burns. We have one hundred and fifty novels to read, and I have brought some of my veterinary textbooks, which I had never read while I was in veterinary school. Phil has computer books to read– thicker than any phone books.

We buy as much fresh fruit and vegetables as the icebox can carry, then, holding our breath, take the plunge and sail off the cliff.

Four hours on, four hours off, twenty-four hours a day. For two weeks, we move along at a steady pace without making adjustments to any of the sails. Minor course changes are "clicked" into the autopilot—two degrees port, one-degree starboard maintaining the "rum line" to the Marquesas.

Our world is reduced down to three colors: blue, white and black. We see no other ships, airplanes or wildlife. No fish, no birds, no people. But one day I do see a large green trash bag floating by—some other ships answer to dealing with the waste that is generated on board.

"What on Earth are you doing?" Phil asks me early one afternoon.

"Jesus you scared me! I am peeing. What are you doing awake?" I ask.

I have recently abandoned using the head while at sea. Instead, I put on my harness and hang out over the bulwark on the lee side—for everything. There is really nothing quite like it, the whoosh of the waves, the complete sense of utter freedom, the knowledge that I alone am responsible for my own destiny. One wrong move and I could fall overboard, while taking a poop, is as much thrill as I care to experience in life.

"I can't believe you are doing that! You who insisted that we have a full bathroom on board! And you who would never use a bucket at sea!" Phil cries.

"I still wouldn't use a bucket. This is infinitely preferable. I don't get seasick this way. Besides I don't wake you up, crashing around in the bathroom."

"Well don't ruin Iwalani's sides."

"For Pete's sake, it all gets washed off even if I do pee on the paint."

Phil comes over to look at the leeward side, upwind of me. "Holy shit! Look at that!" he says pointing."

"Look at what?"

"Goose neck barnacles."

"What?"

I peer over Iwalani's side. Attached to the hull for her entire length and well below the water line, are thousands of tiny, dark colored penises, complete with scrotal sacs and testicles.

"Those are disgusting."

"See what your going to the bathroom over the side is doing to the boat?"

"I didn't do that!"

"How do you know?"

"Oh come on, for crying out loud! There is no way I am going back to using the head while at sea, and there is no way I am responsible for all those penises."

"Goose-neck barnacles."

"Yah, whatever."

"That explains why our speed has been dropping. We have a shag carpet growing on our hull." Phil shakes his head. "We'll be out another two weeks at this rate."

"You've got another hour to your watch. How come you woke up?" I ask.

"I couldn't sleep. I realized today is Mother's Day. I thought I would try to call my mother through Sugar Ida Victor on the Maritime Services Radio net."

"Call your mother? Can you do that?"

"Sure. One of the net controllers on the maritime services net calls my mother collect on the telephone and patches me through. That's one of the advantages of having my ham license. What's for supper?"

"Shrimp and Fettuccini in an Alfredo sauce, cucumber salad, and for dessert, lemon meringue pie."

"Sounds delicious. I am going to see if I can hear anything on the radio."

"May-Day, may-day this is Time Trekker, Time Trekker."

"Good Evening, Time Trekker, what is the nature of your distress?"

I marvel at the calmness of the net controllers voice. A boat in distress! Now this will be worth listening to! I throw the roll of toilet paper in our catchall milk crate, remove my harness and scurry down below. We grimly listen to the radio, Phil at his customary seat at the nav station, me on the fold up seat in the galley, Stewart curled up on my lap.

"This is Time Trekker. I am en route to Hawaii from Mexico. Over."

"Thank you, Time Trekker. How many persons on board, and what is the

nature of your distress?"

"There are two of us on board. Me and my doggie. We've been at sea for six weeks. I am running out of food and diesel."

"Thank you, Time Trekker, you've got yourself and your dog on board, you are low on food and diesel and have been out six weeks. What is the nature of your emergency?"

"I told you. I am running out of food and diesel."

"Um, what is your name?"

"My name is Bob, my dog is Alf."

"Your vessel type and registration, Bob?"

Bob gives them the information.

"Is Time Trekker a sailing vessel?"

"Yes. But there has been no wind for two weeks."

"Have you got drinking water on board?"

"Yes. Over one hundred gallons. It's the food I am worried about. I am worried about my doggie."

"What a jerk!" I say to Phil. "He can't be too worried about his doggie, or he wouldn't be heading to Hawaii. I am pretty sure the quarantine period in Hawaii is <u>six</u> months for dogs arriving from Mexico, even if he did start out in California." I scratch Stewart under the chin, and he closes his eyes, purring at top speed.

After confirming his position the net controller tells Bob to sit tight for twenty-four hours, not to use his radio in order to save on battery power until the following day, and to check back in at 0200 Zulu.

"What time?"

"0200 Zulu."

"I am not sure what time that is."

"Time Trekker—just check in at the same time tomorrow."

"Are there really people that numb out here?" Phil looks at me in disbelief.

"I thought I was first in line for the largest vacuum between the ears. I am happy to know there are others in the same contest with me," I say.

Phil finally gets through to the net control and is patched into a phone line. Out in the middle of the South Pacific, one thousand miles from the nearest land, Phil is talking to his mother in New York! It somehow seems surreal to hear her voice in Iwalani's cabin, even if the only thing she could say is "I don't believe it!" over and over. I know Phil made his mother's day.

Now we have three things to look forward to each day—supper, a shining orange light on the Inmarsat indicating we have e-mail (a luxury boats of the past never experienced) and the ongoing saga of Time Trekker. On the third day of the 'Bob and Doggie Show' we listen in while Bob continues on with his whining.

"I've still got no wind. I'm low on fuel, and we are still running out of food."

"I've got good news, Bob. We've got a Russian tanker heading for you. They are going to supply you with a drum of diesel fuel. We've also been in touch with the Coast Guard, and they are going to airdrop a side of beef and a bilge pump. You should be have no problem making it to Hawaii."

"That's wonderful! You people have been fantastic."

At this point somewhere out in the middle of the South Pacific, two loud screams can be heard coming from a boat named Iwalani.

"I can't believe it! Our tax dollars are going to save a complete moron! Why does he need the bilge pump? He's not sinking!" Phil cries while beating his forehead onto the nav station.

I have read a few books about Darwin while in the Galapagos and still have a few more to go. Survival of the fittest doesn't necessarily mean survival of the strongest or smartest, but rather those that are most readily able to adapt to change. Is Bob showing higher adaptability in suckering Russia and the U.S. into helping him? Is he therefore advancing humanity's genes? I overheard that he had been preparing for two years to make his trip. Our preparations began ten years ago. Were we advancing the human genome by carrying everything we would need for one year with no outside assistance, or was he, with his pitiful mid-ocean re-supplying? "These are the kind of idiots that our species is better off letting Mother Nature clean up," I remark.

"Maybe the Coast Guard had a lot of dog lovers on duty."

"They'd be better off waiting a few days in hopes that the dog eats Bob, then they can go in with a clear conscience and rescue the dog and the boat."

"You know what gets me?" Phil continues, pulling on his beard until he has it twisted into a point. "He'll get back to America, write a book about his ordeal at sea, and make a ton of money from book royalties and movie options, while we write a book about how it really is, bore everyone who reads it, and come home to an empty dock."

"Well, maybe the Russians will give him bunker fuel and he'll ruin his engine. While he's working feverishly to get the engine going, his dog will go ravenously mad at the sight of all that raw meat. The dog will eat too much all at once and have diarrhea all over the decks. Bob will slip on the diarrhea in the middle of the night and fall overboard. The dog will still get rescued without advancing Bob's genes."

"You're terrible! Don't forget the engine isn't working, so Bob will just climb back on board. The boat won't be going anywhere."

"No, I'm not terrible, just insanely jealous. OK, so the dog will not allow him back on board, because then he'll have to share the beef with Bob. So Bob paddles around the boat pleading with his doggie. The dog keeps barking and growling. Bob flails around so much that sharks eat him."

"Now you're talking."

"You know what else? He probably lacks refrigeration, has no rock salt on board to preserve the meat, and lacks the know-how to dry it. The meat is just going to rot. A whole cow died to help him out."

"No. Half a cow."

"Yah, whatever. It's still sickening. Some bonehead is getting fed filet mignon at sea with our tax dollars. It's calm enough out here that we could set up the barbeque and have steaks too. Not that we aren't eating well. It's just the principle of the thing. Maybe I should call in and request the other half of the cow to be dropped off at Iwalani." Stewart wakes up from his nap on my lap and looks up at me. "How bout some genuine U.S. grain fed, beef Stew?" He looks up from me to Phil, and then licks his lips. "Sorry, Stewman. It's not going to happen unless you get on the airwaves and tell them you'd like some take-out also. I am not too keen on eating beef at sea anymore. Hopefully it will make Bob sick."

We can't stand listening in to the Bob and Doggie Show anymore. I didn't want to know to what lengths people would go to save such a loser. I content myself with the fantasy that "Alf, the doggie" is a dachshund, a mutant breed truly worth saving, even if his owner is not.

*   *   *

Our world is now more regimented than a U.S. boot camp. We live completely by the ship's bells. My day begins at four a.m., eight bells. I always wake up five minutes before, just in time to hear the chiming. I make a cup of instant coffee with talc-like powdered whitener and heaps of sugar. Ordinarily, on land I can't stand the thought of consuming such a concoction. But at sea strange things happen to your mind and body. In my case, highly processed food cravings take over. At home, Phil and I grow, can, or freeze all of our own organic vegetables, enough to last us one year. At sea, I do a one-eighty shift; the more highly processed and further away from any resemblance to a living object, the better. Corporate food and candy rule.

From four a.m. onward, I read, listen to the radio, and spend time with Stewart. Each half hour listening as the bells add one more ding, until six a.m., four bells, I grab the toilet paper, strap on my harness and head to the bulwark for the morning sunrise. At sea in the tropics, sunrise and sunset are a big disappointment. Only when we are within a hundred miles or so, of land do the bright colors appear. Otherwise it is just a series of grays turning to blues. Soon I am starving and make banana or cranberry-orange nut bread, lemon poppy seed muffins, pancakes, crepes, bacon and eggs, or whatever, for breakfast, being careful not to bang around too many pans and wake Phil.

At seven a.m., six bells, I check in with the "Little Flying Fish Net." We are a group of eighteen or so yachts, with all but two heading to the Marquesas. Most everyone is four days sail ahead of us.

By eight o'clock, eight bells again, breakfast is done cooking, and the smells usually wake Phil up for his watch. I feed Stewart, clean out the cat box, and then sleep for a few hours. At eleven, I usually wake up. By this time, Iwalani is pretty hot from the tropical, overhead sun. I am covered in sweat and feel sticky and foggy-headed.

For lunch, we microwave whatever we had for dinner the previous night, or make fruit smoothies from the ice made while cooling the icebox, blended with yogurt, canned or fresh fruit, soy powder and sugar.

After lunch, Phil does the dishes and then heads to bed, while I study veterinary medicine. I have one hundred and fifty pounds of textbooks I hope to read over the next three years. At two, I take a break. Once the sun is in front of the dodger, I do exercises on deck for fifteen minutes. The rest of the afternoon is spent reading non-veterinary books. At four I start supper. At five, I feed Stewart. Between five and six p.m., the oceans give the most glorious gift of all to those on board a boat. The seas calm down a bit and allow a brief respite from their unending theme park ride. If the wind generator hasn't filled the battery bank account, we run the engine during this hour, charging the batteries and cooling the ice box in the process, while we sit out in the cockpit eating from bowls with spoon—the feeding dish always held close to the mouth while quick bursts of food are shoveled in. Mealtime on Iwalani isn't a pretty sight. At six, I go to bed until eight p.m.

I have the hardest time waking up for this watch. It is usually the clanging and banging of Phil washing the pots and dishes we had dirtied for dinner which wakes me.

On the eight to midnight watch, I read novels or sometimes listen to the radio. At midnight I e-mail my parents our position and the local conditions, take a small bath using a cup of fresh water, brush and floss my teeth, wake up Phil and go to bed until four. This broken up schedule affords nine hours of sleep for me, ten hours for Phil, and a never-ending supply of human contact for Stewart.

During a person's watch he or she is responsible for keeping a lookout. That means a real look around on deck every fifteen minutes, including checking the radar at night. Weather faxes come in at fixed times each day, so the person on watch is also responsible for receiving faxes or doing any necessary radio work. This schedule changes as we head westward, crossing time zones, so one person is never responsible for doing it all. If the engine is running, the person on watch is responsible for checking the gauges, making sure the wind generator is charging one battery bank while the engine charges the other, and switching the fuel tanks just as the last sips of diesel are taken. The person on watch makes sail and course adjustments. From the Galapagos to the Marquesas we never touch the mainsail. If a squall approaches, we reduce sail by taking down the jib.

The only thing not accounted for in our routine is sex. This is difficult at best for me at sea, as my own human-ness make me seasick. I can spend all day cleaning animal waste in the roughest weather, but when it comes to anything that wafts, drips, squirts, or projectiles out of my own body, or anyone else's for that matter, I get very sick indeed. And this is beginning to have its effect on Phil.

"You didn't even notice the anti-barnacle rig," he says to me one evening at dinner, our third week at sea.

"The what?"

"I ran a line from the bow to the stern on the lee side. It seems to be working. It is scraping the barnacles from the hull, but it's not doing anything for the goose neck barnacles beneath the waterline."

"Our next boat is going to be entirely painted with bottom paint," I add.

"Our next boat won't be sailing for weeks at a time on one tack. One thing is for sure; I am never going to do this again. I had no idea how bored I would be out here," Phil says.

"I know what you mean. I am kind of getting sick of reading. Plus, I am running out of books. I've been reading a book a day."

"I just feel like my mind is going to waste out here."

"I feel like my entire life is going to waste. Do you realize your birthday is in a few days? What would you like for a present?"

"A day of sex," Phil growls with a voracious look.

"How 'bout a back-up plan?"

"Hmmm. I would like to go out to a really nice French restaurant, and then go to a play or maybe a movie. People have no idea how lucky they are to have the choice of what they are going to do. Sit home watch the TV, go out to a movie. I would give anything to be able to see a movie…"

*　　　*　　　*

On my eight to midnight watch, while reading in the cockpit I hear a voice off our aft port quarter. I look up from my book and stare out into the black night. I hear it again. It sounds as if someone is saying, "Are you sure that's right?" I drop my book, stand up and stare into the darkness. I hear nothing but the waves rolling from behind and rushing under our keel. "Hello?" I call out.

Nothing. I feel as if I am being watched. I sit back down and pretend to read my book.

The next thing I know I am showered with a fish smelling salt spray. Whales. I quickly mobilize, diving for the aft part of the cockpit well. Ducking below the tiller, I turn the engine on. Once I get it running, I run down below to turn the stereo on and play Vaughan William's "The Lark Ascending".

"What's going on?" Phil asks trying to rub the sleep from his eyes. "Jesus, what's that smell? Why are you all wet?"

"We are surrounded by whales," I reply.

"Why did you turn the stereo on?"

"If we are going to have an angry whale try to sink us, I am going to do the Titanic thing, and go down with good music. I am also hoping the engine sounds and soothing music will scare them away."

"I think Pearl Jam would have been a better choice," he says as he heads back to the bunk.

The following day, at eight a.m., Phil is still in bed. I feed Stewart and make coffee. I wait until eight thirty. No Phil. I feel guilty about waking him the night before with the stereo and give him another half hour. At nine, I go forward to wake him. Stewart is grooming himself lying on top of a pillow which Phil's head is under.

"Honey? Wake up its almost nine o'clock. Don't you feel very well?" No answer. His legs are warm so I know he is still alive. "What's the matter?"

"I have exceeded Nathaniel's Tetris score by several thousand points," is the muffled response from underneath Stewart.

"That's great. You should be happy. How many other forty something-year-olds do you know that can beat their children at computer games?"

"Hmph."

"Is that all that's bothering you?"

"Hmph."

"What else?"

"You don't love me anymore," he says from under the pillow.

"Oh for Pete's sake. I love you more than anything in the universe."

"Our sex life sucks."

"No, our sex life is stuck. At sea. You'll just have to wait until we get to land."

"That's the other thing."

"What?"

"We won't be getting to the Marquesas until after my birthday."

"I know. We'll just celebrate it at sea," I say while rubbing his legs. I have already figured this depressing fact out. We have four hundred miles left to go and the winds are getting lighter. I had counted on arriving in the French territories for Phil's birthday and have absolutely nothing to give him for a present if we are still at sea. Consequently, I have been spending all my watches making little gifts, which fortunately, the less boisterous sea conditions allow. I painted him a view of Iwalani and am now working on a book of dirty limericks and small paintings, Twenty Six Days of Sea, which is also keeping me from going stir crazy.

On the day of Phil's birthday, I make him some chocolate fudge and whoopee pies in lieu of a cake. It is calm enough that we can set up the VCR and TV so he can watch his favorite movie, *The Right Stuff.* It isn't exactly a movie theater and French restaurant, but it's not such a bad day after all.

Chapter 9

Islands with Spires

Marquesas
May 2001

On our twenty- sixth day at sea, the wind drops to a whisper as we motor the last few miles to Nuka Hiva. At six a.m. on my watch, I am finally treated to a picture postcard sunrise. The early rays project a spectral kaleidoscope on the cloud-shrouded peaks, ten miles away. I bring out my colored pencils and draw the scene using every available color. I don't have to worry about the pencils rolling off the cabin top. It is too calm. Phil comes out before his watch to join me.

"Wow! That's pretty impressive," Phil says admiring the spectacular landfall. "It really does take your breath away—just like the books describe."

"Speaking of breath being taken away, have you smelled something gross down below?"

"I did, but I didn't want to say anything."

"I smell it, especially at your nav station," I add.

"I think it's coming from the bilge and your cat," he says.

"My cat? I thought he was our cat. Maybe. But I doubt it."

We go below, open up the floorboards and are met with dark colored, foul smelling, bilge water. I head up into the bow, where we stored our two hundred cans of Pepsi under the floorboard in plastic bags. Phil had supposedly drunk the last can two weeks ago. "Hey look what I found!" I yell to him. "Two more six packs of Pepsi- only one can has leaked out."

"You made my day!" he reaches with glee for a can.

"Don't you feel excited about seeing your first South Pacific landfall?"

"Not as excited as seeing this! No, I'm only kidding. But I don't feel like I thought I would. I'm more excited about finally going to bed with you. I'm getting a headache from the smell down here."

"Your headache could be from T.S.B.U."

"T.S.B.U?" Phil asks.

"Toxic semen build-up."

"And what exactly is that?"

"It's a term classmates and I made-up for a cantankerous professor of ours in Vet school who was going through a horrible divorce. We attributed his rather unpleasant personality to TSBU. Don't worry. In another hour we'll have the anchor down and can finally go to bed together."

"I can't wait," Phil heads up on deck with the French courtesy flag.

"Since it's Sunday, we won't be able to check in or legally go to shore. "

"Do you hear me complaining?" he calls down to me.

*   *   *

It is believed that Polynesian explorers settled the Marquesas around the time of Christ. They arrived in outrigger canoes loaded with everything they would need to establish a community. At the time of Captain Cook's arrival in 1769, the

Marquesas had reached a population high of one hundred thousand people. From contact with white men and the spread of disease over the last three hundred years, the population has dwindled to six thousand or so inhabitants for the entire island group. Many of these are French expatriates who have succumbed to the calls of paradise.

Taiohae Bay, our first landfall, in Nuku Hiva, is the official port of entry for the entire Marquesas group. The radio nets clutter the airwaves with complaints of too many cruising boats, squally weather and unreliable holding in all of the other islands. I feel bad about sailing by some of the beautiful tall peaks and landing at the largest island furthest downwind, because there will be no going back to revisit any of the others. Phil is adamant about following French laws and clearing in at Nuku Hiva, and it is best to give in to one's husband, every once in awhile.

Tall green, bony mountains surround the bay. These are not the gentle slopes of a sleeping giant draped with soft flannel but are the angular spines of a grazing stegosaurus covered with a green tarp. These mountains look as if they can move.

The harbor has the appearance of a large uneven soup bowl and numerous cruising yachts are but small bits of macaroni floating on the broth. A small opening etched away between tall stone spires, provides the doorway to the harbor. Waterfalls cascade down the steep verdant sides in every direction. The harbor water is dark and makes perfect reflections of the surrounding hills. A thin rim of light brown sand surrounds the shoreline. There are a few houses scattered around the shore and a few more up into the hills, most with traditional pandanus roofs, the preferred roofing material of all French Polynesia. Stronger, more durable and less likely to rot over palm frond materials, pandanus trees were brought in dugout canoes with the original settlers. There are many churches with high steeples, but no high-rise hotels in sight. The only marker for the twenty-first century visible from Iwalani, is a "Total" gas station sign at the trader docks and a helicopter pad on a small carved niche above it.

We anchor in seventy-five feet of water. Because the islands are still too young for a barrier reef, a gentle swell necessitates the use of a stern anchor. When we are finally finished securing the boat, I notice a small skiff rowing over to us.

"Hurry up!" Phil yells from the forward bunk, "I'm ready for the rest of my birthday present! I've been twenty six days without sleeping with you, and it's killing me."

"You might have to wait a bit longer. Someone is rowing over to us."

"You're kidding! A local or a yachtie? "

"He came off a tiny little sail boat with an American flag."

Phil comes up on deck tying the string belt on his bathing suit and grabs the binoculars from me.

"We sail twenty-six days to paradise to be boarded by some scrawny American? He'll be here in three minutes. That's just enough time for a quick one."

"How can you stand the smell down there? If we're lucky our bilge smell will drive him off."

Jim from "Second Chance" arrives sweating and out of breath a few minutes later.

I know Phil is tearing at the sheets so to speak, down below, so I offer Jim a cold glass of water, rather than a cold beer.

"Wow!" he says after he takes his first timid sip. "This is cold and doesn't taste like boat water. How did you get cold water like this after a month at sea?"

"While we may look like an old clunky boat, you should remember that looks can be deceiving," I say to him. "Our desalinator makes the water from the sea."

His real mission is revealed after he opens his backpack. "Got any books to trade?" he asks. His collection, cheap novels mostly, is tattered and frayed. I feel sorry for him having to peddle off romance novels, so I load him down with more substantive works, and some old magazines, which for him carry recent news. He is gone within minutes.

"Now are you coming to bed?" Phil asks.

I race forward. No sooner are we in the throes of a long overdue embrace when a shrill alarm goes off. Not the kind in your head, but the ear piercing, time to get moving, imminent danger kind of alarm.

"What the hell is that?" I shriek to Phil over the blaring siren.

"It's our bilge alarm. We are leaking gas in the bilge!" Phil jumps out of bed forgoing his swim trunks. "Iwalani is going to explode!" Phil runs out on deck to shut the propane tanks off while I lift the floorboards up. "Whatever you do, don't make a spark," Phil yells down to me.

"What if the bilge pump comes on?"

"Turn it off before it does. I don't think it will though. We haven't been leaking any water. In fact, I think that is what the main problem is."

"It doesn't smell like propane down here. It smells like hydrogen sulfide gas and methane. I can't believe that this is from Pepsi," I yell up to Phil.

"I think it is from stagnant bilge water." Suddenly, the alarm stops, but the echo of its din continues to reverberate in my skull. "Iwalani hasn't been leaking enough; and for the last two days we haven't been moving as much, so the bilge hasn't been sloshing around. We're going to have to clean this bilge out."

"Right now?" I ask in disbelief.

"It's either the boat exploding or me. Which would you prefer?"

"Ok, fine. I get the picture. I'll hook up the hose."

I put the saltwater wash down hose into the bilge and run the bilge pumps, but the pick up hoses are situated in such a way that the last few inches of bilge water are left behind. We get baling cups and scoop the last bit out into a five-gallon bucket of water.

"I can't dump this overboard," I say shaking my head and looking at Phil.

"Why not?"

"What if someone sees me? It looks like crude oil."

"I've checked the engine. We are not leaking oil. Nor are any of the spare containers leaking oil."

"Yeah, but anyone seeing me doesn't know that. It still looks like I am dumping crude oil over board."

"You worry too much what people think."

"I am going to dump it in the sink. It will still end up in the same place."

I begin pouring the bucket down the sink, then pause. "It sure looks like oil. Look at the silver sheen on it. What the heck is this stuff?" I take ten Pyrex cups from the shelf and pour the remainder into them.

"Now what are you doing?"

"I'm going to conduct some experiments."

I go forward and untie the case holding my microscope from its resting place over the forward bunk, plug it in, and put a small amount of the black goo onto a slide, stepping around Phil who is still head first in the bilge.

"Look at this- it's an organism."

"Can you get me the scrub brush on deck?"

"This is really cool. It's a protozoal organism, or a unicellular zygote from some larger creature. They all look the same. Half of them are dead."

"While you are up there, do you mind getting a piece of Scotch bright pad?"

"Hm. What did you say, dear?"

"Are you helping me or not?"

"What do you think about the possibility that there is plankton that manufactures crude oil? What if this plankton feeds on wood, which is maybe why no one has discovered it up until this point because most boats now days are steel or fiberglass? One hundred years ago when wooden boats sailed these seas no one was paying attention to oil. What if oil is really from these creatures and an organic substrate and not from the decay of organic material and high pressure from millions of years ago? What if this plankton eats wood thus creating crude oil as a by-product of cellulose degradation? What if, when the oceans covered most of the earth, the forests were eaten by this plankton creating crude oil and then they dried up leaving the deserts behind and the oil deposits beneath? Maybe Iwalani has solved the whole global oil crisis. Maybe that's why people keep finding more oil in reserve because it's actually still being made."

"I hate to burst your bubble but there is also a perfectly logical explanation for the oil."

"I thought you said it wasn't leaking from the engine."

"It's not. But you forget that I filled all the pockets in the bilge with pitch so water wouldn't lay in them. It's probably so hot from the tropics that the pitch has melted into the bilge."

"Then wouldn't we see streaks of it running down into the bilge?"

"Are you getting me the scrub brush?"

"I like my explanation better. I'm still conducting experiments. Wait a minute. I'll get you the brush."

We, well Phil mostly, scrubs the bilge using dishwashing soap and rinses it with salt water. When we are finally done, we take showers and head forward to get back into bed.

"Did you hear something?"

"No."

There is a very sharp knock on the hull.

"Iwalani. Iwalani. Anyone home? It's Sunbow."

"Don't worry. I'll go talk to him."

I throw on some clothes, go up on deck, and tell Ken we have been cleaning the bilge and are only now getting around to other things. Most cruisers are pretty good about giving new arrivals a discreet time to get unfinished business taken care of.

After Ken leaves I go forward. Phil is fast asleep.

*   *   *

The following morning I am still on my watch schedule. I lie perfectly still hoping not to wake Phil, or Stewart who has climbed between us during the night and has his paws wrapped around my neck. Stewart is snoring gently into my ear.

"You awake?" Phil asks.

"Yes. I have been for awhile."

"I am so used to life compressed into four hour sound bites. I'm not used to sleeping one whole night."

"I would have had two cups of coffee by now and read one book."

"Too bad we couldn't get someone to make coffee for us right now and bring it up here," Phil laments.

"Plus a chocolate croissant. Fifi should be up by now."

"Fifi?"

"Fifi- the French exporn star- now turned boat maid, girlfriend of Lars, the bronzed Norwegian hunk with rapacious strength and penurious wit. He sometimes helps me with the sail handling and doesn't ask any questions because he can't. He's too dim witted. They joined us somewhere along six degrees south and one hundred and twenty west."

"I see. And what does Fifi look like?" Phil asks with peaked interest.

"What would you like her to look like?"

"Well she must wear a French maids uniform or nothing. She has long blond hair and blue eyes. She's tan and slim."

"Hmm she can't be too good looking-otherwise I'd worry about you running off with the help."

"Alright. She has a rather awkward looking nose. Distractingly so."

"That's better."

Later, we walk along the cement road following the shoreline. Beaches, some stone, some sand, are interspersed with the remains of large rectangular ceremonial areas called marae. To make the marae, the ancient Marquesans built dry stone beds and surrounded them with stone walls. Altars of stone are situated in positions not unlike church altars of today. Seating areas are constructed along the periphery, with a long stretch of middle ground left open, presumably for dancing. Large stone tikis, which celebrate the phallus, are scattered here and there. A few well-endowed gods are left intact, but most have been amputated by the missionaries. The interior was filled with dirt and over time has now been covered in a soft green carpet of fine bladed grass.

The first American writer to describe the Marquesan islands was Herman Melville in his book Typee. Melville arrived on board the whaling ship Dolly, at Taiohae Bay, Nuku Hiva, in 1844. The French had claimed the Marquesas in 1842 and six large French frigate ships were moored in the harbor. All ship's cannons were aimed at the small palm-fronded huts to ensure there would be no uprising. The militia brought horses on shore and the ship's officers cantered up and down the shoreline to the captivated amazement of the Marquesans. The "puarkee nuee" (big hogs is the literal translation) were an instant hit.

Today we see many puarkee nuee grazing in the abandoned marae. Most have halters and six-foot lead lines dragging in the well grazed green grass. They appear to be communal property for the less prosperous islanders. If someone wants to get to the other side of the harbor, they grab a horse, swing up and canter off to their destination.

If one looks at the shoreline side of the road, one can see the Marquesas of long ago. The marae, the Marquesan men with long black hair and cut off shorts, barefooted and barebacked, galloping by on the small horses. Outrigger canoes, mostly fiberglass now, line the beach. On the inland side of the single street are a few pizza parlors, one bank and two small grocery stores, bringing Nuku Hiva to the present.

In the nineteen eighties scientists claimed palm oil was detrimental to people's arteries. As a result, the copra industry throughout the South Seas suffered. How could people make a buck off an unsuspecting, suddenly health conscious culture? The Marquesans looked no further than their front yards. Present in sloppy, stinky, copious quantities is a tree called the "nono" and considered of little value to the islanders. Related to the soursop tree, it bears fruit high in antioxidants. Overnight, "nono" became "noni" simply by changing a vowel. Noni is being marketed as the new invigorator for a health conscious American culture. Most Marquesans are now wealthy enough to be driving air conditioned Range Rovers, a fact that is not missed by me as I gasp in the exhaust along the road's edge, the few times a large SUV whizzes by us.

After we clear in, we meet up with Ken from Sunbow. Judy has already flown out of the Marquesas for Tahiti where she is to fly back to the US for the birth of their first grandchild. Because they have been cruising for years and are pros at it, and because I am always impressed with the fresh foods they have on board, I wrangle Ken into educating me on the finer points of bartering for food. We have been almost a month without re-provisioning our fresh vegetable supply. A few onions and Galapagos potatoes are still left, as well as Iwalani's jarred garden of bean sprouts, but we used the last cabbage a week ago. We long for something green and crunchy and have the most incredible craving for celery!

Phil leaves us and heads to the internet cafe, while Ken and I meet up with Andy, a two hundred pound Marquesan whose body is covered with tattoos. The Marquesans were among the first cultures to practice tattooing. They burned the nut from the candlenut tree, mixing the soot and sap to produce the blue color of all Marquesan tattoos. The tattoos are highly stylized depictions of humans, animals, patterned checks and diamonds, battles fought and won, or recent victims eaten. The Marquesans were among the last of the Polynesian people to give up

cannibalism. In 1930 a little old woman was convicted of eating her granddaughter, the child murdered on the guise of fetching some fruit off a tree. "Just a little further out dearie, just a wee bit more." Crack, splat, and into the pot. It makes Hansel and Gretel seem almost believable.

"She is looking for some vegetables," Ken says to Andy while pointing at me.

"What have you got for trade? Cigarettes?" he asks me with eyes lighting up.

"No," I say shaking my head.

"T-shirts?" he asks.

Andy stares down on me with terribly fierce dark eyes. I imagine him to be thinking what sauce would go best with my fatty white flesh.

Our bartering box is pitiful. My mother always told me to leave a place better than when you arrive. This can be challenging at times. As a result, I can't bring myself to carry the tacky T-shirts that lie unworn in the bottom drawer at home. There are many garish T shirts with sayings like "Sluts on Wheels," "Eat it Raw," or "Babes on Bikes," gracing the backs and fronts of many native populations. These are hot trade goods, but I just can't seem to be responsible for trashing the local scenery with such crap. I am a snob, I admit it. Our trade goods box has none of the objects on Andy's agenda.

"No T-shirts," I say shaking my head. I actually do have the supplies to make people customized T-shirts with photos of their choice rather than garish logos, but my computer died while we were at sea. There will be no custom manufactured T-shirts.

"You have no T shirts?" Andy asks completely incredulous. "Rum? You must have rum."

I shake my head. "Money. I have American money."

"Maybe I trade tikis for money," he grunts.

He turns and whispers something to his sourpuss wife who has been sitting in the driver's seat of their Range Rover. This should have been a clue to me from the get go. How can I successfully barter with a native who drives a fancier car than I can ever dream of owning?

Before I can voice any objections, they drive off together leaving Ken and me staring at their son, little Andy, who is guarding the vegetables. He is eating, or rather, sucking, the large oversized pumpkin seed-like pit from the inside of a mango. He stares at us, while sucking the mango up then down, up and down, again and again. We stare back, our heads and eyes following the north and south movement of his slurping nodding mouth, his technique, nothing short of porn-star-professional.

Big Andy and sourpuss wife return a half-hour later with a laundry basket full of "hand carved wooden artifacts." Andy reaches into the basket and pulls out a foot high wooden tiki with a six-inch dick that stands fully erect, straight out. It would have made a nice tie rack gift for a detested relative.

"Penis too small," I say shaking my head.

Next he pulls out a carved bowl, which could have doubled as an infant's cradle.

"Too big," I say.

Next, are several ugly wooden beaded necklaces. "Too heavy" I reply.

I can see frustration looming in his eyes as we are nearing the bottom of the basket. He pulls out a wooden hairpin. It would have been nice to use for a set of chopsticks if there had been two. "Need two," I say.

All I really want are some fresh vegetables. Finally, Ken, who has been standing silent this whole time, says in a cooing voice, "She has a cat".

Andy's eyes light up at the thought of fresh feline meat.

I shoot Ken a basilisk glance, "Money for vegetables. No cat."

I pick out two avocados and a cabbage.

"How much for these?" I ask in a high pitched plead. I hate shopping in any form, and want this to end.

"One thousand francs."

"One thousand francs!" Ken barks, feeling a little guilty for trying to sell Stewart. "I paid two hundred francs for a whole wheel barrow full of vegetables on Hiva Oa."

"Yes, well this is Nuka Hiva," says Andy. But you can see the new political conflict developing in his brain. Not wanting to be one-upped by the competing islanders he relents, "OK. I sell you this for five hundred francs."

I agree. As we walk away, I realize I have a lot to learn about this food procurement thing.

"You got ripped off," Ken says to me.

"You tried to sell my cat."

"I was only kidding."

"To a man who probably eats kittens for snacks?"

"Maybe they're good."

"Maybe men from catamarans are better, not as tough as we wooden boat people," I say, punching him in the shoulder.

"Hey, Sunbow is wood, too," Ken says, kneading where I hit him.

"Yah, right."

"No, really. She is strip planked. At the very core she's wood."

I roll my eyes. "Everyone is a wanna-be," I reply.

"Well, you do have an obligation to the cruising community to keep prices low. If one boat pays a lot for something, then everything changes and all the prices go up."

"I hadn't realized I was involved in such an important financial responsibility."

"The worst thing you can do is give gifts—for nothing."

"You mean like a tip? I already know not to tip anyone in Polynesia."

"That's right. It's an insult."

Ken exchanges places with Phil at the single working computer at the Internet café. Phil does his best to hide it, but I can tell we have bad news from the e-mail.

Phil and I decide to go out to lunch before returning to Iwalani. He stops to photograph the school buses as we walk down the street.

"That kid just gave me the finger," he says.

"No, he was waving."

"Waving his middle finger. Why do you have to disagree with me so much?"

"I'm not," I snap back.

"You are."

"Fine whatever."

As we walk down the street, dark clouds blow overhead and effectively seal off all the light, closing in the harbor like a lid on a jar. It is almost as dark as dusk, yet it is still noontime. Before we reach the French restaurant, the heavens open up, and we are deluged with rain so heavy that the drops coalesce into cascades. We are soaked. Steam rises off Phil's back, but I am cold, so I try to warm myself up at the earthen oven used for baking pizza. I had not figured on being frozen in the tropics.

"What's wrong?" I finally ask Phil.

"Just more hate mail from my ex-wife. I really miss the kids. I wish they were here with us."

"Well, you'll be able to fly back in June for Ben's graduation."

"That's the other thing. I looked up the price of round trip tickets from Tahiti. Ben's college tuition is going to be twenty thousand dollars this year. I agreed to pay half of it, while his mother picks up the other half. Then there is the child support and their health insurance. I don't think we can afford it. The airfare for one person is four thousand dollars, not four thousand francs."

"Ouch. I was a few thousand off on my estimate."

"Now do you see why I am so depressed?"

After lunch we walk back to the dinghy dock. The sun is shining, but the air is as thick as jelly.

"Do you see our dinghy?" I ask Phil. The maroon color of the Grape usually stands out from the crowd of gray inflatables.

"It sure looks like it's gone, but it's hard to tell with all the splashing around from all those kids swimming."

"Not all of them are swimming!" I say running to the shore.

"Holy shit! Those little bastards!"

A dozen Marquesan kids are using the Grape as a pool toy. The dinghy itself is sinking and has an inch of free board left. Half the kids are inside the dinghy bailing like mad, while the other half are outside the dinghy throwing water in. Elders sit nearby watching the fun.

By the time Phil reaches to the dinghy he is pretty angry. "OUT!" he screams at the kids.

They pause for a second looking up at him, water dripping from their half-raised arms, then proceed to carry on with the imminent sinking. The outboard engine is just a few handfuls of water away from being ruined.

"STOP" he yells again. He turns his attention to the kids outside the dinghy for they are the bigger pawns in the balance. A few sulk off dejectedly swimming away, while the more earnest young fellows realize there might be something in it for them if they stay and help bail. One boy tries to climb into the boat.

"NO!" Phil screams. Luckily, two boys who remained in the dinghy continue their bailing with renewed vigor, and the scales for staying afloat now tip in the dinghy's favor. We ignore the children who hold out their outstretched hands for financial remuneration.

"Shouldn't we reward the kids who tried to keep it afloat," I wonder.

"What are you, nuts?" Phil asks while bailing. "For all I know they were in this together."

"You're right. This whole kid thing is just one balancing act. No different from training dogs. The barking dog gets positive reinforcement when its owner gives it a biscuit so it will shut up."

"No different."

"But isn't it kind of odd that their parents and family watched enjoying the show while their children destroy private property?"

"You've got to remember we're in a different culture. Everyone here views property as communal."

"So you mean they wouldn't mind if I grabbed one of the town horses and went for a ride?"

"I don't know. I wouldn't want to put it to a test."

That evening we hear drum beats coming from shore, not just the sound of drums made from stretched skins, but an additional sound of hollow logs rapidly being rapped with sticks, all beating in unison. The pulsing rhythm reverberates off the stone peaks of the surrounding mountains, turning the entire harbor into a single amplifier.

"Let's go to shore and see what's going on," I suggest.

In case the miscreants are lurking in the underbrush to ruin the outboard for a second round of "sink the Grape," we remove the outboard from the dinghy and row to shore. After securing the Grape, we follow the drumbeats along the shoreline until we come to the public market grounds, a large pole shed with a cement floor. We avoid the light from the single streetlight and move around in the shadows. Many people are gathered under the roof in the dark: twenty-five drummers, about an equal number of dancers, and the young well muscled coach, wearing nothing but a bathing suit and carrying a whistle. He communicates to the dancers and drummers solely with sharp trills and rapid arm movements. Phil wanders by himself off to the far side of the shed, behind the drummers, so he can get a better view of the dancers.

"Bon soir," a Polynesian man about my height whispers to me.

"Bon soir, monsieur."

"Vous êtes Americaine?"

"Oui."

"Ah good. I practice English. What is your name?"

"Amy. Et vous?

"Thierry."

"Where did you learn to speak English?"

"My father taught me."

"You speak it very well.

"I only get to speak when I see my father."

"Where is he?"

"He lives on Ua Puo. My mother lives on Nuku Hiva."

"Are they divorced?"

"No. That is just how it is."

We stand silently watching the dancers. I don't know what else to say to my new found friend, so after a while I ask, "How do you pronounce the name of this harbor, Taiohae?"

"No. KIE-o-HEY, " he says with a very guttural tone. "You need to say it fierce. It means war."

"Oh, Kie-o-hey," I repeat, spitting on him in the process, quite by accident, but he doesn't seem to notice as he is doing his best to stand upright.

"Would you like a beer?" he asks me.

"No, thank you," I reply.

"How do you like the dancing?"

"Unbelievable," I say. It is true. The entire troupe is working in the dark. The young female dancers are wearing a piece of white cloth tied around their hips. As fast as the human hand can beat sticks on a log, their white cloth is keeping up with the rhythm. Straight black hair cascades down their backs like an unmoving sheet of polished slate. "Those girls have body parts not found on American women. I don't think I have ever seen such beauty in a human body."

He laughs. "This is just the practice. You should be here for the festival."

"Bastille Day?"

"No, I mean, yes. For the French it is Bastille Day. For us it is Heiva. It is like your Olympics- but with dancing, rock throwing, outrigger races, songs, and feasting.

"Do each of these dance moves have meaning?"

"Of course. Each song, too."

It is then I begin to realize that the drums aren't just playing in random jazz riffs, but are orchestrated pieces, as recognizable to a Polynesian as a Haydn or Beethoven symphony is to Western ears.

"This one is about our ancestors coming by boat to the islands and the storms they had on the way," he explains.

Since they had no written word, the Polynesians kept their entire history alive for centuries, through dance and song. I am saddened when I realize the people I come from were the zealots who tried to destroy this culture as being amoral. The dances, the beat, the rhythm were all about fecundity, not just sex: the richness of the land, the bounty of the sea and the final culmination of being at the top of the food chain, women's hips, not their breasts, the most important aspect of child bearing and proclivity. An island crowned with spires. How best to celebrate the glory of god, living in a monastery, whipping oneself for trying not to recognize all human body parts, or living and loving all that is put on this planet?

Phil wanders back to us. "Unbelievable," he whispers to me.

"Yes. Isn't it?

"No, I mean, I leave you for just a minute and already you get picked up by some guy."

"Phil, this is Thierry. Thierry this is my husband."

"Do you have work I can do on your boat?" Thierry asks Phil.

"Phil does all the work on our boat. But there are plenty of other cruisers in the harbor, who might be interested. I'll ask around." I answer.

When the dances finish, we say goodbye to Thierry and return to Iwalani. A lone rooster crows far up in the hills, while the rhythmic squeak of our oarlocks provides the only response.

*   *   *

The following morning we have to return to the gendarme office to fill out more paperwork and buy our stamps for a three-month visa in French territories. As I row to shore, Phil spies a pretty wooden boat, which came in earlier that morning.

"Head over to it for a second, would you? This must be the only other wooden boat in the South Pacific."

"Can you make out the name?" I ask Phil.

"The flag is British. Will-something."

"Willy Bolton?"

"Yup. That's it. How do you know the name?" Phil asks.

"Little Flying Fish Radio net. They sounded interesting. They tore out their mainsail on the way here and everyday sounded cheerful as they hand-stitched away. Well, Kathryn, anyway sounded cheerful. You miss a lot by sleeping through the radio net."

"I don't think so. It doesn't look like anyone's on board, but we should offer to use Beulah and sew their mainsail for them."

As we are walking back from the gendarme we see a pretty woman conducting her two girls down the street like Maria from *The Sound of Music*.

"I bet that's Willy Bolton," I say to Phil. "Lets cross over and introduce ourselves."

No sooner do we say we are from Iwalani when the two girls let out a shriek. "Stewart! You are the boat with the cat Stewart! We have some paperwork for you." The eldest daughter reaches into her backpack and hands me a brochure.

"I am Ellie, and this is Jess. We have started a business called E&J Pet Sitting."

"We could sure use your services. And we might be able to offer some of our own. Have you got your mainsail sewed?" I inquire politely.

All three answer simultaneously. "Yes." "Almost." "Not quite."

"Anthony is finishing the repair right now. However, the stitching on the rest of the sail is suspect," adds Kathryn.

"We have a heavy duty sail repair sewing machine and would be happy to reinforce the stitching," Phil offers.

"Come on out to Willy Bolton this afternoon for tea," Kathryn says while whisking Jess out of the way of a fast moving SUV. "You can have a look at the sail."

"We'd love to."

"Can you bring Stewart?" the girl's ask together.

"By French law he has to stay on the boat," I explain. "But we were thinking about going out to dinner at a restaurant tomorrow night. Would you be able to pet sit him then?"

"Oh, could we?"

"Oh, please, Mum," the girls plead.

"I guess this is the start of your new business," Kathryn remarks.

*   *   *

The following evening we head out to dinner at the only hotel in Nuku Hiva. E&J begin their pet sitting enterprise armed with hairbrushes and combs, bows, cat treats, paper and crayons so they can create cat portraits of their new charge.

Beautiful Polynesians glide to our table bringing us dish after dish of delectable food. "Are you mad at me?" I ask Phil who is more silent than usual.

"Why? Should I be?"

"Great. You only say that when you are. What did I do now?"

"Nothing. But I have decided I can't go back home even for a few weeks. Every man in a four mile radius would be over to Iwalani looking for work or looking for something."

"I think I can handle it. You are way too jealous."

"And with good reason. After seeing you meet up with Thierry on the street and having him slobber all over you. I almost punched him."

"Thank goodness you didn't. Kissing is how the French greet one another. I must admit though that, all the excess saliva did take me by surprise. I think I was even more taken aback to see him in daylight. He's got quite a strabismus," I reply.

"That's what kept me from knocking him flat. After he was done kissing you, I had no idea which eye to aim for."

"I know you have been battle scarred from your first marriage, but you really need to trust me. I try not to get jealous over you and the Bambino boat."

Bambino is a thirty-foot German boat. The German wife doesn't like cruising, so the husband has at least three nubile young women on board for crew. Sometimes his wife flies out to meet him at various places and the bikini-clad crew all mysteriously disappear. Twenty pairs of binoculars are usually fixed on Bambino when she enters a harbor, including a set from Iwalani.

"Have you noticed anything peculiar about our wait staff?" Phil whispers to me trying to change the subject.

"A little flat chested," I say wiping a dribble of coconut milk off the corner of my mouth from the fresh poisson cru.

"More than that."

I look closely at the next person who floats by our table in bare feet. Long black hair is carefully tied back with hibiscus flowers and twine. Dark colored eyes are made up with eyeliner, full lips painted lightly with lipstick. A flowered pareu is draped artfully around the body.

Iwalani's Poisson Cru:
Cut very fresh white fish into 1/2 inch thick strips about two inches long. In a glass bowl combine 2 oz fresh lime juice for each pound of fish and 3 oz (per lb of fish) of coconut milk. Add cucumber, green onions, chives, strips of green pepper, grated lime zest, salt and pepper. Stir to mix and serve immediately.

"Oh my!" I exclaim. "It's a man! They are all men. Well almost," I realize looking about the room. "Do you think we are here on drag night- or is this just the way things are?"

"I think this is just the way things are."

"We've got a lot more to learn about this planet."

　　　　*　　　*　　　*

One week later we take Iwalani to the north side of Nuku Hiva to enjoy what is reported to be calmer conditions away from the prevailing trade winds. Phil and I decide at the last moment to continue on, a little further to the west, to the next anchorage which is free of sailboat masts.

The cruising guide mentions several marae not too far from our private harbor where we might see some hieroglyphs and a sacred banyan tree.

We pack water and cameras and hike up into the hills. A horse grazes in the first marae, and we spy a small overgrown path winding up into the thick jungle beyond it. Before too long we are at the second marae. "I think this

That rock carving is not to commemorate mushrooms and other fungi...

is the sacred banyan tree, only it's been stuck by lightening. Look at what's nesting in the hollow."

I look where Phil is pointing. A long white feather hangs down from a nest.

"What is it?" I ask.

"It's a tropicbird. It's not every day you get to see one of these on land."

I walk through what is left of the banyan tree. The charred core is large enough for a Volkswagen to park inside. The nest has become a roof over the core of the tree. Because the north side of the island is considerably sunnier and hotter than Tahoiae Bay, I am sweating from the hike in. I strip off my dress and bathing suit, happy to be free of clothes.

"Take a look at what I found," Phil says. Near the banyan tree is a stone pot, inside the pot are carved heads, which Phil is busy photographing.

"Nice tribute to cannibalism," I agree.

"What happened to your clothes?"

"I was hot. Plus, they didn't seem appropriate here."

Phil too, throws off his shirt and shorts.

"Much better."

"Come look at the backside of this sculpture," Phil urges.

"Whoo hoo!" I say looking at the writhing mass of tongues and penises, behind a traditional tiki. "This must have sent the missionaries into a tailspin."

"The Marquesans obviously hid this marae from them. It seems as if I am two centuries too late for all that was fun in the world."

I eye Phil's curved rear end, "The missionaries sure put the ky-bosh on a lot of fun. Even cannibalism doesn't seem so bad to me."

"Oh yah- well you've got to catch me first," he squeals dropping the backpack and camera. I chase him around the grass enclosure, too slow to catch him.

"Stop you little pixie- just one bite from your tender flesh!"

"No way! I need my butt for sitting," he yells back at me.

We both fell down panting and sweating on a large stone slab.

"What do you think this was used for?" I ask him.

"Hm, we can conduct a few tests to find out."

"Ack!" I say sitting bolt upright. " I just heard a car door slam!"

"A car door? What are you nuts? You are imagining things."

"No really."

"Uh-oh. I heard it too."

Through the thick brush we can see the tops of several white-hatted heads coming our way.

"Oh no! Where the heck did they come from? My clothes are in the sacred banyan tree."

We scramble off in different directions to find our clothes. When I emerge, a group of eight tourists are being led into the central corral of the marae. Their tour guide seems to be an effective shepherd as the entire group is glued tightly together.

"Bonjour!" the guide calls out to us.

We pick up the backpack and nod to the bunch while slipping down the unmarked path we had taken in, happy we travel in a loosely connected flock, not a herd- the true distinction between cruisers and land bound travelers.

Amy emerges from what is left of the sacred banyan tree.

Chapter 10

The Highway to Tahiti

July 2001
French Polynesia

We spent over one month at Nuku Hiva, hiking, swimming, snorkeling and getting Iwalani ready for the next passage. Phil repaires Willy Bolton's mainsail and those from several other boats. Weeks of constant use and three thousand miles had fatigued a lot of yacht's stitching, fraying both nerves and cloth. With the help of a spare hard drive from Sunbow and Phil's computer skills, Arnold, my computer, is back up and running, but all our digital photographs taken up to that point are gone for good. The pictures uploaded to the internet are all we have as back up. The moon is waxing. Our larders are getting low, and I am failing miserably at the hunter/gatherer role. I finally found one bunch of celery at a small store but inexplicably decided to come back later and buy it. When I returned a half hour later, it was gone. Our new motto becomes, "When you see celery, buy it." It is time for us to move on.

We planned to stop in the Tuomotos on our way to Tahiti. This low-lying group of atolls was a formidable cruising ground in the past and for today's standards, still is. Most charts were drawn in the 1850's with errors of over a mile. GPS corrected charts, with errors measured in inches, have yet to be drawn. With many reefs scattered about, an error in any direction of one mile can put you in dangerous waters. Using the full moon for nighttime illumination helps to lessen the probability of grounding at night; more light means more things like reefs and islands can be seen. We opt for hand drawn charts printed in a book called Charlie's Charts of Polynesia. In some instances, the term "really tall, lone palm tree" is used as an aid for navigation. To say I am nervous using a lone palm tree for navigating is an understatement.

The passage is over five hundred miles. It is to be our first experience with line squalls. During the day, most of the squalls evaporate before they reach us. The skies are blue, the sun is shining and the usual small puffy trade wind clouds follow us, but at night these happy little puffballs coalesce into angry, vindictive and pesky demons. I had read about line squalls from previous voyaging accounts, yet I didn't really understand their true nature. The name fits. At night, the radar picks each one up individually. Sometimes on the radar screen, they look like strips of bacon sizzling in a frying pan. They march along military fashion, huffing and puffing and spitting out rain in perfectly straight lines across the prevailing winds. By judging their speed relative to Iwalani's speed, we get very good at steering around most of them. It is almost like playing a video arcade game. If one can't be avoided, the person on watch drops the jib, keeps the reefed main and full staysail up, closes all the hatches and portholes then waits. Each squall produces at most gusts of twenty-five knots and torrents of rain. They seem to be more of nuisance than a hazard.

One morning, after I make pancakes for breakfast, we take the reef out of the mainsail from the previous night. This is the start of a habit we soon acquire, automatically reducing sail at night. We are beginning to see how lucky we were with our passage to the Marquesas. Full sail up, with no line handling for four weeks, spoiled us. We eat down below, having a civilized breakfast, when I notice Stewart is looking around with a very puzzled expression on his face.

"What's he doing?" Phil asks me.

"He hears something." And then we hear it, too. "Birds? Out here?" I ask.

We leave our plates firmly anchored on the pieces of non-skid we use for placemats at sea, leave Stewart down below, and run out on deck.

"Whales," Phil says. We can see their huge dark shapes swimming hundreds of feet below our keel.

"Aren't you glad I went to such trouble to get green bottom paint now?" I ask Phil.

All the ships attacked by whales in recent years held one thing in common, red bottom paint. In too many parts of the world whale hunting is still legal and most of the attacks happen within a few hundred miles of a whaling operation. Maybe the red bottom paint was coincidental, but I didn't want to take any chances pissing a whale off, and Phil was superstitious about blue paint on a boat, so the only other option was green bottom paint, which was not an easy color to find.

"I don't mind them swimming that far below us, I just don't want one to surface near us. I was due to come on deck and have a look around anyhow. Hey, that doesn't look very good," Phil says.

I follow his gaze to the southwest. In the far corner of our blue world is a band of purplish gray, lipping up over the horizon. "It's just a squall. No big deal. Besides its downwind of us."

"Hm," Phil says doubtfully.

We wait a while to see if the whales re-surface. They never do, which makes one crewmember very happy and one very sad. We go back down below and finish our breakfast and then I turn in for my morning nap.

"Amy, I think you should come up here," Phil yells down the forward hatch to me. I have no idea how long I had been asleep. I look at my watch. Nine thirty. I've been asleep for forty-five minutes. It seems like hours. The squall I had dismissed to the southwest is now fast approaching us. The entire southern sky is smeared with an ugly bruise colored cloud. "We need to put a reef in the main. Fast. This is no squall. This is a front."

We take down the jib and start to put in the reef. This effort usually requires two people. Phil is not one to head into the wind for making any adjustment to the mainsail, preferring to do it on the fly. He is a New Yorker after all, and they are never happy to slow down or alter course. As a result, tying the last set of reef points and outhaul requires him to hang out over the lifelines, practically horizontal over the water, as his long arms reach the dangling ties used to secure the furled sail to itself. I am too short to attempt this maneuver. I hold on to his pants, but if he has no pants on, I make him wear a harness and I hold on to that. Just as Phil starts leaning out, an Antarctic blast of cold wind and rain strikes us. The horizontal rain feels like sleet on our naked skin. Iwalani heals far over. The wind generator begins humming as it whirls around generating twenty amps of steady electricity. We are now on a beam reach and Iwalani is going well over eight knots.

"We need to scandalize the main," Phil yells to me over the roar of the waves.

I go forward and drop the peak halyard while he pulls down on the peak downhaul. The gaff swings down like the broken wing of a shot goose. Iwalani's speed is reduced to six knots; she holds herself upright. Again Phil tries to hang out over the rail. Although the harness is snapped into the jack line, I still hold on to him. He is successful this time and reaches the outhaul and reef points. When he has both feet firmly planted on the deck, I realize we are both covered with goose bumps.

"We're not at the equator anymore, Toto," Phil says to me.

"No kidding. The last creature this wind saw was a penguin."

I still have two more hours until my watch. I go down below and am grateful that Phil washed and put away the breakfast dishes before the front arrived. As an added bonus, Stewart has jumped into the bunk and is keeping it warm.

For the next few days we are plagued with storms or no wind at all. We can't maintain a constant speed as we either have too much sail up or not enough. We maintain regular radio contact with Willy Bolton, who left the Marquesas seven hours ahead of us completely avoiding the bad weather and have been in the Tuomotos for two days. It will not be the only time we encounter dissimilar weather along the same route.

The atolls of the Tuomotos are as distinct from the Marquesas as Kansas is to Colorado. All islands in the Pacific have volcanic origins. The Marquesas, not quite as young as the Galapagos, are still relatively young islands, geologically speaking. The Tuomotos, on the other hand, are ancient decayed grandfathers. The bigger the volcano, the more land mass there is to heat up from the sun, the larger the clouds that are formed over the top of it, the more rainfall there is to carve out valleys. Coral attaches to the side of the volcanoes away from the fresh water streams. As the volcano slowly erodes away from the rain, the coral begins to build up, like tartar on a tooth. The Marquesas are now at this stage; in places along the sides of the mountains away from fresh water, we find very good diving not marked in any cruising guides. But, because there is not a surrounding protective coral reef, the anchorages were uncomfortable from ocean swell.

Eventually the soft volcano erodes completely away, like a rotten tooth, leaving a central lagoon with a coral rim called an "atoll." The coral rim keeps growing and begins to support vegetation. It soon forms low-lying islands called "motu," all that remains of a once high and mighty volcano. Gaps in the coral, called "passes" (probably from the original fresh water streams that flowed down the side of a volcano) are the only way to get into the central lagoon. In some places the passes are known to have currents of up to six knots depending on the tide. Rangiroa was to be our first atoll, and timing our arrival through the pass at slack water was critical.

Willy Bolton radioed us that the current would be going out of the pass until about six a.m. and to time our arrival accordingly. When we are fifty miles away, we realize we are still going too fast. We will not be reaching the pass at the right time. We reduce sail. It still isn't slow enough.

"We'll have to take everything down but leave up the outer jib for steerage."

This is our smallest sail, giving us a sail area almost equal to a man's overcoat held open. "At this rate we will be there by five. Is it light at five?" Phil asks me.

"It is lighter than four, but not light enough to go through a pass."

We change our watch schedule so we will both be up at five a.m. When I finally wake up, it is five thirty. I sleepily climb up the companionway to find out why Phil didn't wake me.

"The wind dropped off at about three," he reports. "I had to put more sail up. We're about three miles away from the pass. The wind just began picking up again. Where the hell is the sun?"

"It's coming. It sort of jumps over the horizon with no great preamble. See how it's kind of gray now? This is pretty much all you get for a sunrise. How come you didn't wake me up?"

"I didn't see any sense in it. We are still a ways off."

Phil heads down below to make coffee and inspect the engine. He cleans the fuel filter and switches the valve over to a full fuel tank while the water boils.

As it gradually becomes lighter, I realize a large squall is bearing down on us from the northeast. We are about a half-mile from the entrance and it is almost six o'clock. According to my calculations, the squall will hit us just as we are in the pass.

"Phil? Come up here for a second. We have an uninvited guest."

"What?" he asks as he pokes his head up the companionway. "Oh shit," he says when he sees the black sky behind us.

"What should we do? Hang around out here until it goes by?" I ask him.

"No, we will miss slack water in the pass. We've got to take a chance and get to the pass first and try to get through even though the current might still be going out."

"Why don't we just skip the Tuomotos and go to Tahiti?"

"No way. We got this far, we're going in," he says. "We'll keep the sails up until the last possible moment. Then we'll take the sails down but leave them loosely furled so we can raise them in an emergency, if we have to. In case the engine dies." He adds as an afterthought while heading back down below.

We line ourselves up with the range markers for the entrance, and I take all the sails down. The sun rises up over the horizon turning the underside of the squall to a copper color.

"We're not into the pass yet and we are early. The current is still going out. Remember what I told you about the wind against the tide at the entrance to the Kennebec River?" Phil asks me.

"Sure. Big waves."

"Whatever you do, don't look back," Phil replies.

A six-knot current rushes out of the narrow entrance. As the outgoing current whizzes by, the water swirls into a turquoise cauldron. Dolphins leap out of the waves like winnings from a slot machine. Schools of lagoon fish are swept out into the mouths of bigger fish. Sharks, I am sure, are lurking just below the waves.

Sleepy eyed people come out of their houses with anxious looks on their faces. Some have bags in their hands for collecting salvage from the wreck of Iwalani. Phil holds on tight to the tiller.

"Whatever you do, don't look behind us," he yells to me for a second time. I can't help it. I look.

The squall is right at the back of our necks, blowing its ugly wet breath on us for a few weak puffs. But then, for some inexplicable reason, it veers away, back to the east like a kicked dog. We are free of its menace.

"I have never seen anything like that," I say to Phil.

"Me neither. Someone is looking out for us."

We have been told and have read that running these passes is a little like shooting rapids in a river. Only, instead of a kayak, we're maneuvering a forty-two thousand pound boat. We head toward the opening, pushed forward by ten foot breaking seas, which are rolling straight into the pass. We have reached the point where we can't turn back if we want to. The waves would roll Iwalani around like a baker kneading a loaf of bread.

"Surf's up dude!" I scream as a huge wave breaks behind us. It parts like a hot knife through soft butter when it reaches Iwalani's pointed stern.

"I thought I told you not to look behind!"

"You ain't the boss of me!"

"Oh yeah? What day is it?"

"The seventeenth of June," I say. "I am the boss of you."

"Well, since it's your day to be captain, you should be manning the tiller."

"No way," I reply. "As captain, I appoint you as helmsman."

"What time is it?" Phil asks me.

I look down below at the clock. "Almost seven. Is that so you can record the very second of our demise?"

"Is there a time change here? I am just wondering why the current is still going out.

"I didn't think so, but there must be. The sun is in the six a.m. position."

For ten minutes we are stuck at the entrance to the pass, hung in a swinging balance. We are sucked back by the current and then pushed forward by each breaking wave.

Phil pushes the throttle wide open. The Westerbeke makes a high-pitched scream.

"What is that?" I ask horrified.

"Don't pay any attention," Phil says. "It's just the fan belt on the alternator."

Gradually, I notice that we are beginning to move ahead. Each huge wave lifts Iwalani up and deposits her one foot forward. The current cannot push us back to sea, try as it might.

The scavengers on shore grow bored watching us suspended amidst the raging seas. When they see we are actually moving ahead they begin to lose interest. Some go back to fishing; others wander back into their houses. It takes us an hour to make it through the thousand-foot long pass, not an impressive record.

We call Willy Bolton on the radio to get instructions into the anchorage. They tell us they are wrong about the time of slack water in the pass. Jess has been up for the last two hours anxiously waiting by the radio, worrying for our safety. We laugh and tell them we are fine and that we found out the hard way about entering the pass. Their directions to the anchorage correspond with the cruising guide. One thing I learned from Phil is to use all your available resources. Too often people are embarrassed to ask for directions because it makes them look stupid; I can care less how stupid I seem, I already know it as fact, but, Phil is the only man I know who doesn't mind asking for directions.

The calm anchorage is nestled behind a curved elbow of land. A steady trade breeze spins the wind generator with electricity producing vigor. The water is crystal clear and the color of "Berry Blue Jell–O." It is like no other color of ocean we have seen to date and certainly unlike any color I have seen in nature.

We anchor, clean up the boat, take showers, and decide to go to shore for lunch. Looking through the binoculars, we decide we have two options, a fancy hotel on one side of the lagoon and a smaller café overhanging the water next to a ferry dock.

Throughout Polynesia men and women travel over the water in fast motorboats that have a steering station in the bow and make them look almost like human-boat centaurs. We call them homme-bateaus. These boats are replacing the traditional outrigger canoes that are now made of fiberglass and used mostly for recreational paddling. After seeing several outboards driven by beautiful Polynesian women heading over to the café, we have no choice but to follow them.

"I sure hope they take credit cards as our supply of Polynesian francs is low."

"They do," Phil says pointing to the Visa/MasterCard emblem.

We order the *plat du jour*, but the waitress is unable to understand our queries as to what we were actually ordering. A dish heavily laden with gravy arrives a few minutes later.

"It's good, whatever it is," Phil remarks between mouthfuls of stew.

Kitchen scraps fly out of a window behind us. Suddenly, hundreds of tropical fish appear from all directions to devour the waste that lands in the water.

"Look at all these fish!" Phil points his fork at the water.

"Very pretty," I say carefully dissecting what is hidden under mounds of red wine laced gravy.

"Who needs to get wet to see such spectacular fish? Hey, what's up Doc?"

"I'm not sure. I'm trying to figure out what we are eating. Mushrooms, stewed prunes and some kind of meat." I pick up a small, thick bone and lick it clean.

"And?" Phil asks.

"It appears to be a femur, but not from any type of bird. It doesn't look like a pig. It's young because the growth plate is very much open. It looks like a femur from a chondrodysplastic dwarf. See how it is so curved?"

"Did you say chondrodysplastic dwarf'?"

"Yes. I did. Exactly."

Phil, Ben and Nathaniel knew full well what a chondrodysplastic dwarf was, ever since I had used that term as a clue on one of my infamous birthday treasure hunts: *"You must seek out the chondrodysplastic dwarf."* I wrote, and hid the next clue on my dachshund Polly, a breed representing the quintessential chondrodysplastic dwarf.

"You don't think…?"

"I don't want to know."

"When in Rome, do as the Romans do or eat, rather."

"Just don't tell any of my patients."

The waitress arrives at our table and slides our credit card through a wireless handheld machine. Paying the bill is easier than anywhere at home.

We are the last patrons to leave, and as we walk out into the bright sunshine I see a small corgi-like dog hanging around the back door of the kitchen whining and fussing. Her teats are heavy with milk, but no puppies are in sight.

"I guess that's our answer, or maybe it is just coincidental and I am being overly paranoid," I hope.

"Maybe. Maybe not. Does it make you feel sick though?"

"No. Not at all. If it was puppy stew, it was pretty good. My whole view on cannibalism and eating meat is changing. It could be an effective means of population control, but maybe I should offer to spay the dog."

"That might cut into their supply of '*plat du jour*'."

"Who do you think will be in the "*plat du jour*" tomorrow? They only get two litters a year from the corgi mongrel if they're lucky."

"American Tourist disappears from the atoll of Rangiroa, next up on Frontwhine," Phil says in a mock announcer voice.

"Maybe next time we should eat at the hotel restaurant on the other side, sort of spread the wealth around?"

"Sounds good to me. I still can't believe it though. Here we are in an atoll in the middle of the South Pacific and we paid our bill with a wireless satellite uplink. You'd think they'd make a TV commercial out here."

"Pay for your puppy platter with Visa? It's everywhere you want to be."

"Or maybe, it's everywhere you may not want to be," Phil adds.

"Don't you like Rangiroa?" I ask.

"So far it's about as close to paradise as I've seen. I'm just missing the kids."

"No, you are just suffering from post-prandial puppy depression."

*   *   *

That evening we sail the Grape over to Willy Bolton for a dinner engagement.

"Don't say anything to the girls about our lunch," I remark to Phil. "They might not let us on board if they know we are now caninophages."

"Don't worry. I won't tell a soul."

We round up, drop the dinghy's sails and come alongside "Willy Bolton." No sooner have we stepped aboard when we are met with four anxious voices speaking simultaneously.

"Glad to see you again. We've been terribly busy doing the wash. Please excuse the clothing on the railing. It's been absolutely mad here trying to do repairs, go shopping and get some schooling into these girls," Kathryn says while grabbing some towels off the boarding ladder.

"You must have had an interesting trip, weather-wise. I'm still having trouble with our generator. It is still over heating," Anthony says with his proper British accent.

"YOU REALLY MUST GO SNORKELLING WITH US TOMORROW AT THE AQUARIUM. IT IS REALLY THE REEF OVER THERE- BUT IT IS CALLED THE AQUARIUM . IT IS REALLY LOVELY," SAYS EIGHT YEAR OLD JESS.

"How is Stewart, the Kitty King ?" asks Eleanor.

"The Kitty King is fine. We'd love to. Need some help? Don't worry about it," we say to the barrage of questions.

"It is terribly frustrating really. I've noticed your wind generator spinning when none of the others are moving. Is it producing sufficient electricity?" Anthony asks.

"Can I get you a glass of wine?" Kathryn asks. "There is a small store across the pass on the other motu. It has mostly eggs and fishing gear, but I did find some corgettes and an aubergine. The main store is on the far side of the island. We are thinking of riding bicycles tomorrow. Would you like to come with us?"

DID YOU KNOW THE FAMILY ON THE DANISH BOAT OVER THERE ARE ALL SICK WITH DENGUE FEVER? THEY WERE IN THE MARQUESAS THE SAME TIME WE WERE," SAYS JESS.

"You would not believe what we saw in the store for people to eat! Packages of nests and eggs!" cries Ellie.

"No we didn't, that's awful; that makes three boats that have come down with dengue. Did you see any jars of frog legs or puppy tails? In about ten knots of wind it puts out an average of five ten amps. We'd love to go with you, and yes, we'd love some wine," Phil and I say together.

"Just a moment then, I'll be right back," Kathryn says disappearing in a fast moving blur to get us some wine.

"Well you know, so many of those wind generators make such an infernal racket. It seems to make little sense having one on a boat if you were to keep it off all the time for the noise; but, yours does seem to be much quieter," Anthony says.

"YOU KNOW THE FRENCH EAT SONG BIRDS DON'T YOU? THEY EAT ANYTHING THAT MOVES! EAT ANYTHING JESS SAYS.

"Would you like to see our collection of stuffed animals?" Eleanor asks.

"Sure. Speaking of stuffed animals, you wouldn't believe what we had for lunch today," I say to the girls.

"It's a land based wind generator. Unfortunately the company went out of business. Hey! I thought we weren't going to tell them?" Phil chides me.

"Yes, you are right. I won't. I'll be back," I say to Phil as I go on a tour of the

146

Willy Bolton stuffed toy menagerie.

Later that night, while trying to sleep, I sort through the quadraphonic conversations from Willy Bolton and remember what little Jess had said.

"What's the matter?" Phil asks me.

"I got to thinking about dengue fever," I say while moving Stewart so I can get out of bed.

"What? Come back to bed…"

"In a minute. Dengue is caused by a virus with an incubation period of three to fifteen days. The virus can cause an acute fever, with headache, severe joint and muscle pain and then a rash after a second feverish period."

"Don't tell me you're feeling sick?"

"No. I feel fine, other than the fact that I will have a headache tomorrow, but that's from too much wine, not dengue."

"So what's the problem?"

"The Merck manual specifically states that it is caused by the bite of a mosquito. That's what I've been thinking about. All of us cruisers, except you, are very good about spraying mosquito repellant all over our skin. Everyone has gone to the same places, for the most part, but we may go further a field. The one thing that separates us from the boats with dengue is that the non-infected boats have water makers. Maybe people get dengue not just from the bite of a mosquito but also from drinking water infected with mosquito larvae."

"I am sure someone would have discovered that by now. You know what I say, there is no original thought. Stop scratching those. You'll get them infected," Phil reprimands me.

I was severely bitten by no-no's while in the Marquesas. This name is given to many things in Polynesia, the most evil of which is a species of small biting fly. These little devils can elicit an intense allergic reaction, somewhat similar to black flies in Maine, only the welts and itching lasts for several weeks, not days. Despite having used one whole can of spray insect repellant, I was severely bitten on a hike we did up to one of the "largest" waterfalls in the world.

"Why don't you look up some way to cure your skin before you start getting tropical ulcers? Quit worrying about dengue. You are starting to look like you've got leprosy."

"Thanks. If I were a dog with a flea bite allergy, I'd use antibiotics and cortisone."

"Well since you are a dog, or are partly anyhow, technically speaking, after our lunch today, as you always say, you are what you eat, go for it. Your scratching has been driving me crazy."

"Fine," I say rummaging through the boxes of drugs. "Once a dog always a dog."

"Just don't start barking or chasing cars."

The next day we bring our bicycles to shore and venture off with Kathryn, Ellie and Jess to the hotel so they can rent children's bicycles. Anthony stays on board "Willy Bolton" to fix their diesel generator. We don't get fifty feet down the road when my tire blows out. We pull over and Phil pulls out a two-inch long thorn from the rubber.

Willy Bolton's crew

"Look at this baby!" he says proudly holding the spike-like thorn up.

"Wowza- that must have been from the Galapagos. No wonder countries are so worried about rubber tires bringing in strange plant life. My tires looked completely clean," I remark.

We return to the hotel so I can rent a bike. By the time we get on the road again it is almost noontime. "I'm sorry, Kathryn," I say apologetically. "We'll never make it to the far end of the island before the banks close for lunch."

"Don't worry a moment about it," she replies cheerfully and leads us back out on to the road while Phil brings up the rear.

The island of Rangiroa is fairly populated with about fourteen hundred people. The houses are single story, cement block covered with stucco, and have corrugated tin roofs. The yards are clean and neat. Most everyone has some sort of flower garden. Hands are raised in greeting, instead of the middle finger salute we received in the Marquesas. Everyone waves with genuine affection at us- but who wouldn't, since we were traveling in the company of two adorable children?

When we finally arrive at the bank, the sign on the door announced it is closed on Wednesdays. "See," Kathryn points out. "All those worries for naught. It's closed today anyway."

We head back to the boat, stopping at the local pearl farm along the way. Phil and I look in silk bag after silk bag, from drawer after drawer, at some of the most beautiful oyster "abscesses" (for that is really all a pearl is) in the world. We finally settle on five perfect pearls to the tune of $250.00 U.S. We keep two and decide to give the rest to our mothers.

"Jess and I formed an organization called Niss Piss," Ellie says to me as we climb back onto our bikes.

"Niss Piss?" I ask her.

"NSPSC- the National Society for the Protection of Shelled Creatures."

"And what do you do exactly?"

"We would like to make it illegal to take the life of any shelled creature just for the sake of collecting its shell."

"That's a wonderful idea!" I exclaim. "Sign me up. I am saddened to see how few shelled creatures there are left in the world."

"We know cruisers who, when they find a really pretty shell, will soak it in a bucket of bleach to kill the creature. You haven't done that have you?" asks Ellie somewhat nervously.

"Maybe a long time ago when I was a kid, but now I think that is akin to murder. Even when you eat meat, you are doing it to survive. Killing something just because it is pretty, and you would like it for decoration, that's pretty awful."

"Good. Then you must become a charter member of NSPSC!"

*   *   *

The following night we head off for Tahiti, one day's sail away. During my watch from eight to midnight, fifty miles above Makatea Island, the prevailing winds carry the scent of frangipani, and tiare Tahiti, the small white flower indigenous to the islands. Possessing a fragrance stronger than gardenia and orange blossoms combined, these tiny blooms perfume the entire ocean. The scent of tropical flowers indicates that land is nearby. And it is, relatively speaking. Yet for most land dwellers we are still fifty miles out to sea, not exactly the average persons concept of sailing close to land.

The moon has not yet risen. It is difficult differentiating the horizon, as the reflection of stars on the water is just as bright as the stars themselves. Iwalani is under sail, making the small creaks and groans of a well-tended boat. Three unidentifiable sound components and the fourth, a water glass hanging on a hook over the sink together produce Iwalani's six-knot theme song: C-F-C-E.

Each time we get under way is no different; no matter how short the passage, or how long the interval on land. It involves the same inner ear habituation, the same internal clock adjustment. For a brief time, I lie in the cockpit confused. For all intents and purposes I know I am at sea, yet the weightlessness of the water and spherical view in all directions of nothing but blackness and brilliantly lit stars makes me feel like I am in outer space, not out at sea, creaking and groaning along in a gypsy-space-ship-caravan. Infinity suddenly feels palpable. The universe is not expanding at an unimaginable rate but is here and now, and I am at the center of it. It is clear how our ancestors thought stars were not heavenly bodies, but small tears in the fabric of the universe letting in pinpricks of light. My world is just a forty-two foot boat suspended in a black box with holes. Only the occasional whiff of flowers brings me back to reality.

"Are you asleep?" Phil yells into my ear.

"Of course not! I am on watch," I mumble.

"You sure sounded like you were asleep. You were snoring."

"Asleep on watch? Me? I was just lying here pondering life, the universe and everything."

"I hate to bring you back to reality, but we are almost at Tahiti and there are lots of boats in front of us," Phil chastises.

"What time is it?" I ask.

"Ah-hah! Just as I thought! You were asleep. It's almost eleven p.m."

"Hm. Maybe. I did hear five bells though."

"Jesus Christ. You're going to kill us," Phil

A Japanese man named Mikimoto invented the techniques for producing today's cultured pearls. Pearl farming is a mix of scientific surgery and fish farming. The live oyster is held in place with elaborate clamps, while the two halves are gently pried open. Using dissecting microscopes, the pearl surgeon implants a small piece of mantle from another oyster along with a tiny plastic bead, around which the nacre, or pearl material, will form. Groups of oysters are then suspended in net pockets around the lagoon. Within two to five years, depending on the size of the pearl desired, the oysters are brought in and the pearl surgically harvested. If the oyster is a good pearl producer another implant is placed and the whole cycle is repeated. This process can be repeated up to four times before the oyster finally dies a natural death. Despite one third dying, one third rejecting the implant and thus buying their freedom, the remaining oysters produce pearls. Of those, less than five percent are of marketable quality.

Before cultured pearls were invented, divers harvested wild oysters. Only a very small percentage had pearls in them. Depending on where the pearls were growing, it could be as low as one in ten thousand oysters, which would naturally produce a gem quality pearl. The old search and destroy technique resulted in a lot of shell heaps, a lot of oysters killed, and very few pearls.

Black pearl oysters, named after the black rim surrounding the inside of the shell, can create pearls in any color but true black: dark green, silver, purple, mauve and any shade in between. They are fantastically beautiful, with prices to match.

mutters.

"What's that smell?"

"You mean the smell of trash burning on Tahiti?" Phil asks.

"No, something else."

Stewart smells it too. He jumps off the settee and sits at the bottom of the companionway ladder, his nose pointed upward.

"French fries!" I cry.

"MacDonald's! Yahoo! Civilization ho!"

The Kitty King adjusts to his new crown.

We introduce Willy Bolton's crew to the healthful benefits of Marshmallow Fluff

Chapter 11

All that is Good in the World

July 2001
Papeete, Tahiti

"Listen to this, there's an entire VHF radio net for cruising boats. This guy sounds like he's some sort of American DJ or something," Phil says turning up the volume so I can hear.

"Good morning, Maeva Beach. It's another beautiful day in paradise. This is the "Same Thing 2" net. We're here to take any call ins, boat to boat traffic or just early morning chatter."

"Same Thing 2 this is Cosmo Girl. I heard from Tiki and they are still in the Tuomotos helping some natives re-wire their house."

"Thanks Cosmo Girl, I wondered what happened to those guys. They must be having a great time."

"Same Thing. This is Decadent. I just wanted to tell everyone how cool it was to go rowing in one of these outrigger canoes. I got to row with a bunch of guys yesterday who were practicing for the races, and I have to hand it to them it's a lot of hard work. More work than childbirth even."

"I sure hope she didn't actually try to row an outrigger canoe," Phil says.

"Paddling, rowing. You think she knows the difference?"

"Obviously not," Phil continues. "This whole cruiser thing is starting to get under my skin. It seems like we are all trying to find the most primitive culture, the cannibal with a bone through the nose kind of thing, so we can put a bone through our nose and play cannibal for a day. It's become the Native Experience Game."

We stay in Tahiti for a week, see some incredible dancing at the Haeve Festival and watch the parade in Papeete celebrating Bastille Day. We restock the larder at some of the best grocery stores in the world. Misconception number one of my sheltered existence was thinking that Americans had better food and better grocery stores than anywhere in the world. How quickly that notion is dispelled after a trip through the grocery stores of Tahiti.

Stewart is "examined" on board Iwalani by the French government vet, not really an examination but a scan, literally, as she is more interested in getting a readout from his implanted microchip, than checking him for infectious disease. She realizes, rightly so, that

long passages through the South Pacific, where rabies hasn't yet spread, is a forced quarantine of sorts. As she passes the scanner over his shoulders, I am a bit nervous that the chip I was sold in America might not have the international frequency necessary for her scanner to read, but it beeps and she nods approvingly. She looks at Stewart's file and says in impeccable English she wishes all the boats cruising with pets were as well prepared. I hope getting Stewart into Australia will go as smoothly.

The "Kitty King" gets examined by the French Vet.

We hike, shop, rent cars to tour the entire island of Tahiti, eat at MacDonalds, or try to anyways, for here, topless above the turquoise waters filled with brightly colored fish, are some of the most beautiful men and women on the planet, delicately eating French fries and hamburgers, with not a tourist, camera, or fat roll in sight.

*   *   *

We slowly made our way up through the Society Islands, with each stop more beautiful than the last, arriving in Raiatea for Iwalani's scheduled haul out, so we can repaint the bottom and inside of the bilge with French bottom paint.

In his logs Captain Cook wrote about the incredible boat building skills of the Raiateans. Not much has changed since then.

"What the hell is that?" I ask passing the binoculars to Phil as we approach the anchorage.

"It looks like an aluminum catamaran."

"It's incredible. I've never seen anything like it. It must be at least ninety feet. It looks fast just sitting still!"

We anchor Iwalani among some smaller catamarans and then row to shore to find out about our haul out.

We wander around the seemingly deserted boatyard until we find a shed with human voices inside. Peering through the opening, we see several Polynesians working on a large aluminum wing. Suspended over their heads is a traditional outrigger canoe. I can't resist and pull out my camera to take pictures of new replacing old.

"Non! Non pas du photograph!"

"Excusez moi," I say putting the camera away.

"Ah, you are American," a small French man says emerging from the shadows, wiping his hands on a cloth rag.

"I am sorry," I say. "What is this?"

"Thees is a fixed wing for the catamaran at anchor."

"Oh yes we saw it. It's incredible. Is this a secret military boat?" I ask.

"Non. It is a boat for a pearl farmer. He wanted a fast way to get pearls from the lagoon to market."

"It sure looks fast."

152

"We are looking for Dominic. He scheduled our haul out," Phil explains.

"He is on Huahine, salvaging a boat on the reef."

"We saw that boat! It looked like it was a total loss. There was a hole in its side big enough to drive a truck through," I exclaim.

"Ah non. Thees is not a problem, she will float again."

"What happened? All anyone could tell us was that it ran up on the reef the day before we got there," Phil says.

"Oui, it belongs to a seventy year old woman. She does much single-handling in thees area. It was very rough. She sailed too close to the reef and a big wave picked her up. She turned on the engine and tried to back up, but she should have tried to sail off, go forward."

"Is she OK?" Phil asks.

"She is fine. Just mad now because we have to fix her boat."

"It looked like no one could fix it. When we saw the boat, it was high on the reef- very far from water," I say.

"We can fix or build any boat."

"Looks like we came to the right place," Phil laughs.

"Is your boat the gaff rigged cutter? She is very pretty for a heavy boat."

"Thank you. She is very safe."

"But slow? Why go slow when you can go fast! Who designed her?" he asks.

"She is mostly our design," I say.

"Oh by the way, I am Ariel. You will be hauling out to paint the bottom? Yes?"

"Yes, and we will need some bottom paint."

"We have very good French bottom paint, and it is environmentally friendly."

"Rats!" I whisper to Phil. "I was hoping for something enriched with uranium, so we could paint the bilge and finally kill the swamp gas producing organism."

"It is very good paint. I have it on my boat. I painted it two years ago and it is still free of growth."

"Which is your boat?" Phil asks.

"The red catamaran. It is a Dick Newick. He is good designer, even if he was American," Ariel says with a twinkle in his eye and a sideways glance at me. He had obviously heard me kidding to Phil about the radioactive French paint.

"Hey! There are lots of Americans that have invented pretty neat things! Bill Gates, George Lucas, Mr. Noyes at Intel."

"Yes, but they did not invent these things, they took these things made by others and made them better. Like Scrabble this is also a very good game but it was French first."

"It was? Well, you guys do the same thing. Catamarans weren't exactly invented by the French."

"We improve things too. Thees is not a bad thing."

"Well I know one thing you could improve—the French keyboard—you have no '@'!"

"Yes, but you Americans have not got thees," he says reaching into his wallet and pulling out a credit card.

"A credit card! Of course we do! What do you think we pay with, wampum and glass beads?"

"Ah, no, you do not have thees credit card." Ariel flips it over revealing a microchip instead of the usual magnetic strip. "Thees can be used in any phone too. If you need to make a call, you put it in and 'Voila!' you make call and pay when you get the bill."

"OK! OK! You win. That is much better than anything we Americans have. A Trump card hidden in your wallet!"

Our haul out, despite coinciding with torrential downpours, goes well. We have serious apprehensions at first, as the gearbox of an antique Fiat tractor balances all forty four thousand pounds of Iwalani.

We leave Raiatea and sail to the high peaked island just to the north, Bora Bora. After moving to our own anchorage on the eastern side of the island, we finally find out why paradise gets such rave reviews. We rent and borrow DVD's to watch at night, buy pain au chocolat for breakfast- probably the best invention by any chef anywhere, delicate croissant pastry filled with semisweet chocolate. We snorkel and dive with manta rays and lie perfectly calm at anchor in ten feet of crystal clear water, while the wind generator hums away giving us enough free electricity to live in the twenty first century. With the boat desalinator working off the wind generator, fresh water is free and plentiful.

Our creative juices flow as we write, paint, eat, swim when hot, shower to get the salt off and live totally for the moment. Stewart, too, enjoys the perfect temperatures and French cat food. Living on Iwalani is like vacationing in a private villa surrounded by an architects award winning swimming pool with the backdrop of swaying palms from the motu in front of us and Mount Otemanu rising up from the turquoise waters behind us.

Cyclone season is but three months away, and we still have half the Pacific to cross in order to make it to Australia before bad weather sets in. Life is grand, yet short lived, our visas allow us only ninety days in French Polynesia, and we are up to eighty-three. We have to keep moving west.

Iwalani gets hauled out

Chapter 12

Too Much Humanity and Too Few Humanitarians

August 2001
Suwarrow, South Pacific

The blue highway forks at Bora Bora. Most cruisers take the Southern route to Niue and Tonga; we decide to take the Northern passage to Pago Pago, Samoa, stopping at an undeveloped atoll called Suwarrow along the way. Originally discovered by a Russian vessel named Suvarov in 1814, this atoll has remained relatively sterile and off the beaten path, as it offers little that humans can exploit, but sand, coral, a few palms and very aggressive sharks.

"Admit it. You've got a crush on him," Phil says to me during our dinner break in the cockpit.

"No. No, and no. He is good looking and funny- but I don't have a crush on him. Natalie and Paul have been married since they were children in second grade. You have nothing to worry about," I respond to Phil, while pouring more Worcestershire sauce on my baked potato.

We are one day's sail from Suwarrow, an atoll managed by the Cook Islanders under the jurisdiction of New Zealand. We met Paul and Natalie while in Moorea just north of Tahiti. Originally from Pennsylvania, they sold the farm and bought a boat to sail around the world in, figuring they world learn how to sail as they went. Paul had worked and saved money buying, repairing, then selling used cars. Their boat Renegade is fast, big, and totally scary for just two people.

Paul filled an aft stateroom on Renegade with welding equipment. As a result, his skills are in high demand wherever he goes. Both he and Natalie gave up on alcohol-which suits us just fine as too much focus gets put on "sundowners" and cockpit cocktails parties with many of the cruisers. We enjoy their company, as they are unpretentious, self-made and immersed in the cruising life like no other couple. Paul had rigged an electric winch for the mainsail by using an electric drill with a modified bit that fits squarely into the hole of the handle slot on the winch drum. With a press of the trigger- presto, whizzbang, their sails are up. He isn't scared to try new things even if they are slightly unconventional.

"I do worry, constantly. That's what happens out here with these cruisers-everyone swaps partners," Phil continues.

"Ick. Let me tell you something. Remember when you left the boat in Bora Bora on my birthday to go shopping for a present?" I ask Phil.

"How can I forget? I didn't know about the password thing on the credit cards. What a disaster."

"Exactly. Do you realize that was the first time we had been apart from one another for over a year? I felt physically sick watching you leave in the dinghy."

"I didn't want to leave without you either," Phil says.

"We have become more than a partnership. You are the right half of my inept whole."

"Don't forget Stewart. He's part of the team too," Phil adds.

"I could never forget Stew. You might be the anchor that brings me back to earth, but he is the balloon that lets my imagination escape."

"So I have nothing to worry about with Paul?"

"You don't have to be jealous about anyone. Well, except Stew."

*   *   *

The following day we arrive at Suwarrow with no time to spare. Paul flies out to meet us in his inflatable dinghy. Possessing an outrageous outboard with sixty horsepower, he is hydroplaning on top of the waves like an oversized seabird.

"Hey, Hey! I didn't think you'd make it in time!" Paul hops on board and ties off his dinghy like a cowboy tying his horse. He points to the opening in the pass, "It's not really very hard, but we don't have much time before the tide changes," he says with his New Jersey accent, "Amoha got here yesterday with no rudder. I had to tow them through."

"I heard about that on one of the nets," I say to Paul. "They weren't the only ones that lost a rudder. Another boat also lost a rudder."

"Don't get me started on spade rudders and fin keels," Phil says. "They're for racing boats. They shouldn't even be out here."

"Yeah, but imagine sailing without being able to steer!" Paul exclaims.

"I sure wouldn't want to do it," I agree.

"We do it all the time with one of our ice boats back home!" Phil reminds me. "It's called a scooter. It goes about forty miles an hour- you just trim the sails and shift your weight to steer- though it is a bit out of control. We have another iceboat that you can steer with a wheel like a car. It's much less fun than the scooter."

"No its not. It goes twice as fast, and you stay in control," I add.

"You should have seen Amy when I told her we were going to jibe, I thought she would have a heart attack!"

"That was my first lesson with apparent wind, real wind and boat speed."

"Yeah, well Nat and I are still learning all that," Paul says.

"So what's it like here in Suwarrow?" Phil asks.

"It's true paradise!" Paul beams. "I went fishing with John, one of the caretakers, and we caught three jacks. There's no ciguatera here and lots of fish. The only problem is the sharks."

"Are they really that bad?" I ask.

"Worse than bad. God n' Plenty caught a fish in the pass and brought it onto the gunwale of their inflatable. A big shark came out of the water after the fish and bit the pontoon. They took off back to their boat like a deflating balloon, which they were, with the shark swimming after them!" Paul chuckles and wipes his hand through his short hair.

"I bet there was some heavy duty praying going on in that boat," I say.

"Jesus, have you heard? I was told they had altars all over their boat."

"Really? Well they never invited us on board, we were always relegated to side-hanger status," Phil says as he turns off the autopilot and takes control of the tiller.

"That's more than Nat and me!" Paul laughs.

Paul leaves us when we round the corner. We drop the anchor among seven other cruising boats. I long for my customary dive into the water to check the anchor and remove the stale feeling of a passage, but I think better of it after hearing about the sharks.

"I'm not happy about having a coral reef as a lee shore," Phil says.

"Not much of an anchorage, but it's still better than some we've been in."

A dinghy we don't recognize rows over to us from shore with a man, woman, and young boy. The man rows alongside, stands up, and hangs on to Iwalani's sides while he introduces his family. "I'm Bill from Queen Jean. This is my wife Mary and son Jasper," he says pointing to the others in the dinghy. "We heard you are a veterinarian?"

"Daddy, can I row now?" his son interrupts.

"Shut up, Jasper, I am talking."

"Yes, I'm Amy, and this is my husband Phil," I say looking them over for obvious ailments; it won't be the first time on this trip I have been called upon to treat the talking primate species.

"There are two cats on shore. They are really friendly. One of the caretakers is going to take them out and drown them. One of the cats is pregnant," Mary says with a real urgency. "You've got to do something to save the cats."

"Daddy! Please! I want to row!" Jasper whines tugging on to his father's shorts.

"I'm sure the caretaker won't drown them. People aren't usually that mean. Sometimes they just say that in order to get other people to take action. I'll do what I can to see that no harm is done to anyone. It would be no problem for me to neuter them."

"Really? You could do that? Oh please let us know. I would really like Jasper to watch the surgery," Mary says.

"Dad-dy!" Jasper starts to rock the rowboat from side to side.

Suddenly Bill swings his arm back as if he is gearing up for a fastball pitch and hits Jasper squarely on the head. Jasper starts to whimper but remains relatively quiet. I stand in shock, unsure whether I had just seen a man wind up and hit his kid or wind up to save himself from falling overboard, resulting in an accidental smack to his obnoxious offspring.

"Shut up!" Bill snarls. "Or I'll hit you harder!"

I look at his wife Mary for any signs of fear, spousal abuse, or retaliation. She smiles up at me. "Thanks, I don't want to see the cats suffer. Will we see you on shore? There's a cookout every night," she says pleasantly.

I can feel the anger well up in Phil, as he would never consider striking anyone, especially a child. I am worried that his normally mild demeanor could change and he would grab something and hit Bill back.

"Maybe. But we've got some things to do on board first," I say.

"Okey dokey. Well nice meeting you," Mary replies as they start to row away.

"What an unbelievable asshole," Phil says when they are out of earshot. "I came so close to hitting that jerk and saying 'How did that feel? Want me to do it again so you can decide better?'"

"Well, their kid wasn't any picnic either."

"Gee, I wonder why, with parents like that."

We row ashore once the boisterous winds drop a bit.

"Welcome to Suwarrow!" a smiling bronzed man says extending his hand to me. "My name is Tom. I am the warden for the Cook Island National Park Association. I'll give you a quick tour."

He points to a house on the highest ground of the atoll which is still only about six feet above sea level. "This is the original house of Tom Neale, the cruiser who came here from New Zealand and wrote the book, *An Island to Oneself.* It's been fixed up a bit here and there."

"Are you here year round?" I ask.

"No, John and I come by freighter in May and leave by November in order to avoid the cyclone season."

"Where is John?" I ask.

Tom points up a palm tree. Several coconuts began raining down not far from where we stand. Shortly afterward a small wiry man slides down the tree.

"Have you ever had any good drinking nuts?" John asks us wiping his hands on his shorts. Phil and I look at one another shaking our heads. "I'll show you how to open them with just a penknife."

John takes out his knife, picks a three-foot stick off the ground and whittles it to a sharp point. He jams the blunt end of the stick into the sand and then grabs one of the coconuts. Holding the coconut between his hands, he slams it down hard on the pointed stick. The husk breaks open and he removes the nut. With his knife he drills a small hole in one of the eyes and hands it to me. "Try this," he says grinning.

I tip the nut back and drink the sweet milk. "Delicious," I wipe my mouth and hand the nut to Phil. "I could live off that."

I feel something rubbing against my legs. I look down and see a very pregnant black cat.

"That's Missy," John says, "and her brother Pete is asleep under the picnic table."

"How did the cats get here?" I ask while bending down to pat the cat.

"A cruiser dropped them off. They were here when we arrived," Tom says with disgust.

"I heard from Queen Jean that you were going to drown them. How 'bout if I neuter them instead?"

"I don't know," says Tom, "they will have to fend for themselves over cyclone season."

"I might take them when we leave," John answers softly.

Tom scowls at John. "If cats overrun the atoll, it could destroy the whole ecosystem. Suwarrow is one of the most important breeding grounds for pelagic birds on the planet."

"I doubt they would swim to the islands where the birds are nesting. Besides, if they tried, they'd be eaten by sharks," I say.

"You've got a good point. I suppose it wouldn't hurt to have you neuter them. We are having a bit of a rat problem here," Tom finally agrees.

"Good! If they don't survive the surgery, then it was meant to be. I'll come back tomorrow morning at ten o'clock and spay the female and castrate the male."

John winces. "Don't worry," I laugh. "You won't feel a thing."

The following morning I get up early to gather all the equipment I need. I re-sterilize my surgical pack in the pressure cooker, measure anesthetic and pain meds, subcutaneous fluids, organize the emergency meds box, (should something go wrong). I package up gloves, surgical scrub, alcohol, surgical solution, scalpel blades, suture material, spare clothes line, nails and a hammer.

"What are you doing? Crucifying the cats?" Phil asks horrified.

"You'll see. But, I am going to need to shave the female's belly. Without electricity on shore it will be hard. I wish I had brought cordless clippers with me."

"You thought you'd be doing all surgeries on Iwalani where we have all the electricity you could want," Phil answers.

"I suppose I could do them out here, like we did with the others in the Galapagos, but it would be violating the quarantine issues for Stewart's entry into Australia. Still, I wouldn't let him have direct contact with these cats. Who knows what diseases they may carry?"

"Don't do it. I don't want Stewart catching anything. We can use scissors and a razor on shore."

"I guess we'll have to. I'm ready to go."

"But it's only eight o'clock!" Phil exclaims.

"You don't actually think I am going to do this with an audience? The last thing we need is ten people and one obnoxious kid chasing the cats. We will have only one opportunity to grab them, after that forget it. You are going to think I am nuts-"

"I already know you are nuts."

"Yeah, right. OK. You have to empty your mind of all imagery of what we are about to do."

"Why?" Phil asks.

"Because some cats can read minds! If they know that we are going to operate on them, they'll hide for days and we won't be able to catch them. When I say 'now', bend down and pick up the cat like you are just being friendly. While you are patting him, gently grab onto the scruff of his neck. I am going to grab the female at the same time, inject her first, then come over and inject the male. It's more important to get her done- since she's due to have kittens any day now."

"Yup, you are nuts!"

"Isn't that why you married me?' I ask.

We row to shore, and I unload the boxes onto the picnic table, like we are getting ready for a big lunch. The cats are right there with us, curious about what we have brought.

I nail four sixteen penny nails into the underside of the picnic table, then tie pieces of clothesline to each one.

I reach down and pick up the female and say to Phil as nonchalantly as I can, "OK. Now."

He bends down and picks up the male. Once I see he is secure in Phil's arms I inject the female, she looks at me with a flash of surprise but doesn't make a sound. I gently place her in an overturned crate while she gets drowsy. Then I inject the male. "I hate needles," Phil says closing his eyes while gripping the cat harder.

"Don't watch then."

The male is asleep before the female, so I stretch him out on a coconut stump, put ointment in his eyes and have him neutered in less than a minute.

"Wow, that's fast!" John says as he comes out to see what is happening.

"See why I live with deep respect for this woman," Phil says, " I realize that in the wink of an eye, she can do the same to me!'

"Yup, that's right! All of you fellers better watch out- or you might be next. Spaying is a bit more involved than castrating though. It'll take me twelve minutes, maybe a few more, since I am rusty and she's so pregnant."

I place the male under the overturned crate and lay the female on her back. With the clothes lines tied to the nails, I tie her arms over her head and her legs straight out like a trussed roast on the picnic table.

"Why are you doing that?" John asks.

"See how limp she is? If I don't, her arms and legs will keep flopping in my way," I say applying ointment to her eyes.

"What's that for?" John asks.

"While they are under anesthesia they can't blink. The ointment is to keep her corneas moist so they don't dry out."

I check her heart rate, shave her, scrub her belly, get the surgical pack ready, open a pack of surgical gloves and then scrub my own hands.

"This will have to be the world's shortest three minute scrub. Can you squirt some alcohol on my hands?" I ask Phil.

I dry them in the air, put on the surgical gloves and head over to my patient. I feel naked not wearing a cap, mask and gown for surgery.

Covering the sleeping cat in a sterile drape, I make the incision, careful not to knick her enlarged mammary glands. The sun gives better light than any surgical lamp. It is warm, but not hot, an ideal ambient temperature for surgery.

"I could get spoiled doing surgery in these conditions. Anyone care to be next?" I ask waving the scalpel at Phil and John.

I lay her uterus out on her belly, clamping it off at the cervix, then tie off the blood supply to both ovaries, removing them with the uterus. Its purple balloon-like sacs are filled with four well-developed kittens.

"It does not bother you to murder kittens like this?" John asks me.

I look at this small Cook Islander with surprise. 'Not one day ago,' I think to myself, 'you were going to drown the whole lot'. But I realize it is Tom who was going to do the dirty work. John is very attached to these cats.

"No," I respond. "My own religion believes that your soul doesn't get into your body until you take your first breath. That is why when you die and you have taken your last breath, your body becomes lighter. I think that's when your soul leaves. Why wouldn't birth be the same as death? As long as these kittens never breathe oxygen, they will remain soul-less. I'm not so sure it is murder, if there is no soul," I say closing the incision.

"And what exactly is your religion?" Tom asks as he walks into the clearing.

"I come from the ultimate tree huggers, the druids. I worship anything that makes oxygen."

"That's not a bad belief system. But weren't they into sacrifices, too?" Tom asks.

"Perhaps. But I think a lot of misconceptions and fantastic myths came from Christians who were trying to elevate the status of Jesus and mire a lot of pagan beliefs."

"Who is going to take the stitches out?" John asks.

"No one. I always bury them with absorbable suture. You won't have to do anything for either cat."

I give the female some subcutaneous fluids.

"Why are you doing that?" John asks.

"Boy, you're almost as bad as a nine year old," I tell him.

"Not that one from that boat Queen Jean! I head up into the coconut trees each time I see that one coming to shore," John says.

"You got room up in those trees for anyone else?" Phil asks him, "Because they're rowing to shore right now."

"What should I do with the uterus?" I ask John.

"I'm burning brush at the end of that path," he says pointing.

"Good. That will do. I'm outta here." I untie the female and put her under the same crate with the male. Then run down the path with the remains of the four kittens and Missy's queenhood.

I remove the hemostats then place the uterus on a burning log, where it spatters and sizzles. The smell of cooking flesh fills the air.

'*Such a strange thing to be doing in such a far away place,*' I think to myself. In order to avoid the family from Queen Jean, I debate about hiding here until the remains have burned completely, but I feel guilty about leaving Phil, so I finally head back to the beach.

"Hey! I can't wait for Jasper to see this surgery!" Mary says to me as I remove my gloves.

Jasper is using a small stick to poke at the cats that were now waking up under the crate.

"You're too late." John says. "They're already done."

"Already done! But it's only nine, and I thought you said ten," Mary whines pouting her lips.

"I decided it would be too hot for them to be under anesthesia at ten."

"Oh, well. Look at the sleeping cats, Jasper!" Mary says distractedly.

"Um, if you wouldn't mind, they probably don't need to be poked with a stick, " I pry the piece of wood from Jasper's small fingers.

He scowls at me for a moment, and then looks up at his mother who is watching Paul and Natalie pulling their dinghy up onto the beach. Mary arranges her hair and tucks her shirt in.

"Hey, did we miss it?" Paul asks.

"No, you're just in time. I'm all through with the cats, but if you want to step right up, I can give you a soprano voice!"

"She can do it, too!" John cries as he climbs up a palm tree like an acrobat.

"I was wondering if you guys wanted to go in our dinghy to explore some of the islands?" Paul asks us.

"Maybe you can help clean up the trash on them," Tom suggests.

"They don't have to do any work here as far as I am concerned. What she has done is good for Suwarrow," John yells down pointing to me.

"With all the tree cutting Paul has done- this place should survive any cyclone," Tom adds.

"You don't have a chain saw do you?" Paul asks, looking at Phil.

"I wish we did. It is the one of the things we should have brought, but didn't."

We stop at Iwalani long enough to drop off the veterinary equipment and reassure Stewart that we will be back later, then head with Paul and Natalie to the opposite side of the lagoon.

Despite the connotations of quiet and still waters, lagoons, in actuality, are much wider and more boisterous than the projected mental image. The lagoon at Suwarrow is close to six miles across. From our position at Anchorage Island, situated roughly at one o'clock on the clock face, you can see the motus at noon and at two o'clock, but none of the others. We decide to explore the motus between seven and nine o'clock.

It is a little disconcerting heading off in a rubber boat into fairly choppy conditions to an island you can't see (with no charts, compass or survival gear) but we do it nonetheless. From habit I bring our backpack containing water, a knife and matches, but that is it. Because the only way into or out of an atoll is through the pass,and Suwarrow only has one pass, the chances of drifting out to sea forever is nearly impossible. The Polynesians criss-crossed the Pacific with far less knowledge and equipment, or so I have to keep telling myself.

We arrive at the first motu and carry the dinghy high up onto the sand. The beach is littered with the castoffs of human civilization: empty glass bottles, which had once contained cough syrup, fluorescent light bulbs with glass tubes still intact, flip-flops, with the molds from which they were cut and everywhere, plastic trash—jugs, tubs, bottles, cups, plates and buoys.

"Wow! Who would have thought there would be so much stuff so far from anywhere," Phil says while admiring a particularly attractive radio beacon, some lost equipment from a sophisticated fisherman.

"Did you know that there is supposed to be buried treasure here?" Paul asks.

"Every protected anchorage off the beaten path is supposed to have buried treasure," I say sarcastically.

"No really. John said a chest of coins was found not too long ago."

"Now I wish we brought the metal detector as well as a chain saw," Phil adds.

"Look at this!" I exclaim in utter amazement. I step on a red plastic jug that could have been a bottle of "Tide" laundry detergent in a former life. Plastic is no longer a suitable name for the material the jug has become. It has gone beyond brittle and explodes into a pile of red dust. "Look at what exposure to extreme sun has done to the plastic! It has disintegrated to powder. And here I thought plastic was supposed to survive for millions of years," I say while pummeling it with my foot.

"Yeah, the glass is more of a problem."

"How do you reckon the fluorescent light tubes survived the sea and washed up on a rocky coral beach without breaking?" Phil wonders.

"It seems pretty weird to me. Anyone need some electrical wire?" Paul asks

Natalie on a bird filled motu.

holding up a large spool.

"You're already wired," Natalie exclaims.

"Yeah for 220! That's two twenty year olds," Paul kids while putting his arm around his wife. "Time for us to move on to the next island."

"I didn't find a single shell," Natalie laments.

"It's been eye opening to me," I agree, "how there are so few shelled creatures left on this planet. It seems as if they are becoming really endangered."

We get back in the dinghy and move one motu over. Paul stops the outboard motor and slips his snorkel and mask over his face, leans over the side of the dinghy and sticks his head in the water. The rest of us follow. Suwarrow has some of the clearest water on the planet. Below us millions of tropical fish hover over colorful hard coral.

"I can't stand it," I cry. "I am going in."

"Me too," Phil says.

"I wouldn't recommend that," are Paul's last words as we both go overboard.

The fish sway like flowers in a breeze over their individual patch of coral. They seem close enough to touch because of the magnifying effects of such clear water.

And then like a flash I see it. Before I can get my arms onto the side of the inflatable, Phil is already in the dinghy. But I don't have my flippers on. In fact I have on plastic "jelly" sandals, which are slowing me down. I can't kick my fat carcass up out of the water fast enough.

Twenty feet away and closing in fast is a ten-foot tiger shark, not a behemoth, but still larger and more dangerous than a toy terrier yapping at a mailman. It is angry and aggressive enough to remove big chunks of important body parts, and half of mine are still in the water.

Paul reaches down and grabs on to the bottom of my bathing suit and helps me flail into the dinghy like an injured seal.

"Jesus Christ!" he cries. " I didn't think it was a good idea to go in the water."

"You saved my life," I say jokingly, "Great! Now I am forever in your debt and will have to be your foot servant."

"I don't think so!" Phil mutters.

"I told you these mother fuckers are mean," Paul says.

"That is an understatement!" I wheeze.

We travel to all but one of the motus on Suwarrow. Two of the islands are home to millions of nesting pelagic birds. Terns and boobies are so prolific that in places one has to step carefully to avoid crushing an egg. For the next two days we do little but snorkel in shallow waters where sharks aren't a problem, hike the beaches, and play card games at night with Paul and Natalie.

On our third night in Suwarrow we go to shore for a potluck cookout. We bring coleslaw, bread and cookies, while Tom and John prepare fish wrapped in palm leaves over fire.

"Since this is your first cookout on Suwarrow, I need to tell you about a few things," Paul warns us.

"Like what?"

"Well, it is custom for Cook Islanders to prepare a feast and then not eat it with their guests."

"I have read about that in old cruising books. You mean they still do that?" I ask.

"Yea, so we'll eat, and then Tom and John eat what's left."

"That's too weird. Can't we tell them it's time to update their customs?"

"Now you're sounding like an American," Phil says to me.

"Well maybe they would think we were weird if we didn't say something to them. Is it too American to feel like everyone should be treated equally?"

"Just don't say anything. If it is their custom, we should respect that," Phil adds.

We sit around in hammocks and on stumps, watching the sun set over the calm waters of the lagoon, waiting for the fish to cook. Tom sits on a picnic bench with a large glass of rum in his hand while John sits in a wheelbarrow playing a small ukulele. Together they serenade us with gentle songs of the islands.

"We are leaving tomorrow," I tell Tom and John when they pause to drink.

"That's too bad. It seems as if you just got here."

"We need to be in Australia before December," Phil explains.

"Do you need anything here? We pretty much have almost everything on Iwalani," I ask.

"Well, maybe," John pauses. I was afraid he would be asking for liquor, which was something we don't have much of. "You wouldn't by any chance have some plant fertilizer? Our vegetable garden is not doing very well".

"I've got a ton of fertilizer. I'd be happy to give you some."

"Great. Then we will be set until we get picked up in November," he says staring out to the anchorage.

John preparing the fish.

"Who's the new boat?" I ask them.

"It is a boat named Dessert First," Tom says while taking a swig of more rum. "A woman in her sixties sailed solo from Raiatea. We helped her through the pass this afternoon while you were off exploring. She is bringing food and parts for Amoha."

A silence falls upon the group. Amoha has been lying at anchor amidst the rest of us since the day before our arrival, after they had been towed in by Paul.

"Does he need help?" I ask, ashamed that we had not thought they might need food, or equipment too. Iwalani is so well provisioned and lacks nothing. I never thought others would be any different. Suwarrow, too, has plenty to offer for provisions, coconuts, crabs, lobsters, fish, and because of Paul's tree cutting, hearts of palm, a delicious delicacy but abhorrent to true Druids.

"I asked him a few days ago if he needed help with his rudder," Paul says looking across the anchorage to Amoha. "He said he had everything under control. He didn't need anything."

"That may explain why they don't come to shore for the cookouts. He may be short on supplies," I say.

"They probably just want to stay to themselves, away from all of us noisy Americans," Natalie adds.

Later, as we were rowing back to Iwalani, I whisper to Phil, "Tonight we should surreptitiously drop off some extra supplies to Amoha. That way they won't feel embarrassed to take them, or obliged to pay us back."

I lean back against the stern of the rowboat, admiring the view of Iwalani and my husband in the moonlight. "I feel pretty awful being so hung up on the cats, we totally neglected some people who may need help."

"We're just typical Americans. No one exists but us," he says between strokes of the oars. "Just don't give away any of my Pepsi."

We gather together a bag of canned goods and silently row them over to the Italian boat. We aren't the only ones feeling guilty. I have trouble finding a spot for our bag on the side deck, as the others were there before us making clandestine donations to the small boat.

The finished product

Chapter 13

All that is Bad in the World

September 11, 2001
Apia, Western Samoa

"This is quite a bit different than Pago Pago," Phil says, as we get ready to check in with the officials at Apia, Western Samoa.

"I'll say. I'm not sure I like it," I wince while struggling to put on a long dress.

"It's too bad the missionaries got to them, too," Phil scowls as he watches me put on more clothes.

"I know. It's too hot for all this."

"Don't offend the locals. At least you can wear sleeveless dresses here. When we get to Muslim countries, you're going to have to cover your shoulders, too."

"What's that?" I pause while hearing a musical commotion on shore.

"It says in the cruising guide that every morning a police band winds its way to the city's flag pole for the flag raising ceremony. All traffic stops while they play the Samoan National Anthem."

"Every day?"

"Every day."

"Even Sunday? I thought all things stopped here on Sunday."

"It doesn't say."

"Well, I am ready now." I grab the backpack snagging my full-length dress on the bedroom door latch.

We are tied to the outside of a tug at the customs and port captain's dock. We had a short overnight sail from Pago Pago, American Samoa, where we spent five days exploring, shopping and meeting the local veterinarian. Our trip from Suwarrow to Pago Pago was fast and full of wind. Stewart had not been doing well, and I had hoped to restock our larder of prescription cat food, but to no avail.

We had been in touch with Willy Bolton by radio and discovered they had picked up a package I missed in Bora Bora. Their engine regulator was also on the fritz, and we happened to have the spare they needed. A trade agreement was reached over the airwaves and a short diversion to Western Samoa plotted into the course.

"Do you think anyone is even in the office?"

"We'll find out."

I follow Phil up Iwalani's ratlines, hand him the backpack containing the valise of ship's papers, and then ease myself down to the tug.

"It looks as if everyone's still asleep here."

We tiptoe across the bow of the tug. Proper etiquette requires anyone crossing over a boat should only go in front of the mast, never behind it. On the ship's starboard side, I stop and survey the new situation we are in. The wind is holding the tug five feet away from the pier.

"I can't get across this," I say to Phil.

"Sure you can. I'll throw the backpack across, pull us in with the bow line and then jump. Then I'll pull the tug in so you can do the same."

"But it's twelve feet down to the water."

"You're not going to the water. Just don't look down."

Phil handily jumps across and pulls the fifty-ton tug in close to the dock. "Hurry! I can't hold it like this forever."

I look at him and then look at the distance that is now beginning to increase between the tug and the pier.

"Any time now!" Phil says between clenched teeth.

"I can't do it."

"Why not?"

"Because in this dress I can't separate my legs far enough to jump."

"Oh for God's sake. Then stay there."

"No. I'm coming, too," I say as I pull my dress off over my head.

"Amy don't!" Phil screams, not because he was worried about me jumping, but because he was worried about what was underneath my dress.

It can be argued that the ability to clothe oneself and present an attractive exterior appearance is a genetic trait. My grandfather possessed one of the keenest financial minds of the twentieth century. He, along with his partners, developed mutual funds in America. Alone, he built up the endowment of Harvard University to obscene levels. But one thing he did not possess, despite my grandmothers assistance, was any sense of fashion. It was rumored that one day in Boston, while conversing with some friends at a corner in the financial district, he paused for a moment and removed his threadbare fedora to scratch his head. No sooner were fingernails making contact with balding scalp when a foreign tourist walked by the group, and misperceiving the impoverished nature of my grandfather's wardrobe, deposited a few coins in the overturned hat. These are the clothes genes I have inherited.

Now I must report that I have a collection of frilly girlie undergarments and have on occasion actually worn them, but one must know that for sheer comfort and price in the tropics, nothing beats a pair of men's briefs. On this particular day in Apia, I had chosen none of the above, but had wisely gone with sensible attire for unknown explorations in tropical latitudes, a one-piece bathing suit.

"For crying out loud, no one is around," I say while neatly landing on the ground.

"That's what you think. The captain of the tug was in the wheel house—up until a few seconds ago, at which point he mysteriously disappeared when your dress went over your head. I believe he fainted, but he is now back upright, rubbing his eyes, with binoculars in hand. Please, Honey, you are embarrassing me!"

"Jeepers. Fine. I had to do what I had to do. I'll put my dress back on."

We follow the signs to the Port Captain's office. In a small anteroom a dozen men are gathered leaning against the walls, none of them with gold braid or white uniforms, all of them looking as if they cleaned their teeth with a pocket knife. I nervously lean up against the wall, too, while Phil stays outside. Twenty-four pairs of eyes are fixed on me. As if on cue in a Broadway musical, one dozen arms open up, pointing the way for me to a small door that is creaking open. They are letting me cut in front of them. I feel badly for thinking the worst of them, thank them profusely, grab Phil and enter the port captains office.

We introduce ourselves to the man behind the desk and hand him our ship's papers, including the clearance from Pago Pago, American Samoa.

"Why are you in Western Samoa? You are cleared for Fiji," he growls.

"Yes, well." I begin, "We were going to go to Fiji- but we were in contact by radio with some of our friends who are here in Apia, and they said how nice it was and that we should stop here."

"You can not just divert your plans based on whim," he says condescendingly.

"We are in a sailboat. We are at the whim of the winds, the seas and demands of the boat," I reply.

"This doesn't mean anything to me. You must go where you are cleared to go. These papers are for Fiji."

"We were in contact with our friends on the radio. Their engine is broken and they needed a spare part. We had exactly the spare part they needed and brought it to them," I say. Phil's hand tenses on my knee.

"What! You must give us this part!" the official howls.

"I can't. I imagine it's already installed on their engine."

"You mean you have given them the part already? You are not allowed to leave your boat until you have been cleared in."

"We didn't leave. They rowed over to us late last night to say hello, give me my mail that was left in Bora Bora and tell us where we where to tie up-"

"That is illegal trading! You must pay import duty on any items coming into this country. Where is this boat? We must speak to them. This is highly irregular. You must come back at one o'clock and see the supervisor."

"We are terribly sorry we have violated any laws. We gave our friends the engine part as a gift. We did not have any money exchanged for it," Phil explains. "Perhaps it would be best if we left for Fiji. We really didn't mean to cause any commotion."

"We just heard how nice it was here," I add. "And wanted to eat at restaurants, go to Aggie Grey's, visit Robert Louis Stevenson's house, buy some souvenirs, visit the Internet café, you know, do the usual tourist thing of throwing money around. I am sure Fiji will do just as well in that regard." I say.

"No, no, no. Do not leave. We will try and work this out. Just come back at one. You may go and anchor out in the harbor."

That afternoon at one o'clock we are escorted to a room containing two chairs and a light bulb dangling from a long cord, the proverbial interrogation room, the existence of which I thought was only on celluloid.

We explain what we had done once again, this time to a white uniformed man with more gold braids than all the girls in Switzerland. Convinced that we are just stupid and not entering Apia with criminal intent, he stamps the customs forms and lead us to the immigration department.

An incredibly large man rises to greet us wearing the traditional lava lava, or wrap around skirt. Samoans are big boned to begin with, but this man fills a room like Victorian furniture.

"My name is Samson," he ushers us to two chairs. "I heard you were in a bit of a pickle with customs."

He looks our paperwork over, nodding approvingly at Stewart's file.

"I have thirteen dogs and four cats myself," he says. "I can't imagine going anywhere without them."

"Stewart was the only one of my pets that passed the boat test. The rest were too scared or too sick and are still at home in the USA."

"I don't think any of my animals could handle a yacht. I don't think I could either."

"It does take a little getting used to."

"I hope you like Western Samoa. Let me know if I can do anything to help make your visit more pleasant," Samson says.

"Thank you. Well there is one thing actually. I read about a rain forest canopy walk on the island of Savaii. Do you know anything about it?" I ask.

"I have heard about it, but I have never gone there. Can't go anywhere with all my animals, but, I will get the paper work rolling so you can go. You will need a special cruising permit. I can have one ready for you when you clear out."

"That's wonderful. Thank you very much," I tell him, "and if you need any help with your animals, call me on channel 16."

"Perhaps you would like to meet with the veterinarian here? Exchange war stories and that sort of thing?"

"That would be great. I have been trying to introduce myself to every veterinarian wherever I go. It's been eye opening."

When we leave, Phil turns to me shaking his head, "I never would have believed it, but you are right, the people who own animals are the nicest to deal with."

"I think there's a logical explanation for it. Owning and loving a pet teaches you tolerance, patience, love and respect for a living thing different from yourself. Animal owners are more likely to be thankful for each day we have on the planet, since we see how short dogs' and cats' life spans are. Of course, they can also be a teeny bit more whacko too."

"Speaking of pets, have you told Stewart we are going out tonight?"

"No, but the Willy Bolton girls are going to pet sit. They are all geared up for it. They have art materials to do Stew-portraits and the usual Stew-parlor, which he barely tolerates, combing and brushing and lots of fussing. They think it will be the last time to pet sit him. He'll get more attention than he has in weeks."

That evening for dinner, we join Paul and Natalie who arrived in Apia ahead of us, bypassing Pago Pago. They invited Converse and Liz to join us, another couple from Maine, from a boat named Whip-'r-will. Before we left home, my mother informed me that Converse and I were cousins of a sort and urged me to phone them. They had done one circumnavigation already, and Phil and I were hoping to get some tips and much needed answers from someone who had done this all before, while we were still back in Maine. "Too busy," they told me over the phone, "We're leaving in a couple of months, and we have no extra time to talk." I practically begged them for just a few minutes of their time, but they blew me off. I am still carrying the bruised ego and hurt feelings all the way to the other side of the planet.

"Gall dang it," I scream as I slip down the companionway and nearly crush

Stewart sitting at the base of the stairs.

"Are you OK?" Phil comes running when he hears the crash. Paul and Natalie are taking us to shore in their dinghy and are hanging on to Iwalani's topsides.

"No. I nearly killed Stewart though." I lift up my skirt and show Phil an enormous bruise beginning to form on my side.

"It looks like you nearly killed yourself too."

"What happened?" Paul asks from behind Phil.

"Stupid long skirts, I stepped on the hem and slipped down the companionway. I almost knocked my front teeth out too."

"Do you want to do this another night?" Paul asks with concern.

"No. Darn it! I'm all gussied up, and I'm going to have a good time, even if it kills me."

"At the rate you're going, that shouldn't be too hard," Paul mutters.

After settling the Willy Bolton girls in for a night of "Stew sitting," we meet Converse and Liz on shore and walk along the main road bypassing many restaurants catering to tourists. Loud American pop music pours out of the open doorways of several bars. We settle on a quiet place at the far end of the street with sand floors and lots of tropical plants. It is hot inside as the setting afternoon sun streams through hanging beaded curtains.

"So tell us about the arm pit of the Pacific," Converse says while sipping a gin and tonic.

"What armpit?" I ask.

"What other armpit is there? Pago Pago!"

"I wouldn't exactly call it an armpit," I shoot back.

"I hear that Starfish Tuna dominates the place and pours an oily sludge into the water. The whole place is a filthy hell hole," Converse says.

"It's not a tourist trap, that's for sure," Phil declares.

"We arrived at night," I interrupt. "It was completely calm, no wind, so we motored in. No smell of French fries or burning trash like the rest of Polynesia, just laundry soap and hot jungle. The tuna fleet was all lit up, bright orange and white lights. No high rise hotels, no bars playing plinky plunky music. Lots of old Somerset Maugham-type architecture. The harbor is shaped like a hex key. We anchored at the far end. The sides are so steep that the buildings are only one width deep along the street. The sun only shines in at high noon. The steep hills keep it out the rest of the day."

"Then there were the American cruising boats. Some of them looked like the jungle had been creeping on board for years. About a dozen or so, of the most unseaworthy looking vessels imaginable," Phil adds. "One boat had a tree growing out of the deck, its roots buried in the ooze."

"It's a shame how corporations ruin a place," Converse nods his head.

"I wouldn't say Starfish has ruined Pago Pago," I say. "What is eye opening to me is the extent to which the world's fishing fleets are prepared to decimate everything in the ocean. The ships could pass for navy ships. Each has helicopters, sonar, radar, and more technology to locate fish than most countries have to wage war. It is no wonder the oceans will soon be empty. The fish don't stand a chance."

"Well Starfish still shouldn't be dumping effluence into the harbor," Converse says while leaning back in his chair nursing his drink.

Pago Pago

"I didn't see that they were," I reply. "There are huge fish with enormous wide mouths swimming throughout the harbor like giant vacuum cleaners. It wasn't too polluted for them. The oily sludge is at the bottom of the harbor. It was like anchoring in a can of lard. We dragged three times and each time we pulled up the anchor it was covered with trash, wires, cables, even a musical keyboard. I wouldn't blame that on Starfish."

"We rented a car and drove around as much of the island as we could in search of flying foxes. Tutuilla is beautiful," Phil says. "America did one brilliant thing, and that was to lease the land for the National Park. Our country spent god knows how many tax dollars on a first rate beautiful library, which is under lock and key, and then spent more money on a billboard sign out front, which says: 'Come in, learn to read, enjoy your library.' What's wrong with that picture?" Phil asks laughing and shaking his head.

"Huh? What is wrong?" Converse asks. "It sounds to me like the American government is at least trying to help the locals."

"Well, if you can't read, how would you know from the sign that you are supposed to come into the library, learn to read and enjoy it?" Phil points out.

"What about the stench? We heard on the radio from Queen Jean that they had to keep clothes pins on their noses," Converse says changing the subject.

"What drove me mad was the non-stop noise of the turbines from the electrical power plant. The smell wasn't bad at all, a little like cooking cat food, which is what it was actually. Kitty King tuna and Cheese, seven cents a can. It was too bad it made Stewart sick," I say.

"How is Stew?" Natalie asks.

"Better now. He did have trouble urinating, but once I figured what his problem was and treated him, he's been fine. He's happy to see the Willy Bolton girls again."

"You wouldn't have believed the only vet on the island! We tried to get more prescription food for Stew," Phil says.

"Iwalani was better equipped than his hospital," I interrupt again. "He had a gurney, a desk and a wastebasket. That's it. He wanted me to give him drugs for anaesthetizing animals, and I almost did because the island is overrun with copulating dogs, but then he said he would be cropping dog's ears for fighting, not neutering. I told him I'd have to think about it."

"Well I still think it is too bad that Starfish dominates there," Converse says.

"Jesus, Converse! Quit ragging on Starfish!" I retort. "I don't think it's fair for you to be so critical when you never even went there." Phil kicks me under the table and I turn to stare at him. "Pago Pago is a lot like Rockland, Maine, before Rockland was ruined by that credit card giant," I remark. Phil rolls his eyes as if to say 'here we go again.'

"Ruined? You're nuts! What the credit card company has done in Rockland is fantastic, cleaning up the waterfront, teaching women how to answer phones instead of canning fish." Converse leans forward and tries to stare me down. "Now women can get their nails done, dress well and feel good about themselves."

"Cleaning?" I retort. "They did more than clean, they sterilized. No more run down fishing shacks, women getting their nails done? What the hell is that supposed to mean? I shouldn't complain about Rockland, as I made a lot of money selling paintings in the new art galleries, but, the only real thing left in Rockland is Seagrow."

"Oh Jesus- they should be closed!" Converse wags his finger at me. "What a travesty! They are the biggest polluters in Maine," Converse cries.

"What the hell is Seagrow?" Paul asks innocently.

"They process seaweed for carrageenan. They make a teeny bit of a bad smell in the process, but it's Rockland," I explain to Paul.

"I can't believe you are defending them. The smell that comes from the plant is wretched–the government should close them down," Converse screeches.

"I'm not defending them," I say trying to remain calm. "I just think a town built on a credit card industry is a town literally built out of cards. If America loses all its industries, we will have a country of nothing."

"It's entirely possible to have a service based economy."

"It's also possible to have industry and keep the environment pristine."

"I'd like to see it," Converse mutters.

"What about your own boat building business? I bet you generate a lot of toxic waste?" I ask Converse.

"And my company spends a lot of money handling it responsibly. Seagrow doesn't," Converse says.

"Well there," I say. "Your own company must be a good example of an industry that exists and can still keep the environment clean. I am sure the government isn't allowing Seagrow to dump hazardous stuff into Rockland harbor-"

"I am not so sure about that," Converse interrupts.

We glare at one another while Converse takes another sip of his gin and tonic. I turn and look at poor Natalie and Paul, who have been wiggling around on the chairs like they are sitting on fire ants, yet they have been uncharacteristically silent. I feel bad that I am ruining dinner for everyone by being so combative. It is ridiculous arguing over a place on the other side of the earth! Home. Phil's home, my home. Our home. Suddenly I miss it like crazy. All of Maine, even stinky old Rockland!

Converse orders another gin and tonic. I haven't even begun my pina colada. I can't believe I am arguing for industry. Each time I turn to look at Converse I think up one more thing to yell at him about.

"What's up with your not flying an American flag? Why do you tell people you are a boat builder? You paid others to build your boat. You didn't lay up the frames yoursel—screw in each plank with four inch screws and a forty pound screw gun; stay up until three a.m. to paint the interior because it was 20 degrees Fahrenheit outside and it took you that long to get the barn above freezing in order to stir the paint..."

My side begins to thob. "How are you two related?" Natalie asks pointing her fork at Converse and myself.

"We're not!" we both answer simultaneously.

"No? You sure fight like relatives," Paul says and we all laugh.

The following day I wake up covered in sweat, with a bruised aching side and a pounding head. Phil is already up, busy about the boat doing small repairs and starting the laundry.

"What's the matter?" Phil asks, handing me a cup of coffee.

"I feel like I was hit by a 747. I'm hung over, I guess. Homesick too. I'm sad about last night. Why can't I be normal? Why am I always such a jerk?"

"You're not a jerk. Your cousin is a jerk."

"He's not my cousin."

"Better put your clothes on. Someone's here."

I throw on a dress and follow Phil up the companionway.

It is Paul. We sit in the cockpit while he climbs aboard. His face looks like it is chiseled from marble.

"Look Paul," I start. "I want to apologize for last…"

"Terrorists took down the twin towers in New York."

"Yeah. Right," Phil laughs.

"No, I am serious. Two planes flew into the twin towers. They're gone. I'm not kidding."

I look at him at him for any sign of his usual jesting. "Paul's telling the truth," I say to Phil.

"How did you find out?" Phil asks.

"One of Converse's sons called him on his satellite phone last night."

"Jesus. What about Roger," Phil says to me.

"Who's Roger?" Paul asks.

"Phil's very good friend, he's a fireman in New York City. He works on the fireboats. I am sure he's OK," I say to Phil.

"I've got to run. Nat is freaking out," Paul says while leaping over Iwalani's bulwark back into his dinghy. "I just thought you should hear it first from me."

"Thanks for telling us."

Phil and I head to shore and wordlessly join the throngs of people walking the streets. Apia, Samoa, is like a zombie movie set. Bars, store front windows and restaurants, all have TV sets tuned to the same picture repeating over and over, two planes flying into the twin towers. And yet, repetition does little to drive home the image, which to us, looks like a scene crafted in some Hollywood back lot.

We get e-mail from Roger's wife. He is OK, but working non-stop. Everyone we know is OK. All the people we come across, including complete strangers, tell us how sorry they are for our country. We feel as if we have lost a great aunt, nothing more. Somehow we seem unconnected, unattached, to the suffering being felt at home.

We walk over to the government building to get our clearance and cruising permit for Savaii and the rainforest canopy walk. Samson is in his office. His dark cheerful face is buried deep in his enormous hands. "I am so sorry about your country," he says looking up. "Come, sit down." He gets up and retrieves our cruising permits from the top of a filing cabinet. "Our country too, lost many people. My supervisor was in the South tower with other dignitaries for an annual meeting. He was killed along with twelve Samoans," he hands the paper to Phil.

"I am sorry to hear that," Phil says. "The people that did such an atrocity-they have no idea how far beyond the American borders their actions extend."

"It is sad but very true," Samson says while shaking his head.

*　　*　　*

After we say our goodbyes to our friends, we head over to the island of Savaii. We depart at five minutes before midnight Thursday so as to avoid leaving on a Friday. We feel no need for testing Phil's superstitions about a Friday departure.

We arrive at daybreak. The entrance to the harbor is not corrected by GPS. We follow the reef until we come to some stakes marking the channel. After anchoring, we load our bikes into the Grape and head to shore.

Traditional Samoan fale

"Good bye! Good-bye," several children yell to us as we peddle by their house. It is almost ninety degrees out, and we are still a long way from the rainforest walk. We are bicycling uphill past many affluent houses perched on the steep hillside overhanging the ocean. Throughout most of the Samoan islands front yards are adorned with large white cement sarcophagi housing the mortal remains of grandparents and other relatives. They are often in front of the fale, or main gazebo-like entrance to a traditional Samoan house where guests are received, so that the living will always be reminded of the dead. But here, on this part of Savaii, the front yards are largely unadorned with traditional fale and white sarcophagi; these houses look more like the upper middle class neighborhoods of California.

"I think they mean to say 'hello', don't you think?" I ask while gasping for breath. "When is this hill going to end?"

"I get the feeling we aren't really wanted here. Take a look at this."

I dismount from my bicycle, grateful for the chance to catch my breath and walk over to where Phil is pausing.

Written in white paint on the road are the words "Long live Sadam."

"Maybe it's the name of some leader on Savaii, not the Iraqi Sadam. Lots of people are called Sadam. It's like Bob-"

"How 'bout this? U.S.A. with a slash through it?"

"That's not good. But praising Sadam? He's just a two bit punk."

"Good bye! Good-bye!" several more children gleefully wave to us from a small house set back from the road.

"This rainforest walk better be worth it. I am not getting a very good feeling about all this."

"Me neither. I think I've got to walk my bike up the rest of this mountain. I'm dying here," I gasp.

"Just think how good this will be going back."

"Assuming I make it that far. I've gotten very soft living on a boat."

"I can't believe you were checking your pulse this morning."

"Hey, just making sure all my systems are working," I respond.

An hour later we arrive at a sign announcing the "Rain Forest Canopy Walk." We leave our bikes in some tall bushes and approach two men sleeping on a mat under a miniature fale.

"Hello," the taller of the two says rubbing his eyes. "Are you lost?"

"We hope not," Phil replies. "We want to see the rainforest walkway."

"You do?"

"Do you know where it is?" I ask.

"It is here. But it will cost you ten tala," the first man mumbles.

"Each," the second man adds. "If you want to see the beach, that is an extra seven tala."

The night of our dinner fiasco, Paul joked that Samoans speak like they have lettuce in their mouths. These men sound as if they have the whole salad bowl. It is difficult understanding what they are saying.

"No," I reply, "We'll pass on the beach, we just want to see the rainforest."

The two men look at each other but say nothing as I hand them the money. "Follow me," the first man mumbles. "I will take you in." The path winds downhill through sun-dappled shrubs until ending at a tall chain link fence. Our guide withdraws a key from his pocket, un-locks the padlock, and then swings the gate open. Two tall trees are caged inside the enclosure. At the base of one is a wooden staircase. The rainforest is nowhere in sight.

"What happened to the rainforest?" I ask.

"This is all that is left," he mutters.

"Two trees?"

"And the walkway. Our school built this as an engineering project. A neighboring village thought our village would get money from tourists. We had a bad fire. Our village fought the fire, but all we could save were the two trees."

"That's terrible!" Phil and I cry in unison.

"The walkway is still very good. Go up those steps. I will wait down here for you."

Phil and I walk in silence up the solid wooden staircase that winds around the huge tree like something from a child's picture book. "This really is an engineering marvel," I say looking at the impressive system of ropes, cables and turnbuckles. Interspersed at different intervals are lookouts. When we finally got near the top we cross over to the other tree on a steel cable bridge. From the second tree we head even higher until we reach the top that affords 360° views.

"It's been burnt out alright," Phil says. Like charred sentinels, the weathered gray branches of hundreds of tall trees stand above the green carpet of the redeveloping forest.

"It looks like it happened awhile ago. I am surprised that no one told us anything about it," I say.

"Hello?" our guide yells from the ground. "Everything OK up there?"

"Yes, we are fine. We are going to have a picnic though," I yell back down to him. "We're not ready to come back down yet. Care for some nuts?"

"No, thank you," he hollers back up. "I'll be back later."

"Might as well get our seven dollars worth," Phil says leaning back against the wooden parapet. "We'll just pretend we are in a rainforest. I hope you brought something better for lunch than that picnic we had in Huahine."

"That was fancy paté de foie gras."

"It tasted like cat food."

"And how exactly would you know what cat food tastes like?"

"I've learned a lot from Stewart."

"I see."

"What's bothering you?" Phil asks.

"I'm just wondering whether we are doing the right thing by heading to Fiji."

"What else can we do? Head to Tonga and New Zealand with everyone else and spend a whole additional year out here?"

"You're right. I am being paranoid. We've been fine up to this point on our own," I say. "But we've got some good friends out here and it just seems a shame to lose them." I hand Phil a sandwich.

"You won't lose them. You can still keep in touch over the radio. And besides, we've still got half the world to meet."

"I know. That's what I am worried about. You don't think we are in any danger because we are American?"

"No more so than if we were at home. You worry too much."

"I know, it's my job."

frigate bird

The Galapagos

Phil, as we approach
Kicker Rock (nice cracks!)

LEFT:marine iguana, ABOVE: sea lion

Marquesas

Top row left to right:
Trade wind sailing-3000 nautical miles to Marquesis; horse and rider in Nuku Hiva; first land fall Nuku Hiva early morning;
Middle row: Stewart with his pet sitters: Ellie and Jess off of Willy Bolton; Iwalani looking tired after 3000 miles on port tack; Tiki in Taiohea Bay,
Bottom: Taiohea Bay Nuku Hiva

Clockwise top right: *clouds and rocks, another Tiki, Phil manning the tiller on The Grape, Bay where Melville's book "Typee" is based, stone pot of human heads, Amy pointing to world's longest waterfall, pandanus roof and bougainvilla, marae enclosure*

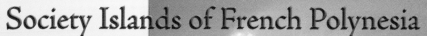

Society Islands of French Polynesia

Clockwise top right:
surfer accompanying
Iwalani through a
pass; Amy blowing
conch horn inBora Bora;
Phil wasn't the only one
using the binoculars;
Vahines on dock, Phil
underwater in the Tuo-
motos, Phil holding The
Grape east side of Bora
Bora, homme-bateau,
watercolor by Amy

Clockwise from right: *Iwalani at anchor in Moorea, Phil repairing folding mountain bike, bread box Polynesian style (yes they deliver baguettes!); Iwalani arriving at Bora Bora, "Tiare Tahiti", Le Truk" public transportation in Tahiti, boat house on Huahine, workmen building the stationary wing mast in Raiatea; background: more Tikis*

TOP AND BOTTOM
The Birds of Suwarro
MIDDLE:
John and Tom- Cook Islanders ,
the caretakers of Suwarro in 2001

FLOWERS
IN
PARADISE

CLOCKWISE FROM LEFT
*Pago Pago fishing fleet,
underwater world of New
Caledonia, Fijian police,
flying fox, red footed booby
hitching a ride, Fijian market,
APW painting of New
Caledonia*

Chapter 14

A Day is Lost, but not Iwalani

October 2001
Fijian Islands

A boat is the muscle and skeleton of a strange seagoing beast and its human crew the twitchy nervous system that controls it. Iwalani has become a creature from a science fiction writer's imagination. She sings her strange song when she is content, roars like a freight train when we have too much sail up, and makes a strange mouse squeak if we are going to have an imminent jibe. Each one of us, Stewart included, has a part to play in keeping her happy and moving forward. Iwalani also begins to take care of us.

On our passage from Savaii to Fiji, we have completely abandoned paper charts, relying instead on a pirated Russian software program called C-Map. When it was first given to us in Polynesia, we had pooh-poohed the software for two reasons. First, it was pirated; Phil and I are adverse to Xeroxing charts, burning copies of someone else's CD's, or installing pirated versions of software. Secondly, we are old dogs; abandoning the comfort of a large paper chart is too new a trick. We start easing ourselves into this new mode of navigating by plotting the course on the computer and then printing the salient features, usually those involving land, onto 8" x 11" sheets of paper.

"What's going on?" Phil says rubbing his beard as he emerges early for his four o'clock afternoon watch.

"Not much. I've been trying to study veterinary medicine. Take a look at this weird stuff on the water. We've been sailing through it for the last hour. I can't figure out what it is."

Phil leans over the bulwark on the leeward side and runs his fingers through the water. Unlike the rest of the South Pacific, where sea and sky are a cheerful bright blue, we are now passing through several convergent zones. The weather is gray, cloudy, damp and unpredictable, the water it's mirrored reflection.

"It's pumice," he says.

"Pumice?"

"From a volcano. I wasn't going to tell you this because it will only add to your worries, but several days ago we went over a seamount that is actually an active underwater volcano. The Inmarsat bulletins said it has now formed an island."

"You're kidding! You mean an island just formed out of nowhere?"

"Well, not actually nowhere. Look at the chart and you can see seamounts all around here. We are in the Pacific rim of fire now. Most of the active volcanoes are underwater."

"You mean we could have run aground on a newly formed, uncharted island?"

"Unlikely. A more likely disaster scenario would have been disappearing in a giant gas bubble."

"A volcano fart?"

"Yup, the boat no longer maintains its buoyancy in a bubble. It would drop down and become swallowed up by the sea faster than you could blink."

"Great, one more thing to worry about."

"Don't worry, we are well out of the active area."

"What about tsunamis? I thought they came after volcanic eruptions?"

"Rarely. They come from tectonic plate activity, underwater earthquakes. As long as we are at sea we should be O.K. In deep water a tsunami would just roll under us as a big swell. We probably wouldn't even feel it. But, if you're ever on a beach and the water goes out to sea quickly, run like hell to high ground, because that means a tsunami is going to hit. Would you like me to make pizza for supper?"

"I was going to make you macaroni and cheese. I don't want anything. I'm not feeling very well."

"Seasick?"

"No. Yes and no. I think my Bartholin's gland cyst is abscessed."

"Oh, great. No sex in Fiji," Phil mumbles.

"I hadn't thought that far ahead. I was trying to figure out how to deal with the here and now. I may need you to lance it."

"No way! Did you see the e-mail from your father?" Phil asks desperately trying to change the subject.

"No. I'm having a hard time sitting. I get too sick down below."

"We didn't realize how good we had it going from the Galapagos to the Marquesas," Phil laments.

"The Savaii fruit washed overboard. I saw it happen hours before it went. And what a job we had bartering for it! Gone. Just like the time the fishing gear was carried off. I didn't do anything about it. I had all I could do to take the jib down during the last squall. I just couldn't figure out where to go with the fruit."

"Don't worry about it. I don't think it would have ripened anyway. It's so wet it would have rotted first."

Later that night, during my eight to midnight watch, the rains let up. It is too painful for me to sit, so I lay in the cockpit covered with our watch blanket. I am having a hard time staying awake. Lying down makes me fall asleep; sitting upright is too painful. I am feeling too sick to read. I turn the light off. I start to fall asleep. I turn the light back on.

'Try to stay awake,' I say to myself.

I stand up and take a look around. Nothing but pitch black. The sky and water are indistinct. Iwalani is floating in a black void. The only sounds are of waves rushing up from behind, the burble and gush of water hitting a wooden planked hull, the plaintive violin scratchings of the glass handled cups hanging on the brass cup hooks down below, the occasional clack of the wooden blocks on the mainsheet, the creak and groan of the Dacron preventer holding the mainsail out. I lie back down, covering all but my face with the watch blanket. We are miles from anywhere.

I hear a small squeak. Two large black eyes the size of dinner plates, peer over the bulwark at me. It is a giant squid holding on to Iwalani's stern. We are not moving forward. He has a beaked mouth like a parrot. The mouth opens and closes with a rusty squeak. Strange. Who would have thought giant squid make noise?

A twenty-foot tentacle reaches up from the oily black water surface. It stretches over the bulwark, dripping seawater on the deck. I am too scared to move. I cannot scream. The tentacle slaps me in the face.

"Jesus Christ!" I scream.

I had fallen asleep. A flying fish flaps madly on my belly. Fish scales start rubbing off all over the blanket. I grab the fish and throw it overboard. Iwalani slams over hard on the wrong side. We have jibed.

Phil charges up from down below. "What's happening up here?" he says while pushing the off button on the autopilot. "Did you fall asleep? Couldn't you hear the preventer squeaking? I've been waiting for ten minutes for you to do something about it. Take control of the tiller. What are all these fish scales all over everything? What the hell have you been doing up here?"

I throw off the watch blanket and grab hold of the tiller. Like a bug-splattered windshield on a hot summer night, sleep has clouded my ability to think and see. The boom and mainsail are pressed hard against the backstay. Instinctively I pull the tiller to port. Iwalani hesitates for a moment, then rights herself, the large main swings back out to its correct position.

"I was being attacked by a giant squid," I say to Phil.

"Glad you are still alive. Pay attention next time! You are going to kill us. See you at midnight, when today won't be tomorrow but the day after tomorrow."

"What are you talking about? I'm not the only one hallucinating."

"Just as I thought! You were asleep! Otherwise you would have seen on the GPS that we are a few minutes, and I mean the degree kind not the time kind, away from where the east meets west."

"I'm sorry, but I am a bit preoccupied with what is happening to my south."

"Huh?"

"The abscess between my legs, which I still need you to drain."

"Me? We're almost in Fiji. We'll find a gynecologist there."

Phil lets me sleep in for my four a.m. watch. When I wake up it is already light out. I can't stand the pain between my legs and grab a scalpel blade out of the surgery box. I carry the metal envelope with the number ten-size blade and stagger out into the cockpit with a hot water compress.

"Thanks for letting me sleep in," I say to Phil.

"No problem, you didn't look very good at midnight. We should be in Savu Savu this afternoon. What's with the wash cloth?"

"Hot compress. Can't you please help me with this?"

"Just wait a few hours, I really can't do it. It is too gross, and I hate needles."

"You won't need a needle, you just stab me with a scalpel blade."

"You've got to be kidding! Forget it. I'm heading to bed."

I stand out in the cockpit with the washcloth between my legs. The sky is damp and rainy and the wind has picked up. We have a single reef in the mainsail, no jib and full staysail. Phil reduced more sail while I slept.

I am not particularly enthused about having a Fijian doctor attend to my privates. I sit painfully down along the leeward rail resting my arm on the bulwark cap and look around, the surgical blade is still in my hand safely wrapped in its envelope. All about me is gray, the sky, the sea, Iwalani's decks and bulwark rail, my mood. I decide it is now or never. I open the blade packet making a makeshift handle out of the metal wrapper. In vet school we were taught never to do this, it is just not proper. I don't give a damn.

The seas are erratic. Iwalani is rolling around like a metronome with a lost beat. I spread my legs open and can see the abscess as big as a tomato, and much the same color. Gently I hold the blade to the surface. On animals, I usually surgically scrub anything before approaching with a scalpel. I am too painful and feel too sick to go through all the formalities. But just positioning the blade on the tender surface brings me to tears. I can't do it. It hurts too much to stab myself. Suddenly Iwalani lurches, the blade slips, and I have an inch long incision through the abscess. I inhale sharply from the sudden pain and appearance of strange colors now flowing from my body: red, yellow and green, so out of place at sea. Waves lick up through the scuppers and wash the mess away. The clean ocean floats about me like a sitz bath. Once the shock of what has just happened wears off, I feel better within seconds. With a lurch and a sway, the boat has done for me, what neither Phil nor I could do.

In the time it takes Iwalani to bound from the crest of one wave to the trough of the next, we leave yesterday and enter into tomorrow. The time of day is still the same, the sun never bats an eyelash at the imaginary line slicing through Earth from pole to pole as we cross the International Date Line. Thursday night becomes early Saturday morning. Friday, September 21, 2001 never exists for us.

"What's up with Stewart?" Phil asks.

"What do you mean?"

"He is limping around down below."

Now that I am feeling better I quickly go below to check on him.

"It could be quite serious," I tell Phil when I return. "His left leg is very painful, his foot is cold and I can only feel a weak pulse. It could mean that he might have a saddle block thrombus."

"Translation, Doc?"

"A blood clot to his leg. I gave him a quarter aspirin and some Heparin."

"Will he be alright?"

"I hope so. But it might mean he has underlying heart disease. I also might need more Heparin. I only brought a little bit, just for preventing blood clotting in the syringe. I wasn't thinking about blood thinning for living creatures."

"I was listening to the radio last night. There's a cruiser on the way to Tonga who was having a heart attack. Another cruiser, a doctor, was talking the man's wife through it all. The wife sounded like she barely knew how to run the radio- let alone the boat. The worst part of it was she didn't have aspirin, she had just about everything else but no aspirin,"

"Too bad he wasn't closer to Iwalani, we've got a ton of aspirin,"

"Speaking of illness's, you seem a lot better this morning."

"You're off the hook as my surgeon."

"Why?"

"Iwalani took care of it," and I tell Phil what happened.

"It only confirms what I've said right along; we're all in this together."

We arrive in Savu Savu, Fiji that afternoon but have to remain on the boat until Monday morning to be cleared in. Two days later, five officials come alongside in an outboard with no steering. The captain pilots from the stern with twin pieces of rope. Left, right, port, starboard he pulls the ropes looking like a puppeteer as he expertly maneuvers a small army of Fijian officialdom wearing white shirts, black pants and heavy black-soled shoes onto our world. We introduce them to cranberry juice, which they sip politely with puckered faces, while Phil and I fill out form after form, in triplicate. The Fijian health inspector also takes a look at Stew, but doesn't realize he can't use his back legs as Stewart remains on the settee cushion examining him back. When they leave, they imprint their rubber stamps in our passports and their waffle shoeprints on our decks.

For the next week we explore the area on foot and by bus. We tour the local sugar mill where only a few weeks before a Japanese tourist had gotten caught in the grinding wheels and was turned to human flavored sugar syrup. Not wanting to succumb to a similar fate, I make sure that the long skirt I am wearing has an elastic waist for quick exiting. My preference would have been to wear shorts, but we are still in Missionary territory and too much skin is frowned upon.

We visit the local doctor and attend to Stewart's needs, exchanging Iwalani's store of valuable antibiotics and ophthalmic ointment for a small vial of Heparin, which the Fijian Doctor says he cannot use. I see the exam/operating table behind an orange curtain, the only thing separating the patient from the waiting room. I silently thanked Iwalani for sparing me the embarrassment of having to lie spread eagled with only a flimsy piece of see-through fabric, separating me from downtown Savu Savu.

After one week of living on a boat at anchor, where the water stays in the glass, the glass stays on the counter, and we all sleep together on a bed that doesn't roll, Phil announces it is time to get moving again. We receive our clearance from Savu Savu for the large city of Suva, restock the icebox with plenty of fresh fruit and vegetables and become mentally prepared to leave.

"Hello, are you Philip?" a smiling Fijian woman calls out to us as we exit the yacht club front door.

"Yes."

"I was told you were good at fixing computers."

"Sometimes."

"I have a computer which needs to be fixed. Could you do it?"

Phil inhales, looks at me, then replies, "Sure, I can try."

Alitia lives at the mouth of the well-protected channel that leads to the village of Savu Savu. Her house is on our way out, so we arrange to meet her after church. Working on Sunday in Fiji is frowned upon, so we assure her Phil will just take a look at the computer and not really work on it. We anchor Iwalani in a protected arm of the cove and row to shore. Roosters crow in the hills while gray rain clouds roll like swirling cotton candy over the tree covered hills. "It's not really great weather to leave anyhow," I say to Phil as we carry the dinghy up the rock-strewn beach.

A small boy appears from behind a large bush. "I'm Kenny," he says. "I'll take you to our house." We follow him up the dirt road until we come to a driveway leading up the steep hillside. Behind a once blue colored tumbled down shack is Alitia's house. "I work in the office at the yacht club," Alitia explains to us as we enter the house. "A cruiser gave me this computer."

The computer sits upon a table with a pink tablecloth in the main part of the house, which is comprised of kitchen, living room and dining room. Alitia turns it on. It flickers a moment and then shows the blue screen of death. Phil immediately sits down in the white plastic chair and punches keys. Alitia brings us some tea.

I awkwardly sit next to Phil but soon realize I am no help to him.

"This is a lovely house," I say to Alitia.

"Thank you. We used to live in front. But we rent that to..."

"What's going on?" a pretty teenaged girl asks as she emerges from a door leading down a hallway.

"This is my daughter Rosie. Phil and Amy are fixing the computer."

"Oh how wonderful!" she dances with delight. Rosie comes in the kitchen and takes a bowl off the shelf and spoons a brown stew from a pot on the counter into it. She eats while standing, and then throws the bowl into the sink. "Bye, and good luck" she calls out to us as she runs out the door.

Alitia rolls her eyes, "Teenagers…"

Kenny comes out from a back room and stands holding a small plastic army soldier. He crosses his small brown legs and stands staring at us while leaning up against his mother.

"How old are you, Kenny?" I ask him.

"He's eight," Alitia answers. "He uses the computer more than the rest of us, so he will be very happy if you can fix it."

"Did the cruiser leave you any software or manuals?" Phil asks her.

"No. Just the computer."

"Hmph," Phil replies as he continues to pound computer keys.

"Where are you headed after you leave Fiji?" Alitia asks while sipping her tea.

"We are trying to get to Australia by November."

"I spent five months in Australia two years ago."

"Really? Where were you?"

"Melbourne."

"Did you like it there?" I ask.

"Oh yes, very much. I didn't want to come

back," Alitia says placing her cup on the table.

"Why were you there?"

Alitia pauses for a moment, then picks her cup back up. "I went on walkabout," she says.

"Walkabout?"

"It's an Australian term for a journey of sorts. I just wanted to leave Fiji."

"What about your family?"

"My husband took care of everyone, his parents, too."

"Oh," I say. "Why did you come back?"

"My visa expired. I was not allowed to stay."

"There!" Phil cries in triumph. "I think I did it."

The computer beeps and wheezes, then Bill Gate's waves his magic wand over the small Fijian island and "Windows 95" comes to life.

"Oh that's wonderful!" Alitia exclaims.

"I'm not sure I fixed it. I'll come back tomorrow to check. If it goes back to blue screen, I will have to reformat the hard drive."

"What does that mean?"

"It means I take all the software off and then re-install it. But I will have to use Window's 98, which is what I have. You would lose any files, letters or anything stored on the computer."

"I don't have anything on it anyway. I just use it to write letters."

"Do Rosie and Kenny use it for schoolwork?"

"Rosie does. Kenny just uses it for games."

"Tell her to save anything onto these floppies. That way you will have a back up."

As we are leaving Alitia hands Phil a large bundle wrapped in a trash bag. "Here Philip, this is for you. My mother made it." Inside the bag is a beautiful hand woven Fijian floor mat.

"I can't take this." Phil says.

"Yes please, I insist."

*   *   *

Monday morning Phil and I row to shore so he can re-check his patient.

"Any bets if it's still up and running?"

"I say "yes" and you won't need all this stuff."

"Hm. I say no, which is why I am bringing these manuals and software. Do you think I should give her the mat back if I don't fix it?"

"Boy, I don't know what Fijian etiquette would dictate."

We can tell by the crestfallen faces when we enter the house that the computer is dead again.

"I have to go to work. Do you mind staying here by yourselves to work on it?" Alitia asks us.

"Not at all, if you don't mind us

Alitia with Phil's patient.

being here. Did you get stuff saved?" Phil asks.

"Yes. Last night. It's all set."

Phil begins reformatting the hard drive. I wander around outside, taking a walk down the street and exploring the peninsula. I walk back into the house two hours later.

"How's it going?"

"So far so good. It's a lot of waiting around for stuff to load."

I look at the kitchen, which appears exactly the same as it did yesterday, only with a higher pile of dirty dishes in the sink.

"Do you think Alitia would be mad if I cleaned up for her a little bit?"

"I don't know. What would local custom say?"

"Who cares about custom? I am just sitting around and it would be nothing more than one woman helping out an overstressed working mother."

I begin by heating up the water in the electric kettle and then work my way through a pile of crusted over dishes. When I am done I go back and sit next to Phil.

An elderly woman walks into the house and shuffles over to the now clean sink. Phil and I say 'hello,' but she just stares at us, stares at the sink and then shuffles out again.

"Isn't this kind of weird?" I ask.

"How so?"

"Here we are on a small island in Fiji; palm fronds are scritch-scratching on the tin roof, roosters are crowing, sitting in a house with cold running water but no telephone, no car, and we are working an a native Fijians computer? I mean aren't we supposed to be drinking Kava and bowing to the chief in a Sevu Sevu ritual?"

"It sure beats working on a computer in a grimy basement in Boston."

"I suppose you are right, but it just wasn't what I expected when we were back home."

"That's why we went on this trip. We didn't know what to expect," Phil says pounding the computer keys.

Later that afternoon Phil has the hard drive reformatted, and the computer is up and running. Rosie rows out to Iwalani with us so we can show her the boat while we make back up CD's. "I would love to live on a boat," Rosie says while settling back on the settee and patting Stewart who is now back to normal.

"It can get pretty boring," I respond.

"Yes, but think of the places you can go and the things you can see. I can't wait to get out of here."

"Fiji is pretty nice," I say.

"Yes, but I would like to go to England and study."

"Why England and not America?"

"America is not safe. Everyone there has guns, and there is too much violence."

"I think you have been watching too many American TV shows. It's not really like that," I say while rolling out the crust for a quiche.

"And how would you know?" Phil asks. "Amy doesn't even own a TV."

"You don't? We do!" Rosie exclaims. "I like Dallas and the Simpsons."

"What would you study if you went away to school?" Phil asks.

"Computers."

"Do you use them at school now?" I ask her.

"No. We have a whole computer room, but none of the teachers know how to use them, and they won't allow us to touch them."

"Well, then, I don't feel so bad about giving you these," Phil says handing her our back up version of Windows 98 and some game CD's. "You must promise to learn enough in college that you can come back to Fiji and teach everyone else how to use the computers."

We introduce Rosie to quiche and after eating, we row her to shore. On our way back to the boat Phil becomes wistful. "I wish Ben and Nathaniel were here. Imagine what they could teach Rosie in just a few days time."

"Don't you think the education would be both ways?"

"You're right about that."

We both go to shore on Tuesday morning, before Alitia heads off to work, to check one last time on the computer and give her some hints on using it. Dark rain clouds scud over the hills, but where we lay at anchor all is peaceful.

"Please, you must stay for breakfast," she says as we walk in.

Not wanting to offend her, we both say "Thank you," and sit down.

"This is my husband," she waves her hand at a man emerging from the bathroom taking a seat at the head of the table. He nods to us and sits down to a big plate of the brownish-yellow stew that I had seen Rosie eating a few days ago. "Where are you heading now?" he asks us.

"Namena Island. I'd like to do some diving before heading to Suva" I answer.

"It's not much of an anchorage," he says between mouthfuls. Alitia heaps large spoonfuls of yellow stew out of the pot onto two large plates.

"Don't you like goat curry?" she asks.

"Oh yes! I love curry," I say trying to sound enthusiastic.

"I cook this curry in the hot springs on the way to work. We just leave a pot full of food in the ground, and by the time we walk by in the afternoon it is all cooked. Here," she says passing us a plate full of white circular discs. "This is fried taro. You eat it with the curry."

I take one of the discs and bite into it. It is a little like eating a missing part from an incomplete brake pad assembly. I manage to swallow almost everything though, despite the fact that the curry is at room temperature, and leave only the bones of some old goat in my dish.

"More?" Alitia asks.

"Oh no, thank you. We have eaten way too much already."

We say our good byes and row back to the boat.

"I'm not so sure that was a going-to-sea breakfast," Phil says to me while I get things ready to hoist the anchor.

"We haven't got far to go. Namena is only a few hours away," I add.

"It might be a little rough getting there, but at least it's a fair wind."

And it is rough. We had become complacent sitting far up the inlet in the well-protected town of Savu Savu. We were unable to receive radio or fax broadcasts due to propagation and the other vagaries of radio waves and laziness. Our weather information came from a small printed picture next to the comics in the Fiji Times. While we were anchored off Alitia's even that bit of information had lapsed.

Taro and goat curry are a combo that even the most adept gourmand would have felt queasy dealing with during the best of circumstances. Getting reacquainted a second time in six-foot seas is far worse. "I think I just threw up my liver," I moan to Phil, as I lean out over the leeward bulwark.

"Hang in there. I sure hope this Russian C-Map program is accurate because it looks as if we are going to have to surf in. If it's wrong, we'll be on the reef for sure."

I lie praying for a new stomach while Phil takes control of Iwalani and anchors us in the island's lee side.

"We should have paid more attention to Alitia's husband," Phil says. "This isn't an anchorage."

"We'll just stay for a day or two, long enough to see some fish."

"You can't exactly go diving in these conditions."

I look around at our surroundings. Namena seems to be a rookery of sorts. Hundreds of seabirds are in the trees, on the beach, and flying low over the water for fish. Despite being anchored in the lee, Iwalani is rocked by the wind howling over the island. The surrounding reef is blocking most of the seas, but there is still a two-foot chop around the boat. The dark clouds cast a gray pall on everything. The visibility won't be very good for diving.

"Hopefully it will clear up tomorrow," I say.

Phil makes pizza for supper which we eat together in silence.

"Once I do the dishes, I'm heading off to bed," I say.

"I'm going to sleep in the cockpit to make sure we don't drag anchor. I don't have a good feeling about this," are the only words Phil says all evening.

"You worry too much," I chide him.

Stewart and I head forward and fall asleep. Phil joins us at around midnight. "The wind has dropped off," he says quietly.

"Umm. It's nice and calm," I drawl back.

I fall instantly back to sleep.

"Now where are you going?" It is light outside. I don't know how long I have been asleep.

"I'm going up to check on things. I don't like the sound of the water lapping against the hull."

I watch Phil head up the companionway. His naked body is tan all over. I am lusting over my own husband, mentally trying to lure him back to bed.

"Amy! Get up here now!"

I sit upright bumping my head on the kerosene lamp. "I have to pee."

"You have no time. I don't know what this is, but we are going to die."

I scramble out of bed, leaving Stewart confused and wiping his whiskers with his paws.

When I get into the cockpit I look to the west. "What in god's name is that?"

Phil has already gotten the engine going. "You've got to get the anchor up."

Fast approaching us, from the opposite direction of last night's wind is an enormous, moving, dark gray wall. At first I think it is a tidal wave. I stand mesmerized, unable to comprehend the enormity of our situation. It looks like a special effects scene from a disaster movie. And then I hear it. A roar so loud that suddenly Phil's voice just five feet away becomes incomprehensible, "Now!"

I run to the bow and step on the button for the windlass. Slowly, link-by-link, the anchor starts to come up. The black wall hits us. This is no tidal wave, but a wall of horizontal pellets of rain and wind like we have never seen before, nor want to see again.

The seabirds we watched yesterday roll past us on top of the waves like feathered bowling balls. Wings outstretched, feet paddling, their plaintive cries turn to gurgles. Hundreds of them roll by, onto the shore, and up into the woods.

'We will be next,' I think to myself.

The windlass strains. The anchor stops. It will come up no more.

"It's holding. Why move?" A coral outcropping on the eastern side of the shore is still a hundred feet away. 'But what is this wind? What if it gets even stronger?' The island is now a lee shore; Iwalani could be carried up like the rolling birds and deposited so far inland that she will become a tree house. We have to get her to the opposite side of the island.

The rain drives into my skin like bullets from a machine gun. Scabs on my legs are blasted off and start to bleed. There is no air to breathe, only water. Only by turning my back to the wind and keeping my head down can I find small pockets of air to inhale.

Iwalani's bow is pointing downwind. Phil is yelling something to me but I can't understand what he is saying. Holding on to hand rails, I make my way back to the stern crawling most of the way. If I let go of the boat, I too, will be carried off by the wind like the tumbling seabirds.

I stand inches away from Phil as he yells into my ear, "What do we do?"

I stare at him. *'What do we do? You're asking me for advice?'*

"I've got the engine in full reverse. The wind is too strong to turn her around. We don't have the horsepower to back up. What do we do?" he shouts at me again.

"The only thing we can do. We'll have to go forward and hope that we have enough time to turn and clear the reef and head east. We have to make our way to the other side of the island. The anchor is stuck on something, but I'll try one more time to free it. I'll raise my arm when we're off. Put Iwalani in forward gear, give it all she has, and steer hard to port," I scream back.

Traveling with the wind, I have a much easier time making my way back to the bow. I step on the windlass button and the chain starts to come up. I raise my arm, signaling to Phil we are free, praying we really are free and that the weight of the remaining chain and anchor are enough to avoid getting carried astern and caught in the propeller. But then I see the anchor just ten feet below the surface. It makes its way up into the roller where I quickly secure it. We skid past the end of the reef as fast as a roller coaster, leaving about twenty feet to spare. I slowly make my way back to the cockpit.

"I need a chart. I don't know what's over here," Phil still has to yell at me, but not as loud since we were now going with the wind.

"I looked at it last night. You should be OK, but I'll find the chart anyhow." I move the soaked cushions out of the way and head down below.

"I had to pile those there. Water was pouring in down below. I didn't have time to get the drop slides," Phil says.

I pass the chart up to him. Thankfully, while we were still in Savu Savu, he had printed out a sheet of paper detailing the island from the C-Map program and had placed it in a protective plastic sleeve. Water is everywhere down below, covering every possible surface, including Phil's laptop computer and Stewart. "You should have stayed in bed," I say to him.

"Don't turn off the computer," Phil yells down to me, "It got a little wet."

"A little?" I pass up a towel and his foul weather gear.

"I'm not ready for that yet. Hold us into the wind while I drop the anchor. This is as much in the lee as we can get."

I throw on my raincoat and head into the cockpit. Phil goes forward and drops the anchor. It sets instantly, but we are far from settled. The boat bounces up and down like a six year old on a school bus seat.

"We'll have to keep it in forward gear," Phil says to me when he returns to the cockpit.

At least the birds aren't tumbling by us. A few that had rolled by the island are struggling against the wind to make their way to the relative protection of the shoreline, or onto Iwalani's lifeline and rigging. The sustained winds have now dropped down to a safer forty knots.

I go down below while Phil finally puts some clothes on. His lips are blue so I make him some cocoa, getting sick into the sink in the process.

I turn the VHF radio on and listen to the Fijian weather forecaster, while Phil stands in the cockpit wearing his heavy Maine winter coat and foul weather gear.

"Verrrrrrryrrrrrroughseas, Verrrrrrryrrrrrroughseas, windsnorrrrrtheast, winds norrrrrtheast, twenty to thirrrrrrrrty knots, twenty to thirrrrrrrrty knots," the broadcaster reports rolling his "r"'s with more virtuosity than a purring cat.

"This guy needs a window," I say to Stew, "or at least a weathervane. These winds aren't northeast."

I switch the channel to sixteen.

"I'm in a Dehavilland Beaver. I'm part of a film crew. We are looking for Koro Island," says the American voice over the airwaves.

"This is sailing yacht Valliant. I am at 17°12 s and 179°e. I don't hear your engine, sorry."

"Jesus," Phil calls down to me, "There is some crazy fool flying a single engine airplane out here."

"Really? I hear him on the radio, and he sounds lost. There is also another American boat out here, too," I say.

I pick up the microphone. "DeHavilland Beaver, Dehavilland Beaver," this is sailing vessel Iwalani. I think we may hear your engine."

"Go ahead, sailing vessel."

"Can you see an island below you?"

"Yes!"

"Fly east, you should see a gray and maroon sailboat, the only one anchored at the island on the eastern shore."

Suddenly a yellow airplane flies overhead and waggles its wings.

"I see you at anchor. But I don't see the landing strip."

"You are flying over Namena Island not Koro; I repeat, this is Namena Island," I say into the microphone.

"Ah Roger that, thank you, sailing vessel."

"This is the yacht Valiant. Repeat your name sailing vessel please."

"This is Iwalani."

"Did you say you were at Namena?"

"Roger Roger," I answer.

"You must have had an exciting time the last few hours."

"You could say that," I reply.

"We were heading to Musket Cove but got word from friends there that several boats went ashore. I guess it's mayhem there, so we stayed off."

"What was this storm? Did any of the forecasters predict it?"

"I don't know. No one predicted it. We had sustained winds of sixty knots with higher gusts. And you? What size boat are you?"

"Forty two feet on deck."

"Valiant is an eighty foot ketch."

"Oh," I say feeling rather small.

"This is Namena Island. Could you please go to channel 72?"

Another American voice. I switch the dial, feeling foolish that I have been blocking the emergency frequency for small talk.

"Namena Island, this is Iwalani."

"Do you need any assistance? I can send my man out to help you anchor."

"No, thanks, we are fine. I wouldn't want to send anyone out in this weather," I respond. "But it's nice to hear so many American voices."

"My name is Joanne, and I own a resort here. My man knows the underwater parts of this island like the back of his hand. But he says you have anchored in the two best spots already. You are welcome to come ashore when this clears off."

Just before dark the wind drops off and goes back to the northeast, so we move over to the original anchorage.

The following morning we launch the dinghy and row to shore. I step over the twisted remains of a wooden sign stating that landing and coming ashore is not permitted while Phil bends down and picks it up, attempting to stand it upright again. We come to a path through the woods that is littered with more debris from the storm. Branches, uprooted trees and palm fronds criss-cross the forest floor. It is only when we get close that we realize scattered amidst the debris are the remains of the tumbling boobies, terns and frigate birds. Some are still alive but are very weak and unable to fly with multiple wing and leg fractures.

"Holy crap," Phil says.

"I can't help all these birds!" I wail.

"Nor should you."

"I suppose you are right. I know my Uncle Charlie would agree."

"Which uncle?"

"The head of the Ornithology department at Cornell. He was aghast when I told him I rehabilitated everything from pigeons to eagles. I told him I tried to take care of everything when possible because I learned techniques from the most common of species, which can help me when I get rare birds in. He thinks they are better off left alone, survival of the fittest, that sort of thing. I disagree with that

197

totally when it comes to problems we humans have created for birds. I might agree with him when it comes to natural disasters like this. But what should we do? If we stayed to repair their fractures, it might take as long as eight weeks. We don't have that time to spare; we'd be caught here in cyclone season. I can't euthanize them, because I don't have enough of the drug, as there was a manufacturers back order when we left. I only have enough for Stewart, which I hopefully will never have to use. I suppose we could chop their heads off with my machete and your hatchet."

"No. We should leave them. Let Mother Nature take care of it."

"Don't you think they are suffering?" I ask.

"Do you?"

I look about me at the sun dappled forest floor. It is remarkably quiet. The birds, perhaps one hundred of them, are scattered like cast off clothes in a teenager's bedroom. Dead birds hang from tree branches like old sweatshirts. Those still alive are resting contentedly in the leaf litter, their eyes barely able to stay open.

"I don't know anymore," I finally say. "Before this trip I thought I knew what suffering was. Now I am not so sure. They seem like they are at home and are happy. Would I want to endure this if I were them? Having just a few more hours of this peaceful place? Yes, I think I would."

We step around the birds and continue down the path, to find Joanne in the main building of her resort. All of the little "bures" are empty, not a tourist in sight.

"Business has been bad since 9/11. Just about all of the reservations have cancelled. It's just as well, I guess with a storm like that. We'll be weeks cleaning up around here."

"Do you have that kind of weather often?" Phil asks.

"Not since I've been here, and that is almost fifteen years. We had a steady sixty knots of wind yesterday. At least that was what I saw before the storm blew the wind speed indicator off the building. I am sure it was more than that, as the storm hadn't really picked up at that point. Twenty years ago there was a cyclone with two hundred knot winds. Little survived."

"I can't imagine that. It would be enough to rip a person apart," I say.

She says she has much work to do but invites us to take a look around her island. We continue walking along the perimeter until we get to a long strip of beach.

"Thank you for being so vigilant," I grab Phil's hand. "We were pretty lucky. If it hadn't been for you, I am sure we would have lost the boat."

"From now on I get to pick the anchorages."

"I still want to go diving before we leave here."

"Count me out. My ear is really bothering me."

"I'll take a look at it when we get back to the boat. But you know what I have decided?"

"What?" he asks.

"If that was only sixty knots of wind, I sure don't want to be anywhere near the cyclone belt during cyclone season. Count me out of going to Brisbane."

"That leaves Sydney as the only other port we can enter for Stewart's quarantine, and that is nearly impossible to get to with the prevailing winds."

"Maybe Stewart won't have to go into quarantine."

"Amy, you know full well the Australian laws. He'll be lucky they don't force a six month quarantine on him."

"The website said thirty days, since he's been in the South Pacific so long where there is no rabies. Maybe he can be quarantined on the boat."

"Wouldn't that be nice? Do you see what I see?" Phil lets go of my hand.

"I sure do."

Lying in the sand is a perfect chambered nautilus shell, a gift to Iwalani and her crew from Neptune and the sea.

Chapter 15

The Mark of Zorro

December 2001
Off the eastern coast of Australia

"Oh my god, don't ever do that to me again," Phil says while grabbing his chest and falling over in a mock heart attack. I am lying up in the bow of the boat, shaded somewhat from the hot afternoon sun by the small jib, reading one of the few remaining books on board that I haven't read, a mystery novel obtained in a yachtie book exchange in Fiji. We are on our way to Australia from New Caledonia, where we spent several weeks trying get the paperwork done for Stewart's forced quarantine, in between land and underwater explorations of unparalleled beauty. For the last two days the winds have been light, so we are motor sailing.

"Do what?" I ask.

"I thought you had fallen overboard. I didn't see you up here."

"Come sit up here next to me. It's relatively cool."

"It's really hot down below. I can't sleep."

"I sure am going to miss New Caledonia. I think I must have gained twenty pounds. I thought pastries like that only existed in fairy tales."

"Yeah. I think Australia is going to have to be pretty special to beat New Caledonia. Especially after such cool nights and no bugs."

"Don't forget the orchids and snorkeling. And to think we nearly passed it by because it lies like a nematode on the chart," I say placing my book down.

"A what?"

"A nematode, a flatworm. It's got an ugly shape on the chart."

"I see. I didn't know we were discriminating places because of the shape of their land mass. Did you get the afternoon weather fax?"

"I tried to, but the frequency seems wrong."

"Did you lower it?"

"I thought so, but it's all static."

"That's too bad. We won't get anything again until tomorrow."

"You know we will have to pay for this kind of weather."

"Don't say anything. You'll jinx it. What about the Mamba radio net?"

"All the boats but us, are in Brisbane. No one can understand me; they complain about a carrier tone and say I'm off frequency. They say I sound like Mickey Mouse."

"I can't do anything else to fix it. We'll have to send the radio back to the U.S. when we get to Australia. The problem is with the microprocessors, one of the drawbacks to an all digital radio."

"That radio's never been right. I'm not sure anyone will be checking in with us tomorrow."

"Well, in another three days we should be in Sydney, but we have to get the next fax that comes in."

"We are the only boat heading that way."

"We are the only boat with a cat. We could have gone to Brisbane with the forty-five other boats."

"No way. It's still in the cyclone belt."

"Going directly to Sydney with prevailing headwinds is nearly impossible," Phil reminds me yet again.

"What did you tell me about impossibilities? Nothing is impossible. Would you have allowed me to bring Stewart knowing all you do now about the hassle of importing a cat to Australia?"

"Of course! I wouldn't have wanted to miss the last two weeks of telephone nightmare. Watching you deal with a French telephone operator and Australian customs has been very entertaining."

"It's not over yet. We're still not in Australia."

"And, by the way, you are going to have to dump your Jamaican marijuana overboard before we get there," Phil chastises me.

"No way! I spent fifty dollars on it!"

"Had I known what you were up to, I never would have allowed it! If we get caught, they'll throw us in jail. I've heard they even send beagles up to the top of the mast to sniff around for drugs. It's got to go."

"Think of what you'll be missing!" I make a deep predatory growl, lunge for Phil and plant a big kiss on his lips. "I have figured out the perfect place to hide it."

"Oh great-where?" Phil says wiping his mouth.

"Inside a six inch piece of garden hose. I'll stopper the ends with cork, then stick the hose inside the charcoal filter in the water maker. Not only will it be immersed in water, but it will be enshrouded by charcoal, deep within the watermaker, in an uncomfortable spot in the hot diesel smelling engine room. I defy any dog to discover it! No customs agent will take the water maker apart. After they remove the first filter, the rotten stench of sea water will stop them."

"No."

"What do you mean 'no'? It's perfect."

"I will not have it. It's bad enough having Stewart in quarantine. I can not handle you in jail as well."

"O.K, fine."

"I'm going back to bed."

"See you at supper. We're having spaghetti and the last of the blueberry pie."

"My favorite, but buttering me up won't work. Throw the pot overboard."

December 5, 2001 APW Personal log

0000: My watch has just ended. I climb out of the watch blanket/sleeping bag in the cockpit and look around. No stars. The moon not up yet. Motor sailing, winds NE 8 knots. Starboard tack. Unusual. Most of our sailing to date has been on port tack. I scan the horizon. Dark clouds ahead. Radar on. Watchman set for twenty minutes. Guard zone alarm goes off. Rain three miles ahead and lots of it. I close the aft lazarette hatch, which we usually keep open to ventilate the engine room. The staysail is loose. I go forward and adjust it. Close the galley hatch on my way by. Go down below and turn on the computer. Bring up Galaxy program for Inmarsat and download EGC's- free weather bulletins, piracy reports and worldwide news. No e-mail. Write my Dad and give him our position:

28d05S/159d33EMotoringNoWindOkByMePieAllGoneThanx4InfoIHa
dItRightGrammyToldMeAll1NightLMacquaryIsBigDealAcc2BillBryson.
PerhapsOzWillTreatDescendantsOkStewIsThrivingOnFrenchFoodIfHeIs
MacquaryCatMaybeTheyWontThrowHimInJailIfHepaysCash4JailTimeX
XXAP&S

    I go back into the cockpit and bring the sleeping bag and Phil's Gameboy down, so they don't get wet. Floss, wash my face and brush my teeth. Record position in ship's logbook and plot it on the chart. We had been way off course. Iwalani was trying to go south, not southwest. We are coming back on course- so I make no adjustment with the steering. I go forward and wake Phil and tell him his watch is going to be wet. Rain is starting to come through the forward hatch. Phil has a hard time closing it as staysail sheet got caught in it a couple of days ago and bent the hinge.

    Phil puts on foul weather gear and decides to take all sail down. It is now his watch and I help. Our rule is, whoever is on watch is in charge. Ultimate decisions are made by whoever is captain and that depends on the day. It is wet. I towel myself off then go forward with Stewart to sleep. The motion forward is uncomfortable. I come aft with pillow, sheet and cat, we sleep in starboard pilot berth.

    0400 Iwalani is now bucking into head winds. Sometime during the night Phil has put all the sail back up. He downloaded EGC's. A low we had been watching west of Sydney is now a gale. Winds are directly on the nose from the SW. We are Motor sailing. Phil has changed course to Coff's Harbour—a few degrees off the wind and to the west. He's grumbly.

    "We'll just stay on the boat. So what if we can't get Stewart to quarantine. Fuck them. So what if we can't make repairs to the boat. Hopefully we'll sink in their precious Great Barrier Reef."

    I say nothing while he heads off to bed. I make instant cappuccino which I can only drink at sea- along with all the other corporate chemical foods, which can only be eaten, and or drunk while conditions are rough. It has cleared off but we are still motoring into head winds. I start rereading Bill Bryson's In a Sunburnt Country, *it makes me laugh.*

    0500 I go down below and get weather faxes. The radio reception is terrible- all crackly. I can't get a clear signal on any of the frequencies from Honolulu. Phil pulls back the curtain in the pilot berth and offers some suggestions, none of which work. Stewart is hungry and eats all his breakfast. I clean the litter box.

    0600 Australian faxes even worse. Totally unreadable.

    0700 Next ones still bad. I set out the fishing lure. Still haven't caught a fish.

    There are two sets of swells. A large one from the SW and a lesser one from the East. It is hypnotizing watching both sets converge and move through each other. Iwalani bisects a large wave and is agitated around like a rug shaken out by a cleaning woman.

    0800 Turn on radio to Mamba net. Danza touched bottom going into Brisbane all boats but us are in. One boat is at Lord Howe Island. Not allowed to anchor. Moorings cost $23.00 a day. Almost as expensive as back home, but we have half priced sale with low Australian dollar. They are in the middle of the low. Winds 40k. They couldn't hear us check in and are worried about us. We have 300 miles to go if we continue to Coffs- 460 if we go to Sydney.

    I switch to second fuel tank. Not making much progress. Speed four knots at best. Phil wakes up and says we are definitely not going to Sydney. I go to bed. I did not make him breakfast.

    1130: No wind still motoring. I went to the cockpit. No Phil. He's not on deck, not in the crow's nest. I didn't pass him down below. My heart starts racing. He's not in the head. I find him napping forward in our bunk with radar guard zone on. He's curled up in the corner where I couldn't easily see him. I think he was deliberately hiding to pay me back and scare the beejeezus out of me. It worked. We are both cranky and pissy about Australia's problem with Stewart. I heat up leftover pasta for lunch and drink my last "V"-perhaps the world's best soda. It will be two days before I can get more.

It has cleared off. No rain. High thin clouds.

1300 more faxes come in. Finish Bryson. Phil is reading computer tome again.

1500 Take a shower. Haven't bathed in three days. Hair feels like coleslaw. I was beginning to smell like a dead mouse in the wall- or worse, a perfumery trying to hide the smell of the dead mouse in the wall. Phil wakes up briefly and we go over faxes together. Tomorrow morning we should have a better idea of where the low is going to go and will decide if we head for Coff's or Sydney.

1600 Stewart is at the bottom of the ladder waiting to be fed. Seas still confused. Slight head wind. No fish. Rain. I go down below to feed Stewart. E-mail light is on. Letter from friend in Maine. Nice to get e-mail on passage.

1630 Phil gets up. I make supper- sweet and sour stir-fry. Phil sees ship to the SE. Radar shows it six miles away. I can just barely see it. It disappears. Phil has a headache and ear is ringing. I give him two Advil, surprisingly he takes them.

1800 Talk to Willy Bolton on radio. Kathryn says they have been visiting a farm belonging to one of their relatives. They are in Napier, heading to South Island in 10 days. Renegade made it to Auckland with no problems.

1815 I take a nap.

2000 Wake up. No wind. Phil and I look at where we are. Six days from Sydney at current course and speed. Three days from Coff's Harbour. Our chart is beginning to look like the mark of Zorro with all the forced course changes. We have enough fuel to get to Sydney but Phil wants to go to Coff's. We will have to remain on quarantine buoy with Stewart. Phil is hoping we can quarantine Stewart on the boat. I don't see that happening. We start heading for Coff's. At the very least we can refuel. I think Phil doesn't feel good which is why he wants to go to Coff's. Phil goes to bed. Rain showers ahead on radar. I close all hatches leave portholes open.

2230 Lots of rain. Steering North of Coffs Harbour now. Hopefully Australia's south setting current will push us down. Wind and seas pick up. Can't see anything on radar. Start making securité announcements on channel 16. Wait for my watch to end.

"Now what are you doing?" Phil's voice sounds muffled coming from the forward bunk.

"I turned off the engine because we weren't getting anywhere. We have head seas, no wind and we were only making one knot. I couldn't justify burning that much fuel. Besides I am hungry. I thought we might as well just hang out and have a good breakfast. I'm making scrambled eggs and bacon."

Phil gets up and the three of us eat at the table, civilized fashion, Stewart included, with his teacup saucer dish. After breakfast Phil heads up on deck for the start of his watch.

"It looks like some wind is coming. I'm putting the sails back up."

"Do you need any help?" I ask.

"No. I can manage."

I put the last fork away and then head up on deck. In front of us is a dark gray cloud. "Jesus, Phil, I think a double reefed main is …" Just then a gust of wind hits Iwalani hard. We heal so far over the cabin top submerges. I have seen this wind before- in Fiji when we nearly lost the boat to the island of Namena. "...too much sail," gets carried off in forty knots of wind.

"Hurry!" Phil yells at me, "We've got to get this sail down fast!"

We both head to the starboard pinrail on the leeward side. We are standing knee deep in water.

"Should I get our harness's?" I yell to Phil who is standing two feet away from me.

"No time. We are just seconds away from a complete knock down."

Water completely fills the leeward side deck. Iwalani's boom is in the water. We are walking on top of the sidewalls of the bulwark. Iwalani is foundering.

I automatically drop the staysail while manning the peak halyard. I had no time to say The Shepard's prayer, Alan Shepard that is, 'Please, God, Don't let me f#@! up.'

"Get the peak downhaul. Now!" Phil screams.

My brain hesitates for a second as I am still holding the peak halyard. I have been so ingrained after thirty years of sailing, never to do the unthinkable, which is to let go of a line leading aloft without first securing it to something. Though the bitter end has a stopper knot through the cleat, there is still a long loop of loose line that can find trouble hanging up on something. To secure the peak halyard means to go forward. To get the peak downhaul means to move aft. I let the halyard swing out with the wind, knowing full well I am doing a really stupid thing and head aft.

I start to pull on the peak downhaul with every ounce of strength I have. Phil hauls too, but the wind is so powerful that it has effectively fused the mainsail to the shrouds and ratlines.

"Promise you'll forgive me for putting all this sail up?" Phil yells into my ear.

"You never do anything wrong, so it's nice to see you do something every once in a while that's a little more human. Promise me you won't be mad when I tell you about the equally stupid thing I did?"

"How could you have done something as dumb?" he pants between pulls on the downhaul.

"We can't get this sail down because I let go of the peak halyard. It's caught somewhere."

The lower belly of the mainsail is now in the sea and is quickly filling up with water. "Jesus Christ! I'll say it's caught. Look at where it is. That's a Murphy point that's probably going to kill us. Get the boat hook." The peak halyard has looped itself around the outermost end of the boom, a nearly impossible place to reach under sail.

I slosh my way through the water, vaguely aware of the strange sensation that the world I have become so familiar with, has now completely turned on its side. I start worrying about how much water is rushing in down below. Are the port lights closed? I pass the boat hook to Phil and support myself on the bulwark and stanchion., while he perches like a giant bird on the uppermost lifeline, toes curled for security. I hold on to his naked legs as he reaches far out with the boat hook to free the snagged peak halyard. He frees it on the first try.

"Yahoo!" I yell to the wind.

"We still haven't got the sail down."

I pull on the downhaul and Phil grabs the leach of the mainsail and pulls with me. Slowly it begins to come down. "The wind is slacking a bit," Phil yells.

"Promise me we will add a throat downhaul in Australia?"

"Just be thankful this isn't a marconi rig. We would have a much harder time getting the sail down."

With each foot of sail pulled down toward the deck, Iwalani raises herself from the tumultuous seas, dripping water like a tackled football player shaking sweat and grime from a muddy playoff field. Once we have the sail secured and lashed to the boom with sail ties, Phil heads forward and puts a reef in the staysail. We raise only fifty square feet of sail, yet it is enough to carry Iwalani downwind at eight knots.

"You mother fucking, cunt assed, cocksucking bitch!" Phil yells into the wind. "This isn't necessary!"

"This is fun," I holler to Phil. "Now we are heading back to New Caledonia!"

"I thought I heard you say you wanted more chocolate."

"I take it back. I'd like to see kangaroos."

I head down below to check on Stewart and see what kind of disaster awaits us.

"We've got water over the floorboards," I yell up to Phil. Stewart is stranded on a settee island. His usually dry and comfortable world is now flooded. I manually turn on one of the electric bilge pumps. Thankfully it pumps for a bit, then stops. The automatic bilge pump switch must be broken. Small pieces of newspaper float around my legs. "Where the hell did all this paper come from?" I ask Phil. "It's clogging up the pump." I grab one of the strainers off the hook and start scooping the surface of the water like a Los Angeles pool cleaner. Phil manages to pull the floorboards up and we are shocked to see even more paper floating around.

"Now do you see why I had you take all the labels off the cans, and write the contents on the outside before we left?" Phil holds up a petite pois label from the screen of the bilge pump.

"Where did that come from?" I ask.

"Some French territory would be my guess."

"No I mean, I haven't been keeping canned food in the bilge since we left."

"Well it just floated by."

"I guess I've gotten kind of lazy. After a year of having the water on the outside of the boat, I just never thought we'd be wading around down here."

For just this reason, we had been so careful about making sure that every speck of sawdust had been cleaned out of every nook and cranny during Iwalani's construction. Every can stored in the bilge had all labeling removed. But, a few months ago, I put the Fiji Times newspaper under the cans in one of the lockers behind the settee as a sort of shelf liner. I never considered water would get three feet above the floorboards, but it had. When we were knocked on our side, vertical distances had no meaning. After living on the boat for over a year, I had forgotten the number one rule about paper on a boat, it doesn't matter where it is, it can become a problem.

"I did want to clean out the bilge, but this is a bit premature," Phil laughs.

"You know how many people would freak and get on the radio to call for an immediate airlift at this stage of the game and here we are wading around cracking jokes? I probably would be scared if this were at night though,but at least the water level isn't rising very fast."

"There!" Phil replaces the pump down into the bilge. "Try it now. Don't forget we have three other bilge pumps, one of which pumps hundreds of gallons a minute."

"Don't forget the best pump of all, a scared man and a bucket!"

"Our manual pump can still do more than the most scared man."

"Not if it is clogged," I say putting the small food strainer in the sink and flicking the pump switch at the nav station. It begins pumping again. "Did all of this water come in from the portholes?"

"Must have, but I think we are going to have to get Iwalani hauled out and check her over."

"That means that we have no option but to get Stewart to quarantine."

"That's right, but first we have to get there."

*   *   *

"You've got to throw it overboard."

"Fine. But we need someone to play taps or at least hum a death dirge. This is such a waste."

"Overboard."

I insert a tiny note into the six-inch piece of garden hose stoppered at both ends with cork. '*Dear Surfer Dude, inside lies the quintessential cannabis experience, fresh from the shores of Jamaica. Best Wishes, a new arrival.*'

Reluctantly, I throw the tube far from Iwalani, where the currents will carry it off to the South and then to the west, hopefully hitting the surfboard of some New Zealander.

"Thank you, it has bothered me having that on board. It's bad enough having a boatload of legal veterinary drugs, much less the illicit kind," Phil says.

"Well, you know what? I don't want it anymore anyhow. Does that mean I am grown up and don't need artificial stimulants or aphrodisiacs? But I still feel like I have thrown away the last piece of my youth. Now it's your turn."

"My turn?"

"Popcorn. You've got to get rid of your precious stored popcorn."

"No way."

"Yes way. It's on the list of Australian taboo items."

Phil slumps off to get close to ten pounds of un-popped popcorn. "This is awful."

"Now you know how I feel."

Phil spreads the yellow kernels over the water as if he were scattering ashes of a beloved relative. "I suppose now that we are all legal, we should announce ourselves to the Australian authorities. It's your day to be Captain."

"What day is it?"

"Sunday, December 9th,."Phil responds.

"As Captain, I nominate you as radio operator."

"Ok, fine, but as radio operator I get to stay down below while you bring us through the entrance to Coff's."

"Alright, I'll call them. Both of us need to be on deck when we make

24' North Coast Pocket spot
Fish 26 Degree Deep Vee
Outstanding Sea Boat
Twin Evinrude 350 HorsePower OF
h/ InBoards
Stainless +Half-Tower w/Hardtop

Radar - GPS Excellent
Running cond Bottom Paint More

landfall."

I head below and pick up the mike for the VHF radio. According to the cruising books, we are supposed to call Coastal patrol when we are twenty miles out. I report our boat's name, spelling it phonetically, give our position, expected time of arrival and request that customs and quarantine be notified as we have a cat on board.

"*Romeo, say again your position?*" the Australian woman asks.

"Harbor Patrol this is Iwalani, we are at 30 15' S. and 154 22 E"

"*Romeo, and when do you expect to arrive?*"

"Coastal Patrol, this is "I-W-A-L-A-N-I". We expect to be in Coff's at noon local time."

"*Romeo, please call back when you are one half hour out.*"

"For Pete's sake," I yell up to Phil, "She's beginning to get on my nerves. Is she deaf? Why does she keep calling Iwalani, Romeo?"

"I believe she's saying 'Romeo' like we say Roger," Phil chuckles.

"Uh oh. I think we are going to have major language problems in this country."

*   *   *

A half-hour out, I call Coastal Patrol again and am told to pick up the quarantine mooring buoy in the outer harbor. Customs will meet us at the marina Monday morning.

A "southerly buster," the Aussie term for gale force wind from the south, is due to arrive that afternoon. After securing the boat and raising the "Q" flag, we sit in the cockpit staring through binoculars at the Australian shoreline. Small hills sleep quietly around the harbor with modern houses perching on their slumbering sides. Beyond them, taller hills rise gently covered in lush tropical greenery. White sandy beaches completely surround this part of Australia, where some of the best surfing in the world can be found. Black cockatoos and rainbow lorikeets fill the trees along the shore. "What on earth is that sound?" I ask Phil. "It's worse than the electrical generators in Pago Pago."

"Maybe so, but it's all natural."

"What is it?"

"Cicadas."

"How is anyone supposed to sleep?"

"Well, we have nothing else to do. Let's go lie down and test it out."

We head down below, and within an hour Phil is fast asleep. I lie next to him with Stewart on my belly, listening to the cicadas over his purring and Phil's gentle snoring, while watching through the companionway as children take running leaps off the jetty.

As I watch I become vaguely aware that our stern is getting closer to the pilings. I turn to look at Phil. He is still asleep. A half hour passes with me staring at the jetty with Stewart on my belly. We are definitely getting closer. The wind has picked up, and the halyards are starting to womp against the mast. Finally when we are within twenty feet of the jetty, I wake Phil.

"We have a problem," I say nudging him and upsetting Stewart.

"What?"

"We are dragging the quarantine mooring across the harbor and are about to crash into the jetty."

"Why didn't you wake me sooner."

"You were sleeping so peacefully. I'll get on the radio and tell Harbor patrol we're leaving the mooring and are anchoring out."

"*Romeo, Iwalani. But you can not anchor in the harbour.*"

"Why not?" I ask.

"*Because it is not good holding and with this Southerly buster you will drag onto the beach. You must come into the marina.*"

"But we can't come into the marina. We have a cat!"

"*You will have to keep the cat locked on board,*" the woman says.

We drop the mooring pennant and reluctantly motor into the marina. The wind is blowing thirty knots and maneuvering Iwalani into a tight slip is no easy feat for two sailors who have been in a marina slip only one night out of the past five hundred. But thankfully, we have lots of help from other cruisers who have terror and panic furrowed into their brows when they see forty four thousand pounds of two-inch thick wooden boat barreling toward their floating homes at breakneck speed. It is a situation where easing ourselves in slowly would cost us maneuverability, and we would have been at the mercy of the crosswind, so in typical Phil New Yorker fashion, he rides Iwalani into the slip at a full gallop, then pulls hard on the reins getting her to stop at the very last second.

Once we are tied up, the crowd disperses, with shaking heads, trembling hands, and awestruck eyes. We head below and with the wind blowing through the rigging of a hundred docked sailboats like banshees in a grade B horror movie, the three of us fall fast asleep, oblivious to the cacophony around us.

The following morning a sharp knock on the hull announces the arrival of customs. "Iwalani! Do you know you are in violation of Australia's strict quarantine laws?"

"Well not exactly," I say to the man clenching our lifelines as if he was grabbing hold of a live 110 wire. The veins on his neck pulse like striking snakes. "We were only doing what Coastal Patrol told us to do," I respond.

"Is your moggie tightly sealed below?"

I stare for a second at the official, not quite sure what he has just asked me.

"Your cat. Have you sealed it up below?" he repeats.

I tell the two officials, (Peter and Rebecca to us, as everyone is immediately on a first name basis in the land of Oz) that Stewart is crippled from arthritis and can't climb up the companionway ladder, much less jump off the boat.

"Give me the cat's paperwork. I must go make some phone calls," Peter states, his official work done.

Rebecca comes on board with the usual entry paperwork and plethora of forms to fill out. Coff's Harbor has no quarantine officials yet still is considered a port of entry. The customs officials are made to do the quarantine officials jobs and Rebecca apologizes to us, for she has no idea what she should be looking for in terms of animal disease. "I am not trained to know whether a pet is crook. What's worse, I will still have to levy you a fee, despite my being just a wanker."

I look at Phil to see if he understands what she is saying.

"Everything seems on top. Your moggie though, what did you say his name was?" she asks donning some latex gloves. Like a genteel lady doing a white glove test, Rebecca swoops around Iwalani with four different small cloth wipes, rubbing the surface.

"Do you mean Stewart? What are those?" I ask pointing at the swipes.

"I am wiping the surface for narcotics."

"Does that test for residues of marijuana?"

I hear Phil inhale sharply.

"No, we are only testing for narcotics. We'd have heaps of problems if we tested for everything. We'd have to arrest every third man, woman and child in Australia. A tiny amount of marijuana for personal use

"Crikey mates! These Yanks on Iwalani have a bloomin' cat!"

results in a fine, not much more than a speeding violation really."

She puts all our garbage in a huge bright yellow heavy duty bag, something I am happy to see, as I think it highly suspect that all of the other countries disappear with our perfectly good fruits and veggies but have no interest in properly disposing of our garbage. She takes our unopened mayonnaise, sprout seeds, French cheese, Stewart's cat food, except for the two cans of French Sheba, which he has become very fond of and we both beg her to leave. She also tries to take my hard boiled eggs, which I tell her we will be eating for lunch. None of our wooden artifacts are asked for, and none of our shells looked at. We had heard from Willy Bolton that the New Zealanders took their giant clam shells, so we sent ours back to the U.S. from New Caledonia to the tune of seventy U.S. dollars.

"Don't you want to look in the engine room?" I ask her.

"No, that won't be necessary."

"What about the head and the anchor locker? That's where we keep the Chinese boat people," I tease.

"No worries," she says laughing.

"How bout the bilge? That's where we store our rocket launchers, oozies and hand grenades."

Phil gives me a sharp look.

"I'm only kidding," I respond.

Just then Peter returns. "I spoke with Eastern Creek Quarantine. They said you were supposed to arrive in Sydney."

"If you could stop the southerly busters, we would be there now," Phil counters.

"You will have to leave the marina and anchor out in the middle of the harbor," Peter growls.

"Coastal Patrol said there isn't good holding out there. Won't we be a hazard to navigation if we are in the middle?" I ask petulantly. Both officials ignore me.

"What happens if we don't import Stewart and he doesn't go through quarantine?" Phil asks trying to bring some calm to the potential storm that is brewing between the officials and me.

"You will need to anchor in the middle of any harbor or in the middle of any river. You may not come into a marina. Anytime you need to bring the boat in for fuel, you must first call quarantine or customs, so an official can come down and make sure your cat does not go to shore. In addition you will have to pay for quarantine inspectors to come weekly and inspect him. "

"And hauling the boat out to repair and repaint it?"

"It would not happen."

"Then we'll have to figure out a way to get Stew to quarantine," I say resigning myself to the fact he and I will be separated for thirty days.

Rebecca pulls a camera out of her customs bag.

"What's that for?" I ask.

"We need to photograph Stewart."

"There are plenty of pictures of him at our website."

"We need to take some of our own."

"Do you need head on views or just side views?"

"Both actually," Rebecca responds.

"And fingerprints? I mean paw prints?"

"The microchip will do."

Stewart always has loved to have a camera aimed at him. He regally poses on the settee for Rebecca, while I try to distract him, trying to make the pictures poor quality. I have alternate plans for getting him into the country, and they didn't involve mug shots taken by customs officials.

"That's it then," Rebecca says while checking the thumbnail pictures on her digital viewer, then packing the camera away. "Do you mind if I give him one of these?" she asks holding up Stewart's cat treat container.

"No, go ahead. Just be careful, as he loves those…"

"Ouch!" Rebecca cries. "He bit me!"

I look at Stewart, who is greedily devouring the cat treat, completely ignoring us. A feeling of dread overwhelms me, as I know what could happen next. The main reason for animal quarantine in Australia and New Zealand is to prevent the introduction of rabies, a disease not found in the South Pacific. Any animal in the United States that is a rabies suspect and has bitten a human is automatically euthanized to have their head decapitated so the brain can be sent away for testing. This is the only way, at present, to test for the disease in animals. Would the Australians automatically take Stewart away, give him a lethal injection, and then decapitate him in order to send his brain away for rabies testing because he bit the customs officer?

"Did he break the skin?" I ask my voice shaking with panic.

"Naw, it's just a bit of a scratch, really."

She holds out her hand for me to examine. The tip of her finger is indeed red, but thankfully the skin is not broken.

"I'm sorry about that. I tried to warn you about his greedy habits when it comes to those treats. He is not delicate when it comes to food."

"No dramas. But you must leave the marina at once."

We leave the other peaceful yachts tied like contented horses in a stable and motor to the outer harbor.

"Well, then," Phil says. "Where should we anchor?"

"I suppose right in the middle as they requested, but I would prefer off to the side so we don't get run over by a fishing trawler. Anywhere but where those surfers are."

"We'll have to put the one hundred pound storm anchor out."

"Lovely. I'll put it together if you set it."

"It's going to take both of us to put it together and both of us to set it."

No sooner have we gotten the pieces for the large, heavy anchor pulled out of the forward anchor locker, assembled and set in the sandy bottom when a launch pulls along side.

"Sorry mate, but you can't anchor here. You're right in the way of the paragliding tours."

"No problem," Phil says with remarkable restraint. "Where would you suggest we anchor?"

"Right over there would work for us."

"You mean where the people on the surfboards are drifting?"

"Yea, that's it."

Using most of the sixty three-horses powered in the engine, we succeed in lifting, then resetting, the anchor. Afterwards, we retreat below for iced tea.

"Hopefully we don't have to move again," I remark.

"I've been thinking," Phil says while grabbing his glass before it slides off the counter.

"Nice catch."

"How would you feel about renting a car, driving to Sydney and looking at the facility before we commit Stewart to it?"

"Are you kidding? That would be wonderful. But let me tell you about my plan for Stewart and quarantine."

"Oh, brother! Now what?"

"Well, we don't have any objection to paying the thousand dollars to put him through quarantine, maybe more with this little jaunt added in. Right?"

"No, we made provisions and budgeted for this all along."

"I was thinking about going to the humane society in town, adopting a brown tabby cat, bringing him back to the boat, removing Stewart's microchip, which I can do without any anesthetic, sterilize it in the cold pack, and then implant Stewart's chip into the new cat. Then we send the adopted cat, which is already used to living in a cage, off to quarantine while Stewart stays on the boat. If anyone asks who Stewart is, we say we just adopted him. After a month we pick up the adopted cat and Stewart will have a companion."

"And what about the pictures Rebecca took?"

"Well, we need to find a cat that looks just like Stew."

"Too obvious. These Australians know you're a veterinarian; they might be suspicious of such a plan. If they caught you, you'd probably lose your vet license, and they'd probably kill Stewart. It's too much of a risk."

"Putting him into quarantine is too much of a risk."

"Amy, you've known about this for four years or more."

"I know, I just figured rabies would show up in Australia by now."

"How could that happen? You said yourself a sailboat is the perfect quarantine station, since it takes so long to sail here. An animal with rabies would die before it got here."

"It's bound to happen, sooner or later. Not from a sailboat, but more likely a cargo ship from China, India or Ecuador, leaving at night, a small rabid bat hitching a ride with a container on deck. The faster the ship, the less time there is for the bat to die en route. Globalization is going to make all continents at risk for every disease. I'm just worried about him picking up a disease at the quarantine station. It's going to be a stinky Christmas without him—that's all."

Chapter 16

Down in the Dumps Down Under

Coff's Harbour
New South Wales, Australia
December 2001

The following day we rent a car and head south, leaving Stewart in charge of the boat. We drive parallel to the coast on a two-lane road, through small towns and past farms with fat cows. It is hilly terrain and green, not at all like the pictures in coffee table books about Australia.

Claybucca, Nambucca, Kempsey, home of the late great Slim Dusty, with his hit, "The Pub with no Beer," we whiz by them all at death-defying speed. Sixty miles an hour seems like warp ten after a yearlong pace of five knots. Seven hours later we arrive outside of Sydney at the Eastern Creek Quarantine station wedged between the highway, an Arnott's Bakery and an amusement park.

After a tour of the facility, we meet with the people who will be taking care of Stewart. Since Stewart had been in the rabies free South Pacific for the last six months, he will only be in quarantine for thirty days. Had he arrived by plane from the U.S., the quarantine period would have been six months. The cages are at least ten feet tall with platforms connected by climbing ladders to an open caged turret at the top, where young cats can sit and watch birds fly by (and pick up avian-born pathogens!) The pens would have been nice for an ordinary cat, but since Stewart is no ordinary cat and cannot climb, he will be relegated to living on the four-foot square cement floor.

The director of the facility helps us make arrangements so I can fly with Stewart from Coff's Harbor to Sydney on the domestic Qantas airline. The problem is arriving in the non-international side of the airport. The Australians are not set up to deal with a quarantine bound animal on the domestic side. Stewart is posing a security risk to the entire Australian country.

"What would have happened if we had driven down with him today? I ask the director.

"Oh my! We would have euthanized him immediately on arrival."

"What would that accomplish?"

"Then we would test him for rabies."

"That wouldn't solve anything. It wouldn't tell you who or what he had been exposed to, it would do little to save Australia from rabies, and it only would piss people off, me especially. How many animals have turned up with rabies after the quarantine period?"

The director glares at me. "None. We thought we had one last winter but it turned out to be a brain tumor."

"I know you will think I am a smart aleck American, but I don't care. Stewart is as close as I will get to having my own offspring. I think your quarantine system is actually a good thing. I just think the length of time is a bit excessive. Most viral diseases show up within a two-week period. Pets coming from affluent countries are vaccinated, the vaccines work; I have never seen rabies in a properly vaccinated pet. In addition to all the other import requirements now present, why not have just a ten-day quarantine period, coupled with a thousand dollar import duty on each animal? Anyone who can afford to pay that much would most likely have a pretty well cared for animal. You would still get the income, but have less overhead as animals would be here for a shorter time. So there would be a greater profit margin for the Australian government."

The director continues to glare at me, "You'll have to talk to the people in Canberra."

We drive back up to Coff's Harbour that night.

"You shouldn't have pissed him off. He was only trying to help," Phil remarks.

"I know. I couldn't help myself. Amy the American asshole strikes again." I say while flipping the stalk for the windshield wiper instead of the turn signal. "But you know, this quarantine thing is making me sick."

"Uh, maybe I should be driving. We are going to have the cleanest windshield in Australia. That's the third time you've used the wiper instead of the turn signal."

"Give me a chance. I'll get used to this wrong side driving eventually. I did get a little nervous when I looked to my left and saw you flipping through papers. I thought to myself, 'what the heck! How can he do paperwork while driving?'"

"Oh, great. I think I should point out that you are behind the steering wheel, not me."

"I'll catch on. I'm not exactly feeling great. Do you know that we passed seventy three squashed animals along the road on the way down here?"

"Seventy three, huh? It did seem like a lot. It must be that the drought has made animals move around more. I was reading in the guidebook that most Aussies don't drive at night because of the likelihood of hitting a kangaroo. Maybe we shouldn't be driving either," Phil suggests.

"Don't be a wuss-ass. I want to get back to Stewart. I sure can't wait to see a live kangaroo though. We've passed about fifty dead ones."

At that very moment a huge black object appears in our headlights. I swerve to the right to avoid hitting it.

"What the hell was that, speaking of dead things?"

"Jesus, that was close," I say, my hands trembling. "I would have flipped the car if I had driven over it. That was either an eight hundred pound kangaroo or a dead cow."

"Thank god, no one was coming the other way."

"OK, your turn to drive. That's enough excitement for me."

*   *   *

Monday morning we once again leave Stewart rolling around on Iwalani and walk up to the center of town. Lorikeets, cockatoos, and lizards the size of dachshunds, are intent on gathering food from the profusion of flowering plants along the way.

"My god, this sky is blue! It's bluer than the sky at sea," I exclaim.

We go to two veterinary clinics and introduce ourselves. Neither clinic seems very busy, and the veterinarians are puzzled as to why I am asking so many questions about diseases in Australia and the whole rabies issue.

At the third veterinary clinic we meet a doctor named Lyle McLaughlin. An animated man with curly hair and a port wine birthmark between his eyes, he has sailed to Fiji and wants to hear about our trip. I tell him I am anxious to do some veterinary work and attend some conferences. Lyle had been the past president of the Australian Veterinary Association and is the man in charge of licensing for all of New South Wales. I can tell he is sizing me up. I get the feeling that the whole of America's veterinary reputation is being carried on my shoulders. He says he'll be happy to help me get an Australian Veterinary license, perhaps even let me work a bit at one of his hospitals.

"How would you like to perform a necropsy on a koala?" he asks us.

My excitement extends over to Phil.

"Well, legally, you can't do anything without an Australian license," he adds, "but I might make an exception, this once."

We return that afternoon, and Lyle shows me the outside area for the necropsy. I quickly don my scrubs and gloves while Phil sits poised with pen and paper for taking notes.

"I haven't seen you this happy in awhile," Phil says to me.

"This is a koala!" I pull the stiff male from the plastic bag. "Is this cool or what? The best part is, not having to worry about rabies. I hate doing necropsies at home where I have to behead the animal. I never would have made it in the guillotining era, I have a problem with heads separated from bodies." I examine the eyes and ears, mouth and tongue. "O.U. purulent discharge."

"What?"

"Just write what I say, don't worry about the spelling." I hold on to the small padded hands, prying open the fingers that are perfectly crafted for grabbing branches. I can find no other external abnormalities.

I make a full-length incision into its abdomen.

"Wow, that smells like Vick's Vaporub," Phil says while peering over the clipboard.

"Nothing like a diet of eucalyptus."

"Oh crikey," Lyle exclaims as he blasts full speed through the swinging door. "I forgot to mention you have to remove the head so we can send it to Sydney for a chlamydia study."

"Darn. I was hoping for no beheadings."

"Heaps of koalas in this area have chlamydia. It causes eye infections and reproductive problems. All of the autopsies are tested."

"I have to say this is the best smelling necropsy I have ever performed."

"Fantastic isn't it?" Lyle agrees. "It's no wonder all koalas seem so content and docile. They spend their time high on phenols."

* * *

That evening we stay out late going to the movies and shopping. We return to the boat where I begin to get very sick.

"You're just seasick. Put on a scopolamine patch," Phil says to me. "We are all sick anchored out in this surf. This isn't an anchorage!"

"I'm not so sure it's seasickness."

"You probably caught something from one of the didgeridoos you were testing out in the tourist shops," Phil chastises.

The following day I am worse. I have a high fever with severe vomiting and diarrhea.

Customs contacts us and says final arrangements have been made to get Stewart and me to Sydney on a domestic flight the following day. At exactly eight a.m., we are to bring Iwalani into the dock where the customs agent will meet us and lock Stewart into a cage. The whole thing will be cancelled if any other Australian pets arrive at the airport.

Phil buys the tickets and makes all the final arrangements while I lie in bed with Stewart wishing I were dead. The following morning the GI problems have abated somewhat, but I am now suffering from a tremendous head cold.

"I'll be glad to finally sleep in a bed we don't roll out of," Phil says. "I think I am getting your gut disease. You don't suppose we caught something from the koala?"

"Who knows? It may just be the flu, or our unchallenged immune systems are sitting ducks for Australian viruses. That's why I am really worried about Stew. It's possible every disease in the world is concentrated at the quarantine facility."

While I carry around a roll of toilet paper to stem the flow from my nose, we hoist the anchor and motor into the marina. The customs agents are standing on the pier ready to take action lest Stewart becomes an illegal immigrant by jumping ship. Rebecca climbs on board with the customs cat carrier, and I place Stew inside. Then she secures the door with a bright yellow heavy-duty cable tie and multiple pieces of yellow customs tape; at least there are no steel locks. I don't like the idea of any animal being trapped behind a lock requiring a key.

It is difficult for anyone to tell whether my sniffling is from disease or anguish. It seems ludicrous that the healthiest member of our boat is being carted off like a criminal to a quarantine facility.

Phil and I follow in our rental car behind Rebecca and Stewart to the airport. When we arrive, she explains to the Qantas people about the cat in the sealed cage. There are no other pets flying to Sydney, until a man walks through the double door with a cardboard carton, full of pigeons '*Uh, oh,*' I think to myself. '*He wants to put a dozen pigeons on Stewart's flight.*'

"It's a good thing birds can't get rabies," I blurt out to Rebecca. "Otherwise we'd have to get a later flight."

"Birds don't get rabies?"

"No. Only mammals."

"Right then. We'll just carry on."

I kiss Phil goodbye and followed the cart containing Stew and the nervous pigeons out to the tarmac.

"Don't worry, Stew!" I yell. "It's just an airplane. Kind of like a noisy car. I'll be sitting in a chair right over your head."

He looks at me and meows, but the roar of the jet engines carries the sound away.

*   *   *

When we land in Sydney, I watch through the window as they unload the baggage and finally Stewart and the pigeons. I cannot get his attention as I tap

216

wildly on the airplane window. His gaze is fixed on the airplanes on the runways. He is sitting bolt upright straining his neck with an amazed sort of look on his face as he stares at the airplanes flying, landing, and taking off. He then turns and looks at where he has just emerged from. Finally my frantic waving catches his attention. He looks up at me and hisses.

"Same to you, too, bub," I say. "You have no idea what we are going through for you." I look down at him and begin to cry, feeling horribly guilty. "I'm sorry to be so selfish and drag you through all this, Stew. You could be sitting behind the woodstove with our house sitters taking care of you. Their grandchildren would be climbing all over you, pulling your tail, braiding your whiskers. I am just selfish and heartless." A few passengers in the plane turn and stare at me. "My cat. I am just talking to my cat," I say blowing my nose into some tissues.

He disappears with a baggage handler. I make my way to the train station and take the Blue Mountain Express westward. I am thankful we had made the earlier recon mission, as the quarantine facility isn't easy to find from the train station. Four hours later I am blowing my nose and reading a book on the cement floor of Stewart's cell. All the cats have plastic sleeping huts with fleece lined electric heating pads placed on the shelf above the floor. I move Stewart's down to floor level. He is still very "hissed" off at me.

"What's the matter Stew, cat got your tongue?" I taunt him.

At closing time I grab my pack and head to Minchenbury in search of a motel, walking along the side of the highway like a homeless person. I find one named "The Voyager" almost abutting the quarantine facility land. I climb into bed sniffling and sneezing, feeling very much alone and wanting desperately to feel the purring warmth of our cat.

The following day Phil drives the rental car from Coff's Harbour to the quarantine facility.

"What happened to you? I ask when he enters Stewart's jail cell. He has black circles around his eyes and looks awful.

"I've got the disease. I barely made it down here."

At the sound of Phil's voice, Stewart comes out of the plastic hut and rubs his face against Phil's legs, still completely ignoring me. "How are thing's going down here?"

"Not good," I say blowing my nose. "Stewart hates me."

"Stewart doesn't hate you. He's just upset. He'll get over it."

The next five days are spent living in hotels, touring Sydney, traveling to Canberra to talk to the government officials about their quarantine laws, and visiting Stewart. Phil recovers from the dreaded disease, while I remain sick. Stewart is still not talking to me. The quarantine facility is closed to visitors over Christmas, so Phil and I decide to go back up to Iwalani. We arrive late Christmas Eve back at the marina, thankful we don't have to row out into the harbor.

As we are walking on the dock a three-inch long cockroach scuttles in front of us. I make a dance move to step on it. It snaps and explodes like a helium balloon. "Quiet," Phil whispers, "You'll wake everyone up."

"We had these cockroaches in the lab animal facility basement at my college. They told us they were from Madagascar and had escaped from a researchers lab. I didn't think they were from Australia. What happens if they come on the boat?"

"That's why we are at the end of the pier."

Christmas Day we are invited for a dinner party at Lyle and his wife, Kim's, house. I make a concoction of all the cold remedies on board the boat, gulp them down and hope I will be able to attend the late afternoon event. By 2 p.m. I have a high fever and am completely loopy. Phil takes a small gift and heads off to the party by himself.

When we initially arrived in Coff's Harbour, the winds had been blowing either from the south or the northeast, but by Christmas afternoon they are blowing from the west and blow fiercely, with hot dry exhaust from the Australian desert interior.

I lie in the bunk blowing my nose and feeling sorry for myself, for no good reason other than I miss Stew and wonder why he is so mad at me. It is Christmas, and I have much to be grateful for. We have arrived safely, things are going relatively well, and people, for the most part, have been very helpful. I try not to think about my family at home, gathering at one of my sibling's houses, watching quiet flakes of snow falling, eating roast beef, with my mother's traditional angel food birthday cake for dessert. Christmas is her birthday, which is what we really celebrate, not the more famous birth. Everyone would be laughing, opening presents and having a good time. I think about Phil's boys. Where are they? They told Phil that airport security was too much of a hassle; they didn't want to come to Australia.

The banshee screaming from the other yacht's rigging takes on a more sinister tone. It becomes a thousand violins playing a long drawn out version of the shower scene from *Psycho*. I want to cry but have run out of tears. I have a craving for ginger ale. It soon goes beyond a craving and becomes an obsession. I know there is one bottle in the bilge, but how to get to it? I can't even lift my head off the pillow let alone lift up the floorboards. I have never wanted anything so much in my life. For the next two hours, getting the ginger ale out of the bilge becomes my entire focus. I forget about Christmas and falling flakes of snow. All my mind sees are effervescent bubbles from freshly poured ginger ale, lifting like tiny little angels from an ice-filled glass.

I finally tell myself to stop being a jerk and just get out of bed. Anyone who can sail halfway around the world, can get out of bed. I spring up from the mattress not realizing I have become weightless. I feel as if I am vacationing on the space shuttle. There is no need for my legs to support a weightless object and they dance kick themselves out from under my torso. Luckily, I fall right next to the very floorboard I need to lift up. I curl my fingers into the finger hole and begin to lift. It comes up easily, perhaps too easily, as the dry searing winds are starting to shrink the floorboards into light tinder. Like a piece of street paper caught in the wind, the floorboard flies away from my hands and hits me in the chin. I don't care, for there lying nestled between the stringers, like the holy grail kept for centuries in a forgotten treasure chest, is a bilge stained bottle of golden ginger ale. I drink the entire liter without pausing to breathe. It is a Christmas I will never forget.

*   *   *

The next day I wake up smelling smoke. "Fire!" I cry as I jump out of bed. "Oh my god. Stewart! Phil wake up, Stewart needs us!"

"I see you're feeling better," Phil says not wanting to get up. I run aft to see where the fire is, but can find nothing.

"It's bush fires," Phil replies. "Everyone at the Christmas party said they happen this time of year and are a normal fact of Australian life."

"But Stewart!" I wail. "We need to drive down to Sydney."

We find out that the fires are in the Blue Mountains west of Sydney, and are worse than normal because it has been so dry. They are heading toward Sydney, with the prevailing hot westerly winds, at an alarming rate.

The real cause of bushfires

Phil and I get dressed, hop in the car, and drive south as quickly as we can. Smoke lies in the air like a heavy wool blanket. In some areas we have to drive through smoldering embers, but fortunately, the road is open and still intact. We reach the quarantine station in six short hours. They open the gates for us after we plead into the little black speaker box separating us from Stew.

Phil and I run to his cell. He practically leaps into our arms when he sees us. Small fluttering pieces of burnt ash fall down through the open turret at the top of his cage and settle on us like snowflakes. I take his water dish out and refill it, as it too, is filled with floating bits of ash. I open an illegal can of French cat food, and surreptitiously hide the empty can under paper in the trash barrel.

At the sink, I run into his caregiver Mike, "I hope you had a great Christmas," I say to him, realizing in our haste to get down here, I forgot the Christmas present I bought for him and Lani, Stewart's other caregiver.

"It was alright, I guess," he responds. "Though I wish I had today off too."

"What exactly would happen if the bush fires made it this far? What would you do with the animals?" I ask.

"No worries, the firees would put the blaze out."

"But what if they can't? Do you have vans to put the animals in?"

"No, nothing like that. We'd turn the sprinklers on and run."

I take the water dish back to Stewart's cell. "We have to stay down here until these bush fires are under control," I report to Phil. "We need to be ready with a big blanket, so we can climb over the barbed wire at the top of the fence, in case we have to rescue Stewart. These locks on the cages are easy enough to pick open. I suppose we should get bolt cutters though, just in case."

"No problem. What about the other cats here?"

"I suppose we could open their pens and let them go, if we had to. They might get killed by cars though, since this place is surrounded on all sides by highway. And we'd be doing a really bad thing as far as every Australian is concerned. Let's not think about that." I give Stewart his French cat food, which he devours. When he is finished I burrow my face into his fur smelling strongly of smoke. He purrs, then gives my face a lick. Everything is back to normal.

Chapter 17

At the End of a Dockline, the World Binds with Us

January 2002
Eastern Australia

The bush fires finally get under control with the arrival of Elvis, an American helicopter capable of dumping over 2000 gallons of water at once. Stewart is no longer in danger while in quarantine, and with Iwalani safely in a marina, Phil and I take advantage of our freedom and explore the Australian countryside by car. When we see the online credit card bill for car rentals, we buy a 1985 Ford Falcon station wagon from a rather disreputable used car dealer. We name the car after the conductor Neville Mariner, because it makes such a symphony of sounds clattering down the road. We buy camping gear and, using the GPS and moving map programs, head off into the unnamed places of Australia.

"Aren't you afraid of snakes and spiders in the bush?" people would ask when we tell them of our desire to head out into the middle of nowhere. We have a few close calls but none as close as the encounter I had while snorkeling in a remote reef in New Caledonia. Phil had been trying to warn me with wild gesticulations and

Sailing the Grape in Coff's harbour

muffled snorkel screams of what sounded like 'fish fight!' Fortunately he grabbed my flipper and pulled me backwards before I came to an untimely death. Hanging down from the surface and camouflaging perfectly with the sun dappled wavelets was one of the most deadly sea snakes in existence, just one stroke away from my arm and two days sail away from any hospital. "Sea snake" sure sounds like "fish fight" in snorkelspeak.

Most of the dangerous land snakes we see in Australia are lying along the side of the road soaking up sunshine on the black pavement. Often times we would return to get a photo, only to find the snake run over, a driver deliberately steering the vehicle off the road to hit them. I even spend time looking under rotting logs for the famed funnel web spider but never find one. Yet, I nearly have a heart attack from excitement when I saw my first kangaroo bounding about the bush. Dangerous animals are only a matter of perspective.

Iwalani rests very comfortably at the end of the pier, waiting for Stewart's jail time to pass. Despite the long walk we have to the bathrooms and showers, Phil and I settle in, too. Our plan for Iwalani is to get her hauled out so we can get her bottom repainted, and do necessary maintenance over cyclone season.

Phil has the Telstra Phone Company come down and look at a phone line he finds lying under the pier, like a barnacle covered sea snake. Now that the boat is stationary for a few months, he hopes to be connected to the Internet via the phone. When the phone technician sees the line, he shakes his head and says 'No joys mate.' Phil practically clings to his pant leg, pleading with him to at least test the line, which the technician finally does. To everyone but Phil's amazement, the line is useable. That evening Phil is surfing the web and I am phoning home, as an hour long call to the US is only $2.50.

When Stewart is finally released from quarantine, we take him to a fancy hotel to celebrate and then to the University of Sydney Veterinary School for an echocardiogram. A great French veterinarian in New Caledonia let me borrow his ultrasound to test Stewart's heart, but I wanted a second opinion, as I could find nothing wrong. I was worried about the blood clot he had in developed in his leg while we were in Fiji. The Australian vets find no evidence of heart disease either; severe arthritis is their diagnosis.

Phil is the first to notice that something is not right with our crewmember, when Stewart returns to the boat. He is more aloof, spending time sleeping in the engine room and not with us in bed. I chalk it up to his being angry over the whole quarantine issue. I don't want the Australian vets thinking I am completely wacko if I explain to them that our cat isn't talking as much. I tell Phil not to worry.

In the last half of January a modern sloop moves onto the adjacent slip on our pier. Malahini is owned by Alison, an aboriginal artist, and her boyfriend Michael. They have an Australian cattle dog named Mags and have hopes of one day sailing around the world. Alison made a large amount of money selling prints of her artwork during the Sydney Olympics. She paints the large canvases in the small confines of their boat, has them digitally photographed, then makes prints on archival watercolor paper from her Epson printer, which she sells to museums and gift shops. She teaches me the finer points of using Photoshop and how to change the settings on the printer for the thicker paper.

Coff's Harbour is home to shrimp boats and has a great fish store near the marina showers. We dine almost daily on prawns, Morton Bay bugs and other delicacies of Australian waters. One night we have Alison and Michael over for dinner where we cook shrimp Creole and, for dessert, Phil's homemade vanilla ice cream

topped with Vermont Maple syrup.

"You know you really aren't so bad for Bush Turkey American planetary polluters," Michael says to us with a sparkle in his eye.

"Gee thanks. I'll take that as a compliment." I say.

Amy and Alison

Michael inhales deeply and puts his hand on Alison's knee. "It's too bad, what happened on 9/11, but you Yanks had it coming. You ignored the experts readouts of all the crystal balls."

"Innocent people killed while at work? I don't see how they deserved to die," Phil says while clearing the dishes from the table.

"It was symbolic. The World Trade Towers were the symbol of capitalism and financial power. It was a strike against the consumptive mentality of American corporate greed."

"But it wasn't just Americans who were killed," I remind everyone.

"True. But everyone in the buildings had the American consumer mentality and was contributing to the American corporate powerhouse. Consume, consume, consume. You Yanks use more of the world's resources, produce most of the world's pollution and trash, and, yet, when your president is asked to attend a global conference and sign a treaty which would limit greenhouse gas emissions, conserve water or other resources and help make the planet a safer place for us all, he walks away. It is no wonder you are the world's villains."

"Hey, wait a minute. We are the villains? As I recall Australia didn't sign the Kyoto Agreement either."

"Of course! What you do, we do, or don't do. But America is still at the top of the food chain, not to mention the tail that wags the dog for all the political coups around the world. Removing a country's leader because you don't like him, then placing a dictator in charge as a puppet for your president. I don't think Australia will ever forgive you for replacing our prime minister, but what bothers me about my country is that we just follow in your footsteps."

"At least we are independent," Phil remarks.

"Independent? You are completely dependent on foreign oil."

"No I mean from England. You guys never had a Boston Tea party. What's up with the British antipodean apron strings? What's up with the Queen of England blessing the Sydney Opera house? When you have elections and vote for your prime minister, he or she isn't really in charge of Australia. The governor general appointed by the Queen of England has ultimate authority, because the governor general can overthrow the Australian prime minister," Phil says.

"It's a crook system, I admit," Michael agrees. "That's basically what happened in the seventies when America overthrew Whitlam."

"Who?" I ask.

"Our elected Prime Minister Whitlam, was dismissed by the governor general in the mid seventies. Australians think America was always behind it," Michael says.

"But why?"

"Because he wouldn't bend to your country's foreign policies. That was also around the time we whites were still doing really horrible things with the aboriginal people. So we really aren't much better. At least America's excuse for slaughtering the red men of the plains was that it happened a long time ago. Australia can't say the same thing."

"Slaughtering aboriginals?" I look at Alison, who nods her head in agreement.

"And Worse. Those were the lucky ones," continues Michael. "Some of Alison's family were buried in sand and then had their heads used as golf balls. Aboriginal families were separated, children forced to live with white families."

"In the nineteen seventies?" I ask completely incredulous. "That seems a bit farfetched."

"There's a lot you in America probably don't hear about that happens in the rest of the world."

"That's an understatement," Phil and I say simultaneously.

After they leave, I help Phil do the dishes.

"Michael is right about us Americans and our propensity for being so wasteful."

"Maybe. But I am still homesick for America. I miss flying full scale planes and RC models. I found a local control line club on the Internet. I also found a local ham radio operator named Buck Rogers. I'm still hoping to find a way to get satellite pictures on the boat. I don't want a repeat of our trip here from New Caledonia."

"That makes two of us," I say. Stewart wakes up and yawns. "Does his vote count? All three of us are in agreement. No more repeats of not knowing what weather lies over the horizon!"

*   *   *

For the next few months we continue to travel and make improvements to the boat, replacing worn gear and buying electronics. We remove all the sails and attendant lines and store everything out of the sun under an awning we make which covers our decks. We sand and varnish the spars and take all of our anchor chain to a town outside of Sydney to be re-galvanized. Phil drags all the precut curved pieces of cherry trim from the aft lazarette and installs them down below. Officially, we have finally finished building the boat, now that we are halfway around the world.

Twice a week we run all the electronic equipment on board whether we need to or not, in order to prevent the sad but true axiom "use it or lose it." We purchase a step down transformer to convert 220v Australian current to North American 110v. After learning from Phil's new electronics friend, Buck Rogers, I become adept at soldering the circuitry. Each time the electricity is interrupted to the boat, either through a power outage or a cruiser unplugging us from the box, the resistor on the transformer overloads and burns out. It becomes a weekly occurrence, until we finally get smart and duct tape our plug to the dock outlet.

In March my parents come for a three-week visit and spring for a trip for the five of us to go to New Zealand. I planned to fly Stewart with us, but we decide

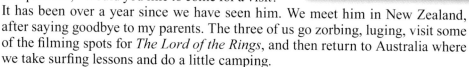

against it, when we find out he would have to fly in the belly of the plane, not under our seats. I feel safer boarding him at the University of Sydney Veterinary School. I am not sure he is happy with the arrangement.

Phil's youngest son, Nathaniel, surprises all of us by responding with an "OK" to the now age old question, "Would you like to come for a visit?" It has been over a year since we have seen him. We meet him in New Zealand, after saying goodbye to my parents. The three of us go zorbing, luging, visit some of the filming spots for *The Lord of the Rings*, and then return to Australia where we take surfing lessons and do a little camping.

The best spot for kangaroo viewing in the entire Coff's Harbour region is at the local gun club. One afternoon, we drive Nathaniel there so he can watch the Eastern gray joeys jump in and out of the mother's pouch while the older kangaroos graze in the field and scratch their armpits. Nathanel sits in the car playing his GameBoy while Phil and I photograph and sketch the hundred or so, kangaroos.

"I am worried about Nathaniel," Phil points the camera at a young joey.

"Me too. Maybe he is just anxious about going home."

"I wish he would stay with us on the boat."

"All we can do is keep asking him. He's old enough to make up his own mind, but we have to realize his interests aren't the same as ours," I say.

A van drives up and a tall man wearing loose pajama bottoms jumps out. He opens the back doors and removes a large-scale model of an RC helicopter. Phil is nearly as excited as I was when I saw my first kangaroo. This is his favorite hobby at home, and I know he is really missing it.

Joseph built the large model from real helicopter plans. The hand machined, intricate details of fuselage and mechanics are incredible. The tiny sculpted pilot even has a little handkerchief in his pocket to wipe his plastic brow. We watch, along with the kangaroos, as Joseph hovers and flies the large model in small circles. Nathaniel stays in the car.

We tell Joseph how we got to Australia, and he becomes very excited when he sees a picture of Iwalani on our "boat card." He tells us he is an artist and makes his living doing marine related art; he promises to come visit us at the marina.

We are not nearly so exciting to Nathaniel. He continues to shake his head and mumbles "No thanks," whenever we ask him about continuing on with us. On the day of Nathaniel's departure, Neville bounces and jounces and makes his usual racket going down the road. The rest of us sit in silence. Stewart, too, rests next to Nathaniel, not purring. Once Nathaniel is in the air, Phil and I set about getting home with renewed vigor. Both of us sense something is wrong though Nathaniel had never said a word.

Mrs. Wally Bea demonstrates the benefits of marsupialization to the North American backpackers convention

Nathaniel and Phil

* * *

Accurate weather information is one of the most critical aspects of safe voyaging. Buck Rogers shows us how to get satellite images from an inexpensive setup using a homemade quadrifilar helix antenna (resembling a giant mixer beater), a hundred dollar police scanner receiver, a laptop computer, and a free program off the Internet. Together we assemble the components and soon begin to get "real-time" satellite images. We now have the ultimate crows nest. Polar orbiting satellites appear twice daily. Our favorite, an aged Russian satellite named Meteor, is higher than the U.S.'s NOAAs 12 and 15 but only broadcasts during daylight hours as it has no infrared band nor power for night passes.

We have been aware of these satellites long before they became an important part of our lives. At night, we would see them speed by like electrons around our cockpit nucleus. Often times, far out to sea and away from the shipping lanes, with no airplanes overhead, they are our only connection with civilization. But how do we interpret their images? Neither of us are trained weather forecasters. With the help of the meteorologists at the airport, books and the Internet, Phil and I start studying weather patterns. Soon it becomes second nature differentiating between fronts, lows, highs, ridges and troughs. When we disagree on what the spinning swirls of clouds or clear patterns actually are, the weather faxes settle the argument.

I decide that we need to get rid of the cloth dodger and replace it with something more substantial. Phil agrees. Our research warns us of the boisterous conditions in the Indian Ocean; we will need more protection from the elements than aluminum pipe and fabric. In three days Phil designs and builds a rugged "hard" dodger made from inch thick MDO signboard and fiberglass. We even put in bulletproof Lexan windows.

* * *

"Hello, Ameri-cans!" a loud voice calls from the dock. We are having the first day of rain in Coff's Harbour and are down below doing rainy day projects. I am building miniature dollhouses for the girls on Willy Bolton and Phil is building a balsa wood and tissue paper airplane to mail back to Nathaniel. We had hoped to start painting the decks on Iwalani, our last chore still to be accomplished before departure, but we saw the rain coming from the satellite pictures and altered our plans.

"Hello? Americans! It's Joseph the Artist."

"Joseph! Come on down. It's a mess down here, but it's dry."

Joseph takes off his anorak in the cockpit, shakes it out, bends his large frame under the newly constructed hard dodger and bangs his head.

"I told you I would come for a visit. I had trouble finding you. I asked where are the Americans and no one seemed to know. Then I showed picture of your boat and they say, 'No they are not Americans. The woman is Australian and the man never speaks!' It is incredible you live here, such a small space. How do you not kill each other?" Joseph's exuberance begins to fill the small voids of our ship.

"It's boredom that tries to kill us, especially at sea," Phil responds.

I clear the table off and make a pot of coffee.

"I do not know how you do it. I would go crazy, but I see you have many things to keep you busy."

"We have everything you could want or need on this boat. So when we are at anchor, we are never bored. But at sea, you almost always feel just a little bit sick, like you are recovering from the flu. It is much harder to do anything other than cook, eat, sleep, read, write, or knit," I say.

"What is this?" he asks pointing to the woodstove. "A combustible?"

"Yes, we use it to burn wood for warmth, sometimes to burn trash."

"And the windmill? Do you use it too?" he asks pointing to the wind generator in the stern whose blades are tied off while we are hooked to shore power.

"That is a land based wind generator," Phil explains. "It makes electricity which gets stored in four huge Lifeline AGM batteries, the kind found on military helicopters. They don't vent hydrogen and can go through hundreds of cycles."

"What about your engine?" Joseph asks.

"We have a Westerbeke diesel 63 horsepower. We carry enough fuel to motor one week."

My only regret," I add, interrupting Phil, "is that we didn't know about using fry-o-lator grease in the engine before we left."

"Could you do that?"

"Sure," I exclaim. "We'd have to filter the grease first, but I'm sure it's hot enough in the engine room that we wouldn't have to preheat the grease while we are in the tropics."

"Where would you get the grease?" Joseph asks.

"The second smell that greeted us in Tahiti was French fries. We would never have had to buy fuel!" Phil responds.

Joseph and Phil launch into a long conversation about RC helicopters and fuel. I lean back, listening, and then begin to watch Stewart. He is wandering around the cabin floor as if he were lost. We are keeping his bed on the floor ever since we came back from New Zealand because he did not want to jump up on the settees or get into bed with us.

"How did you end up in Australia?" Phil asks Joseph.

"I moved to Australia seventeen years ago from Czechoslovakia. I came here and learned English while working as a plumber's helper, and I did paintings on the side. I sold my first painting in a friend's gallery. After a few years I realized I was making more money from my artwork than from plumbing, so I quit and bought my own gallery."

"Do you like living in Australia?" Phil asks.

"It's great. The weather is good, though around here it gets cold in the winter, sometimes as low as 6 degrees C. The people can be a little…"

Stewart wanders his way into the corner of the galley and then stops. His tail jerks back and forth like he was pissed off at something but doesn't know what.

"A little what?" Phil asks.

Joseph shakes his head. "Oh, I don't know the word. They are just different."

"The more I travel the more I realize that people are who they were. There is no escaping our roots," Phil adds.

"How do you mean?"

"Well, for instance, the Australians. Since the country was initially established as a penal colony, most of the original inhabitants were either guards or prisoners. I have never seen so many security cameras in a country anywhere, on the highways, in the bathrooms, at vet's offices. Customs has one aimed at us 24 hours a day."

"They were put in for the Sydney Olympics," Joseph explains.

"Customs is still filming us?" I ask. "I knew they had one on us when we anchored out."

"Take a look at it. It's turned in our direction at the dock."

"But Stewart is legal."

"We are the only American flagged vessel here, even if we aren't flying the flag. I am hoping they are watching for terrorists who might do us harm."

"We get lots of hate mail from our website," I tell Joseph.

"Mostly from Australians who hate cats!" Phil adds.

"Ah yes. That is a big majority here. I, too, have a pussycat. The Australians are very protective of their wildlife. And you are a vet?" he asks me.

"Yes, and though it may not look like it right now, this boat is better equipped as an animal hospital than many of the clinics we visited in the South Pacific, including the human ones."

"Did you make it to New Zealand?"

"Yes. It's intensely beautiful," I say. "But I didn't like it as much as Australia. We flew there and did the tourist thing with my parents. It gives you a completely different impression of a place, rather than traveling by sailboat. I am not sure you really know a country until you have to buy toilet paper and food at a grocery store. Staying in hotels and bed and breakfasts is a more insular way of visiting."

"Yes, but please take no offence," Joseph hands me the empty coffee cup, "I'd take that any day over sailing in a little boat at sea."

*   *   *

In early June, Phil and I finish provisioning the boat and are ready to begin the long trip up the East coast of Australia and over the top. We only have to sell Neville, the car, and clear out with customs.

Stewart is getting more and more quiet. We take him up to Lyle's Veterinary Hospital for more tests just before we leave. When I pull him out of the cat carrier and put him on the floor to walk around, he makes a small semi-circle and then walks face first into the leg of a table.

I know instantly what is wrong with him.

"Crikey, Amy, he's as blind as a bat!" Lyle crows.

"I see that. That's the problem with living on a boat. It's too familiar. He has memorized most of the floor space on Iwalani."

Lyle repeats the tests done at the University of Sydney, with no significant changes. "You know, Amy," he says, the birthmark between his eyes pulsing, "it might be time to think about putting him to sleep. He really must be suffering with that arthritis. It must be torture for him to live on a boat."

I thank Lyle for his help, pay my bill and put Stewart back in the carrier. The three of us drive back to Iwalani, not saying a word.

"What should we do?" I ask Phil later after we have cleared away the supper dishes. "Lyle's not the only one who thinks we should put him to sleep. My mother thinks I should too. I don't want to be one of those pet owners who keeps an animal going for selfish reasons. Am I being selfish?"

"Look at him. Does he look like he's suffering?"

Stewart is curled up in his bed asleep, exhausted from all the poking and prodding. I go over and pick him up and he begins to purr.

"I don't know what suffering is anymore. This trip has distorted all my values. I was trained to prevent suffering, but after seeing the dogs and sea lions dying of distemper in the Galapagos and the storm destroyed seabirds in Namena, I can't say anymore what suffering is. I feel like I must prevent waste, not suffering— wasted lives, wasted food, wasted fuel, wasted resources. Is Stewart suffering? I just don't know. anymore."

"Don't cry," Phil says holding us both in his arms. "You've got me crying now too."

"What are we doing out here? He needs an MRI, and he needs to see Dr. Potthoff in Maine. He is one of the best veterinary neurologists I know. But if we send him back home by plane we won't be able to pick him back up in Australia. He'd have to go through quarantine all over again. This time for six months."

"What do you think is wrong with Stewart?"

"I don't know. His blindness could be from hypertension, from inflammation, infection, a tumor. I got e-mail from a vet school classmate who said it could be from an antibiotic injection I gave him, too."

"Is there anyone in Australia that can do the tests?" Phil asks.

"I called around. Their best neurologist is out of the country for three weeks. They can do CT scans but not MRI's, yet."

"We need to leave, it's already late. I was hoping to leave Coff's Harbour a month ago. If we don't leave now we will be in the Southern Indian Ocean in cyclone season, but Stewart is our best crewmember and he deserves the best care. What if we flew him home from South Africa?"

"That might work. I don't think he would have to go into quarantine if he flew back to the boat. But I don't know. South Africa has rabies, so probably not."

"Well, it looks like we have to get to South Africa as quickly as we can."

Chapter 18

The Cussedness of Inanimate objects

June 2002
The eastern coast of Australia

Inch by agonizing inch, we slowly grope and crawl our way northward along the east coast of Australia. Winds are light, 15 knots from the north or sometimes the more favorable northwest. The seas are calm, since the wind is basically going in the same direction as the strong south setting current, Australia's equivalent of the Gulf Stream. We could do what everyone else does, head up a river and wait for the winds to change to a more southerly direction, but Phil and I can be very stubborn, and we are anxious to keep moving, even if it is backwards for a short time.

The old Westerbeke huffs and puffs, trying to push us uphill while heating up the aft cabin where Stewart lies huddled sucking warmth from under the engine room door. We keep the third reef in the mainsail, not because of strong winds, but because this configuration gives a flatter shape for doing windward motorsailing.

For the first few hundred miles the scenery varies little from Coff's Harbour—long stretches of deserted sandy white beaches, undulating hills, and an occasional jagged peak punctuating the landscape. There are few houses on shore. Every once in awhile, clusters of lights indicate a small coastal town. Of the eighteen million people living in Australia, most of them live within one hundred miles of the coast, and most of those live near the larger cities.

At Coolangatta, south of Brisbane, the mountains begin to disappear and are replaced by high rises and condos. Because of our seven foot draft, we opt for traveling on the outside of the barrier coastal islands, thereby avoiding the pitfalls of threading our way through shallow water and the tidal flows of the inside bays. We are now officially inside the Great Barrier Reef.

Our trip north coincides with the annual northward migration of the humpback whales. We see nothing, not even a plume in the distance. I also continue to drag my fishing lure for hundreds of miles, hoping for just one fish, but I don't even get so much as a nibble. While reading a book in the cockpit during the eight to midnight watch, I am hit a second time by a flying fish which I chop up and feed to Stewart in the morning.

We wait until we are four days out of Coff's Harbour to start up the water maker and find to our dismay that the end pieces are cracked and the whole assembly is showering the engine room with salt water. The weather is due to go

229

downhill with headwinds of 20 knots from a forming trough. We are not used to the four hours on, four hours off schedule, as we have had a six-month reprieve. So after motoring for six days straight, we decide to give the engine a break and stop at Great Keppel Island. We anchor, take the dinghy to shore, and land on the beach amongst thousands of cuttle bones.

"Too bad we couldn't package these up and sell them at home to pet shops," I say to Phil. "Where are they actually coming from?"

"The cuttle fish."

"Are they giant fish scales or what?" I wonder while beginning to fill my pockets. "Why did they all die?"

"Cuttlefish are related to squid and octopus. These 'bones' are part of their internal skeleton. I am not sure why they all died at once."

We find the resort and it looks a bit like a run-down college campus. Few people are around; the beach holds empty lawn chairs forlornly staring out to sea. After finding a phone, we order the parts we need for the watermaker and have them shipped ahead to us in Cairns.

We have lunch at the resort's outdoor grill. We sit down by ourselves and greedily "tuck" into hamburgers, as the Australians would say. All of a sudden, a kookaburra swoops from a branch and knocks the hamburger from my hand. While I am busy trying to compose myself, a second kookaburra comes from the opposite direction and grabs the hamburger patty.

"Hey, you beef thief," I yell, upsetting my chair as I rise to retrieve my lunch.

The kookaburra is incredulous that a human is actually giving chase and drops the hamburger patty on a nearby chair. Flying in a tumbleweed pattern and keeping one eye on me, he lands on the branch of a nearby eucalyptus tree. I pick the hamburger up, shake it off and return to the table to reassemble my lunch.

"That was a well coordinated attack," Phil remarks.

"Too bad they didn't grab the beet. You know, after several months in this country, I'm still unprepared for the unexpected gustatory experience of biting into a beetroot garnished hamburger. Here, you fine feathered fiends, take this!" I fling the sliced beet off toward the marauding birds like a miniature Frisbee.

"Oh god, Honey, not New Caledonia all over again."

"What do you mean? There's no one around. Boy, you're never going to get over that," I say wiping a bit of dirt off my hamburger bun.

"It was embarrassing."

"Well, what was I supposed to do? I saw that three-inch cockroach crawl over that skinny French lady's high-heeled toe heading directly toward our table. Of course, I had to kill it."

"I think the entire restaurant could have done without the Japanese Ninja sound effects."

"It added to the moment. How was I to know that when I jumped on it the cockroach would explode like a firecracker?"

"Even the violinist stopped playing."

"Not out of respectful reverence at the demise of such a creature, I might add."

"I sure miss New Caledonia," Phil says shaking his head.

"Remember that patisserie and how we would each get one pastry, a work of art, and how they wrapped it so delicately in tissue and nestled it in the fancy box with all the artwork? And the ribbon tying it up on the outside? Such beauty!"

"So delicious! Remember the pop of the cork on the magnum champagne bottle as the chef poured it into the chocolate?"

"Ah, never to be forgotten. The French, thank god for them," I swoon.

"Sorry to break the spell, but we've got to leave if we are going to get back before dark," Phil says.

We circle around the island arriving back at Iwalani just as the sun is setting. The wind has picked up and heavy surf is now pummeling what is left of the beach where we had tied the dinghy above the high tide mark. There isn't a cuttlebone in sight.

"So much for my get-rich-quick-scheme," I lament.

"We have enough junk on the boat."

"Junk! I call it all highly prized natural artifacts."

"Plants, shells, bird's nests, skeletons, dead insects, not to mention a bilge full of rocks. Junk! We'll have to row out past the surf line and then put the outboard on," Phil calls to me.

"That sounds O.K, but how do we get past the surf line?"

"Timing. We'll walk the dinghy in. When I say 'get in' jump into the dinghy, and then I'll row like mad. Remember how we did it in Las Perlas? Same idea. This looks like a good time. Go!"

"Shit!" Instead of neatly landing in the dinghy I land completely in the water.

"You row!" I yell to Phil. "I'll swim. I'll meet you beyond the surf."

"What about salt water crocs? This water is cloudy," Phil yells to me while pulling hard on the oars.

"Never mind them. It's too rough for crocs…I hope."

When we get out to the boat Stewart is anxiously waiting for us. I long for a hot shower to warm myself up but have to settle for a sponge bath using a cup of precious hot water.

Phil reads the weather report which came in over the Inmarsat, while I light the woodstove. "We have to leave early tomorrow. A gale is expected to form south of 26° south. If we get far enough to the north, we should be OK."

*   *   *

"I thought you said this cruising up the inside of the Great Barrier Reef was going to be like cruising at home! What the heck is that?" I yell to Phil at the change of our shifts at four in the morning. A large twelve-foot following wave crashes over our stern.

We had sailed northward the day before, leaving Great Keppel Island with a steady following breeze of 25 knots. We are quite a bit above 26° south, but the gale knows nothing about latitude and weather forecasters and decides to follow us. The wind has increased, and we are soon in thirty-five knots of wind, with steep short seas.

"It's going to be a bit tight going around this lighthouse. I'll stay up until we round it. We may need to jibe for the new course."

"Great. I love jibing in gales. What the hell is that?" I say looking at some confusing lights.

"It's a ship on a reciprocal course. I've been watching them for the last half hour on radar."

"If they are on a reciprocal course, why am I seeing red and green lights?"

"What? That god damn bastard! Get on the radio. We are on a collision course! We have no maneuvering room to port. There's a reef."

I do everything I can think of to get the attention of the ship. They will not answer my hales on channel 16. What if the VHF radio isn't working for broadcasting? The receiver has been working fine, but we did not do a radio check for transmission before we left Coff's Harbour. How comfortable we had gotten with the marina life. I quickly broadcast a radio check.

"Your radio is fine," a French sounding woman responds.

"We are two miles southwest of the light north of Break Sea spit. There is a ship heading south on a collision course. I was wondering if you could try reaching them? They don't answer our call."

"You mean the light on Frazier Island?" the woman asks.

"No. The light north of Frazier Island, just north of Break Sea Spit. It has no name on my chart," I answer.

"But that must be us!" the woman says with panic. And then the radio goes dead.

"Now what the hell are they doing?" Phil yells down to me.

"Why? What's happening? Where did she go?"

"The ship is turning on every single light on board."

"Hello? Southbound ship, this is sailing vessel Iwalani at 24°25'S and 153°14'E. We see you fine. Can you see us?"

"Non, not even on radar," the woman responds.

"We are a forty-two foot sailing vessel. We probably look like sea clutter. We have a spotlight on our sails. Do you see us now?"

"Non. We see nothing. Say your position?"

"We are one mile southwest from you at, 24°25'Sand 153°14'E. If you alter course twenty degrees to port, you will not run us over."

"Yes, good. We are altering to port."

"Thank you, southbound ship,"

"I see only green nav lights now. We will be fine," Phil calls to me. "But, the wind is picking up. We need to take the mainsail down and go with just the jib."

"Ok with me," I say hanging the microphone up. "Jibing the jib is no big deal. God, I love these early morning "Custerflucks". Who needs coffee to stay alert?"

*   *   *

A few days later, while at anchor in the northern end of the Whitsunday Islands, Iwalani finally is at rest. We have gotten the parts for the watermaker and have made repairs. There are no other boats or houses in sight for many miles. We go snorkeling, come back to the boat for warm showers and while a chicken roasts in the oven, I sit out in the cockpit with a chilled glass of Australian chardonnay.

Sulfur crested cockatoos sit on branches in the darkly forested hills towering above Iwalani. Their pure white bodies stand out like brides resplendent in wedding finery, cloistered in a dark cathedral. Sounding like prehistoric dinosaurs, they shatter the still air with ear splitting screeches. This is what cockatoos are designed for, not living in some trailer in northern Maine with a chain-smoking truck driver.

"Are you coming up here? Do you realize this is the second time of this whole trip I have been able to sit out in the cockpit and watch the sunset? This must be why people go cruising," I lean down through the companionway and say to Phil. "This is very nearly idyllic! Hurry up! And bring Stew, this is too nice to miss."

"We'll be there in a second. I'm downloading the EGC's."

"I'm not sure I can ever be an avian vet when we get back."

"No? You have to. You've seen how birds should be living. It is up to you to make sure they are well cared for back home."

"I suppose you are right. But maybe we should just stay right here. I have never been to a place with such enjoyable bird sounds. I could live here forever. This is my idea of paradise. You've got to come up here and listen to this," I settle back against the cockpit coaming listening to the chirps, twitters, trills and screeches surrounding the boat.

"I want to get home. I miss the boys too much," Phil says.

"Now what are you doing?"

"I decided that since it is so calm, I ought to check the engine valve lash. Here's Stew," Phil stands on the bottom step of the companionway passing him up to me.

"Thanks. Are you crazy? Supper will be in a few minutes."

"This is only a five minute job."

"I've heard that one before."

Stew sits purring on my lap, listening to the bird calls in the hills, while the sun slowly sinks behind the mountains on the mainland. Two kookaburras add their farewells to the setting sun. A lone cockatoo gives a few more screeches, and then all is quiet.

"Mo#$&! F&#!#4@!g, suck wadded c!#$ breath!"

"Uh-oh, Stew. Do you need some help?" I reluctantly yell down to Phil.

"No! I forgot the refrigerator compressor has to be removed."

"Give it a rest," I say carrying Stewart down the ladder.

"I can't give it a rest. Who else is going to do this stuff?"

"Get Lars or Fifi to do it. Can't it be done tomorrow?"

"No. We will never make it over the top. It's almost July."

I quietly put the salad on the table, mash the potatoes, make hollandaise sauce for the steamed broccoli, carve the chicken, and then serve it all up. I put Stew next to me on the settee, just as a large crash of tools sounds from the engine room.

"You god damned ass f!#@%, shit eating, tit sucking, liver lipped, mealy mouthed bastard."

"Supper's ready."

Then come the fake sobs. "Why me? Why the f#!@ me? Just eat without me."

"You know, Stew," I say, "this is why two boats cruising the exact same course, at exactly the same time, can have completely different experiences. Even

why two people on the same boat would have different versions of the same event."
Stew eats a bite of the chicken and curls up next to me. I eat my dinner in silence
as the aft end of the boat heats up from Phil's torrent of swears.

"Are you sure you don't want some help?" I offer.

"Son of a bitch. The god damned cussedness of inanimate objects. You
fu!@#$g dickhead. You bastard suck wad. No. I don't need any help. Does it sound
like I need help?"

"Do I have to answer that?"

One can only marvel at the complexity of his combination of vulgarities. I
eat in silence, trying my best to stifle a chuckle at my otherwise silent husband's
professional skill with profanity. Fantastic combinations of words are preceded by
the clatter of a tool falling into the bilge or punctuated by the bang of a wrench
against wooden floorboards. I have learned over the years that sometimes staying
out of the picture is the best help I can give.

"I'm sorry to be such an ass. Look at this dinner you made," Phil says a half-
hour later as he emerges from the engine room covered in sweat.

"It's no big deal, nothing the microwave can't bring back."

"You've got to come look at this."

I look in at the red engine that is really the heart of Iwalani. Yes, she is a
sailboat, but sails only take you places when the winds blow; an engine can take
you where they don't.

"Oh, my god! I wasn't expecting this."

The entire top third of the engine is removed, and like a doctor doing brain
surgery, we are looking down into the open cranium of the Westerbeke.

"Do you see it?" Phil asks.

"I'm not sure <u>what</u> I am supposed to be seeing."

"Rust. Everywhere. All eight of the valve springs are broken and rusted."

"Oh," I say trying to take it all in. "What does that mean?"

"What does that mean? We aren't going across the Indian Ocean like this."

"But, the engine is working fine."

"That's because it is a really good engine. Salt water must have gotten in here
somehow when the water pump broke in Jamaica. It's probably been like this for
a while."

After wasting a day trying to order the valve springs over the phone at a
snooty resort, we e-mail our friend Rick back in Maine in desperation. Rick
immediately e-mails back that the parts are ordered and will be shipped ahead and
will meet us several days sail away in Cairns.

When we finally arrive at Cairns in the early morning, we anchor up the river
away from the fleet of cruising boats. We pick up the engine parts on shore and
return to Iwalani.

"We've got to get this over with now," Phil says. "It's going to take two of us
to do this job."

"But it's so hot! I had hoped to go croc hunting in the dinghy."

"The sooner we do it, the sooner we'll know if anything else is wrong. We'll
go croc hunting as a reward for getting the engine fixed." Phil preps the patient for
surgery while I strip down to my underwear. Reluctantly, I wedge myself into an
L-shape on the engine room floor, while he stands naked above me.

"OK, here's the deal. I'm going to use this lever along with these socket wrenches positioned just so, to compress the old spring. You need to pull the keepers out with this magnet and a pair of hemostats, once I get the spring down. OK, Ready?"

"What the heck are the keepers?"

"Little wedge shaped pieces that together form a cone. They keep the spring in place."

"You're in the way. I can't see what I am doing."

"You'll have to do it by feel. Hurry up. I can't keep pressure on this forever. Whatever you do, don't drop them down the hole or into the bilge."

"But the lever is in the way."

"Bastard." The two rounded sockets Phil is using as both fulcrum and pusher for the lever, fall off the engine. Phil repositions them. "I can see this is going to take awhile," he says dripping sweat on me.

"Shit," I say.

"What?"

"I was just trying engine room language out."

"It helps, believe me."

"Mother fucker," I say while struggling to remove the keeper.

"Good. You got one of them. Careful with the other. Excellent. Now we can put the new spring on," Phil says.

"Dick head pecker wart. That only took fifteen fucking minutes."

"They'll go faster from now on."

"This is fucking bullshit. You'd think there was a god damn better way."

"There is," Phil says repositioning his pry bar and sockets.

"There is?"

"Sure. They make a mother fucking tool for this," Phil admits.

"You're kidding. Why don't we have the fucking thing?"

"Because, we are out in the middle of the god damn Indian Ocean and there is no hardware store out here."

"No we aren't. We are in the middle of mother fucking Cairns, and the fucking hardware store is right around the corner," I point out.

"Humor me O.K.?" Phil asks.

"Fucking ass bashing blasted bastard banger. Hey, you know it really does help. I could enjoy fucking talking like this. I can see it now, when I get home, 'Excuse me bitch, shut the fuck up, I can't hear fucking Fifi's heart with your mother-fucking blabbering."

Two and a half hours later we are finished. I have my backpack ready and am in the dinghy before Phil.

"What's with the machete?" he asks me.

"In case we get attacked by a croc."

"We won't get attacked by a croc," he says.

"They can jump far out of the water, and, what's more, the rumbling of an outboard sounds like a male croc, so they can get territorial if they think their space is being invaded."

"Great."

Cairns is built on the west side of a northward flowing river (which may have been the reason for my profound loss of any sense of direction on this one spot on the planet) next to hungry catamarans tied to the wharves anxiously waiting to take pale, soon-to-be-seasick snorkelers out to the Great Barrier Reef. Yachts cling like parasites to the mangroves lining the eastern shore, anchored or tied to pilings of dubious durability. The tourist section gives way to the Navy further up river; yachts give way to the faded dreams of retired passage makers, and these ghosts finally give way to the swamps.

We motor slowly up river and encounter a nautical assemblage of various marine store sale parts, fashioned together haphazardly, resembling nothing remotely seaworthy—a floating ghetto. These craft are treading water with varying degrees of success. Most are succumbing to a gentle snooze broadside in the muck, or nose first in the mangroves,

Amy the Croc hunter

or, sadder still, just barely visible from our dinghy, the gray faded nautical remains of a cyclone-sneezed vessel, left deep in the mangrove interiors like discarded tissues.

The mangroves in the fading light of day give a morgue-like feeling to the scenery. The branches and root system, twisting and tortuous, have equal parts above and below the waterline. Their circulatory system lies exposed to the casual observer like a half completed autopsy. The remains of pastel colored shopping bags hang in the branches like tattered hospital gowns. Popping sounds come from deep within the mangrove forest like a loud tap on a hollow bone. Beside our outboard, it is the only sound we hear.

Historically, mangroves have long been the bane of humanity, home to muck and mud, mosquitoes and crocodiles. When man looks at mangrove swamps, he automatically thinks of backhoes and bulldozers. Yet, they are very important for the health of our planet. Mangroves are a nursery for young fish, as well a natural air and water purifier for pollutants. They also act as a buffer for high wind or water during cyclones or tsunamis. For yachts of any size, their intricate root system is the anchor of choice in a cyclone. Fortunately, Cairns has left a lot of theirs alone.

Not one croc is visible, so we dejectedly head back to Iwalani. In the Australian winter the crocs are less active, preferring to snooze in the hot sun on a mud bank, but where they would venture in late afternoon during winter is anyone's guess. During the heat of summer they have been known to cruise out to the public beaches and terrorize the bathers. Usually the beaches are closed at the first sight of a croc. The water, heavy with river silt, is guacamole colored and almost as thick; how anyone can sight a croc seems quite a feat.

Stewart is happy to see us when we get back but doesn't want any supper. The further north we go, the further downhill he seems to be sliding.

"I'm giving him prednisolone and blood pressure meds. If his problem is arthritis or just inflammation he should be getting better, not worse."

"Well, he definitely seems a lot worse to me."

"Me, too. I doubt very much if he has high blood pressure. Somehow we have to find someone with a sphygmomanometer," I say to Phil while digging through the cat locker, looking for the secret stash of French cat food I had been hiding from the Australian authorities. "I'll stop the prednisolone and blood pressure medicine and start him on an antibiotic, one specific for toxoplasmosis."

"What's that?"

"A protozoal parasite he has had a slight titer to in the past."

"Translation?"

"It's an organism cats can get from eating mice or raw meat, as may have been the case with the raw lamb cat food I gave him. It can get in the brain. I think that it may remain dormant in tissues, and during periods of stress come out of dormancy, and start to multiply."

"But Stew isn't under any stress."

"Not now. But he was while he was in quarantine. With me giving him steroids, I only suppressed his immune system further."

"How long have you been giving him steroids?"

"Just the prednisolone, every other day, for two weeks now."

That night we run the engine to recharge the batteries, as there is little wind upriver for the wind generator. Afterwards we leave the engine room door open to warm up the cabin, which gets a little chilly at night even this far north. The following morning we can't find Stewart anywhere. I panic. I know it is impossible for him to climb up the companionway ladder, besides we have screens over it to keep the mosquitoes out. How could we lose him?

I search the engine room and find him wedged under the propeller shaft. Our stuffing box continuously produces a small but steady drip of water and Stewart is lying in the pool of bilge water under it.

"He's dead!" I scream.

"No way!"

I reach in and pull him out, sopping wet. He chirrups in his usual Stew fashion, alive, but very cold.

"I think he got confused, and, since he can't see, he just got lost."

I fill the sink with warm water and give him a bath, which he enjoys very much. He slowly comes back to life. I think about many of my former patients who would follow the call of a long dormant instinct to head to the swamps when they are about to die. Was that what Stewart was trying to do? I give him the new antibiotic and carry him up into the cockpit where the hot Australian sun is shining. We lie out for a few minutes until I begin to feel my flesh sizzling like a side of bacon.

We can find no veterinary clinic equipped with the necessary blood pressure cuff for cats, so we continue northward. I stop all the medication except the new antibiotic. Gradually Stewart starts to improve. He is nowhere near normal, but at least he is eating and moving around more with his purr motor in high gear.

For the next few weeks we continue to work our way up the Great Barrier Reef. We are now in the routine of sailing sixty kilometers by day and then anchoring for the night. The cruising guides describe the majority of anchorages as "lively." This is not referring to the nightlife, but the overall sea conditions. By day, we are under the influence of the prevailing southeasterly trade winds. By night, the sea breeze drops off, only to be replaced at two in the morning by the potent land breeze from the heated desert interior. As a result, the boat swings around into the new wind direction, sometimes trying to dislodge the anchor. None of us gets much sleep; one of us is always popping out of bed to check the anchor throughout the night.

Often times it is too cold and windy to do much underwater exploring. Instead we make many trips to shore armed with my machete to explore the interior of islands. We see many goanna and tracks from crocodiles but, alas, no actual crocs. On one island we find a huge mound of decomposing leaf litter with some suspicious freshly dug holes which look like the croc nests I have seen in nature shows on TV. At anchor, I hang chicken carcasses off the stern and repeatedly whack the surface of the water with a seat cushion. As my attention span is nine and a half minutes at best, I'd give this up perhaps too early and anxiously scan the dark surface of the water with a flashlight looking for two beady eyes. Nothing.

"I think it's too cold for them," Phil says late one afternoon as we are returning from exploring a completely deserted river.

"I suppose it's a good thing we haven't encountered one, as we really are woefully unprepared to deal with an attack. My machete would probably just bounce off its snout."

"There's that boat again."

"What boat?'

"The pretty red ketch. A Colin Archer type. It's called Northern Light. I've been seeing it here and there since the Whitsundays."

"I don't see it."

"It's sailing behind that island."

"Wow! It sure doesn't look Australian."

For the past few weeks we have been seeing many peculiar boats with a box-like structure overhanging the stern, almost as if someone decided to build a screened-in porch off the transom. Many of these boats are ill equipped for ocean travel and barely look like they can travel more than fifteen feet let alone fifteen miles. They are the homes of the uppermost tier of the corral reef, the human live-aboard.

With world cruising, unlike coastal cruising, the boat one lives in becomes the label of who you are. The boat's name becomes your last name, your religion, your country, and your world. The boat takes on a persona of its own. We avoid a boat and its people if it has a cutesy name, unsafe clutter on deck, poorly maintained topsides, or is erratic underway. Everyone has his or her own set of standard discriminatory units; that's what makes cruising interesting. I am sure Iwalani has many points against her, not only because we are made of wood, but also have a gaff rig. 'Wackos!' I am sure a lot of people think, as we sail by with our steering remote in one hand and a dish of ice cream in the other. 'They probably don't have a toilet on board either,' is the collective thought emanating from Iwalani's antagonists. We even have met people who discriminate against people over the price of a boat. But neither Phil nor I have any idea of the price tag of any of the boats manufactured after 1975, let alone the name of the manufacturer. A Halburg-Rossi, Hinckley, or Hog's Head, they all look the same to us, always possessing a sloop rig, white topsides and blue sail covers.

But here is a boat unlike the regimental battalions: red topsides, outrageously tall masts and spartan uncluttered decks. After keeping pace with the Northern Light, we finally run into the owners on a steep trail on Lizard Island. Phil and I are hunkered under a bush waiting for a sudden rain shower to pass, contemplating what sorts of sex acts we could pursue, when I look a little further up the steep slope, and see two other people similarly hunkered under a bush.

When the downburst gives way to showers, we meet the couple half way on the trail. Deborah is American with wild hair that cuffs about her head like a young bear cub. Her husband Rolf is Swedish, and we find out later, quite a bit older than she, though his spry joints and lack of facial creases never reveal that secret. They have been married several years and have been cruising for a few more. That morning they have already sprinted to the top, traversed the upper ridge, crossed over the entire island, and are returning to their boat for breakfast.

"Best to watch your step above." Rolf says to me. "The rain has made the rocks very slippery."

"Maybe we should go snorkeling instead," Phil says to me.

I turn and look at him. "But it's raining."

"So? You have to get wet anyhow!"

"Come on out to Northern Light for coffee afterwards," Deb says trying to bat down a bear leg of hair clawing her in the eye.

Phil and I return to Iwalani and put on our bathing suits. The rain has let up, but it is still gray, blustery and cold. The fresh water runoff from the rains has brought out thousands of fish seeking a quick meal. The underwater world cares little for the bad weather above. I finally see my first cuttle fish, home to the infamous birdcage cuttle bone.

"This isn't so bad," I holler over to Phil, trying not to aspirate a mouthful of seawater from the boisterous waves in the process.

"Look at the size of these giant clams! I haven't seen them this big since Fiji. Now I see how people can get killed by them."

"I know. Their open maw just begs you want to stick your flipper in for a quick tickle."

"Please resist the temptation! I'm getting cold. I think it's time to go back," Phil says.

"You can take the dinghy. I'll swim back. This is great. I think we need to take Iwalani out to the main reef."

"No way. It's too rough and far too dangerous," Phil shivers.

"OK fine,"

After hot showers on Iwalani, we get back in the dinghy and motor over to Northern Light. "Sure am glad we got all cleaned up," Phil says to me as a wave hits the "Grape" broadside and drenches both of us.

"Sorry about that. I'll drive a little slower."

We reach Northern Light and are given a quick tour. She is flush deck and completely devoid of any clutter. No dodger, bulwarks, or deck gear. The only thing rising from her deck like a tiny pimple, is a small bubble hatch located in the aft section so the person on watch can look around in foul weather without getting wet. While her basic DNA blue print came from the same lineage as Iwalani, she is completely a boat of the twenty first century, rod rigging, roller furling and a carbon fiber mast, replacing dead eyes, lanyards and Douglas fir.

"This is a prototype for a rigging company in Sweden," Rolf says pointing to a system of roller furling for the mainsail. "They pay us to field test their equipment and report back. It's a piece of shit really, no one seems to be able to manufacture it right."

"Northern Light had a total refit a few years ago," Deb explains.

"Yes, I put in the carbon fiber masts, making them taller. To compensate we put on a winged keel," Rolf adds.

Deb and Rolf

I look up at Northern Light's mainmast. It seems twice as tall as Iwalani's. "She must roll like crazy downwind," I say.

I had just breached the limit of boat etiquette. Asking about rolling in a boat is a little like asking a couple how many times a week they have sex. It's just not polite. Every boat rolls downwind; it's just the frequency and degree that is never discussed.

"We don't ever go dead downwind," Deb concedes.

"But look at the leading edge on the main and mizzen," Phil observes. "She must go to windward like a bastard."

"Better than that," Deb chides.

Down below Northern Light is also well thought out for serious cruising, no wide open spaces where you could get thrown about and few things left loose.

"I just got this espresso maker at a yard sale," Deb says getting the canister out of a closet. "Hope you like espresso."

"Love it," Phil and I say together.

"Where was this taken?" I ask Deb while looking at a picture of Northern Light frozen into an ice and snow filled landscape.

"Antarctica," Rolf responds. "We've been there twice."

"Rolf, show them the book," Deb suggests.

Rolf hands me a beautifully bound coffee table book.

"Jeez, Phil," I say winking at my husband. "We are in the company of professional cruisers."

"Don't hold it against us!" Deborah cries from the galley.

"Just as long as you don't write falsehoods," I comment.

"Well…" Deb begins.

"Falsehoods?" Rolf asks not grasping the English phrase.

"Stretching the truth. Like the writers who go on and on about the cocktails in the cockpit, watching the sunsets in exotic locations, snorkeling all day, the wonderful native people," I remark.

240

"We have a web site and update the log page weekly," Phil explains. "We tell it like it is. It pisses a lot of people off."

"In one of my articles I did write about the truth of passage making and cruising," Deborah admits. "The editor wrote me back and said I had to change it. They didn't want to print any of the bad stuff because then, no one would want to go cruising and they wouldn't sell magazines. They would also lose advertisers, and so on."

"A whole industry is buoyed up on half the story," I say. "You didn't comply, did you?'

"We have to eat," Deb confesses. "Besides, this life really isn't so bad."

"Bad? It's wonderful. I would not trade a life on passage for any other," Rolf exclaims.

"I would not trade our memories of the first trip to Antarctica for all the tea in china," Deb laments putting the steaming espresso cups on the table.

"We froze ourselves in for the winter. It was incredible," Rolf begins.

"One bright sunny day we had several Adele penguins come visit. We had several lines running to shore essentially tying us in place so we would freeze solid with little movement. The first penguin came to the taut line and tried to jump over it. He fell flat on his face. He had never seen such a thing in his world. The rest of the penguins that were standing behind him, actually started to mock him. I'm not kidding. They were laughing at him. That was how they all learned to walk around the line," Deb says.

"And the shadow," Rolf says while sipping his espresso.

"Because they are not used to shadows, they actually walked around the shadow of the line, too. It was unbelievable."

"And what happened with the second trip?"

"Ah…"Rolf pauses. "Our own undoing."

"This was after our books and the articles. We were frozen in with another boat," Deborah replies swiftly. "It was a lot different."

"It sounds like hell," I speculate. "Going to a place to escape humanity so you can be responsible solely for yourselves and suddenly having another boat to deal with."

"Yes," Deb says passing me a brownie. "Well, it wasn't exactly hell, but not what we expected either."

"Well, is any of this?" Phil asks.

Chapter 19

Over the Top

July 2002
The very Northeast corner of Australia

At Cape Melville we anchor in five-foot seas that keep the bow and stern soaked as Iwalani bounces up and down like a terrier tethered to a leash. The grass-covered bottom is great for dugong but not great for anchoring. We plow our way backwards for one half mile until the anchor is polished to a brilliant shine. Thankfully we are in a wide-open bay with plenty of leeway, no other people for miles.

An adult dugong appears off the stern, floating upright in the steep waves. Smaller than a manatee, it turns its old man face to look at our stern. We turn to look too. In the process of moving backwards in such boisterous seas, considerable strain is being put on the tiller arm for our autopilot. We back into a steep wave, the stern submerges, the autopilot overextends, a strange gasping sound comes out

Phil repairs the autopilot

of its tubular body and then it snaps in two. After I shriek, Phil makes a quick move grabbing the pieces before they disappear forever in the murky water.

The result is a day going nowhere while making repairs. Using plastic epoxies, spice bottle caps for molds, stainless steel wire and a bit of good luck, Phil operates on the arm that keeps us from having to man Iwalani's monstrous tiller. His rebuilt autopilot looks pretty good, actually, and seems to work even better than the original. The dugong, however, never makes a return appearance.

"You look awful," I remark to Phil when he comes up from napping during my afternoon watch. We stopped the night before at Morris Islet, an even worse anchorage than behind Cape Melville. Morris Islet is a tiny island like the kind in shipwreck cartoons with a single palm tree and one kapok tree and not much protection from either the trade winds or the nighttime land breeze. Phil was up and down all night like a nest-building wren, worried we were dragging anchor.

We decide to sail through the night to the Escape River, as the anchorages have become more stressful than just moving forward. The trade winds are blowing a steady twenty knots, which makes Iwalani happy and keeps us heading northward, but provides for little sleep when we stop, especially when the trades drop off at night and are replaced with the "land bullets," the wind that appears from the hot Australian interior, always from the opposite direction.

Phil says nothing as he leans up against the bulwark on the leeward side to pee.

"Pretty gloomy weather," I comment. "Are you OK?"

He still says nothing.

"What's eating you?"

"How's the autopilot behaving?" he finally asks.

"Fine. It makes more noise than it used to, but, actually, I like that. It reminds me that it is still there, working away. What is bugging you?"

"The Torres Straight."

"What's the matter with the Torres Straight?"

"Well, for one, it is the graveyard of a thousand ships. Imagine taking the entire swirling volume of the Pacific Ocean and funneling it through a bottle neck no bigger than a few miles across. Add to that, the worry of pirates waiting to pillage any boat that runs aground on the numerous reefs. That's what's bugging me."

"We'll do fine. The Great Barrier Reef has been more stressful than I thought it would be. Like for instance, right now-smell that?"

Phil stands like a hunting dog, nose pointing to windward. "Yup. Old Spice."

"I'll go look on the radar and see where they are."

"Don't bother. They are coming up over the horizon pretty damn fast. It's a container ship."

"I'll go grab some clothes."

Within a few minutes the ship squeezes between us and the outer reef. Two white uniformed crewmembers wave to us from the bridge, disappointed we have put our bathing suits on.

"You'd think the Australians would make those ships go outside the reef. Look at that rust bucket. Can you see what its hailing port is?" I ask Phil.

"Monrovia," Phil replies while handing me the binoculars.

"That ship looks like it would break apart in seconds if it ran aground."

"There should be a speed limit at least. These ships never obey the buoys, always taking the shortest route between reefs and islands if necessary," Phil says.

"It's Indian territory up here, that's for sure. Maybe we should not continue on tonight. I looked at C-Map earlier, and we can stop at a place called Portland Roads. It looks like a better anchorage than we've seen for some time."

"I thought we agreed to keep going?"

"I'm changing my mind," I admit.

"You can't do that!"

"Why not? Since it's my day to be captain, we're stopping. All three of us need some sleep."

"Look at the chart—steep hilly terrain, that means more wind bullets. If we keep going, in just one day we'll be over the top."

"Nope, we're stopping." We arrive at Portland Roads with a half hour left of daylight. A small enclave of houses is visible, the first we have seen in days, many fishing boats, and a handful of yachts. I pick out the best spot to anchor, away from the yachts and nearer the fishing boats.

Our usual method of anchoring is for me to stand in the bow and give Phil hand signals, indicating when to stop, back and hold, or which direction to head. We get to the area I had indicated, and Phil begins backing before I have time to get the anchor over.

I walk back to the cockpit and say quietly, "Hey, you began backing before I was ready."

"Sorry," Phil confesses. "Where do you want to drop it?"

"Further forward than where we just were."

"If the wind shifts, we'll swing into the fishing boat."

"By the time I put out 120 feet of scope we'll be well behind it; besides, it's on an anchor not a mooring. The fishing boat will swing too."

We motor ahead to the chosen spot. I let the anchor out and then indicate for Phil to back up while we set it. Nothing happens. We aren't going in reverse. Iwalani's bow is soon caught by a gust of wind and since it is her nature to swing away from the wind, we begin turning around. The anchor isn't holding.

I push on the windlass button to pull it back up.

"What the hell are you doing?" Phil yells at me.

"Getting the anchor back on board."

"What the hell for?"

"Because we need to do it all over again," I hiss between clenched teeth.

I don't have the hose hooked up to the salt-water wash down pump and the anchor chain is covered in foul smelling mud, which soon covers the deck, like frosting on a chocolate donut. Phil slams Iwalani into forward gear and makes a wide circle around the anchored boats, while I try to look invisible on the foredeck.

I walk back to the cockpit covering the side deck with my muddy bare feet.

"Can I ask what you are doing?" Phil asks me.

"Maybe I should ask the same thing," I say.

"I've been anchoring my whole life," Phil begins.

"Ya well, and you still don't have it right," I stab.

"F!@# You!"

"No, **F!@!** YOU!"

We stand staring at each other while Iwalani continues to make wide circles around the other anchored boats. I consider taking a handful of mud off my feet and smearing it on Phil's face. Phil is entertaining thoughts of tying me to a line and dragging me behind the boat. We both stare at one another for what feels like an eternity. Being angry with Phil is about as productive as taking a heavy anvil and dropping it on my right foot, then picking it up and doing the same thing to my left foot. No matter how hard I tried to stay angry with him, it never lasts longer than about two and a half minutes.

"Let's try it again. This time I'll drive. You be the bow guy," I suggest.

I slowly motor Iwalani to the original spot. Phil lets the anchor out, and I slowly back down on it. It doesn't hold. Phil walks purposefully back to the cockpit. "May I make a suggestion?" he asks.

"Sure, what?" I say looking anywhere but at my husband.

"I suggest we anchor over there," he says pointing to a spot closer to shore, well away from everybody. "This obviously isn't working."

I motor over to where he indicates and within a few minutes we have the anchor down and don't drag after using all of Iwalani's sixty three horsepower to back down on it. I go down below to check the chart. It seems like an OK spot so I bite my lip, feed my cat, and take a shower.

*   *   *

"Is this great or what?" Phil yells up to me a few days later. He is down below dancing naked and singing to U2, "It's a Beautiful Day." We have just written the new compass heading in our logbook: 256°. We have made it over the top and are now sailing in a westerly direction, the first time in a long time.

After getting a good night's sleep at Portland Roads, we sailed straight through the night and made it through the Albany pass, a narrow channel that runs along the inside of the Australian coast. Rather than heading further north and stopping at Thursday Island, we decide to stop at Possession Island and stretch our legs, hoping to meet up with Northern Light. We have timed the currents perfectly. The sun is shining, the wind is steady and plenty of electricity is coming out of the wind generator and getting deposited into the battery bank account.

I am not exactly sure what we will encounter in these parts, so have donned a pair of Phil's briefs and decide to spend my off watch reading in the lee side of the cockpit. I do a quick look around for Phil who is still euphoric down below, cooking French toast for breakfast. Seeing no other ships or hazards, except a large Australian customs boat a few miles away in the lee of an island, I settle back to enjoy reading in the warm morning sun.

"Do you want one piece or two?" Phil sings up to me.

"One. Thanks."

"How come you're wearing my underwear?" he adds in tune.

"Mine are all dirty."

"Time for me to do the laundry. I'll make water after breakfast."

I realize I am not going to get much reading done so lie my book down on my belly.

"G' day!"

'Huh? Who said that? I am definitely hearing things,' I think to myself.

"G'DAY!" I look up.

Perched on the high side of the bulwark is a smiling man's head wearing an Akubra hat. It takes a second or two for me to realize that I am not hallucinating and the head is connected to a neck, which is connected to a man, who is standing in an outboard, while hanging onto the windward side of our boat.

My book falls into the cockpit as I make a lunge for the companionway.

"Yikes!" is all I can scream.

"What's wrong?" Phil asks holding the spatula in mid air, like a tennis player ready to serve.

"There's a man up there! It's your watch; you deal with it."

I take off Phil's underwear and throw them over to him.

"No thanks. I've got my bathing suit," he says turning the stereo off.

I stop shaking long enough to find a shirt and some shorts and join Phil in the cockpit. A semi rigid inflatable with six Australian customs men is following us at a discreet distance in Iwalani's wake. When they see that we are both decent they come back alongside.

"Have you been to Thursday Island?" one of them asks while holding onto a clipboard.

"No. We sailed through the night, and just came out of the Albany Passage," Phil responds.

Are you going to Thursday Island?" the man at the motor asks.

"Uh, no."

"Where was your last port of call?"

"The last place we anchored was Portland Roads," I answer.

"Have you cleared into Australia?"

"Yes, many months ago, in Coff's Harbour."

"Right then. G' day to you both."

I can tell they are trying hard to keep a straight face. Phil is still holding the spatula, and my clothes are all inside out.

*   *   *

Two days later we make it through the Endeavor Straight, and spend some time with Deborah and Rolf from Northern Light. Then we head to Gove, through the Gulf of Carpentaria. The books all describe the winds in this part of the world as unrelenting and boisterous.

We spent seven months in Australia combing through bookstores buying enough books to get us at least to South Africa. Our stock is bountiful, varied and thoroughly engrossing. "I hope I am not disturbing your reading," Phil says just before my midnight shift ends. "But, have you been paying any attention to where we are going or what the wind is doing?"

"Hmph," I snort.

"We happen to be five degrees off course, and in case you haven't noticed, the wind generator is screaming and we are careening along at eight knots."

"Great isn't it?" I acknowledge not putting my book down.

"I think Amy Tan can wait a bit. Iwalani needs help."

"OK fine." I put the book up on the shelf under the dodger and stand up in the cockpit to look around. Despite the full moon, the ocean is lit up from a million stars that seem to cover the night sky. The crests of the waves look like eighteenth century dancers swirling in dark blue skirts edged with lace, each one touching the void of the ocean's dance hall.

"Click in five degrees to starboard," Phil yells up to me. "Otherwise we'll be going aground."

"It is a bit windier than I thought. Now that we no longer have the cloth dodger, I wasn't aware of how the wind has picked up. Before, the dodger used to make such a racket rattling in the wind. I knew when it was getting bad."

"Excuses. Excuses."

"I guess we should put in the third reef."

"No argument here," Phil agrees.

We head out on deck strapped into our harnesses. I drop the peak and throat halyards while Phil pulls on the peak downhaul. I climb onto the overturned dinghy and sit on its slippery surface in order to tie down the tack, while Phil starts to reach for the third reef outhaul.

"Holy Shit!" he yells up at me. He is standing on the leeward deck just a few feet below me. "Hold on as tight as you can to the mast!"

I hear it roaring upwind of us. A huge monster that blocks the light of the moon as it approaches. I wrap my arms and legs around the mast, hugging Iwalani with all my strength.

"This is it," I think to myself. *"The end. No one will know what happened to us; where we disappeared or how we died."*

A huge wall of very hot water breaks over us. Within seconds it is gone; the monster wave roaring its way off to the northwest.

"Are you OK?" Phil yells to me.

"Thank god, you are still here. I saw things float away on the leeward side."

"Your cabin top herbs, I'm afraid, are history. The window box is still tied in, but the dirt and plants- gone, washed away. One of the life rings is gone too."

"What was that, a tsunami?"

"No, a rogue wave. A very big rogue wave."

"Why was the water so hot?"

"That I don't have an answer for," Phil says. You better go down and check on Stewart. I'll tie in the reef points."

"What if another wave appears? I can't believe there is only one."

"Look behind us, everything looks normal."

The hatch over the galley is open, as well as all the portholes on the leeward side. Stewart and his bed are soaked. Most of the water came in through the galley hatch; not much made its way in through the leeward or windward portholes. I close everything up in case the rogue wave has siblings and then give Stewart a bath. I rinse everything down with fresh water, wrap Stewart in a towel and take him to bed with me.

We arrive in Gove, or Nhulunbuy, the next day. Gove is a mining town established in 1973 by the Alcan Company, who moved in and started taking the ochre colored dirt and processing it into bauxite for aluminum cans, while leaving piles of red toxic dirt behind. The local Yolngu people opposed the mining operation but lost in a famous court battle. They still own the land but lease it to Alcan. This led to the signing of the Northern Territory Land Rights Act, which requires permits for any white person entering aboriginal lands and gave 42% of the northern territory back to the aboriginal people.

The harbor of Gove is well protected and dominated by two buildings, the Alcan smelter and the yacht club. We stay almost a week, provisioning and preparing for the 2,300-mile trip to Cocos Keeling, an atoll belonging to the Australians. We check and recheck equipment and rigging aloft and run through disaster drills, sinking, holing, fire and the like, preparing Iwalani and ourselves for every possible disaster. The signs posted along the beach and shore, warning of the dangers of swimming, scare me away from checking the underside of Iwalani. There are crocodiles year round and deadly jellyfish in the summer.

On our final day we row to shore hoping to spend some time at the Arafura Festival. We decide to walk to town, but no sooner have we gone a few hundred yards when we are picked up by a white ute, the modern day replacement for the cowboy horse. All throughout Australia utes, or sport utility vehicles, are the main mode of transportation. Most of them are just small, four door, Toyota pickup trucks, sporting stainless "roo" bars on the front and the typical Australian cattle dog panting in the pickup bed. "Care for a ride to town?" the driver yells at us.

We climb in and sit in the back seat. "Thanks," we both say. "It is pretty hot on the road."

"Always try to help a fellow yachtie."

"What boat are you from?" I ask.

"Six Pack. It's a motorboat. I am doing a circumnavigation of Australia. The Matthew Flinders thing, the wrong way, by myself. That's why I am holed up here, waiting for the wind to die off a bit so I can continue east. My wife meets me every once in a while but only when I'm at five star marinas. I'm borrowing this ute from the owner of the marina, otherwise I'd go completely wankers. What boat are you on?"

"Iwalani, the gaff rigged cutter," Phil says.

"Bloody balmy, just the two of you sail that thing?"

"Yes, just us and our cat," I respond.

"Bugger! I hate bloody cats."

"Well you know," I begin, "if you are really doing the Mathew Flinders thing, in honor of the continent of Australia's most famous circumnavigator, it would be important to have a cat on board too. Your explorer Flinders, had one of the most famous boat cats of all time, named Trim. He was a really important member of the crew. Have you ever seen Trim's sculpture in Sydney?"

"Christ no. You aren't one of those know-it-all females are you?"

'No,' I think to myself, *'if I was, I would have a really snappy come back to such an asshole remark. We did see Trim's sculpture at night where it cast a fifteen-foot shadow on the library building in Sydney. It is very impressive actually. Too bad you are a cat hating jerk who wouldn't appreciate it.'* But, I keep my mouth shut.

Just then an aboriginal man walks in front of the car gripping a Victoria Bitters Ale can. "Bloody blacks. Think they own this town," our driver barks.

'Technically, they do,' I think to myself.

"This savo you should go to the Arafura festival," the driver suggests.

"That's where we are headed. We saw the signs at the marina."

"I'm going, too. I'll take you there. My name is Bill."

"Phil and Amy," Phil replies.

Bill drops us off and heads to the parking area. The majority of the four thousand inhabitants of Gove are present at this festival. What exactly they are celebrating, we can't quite figure out. Most everyone has been partying for three days and has reached an inebriative plane on a level out of our reach. On the platform stage four white males are cavorting around in nun's garb singing a rendition of a song known to the rest of the audience, as they, too, are chiming in.

We head over to a beer stand and Phil buys two Victoria Bitters.

"When in Rome," Phil extends a plastic cup to me. "Cheers!"

"Let's put as much distance between us and Bill as possible," I suggest.

"Hey, you sound American," a man exclaims reeling into us with his two daughters. "I'd like to thank you for your country's help."

"Help?" I ask.

"Yeah, you know most Australians right now are really down on you Yanks and what Bush is doing, but not me. I'd like to shake your hands. Owen's the name, mining's the game."

"Nice to meet you Owen. Phil and Amy," I say to him.

"And these are my daughters. Someday we're going to Disney World."

"I hope you aren't disappointed. As Australians you might be. Your whole country is like a giant theme park, no trash, filled with interesting animals, the threat of life taking dangers lurking at every bend…."

"You like Australia?" he slurs.

"Love it. It's ironic that the British relegated the best of the crown's possessions as a penal colony," I tease.

"And America, too," Owen offers splashing beer on us as punctuation. "We weren't the only ones used as a dumping ground for British convicts."

"Let's make a toast to the outcasts of British society," I suggest.

"I'll drink double to that. Bloody Poms!" Owen raises his cup.

"What do you do for Alcan?" Phil asks.

"Crane operator. Would you like a tour of the facility?"

"We'd love it," Phil answers. "But we are leaving tomorrow."

After no more acts appear on stage, we come to the realization that the nuns were the grand finale. Owen tells us there are holding pens in Gove Harbor for trapped crocodiles, which are then moved past the marina to a small aboriginal settlement. This seems like the last opportunity I will have for seeing an Australian crocodile, almost in the wild. He gives us a ride back to the marina where we decide to walk down the road to check it out. But, no joys, not a soul, nor a croc can be found in the entire community.

"You seem kind of depressed," Phil observes as we walk back to the boat. "I didn't think seeing a croc was that important to you."

"I'm homesick, I guess. Or maybe it's my birthday coming up. I can't even remember how old I am. That's pretty bad."

"We can figure it out if you want."

"No, I'd rather stay in the dark. Thanks for the didgeridoo though. It's the nicest I've seen in all of Australia." Phil bought it for me at the local Gove art center which supports aboriginal people by teaching them marketing and how to sell their crafts. It is painted flat black and has three bands of yellow, white and red stripes. I picked it out after seeing and testing out literally hundreds over the last few months. It looks like a didgeridoo should look, not a shiny tourist trinket.

"I'm beginning to think the worst about Stew."

"Why? He seems to be doing better."

"Maybe I am sad about leaving Australia too."

"Not me. I am ready to go home. Don't you miss being able to swim?"

"Yes," I say looking at the vast expanse of turquoise water in front of us. "This is torture. I can see why it's so dangerous though. It's like cream of tropical soup, so cloudy. It's impossible to see a croc coming. Do you think that's from the mining?"

"Probably not, but I don't know," Phil says.

The following day we clear out of Australia and begin the long trip to Cocos-Keeling, a small atoll in the Indian Ocean. The winds are abaft the beam, fifteen knots. We have fresh food to last a month, enough dried and canned food to last a year. The boat is ready. We are ready. The only dirty sock in this neatly stacked laundry pile is Stewart, who is hanging to life by a clothespin. His appetite dropped off the day before we left, and I am resorting to giving him subcutaneous fluids, injectable pain meds and antibiotics. I resign myself to the fact that we might not get to South Africa in time to fly him home.

"It's going to blow over thirty knots tomorrow," Phil reports.

"On my birthday? I don't think so. I would like it sunny, with five knots of wind, no seas. An engine day."

"Not going to happen. We'll have to reef down tonight."

My birthday arrives with full sun, calm seas and little wind. The gale warning is cancelled by eight a.m. so Phil makes me sticky buns, the best on the entire planet. He also gives me two DVD's, which, since it is so calm out, I plan to watch later that night.

"Thanks for giving me such a great birthday at sea," I tell Phil.

"But…"

"But what?"

"Something else is bugging you."

"Well, yes," I say hesitantly.

"Stewart?"

"Yes. I'd like to run more blood tests on him."

"So, do you want to stop in Darwin?"

"Can we? We've already cleared out of Australia. Will they freak out?"

"I didn't realize until I looked at the chart how far to the west Darwin is. You know this is one hell of a big country. It's not out of the way at all, really. We can say we have a medical emergency. Which is true"

"We just won't utter the "C-A-T" word."

We stop for a few days in Darwin and have no trouble with the authorities. In fact we meet some great female veterinarians at a pet hospital as well equipped as some of the teaching hospitals in America. They go out of their way for Stewart. They just bought the instrument to measure cat's blood pressure and need help using it; Stewart and I are more than happy to oblige. Unfortunately, his blood pressure is normal. We run more blood tests. Stewart has a very high white cell count. I send his smear off to a pathologist who says it looks like overwhelming infection is more likely than a tumor. The Darwin veterinarians promise to e-mail our friend Rick in Maine, who will relay to us the results of a thyroid test and a toxoplasmosis titer.

My computer also decides to auger in, again. Luckily I had bought the extended worldwide warranty before we left Maine. We find a Compaq dealer and a longhaired technician munching chips and drinking "V' soda, who tries to bring him back to life, but to no avail. He cannot figure out what is wrong.

On our last trip to shore we pick up five ten-pound rocks. Silently, Phil and I stow them in the bilge, knowing in our hearts that these pieces of Australia may never make it back to Maine.

Australian Icons

CLOCKWISE FROM RIGHT: *Sydney Opera house, eastern grey kangaroo, red kangaroo, Uluru rock, Emu, koala*

THESE PICTURES AND RIGHT: Australian outback from the air and from The Ghan Train, Alison Buchanan working on a painting on board her boat.

ABOVE: Amy in the Australian bush
RIGHT: Sydney Harbour from our hotel, and the same view one week later hidden in bush fire smoke

AUSTRALIAN BIRDS DECORATE
Iwalani and the landscape like festive
party ornaments.

Half a world away but getting closer still
I hear the screen door slam
and smell the damp fir feet
heavy fog soaked leaves drop moisture down
on me
I'm in a sunburnt land with parched and
crumbling hills
raucous white birds scream through thirsty
parrot bills.

-Stewart

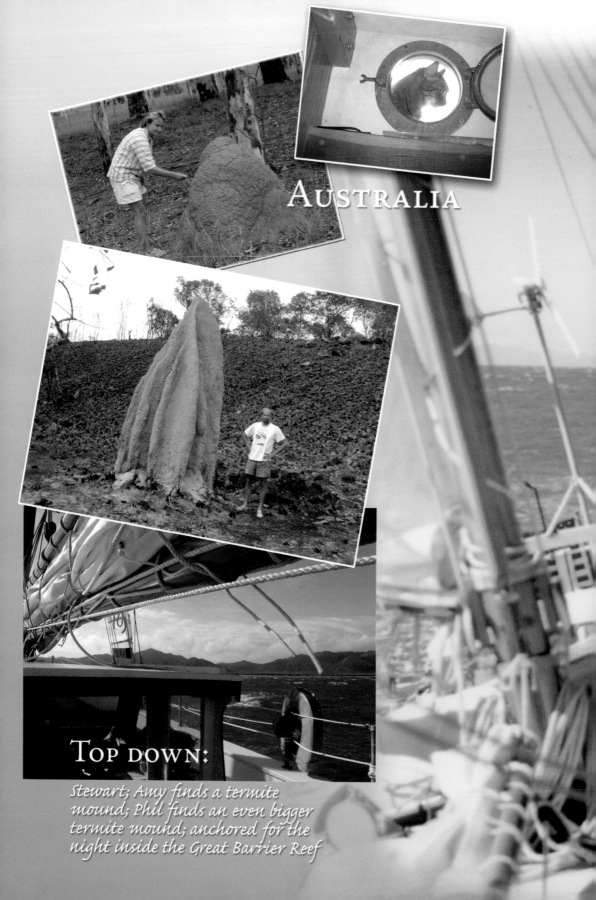

AUSTRALIA

TOP DOWN:

Stewart; Amy finds a termite mound; Phil finds an even bigger termite mound; anchored for the night inside the Great Barrier Reef

Fair Winds
&
Peaceful Holidays

S/V
TWALANI

worldvoyagers.com

Oh, so very hot
down under!

Indian Ocean Landfalls

Clockwise from Above: *Iwalani anchored in Grand Baie Mauritius; motu on Cocos Keeling atoll; roadside sscenery in Reunion; our sign for Direction Island hut; Russian sailing vessel SAID arriving in Cocos Keeling*

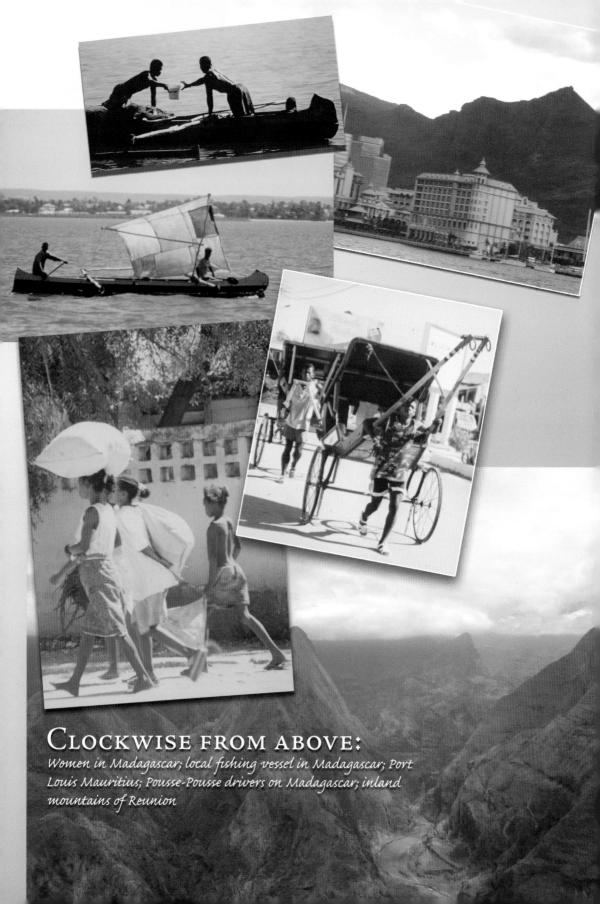

CLOCKWISE FROM ABOVE:

Women in Madagascar; local fishing vessel in Madagascar; Port Louis Mauritius; Pousse-Pousse drivers on Madagascar; inland mountains of Reunion

MADAGASCAR
CLOCKWISE FROM BELOW:
Woman and child; Iwalani tied to Ukrainian fishing vessel, "We will follow you to Africa!"; oxcart transportation

Chapter 20

Indian Territory

August/ September 2002
Eastern Indian Ocean

We leave Darwin with fifteen knots of following wind. As the day wears on, the seas became rougher, the winds greater. None of us feel very good. Stewart is no longer eating and is acting very uncomfortable. I am giving him daily injections for pain. I make the decision that if he still hasn't eaten by August 17, two days away, I am going to euthanize him.

The evening of August 16 is still very rough. It takes what little energy I have to get a can of chicken noodle soup open for supper. Because we have gone back to taking labels off cans and writing the contents in indelible marker on the outside, I am surprised when I open the slightly rusted can to see that I had bought *cream* of chicken noodle soup. *'One of us must have made a mistake at the store',* I figure. It looks positively repulsive. It doesn't smell bad, so I stick my finger in for a taste. It tastes slightly metallic, but not bad.

I had just gotten through reading a book called <u>The Galapagos Affair</u>. It went into great detail about the soap opera story of the Floreanna Island inhabitants. The vegetarian dentist, Dr. Ritter, was accidentally poisoned from home canned botulism-tainted chicken soup. I look at the inside of the can again, then at the rust on the outside. It isn't worth the risk. I toss it up the companionway where it flies over the lifelines and lands with a dull smack onto the sea. But what about the small amount I have just tasted? Exactly how toxic is botulism? Surely a lick from the end of my finger won't kill me. Or will it? I go into the pharmacy locker and bring out a bottle of activated charcoal used for poisoning in animals. I shake it up and drink a half-cup of the vile liquid. Then I decide to go out in the cockpit where Phil is spending his watch.

"I hate this. Don't bother with supper," he mumbles to me.

"It's always the first five days of a passage which stink," I respond.

"What the hell happened to your teeth?"

"Huh?"

SPECIAL EDITION | **JULY 31, 2002**

GOVE GAZETTE

STEWART THE CAT SUES FOR DAMAGES

How much would you pay for a cat that could write and communicate in English? This is a question a US jury must decide sometime in the not too distant future.

A U.S. cat, recently visisting Australian waters became the focus of a controversial potential law suit. Stewart P. Wood, a twelve year old tabby, recently released from Australian quarantine, has been the author of "Stewart's Log" on the worldvoyagers.com website. An injection of an antibiotic manufactured by the Bayer Pharmaceutical Company has left him legally blind and with a debilitating neurological condition. Through his spokesperson, Mr. Wood claimed that the veterinarian who gave the injection at the recommended dose should have been current with the American Board of Veterinary Ophthalmologists, who have issued a statement that Baytril not be used in cats due to permanent blindness.

Mr. Wood is sueing the veterinarian for malpractice. Not very surprisingly, the veterinarian, Dr. Amy P. Wood, is also Mr.Wood's owner. "Does this present a conflict?" we asked Dr. Wood. "Not at all." she replied, while onboard Iwalani, their US registered sailboat.

"Stewart is entirely within his rights;" Dr. Wood is considering her own seperate lawsuit against the Bayer company who have still not withdrawn the antibiotic for use in cats. "What I did was wrong, but what Bayer is doing is worse still. The drug should not be approved for use in cats."

When asked why Mr. Wood was waiting until he returned to the US to pursue his lawsuit he replied "Aussie people love their dogs and they love their birds, but they are still some people in their country who would consider a blind cat a good thing."

A spokesperson for Bayer was not available for comment. Already thin and fragile, Mr. Wood may be taking considerable risk in delaying the lawsuit. "It's a risk I've got to take; each day that goes by, closes the curtains further on my eyesight and abilities. The longer I wait, the more my disability becomes apparent-soon I will be reduced to not being able to read, write or even issue any statement at all."

With his world tour on board Iwalani- Mr. Wood had hoped for revenue from a childrens book and the sale of his own "paw" written log book- valued in the thousands, not to mention the potential revenue from television appearances and lecture tours. His disability could be worth millions. How much would you pay for a literate cat?

"I'm pissed" said Mr. Wood,
"Corporate drug companies need
to have some accountability even
if it is 'just a cat' who's the
injured party."

"Your mouth. It's all black. What have you been doing?"

"Oh. I think I may have eaten some botulinum toxin."

"WHAT? We better go back!"

"I'll be fine. I just drank a ton of nasty tasting charcoal to adsorb it. Besides, we have big brother out here if I start dying."

Every day at varying times the Australian authorities fly overhead and check in on channel 16 with all the boats in the far offshore waters of Australia. If the boat doesn't answer back on the radio, they will keep flying over, each time lower and lower, until they practically tear the mast off.

August 17 arrives with little change in the rough weather from the preceding days, except I have a whopper of a headache coupled with double vision. Stewart is still not eating, so I decide to put him to sleep at the end of my noon to four watch. I have been sewing the large bag we will slip his body into, along with the fifty pounds of Australian stones to weight the bag down. The bag is hand painted with Stewart's birth date, August 13, 1990, leaving only his date of death to be filled in. I go down below to complete the task and draw up the injections I will need.

I look over at the two Stews. They are stretched out barely moving in the twin cat beds. Both are comfortably sleeping off the injectable pain meds.

I vomit in the sink. Am I suffering from seasickness or poisoning?

"I can't do it," I cry to Phil. "He's not ready. I can't see which cat to inject. My head hurts."

"You can't schedule death."

"You can't? Lots of people do it. It's sometimes a very hard part of my job."

"Maybe so, but this time it is out of our hands. You've got to let the Big Cheese decide."

I hear crackling on channel 16 of the VHF radio, then a deep male voice fills our cabin, *"Schooner with red sails, schooner with red sails. Come in, please."*

I scream and jump in the air. "Jesus Christ! That's not for us. We don't have red sails, for a moment I thought that was the Big Cheese calling."

"We're not a schooner either. God doesn't make mistakes," Phil says.

"Schooner with red sails, this is Coastal Patrol. Come in please."

"Listen, Coast Patrol, I'm fed up with your annoying harassment. We are an American yacht in International waters and you should just fuck off."

"Wow. That guy's having a bad day."

"Which one?"

A few moments later the plane flies over us. *"Grey yacht with maroon stripe, this is Coastal Patrol."*

"Hey there. How are you guys doing?" I say into the microphone.

"State your vessel's name phonetically and your destination."

"India-whiskey-alpha-lima-alph-november-india, heading for Cocos Keeling. I enjoy having you guys out here. One of our crew is really sick. I was wondering if you could do me a really big favor?"

"We can try."

"Would you be able phone this number and ask Dr. Sherman if the lab results are back?"

"Be happy to, Ilawani. Do you require emergency evacuation?"

"That's Iwalani. No, thank you. It's our cat actually that is sick."

"Stand by one."

"Roger that. I mean, Romeo that."

A few minutes later they fly over again.

"Iwalani, we talked with Dr. Sherman. The results will be e-mailed to your friend in Maine. He should have them soon. We hope your cat gets better."

"Thanks for all your help. We'll talk to you tomorrow."

"Be careful out here. Coastal Patrol, clear with Iwalani."

That night I feel much better. The rough weather finally subsides and Rick e-mails us Stewart's test results. Stewart's thyroid is normal, but his titer for toxoplasmosis is very high, indicating an active infection. Am I responsible for this, since I had fed him a package of Australian raw meat cat food, or was this a reoccurrence of an infection he got in Maine? I decide not to put Stewart to sleep, but to try and lick his infection.

*   *   *

For four days we have no wind and motor along in glassy seas. The air is finally getting clear of the hazy smoke of aboriginal burning in the Northern Territory.

"Do you realize we still haven't gotten halfway around the world," Phil comments at breakfast.

"We should be getting close, though."

"Tomorrow, as a matter of fact."

"Let's celebrate today. It's a perfect day for a party. We can have barbecued spare ribs, potato salad, corn on the cob, blueberry muffins, and for dessert, pecan pie with cold whipped cream," I suggest.

At noontime we shut the engine off. Iwalani coasts for a long time and then stops. The silence and vastness of the ocean feels as if a glass lid has been placed over us.

"HELLO! ANYONE OUT HERE?" Phil screams into the thick air. The words fall a few feet away, muffled by the stillness.

"Since we aren't moving and there are no weather dangers, can I make some gin and tonics?" I ask while setting up the barbecue.

"Sure, what the hell. I don't see why not."

"I'll get on the radio and see if anyone else wants to come over."

"You better not get any response. I have other things in mind after I change the engine oil," Phil says while pulling a new gallon of oil from the lazarette.

I cook and we drink. And then we eat the most scrumptious meal ever eaten at 12°23′S and 115°E. Stewart too, eats all his cat food as well as some spare ribs. We are a thousand miles from Cocos, five hundred miles from Darwin, but just a few hundred miles south of Jakarta, Indonesia. Still, it seems as if we are the only people on Earth. Iwalani is drifting with an unseen current at a half a knot in the right direction. We keep all sail up even though there isn't a breath of wind. Usually in light airs we take all sail down, as there is enough movement in the ocean to make the sails slat around. Not today. Iwalani stands like the proverbial painted ship upon the painted ocean. The three of us lie in the cockpit listening to the only sound for hundreds of miles, the squeak of the mainsheet's wooden block and leather chafing gear wrapped around the boom.

"Can I put my head in your lap?" Phil asks.

"Sure." I lift Stewart up and place him next to us, then maneuver myself on the settee.

"What do you miss most while being out at sea?" Phil asks.

"Oh, I don't know. I miss a lot of things, but I have them stored in my brain and can replay them over, so it's not so bad really."

"Like what?"

"The smell of a bald eagle, the sound of a stable full of horses munching their grain. The sound of snow falling. Dumb stuff," I say.

"Well, besides the boys, I miss walking to get the mail, and the silence of home. If anyone had told me how noisy it was sailing around the world, I never would have believed them. Except for today. And the smells. I didn't know that the middle of the ocean has no smells."

"What smells do you miss?" I ask.

"Castor oil from the fuel in my model airplanes. Christmas trees."

"I can solve one of those." I go down below and bring up one of the pillows I made back in Maine. I had sewn a pouch of balsam fir needles into the center of all of them, which only have to be crumpled to release their odor.

"You're crazy. I had forgotten you did that," Phil says as he takes a long whiffs of the far away scent. Later that night we watch a movie, hooking up the speakers that give us surround sound. The only wind for miles comes from the in and out puffing of the woofer speakers.

*   *   *

After the movie I go out on deck to look around and see lights off in the distance. A small vessel not much bigger than us purposely moves in our direction. "Fishing boat heading our way," I say to Phil.

Phil comes up and takes a look at it through the binoculars. "I don't have a good feeling about them. I am going to do something I have never done before, nor thought I would ever do."

"What's that?" I ask.

"Turn all our lights off. We should take down the sails, then we'll motor with no running lights."

"Our biggest problem is going to be the moon," I say.

"I know. I'll check the oil, you can start the motor."

"Fire in the hole," I call down after Phil says all is O.K below.

Later that night, after one week of calms, the wind starts to pick up. We raise sails, step off the Timor Shelf and are officially in the Indian Ocean.

I have been maintaining regular radio contact with Northern Light, who is sailing down the west coast of Australia hoping to reach Tasmania from the west. We develop a method of playing Scrabble at sea, which keeps both of our minds occupied. While we were in Darwin, Phil and I met several other boats also heading to Cocos, and I try to maintain a regular radio schedule with them, but it is getting difficult, as none of them have left Darwin yet.

The Indonesian fishing boats very quickly become a source of frustration. At night we continue to sail with no lights. If we are spotted, they make a beeline for our boat and try to cross in front of our bow. Made of wood, san pan style, with little metal on board, they make poor returns on radar.

One of the boats in our radio net tells me not to worry; it is an Indonesian custom for a boat to cross in front of the bow of another vessel. The Indonesians believe that the evil spirits will jump off their boat and become established on the other boat. They evidently aren't worried about catching evil spirits with this daredevil maneuver, only in passing them on to us.

At nine o'clock, on the night of the full moon, I see several fishing boats clustered off to the northwest in front of us. Because we are going downwind, and are on a port tack, I have plenty of maneuvering room to the south. I keep a wide distance between us. Even with us "sailing silent," as Phil has termed this new procedure of sailing without lights, a fishing boat manages to see us coming and performs the customary suicide move in front of our bow.

'Fucking lunatics!' I think to myself. 'We must have every bad joo-joo and evil spirit in Indonesia on board Iwalani now.'

The seas soon build to ten feet; the wind is steady at about twenty-five knots. Night and the wind whipped waves become the color of sterling silver.

I see another fishing boat off our starboard bow. Wanting to avoid it completely, I begin nosing Iwalani's bow up into the wind to make a wide arc around the boat. It, too, begins changing its course in order to maintain an imminent collision. Are they trying to protect a net they have set? I can't believe how persistently they make course adjustments in order to try and cross in front of our bow. I continue making corrections but cannot avoid them. I veer Iwalani as far as I can in one direction without jibing and then tighten sails and sheets to head up into the wind in the opposite direction. I get as dizzy as a dog chasing its tail, while I snake Iwalani downwind. For over an hour we play this cat and mouse game, until I finally give in and let them empty their boat of its evil spirits.

As they approach, I realize they are not trying to cross our bow but are trying to come alongside. I quickly cover the radar and cockpit instruments with cushions and our watch blanket. The green glow of the high tech instruments would advertise Iwalani as a ship full of Yankee dollars.

Two men stand in the stern of their boat, the sides of which are festooned with lines of laundry flapping in the breeze. One is holding a spotlight, which he shines all over Iwalani, focusing on our name and hailing port. The airing laundry makes me think these men can't possibly be dangerous. How could people who worry about clean clothes be up to no good? The man standing next to the spotlight holds a long coiled rope with a huge grappling hook on the end. When I see the size of the hook, I realize they may be fishing for sea creatures of a more human variety. I stand transfixed in the cockpit shining a flashlight on our sails, hoping the wooden gaff rig will look anything but high tech and certainly not worth pirating.

"Phil!" I yell down the companionway. "You need to get up here fast!"

A huge wave passes under our stern. As it moves forward, Iwalani's bow rises up like a Lipizzan in battle, her bowsprit poised like a hoof ready to strike. She comes down with a crash. Forty four thousand pounds of boat displaces enough water to send a wave that rains down on the marauders as we fly by them. They realize the enormity of our hull and weight and how, if they get too close, Iwalani will crush them like a paper cup. But they don't give up. They spin around and begin motoring in our wake.

"What's going on?" Phil asks.

"All night I have been avoiding swarms of fishing boats. This one I can't shake. It's not acting like the others. I think they were actually trying to board us."

"Shit. We've got to turn the engine on to outrun them."

The Westerbeke quickly starts, and Phil throws the shifter forward, full speed ahead. While turning the autopilot to standby, he grabs hold of the huge tiller. Iwalani picks up speed as if Phil had cracked her with a whip.

I watch the silver backed waves which usually roll under us, become frozen in mid air. Then they are left behind. We are going faster than the seas.

"Ha, Ha! You assholes," I yell into the wind. "Try to keep up with us now!"

All of a sudden Iwalani starts to stumble like a horse unable to clear a jump. She starts swinging around, trying to push her nose into the wind, faltering, out of control. She is going to broach.

I sit paralyzed with fear. Phil braces both of his legs in the cockpit well as he uses every ounce of strength to regain control of Iwalani. The marauding boat is well behind us, unable to keep up as we careen away at break neck speed. I come to life when I realize the danger we are in. We were going far too fast and are completely out of control. I quickly dive under Phil's legs, into the cockpit well and under the tiller. I push the throttle back to idle. It is just enough to slow us down, so Phil can retake control. Then I shut the engine off.

"Whew! That was scary," Phil says with amazing calm in his voice.

"Lets not do that again. I don't have enough underwear for maneuvers like that!" I gasp.

"We outrun pirates only to sink in the process! I think the only thing that saved us from being boarded were the rough seas," Phil adds.

"I also think not flying the American flag helped. Plus, our name and hailing port; Iwalani doesn't sound American, and Georgetown is a Port in Malaysia."

"We were lucky," Phil says as he turns the autopilot back on. "We must not have picked up too much bad joo-joo after all."

*   *   *

The last few days at sea are rough on us all. The three of us spend most of the time stacked like coins in the cockpit, either trying to rest, or keeping watch for more fishing boats. When the weather got rough, Stewart went downhill. He delicately lapped at canned food, but that was it. Iwalani sailed by islands of flotsam, empty rafts made of bamboo and poles lashed together, and miraculously avoided hitting any of it. Fortunately, the closer we got to Cocos, the less run-ins we had with fishermen wishing to rid their vessels of spiritual waste- or worse.

On day eighteen we arrive at the atoll of Cocos Keeling. We anchor in the required spot off Direction Island and wait for Australian customs to clear us in. Cocos-Keeling is Australia's furthest outpost and once served as a quarantine spot for any biologicals heading for the continent. I dive into the water of this idyllic island as soon as the anchor is down. There are no crocodiles or poisonous jellyfish here.

After showering the salt water off from my swim, I give Stewart a complete physical and am shocked to find his lymph nodes have become the size of walnuts, which is making swallowing food difficult. Convinced he now has lymphoma, I cloak my depression with a wall of thirty veterinary textbooks, piling them around me like a fortress. After customs clears us in, I plan on anaesthetizing Stewart to biopsy a lymph node. I don't want officials arriving while Stew is under anesthesia and have to explain to them what the heck I am doing to my cat.

A dinghy passes by us at full speed, causing Iwalani to rock just enough to topple the smallest book on top of the stack. It falls to the floorboards and lands open to the section on toxoplasmosis. I pick it up and begin reading. This book recommends twice the dose of Clindamycin. It is such a large amount for such a small cat that I have to get the necessary capsule from the human pharmacy box. It seems worth a try and none of us has anything to lose. I grease up the enormous capsule with butter, and then fire it down Stew's throat.

With a loud crash into the side of Iwalani's hull, Australian customs agents arrive at our boat two days later. Phil has just removed another batch of sticky buns from the oven.

A man and a woman take their shoes off, before coming on board to look our paper work over. These are the first officials to obey the unwritten custom of cruising yachts.

"You have no dogs on board?" the woman asks before stepping over Iwalani's lifelines.

"No. Just a cat."

She looks relieved. "That's good. The boat over there has a very big black dog which jumped all over me."

"Sammy?" I ask. "On Cornelia? She wouldn't hurt a fly."

The man answers for her, "Maren is Muslim. It is against Islamic law to touch or come in contact with dogs."

"Oh," I respond. "I didn't know that. I guess there is much I don't know about Islam. I thought women had to cover their heads, too?" I ask looking at her well-tanned face and dark hair.

"No, women have a choice to wear the hijab or not. I choose not."

Despite their having rammed headlong into Iwalani, Phil gives them some sticky buns.

"These are delicious," Maren says. "Did you get these at a bakery?"

Phil and I look at each other and laugh.

"No," I answer. "When you are sailing on a boat like this, you learn that if you want something, most of the time you must make it. My husband actually made these."

"It is not a life I could lead," Maren pauses. "Did you see anything suspic… um, did you have any problems with fishing boats coming here?" She glances over at the male customs agent, who gives her a sharp look.

"Did we ever. I think some of them were definitely doing something other than looking for fish," I exclaim.

"The United States Embassy has just been closed in Jakarta, due to terrorist warnings," the man says shuffling some of his papers. "There are some problems."

"The Australian Coastal Patrol found an Epirb floating five hundred miles east of here," Maren explains.

Phil and I look at each other. That was where the fishing marauders were trying to board us.

"When?" Phil asks.

"A few days ago. You were very lucky," Maren says. "One of ours was not."

"Was the Epirb off an Australian yacht?" I ask.

"We can not tell you any more than that," Maren answers.

"Here," the man says handing me a piece of paper. "These are some of the things you must be aware of while visiting Cocos-Keeling. Because half our population is Muslim, we ask visitors to respect their ways. Mostly it is to avoid wearing bathing suits and shorts on Home Island."

"Yes, we will be respectful. Thank you," I say.

"No, thank you," Maren says. "We have not had such good pastries in a very long time."

*   *   *

Crescent shaped, palm-covered Direction Island arcs around the boats at anchor like a protective arm. A long stretch of white sandy beach curves along the shore. The native Muslim school children come from Home Island a few times a week by small ferry to have swimming lessons, fully clothed. On shore, an open sided hut with corrugated tin roof covers two picnic tables and an assortment of weathered plaques made by visiting yachts with the ship's name and date of arrival. The tin roof serves as a water catchment for laundry water. A phone nailed to a post under the palms takes Australian phone cards, so cheap calls can be made to anywhere in the world.

Phil phones his sons and afterwards decides to phone Nathaniel's guidance counselor, as Nathaniel is even less communicative than usual. While Phil is on the phone, I wander around the island. It is very early and the sun is just starting to make its appearance over the eastern horizon. The coconut palms are so dense in places that they have become thick forests. Ethereal branches arch church-like overhead. Patches of filtered pink light sift down through the fronds as if they were Venetian blinds. Under my feet, the spongy litter is damp and earthy. In the distance the ocean makes its usual racket on the windward beach, destroying the forest solitude.

I come across the local "tip" an inland pit with a steel drum of kerosene so yachties can burn their trash. If we have to, I figure, we could burn Stewart here, and take his ashes with us. But it is now looking like it won't be necessary. He is acting much better on the high dose of Clindamycin, and his lymph nodes have actually halved in size, making the biopsy unnecessary, for the time being.

When I return to the telephone hut, Phil is pacing up and down the beach.

"What's wrong?" I ask.

"Nathaniel's counselor said something was very wrong with Nathaniel. A friend told his parents that Nathaniel was talking about suicide."

"What? Suicide? What should we do? He seemed quiet when he was visiting us. We both thought something was very wrong, but suicide?"

"I just wish he had stayed with us," Phil says while picking up a shell containing a hermit crab.

"I do, too. But wishing for things doesn't help solve anything."

"What can I do? Here we are stuck in the middle of the Indian Ocean," Phil laments.

"Keep the channels open so that he knows we care about him, and he can come live with us whenever he wants," I say. "Don't be like that little crab in your hand and hide deep within your shell. I don't know what else we can do. My previous experiences with suicidal people have never ended well. It's not a condition I can relate to. Life is too short as it is, why would anyone want to make it any shorter?"

*　　*　　*

Four days after being on the really high dose of Clindamycin, Stewart's lymph nodes shrink back to normal size and he becomes ravenous.

"You know, I think Stewart can see!" I yell down to Phil one morning while Stew and I hang clean laundry on the lifelines to dry.

Phil is at the sink washing the clothes and mumbles something back.

"What?" I ask. Stewart looks around at the beach and other boats and his gaze follows a man as he gets in his dinghy. "I still can't hear, you."

"I said, I THINK YOU ARE GOING DEAF!" Phil passes more clothes up to me.

"No kidding. For the last few weeks at sea the ocean has been deafening. I can't hear a thing!" The dinghy heads in our direction. "Company's coming," I call down.

The boat comes along side and a young American man introduces himself. "I am Bernie from Blackbird. I heard your cat was sick and thought you might like some fish for him." Bernie says holding up a plastic sandwich bag.

"That's very nice of you, Bernie. Come on aboard," I reply.

"Is this the famous cat?" he asks bending down to give Stew a pat.

"Yes, his name is Stewart. He really is quite famous. He gets lots of e-mail from people all over the world. Celebrities, politicians, physicians, he converses with them all. "

"How come?"

"He's pretty smart and has a really good view on life."

Stewart is lying with his back against a my sweater and winks at Bernie.

"Have you been snorkeling in the rip?" Bernie asks.

"Not yet," I answer.

"It's great. You'll never see such big fish. One grouper is at least one hundred pounds. Of course I didn't spear gun these fish from the rip," Bernie says holding up the bag again. "That area is protected. I got these near the entrance, but I always get way more than I can use myself. It's like shooting fish in a barrel. Mostly this is grouper, I got a small one only about twelve pounds!" he hands the bag to me.

"Thanks! Stewart will appreciate this."

"There is going to be a potluck dinner on shore tonight. All the yachts are invited."

"What time?"

"Well, everyone usually goes to shore around three every day, or after the ferry takes the schoolchildren back from their swimming lessons. We play musical instruments or whatever, so anytime around then or later. Well it's nice meeting you Stew. I've got to spread the word around about the dinner. I hope you enjoy the fish." Bernie gives Stew a scratch under the chin before getting in his dinghy.

After Bernie leaves, I carry Stew back down below and give him some of the fish, which he piles into with gusto.

"Now that's a nice man, don't you think, Stew? But spear fishing? Not to look a gift horse in the mouth, but he needs to learn the rewards of giving life back to an animal, not from taking it away."

"Sounds like he already has from the sounds of Stewart pigging out," Phil says.

We make lasagna and bring it to shore. After introducing ourselves, we sit at a table next to a man who is using a hand crank sewing machine to repair his jib. "Want some help?" Phil asks.

"No thanks," he replies. "I have a system."

"Has anyone met the people from Sallymander? someone asks.

"No. They stay on board a lot," I answer. "They aren't really anchored either. I snorkeled over their anchor and it's just lying on its side in the sand. As if it was thrown over in a hurry but never set."

"I went over to tell them about the party," Bernie confides. "The wife was down below playing solitaire on a computer."

"Imagine that, sailing around the world and spending the whole time on a computer," one of the Germans snickers.

"Maybe they are spies," someone else says laughing.

"Maybe they have a really great sex life!" Bernie suggests.

The hand crank continues to turn, but the operator definitely has a problem.

"Uh, excuse me. You ran out of bobbin thread about three feet back," Phil says.

"Oh, thanks, I guess I don't have much of a system."

"If you would like, we could sew it with our machine," Phil offers.

"No that's OK. I rather like doing this."

"Did anyone else have problems with pirates on the way here?" Bernie asks.

"Pirates?" Sjany from one of the Dutch boats asks in disbelief.

"Well, fishing boats, technically. But they were insane, coming right up to me in the middle of the night," Bernie says.

"We wouldn't know. We were in bed."

"You don't keep watch?" Bernie asks.

"No, not at night. Our boat, Red Oranda, sails itself."

"How many people here have a person on watch all night?" he wonders. Three quarters raise their hands.

"How many people don't keep running lights on at night?"

Only half raise their hands. "We don't have the battery power," one English couple admits.

"I sailed in the dark coming here after those crazy fisherman appeared," Bernie confesses.

"We did, too!" I add. "How many carry a gun?" I ask. All, but the three of us American boats raise their hands. "Wow, there's a switch for you," I say.

"We hide it. We don't declare it," a man off one of the Dutch boats confesses.

"Would you bring it with you again?" I ask.

"Definitely. I used it once, in the Caribbean. A boat approached us in very rough weather. I fired at them and kept going."

"Did you kill anyone?" one of the Swedes asks.

"We didn't go back to find out, just kept sailing."

"Here comes Tom from Mermaid," Sjany says. We all turn to watch a small dinghy row to shore. "Have you met him?" Sjani asks me while picking up a well-worn shell barely containing a bulging hermit crab. "Mmm, this will be a nice addition to my collection."

"Isn't he on the boat with the Chihuahuas?" I ask.

"That's right. He's Australian. His wife left him at Christmas Island. He's single handing now."

"A very elite club, single handing," Bernie comments.

"G'day," Tom says to everyone while we make introductions.

"Which way is everyone going from here?" the Frenchman asks.

"We are going to Chagos, and then the four of us," one of the Brits remarks while circling his hand indicating the other British boats, "are going as a convoy up the Red Sea to the Mediterranean."

"Whewie, it's going to be a political hot zone," Bernie says.

"It's shorter for us. We are anxious to get home."

"But dangerous," the Frenchman adds. "I would rather take my chances with the Aghullas and bad weather off the Cape of Good Hope than get caught in a potential war zone, with hot blooded Arabs."

"I have a list of all the broadcast frequencies for the weather faxes compiled for the Indian Ocean. If anyone would like a copy," Phil offers. "It should help us with weather around the Aghullas."

"No, thanks," one of the Germans says. "I don't bother with weather reports, since you can't do anything to change it anyways."

"Sure you can!" I exclaim. "You can alter course, or make preparations ahead of time."

"I just take what comes along."

"I still like to know beforehand what's coming. You should see the satellite antenna Phil made. We get incredible real time satellite images! It is the ultimate crow's nest," I gloat.

"How do you interpret them?" one of the British women asks.

"It's not hard. The cloud patterns are pretty distinct. You can usually differentiate fronts, lows and highs with no problem."

"I don't know. I would still need someone to interpret it all for me."

"Which way are you going to South Africa? Down the Mozambique channel or under Madagascar?" Sjani asks Phil.

"We haven't decided yet. Whichever way affords the best chance at really great French territories."

"What is so good about the French territories?" the German asks us.

"They're the best," Phil responds. "Unbelievable pastries, pain au chocolat, high speed internet, good DVD rentals. We learn a lot about a country by renting DVD's. It's the first thing we try to do after we clear in. The larger the deposit the proprietor wants, the more potential for crime and dishonesty we assume there is, and the more careful we become. The best place for DVD's is New Caledonia, the least expensive, and the widest selection. They even had a drive through computerized rental service. All they did was photocopy our driver's license, not a suspicious person there at all!"

"This is crazy!" exclaims the German. "Renting DVD's? You might as well stay at home!"

"Why? We aren't just making this trip so we can photograph ourselves next to natives who we have to pay to dress up in costumes and stick a bone through their nose," I say. "We want to experience all that each country has to offer. The good and the bad. How the average person lives. How they use technology to carry out the day-to-day things in their life. Museums and zoos are nice, but I'll take a grocery store and a hardware store any day over a theme park. Besides, some of the DVD's we watch can't be found at home."

"Uh, hey guys, I hate to interrupt," the Canadian single-hander asks, while waving his hand in the air. "But just what is a DVD?"

"Mon dieu, Alex!" the Frenchman cries. "You've been out here too long!"

*   *   *

The following day we take the dinghy over to Home Island and find the local Internet café, a small hut with a huge satellite hookup. Several Malay teenaged girls are inside enjoying the air conditioning and listening to music. A few are playing solitaire on the computer.

After downloading all our e-mail onto a floppy disc, to be read back at the boat, we find a local restaurant and have lunch. As the only patrons, we are treated to a feast of fish delicacies whose names I can not pronounce, cooked Malay fashion with exotic spices and flavors. Then we take the free ferry over to West Island, the home of the non-Muslim Australian inhabitants.

I figure a tour of the airport might cheer Phil up, so we hop on the local bus to town. We wander around the tiny airport admiring the huge runway. A man is playing golf along the tarmac. When a loud siren blares, he jumps into a jeep and drives back to the street. A few minutes later a large British C-3 transport plane lands. Several men in military uniform exit the airplane running at full speed towards the small airport building. We follow them inside, hoping to ask them questions about Chagos and any news they might have about President Bush's ambitions to wage war on Iraq, but they disappear into the men's room where they remain for quite some time.

Giving up on them, we walk back to the ferry landing. On the way, we stop at a hidden beach. We find only a few shells, but there are mountains of bleached coral as fragile as porcelain figurines.

When we get back to the boat, I bring the plastic modeling clay out of storage. Stewart curls up next to me while Phil reads our e-mail.

"What are you creating now?" he asks.

"Hermit crab advanced modular prototype housing, HCAMOPH. Want to help?"

"No, thanks."

"Somehow we have to figure out a way to get school children to do this.

270

The plastic shells should be able to float to islands, so hermit crabs can move in. There's too much competition between humans and crabs for shells."

"It's too bad they can't live in flip-flops," Phil grumbles.

"Uh, oh, what are you reading? You don't sound good," I say.

"I finally got up the nerve to read the rest of the e-mail. It's the usual from my ex-wife, blaming me for all that is wrong in America and all that is wrong with the boys."

"I suppose you are responsible for the scarcity of shells too."

"No, just global warming."

I fart. "Better blame that one on me."

"Jesus, Honey, you are disgusting."

Stewart too, gives me a dirty look and tries to move away.

"Boy, I never knew I was living with such sissy-boys," I say grabbing Stew and giving him a big juicy kiss. "Isn't that why you love me?"

Chapter 21

Spits and Spray

September/ October 2002
Cocos-Keeling to Mauritius

"I am not so sure you should write all this," Phil says, while reading over my latest worldvoyagers.com log, which is several days overdue to be posted on the Internet.

"I am sure I will hate myself years from now when I go back and read some of the stuff I wrote, but you said the logs had to be about our thoughts and feelings at the moment. If we edit them too much they won't be realistic and we will be like all the other accounts written by cruisers—sundowners in the cockpit, free trade agreements between wonderful natives, snorkeling, blah, blah..."

"I know, but bashing the U.S. isn't really relative to what we are doing."

"I am not bashing the U.S. I am bashing President Bush. I see why Americans are hated now. I always thought it was because people were jealous for all that we have. I had no idea we were hated because we tell others how they should live, hog all the resources on the planet for ourselves, and give so little to others. I thought America gave more aid to the rest of the world than all the other countries combined. But when I see signs in developing countries thanking everyone but us for the schools, libraries, hospitals, computer centers, it makes me feel odd. Where are the signs thanking Americans? I know individual people are extremely generous in our country, but is any money making it to places where it is needed or is something else happening to it?"

"What about the memorial in New Caledonia thanking the Americans for saving them from the Japanese in World War II?"

"Military aid! That's just what I mean. It's thanking us for killing off a bunch of people. I am sure Bush is going to start a war in Iraq. It is such a waste! Think of all the resources that get used up to raise a person to the age of twenty-one! All the trees that are consumed, pesticides applied, rivers and waterways fouled, oil burnt up, carbon dioxide released in the atmosphere—just to raise one human being. And then Bush just throws that life away! Why? So we can waste more cheap oil from countries containing hot blooded Arabs. And yet, he won't allow frozen embryos to be used to fight diseases of people that have consumed resources to get to adulthood. It doesn't make economical sense."

"Well, other countries aren't without fault too," Phil says.

"That's just my point. Trying to save unborn people is wrong when we can't take care of the people that are already here. I think this is what has been giving me migraines the last few days, worrying about us going to war in Iraq."

"I thought you were worked up over the Indian Ocean and the Agulhas Current?" Phil asks.

"Well, yes, that too. And Stewart. I'd rather leave Saturday than Thursday; it will give him a chance to put on more weight. He seems to be doing so much better now. Besides, it's starting to get interesting around here what with the arrival of the Russian."

"Hard to believe that he built that boat while it was strapped to his balcony in Moscow," Phil says.

"Hard to believe he can fit in it! The boat is only eight feet long and he's no midget. Plus, he sailed it around the Horn."

"It just reinforces the notion that small boats can ride over waves that can snap long ships in half. Iwalani can't be seen by ship's radar most of the time, imagine a tiny boat like that!" Phil says while tapping a pencil on the wood trim.

"I'd still take Iwalani over any other boat out here."

*   *   *

After provisioning, making our sign for the Direction Island hut, repairing the jib, and filling the fuel tanks by jerry jugs, we get back on the high seas highway. The weather is right for leaving, and we are once again behind the rest of the pack. We decide to take the southern route, sailing under Madagascar via Mauritius and Reunion.

For two weeks we sail in a westerly direction, with gray skies and east southeasterly winds of twenty knots. For five minutes of those two weeks, I have to hand steer Iwalani when the autopilot breaks. It is enough of a struggle to make me realize the importance of this small metal tube. Phil straps on his harness and removes the broken autopilot and lashes the back-up arm in its place. Then for the next four hours he disassembles the housing with all of its hundreds of tiny stainless steel balls, greases them all and assembles it back together. It works fine, so he returns it to its base pad on the stern pulpit and puts the new one back in storage. How he accomplishes this repair, from a workstation that is continuously moving, is nothing short of a miracle.

My already foul mood becomes worse with each passing gray day. When the rain comes down in torrents, I improve slightly because thousands of tiny slippery dead flying fish bodies are quickly washed off the decks. Reefing and un-reefing the sail, which we have to do several times a day because of the psychotic winds, is particularly hazardous at night when these miniature banana peels are especially prolific and completely invisible.

Unlike the Pacific Ocean, there are a lot of ships. Most travel between South Africa and Indonesia. Every day we have at least one ship on radar. But by far the worst part of the passage is the fifteen foot cross swell from the South, casually mentioned in one of the cruising guides as "annoying." At least twice a day it slams into Iwalani's side with the force of a small pickup truck driven by a novice high school student. WHAM! The rigging shudders, our teeth rattle, but only twice are we completely

knocked down.

Throughout all this Stewart continues to improve. His foam rubber bed shoots around the salon floor like a pinball, while he lies curled up and sleeping, bouncing off the settee, the table legs, the forward step and finally for extra bonus points, the aft ladder. He eats more than we do, tries to use his litter box, despite the technical difficulties of doing so; often times ending up with "Stew River" flowing down the floorboards. Iwalani developes a malodorous air, comprised of disinfectant, cat piss, stinky wet laundry, stale sponges and rotting flying fish.

The highlight of each day is at five o'clock, when the three of us sit around the nav station while Phil reads the EGC Inmarsat bulletin aloud. He starts with "Team Talk Sat News," which gives headline news from around the world, as well as the weather. The Inmarsat is worth every penny we paid for it.

*   *   *

After averaging 140 miles a day, we finally arrive at the island of Mauritius. I feed Stewart his supper and then try calling on the radio to announce our arrival. After receiving no answer, I trade places with Phil who immediately starts talking to an Indian sounding voice. Port Control tells him that we cannot enter the harbor, as it closed for the night. The radio operator directs us out to the ship's anchorage, where vessels of several hundred feet lie at anchor.

"I just sailed three thousand miles, and you're telling me the port is closed?" Phil says into the microphone in an uncharacteristic outburst.

I think they must have heard the scream that came out of my mouth and echoed for hundreds of miles across the barren hills. A few minutes later the same fellow comes back on the radio telling us we can proceed in with caution. We slowly motor in using the Russian c-map program on the computer, but the data appears to be incorrect.

"It says we are going over land," Phil yells up to me as I slowly steer us in. Rotting heads of cabbage and lettuce float by, along with orange peels and plastic grocery bags.

"Not yet, but I could use some help," I yell down to Phil. "There are so many lights around the city, I can't see the range markers."

"You are way off, that's why. You need to head further to starboard," Phil comes up on deck with our stowed American flag and the Mauritius courtesy flag he made the last few days of the passage. He studies the confusion before us and points. "Head over there."

I change course. "I still don't see them. Are they white, or green, or what?"

"I think that's one on top of the building there," Phil says pointing. "The other is also green and high up the hill. Do you see them now?"

I line the green lights up so that they are on top of each other. "I sure hope you are right," I remark.

"Just go slow. Stay on course," Phil responds while raising the courtesy flag.

An hour later we make it to the head of the harbor. We pass our lines through the railings that encircle the small basin, preventing tourists from falling into the water, just behind the Dutch boat Red Oranda.

Arriving at port, after weeks at sea, is a little like walking into someone's

274

house with a TV blaring when you don't own a TV. Anything that makes noise, flashes lights, or shows vibrant colors, grabs your attention and you have no choice but to stop and stare at the wonder of it all.

Illuminated by the orange glow of many ornate wrought iron lampposts, a brick boardwalk surrounds the waterfront. Many restaurants and shops are just ten feet away from Iwalani. Loud Indian music plays from the Tandoori restaurant, our closest neighbor. Across the basin, tall high-rise hotels stand out like peacock feathers from a Victorian lady's hat. They are all new and modern with ornate, complex architecture.

Beautiful women in saris, holding lightly onto the elbow of their boyfriend or husband, promenade past us. We try to make our way to Red Oranda as they had invited us over for a glass of wine, but we stand transfixed, mesmerized by the glittering gold in the women's saris, the honking horns, the sitars playing, the high pitched female voices singing, the aroma of curry, humanity and street exhaust.

"Hello! Iwalani" Sjani yells to us. "Are you coming over?"

We slowly make our way over to their boat. Sjany and Chris have been married for many years. Sjany is a "petophile" and we share our experiences with humane societies and dachshunds. They made enough money selling their business in the Netherlands to have Red Oranda built. Sjany and Chris raised hydroponic greenhouse-grown vegetables and hatched the idea of putting tropical fish in the warm water to fertilize the plants. The fish part of the business took off, and that was how their boat got its name. Sjany is fluent in several languages, including English. But we mostly liked hanging out with them, ever since our meeting in Cocos, because they, too, are anxious to get home.

"You know Philip," Chris says while taking Phil aside. "We heard rumors that some of the Al Quaeda is here. You should not fly your American flag."

"Have you had any trouble?" I ask.

"No, everyone is friendly," Sjany replies. "But there is no place to do laundry, and the officials seem a bit confused with us. They aren't really set up to deal with us yachts," she hands me a glass of wine. "How is Stewart doing?"

"Better actually. He has put on some weight. Thanks for asking."

"I have something for you," Sjany reaches up and unhooks a decorated tassel hanging from their ceiling, then hands it to me. It has three small beads tied together with macramé string. The bottom bead has smiling cats on it. "It is a Mauritian good luck piece."

"Thank you, Sjany. We need all the good luck we can get."

I look around at Red Oranda. Built in Poland, every part of her is constructed of rugged steel or aluminum, with lots of headroom down below, as both Sjany and Chris are very tall. "Are all Dutch people as tall as you?" I wonder out loud.

"The Dutch are some of the tallest people on Earth," Sjany responds.

"When I think of the Dutch, I think of tulips, canals, windmills, blue delft tiles, chocolate, wooden shoes and fat little boys holding their fingers in dikes!"

"It's funny what you learn sailing around the world," Chris says.

"Everything you think is true turns out to be not quite what you thought," Sjany adds. "We figured Americans were all gunslingers, like you see in the movies. And yet, none of you American boats even carry one gun!"

The following morning we check in with the officials and wander around town in search of a public bathroom. We are now anchored in a harbor with little seawater exchange, so we do not use Iwalani's head and have to rely on the public facilities while we are tied to the quay. I come out of the woman's room but cannot find Phil.

"Phil?" I holler through the men's room door. No answer.

I circle around the small block of shops and head back to Iwalani. He is not on the boat. I see Wendy, a women off the only British boat going to South Africa, sitting on the park bench. Phil and I had nicknamed her "Weepy" behind her back, as she is usually crying whenever we see her. Today is no different.

"Hi, Wendy!" I say sitting next to her. "What's wrong?"

"Its just awful. A man came up and spat on me. He thought I was American. I told him I was British, and he spat again."

"That is awful! But don't take it personally. You just represent the West to him. Uh, you haven't seen Phil anywhere, have you?" I start to worry about the possibility that people here might resort to violence a bit more sinister than just spitting and begin to get nervous about my missing husband.

"No," she sniffles.

"Well, if you see him, tell him to meet me at the boat."

I circle back to the men's room.

"Phil?" No answer.

I look around searching people's faces for an explanation as to why my husband has disappeared. My imagination kicks in and puts all sorts of ideas into my head. My knees start to get weak, and I feel like I am going to throw up. An Indian woman comes out of a shop with a beautiful lace tablecloth in her hand.

"Would you like to see more?"

"It is beautiful," I tell her. "I will come back later to look. Right now I am looking for my husband."

"Is that him?" she points to a Western looking man.

"No."

I wander back to the men's room just as Phil emerges. He has a pained look on his face.

"What happened to you in there? Why didn't you answer me?"

"I thought the toilet was broken because it was missing. Then I discovered that all the stalls are like that. Don't you have the same thing in the women's room?"

It slowly dawns on me what the trouble is. Phil has never been educated on the finer points of Indian style plumbing. Fortunately for me, the ladies room has traditional western appliances, while the men's room does not.

"All I had was a porcelain hole, a bar to hold on to, some toilet paper, but no toilet, and that was it. I got things all coordinated, and then you would holler in to me. It was a disaster."

"How hard would it have been for you to answer me for Christ's sake? You can multi-task enough to at least answer me! I thought you were kidnapped,"

"You worry too much."

We wander around the waterfront looking at the shops selling Louis Viton watches, Ralph Lauren sweaters, Polo shirts, but are unable to find anything that is interesting or worth buying. All we really need are some eggs, cat food and bread.

Shopping in Mauritius is a little like peeling an onion. We have to go through many layers until we finally arrive at the most vibrant part of the shopping districts, the open-air markets. Cars creep along, scooters slip through tiny spaces, and horns honk while we carefully make our way down the rutted street. In some places, the greasy black slime from years and years of car exhaust is as slick as ice. A river of people steadily stream down both sides, while the awning covered produce vendor carts remain frozen to the center, fruit piled in colorful pyramids. Some vendors sell little nervous lovebirds, packed in cages like tiny businessmen in an elevator.

On either side of the median, grocers, shopkeepers and skinny street vendors sell everything you don't need and some things you could do without: plastic world globes, plastic place mats with snow scenes, madras shirts piled three stories high, (which do hide spilled chili sauce when the boat makes an unexpected lurch), hand cranked welding machines, and thousands and thousands of Hindu gods, Buddhas, Jesuses and Pokemons; gold embellished, ceramic effigies of the things we humans worship.

One store is lined with CD's and DVD's just inches away from chickens hanging by their legs and sliced roots of unknown flora. I follow Phil in. Eager patrons crowd around the counter in the back, pointing, arguing and clapping their hands while thumbing through three-ring bound notebooks. When several of them move away, Phil and I take their place. "Pirated software!" Phil says in amazement.

I too, look at the pages of all the greatest software the U.S. has to offer. Microsoft Office 2002, AutoCAD 2002, Adobe Photoshop 7.0, Macromedia Flash, anything and everything that your computer could ever want, is displayed on plastic covered pages for one twentieth the price in the U.S.

"Would you like me to order this for you?" the salesman asks holding up a plastic sleeved edition of Autocad.

"How long does it take to get it?"

"I can have it for you tomorrow."

"I'll have to think about it," Phil tells the man.

We look at the row upon row of pirated DVD's and VCD's, all selling for about two dollars.

I know I cannot bring myself to buy pirated software, but packaged Asian VCD's are an entirely different animal. These are unlike their American original, despite attempts to make them appear from Hollywood. Often recorded from a handheld camera brought into a movie theater, the background sounds, dog collars jangling, chairs squeaking and bizarre English subtitles unrelated to what the actors are saying, oftentimes makes a bad movie more entertaining than the original.

"I don't see how U.S. software businesses stay afloat," I say. "I always thought that pirated software was sold like street drugs, behind the scenes in dark alleyways. I didn't realize you could just go in a store and buy it!"

"Pretty sad, isn't it?" Phil agrees as we hide our recently purchased VCD's of the Indiana Jones movies in the backpack, and rejoin the human stream out in the street.

A few days later we finally find a more Western type grocery store on the outskirts of town. We buy cat food and a chicken not hanging by its legs, but resting comfortably on a Styrofoam bed covered in a clear plastic sheet. As a veterinarian, I sometimes have a hard time eating meat that resembles former patients. Grocery store packaging can be a godsend.

Back at the boat, Phil gets the barbecue going while I take care of Stewart. He had been doing well, until our arrival in Mauritius. Over the past few days he is starting to act like a person with encephalitis. He will raise a paw, almost as if he belonged in the third Reich. Sometimes he will get up out of bed and start walking around with arm outstretched, and then stop mid salute, like he is waiting for further marching orders. I am still giving him the high dose of antibiotic, but I think the high-pitched screeching from the Tandoori restaurant is starting to get to him, as it is to us. What started out as exotic background music has gradually turned into a painful type of hostage torture.

"Bon appétit!" I hear a man say, as Phil grills the chicken.

"Merci," Phil replies. I pause, waiting to see what else will transpire. I know we have just reached the limit of Phil's verbal skills with French.

"You're American!" the man responds with a British accent.

There is a pause and then Phil answers, "Yes."

"Well you are a long way from home. Did you just come from Australia?"

"We arrived a few days ago."

I quietly spoon cat food into the dish while listening in.

"Ah sailing around the world. It has always been my life's goal, but I will be lucky to end up with a small boat to sail around the Indian Ocean. My name is Ian by the way."

"Nice to meet you. I'm Philip. Would you like to come aboard?"

'No, don't!' I think to myself. 'We are inundated with stinky laundry down here, Stewart is doing his Heil Hitler routine while he waits for dinner. My hair is dirty, and the floor is, too. Any other time but now!'

"Can I take a rain check? I am supposed to be home and am running late. How about tomorrow night?"

"Tomorrow my wife and I are going up to Grand Baie. The restaurant music has finally gotten to us," Phil admits.

Ian laughs. "I don't blame you. You are only a few feet from the loudspeakers. Listen, I live very near Grand Baie, actually. Why don't we meet up there? We can have you over for dinner this weekend."

The following morning we make preparations to sail. Several boats have arrived in Mauritius after us and are rafted to our port side. Timing our departure also necessitates the coordination of four other boats.

An Indian man stopped by the boat on the day following our arrival, offering to do our laundry for a few rupees. When doing laundry deals like this, I have learned that it is better to give the laundry person a test batch, sheets, dish towels, etc, to get a feel for the job they will do, and to see if they stick to the agreed upon price. Iwalani isn't going anywhere until he brings our sheets back.

We are busy cleaning the boat down below and have the stereo on full blast in order to drown out the Tandoori competition. I am vaguely aware that someone has stepped on our deck as Iwalani tilts half a degree to starboard, but quickly dismiss it, thinking it is someone probably going across our bow to their boat rafted on the outside.

Phil sits at the nav station reading aloud our e-mail to worldvoyagers.com, while I wash the floorboards. I look up to see a large man wearing black shoes, black pants and a white shirt coming down the companionway, with another man right behind him. Phil looks as startled as I do and quickly turns the stereo off.

"Can I help you?" he asks the intruders.

"I am Special Customs," the man says with a heavy accent. "We are here for roo mahge."

Phil and I look at one another. "Roo What?" I ask.

"Roo mahge."

"Raw meat? I only have a cooked chicken," I respond.

"No! R-U-M-M-A-G-E!"

"Rummage?" Phil asks.

"Yes. We must go through your things," he orders.

"Do you have identification?" Phil asks. The man quickly flashes a gold badge.

"Whatever," I reply. "But I'll warn you now, those green plastic trash bags up forward have really bad smelling laundry in them."

I grab Stewart, hold him in my lap, and nervously sit at the nav station next to Phil, while the two men squeeze forward to "roo mahge." The larger man starts going through the clothes lockers while the second man heads for the canned food lockers. From where I sit I get a good view of what both men are doing.

The first man opens my underwear drawer and begins pulling out panties and bras, examining them like a buyer for an upscale department store checking for sewing flaws. He finds a small pillow under my socks, which I made back in Maine and had stuffed with balsam fir needles. Feeling the needles inside, he pulls out a pocketknife and slits it down the middle.

"Smell it!" I yell up to him. "Those are the "leaves" from a tree that grows where we come from in Maine. It is what our Christmas trees smell like."

Phil kicks my leg under the nav table, but the customs agent ignores me. He opens the locker where I store my shirts, shorts and skirts. Even with much of my clothes dirty and packed in the laundry bag, the locker springs open and clothes burst forth like a stuffed snake jumping out of a joke jar. Early on in the voyage, I abandoned the technique of folding clothes; I also abandoned Phil's technique of rolling clothes into sausage shapes as being too time consuming and impractical. For me, the best method of clothes storage is to just stuff it all into one locker haphazardly. When one particular blouse is desired, the whole mass gets pulled out of the locker then re-stuffed once the desired object is located. This allows for periodic exposure to fresh air and light, and by my lazy reckoning, prevents the growth of mold. Clothes do look a little rumpled early on, but after a few minutes in tropical heat and humidity, wrinkles sometimes give way to a relaxed, casual, creased kind of look.

I am very thankful that just a few weeks before, while we were still in Australia, I came across the plastic baggie of catnip that one of my clients had given me for Stewart. It looked exactly like a plastic baggie of a more illicit variety. Fortunately, I threw it away in Cocos.

"This is weird," I whisper to Phil.

"No kidding. But don't give them a hard time. They are more likely to get bored and leave if we do nothing.".

"But do you see what locker he is heading to next?"

"Yes, we're going to be in trouble," Phil whispers back.

I have learned over the years that most men have peculiarities that are best dealt with through gentle acquiescence. The more fuss that is made, the more angst for everyone involved. A perfect marriage requires a certain amount of give and take, and learning to turn the other cheek, if need be, on occasion, and Phil certainly has to do this on an almost daily basis living with me. But, as perfect as my husband otherwise is, he does have one peculiar streak running through him. He possesses an unrelenting drive and desire to shop for souvenirs in stores with blacked out windows. Most women get jewels, flowers, culinary appliances, or sink faucets for gifts. My husband opts for appliances of a more amorous nature. "Thanks, Honey, that's really great. I know just what to do with it," I'll say. And I do. All these collectables get stored in a plastic bag, waiting the day they will eventually be brought to life. Over eight years of marriage, and two years of cruising, I have amassed quite a collection of "jouets d'amour," from around the world.

All sorts of marriage instruments lie concealed in a white plastic shopping bag just inches away from the customs inspector's knee, directly below the cabinet he is now "roo-mahging" through.

In some countries, especially those with any Muslim population, x-rated magazines, movies or images are hard to find, and, in most cases, possessing them is outright illegal. I am not sure about the laws of Mauritius and whether sex toys count as illicit imports, but I don't want to find out the hard way.

I can imagine the inspector finding the opaque bag, looking inside and then dropping it onto the floor, red-faced and weak-fingered from embarrassment. Before any of us could recover our composure, all the unguents, ointments, oils, beads, batteries and plastic pulsating body parts would tumble out like an X-rated horror movie. Switches would turn on in the process, and all sorts of slithery, snake-like objects would begin vibrating, twitching or writhing over his black-soled shoes.

The only thing protecting all of us from sudden embarrassment, and Phil and me from potential jail time, is the rather large bag of smelly laundry in front of the locker.

"He's picking up the laundry bag," I whisper. "He's undoing it. Oh my. I think he's going to pass out."

At the very top of the bag I had put a few of Stewart's bed pads, which are completely soaked in cat urine.

"That is it," he says coming aft to collect his colleague. "We are done here."

"I am sorry it is such a mess. Would you like to see the engine room? That is where we keep the immigrant families," I tease.

"No that is OK. This is not so bad," he responds laughing slightly. "We take showers after we go on Taiwanese boats."

The two customs officers leave just as the man with our laundry arrives. I come out on deck while he passes the small bag over to me.

"Where are the sheets?" I ask.

"In the bag!" he replies.

I open it expecting only to find the pillowcases, but our entire bed wardrobe is washed, pressed and packed into a tiny bundle, not much bigger than a box of tissues.

"Wow," I exclaim with true admiration. "Nice packing job."

I give him an extra tip and head below. "Look at this," I say to Phil. "I need that guy to pack this entire boat up. He'd be able to fit the entire contents of Iwalani into the dinghy! He did such a good job I am embarrassed to give him our really gross laundry. We'll have to wash it ourselves. Hey, what's wrong?"

"Well, we got over fifty e-mails. Most people are worried about us because you were so late on posting the log, but-…"

"But–what?"

"You got three death threats," Phil says.

"What? Only three? From whom?" I joke.

"It's not funny. They are all American men, mostly in the military. I don't want anything to happen to you. I think you should lay off the political diatribe for a while."

I read the computer over Phil's shoulder and feel a knot harden in my stomach. "Great. If the sea doesn't kill us before we get home, a fellow American will."

*　　*　　*

After jockeying all of the other boats around so Iwalani can leave the dock, we sail to Grand Baie and anchor in creamy turquoise water. We grab our snorkel gear and are out on the reef as soon as the anchor burrows into the sand.

Finally we are free of the screeching Tandoori music. A steady breeze blows across the island giving us plenty of wind driven electricity. Phil volunteers to do the rest of the laundry while I try in vain to bring my dead computer back to life. Later, we find a phone on shore and after several attempts and a not so quick lesson in how many Mauritian rupees are needed to make a local call, we finally reach Ian. We arrange to meet the following day at the yacht club, as he wants to come out for a tour of Iwalani.

The next day, just as night turns to the dove gray of morning, a melodic voice rises out of the waves gently lapping at our hull. Like a dream that slowly materializes into reality, the soft gauze-like shroud of sleep gently peels from our consciousness.

"What is that?" I mumble to Phil. "It is the most beautiful singing I have ever heard. It's putting Pavarotti to shame and that's no easy task"

"The Muslim call to prayer. It is nice. It could make even me get out of bed and become religious."

"Don't you dare! I worship every moment of being able to lie here with you," I whisper.

"Yes, in a bed that's not trying to kill us. Don't worry, I am not going anywhere. Why do you suppose this feels so good?"

"I don't know. But I think this is at the very core of all that humans are seeking. This is what all people are desperate to feel. They try drugs, religion, alcohol, all hoping get this brain chemical released, whatever it is. I think very few people experience love like this. We are just really lucky."

*　　*　　*

Later that morning Phil rows to shore to collect Ian. I make eggs benedict for lunch and have a bottle of Australian chardonnay chilling while I open our last jar of home canned dilly beans.

"Welcome aboard Iwalani!" I say to Ian as he makes his way up the boarding ladder. Phil gives him a quick tour of the boat and the systems, and then we sit down below out of the hot sun for lunch.

"Thank you for inviting me. It is a real treat. This has been my life's goal."

"To eat lunch on Iwalani?" I joke.

"Well, with all due respect, no, to sail around the world."

"Ours too," Phil confesses.

"Has it been everything you had hoped?" Ian asks.

"It is definitely not what we expected. The experiences we have had so far, the things we have found out about ourselves and the planet, they weren't what we thought we would learn," Phil says while pouring the wine.

"Oh, like what?"

"Well, for one thing," I say, "the things environmentalists are squeaking about, what we humans are doing to the environment, are grossly understated."

"Yes, it is very true," Ian agrees. "I am a coral biologist and have just returned from the Seychelles, where there has been a large area of coral bleaching. I am part of a team trying to figure out the reasons why."

"Interesting. What have you come up with?" Phil asks.

"There are probably many factors. In one area of the Seychelles the reef is perfectly healthy. It actually was an area where the water was cloudy. Perhaps this protects the reef," Ian says.

"Isn't turbidity just microorganisms? Wouldn't clear water be an indicator of scant plankton or micronutrients?" Phil asks.

"Maybe. We don't know yet. We are still in the data collecting stages."

"I would think pH and salinity are the most important things. I thought it was a well-established fact that coral doesn't grow where there is fresh water run off. That's how all the atolls formed passes in the first place," I say.

"It may turn out to be a large factor," Ian says while sipping his wine. "Water temperature is also significant, especially with the large scale die off of 1998, when the sea temperature rose to 34°C. Pathogenic bacteria, UV damage, run off from agriculture, even just manhandling can also be factors. Last year we had a massive problem with local fishermen just pounding the reef with heavy pry bars."

"You know Ian, you're on a busman's holiday," I tease. "I have been storing all these questions up for the day when I found the person with the answers. And guess what! You're it! But, if there is anything I can do to help you, please let me know. I'm a vet, and we've been leaving neutered animals in our wake."

"Really? Well we might be able to strike a deal. We have a young male cat that really should be fixed, but my wife doesn't want it to be done because she is worried about the long terms effects."

"No problem. When we come to your house I'll tell her all the reasons why it should be done. There aren't really any reasons not to do it. I'll bring all the instruments and drugs to do a quick- snip-snip," I say cutting the air with my fingers.

282

"It's a deal. What is wrong with your cat?" Ian asks. Stewart has wandered out of his cat bed after hearing the conversations about cats. He stops for a moment under the table, yawns, and then puts his arm forward like he is pointing at something.

"He may have encephalitis from toxoplasmosis."

"Oh my goodness. I won't infect my cats, will I?"

"No."

"My wife is pregnant. Will I make her sick?"

"Toxoplasmosis is the disease that pregnant women have to worry about, but he is not contagious to us. The experts say cats only shed the organism in the early stages of the disease. Eating Stew might be more of a problem."

"Don't worry. I won't put him on the menu," Ian laughs.

"Here Stew, I saved you some fish. I also wonder about the effects we yachts have on coral reefs." I say placing the salmon in Stewart's dish. "Every boat, whether it's a ship or a ten-foot yacht, has antifouling paint on it. Most are ablative, so with every passing millisecond, thousands of toxic particles are being released into the water."

"It is toxic stuff. After just a small exposure, some male species end up with two willies. You could use antifouling paint made from cayenne peppers," Ian says.

"Two willies?" I ask. "Oh, I get it. Yes, cayenne peppers. I have heard of that, but I have never seen it for sale. I am thinking about removing all the bottom paint when we get to South Africa and having the hull sheathed in copper."

"You are?" Phil asks. "That's news to me."

"It would certainly be the best place to do it," Ian responds. "With labor rates being so low there."

"I've also been wondering about spear fishing," I ask. "Many yachts have spear-fishing guns and live a sort of "Rambo of the Reef" lifestyle. Most of them eat the fish, but I think a lot of it ends up in people's freezers and eventually just gets thrown out. Do you think spear fishing makes much of an impact?"

"It certainly does! A good-sized, one-dinner party grouper is about sixty years old! A small, one person, lunch sized parrot fish is about twenty years old."

"And mahi-mahi? How old is a three foot mahi-mahi?"

"They grow pretty fast, actually. That wouldn't be a very old fish."

"I have been dragging a lure for most of the way around the world. It is amazing to me how few fish we catch. I think we have caught more boobies than fish. I just chalked it up to being a lousy fisherwoman. But you know, when we were on the way to Ecuador, I hooked a good-sized mahi-mahi. While I was trying to get the fish onto the boat, another mahi-mahi was circling around and it seemed really agitated. At first, I thought it was a cannibal fish, but now I am not so sure."

"It was no cannibal!" Ian exclaims. "Mahi-mahi mate for life. You hooked either the male or the female and its mate was upset!"

"Great. I don't think I can eat another one knowing that," Phil says. "Even if they do grow fast."

"And Mauritius. Why does it seem to be sort of anti-yacht? It's a bit peculiar since yachts and sailboats have been stopping here for over four hundred years,"

SMOKED SALMON EGG'S BENEDICT

This recipe is a modified version from a restaurant in Sydney. When Phil ordered it, the waitress said it was unavailable because they were out of spinach! After Phil recovered from an attack of the shudders, he said, "That's ok, I can eat it without the spinach!"

INGREDIENTS:

Enough for 2 Americans or 4 French people.

English muffins: 2 cut in half

Juice of 1 lemon

1/4 cup melted butter

Kettle of boiling water

1 package smoked salmon

4 egg yolks (save whites for recipe down the road)

4 large eggs for poaching

-Toast 2 English muffins, spread with a touch of butter, or not, if you are on a diet.

-Lay thin strips of salmon on muffins.

Make hollandaise sauce:
(Iwalani's version has half the butter and twice the lemon juice. It is good with smoked fish)
Boil water first, set kettle aside. Take a small saucepan and using a wire whisk that fits the saucepan, whisk the 4 egg yolks. Turn heat to low. Keep whisking yolks, scraping all the little bits that fit in the nook of the saucepan, for ten seconds or so. Add a bit of boiling water, (a teaspoon or two), egg yolks should start to thicken. Then add juice of 1 lemon, while whisking. (Yes, that's right, ONE lemon, this is not one of those whimpy French sauces)
Add a teaspoon more of boiling water if things look a bit curdly, or too thick. Add the melted butter in a thin stream to the thickened egg yolks, whisking all the time.
I don't usually add salt to hollandaise, I figure the cholesterol will kill you as it is.
Poach the four eggs. This means crack them open (gently) into a pan of boiling water. I like mine done, i.e. no runny yolk, so that's about three minutes of poaching. Fish them out with a slotted spoon and place on top of the salmon fillets.
Cover all with hollandaise sauce. Garnish with a sprinkle of paprika, cayenne pepper or parsley flakes.

I say.

"It's the Indian influence," Ian replies. "In traditional Indian society anyone who has anything to do with the water is from a lower caste—fisherman, boat builders, you yachties. It has only been in recent times that the wealthy Indian population is finding the value of waterfront property. There has been some talk of a marina here, but I think it will be a long time in coming."

"How did you end up here?" Phil asks.

"I am originally from Scotland. I worked as a welder, diving on deep-sea oilrigs in the North Sea. It got a little too hair raising. Then I met my wife. She's a physician originally from Réunion. I decided a saner life was in order, so we settled back here. Where are you heading from here?"

"Réunion. We are leaving on Monday."

"And then where?"

"We have been thinking about stopping at Madagascar, before heading to South Africa. Amy wants to see a ring tailed lemur," Phil says.

"If the political climate allows, I definitely would recommend it."

"What is happening with the Madagascar president?" I ask.

"The opposition has blocked all the roads into the capital, so the president is stuck there, but that should not affect the coastal towns," Ian says.

"What happened?" Phil asks.

"There was some debate about the outcome of the recent election," Ian says while looking at his watch. "Well, I must be off. I have reports to write up. Thank you for the wonderful lunch. I'll be at the yacht club tomorrow around noon."

"Great, we'll be there. Don't give your cat any food for breakfast," I say.

"Right. I'll try to remember that. That will be harder on him than the neutering."

*   *   *

The following day I pack up two bags worth of drugs and instruments.

"I am a bit confused as to why we are getting picked up at noon if we are going for dinner," I say to Phil.

"This is one of those all day events, I guess."

"What about Stewart? We haven't been away from him for longer than a few hours. I sure wish Willy Bolton was here. We need the services of E & J pet sitting."

"We'll leave the light on and give him some extra food."

"Should I turn the VHF radio on too?"

"Why? So he can call out in an emergency?" Phil teases.

"I can take the hand held and call him every once in a while."

"If it will make you feel better, go ahead."

We meet Ian on shore, and he drives us through burning sugar cane fields to his house on the east coast. We cross the island and are well beyond the twenty-mile range for the VHF radio. Stewart will have to do without us for a while.

Ian's wife, a petite Creole woman named Marie, is very pregnant and meets us in their yard. Their bungalow house is situated a few feet from the water.

"Amy is here to neuter Bobby," Ian announces.

"Oh. Why?" she asks.

"Well," I begin, "if he is not neutered, he will grow to be a tom cat. He might start spraying urine in or around your house to mark his territory. Other cats will start doing the same. Conflicts will develop. He will be more apt to fight with cats to defend his territory, which will put him at risk for getting some of the nasty blood born viruses like leukemia and FIV, which is like HIV. He will get more abscess's from fighting…"

"OK, OK, you convinced me. But will it hurt?" she asks.

"I will give him an injectable anaesthetic."

"Which one?"

"Ketamine, a tiny amount of acepromazine, which is a phenothiazine tranquilizer, atropine-"

"And for pain?"

"The ketamine in cats has been found to have analgesic properties. It's more than just a dissociative anesthetic, but, I brought Butorphenol too if he is really uncomfortable. He shouldn't be. I need to use your stove top though to sterilize my instruments in my pressure cooker."

I get everything ready while Marie clasps and unclasps her hands. Within twenty seconds the whole procedure is done.

"Please let me know when you make the incision," she requests.

"She's all done," Ian answers.

"Done?" Marie aks.

"Yes. Look. Here are Bobby's balls," Ian says dangling the two testes for all to see like a pair of baby shoes. "Well done."

I stay in the guest room with Bobby until he is completely awake.

When I emerge, the party is in full swing. For the rest of the afternoon and evening we are fed delicacies prepared by Marie's Indian cook, while I pry information from Ian's marine biologist friends. We don't make it back to the boat until well after midnight.

As we get close I can hear the Inmarsat alarm piercing the quiet night air. "Oh no!" I cry to Phil. "Poor Stewart. That alarm must have driven him crazy."

We climb on board, and I run below to turn the alarm off while Phil takes care of the dinghy.

The sight that greets me nearly makes my heart stop. Stewart is standing on his head, tail in the air, with an electrical cord wrapped around his body and neck. Cat poop is everywhere. He is not moving, but when I pick him up he does his usual chirruping sound.

"Jesus, Stew! What the hell happened?"

I don't know whether to laugh or to cry. So I do both. He is alive, but what did he do to get into such a mess? I look around thinking some person staged this gruesome scenario. Computers, radios and everything else of value are still on board. We rarely ever lock Iwalani, thinking an open door policy is a bigger deterent to thieves than a lock and key. Where did the electrical cord come from? It appears he had somehow gotten tangled up in it and, in the process of getting wound up, became stuck head first in the corner, next to the ice cream machine. Because he no longer has reverse gear, he had no option but to try and somersault out of his predicament. I have no idea how long he had been frozen in that position.

"What the hell happened here?" Phil asks as he comes down below.

"Stewart came unglued. You wouldn't believe the sight I was greeted with when I came down here. You know the movie *Harold and Maude*? Well Stew did an incredible Harold performance, trying to hang himself with an electrical cord. Only I don't think he did it for attention. I think it was lucky we got here when we did."

After cleaning the floor, I give Stew an injection for pain, a warm bath and then bring him to bed with us.

"Do you know what?" I ask Phil.

"What?" he mumbles back.

"Are you asleep?"

"Not anymore."

"I think cats are the highest life forms on the planet. Look at what they have accomplished. They pretty much have humans doing everything for them. They have the finest medical care. They have us build them nice houses, they can hunt if they want, or get fed by us. I really think the Egyptians were on to something when they made them gods."

"Did you look to see why the Inmarsat alarm went off?"

"No. I was too busy taking care of the Stew-god."

Chapter 22

Réunion and Disunion

November 2002
Réunion and Madagascar

After clearing out of Mauritius we head for Réunion, a one-day sail away. We opt for Port Galets on the Northern side of the island. We arrive before the majority of other boats have left Mauritius and tie to a French yacht that looks like it had fused with the quay, a bit like an oversized barnacle. Jacques, an elderly Frenchman is the only person on board. He is recovering from a stroke. On one part of his deck he has been repainting, a few feet away a welding project is underway, and just inches from that parts and pieces of the engine are under repair. He is anxious to get home to his family and France, but he is unsure why.

Our conversations are short and punctuated with lots of pantomime as his English is about as good as our French. He introduces us to a small Belgian man who speaks five languages fluently. Pierre is the quintessential Hercule Poirot and makes arrangements for a rental car company to come the following day so we can acquire a car.

Le Port, the part of the city where we are tied, is in the most industrial section of the island. Jack hammers, turbines and welding machinery serenade us most hours of the day while the orange glow of industrial lighting envelops us at night. The only reminder that we were in an exotic location, and not downtown Detroit, are the tall mist shrouded mountains rising up silently behind the bustling clamor.

"For anyone interested in invading a country, they should first check out how reliable their weather fax broadcasts are," Phil says to me while waiting for a fax to come in.

"Why? What's the matter?" I ask.

"South Africa. Pretoria should have broadcast the fax fifteen minutes ago. When it does come through it's often unreadable. If a government can't send a weather fax on time, how can they possibly coordinate a war?"

I am at the stove stirring a potato water and sugar mixture, Stewart's latest medicine. Since his twisted night on Mauritius, he has started to slide back down the slippery slope. His lymph nodes are getting big again, and he is only interested in eating human baby food. In addition to his other antibiotics, I am adding in a sulfa antibiotic known to make cats drool, and am hoping to avoid the unpleasant side effect, by covering the pill in a heavy candy coating.

"You are like a mad scientist when it comes to that cat."

"Not really. I took an oath to do no harm, and so far I think I have helped him. I am facing the harsh reality though that flying him from South Africa isn't a realistic option."

"I agree. The plane ride will kill him." We both turn to look at him as he sleeps in his cat bed. He is getting thin again.

"Do you want to go to shore for dinner?" Phil asks me.

"I thought you'd never ask, but I haven't seen any nice restaurants nearby."

"We can do what the locals do and try out the food wagons at the edge of the harbor. Who knows? We might get lucky, like we did in Tahiti, and find a really good source of crepes."

"Wouldn't that be nice!"

I change my clothes and follow Phil up the companionway. The sun is setting and casts an orange glow to the west competing with the orange glow from the industrial complex to the east.

We stand together at Iwalani's pin rail surveying the best route across Jacques boat. Saw horses, coils of rope, sheetrock buckets, and a tiny army of tin cans brandishing paint brush swords obscure any clear channel to the rusty ladder up the pier. "Jesus Christ!" Phil whispers to me. "Look at them!"

"I know. I am going to knock every paint can over."

"No! That's not what I mean! The cockroaches!"

I look again at Jacques boat. What I had originally viewed as thousands of rust spots on his deck, are in fact thousands of cockroaches frozen in their tracks, feelers swishing silently, as they stand by, watching us.

"Oh, my god. We're doomed. Iwalani is bound to get infested."

"Can you imagine what they are like down below?"

"No. That's not an image I want to picture."

Phil gingerly steps over Iwalani's bulwark onto Jacques deck. The cockroaches scuttle off to hide under the clutter. I tiptoe behind Phil as he works his way over to the ladder. Quietly we climb up. When we are at the top of the dock we stop whispering.

"We better buy some of those sticky cockroach hotels," Phil says.

"And a gecko. I feel like bugs are crawling all over me," I add.

"They probably are. Up until now we've been really lucky not getting cockroaches on board."

"Well that's about to change. I think Stewart would help if he could see. He used to be the best bug hunter around."

"We can't rely on his skills now."

We arrive at the food wagons and stand in line while reading the menu.

"No crepes I'm afraid."

"I forgot my reading glasses. What is there?" Phil asks.

"Sandwiches on baguettes. Here's one you might like. It's called the Americain; it's got French fries, cheese, and mayonnaise all snoozing inside a baguette roll."

"Yuck."

"Explain to me how French people can eat this and stay so skinny?" I ask looking around at the other patrons, none of them fat.

"What else is there to eat?"

"The U.K, a fried fish sandwich."

"Sounds good to me."

We order two and eat at one of the picnic benches lining the inner harbor, which is undergoing construction for a new marina. After buying some phone cards, we return to the boat.

The following day French officials with only a few words of English at their disposal, attempt to clear us in. With our limited French and a French English dictionary passed back and forth, we are able to get stamped in.

At ten a black Mercedes sedan arrives to take us to the car rental place.

"We're in trouble," I say to Phil.

"No kidding."

We arrive at the luxurious three-story glass fronted building and are ushered into the air-conditioned receptionist office. "Wait one minute and we will be with you," the short-skirted woman says.

Wordlessly, we are ushered into another office where a tall woman in a linen suit sits behind a polished mahogany desk.

"You would like to rent a car?" she asks in flawless English.

"Just a compact car. For five days," I reply.

"Have you got your passports?"

I shuffle through the leather backpack and hand them over.

She opens them both and inspects them with her pince nez. "Licenses?"

Phil and I both reach for our wallets and hand her our Maine driver's licenses. She looks at them both, flipping them over and over, in her well-manicured hands like our licenses are multi-faceted. "These are drivers licenses?"

"Yes. From Maine."

"Where is Maine?"

"It's a state in the United States."

"Nowhere on these does it say when they were issued."

"They have an expiration date."

"Yes but they do not say how long you have been driving."

"Most people in the U.S. start driving when they are sixteen. We have been driving a very long time. What's more we drive on the right side of the road, like you, not like the British."

"You do? I am sorry, but we cannot rent you a car. You must have an international driver's license. These are not acceptable; our insurance will not allow it."

"No problem. Thanks for the ride here."

Dejectedly, we walk back to the boat. "Too bad Fifi and Lars can't row over and pick us up," Phil laments as we look out at Iwalani, a stone's throw across the small basin. We will have to walk several miles around the harbor to get back to her.

"Too bad is right. Say, I've been thinking."

"Oh great," Phil says. "Now what?"

"Since we won't be flying Stewart back, what would you say to using the money instead to fly the boys to meet us in South Africa for Christmas? We can go on safari," I suggest. "Seeing Nathaniel will no doubt cheer up Stewart."

I am sensing that not knowing how Nathaniel is doing weighs heavily on Phil, though we have not been talking about it. Ever since he had been in touch with Nathaniel's guidance counselor by e-mail, the only result has been an increasing torrent of hate mail from Phil's ex-wife.

"That would be too good to be true. But first we have to get to South Africa, which is going to be tricky with no reliable weather faxes. Do you have the French-English dictionary with you?"

"Sure. I don't leave home without it. Why?" I ask.

"I am going to go into the Meteo station and see if they have any better weather fax frequencies broadcast from here."

"This ought to be entertaining."

The Meteo station looks like a blue capped salt shaker sitting on a vast green tablecloth of lawn. Phil knocks on the heavy metal door. We can hear a voice three floors up yelling down to us in French. "Did you catch that?" I ask.

"I think I caught 'entre' in there somewhere."

"So long as it wasn't pas de entre…"

Phil slowly opens the door and calls up, "Nous sommes Américains."

"Hey, not bad," I compliment him.

"You may think I am a moron, but I can learn."

A thin man clatters down the spiral metal staircase like a golf ball down a curved drainpipe. "Bonjour!" he exclaims.

"Bonjour!" we exclaim back.

"Parlez vous Anglais?" I ask.

"Non!" he shakes his head.

The three of us stand staring at one another. "It's all yours," I say to Phil.

"How do you say we are on a sail boat?"

I tell him.

"How do you say, we are wondering if Réunion puts out any weather faxes?"

"Sorry, but that's beyond my eighth grade French."

Phil makes the sounds of a weather fax and undulates his hands like a Hawaiian hula dancer.

The French meteorologist looks at us both as if we have escaped from a lunatic asylum. Then his eyes light up and he runs back upstairs almost as quickly as he had come down.

"That was weird," Phil says.

"I think he went to get something."

A few seconds later he clatters back down the stairs holding a sheet of paper. It is a weather fax.

"Oui," Phil says nodding vigorously at the paper. "Look up how to say schedule and frequency."

"They're not in the dictionary."

"Ah , oui, cinq heurs" the man says.

"Five o'clock?"

"Oui."

"I think we are reaching a roadblock," I admit.

"Does he want me to come back at five?" Phil asks.

"I'm not sure."

We thank the meteorologist and head back to the boat. "I'll come back at five o'clock with my book on weather fax frequencies and see if that means anything to him," Phil suggests.

We meet Pierre on our way back to the boat. "Where is your car?" he asks with a worried look on his face.

We explain to him what happened. "Mon dieu! This will not do. Quickly, follow me and I will take you to where I got my car."

"That's very nice of you Pierre. How can we repay you?" Phil asks.

"You must do the same to any Belgian cruiser who comes to America!"

"That's a deal," I say.

We drive to a much humbler establishment on the main street. The owner, a rather corpulent fellow is also reluctant to rent to us, but Pierre comes to our rescue.

"This is ridiculous! These Americans have sailed their boat more than half way around the world. I will personally vouch for their skills in a car!"

Reluctantly, the rental agent opens a drawer and removes the necessary forms for us to fill out. Within a half hour we are led out back to a small car lot. In the corner, a dejected Renault cowers like a beaten puppy.

"That?" Pierre exclaims. "I would not let my mother-in-law drive that! It is an embarrassment to my fine American friends."

"No, it is perfect!" I cry clapping my hands together.

"Really? Well I am afraid all my best cars have been rented out."

"This is fine," Phil says. "Really."

Phil and I climb in. We agreed that he would be the driver as I am used to driving in Australia, on the left hand side of the road and would be more likely to get us killed. I open up the passenger side, scraping my knuckles on the rusted jagged edges of the door jam as I throw my backpack into the rear seat. I get into the passenger seat and try to find a seatbelt. The next thing I know I am lying on my back as if in a dentist's chair, with my legs up in the air.

"Oh, madame, I am terribly sorry. I just need to make a small adjustment."

I look over at Phil who is trying to stifle his laughter.

"What happened?" I ask.

"The seat isn't bolted down."

I get back out of the car while the rental agent goes in search of a toolbox. Within a few minutes we are back in business and heading out onto the road.

"Look out!" I scream to Phil as a large truck tries to run us over.

"Whoopsie! I'm used to looking the other way."

"I guess we are even," I say.

"How so?"

"Remember the time I nearly got killed in Fiji, when I stepped into the road with a big truck coming the wrong way?" I ask.

"How can I forget it? I thought you were a goner."

We drive back to the boat and retrieve the Admiralty list of fax frequencies.

"Where to first?" Phil asks.

"I don't know. Lets go exploring. Head up that mountain."

"Oh great, another Amy tour."

After an hour of driving up countless switchbacks, we break through clouds and are near the summit of the mountain behind the harbor. We come to a small parking lot with a snack truck selling pain au chocolat and other French pastries. A hiking trail leads up the mountain.

"Do the French know how to live or what?" Phil asks.

I grab the backpack, and we set off up a steep trail covered with passion flower vines and other plants I don't recognize. We follow the path barely scratched into the side of the mountain.

"You won't see this in the U.S.," Phil says.

"How so?"

"The lawyers wouldn't allow it. We'd have guardrails and all sorts of things keeping people from falling thousands of feet down. Lawyers take all the fun out of life."

"Don't forget the missionaries," I add.

"Yeah, them too."

We walk back to the car and buy the last two pain au chocolat.

Phil turns the car back onto the road and I realize we now have a downhill trip in front of us. "Jesus, I sure hope the brakes work in this car," I say.

"Me too. This must be why they are so particular about renting cars. The drop-offs on this island are incredible."

"What do you suppose those little shrines are for?" I ask. Carved in the rocks along the side of the road, every half mile or so, like little altars, are small vases of flowers, Madonnas, candles or all three together.

"Probably a memorial to a person whose brakes didn't work."

"Great."

We squeal our way down the switchbacks, Phil all the while using the brakes only when absolutely necessary. On our route back to the boat we find a beautiful veterinary clinic where I stop to talk to the vets. I have to speak by cell phone to the husband of the wife on duty, as he is the only one around who understands English. They sell me an injectable form of the antibiotic I am covering in starch and sugar. They all wish us well with Stewart.

We arrive back at the Meteo station at five o'clock, but the meteorologist isn't there and everything is locked up. When we arrive back at the boat, Jacques is excitedly waving a piece of paper at us. "Ici, Américains! Pour vous."

I take the paper from him; it is a printout of the day's fax, hand delivered by the meteorologist.

"How did he know what boat we were on?" I ask Phil.

"Take a look a round. It isn't very hard, we're the only Americans here."

"What are we going to do to repay him? He can't come down here every day with weather faxes!"

The following day Phil shows him the book on fax frequencies, but the meteorologist shakes his head. It appears faxes are no longer broadcast from Reunion. The faxes he delivers to us for the next four days come from France via the telephone.

We have the car for two more days, so we spend the rest of the time circumnavigating the island and driving to remote towns in the interior.

"I think I am going to have biceps like a weight lifter," Phil says while negotiating a particularly hairraising turn. "I am now a firm believer in power steering."

"You're taking it pretty well that Ben and Nathaniel don't want to come to South Africa," I carefully broach the subject, which neither of us wants to talk about.

"Appearances can be deceiving," Phil says flatly.

"I can't imagine not wanting to go on a safari."

"I wonder why it doesn't look like many tourists come this way," Phil says changing the subject.

"You're not supposed to."

"What?"

"It's off limits on the car rental map."

"How long have you known this?"

"About three minutes. I didn't look at the map that closely. Three years ago a cyclone washed out most of the road."

"Great. It's going to be impossible to turn around with these corners and drop offs. Another Amy tour."

"Hey! Have I ever steered us wrong? I'm sure they've fixed it by now."

"I can remember a trip through the desert in the Galapagos in ninety degree heat with a pint of water," Phil says.

"Yes, well, we survived didn't we?"

*   *   *

We leave Réunion before Halloween. My last view is of the "Total" gas docks which we pass without a thought. The winds are light and we motor-sail for the first two days. I use a ceramic pumpkin my sister-in-law had given us to ward off evil spirits at sea. On the third day the winds come out of the northeast at twelve knots, so we finally turn the engine off. Phil's weather satellite shows a large low two days sail south of us.

"Stewart's doing better," Phil says to me as he comes up at four.

"I know. Don't jinx him. I stopped all his oral meds. I think it is helping to make him hungry. I have lost hope that I can cure him though. I have tried every thing Western medicine can offer up, short of brain surgery, and I'm not up for that."

"That makes three of us. What's for supper?"

"Szechwan chicken stir fry, rice, fresh fruit salad and brownies for dessert."

"Seen anything interesting while you've been up here?"

"Yea, a large white box the size of a bathtub floated by, and I saw a huge creature I couldn't identify. I almost woke you up, but it swam by so fast and I never saw it again."

"What was it?"

"I'm not sure. It was about thirty feet long, the color of Stew, not dark at all, it had a dorsal fin like a shark that went straight through the water, it didn't swim like a porpoise or whale."

"It must have been a whale shark."

"I don't think so. Remember the one we saw in Maine? That was going slow. This was going really fast. It was only about forty feet away."

"We're supposed to keep an eye out for whales here, because this is their migratory season. Why are you picking your face? It's bleeding."

"I don't know. Nervous, I guess."

"About what?" Phil asks.

"The Agulhas Current, I suppose. I have been having this bad feeling like something really horrible is going to happen."

"You have too active an imagination," Phil assures me. "It kills me to see you do that to yourself. Just wait until we get to Madagascar and you can see your first ring tailed lemur. We can rent a car, go camping if you want."

"That would be nice, but I'm not so sure. Remember when we were at Marie and Ian's house on Mauritius and you mentioned the car rental? They had a queer look on their face."

"I noticed that, too. It's not like we haven't gotten that look before. Remember when we were at Thrumpton Hall and told your relatives that we were going to tour most of England, Scotland and Wales in less than ten days? That was the same kind of look."

"Yea, the, Oh-my-God-these-Americans, kind of look."

Phil unties the mop from the cabin top and begins washing the side decks.

"You're such a housewife," I jest.

"Yea, well Fifi and Lars have become slackers."

"Have you noticed that our speed is down to almost three knots?" I ask.

"There is definitely an adverse current here. We will have to jibe soon. We should probably do it before dark."

"No time like the present," I say. "When someone says reef the mainsail, do it. When you see celery, buy it!"

I remove the running backstay on the port side and wrap it around the shrouds, our method of stowing it when not in use. Then I go forward and unfasten the preventer and walk the line to the pin rail. Phil clicks in the course change into the autopilot and slowly gathers in the mainsail. I pass the preventer on the outside of the pin rail as the sail slowly comes amidships.

As the big heavy mainsail swings around to the other side, I realize we have forgotten to scandalize it. With less sail area exposed to the wind, scandalizing the main makes jibing a smooth operation. As soon as it is amidships, the wind grabs the full belly of sail and slams it hard to port. Phil tried to ease the strain by holding onto the mainsheet but burns most of the skin off his palms in the process.

"What an idiot I am!" he screams.

"No, that's plural. How many times have we done this maneuver and we still screw up? Are you OK?" I ask.

"Don't worry about me! Get the running back."

I run to the pin rail on the starboard side and unwind the starboard backstay from the shroud and refastened it to the windward tackle. "I'll get some ice and burn cream for your hands," I tell Phil.

"Let's hope that was what your bad premonition was."

"I don't think so. I still feel it."

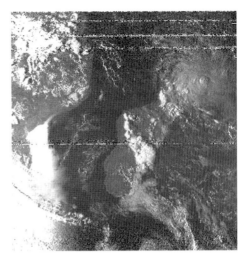

Image of Madagascar from Phil's satellite antenna, with Atang to the north.

* * *

A few days later we round the southern end of Madagascar and make our way up the Mozambique Channel to Tulear. Even though we are a hundred miles offshore, I can smell limes, wet mud, and diesel as a brief shower passes over us. It is overcast, and we are motoring because of light wind. Iwalani is actually going backwards at one point when we are in an adverse current with overfalls.

The weather faxes from South Africa are just barely legible. A tropical disturbance named "Atang" formed to the north, and was the reason for the Inmarsat alarm when we were in Mauritius. We are monitoring it through the South African radio nets: the morning net called Peri Peri, run by a South African named Fred Meyer and the afternoon ham net, run by Alistair Campbell. They assure us that it is very rare for cyclones to form this early in the season. Despite the adverse current and Atang, we continue on to Tulear, Madagascar.

Phil gets a weather fax which shows a front heading our way from the west, due to arrive in 24 hours, with reinforced trade winds after it passes. We predict it will reach us towards the middle of the following day.

That night thunderstorms form all around us, so we take all the sails down. We want to play it safe and not get knocked flat by an errant gust. The following morning we have winds out of the SE at 20-25 knots, as predicted.

"Do you think this is the front?" I ask Phil when he gets up at eight a.m.

"It must be. Did you get another satellite picture?"

"I got two. A good one from Meteor. I've never seen such a sharp leading edge on a front. It's pretty bizarre. You should look at it," I tell him.

"I will, but we need to get the mainsail up."

"I was waiting for you. I didn't want to wake you banging around on deck. Second reef?"

"Yes. We'll put the third reef in before dark."

At noon I wake up and make lunch. It is still overcast, with winds of 25 knots from the SE. I make coffee and store it in a thermos.

Phil heads to bed, but by two o'clock in the afternoon the winds really start to pick up. The wind generator turns itself on, which is never a good sign, as the winds are overriding the magnetic brake.

I go down below to try and shut it off. No luck. I give in and let it make all the electricity it wants and head back on deck. Phil comes up through the companionway. "I think we better put the third reef in now," he says to me.

"Thanks for waking up. I actually think we need to take the main down altogether."

"Don't worry about waking me if it gets bad."

"It's only in the last fifteen minutes the wind has really picked up."

Phil stands on deck. "Christ, it's blowing close to thirty-five knots."

It takes us an hour to get the sail down. We both decide to leave the wind generator on as the alternative is too dangerous. In situations when we have to turn the wind generator off and can't do it with just the switch, Phil will grab a small looped line, hanging off the tail vane, with a boat hook. This is a little like grabbing a loop on a balloon with an oversized crochet hook, a feat which is not easy in heaving seas, with three propeller-like blades spinning madly. Then he hands the boat hook to me. I hold the blades off the wind so they will stop spinning, being careful not to let the wind catch the blades either from the front or worse from the back. Once all is quiet, he shinnies up the wind generator mast and ties one blade to the mast.

"We still have too much sail up. I'm putting a reef in the staysail."

"I think we are still in the adverse current," I respond. "That's why the seas are getting so large."

"The EGC's from this morning said we will have gale force winds in this area. I guess they are right."

"Are you coming down below?" I ask.

"No, I think I better stay in the cockpit," Phil answers. "I need to be here if the autopilot fails for any reason, and to make sure we don't jibe. These seas are pretty steep and I don't want her to broach. I'd like to keep heading for Tulear as long as we can."

We have every hatch and port light completely closed. Because we are making more electricity than we can use, I have every power consuming gadget turned on down below. I can see Phil through the clear lexan of the companionway slide. Every once in a while I hand up mugs of soup, crackers, tea or coffee. I am heating soup in the microwave, not because it is easier, it isn't, as the glass rotating plate tries to kill me each time I open the door and Iwalani rolls or a wave crashes over us. But we need to use up the electricity. We still have an electricity overload and the superfluous power is being turned back into the resistor coils as heat. As a result, it is about ninety degrees down below. I also have the stereo on, hoping Pavarotti can drown out some of the sounds of the screaming rigging and the roaring seas.

We have been watching the movie "Oh Brother Where Art Thou" almost every time we are in port. As a result, we have picked up a hillbilly accent that we have a hard time shaking.

I hand Phil up another mug of tea and he quips, "What'r you tryin' to do? Drown me? As if I aint been havin a hard 'nuff time with the weather."

"How's it goin out there?"

"Juss fine. Now don't you wurry 'bout nuthin'."

"How big'r them waves?" I ask trying to see behind him.

"Well now, we just had an honest thirty footer go by. Keep that slide closed. We don't want none of this here water getting down below."

While we were on our way to the Marquesas, another sailor checking in to our radio net was asked how big the seas were. He replied he had just seen "an honest fourteen footer go by." When we heard that, Phil and I howled with laughter for days, and subsequently all waves in our world, gained "honest" heights.

"What'r you got fer wind?"

"'Bout forty-five knots."

"Is that a real forty-five knots or a Phil Shelton forty-five knots?"

"What do yer think? Don't dally, hurry up with that slide."

Phil always underestimates wind speeds. His main reason for doing this is to counteract all the people who exaggerate. He says it is the only way of maintaining balance in the world. The other reason he does it, though he will deny it, is to keep me from getting anxious. Despite playing Pavarotti at full volume, and despite the fact that we are going with the wind, I can tell from the sounds outside that it is probably blowing a lot harder.

I climb down the ladder and sit at the nav station. Every fifteen minutes I broadcast a securité on channel sixteen announcing our position, heading and speed. We are only moving forward at four knots and I know this is because of the mysterious counter current we picked up, which is also contributing to the tall seas. I am having a hard time not talking in hillbilly speak on the radio.

Stewart walks over to the nav station and meows. I pick him up and hold him while he purrs and sucks on my earlobe. "If it weren't for you Stew, we wouldn't have gotten this far. You've got to hang in there and make it back to Maine. You can beat this infection in your brain. You've got to, Nathaniel needs you too."

Many years ago when Phil was in the middle of his lurid divorce and Nathaniel was showing battle scars of a young child swept up in the maelstrom, we overheard him talking to Stew. It seems that Stew was the only one who really understood him. Oftentimes, Phil and I would use my animals to draw both of his sons into conversation. Stewart, though, had a gift for getting to the meat of any problem, and we have never taken his gifts lightly.

I hang on to him and stand up to check the radar. No other boats at six miles, eight miles, twenty-four miles, thirty-six miles. Stewart's purring is drowning out the storm.

"I hate to intr'upt you two down there," Phil yells through a crack in the companionway slide. "But you don't spose you can mosey into the engine room and open the drain on the muffler?"

"Surely, I can."

"My name's not Shirley."

I put Stewart down on the floor. He walks forward to use the litter box while I latch the engine room door open. One of the toolboxes has decided to eject every tool from its nest. Those that aren't decorating the engine are falling into the bilge. I open the muffler drain and gather all the tools up and lash them into the fixed box. It is hot, smelly and nauseating work. I finish, run up the companionway, and fling open the slide to gather large lungfuls of storm air.

"You OK down there? Did any water come out?" Phil asks, his voice barely audible from the scream of the wind and the roar of the waves rising behind him.

"Your toolbox done come unstowed. I had to gather up all the miscreants and teach them a lesson or two, 'bout how to beehave in a storm. Can't rightly recall if any water done come out the muffler drain. Don't think but a drop, or two. Say, it looks a wee bit nasty out here. Sure you don't want to come down into the cozy little cabin?"

"Naw, it's nuthin but a little drizzle. Don't you wurry none 'bout me."

For the next four hours the winds and seas continue to build. Phil remains outside, taking the brunt of the storm, strapped into his harness, standing or trying to anyways, grasping the hard dodger and staring straight ahead. I stay below, with Stewart on my lap, completely closed off from the fury of the storm. We entertain ourselves by listening to opera, the radio and making our periodic securités. At eight p.m. the Inmarsat alarm goes off. I download the EGCs onto the laptop to read the information. It is just the new position of tropical depression Atang, northeast of the northern tip of Madagascar. It has sustained winds of twenty-five knots.

"Whoop dee do, Stew, what about us? These winds are double that. Think they send off an alarm for us?"

While we are at the nav station, I notice a thin river of water flowing aft from somewhere near the bow. I put Stewart down and head forward to investigate. He just used the litter box, but that is not the source. Water is coming out from under the bathroom door.

Reluctantly, I slowly unlatch the door. Expecting a torrent of cartoon water gushing into the cabin from a broken thru-hull, I am happy to see it is just the toilet overflowing. I had forgotten to close the intake seacock.

At midnight the winds move from the south to a more easterly direction. Iwalani is healed far over to port, with just a reefed staysail. We are no longer in danger of jibing.

"Hows it goin' down there?" Phil yells down through a crack in the companionway.

"Its hot, but I'm not complainin'. Stewart's been asleep on my chest for some time now, just purrin away."

"She's easin' off now. Why don't you go get some sleep?"

"Me? Yur the one that's been up for nye onto one day," I yell up.

"But I'm full o' caffeine. Go get some sleep. I'm doin' fine.

"Well that's might neighborly of yer. I'm plum tuckered out. My heads getting in that painful place, where I don't think straight. I am mighty grateful you are so considerate." For the first time in my life I go to bed without brushing my teeth or flossing.

Just as the eighth bell chimes, I wake up feeling completely refreshed. I hurry aft to replace Phil who appears to be snoozing in the cockpit, though he begs to differ. Phil shuffles forward to get some much-deserved rest. Stewart still wants to be held, so I hold him while I get the weather faxes and listen to the morning radio nets.

By eight a.m. the winds drop off and the sun starts to come out. I take the reef out of the staysail but don't want to wake Phil by putting the mainsail up. Tulear is an hour away but not yet visible. We are in no rush to arrive. Iwalani slowly plods along at two knots.

Stewart cruises around the cabin floor with tail straight up and purr motor in full gear. I fill his dish with French dry cat food, which he digs into with gusto. He looks up at me and meows for more. "Hang on, Stew, when we get the anchor down I will make us all a feast."

Satisfied of my answer, he licks his chops, goes over to his bed and begins grooming himself, a process he usually has little time for.

Phil gets up at nine and heads up to pee over the side. We raise the mainsail and then he lies out in the sunshine while I clean up down below.

"You need to come up here," Phil yells to me. "Bring the binoculars up with you."

I grab the binoculars and come out on deck. I watch as sand dunes and shoreline come into view. We are near the entrance to Tulear, Madagascar. A tall monument marks the starboard side of the channel. It was once monolithic, created of sand, cement, and filigree. But parts of it have disappeared from passing time and storms, leaving only a strange spiral core, not unlike the inside of a broken seashell. Wearing the regal cloak of time, it stands slightly out of place as a harbor marker. It looks more like a monument for a deceased king, world conqueror, or great leader. Thousands of people are standing on the beach, in the shallow water and on the dunes.

"This is why I need the binoculars," Phil says to me. "What are all these people doing? Look at all the ox carts."

"Ox carts? On the beach? Let me look!" He hands the binoculars to me. "Wow, I need to get my telephoto lens."

I go below and grab my camera case from the hook over our forward bunk. As I come aft, Stewart is lying in his bed on his back, legs straight up in the air, a position I have not seen him in for a long time. He has a queer smirk on his face as if he were laughing at some private joke.

"Knock it off, Stew," I say to him. "You'll have to tell me about it later. You won't believe the time capsule we have just entered."

I go back up on deck and shoot roll after roll of film.

"I'm getting hungry," Phil says to me.

"Me, too. I guess I'll go down and make our feast now, as it looks like it will take us another hour to get to the anchorage." I go down below.

Stewart is dead.

Chapter 23

Time Stops

November 2002
Tulear, Madagascar

I lift Stewart's limp body and cradle it in my arms. His lips are still warm. Tears pour from me and fall on his eyes, his fur, his whiskers. How is it possible to love such a small thing so much? I do not need to tell Phil. He knows as soon as he sees my face. Wordlessly, we slowly bring Iwalani about and head back out to sea.

Phil opens the floorboards and brings the Australian rocks out of the bilge. We place them at the bottom of the four-foot bag I had made on our way up the Great Barrier Reef. I start to put his body on top of the rocks, then stop. I know it makes no difference at this point, but it seems too raw, too uncomfortable. I put one of his beds in, a Maine balsam needle pillow, catnip toys, and then nestle him on top, covering him with a blanket.

Phil gets the sail palm and stitches the bag closed. Both of us carry the bag up the companionway. Phil retrieves the varnished mahogany daggerboard from under the dinghy and we stand on the leeward side of our great ship, heaving, sobbing, and holding each other. Iwalani is shuddering, shaking too, as we drift next to the tall monument of Tulear. Thousands of people on shore, with their ox carts frozen in time, stand silent, unmoving, staring at us.

I hold the daggerboard over the side. Phil sets the heavy bag on top and choking back his sobs, can only say three words, "Thank you, Stew." Stewart slides down the board and is swallowed by the sea.

The four of us are now down to three.

A mile long jetty comes out from shore. Two large rusting fishing trawlers are tied to the leeward side, along with three wooden fishing boats from a bygone era. The tide is completely out. Even the sea is drained of tears. There is no room or water, for us and our boat.

Somehow Iwalani chooses a spot in the middle of the vast plain of water, unprotected, exposed, well away from the pier. We anchor and then go below where Phil holds me while we both cry.

"I want to tell you something," Phil says choking back tears. "I always thought an animal was just an animal. I had no idea…"

I am still unable to speak but cling to him tightly. Very few people in life find out that the DNA that winds through all of our nuclei has more similarities than differences as it codes the blueprints and plans for all the species on earth.

*   *   *

We sob and then sleep for what seems like an eternity. I am aware that the anchorage has become very rough. Iwalani is bucking and snorting as the reinforced trade winds blow through the bay.

The Inmarsat alarm starts blaring. Phil gets out of bed to shut it off. "Jesus Christ! We're dragging. You've got to get up, or we'll lose the boat."

"I don't care. I want to die."

"No you don't. Think of Ben and Nathaniel. Think of your family, your work. Think of all you have left to do. Think of me. Think of this boat, she wants to get back, too."

I put my clothes on and drag myself out on deck. "What the hell kind of anchorage is this?"

"We've got another few hundred feet behind us, and then we'll be on top of a wreck," Phil says. "We've got to set the Luke storm anchor." Phil starts the engine and puts it in gear. We are still dragging but not as fast.

"I'll get it," I grumble. I lumber forward and heave the hundred pound pieces out of the anchor locker, then drag them topsides, dropping them with a bang and a crash on the deck, not caring that I am hurting Iwalani in the process. Phil gives me a sharp look but says nothing.

He assembles the anchor while I maneuver Iwalani's bow, with great difficulty, into the wind. I curse us for buying an engine with only 63-horse power; right now we could use one hundred more. Phil gets the anchor down and set but quickly realizes this isn't going to work as the four-foot seas are putting a lot of strain on the ground tackle.

"Can't we use a snubber line?" I ask.

Phil turns his steel blue eyes on me. "Sure go ahead. Do it."

I head forward and look at the bowsprit. Every third wave is burying the bow three feet under water. We are way beyond using a snubber line.

Phil makes a call on channel 16 to see if there is any room alongside the jetty, or if anyone speaks English. The radio seems dead. This is the first place we have been to where channel 16 sits dormant. I can tell he is trying not to cry.

Then, suddenly a woman's voice comes back over the airwaves thick with a Russian accent. "It would please us, for you come alongside our trawler."

"Can you repeat?" he asks.

"Please, come along side our trawler."

I get all the lines and fenders ready. Phil motors us in, both of us praying we will have enough water so we can turn and tie to the trawler port side to. The "chop" in the lee is close to three feet.

"I should have paid more attention to Coast Pilot's description of an uncomfortable anchorage with the afternoon trades. That book is written for ships 150 feet or larger," Phil confesses.

Several men are leaning over the bulwark of the trawler ready to catch our lines as we get close. I heave the bowline as hard and as far as I can, hoping it will arrive somewhere near the man twenty feet above me. He catches it like a trained trapeze artist.

Iwalani fights like a bronco at the thought of being tied alongside a Russian trawler. She bucks and kicks and rams her bowsprit against the steel hull of the behemoth. Nothing happens to the ship, but the railing on our bowsprit fractures.

When we are securely tied alongside, the men disappear. I watch and wait hoping the woman will appear. Her voice over the radio airwaves was like a life ring thrown to a drowning man. Pieces of carbon start to rain down on Iwalani from the trawler's engine exhaust. I go below and make gin and tonics. We have lots of ice left from the excess electricity of the storm. I can't remember when we ate last.

We take our drinks up to the bow where we sit and watch the sunset.

"Remember what you told me about how you thought we are dealt a preordained amount of time on this planet. When your

time is up, that's it. There's nothing anyone can do?" Phil asks rubbing my back.

"Yup," I reply, gulping the cool drink.

"Well, think of it this way. Stewart was meant to die at noon on November 7, 2002. There is a reason for him to die here in Madagascar. Nothing happens without a reason."

"You mean like a recycled soul? He is meant to come back to help the people here?"

"Maybe, if it will help you to deal with it."

"I was hoping to join up again with him in Maine, when he has a new form. Do you remember Stewart and the sauerkraut?"

"Only from what you told me about our first time making it, and how you'd never even smelled it before—and when you did you nearly threw out all sixty pounds! Until you turned around and saw Stewart,standing on his back legs with both paws in the crock, raking it into his mouth. He saved our sauerkraut."

"I know, I was scared to eat it until I saw how much he liked it. I'll never forget one night when I was lying in bed years ago trying to sleep, and I heard this dull 'thump, thump, thump,' coming up the stairs. I couldn't figure out what it was and was a teeny bit frightened, too, so I turned on the light—and it was Stew dragging an uneaten baked potato up into the bedroom for a late night snack."

"He sure was unique."

I choke back tears. "Did you download the EGC to see why the alarm went off?" I ask trying to change the subject and keep my eyes averted from the monument marking Stewart's sea grave.

"Yes. It was an update on tropical depression Atang. It has been upgraded to a cyclone."

"A cyclone? Great. Where is it?"

"About to cross over the northeast coast of Madagascar, then it is supposed to make landfall in Mozambique. I got a satellite picture of it. It's unbelievable. You know the cute little cyclone icon they use on the weather faxes, kind of looks like a kid's flying toy? Well, when you see the satellite picture with the eye and the mass of swirling clouds covering half the picture, it will give you a completely different impression. "

"I'm glad we didn't take the northern route around Madagascar. Most of the American boats are up there now."

"I know. I hope they are alright."

The sun is plunging into the sea directly in front of us. Each time I look to the northwest I see the Tulear entrance monument marking Stewart's grave, and begin crying all over again.

"I'll make pizza for supper. How does that sound?" Phil asks.

"Thanks, it would be nice."

Phil goes down below while I sit on the cabin top watching the sunset. When the sun gets just a few inches above the surface of the water, I watch in amazement at a phenomenon I thought only existed in the reflecting lime from someone's ice cool gin and tonic, the cocktail phenomenon known as the green flash. Like a squeeze of toothpaste, a bright green ray squirts out of the top of the sun. It is no flash, no great heavenly display like the Northern Lights. Nature is reflecting the loss I am feeling—a slow-seeping ooze from a very sad heart.

*   *   *

The following day we have to maneuver Iwalani away from the Russian trawler so their third boat can tie up. We tie to the outside of the new boat and are now the fourth boat from the pier.

We are called into shore to check in. Phil gets the dinghy ready to launch. In the process of maneuvering it, I smash his finger against the cabin top. He lost even more skin from his palms while setting the Luke anchor the day before. As a result his hands are virtually useless, so I row both of us to shore.

When we pass by the wooden fishing boat moored behind Iwalani, several Malagasy fishing men are sitting on the cabin top cooking on an open fire, which they feed with five-foot branches.

"How come they don't burn their boat down?" I ask Phil.

He doesn't answer. When they see a man being rowed by a woman in a dress they all stand up and begin cheering, waving, and laughing at us. I pause for a moment between strokes and wave back to them. "Bonjour, messieurs! Comment ça va?"

Some of them fall over in mock feint, as if they have finally seen everything. I row us to the launching ramp and try to pull the Grape up as far as I can on the slippery surface. The tide is still going out. Construction workers are everywhere, on the pier, driving trucks, moving rocks by hand or with rickety wheelbarrows. Dust blows like brown ribbons, over, under and around all the men. They stop when they see a woman maneuvering a boat.

An official wearing a white uniform comes to greet us. "Hello! Please follow me to the office." We are ushered to a large shipping container. Holes have been cut in the sides for windows. A large desk hunkers at the far end, surrounded by four trembling wooden chairs barely able to support themselves. I start to sit in the worst of the bunch, saving the better chair for the official.

"No, no!" he cries. "Please sit here." He holds out the best of the four for me. "What are you doing in Madagascar?" he asks us.

"We are here for a visit. I want to see a lemur," I reply.

"Lemur?" he asks puzzled.

I take out my sketchpad and draw a picture of a ring-tailed lemur.

"Oh, maquee!" He shakes his head. "That may be hard. It will cost you forty dollars each for visas and about fifty dollars for the port fees, the taxes and departure fees when you leave."

"These lemurs better be worth it," Phil whispers to me.

"How much do we need to pay now?" I ask.

"Eighty dollars."

I look at Phil. He has twenty US dollars and I have ten.

"I will need to row back to the boat." I head back out to Iwalani with the same waves, whoops and catcalls from the male audience. I go below into the head where we store our cash in an empty cold cream container. Before we left, I lined the container with lead and made a false creamy looking inside, so for all intents and purposes it looks, feels and smells like the real thing. We left the US with close to three thousand dollars in cash, stored as fake cold cream. We are now down to two hundred dollars. I take a fifty and row back to the port captain.

He takes our money and puts it in his wallet.

"I am sorry, but the immigration man will not be here until one. You will have to come back later for your visas."

"Can we get a receipt for the money we gave you?" Phil asks.

He gives us a funny look and reluctantly writes out a receipt.

When we return at one, he meets us at the boat ramp with our stamped passports in his hands. "Thank you very much," Phil says when he hands them over.

"What no gift?" the official asks me. "No whiskey? No cigars?"

"They're not good for you," I reply. "I didn't know it was customary to give gifts here. I am sorry. We do not do that where we come from. Do you have a pet cat? Our cat just died and we have lots of cat food we could give you."

The official looks at me as if I was insane.

"You will still need to check in with the Port Captain, who is on the main street," he says. "I must warn you about Tulear. If you leave your boat, you should hire a guard. If you don't, everything on it will be stolen."

"How would we know if the guard is honest?"

"I can arrange for one."

"How much does a guard usually cost?"

"About 30,000 Malagasy francs for 24 hours."

We thank him and then row back to Iwalani. Phil grabs the mop and starts to wipe down our decks from the thick coating of soot belching out of the Russian fishing boat.

"Hello, Americans!" a pretty woman calls down to us from the Russian trawler. "My name is Anna. The owner of our fishing boats, Mr. Vasylyev, would like to take you out to dinner Saturday night. He also wants me to tell you not to worry about your boat. Our men will keep an eye on it. But if you need to go to shore, it is better if you cross over our boats."

Biting a cigarette projecting from the corner of his mouth, a bald man with biceps like hay bales, throws down a rope ladder.

We thank her profusely and tell her it will be an honor to go out to dinner.

"We will meet you on the dock at 6:30 Saturday night," she calls down.

After she leaves, I gather our gear. "Do you think you can do this?' Phil asks me as I begin climbing up the rotting fifteen-foot rope ladder.

"I'm going to have to, there isn't any other choice. If we row to shore our dinghy will be stolen." Once at the top of the ladder I swing myself over the rusted bulwark of the trawler onto the deck. Nets and ropes are strewn about in various stages of repair. I wait for Phil to climb up with the backpack.

Four Russian men, sitting on tree stumps, smoke cigarettes and repair their nets. They immediately jump up and show us how to get to the next boat. We carefully step over the nets and follow in their wake to the far side. One of them picks up a six-inch wide, faded gray plank and lays it across to the bulwark of the next boat.

I look at Phil. "You've got to be kidding."

Despite the fact that the fishing boats are tied together, there is still a twelve foot gap between each of them with heaving frothy seas, churning and crunching twenty feet below the two hulls. Huge tractor tires serve as fenders between the boats, and with each lunge and surge they make a ghastly groan and burp.

One of the Russians jumps up on the narrow plank and casually skips across, cigarette held at his side, as if he were doing a jig down a sidewalk, demonstrating to me how easy it is.

"I'll go first," Phil says as he takes the backpack from me.

"I can do this," I say. "Anna did it. I can do it, despite the fact I am twice her age and about as graceful as a walrus coming out of anesthesia. It's not going to be pretty, so stand back."

I kneel on the end of the plank. I spent an earlier part of my life "tightrope" walking along the top rail of the fence that corralled my horse as a child, but I never was good at it. Planet Earth and my inner ear always seem to be at odds with one another. It was a spinning battle of statiths, otoliths, and other inner ear parts against gravity, with the loser (me) usually ending up festooned in manure.

I decide that the best course of action is to keep low and crawl over like an arthritic inch worm. While watching the energy of the reinforced trade winds frothing in a cauldron twenty feet beneath me, I imagine myself falling and becoming trapped between the two rusty steel-sided, burping death pots, and then fished out with a grappling hook and carted off to a Madagascar hospital with fractures, spinal injuries or bleeding wounds. Instant death seems infinitely preferable.

Once across the plank we navigate over another rope strewn deck to the second obstacle, stepping on a well-worn and shredded tractor tire hanging as a fender on the next boat. The agile acrobat, once atop the tire, merely has to do a hand over hand pirouette onto the next rope ladder, carefully avoiding the wooden steps broken in half, splintered into many fragments or missing all together. Once aboard the final ship it is all downhill, literally! A well-polished gangplank hangs like a sugar shoot and finally deposits my gymnastic adipose tissue in a tourist-togged heap onto the dusty pier.

The Russians on the first boat cheer and clap when they see that I made it. A few, looking despondent, clasp the hands of the cheering section and walk away shaking their heads. "I think I was the source of a small wager," I say.

"Really? Too bad I couldn't have been in on it."

"And how would you have bet?"

"How do you think?"

"Well, I would like you to know that the majority were cheering when I came up from the ground on both legs."

With the ever-present wind whistling at our heels and stirring up clouds of dust, causing us to keep our eyes closed for most of the time, we walk down the jetty and enter the world of Tulear. The further down the pier we go, the faster the years of the last century begin to peel away. We are caught in a sort of time machine and are deposited into another century, in another land far, far, removed from MacDonalds, TV's, Computers and DVD's. The people of Tulear wave and smile as we walk down the road. A few old men straggle from their seated positions on the ground asking for handouts of whisky or cigarettes, neither of which we possess.

Soon we are surrounded by the preferred mode of transportation in Madagascar, the pousse-pousse. Similar to a rickshaw, it is bedecked with ribbons and powered by an athletic two-legged male engine. Since only five percent of the pousse-pousses are in use at any one time, the idle time affords a cleanliness competition between drivers. Pousse-pousses hurry past us, trotting their passengers in reclined comfort to other parts of town. Old Renault taxis, barely wide enough for two adults to sit side by side, vie for their share of road with people, pousse pousses, trucks and ox carts.

Houses, shelters really, consist of sticks woven together and grass for a roof. Small children play with simple toys. A car made from a sardine can has bottle caps for wheels, a land yacht made from sticks has a plastic bag for sails, and cans of various sizes serve as instruments for a one-man band. Children wearing uniforms, their white shirts starched arctic clean, return home from school with workbooks and papers under their arms.

Two foosballs games, set up under a roof are the main afternoon entertainment for small children, the Tulear version of a video arcade at the mall. The little soccer players having long since been be-headed. Kicked randomly by the spinning, carved headless legs, an old golf ball careens wildly about the peeling green playing field.

We are stared at from all sides as we walk down the street. A few small children run up to us. "Stilo, stilo," they cry in unison.

"What gives? Why are they yelling "stealo"? Is this a mass preschooler robbery?" Phil asks.

"No stilo is the French word for pen. Do you have any?"

"If we do, they are in the back pack."

"Lundi," I said to the children, hoping to defray a daily ritual of handouts.

They seem satisfied, nodding their heads and return to their foosball game.

"What did you say to them?"

"I told them we would have pens on Monday."

Two flimsy electrical wires follow the road, but the only sign of electricity is music wafting from a few local watering holes advertising Three Horse Beer on faded cardboard signs. All one needs to open a bar in Tulear is a wattle hut, a plank laid relatively horizontal for the "bar," and a shelf with two or three bottles of liquor.

There is the omnipresent smell of charcoal, as outdoor fires smolder beneath battered pots holding beans, rice and small tidbits of meat. Charcoal is for sale in small pyramids. Real charcoal, not briquettes, is the main method for cooking food. These charred black remnants are the final remains of Madagascar rainforests. Small stands offer grains and meats from unknown body types. The people are friendly, always the first with a smile and a greeting, usually in French. Their colorful clothes are immaculately clean. With little sign of running water, this seems a small miracle. Our own clothes are wrinkled and musty.

Women carry containers of water from the one spigot supporting hundreds of families. Plastic strapping, used to hold together cargo bales, and discarded as trash just about everywhere else in the world, is woven into baskets and carried on top of women's heads; these fragile containers seemingly screwed in place like a cheap wine bottle cap. Other implements, large cans, bales, buckets, or baskets are also carried atop the women's brown hair. Bending down, gliding along, hands always free, these women never spill a drop or kick up a cloud of dust.

Bird song is scarce. It is replaced by the sound of human voices—women singing two, three or more in harmony and children laughing. Content dogs lie in the shade snoring. Cats sit quietly beside the dusty street, washing their front paws clean, while taking in the slow procession of walkers, the soft gentle rhythmic thump-thump of the pousse-pousse drivers feet on dusty ground, ox carts creaking and taxis honking.

We walk with the procession, vaguely aware that we are heading towards something. Some people pass by with bright white T-shirts worn over their regular clothing, a smiling, waving gentleman printed in black ink covers people's chests. I ask a woman in French where we are heading. She answers that the newly elected president is speaking down the road. Phil and I follow at a discreet distance, not sure what kind of reception we are walking into.

Hundreds are gathered, but Phil and I stand apart from the rest, the only foreigners for miles. Loudspeakers play Johnny Cash, which leaves the crowd oddly quiet and vaguely unsettled.

"Gee, I wonder what government backed this president?" I whisper to Phil. "No wonder there is so much controversy."

The president arrives in a Mercedes motorcade. The crowds stand silent as he drives down the street. No waving, no cheering, no jeering. We hang around watching the crowds listen to the speech in Malagasy but get bored after awhile and continue our quest to find ring-tailed lemurs and cash.

We locate a French woman who rents tourist bungalows not far from Tulear, where we exchange some of our American cash for Malagassy francs. She gives us the name of two Italian brothers who might be able to rent us a motorcycle, as there are no car rentals available in Tulear.

The Italians, Mario and Enrico, take our passports as collateral, and we pay the forty thousand Malagassy francs for a twenty four hour rental fee. "Where to?" Phil hollers to me as I cling to his waist.

"I am not so sure about this motorcycle business."

"Hey, you saw me take off down the road on my test drive."

"Yea, Mario said I had nothing to worry about. But it's not you I am worried about."

"Why, what can happen?"

"What if I zig, when you zag, and I cause us to wipe out?"

"Just relax and hang on. Don't worry so much. Where are we going?"

"Mario told me we need to get out of town and follow the river. We need to find trees, which is no small feat, as so much of the forest has been turned to charcoal. He also said Madagascar people eat lemurs. He didn't sound too optimistic about our finding any."

"How do we get out of town?" Phil asks.

"The main road goes straight through town. Not many other options."

"Well this can't be the right way. We are sort of losing the road."

"It looks like we are heading to a college campus."

"We are getting into the poor section of town, if you can believe it." Phil is right. The wattle houses are replaced with nothing more than blue plastic tarps over rickety sticks. More people, animals and pousse-pousses are congealed in the street than the more affluent section. "I think we are going the wrong way. I am going to turn around. What do you think these people do when they have to go to the bathroom?"

Just as Phil turns his head back so I can hear his question, two teenage boys walk in front of us in earnest conversation. They walk to an empty lot, pull their pants down and squat next to a high wall. Still talking, they pull their pants up when they have done their business and walk back in front of us, just as a gust of hot Tulear wind skates across creating a miniature whirlwind.

"It's a good thing it is so dry here. Shit vaporizes to dust pretty quickly. What the hell happens in the rainy season?" I wonder out loud.

"Don't forget this is why we got the watermaker on Iwalani. Yachts are forbidden here when they have cholera outbreaks."

"Go left here."

"Are you sure?"

"No, but it looks promising," I say.

"Didn't you get directions?"

"Sort of. I have a hand drawn vague kind of map."

"I am not so sure an Amy tour is a good idea in this country."

"Trust me. This road looks like it had pavement at one time."

"Don't forget we are going out to dinner tonight with the Russians. We are going to need to take showers."

"No kidding. We'll need lung vacuuming too."

"Now you are sounding like the anal American."

"Just a little worried about what we are inhaling."

We arrive at an intersection with a boulevard. Sod has been laid along the median, but has long since died in the Tulear blast furnace wind and is nothing more than a brown shag carpet. Large gaps in the sod look like empty mortar lines.

"Go right," I say to Phil. "I think this is the main road."

"There's a road block ahead."

Several military trucks are parked a half mile in front of us. Men wearing camouflage uniforms and carrying very large machine guns are stopping traffic.

"Now what do we do?" Phil asks.

"Go with the flow."

When it is our turn, the militia asks for our passports. I tell them in French we gave them to the Italians so we could rent the motorcycle.

The man looks at me as if I were crazy. "Never go anywhere in a foreign country without your passport," he says in perfect English.

I apologize and say we will go back and get them.

"That's going to set us back an hour," Phil says.

We return to the Italians and tell them we need our passports in order to get out of town. Reluctantly they give them back to us. We return again to the checkpoint. Most of the people ahead of us are waved on through. But when we come abreast of the trucks, we are asked to pull over so they can go through our things. I open the backpack containing sandwiches, apples, nuts, two liters of water, our passports, emergency medical equipment, flashlights, duct tape, cameras, matches, rope and the French/English dictionary. Satisfied, he nods his head.

Another man then looks at our passports and wants to know why we are in Tulear and where we are heading. I explain in my best French that we are in search of "maquees" and are tourists off a yacht. I ask him what is going on. He explains that the president is getting ready to fly back to the capitol and they are worried about terrorists. Satisfied that we aren't evil, they finally wave us through.

"Funny, I don't think we look like terrorists," I say to Phil.

"Anyone who looks different is always treated with suspicion. We sure as heck don't look like anyone else here, so people are suspicious of us."

"Don't you wish we brought brown makeup and brown contact eye lenses so we would not stand out so much in some of the places we've been?"

"An invisibility cloak might be better."

We cross over barren hills out of town and then head south on a dirt road toward the river. "You sure this is right?" Phil asks nervously.

"According to my map, we're right where we should be."

We drive for miles on a road made of two parallel strips of concrete. Over the years, the steel rimmed wheels on the oxcarts have carved a furrow down the middle. It is a bit treacherous for motorcycles. We have to drive slowly, and Phil's arms get a work out. His denuded hands are protected by bright yellow rubber dishwashing gloves we had stored on Iwalani. In places, the roadbed is nothing more than boulders and big rocks. Phil doesn't argue with me when I tell him I think it will be safer if I get off and walk in these sections.

After an hour we start to head down hill. Small bits of green are beginning to sprout up in the otherwise brown landscape. Soon we are alongside a verdant river. Crops grow along the shore in organized terraces. Small wattle and daub houses sprout up from the dirt, square and neat, orderly bits of humanity assembled from the chaos of the orange desert earth and twisted sagebrush. A few people sit in doorsteps and wave to us as we pass by. Some people are sleeping under bushes or under empty carts. The houses with no signs of humanity have thorny bushes piled in front of the door to keep the goats out. Even the goats raise their heads, swishing their tails in greeting as we ride by.

We continue on until we get into a more remote area. The fig trees are taller and arch out over the river. A few miles past a convent I make Phil stop so we can have a picnic lunch. This looks like lemur territory.

"Trees. It's nice to have shade for a change," Phil says.

A group of children walk around the corner. They stop and watch as we get our picnic ready. When we have settled onto the riverbank, they walk up to us with hands outstretched. I slice up an apple and divide it among them.

Motorcycle Phil

I ask them in French if they have seen any maquees. They take a bite and run away hollering and squealing.

"I don't think they understood you," Phil says.

"I think we should hide the motorcycle in the bushes and try to hike up a bit into the woods. It's lunchtime so the lemurs have probably been napping in the trees and are waking up wanting a snack."

"How do you know that?" Phil asks.

"Because if I were a lemur, this is where I would live and that's what I'd be doing."

"Not me. I'd be chasing female lemurs around."

"No, you wouldn't. In lemur societies the females are dominant, so they'd be making you bend to their beck and call," I say.

"Doesn't sound too different from life right now."

We wander around the copse, but it's empty. On all sides people are clearing trees, burning them for charcoal and using the arid remaining landscape for goats and Ankole-Zebu crossbreeds—tropical cattle with long horns and big humps bred to tolerate drought, heat and insects.

"So much for seeing a lemur in the wild," Phil says sadly.

"There is no more wild."

"Just wait until we get to Africa!"

We drive back to Iwalani and pay five dollars to have a man on the first fishing boat guard the motorcycle overnight. Then we cross over the Russian trawlers in time to take quick showers on Iwalani.

"How the hell am I supposed to get gussied up for a fancy dinner when I have to cross over the death defying obstacle course?"

"Just don't wear white."

"I'm still in mourning anyway. No problem there," I say.

"You're holding up pretty well, all things considered."

"I try not to think about it."

At six thirty, I slide to the ground in front of Vadjim Vasylyev, the owner of the fishing boats. He is a tall man, tan with brown hair, laughing eyes and movie star handsome. Anna dressed in white slacks, a white shirt and white heels stands next to Vadjim's son, Anatoli.

We introduce ourselves and slip into his Toyota SUV, the largest car in Tulear.

Vadjim can speak some French, a bit more than I can, but we can't understand one another because of our accents. Anna becomes the interpreter for us all, as she is the only one knowing all three languages.

"Mr. Vasylyev asks why you are in Tulear?" Anna asks politely.

"We came to see lemurs in their natural environment."

"Mr. Vasylyev asks any luck?"

"Sadly, no. Too much habitat loss."

We drive to a Greek restaurant on the outskirts of town. The owner Mr. Vaccilly, a large exuberant Greek man, escorts us to a table elaborately set up for our arrival.

"Welcome, my most distinguished guests," he says in excellent English. "Mr. Vasylyev supplies us with our prawns and other delicacies from the deep. He and his friends are always welcome here."

"Thank you very much, this is a great pleasure for us," I say.

"Mr. Vasylyev wants to know how long will you be in Tulear?"

"We are leaving Monday. Cyclone Atang is too close for comfort. We need to get to South Africa. This would not be a good anchorage in a storm," Phil says.

"You needn't worry," Mr. Vaccilly responds. "Cyclones never come down the Mozambique Channel, and none have hit Tulear. Still you are right, it is a bad anchorage. The wreck out there is my boat."

"Your boat?" I ask.

"Yes, I was a sailor, too. I came here twenty years ago from Greece. I lost the boat in a sudden storm. I decided to stay. The boat, I could not salvage. So I started the only Greek restaurant in Tulear."

"Don't you miss Greece?"

"Yes, sometimes, but this is my home now. Excuse me, I will get you some wine."

"How long have you been fishing in these waters?" Phil asks Mr. Vasylyev via Anna.

"We had been fishing in Mozambique. We came here two months ago. That is when the problems began," Anna responds.

"Problems?" Phil asks.

"Yes, trying to find a buyer for the prawns. Our freezers are full. They can remain frozen for three months, and then they are no good. There is much bureaucracy here. Too many people want part of the pie, many forms to fill out and much dealing. The problems with the president and elections do not help."

"Which president was visiting here today? The new one or the old one?"

"The new one. He is backed by your President Bush," Anna replies.

"It must be quite a change from what the Soviets would have allowed ten years ago. Free market, supply and demand, and global economies. Russia certainly has changed," I say to him.

"We are not Russian!" Anna says laughing. "We are Ukrainian. It is a big difference."

"I am sorry. I didn't mean to offend you," I say.

"You didn't. Mr. Vasylyev says he loves how it is now. He was born to be a capitalist. He started out as a very young boy selling fish he had hand caught along the pier near Kiev. It is just the bureaucracies he does not like."

"Bureaucracy is a problem no matter what type of government there is. Give a person authority and watch out," I laugh.

"Are you an anarchist?" Anna asks.

"No. I agree with Mr. Vasylyev. Capitalism and a free market are the way to go."

Mr. Vacilly arrives with our wine, pouring a glass for himself, too. We toast each other while the waitress passes out bowls of Greek salad.

"Mr. Vasylyev had an embarrassing thing happen to him today. Another person thought he was fifty years old. He wants to know how old you think he is," Anna asks me.

I look at him carefully. I am anxious about not starting a new Cold War. I would have guessed 46, but then I think to myself, no better aim lower. But then I don't want to go too low, because then he might think I am just being polite and not up to the task of being truly honest.

"Forty three," I say.

"No, he is forty two," Anna says. "He wants to know how old you are?"

"Ahh," I say sipping my wine. "I honestly can't remember. Tell him it is not the age that is important, but the mileage. And of that, I have a lot. I am a few years older than he is, I think."

Our first course arrives, prawns, caviar, and other shellfish. As we drink more wine, we begin joking with one another over the stereotypes of our respective homelands.

"Vadjim says," Anna is definitely loosening up abandoning the name Mr. Vasylyev, "when he was a teenager, his school took a trip to America, and he could not get over how Americans do things so fast. Even words are shortened, 'thank you' to 'thanks', 'hello' to 'hi', food is eaten quickly, cars drive fast. He thinks you are not typical Americans because you don't have a racing boat."

"No, we are not typical," I say to him. " Our families are though. My sister especially, she is always rushing around, no time to do this, no time to do that. I watch her and think she is like a dog chasing its tail. That is not how I want to live. Life is too short to spend it spinning around in circles."

As the evening wears on, I can tell Anna is getting exhausted with her interpreter role. We invite them to Iwalani the following day for coffee, or lunch, but Vadjim has to leave early for a flight to the capitol of Madagascar. He says he will be back in a few days. We thank them profusely for a lovely night, especially Anna who has to do all the work of translating.

I reach into my backpack and hand Vadjim our last unopened bottle of gin, decorated with a large red bow.

"Too bad we did not have this sooner," he says via Anna.

"No, it is for you. You may need it to get the permits for selling your prawns."

*   *   *

After returning the motorcycle, which had been carefully guarded by the Russians, we head back to Iwalani to get ready for the crossing to Africa. I pull out the eighty-pound sewing machine to put yet another patch on the well-worn stay sail, while Phil sews the South African flag by hand.

"This flag is impossible."

"Do you want some help?" I ask.

"No."

I finish the repair on the staysail, put the sewing machine away, and then go forward to write in my journal. I am really missing Stewart.

"Might as well be single handing," I hear Phil mutter to himself.

"What's the matter now?" I sniffle.

"You could have been changing the engine oil."

"I didn't know it needed it".

"Of course it needs it. It gets changed every one hundred hours."

"How was I supposed to know it was time?" I ask.

"Hello? Don't you live on this boat too?"

"If you want to single hand, fine with me. I've got nothing left to keep me here," I snap.

"Fine."

"Fine." We both sit in silence at opposite ends of the boat. Phil is the first to come up to the bow.

"I'm sorry," he says. "I know leaving here without Stew is going to be hard on you. It's going to be hard on me, too."

Grieve not for me nor the setting sun
Another days journey has not yet begun
The moon will rise the sun will set-
Black hooded oarsmen will always be met.
Life begets death and darkness morn
For each setting son another is born.
Wind whipped waves rage full of despair
Solitary fears perfume the salt air.
A moonchip appears through the round portlight
Brief solace found from the darkness of night.
Gone is the storm that carries life's fears.
Love and its loss fill oceans with tears.
Whispering winds announce days break
Grief and its nets are cast in times wake.
                    -Stewart

"I'm sorry, too. I couldn't leave you or Iwalani. I don't know why I say things just to hurt you. I don't mean them."

"I know. We are both under stress. We've got the mighty Agulhas current still to cross, Atang bouncing around over us, and we both know the superstitions of bad luck when the ship's cat dies. But so far we've had pretty good luck. The Russians, especially, saved us."

"Ukrainians."

"Right. Whatever."

"I'm also worried about money. We are almost out," I announce.

"We've got the credit cards."

"A lot of good that does us here. No one takes credit cards, including the banks. Hell, the banks don't even have Madagascar money. I've never seen a bank that was out of money, much less three banks out of money."

"It's a struggling country, that's for sure. But we've got- hang on a second," Phil says pulling out his wallet. "One hundred and seventy thousand Malagasy francs."

I look at the inch thick stack of very dirty money stapled together into groups of twenty thousand, which we had a very hard time procuring.

"We've got eighty US dollars left after renting the motorcycle," I say. "We need to buy more fuel, pay our exit fees to reclaim our ship's documentation, buy fruit and vegetables for the crossing, and I'd like to ride in a pousse-pousse."

"Fuel is going to be the problem. If we can fill the jerry jugs, that will give us another twelve gallons, beside the fifty gallons in the last tank. That should be plenty to get to South Africa."

The following day we carry the jerry jugs to the end of the pier. For the first time since we arrived, we are not swamped with taxi drivers or pousse-pousse's offering their services. I see a taxi cab cast off to the side of the road next to a bar advertising Three Horse Beer.

The cab driver runs from the bar to the taxi when he spies customers surveying his 1955 vintage Renault. In his exuberance he opens the driver's side door with perhaps a bit too much gusto. It promptly disarticulates from the car at the rusted hinges and lands on the ground with a dull thud while kicking up a small cloud of dust. He looks up with a smile on his face, shrugs, and gingerly puts the door back in place. Future entrances to the cab will be made through the passenger side. When he realizes Phil and I aren't going to fit in the back of the cab with the jerry jugs, he pries open the trunk hatch with care, so it too won't land in the dust.

We agree upon a price of twenty five thousand francs to go to the fuel station, to the tax office and then back to the boat. After much lurching, laughs, waves and pantomimed sign language we are underway for the fuel station.

It takes several attempts to find a gas station that has diesel. I hop out of the car and surreptitiously take photographs of the street life. Phil comes over to me and says we have a problem. His usual infallible grasp of currency and exchange rate has somehow gone awry when we arrived in Madagascar, and he had to start adding, dividing and multiplying with so many zeros. I think the stapled money packets are also throwing him for a loop. The fuel bill is two hundred and fifty thousand; we are short by several thousands.

By now it is 3:30 in the afternoon, and I don't see any way that we can pay the port tax, the fuel bill, and the taxi driver with what we have for currency and time left in the day. Most of the businesses in Tulear are only open from ten to noon, and then again from two until four. Phil decides to stay with the two men who are anxiously hovering around him like pets at dinnertime waiting for their money.

My job is to find more cash. There are no bank machines in Tulear. I grab Phil's wallet, with the small amount of Malagassy money we have left and our remaining eighty U.S. dollars. I have no idea where I am or where the nearest bank is. Two years of ship-board life does not a runner make. I am thankful for all the hiking we did in Réunion as it toughened my legs up. I run and I run, like a fat rat through a timed animal behaviorist's maze, finally finding the town center and a bank. Bingo. The little bell sounds off in my brain, the rat gets its biscuit.

It is now twenty minutes to four. Second in line for the teller, I nervously stand watching the hands on the clock sweep past numbers faster than I can run. Sweat runs off of me in great torrents, making small pools of salty water on the floor. People turn to look at me and then wave me to the front of the line as they think I am obviously a victim of some tropical malady with only hours to live. The teller says she can exchange my American dollars, but she needs my passport. 'I will be right back' I wheeze. She turns to look at the clock and says in French, better wait until tomorrow morning, the bank closes at four. The waves of sympathy really pour forth when I say, "I can't wait until morning", only with my limited French, it comes out as, "I will have no more mornings."

I leave the bank at full speed and, keeping my back to the sun, decide a more direct route to Phil will be through the fruit and veggie market directly in front of me. For some reason the soundtrack to *Chariots of Fire* enters my brain as I run through the market, jumping watermelons, slaloming around mountains of potatoes and nearly coming to a grinding halt when I spy a small mound of lychee fruits in front of me. They are truly delicious and I would love to eat them, but I have no time. Finally, I find Phil standing on the side of the road with a very worried look on his face. He has the passports, fortunately with the ship's papers. So I grab mine and head back through the market. By this time I am beyond being thirsty. My legs are like pulsing bands of sinew and strength, or so I imagine, and I catapult myself forward at hundreds of feet per second.

A man stacking potatoes begins cheering, then another man who is opening bales of Salvation Army clothes and hanging them onto handmade hangers. Soon every merchant joins in, as the strange white woman is making a return trip through the market, running at full speed without a pousse-pousse. Women do not run in Tulear. White women are rarely seen, so a white woman running, is quite a sight indeed. By the time I make it to the bank, I think three quarters of the town is cheering me on. The teller is in disbelief. I am too, as I still have seven minutes left on the clock.

*   *   *

The following day we take a pousse-pousse to town with what is left of our Malagasy currency. The most remarkable thing about riding behind a human powered vehicle is how quiet it is. Throughout all of Tulear, despite the large number of people and the hustle and bustle, the relative decibel level of activity is amazingly low. A person can hear a conversation across the street.

One thing is for certain, our driver is getting a workout for his fare. Other drivers going in the opposite direction call out to our driver saying something in Malagassy, amid much laughter. One doesn't need to understand much of the language to know they are joking about the fat white Americans on board. By the time we reach our agreed upon destination, I give the sweating driver a new T-shirt for a tip, worth more than the entire fare, which he greatly appreciates.

We get our exit visas, buy some fruit and vegetables and walk back to Iwalani. "Are you crying?" Phil asks me.

"No. Maybe. Yes. Could be the Tulear dust in my eyes."

"Or Stewart? Here use my handkerchief."

"Thanks. I can't keep anything from you," I say.

"It's going to be tough going on ahead without him."

"Look! This place takes credit cards," I say trying to forget my grief.

"But what do they sell?" Phil asks.

"Cadeaux, it's a gift shop."

We walk in to a room loaded with wooden carved animals, wooden bowls, little cars made from soda cans, wooden carved boxes with secret compartments, leather bags and beaded jewelry. I could buy the entire place out, but everything is relatively expensive.

"Nothing like spending a little money to make a woman happy," Phil jokes as I walk by him carrying an armload of trinkets for his boys.

I bring them over to the owner. She sorts through everything and makes tallies on a slip of paper. I grab a handful of carved wooden lemurs sitting in a basket on her table. They will make great Christmas tree ornaments. I tell her in French that lemurs are the reason we came to Madagascar, and yet we never saw one.

In perfect English, she tells me to wait a minute, and then disappears behind a curtain to her living quarters. She returns with a ring-tailed lemur sitting on her shoulder. "This is Mascot," she says to us, "He is a pet."

"Do they make good pets?" I ask.

"Oh yes. They are more like house cats than monkeys. They are very sociable.

Mascot is a male, less aggressive than females. It is much better to live with them, than to eat them."

Mascot jumps off her shoulder, poops on the floor and stands staring at us. His ringed tail is erect, resembling a leg off a prisoner's uniform. He seems leery of our skin color but allows me to pat him and hold his hand, which seems more like a koala than a primate.

When we exit the shop a group of children see us and come running up, hands outstretched. "Stilos! Stilos!" they cry. How wonderful to be in a country where the children want gifts of literacy and not money! We hand out pens and paper to very grateful children.

When we get to the end of the street and head on to the pier I start to whistle, the first time I have whistled in several years. Whistling is bad luck on a boat and forbidden on Iwalani.

"I'm glad you finally got to see your lemur," Phil says. "even if it was just a pet, but watch out for that whistling. You may be whistling up the wind."

"Haven't you noticed?" I ask. "We're not choking on clouds of dust. The wind has dropped off. We'll be needing wind now."

"I know. I guess we'll be motoring for awhile."

At the boat, I pack up the gifts in newspapers and foam rubber, stowing them in the bow near the ice cream maker, the area in the boat with the most movement, but the least amount of moisture.

From the descriptions in our Internet logs about our paltry supply of trade goods, our families felt sorry for us and sent us packages of T-shirts, dark glasses and perfume while we were in Australia. I gather together a large package of gifts for every crewmember on both Ukrainian prawn boats, perfume for Anna, a book for Anatoli and Phil's prized possession, a NASA baseball cap for Vadjim.

I crawl up the ladder for the last time and hand things out to the crew. The bald Ukrainian with the biceps like hay bales, rips off his torn, well-worn gray T-shirt and replaces it with one of the Tasmanian devil. Soon the whole crew is bedecked in Tweety Bird, Mickey Mouse, Bugs Bunny, New York Yankees and Red Sox paraphernalia. Vadjim is not back from his dealings at the capitol, but it is time for us to leave, we cannot wait for him to return.

I put together packages for the native fishermen anchored behind us: hooks, lines, shirts, shorts, hats, rope, cloth, empty soda bottles and Ziploc bags. Things that would have been looked at as trash in America have huge value here. They accept everything gratefully. I tell everyone in French, 'thank you for looking after us'.

By American standards, we are now the poorest we have been since starting this trip. Empty hearted, low in provisions, very low in fuel and almost out of cash, we discovered riches far beyond what you can carry in your wallet.

We cast off our lines to the Ukrainians, and amidst loud cheers and waving hands we head back out to sea.

Chapter 24

Thanks and No Thanks

November 2002
Mozambique Channel

For the first two days we motor away from the coast of Madagascar under a blazing hot sun, no clouds and no wind. Atang makes landfall just to our north along the Mozambique coast. She is jammed like a spinning drill bit, unable to punch her way inland, and not wanting to cleave her bond to the sea. Yet, she is still strong enough to steal the wind from our sails.

Our third day out, I sit on the cabin top of Iwalani, my back against the mast, drawing. At times it is the best spot on the boat. The shade provided by the staysail or mainsail, depending on the angle of the sun, and a steady supply of fresh air, keep it cool. We have all sail up yet are making only one knot through the water. I turn the engine off to conserve fuel. We have already gone through twenty-five gallons of diesel, leaving us with thirty-seven gallons on board, five hundred miles to go and the Agulhas Current still in front.

"What are you up to?" Phil asks.

"Working on a design for a solar oven. I figure that if the people of Madagascar used this for cooking, they wouldn't have to cut all the trees for charcoal. It could be made for about twelve dollars."

"You know what I say; if you can think it up, it's already been done," Phil says.

"Maybe, but look. It's collapsible, hexagonal, black sheet metal on the outside, and alternating black and hyper-reflective metal on the inside. With a glass convex dome lid, acting like a giant magnifying glass. Cool huh? It will work anywhere there is sun overhead," I remark.

"You're nuts," Phil says.

"Did you take a look at the satellite image I got? Then you will really think I am nuts."

"Why?"

"The clouds look like a giant cat. There is a big cats paw coming from the south east. It's Stewart. He's pushing us to South Africa."

"I see," Phil says, clearing his throat.

"Look behind us if you don't believe me. Even from this angle the clouds look like a cat," I add.

"Hmm, maybe. If you sort of squint, perhaps a bit." He sits down next to me.

"You might also be interested to know that Iwalani is traveling with a whole school of pet fish," I report while closing my sketchbook.

"What kind of fish? Tuna?"

"No. Far more embarrassing, Sergeant Majors."

"Those are reef fish! I don't believe it!" Phil says.

"Take a look over the side. We are being mistaken for a reef."

"This is really depressing. What I think we need to talk about is fuel management. What are your thoughts on what we should do?"

"I think we are in no imminent danger right now, and we have to save the fuel. I want to have a day's worth of fuel left when we get near the Agulhas, so we can motor into or out of it if we have to. That is why I shut the engine off."

"This drifting is going to drive me crazy."

"This is the way it is supposed to be on a sailboat. We have been the ultimate Americans, consuming fuel to get to places in a hurry," I say.

"If we never used the engine we would still be back in the Pacific trying to reach Australia. You were the one who wanted to be gone three years, and no more. Well, the engine has allowed us to do that," Phil says.

"I know, but now I am feeling guilty," I admit.

"Don't you want to go home and go back to work?"

"Yes and no. I mean I am worried about becoming a space occupying mass. This is a pretty selfish lifestyle. And I do miss work. But this isn't really <u>so</u> boring. I have been able to create stuff. I know it is hard for you, because you make stuff on such an enormous scale."

"Fuckin'-A-Bubba! I can't stand it. I'm ready to get home. A few days in Madagascar has taught me the value of the smallest bottle cap. Living with Stewart has taught me how important it is to live your life to its fullest, never waste a single day. I feel like I am wasting my life out here." Phil pauses while he scans the horizon. "I actually came up here to tell you that you got e-mail from your sister."

"Which one?"

"The one you told Vadjim was like a dog chasing her tail. Whistle's going to meet us in South Africa."

Alistair Campbell at his radio

   *   *   *

For three days the winds blow lightly from Madagascar, and we are able to make forward progress. Phil, with his ham license, converses with Alistair, one of three South African men who every day volunteers his time on one of the radio nets to guide cruisers safely to and around South Africa.

The Agulhas Current whizzes from the Indian Ocean to the Atlantic along the eastern coastline of South Africa. Strongest at the 100-fathom line, it can pick up speeds of six knots. It is probably one of the strongest "rivers" in the world and is known to routinely break up big super tankers. Crossing it is going to be the most dreaded part of our circumnavigation.

We use up the last gallons of fuel in our tanks when we are told a front is coming our way. Getting caught in the Agulhas with a cold front is the worst possible scenario. Frontal passages usually start with twenty-four hours of very strong northeast winds, followed by winds from the southwest blowing twice as hard, which whip up huge waves when they meet the south setting current We are timing our crossing of the Agulhas with the predicted favorable winds. Northeast winds of the first day will be in the same direction as the strong southwest setting current and should keep our passage across relatively calm. We have exactly twenty-four hours to get into Africa before the deadly wind shift to the southwest occurs.

"Hey you know this isn't bad!" Phil exclaims at suppertime. We have eaten our way through all the fresh food on board and are now breaking into the large supply of canned food acquired in the French territories. We are eating canned "Fruits de la Mer Paella."

"Bad? I thought I would be barfing, especially when the little squids fell into the pot," I say licking my fingers.

"How 'bout this? You'd never see this in American canned food," Phil says holding up a chicken bone. "The lawyers would be all over it."

"I see why Stewart was so nutty over French canned food. It's delicious!"

"Speaking of Stew, now it's my turn to be crazy. Did you see the weather fax?" Phil asks.

"Tonight's? No."

"It's weird looking. There is a cat's paw appendage to the Indian Ocean high pushing the cold front that was supposed to hit us further to the south. Even Alistair called it a cat's paw. He says we'll cross the Agulhas in a coastal low, which is safer than a front. The front will hit later, but, we are dead if we aren't in by Saturday morning."

"Is this cat's paw appendage coming from Madagascar?"

"None other," Phil replies.

Fred Meyer of Peri-Peri radio, the other key person who helps yachts get to Africa from the east.

"Good. I'm glad you are becoming just as weird as me," I tease.

"Becoming?"

"So who is this Coco person who came up on the Peri-Peri radio net and said she knew you and was from your home town?" I ask with a tinge of jealousy.

"I have no idea. I've been trying to figure it out. I don't know any Cocos. Which hometown? It's a complete mystery," Phil says licking the last of the canned paella from his spoon. "Tomorrow we will need to pour the jerry jugs into the fuel tanks."

"When I was in the engine room, I heard fuel sloshing around from supposedly empty tanks. The pick up tube is obviously not getting the last drops of diesel. Do you think it would be worth it to manually pump out the tanks?" I ask.

"It might be worth it."

The following day is cloudy, gray, with spits of rain and northeast winds of twenty knots. During my morning watch, we lose radio contact with the South African nets, with no audible relays. By noon we are at the hundred fathom line, the strongest part of the Agulhas. While being tossed around in two-meter seas, we manage to pump out five gallons of fuel from the "empty" tanks. We add this diesel and the fourteen gallons from the jerry jugs to our remaining fuel tank, neither of us spilling a drop. We estimate we have no more than seventeen gallons of usable fuel, which will take us roughly one hundred miles.

By four p.m. the barometer drops to a low of 1013 before it begins to rise. This is an indicator that the winds are due to leave the northeast sector and blow from the south. At five we make the decision to turn the engine on and get well inside the hundred fathom line. By four a.m. Friday, the wind comes out of the south, but even though they are very light, at ten knots, the opposing forces still kick up a heaving sea. With all her inherent luck still present, Iwalani safely gets us across the mighty Agulhas.

*   *   *

By noon time we arrive in Richards Bay and a woman with shoulder length brown hair and doe-like eyes takes our lines and helps to get Iwalani settled into her new stall, the quay at Tuzi Gazi. She is the mysterious Coco from the radio and is the sister of another boat builder from Maine. She hails from our hometown of just a few hundred people, yet we have never met her before.

For the next few months, our stay in South Africa will be restricted to marinas, piers and docks, since anchoring is not allowed. This is going to be the most contact with humans Phil and I will have for a while, and I am not sure I am going to like it.

We rent a brand new little electric green, right hand drive car and begin the process of finding a place that will haul Iwalani so we can repaint the bottom or sheath it in copper. We find a travel lift big enough in Durban and schedule the haul

320

out for over Christmas.

I find a computer place in Richards Bay that will work on my computer, Arnold. It still has one year left on the warranty. I have high hopes for the new "doctor," an Indian, but then I had high hopes for the greasy, long haired "V" drinking geeks in Australia.

We treat ourselves with passes to the game parks and drive our little green car off in search of Africa's big five.

"This is too awesome," Phil says to me as we pass another giraffe. "They wouldn't let people do this at home."

"What do you mean?"

"Letting people loose with their own car in a wild game park."

"It's good, but I thought South Africa would be different."

"How so?" Phil asks.

"I guess I thought giraffes would be everywhere, like deer are at home, or kangaroos in Australia. I didn't realize that, for the most part, all the animals are fenced into these huge reserves. I thought we'd be passing giraffe on the way to the grocery store."

"I think the game parks are more for the animals protection, to prevent people from poaching them. But hippos, if the yellow road signs are any indication, are around loose. And they're supposedly the most dangerous African animal, maybe even worse than the humans!"

"That's it too. Like today when we dropped Arnold off at the computer place. Armed security guards in stores? Having to get buzzed into a store through a two lock system doesn't exactly get you into a spending mood," I reply.

"Well, I have to admit, the amount of razor wire on people's fences and the iron bars on the windows is even worse than Panama."

"And all these security warnings: never drive at night, never drive with the windows open in a city, don't rent fancy SUV's, never stop a car along the side of a road. It's not because of attacks by wild animals, but people," I say.

"Hey look! A real dung beetle!" Phil cries. He pulls the car over to the side of the road while I get the camera.

"We're not supposed to get out of the car," I remark.

"What do you think, a lion will leap out of the bush and attack us?"

"I don't know. I suppose not. There's only one way to find out!"

We quietly get out of the car and look around at the vast savanna in front of us. Spring is in full bloom, and the grasses are a soft green, waving gently in the breeze. Acacias dot the landscape here and there, and I continue to keep a sharp look

CAUTION
DUNG BEETLES
HAVE
RIGHT OF WAY

out for the possible large cat snoozing in their branches or in the shade below. A huge pile of dung has recently been deposited in the road, and the beetles are busy standing upside down on their front legs, while their back legs swiftly spin small chunks of the manure mass into tight billiard-like balls. "Wow!" I whisper. "I had no idea they could make these balls so fast."

"It's impressive. But what's more impressive is the size of the shit pile."

"Probably rhino. It's about half as big as an elephant's," I say.

"How do you know so much about shit?"

"It's my job. That's how you take the temperature of an elephant. You stick the thermometer in a freshly deposited poop pile."

"Nice. I'm glad you shared that with me."

We get back in the car and continue down a dirt road. We see an elephant in the distance performing his ablutions, as the Afrikaners like to call a person's daily wash ritual, at the edge of a curving stream. We continue on in his direction hoping to get a closer look.

"Stop here for a second," I say to Phil. "We are about even with the river by my reckoning. See anything?"

Phil and I both look off to the right. "A path."

I look off to my left at a grove of trees growing up a hill. Some of the trees are uprooted. Suddenly the tree trunks begin moving. "Holy shit," I scream. "Those aren't just tree trunks."

Phil leans over to look out my window. "Jesus Christ, they are heading this way. What do I do? Those elephants are going to walk right on top of us!"

"Back up very slowly and whatever you do, don't spin the tires," I whisper.

We quietly back up to clear the way for five of the largest elephants I have ever seen in my life.

The last male, the largest of the group, stops in the road. He stands in front of us waving his big ears back and forth, staring at our car. He nods his head up and down, brandishing his short, thick dual tusks like a two-handed pirate.

"We're dead!" Phil whispers.

"Don't move. He's looking us over. I think it's the car actually. I bet he's never seen one this bright green color. He must think we are a huge dung beetle."

"Ya right," Phil says.

"You can't drive backwards fast enough to outrun him."

"Wanna bet?"

"Don't do it."

Finally, the elephant is satisfied that we are not a threat and continues on his way to the river.

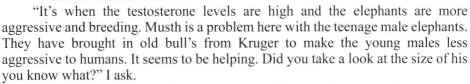

AIRCON OBLIVION   THE EARTHMOM   THE CATTLE CAR

THE YACHTIE

GAME PARK VEHICLE SIGHTINGS

"Talk about a non-nonchalant walk," Phil says.

"I don't think he was in musth. He had no eye secretions. We would have been dead if he was," I say.

"What the heck is musth?"

"It's when the testosterone levels are high and the elephants are more aggressive and breeding. Musth is a problem here with the teenage male elephants. They have brought in old bull's from Kruger to make the young males less aggressive to humans. It seems to be helping. Did you take a look at the size of his you know what?" I ask.

"I'm afraid I was too busy seeing my life pass in front of my eyes to notice."

"Impressive. Very impressive."

*   *   *

Thanksgiving arrives and one of the American cruisers organizes a dinner at a local restaurant for all of us yachties. Tables and chairs are set up on the outside veranda. The American boats make pies and all the trimmings, while the restaurant provides enough turkey to feed seventy-five people and keeps the wine glasses filled with delicious South African wine.

Phil and I sit down at a table with a German couple, a French couple, one other American, two Brazilians and a Uruguayan. The Frenchman had recently been released from the hospital after recovering from injuries he sustained while crossing the Agulhas current the day after us. Their boat was rolled over and stripped of all deck gear and masts. Despite their black eyes and bruises, both husband and wife are in good spirits.

"This is very good, we don't usually eat turkey," the Frenchman says to me, "Even if I don't understand what we are celebrating, I like it."

"Whoa," I say. "You don't know what Thanksgiving Day is?"

Everyone but the American at the table shakes their head while continuing to devour the turkey, potatoes and gravy.

"This won't do," I whisper to Phil. "Somebody's got to say something."

"Who?" he asks.

"I don't know. Somebody."

"It looks like it better be you."

"Me? I hate public speaking. I can't make a speech."

"Sure you can. You've conquered your fears at sea. This is far less dangerous. If you don't do it, no one else will." Phil says, while shoveling mashed potatoes into his mouth.

I stand up and ring a spoon on my glass, while the rest of the tables urge quiet. "I'd like to thank the Tuzi Gazi restaurant for putting on this celebration," I begin. "I'd also like to thank Ann on Serenity for all her organizing, and everyone for coming to help us celebrate a very important American holiday. But I thought I should say a few words about the history of Thanksgiving and why it is important to Americans."

"Here, here!" someone says.

"Shut up, I can't hear her," another voice adds.

"In December of 1620 the Pilgrims sailed across the Atlantic, landing on a rock they called Plimoth, in a land far removed from what they were used to, in the state now called Massachusetts. They were Puritans seeking a place to freely practice their religion. Persecuted in Holland and England, they believed that any person could be and should be knowledgeable about the scriptures, not just the scholars at the top of the church food chain. The established churches didn't agree and wanted this knowledge to be kept strictly with the people in charge of the church, so they booted the Puritans out.

"These Puritans were America's first cruisers. Arriving on the Mayflower, they didn't know what to expect and were woefully unprepared for the winter ahead. The local Indians, tribes called the Wampanoag, Massasoit, and Nipmuck, helped them to get through the first winter by sharing their food. Despite the assistance, many Pilgrims died. When summer came, one Indian named Squanto showed them how to plant American crops and how to fish.

"That fall, the Pilgrims had a good harvest and invited the Indians to celebrate with a feast to thank them for their help the preceding winter. The original meal probably had squash, fish, lobsters, corn and local game birds, turkeys as well as partridge. Not quite what we are eating today, but almost!

"It wasn't until America's Civil War that Thanksgiving became a national holiday. Deeply divided, my country was at war with its self. Not that different from what South Africa went through just a few years ago. Blacks against whites, whites against whites, Northerners against Southerners, America was a huge mess. Abraham Lincoln, our version of Nelson Mandela, was trying to find a way to unite the country. He decided that the last Thursday in November should be set aside for a national holiday called Thanksgiving. Everyone had to stop everything for one day, count their blessings, and be thankful for all those who have helped them. No gifts, no hoopla, no commercialism, just quiet thanks and good food.

"So, Thanksgiving is really the ultimate cruiser holiday! As we feast and celebrate with the different countries and people who have given us help along the way, Thank you!" I fall back to my chair amidst a volley of cheers.

"That was good," Phil whispers as everyone digs back into the feast.

"Thank goodness for all my grade school trips to Plimoth Plantation. Boy, how I thought all that stuff was tiresome growing up—Miles Standish, Abigail what's-her-name, making paper turkeys out of handprints. Funny how you may need the smallest squirreled away bits of knowledge when you get older! Notice how I skipped over the part about what happened the following winter?"

"Can't say as I did," Phil says chewing on a turkey leg. "What happened the following winter?"

"Nothing that won't repeat itself again.That was during King Phillip's war, when the religious zealots slaughtered the Indians because they were heathens."

After the feast, we call Phil's boys to wish them a Happy Thanksgiving. They seem depressed and tell us they are having macaroni and cheese for dinner. Their mother is someplace else.

Worried that something is very wrong at home, a few days later we finally manage to reach Nathaniel's guidance counselor. I stand next to Phil as he talks into the phone while plugging a finger into his other ear.

"Uh, Oh. No! Oh, my god! Transition? What transition? No! I don't believe it! That's outrageous!" he says into the receiver. When he hangs up, he stands for a few moments staring at the telephone.

"What's happening?" I ask. "Where is their mother? Talk to me!"

Phil takes a deep breath and turns to me. "Thanks goodness for Nathaniel's guidance counselor, she seems like a very good person."

"And? What's going on?"

"The boy's mother is on vacation in the Galapagos."

"Boy, am I glad we didn't run into her there," I joke.

"That's not the whole story. The counselor is worried that Nathaniel is having trouble with the transition."

"What transition?"

"The counselor just found out that the boys have been living on their own for the last three years. My ex-wife lost her teaching job and moved four hours away! She wanted the boys to stay in their school and remain with their friends, so the boys stayed in the house, while she came home on weekends. It is basically abandonment, but the counselor says legally it's too late to do anything, since Nathaniel will be graduating from high school in a few months."

"So you mean the boys have been taking care of each other for the last three years?"

"Exactly," Phil replies. "They've been leading a Lord of the Flies lifestyle. Ben hasn't been going to college either. He dropped out of RIT last fall."

"And Ben's tuition money? What's happened with that?" I ask.

"Good question."

"What should we do? We're broke. We can't fly back."

"Not much we can do," Phil says while putting the backpack over his shoulder. "But, no matter what, come hell or high water, storms, tempests and gales, we've got to be in upstate New York for Nathaniel's high school graduation in June. I didn't make it to Ben's, I'm not going to miss Nathaniel's."

Chapter 25

Lion Wars

December 2002
South Africa

When my sister comes to visit she wields a travel guide beneath one arm and a ticking clock under the other. We try to pack as much sightseeing into one week as is humanly possible. We tour the countryside, visit game parks and museums, hike, and get caught up on two years of backlogged conversation, all the while trying hard not to kill one another. Phil and I no longer possess the American pace and often times we don't move as fast as she would like. I barely have time to try on all her clothes, let alone swipe them. She leaves with a much lighter load—minus a few shoes, pants, raw water pumps, light bulbs and magazines.

After leaving my sister at the airport, Phil and I pack up the computer, GPS, our toothbrushes, and then head north. We had received e-mail from an American

follower of our web-logs, urging us to drive to the northern part of South Africa and visit a lion rehabilitation facility where his daughter Kelcey works. Despite having only an electronic connection with this reader, we decide to do it.

Between villages and grazing lands, eucalyptus trees grow arrow straight, planted in orderly rows and harvested like a crop, with leaf tufts and branches sprouting at the top like frayed cigarettes. They are clear-cut, then stacked in rail cars or trucks, and brought to the waterfront next to Iwalani where they are transported off in the hold of big ships to other countries. Where there has been clear cutting, industrious young men pick through the roots and stumps, taking what wood is left and carving it with machetes into animal works of art, which they sell along the road for just a few dollars.

Sugar cane is grown on the land not occupied by eucalyptus. Where there is no farming, there are coal mines, factories, power plants, jails, and many small Zulu villages. Traditional round stone, wattle and daub, thatched roof huts are slowly being replaced with square, brightly painted, tin roofed houses, These modern day Zulu villages, despite the upgrades with electricity and modern conveniences are lacking in character. Young children play along the highway; older siblings stand nearby, selling bags of lychee fruit or golf balls. Women walk along the side of

the road, gracefully, most of the time with large heavy objects perched on their heads. Cattle graze along the edges of the roads, tied (sometimes) with rope. Men are either walking, sitting on the guardrail, or perched on old sofas dragged out for the purpose of watching the cars or trucks go by. People cling to trucks like pepperoni on a pizza. With no public transportation, humans are at the mercy of friends and truckers in getting from point A to point B.

As we drive north, farms of pine trees gradually replace the eucalyptus. A few hours and several hundred miles later, signs of human industry disappear all together, leaving nothing but the rolling hills and savanna grasslands, punctuated with the small, more traditional Zulu villages one usually associates with Africa.

"You're awfully quiet," I say to Phil.

"Just feeling guilty about being here."

"At least now we know what's been wrong with Nathaniel," I say.

"Yeah, abandoned by both parents."

"Look, you have been planning this trip since, when? Since before they were born! They were in diapers while Iwalani was first taking shape. You have always done what you said you would. How can that be wrong?"

"It doesn't matter. I wasn't there for them."

"I think they know how much you obsess about them, even from here."

"You need to turn left up ahead," Phil says while monitoring our progress with the GPS and laptop computer.

He recently bought a cell phone in Durban, and we are both anxious to try it out. "Now what's Mr. Gadget doing?" I ask.

"Trying to e-mail Ben."

"From the cell phone?"

"Yeah, the South Africans are years ahead of the U.S. in terms of cell phones. I'll give it to you when I am done, so you can call Kelcey."

Despite being far from anywhere, we still have good cell phone coverage when Phil hands me the phone. Kelcey answers on the first ring. *"Where are you?"* she asks.

I tell her we are still on the main highway a little over an hour away.

"Make sure you don't stop anywhere along there because of the attacks."

"The what?" I ask.

"Attacks. A woman was raped by seventeen men when she pulled her car over to the side of the road to talk on the cell phone. It happened just a few days ago."

"Oh," I say looking over at Phil who is calmly tapping away on the computer, not hearing the other part of the phone conversation.

"You need to get to the parking area before the sun sets. The woman who will be taking care of your car won't come out after dark. You'll need to leave your car keys with her. Do you have insurance on the car?"

"Yes."

"That's good, because it will probably be stripped."

"Wouldn't it just be better if we drive in to your place?" I ask her.

"It's impossible. The road is nothing more than a dirt track. You need a four-wheel drive truck. It's over seventeen kilometers."

"OK, I'll call once we are in the parking lot then"

"Yes, that's good. Make sure you keep your windows rolled up and your doors locked. But you should be OK waiting in daylight. You won't be seeing me, I am still testifying in Johannesburg. One of the guys will come out and pick you up in the truck. They will be taking care of you all weekend. I won't be back until Tuesday at the earliest."

"That's too bad. I was hoping to meet you."

I hang up the phone and drive in silence staring ahead at the road. What am I getting us into? Kelcey sounded earnest but probably is doing the American thing of supersizing the risks. Still, I feel apprehensive. Testifying? Attacks? We drive by a green highway sign, which looks like state signs everywhere, only this one reads, 'Do Not Stop for Any Reason. High Crime area.' I look around at the surrounding landscape and it doesn't look any different from where we have just been.

"Where the hell are you taking us?" Phil asks as he reads the sign.

Reluctantly I tell Phil what Kelcey just relayed to me.

"I'm not leaving the Dung Beetle in the parking lot to get stripped. I've gotten fond of this car, even if it is just a rental," Phil says.

"I agree. We need to drive it in to their place. If we get it stuck, we'll deal with it. You and I can probably lift this car up and carry it if we have to."

An hour later we pull in to the parking lot. Composed of compacted red mud, well rutted, with washout areas and huge holes surrounded by scrub growth and big rocks, it seems more of a place for heavy machinery than automobiles. Several dirt roads wash down into it, three heading off into higher hills.

"Which is the right road?" Phil asks.

"Good question. There are no signs and I have no idea where this place is. Looks like eenie-meenie-minie-moe. If we are wrong, we'll probably get murdered and robbed for our cell phone and car parts, but oh well. C'est la vie," I say.

We decide to take the middle road heading up into the hills, as it appears slightly more traveled than the other two. For the first seven kilometers it is rough going, with steep inclines and even steeper drop offs, falling into washed out riverbeds at the bottom. Fortunately, it has been relatively dry and most of the rivers have only six inches of water. For part of the time, I have to get out and walk, rolling large boulders out of the way so as not to dent the oil pan on our little car. We are fortunate to have bright sunny weather; I can see that with any type of rain this trip would be impossible.

"How far have we gotten?" I pant to Phil through the open window.

"Twelve kilometers," he replies while steering around a big stone. We arrive at a huge washout. Rainwater has neatly sculpted a steep three-foot wide ravine through the red mud.

"Should we fill this up with small stones?" I ask Phil.

"Big ones to start. Then we'll top it off with little ones."

For half an hour we work together to fill in the ditch.

"That should do it. We should be able to drive across now," I say.

"I sure hope we are going the right way," Phil says.

"Me too. It feels right though."

Before long we reach the top of a breezy hill. There are few tall trees, and here and there small tufts of grass sprout out of crumbly parched soil, but as far as the eye can see Sugarbush Protea bloom indecently; tawdry showgirls flashing legs and thigh on a dry desert dance floor, their insect patrons and audience abuzz about them. "Wow, even if we are in the wrong place, this is pretty," Phil says.

"There must have been a fire here not too long ago. I think Protea plants need fire to grow. How far have we come now?" I ask.

"Sixteen kilometers,"

We continue on a bit further until we come to some barns and farm machinery and a small sign announcing we have arrived at the lion sanctuary.

Mitch and Puppy

We drive in and are greeted by a huge Great Dane, who tries to crush our tiny little car.

"Puppy! Get down!" A tall man with long blond hair tied in a ponytail comes out from under a truck wiping his hands. "I don't believe it," he says. "No one has ever driven a car in here! Follow me, I'll show you where to park. I don't want anyone seeing a car. You have compromised the lions safety. Did you pass anyone on the way in here?" he asks while putting a South African leather hat on over his long blonde hair.

"Early on a few people walking, and at the end a truckfull," I say.

"I'm Mitch, by the way. I'll show you where you'll be staying. These disreputables," he says, pointing to two white men wearing khaki shorts, shirts and leather boots coming out from under the truck, "are Clayton and Vickers. The good-looking one is André. He's a volunteer from England."

"It's just as well you drove in," Clayton says. "We haven't got brakes on the bakkie and don't have parts to fix it."

"Kelcey won't be very chuffed, when she finds out you drove in," Vickers says.

"If she finds out," Clayton adds looking at Mitch.

We hide the Dung Beetle next to the guesthouse where we are staying, pressing it up against the building. The main house, recently built, is composed of tan, river washed stone with tight fitting joints and a stone veranda on the north side. The guesthouse, two bedrooms separated by a bathroom, hooks like a tail off the main house. Electricity is provided by a generator which runs for a few hours each day. A wood-burning furnace gives hot water once in the morning.

Mitch brings us out some cold fruit juice while we sit in the shade of the veranda talking about veterinary medicine and our trip around the world.

"I'm sorry about driving in," I say. "I didn't realize we would be endangering the lions."

"Not to worry. We're all just on edge because of what is going on."

"Oh, I see," I say taking a sip of juice. "What exactly _is_ going on?"

"Aren't you friends with Kelcey's dad?" Mitch asks. "She told me you were."

"Uh. Not exactly. More like electronic acquaintances," Phil answers.

"Did he tell you anything about what is going on here?"

"Only that you have a rehabilitation facility," I respond.

"Do you know anything about the canned hunt business?" Mitch asks.

"Not really," Phil and I both say together.

"Every year over fifteen hundred lions in South Africa are killed by hunters looking for trophies. It is a huge business, and Westerners are willing to pay sometimes as much as one hundred thousand U.S. dollars for the chance to shoot a lion. Most of these are captive bred. Have you ever seen the Cook Report?"

"No," I acknowledge.

"It's a British documentary show which spotlights controversial issues. They did a particularly good piece showing how gruesome canned hunting is. When we get the generator going I'll show a tape of it. To preserve the head, the lions are usually shot in the chest. They die from bleeding internally or from suffocation. The whole safari is a sham. Before going out on the hunt, the lion is drugged and positioned under a tree, the hunter and guides drive around pretending to stalk it. Everyone, except the hunter, knows full well where the lion is."

"Are all safaris like that?" Phil asks.

Mitch nods. "A good many of them are."

"It sounds awful, but I am not surprised really, given human greed. How did you get involved?" I ask.

"I was manager of a private game park, that was where I met Kelcey. She was a tourist from California. She decided she had enough of the corporate world and moved to Africa. We hand raised a litter of cubs, destined for the business. We couldn't let them get killed and bought the litter outright, then bought this old farm and transported the lions here after building a state of the art enclosure. The lion pen is forty acres. We hope to build one that is two hundred and fifty. We are building high end bungalows and hope to tap into the eco-tourist trade."

"So how can anyone fault you for that?" Phil says.

"We angered a lot of people in the process, my old boss for one, who is Afrikaans and is a nothing short of a Nazi. I discovered he was illegally importing cheetah from the north for canned hunts. That was what really pissed him off. He is bound and determined to take our lions away from us and get their heads mounted on some boardroom wall. They are fighting us in court, saying we didn't have the necessary permits for transporting the lions here."

"Did you?" I ask.

"Unfortunately, they were not in our hands at the time," Mitch says.

"So they are getting you on a technicality?" I ask.

"Yes, unfortunately, a mistake I will regret for the rest of my life. The illegal trade of animals brings a lot of money into South Africa. There is also an underground market to move animals out of state game parks for hunting. A lot of money gets passed along through the various channels, even through some people who should know better. Even Kruger gets animals removed illegally for hunting purposes," Mitch says.

"Unfortunately," I say, "the state in America where we come from is almost as bad. Our state biologists and game wardens are in favor of leg hold traps and bear baiting. The bears aren't drugged, well, unless you call an overdose of donuts drugging. They are fed junk food like pets, day after day until they are habituated to human smells. Then groups of hunters pay money, get a guide and come in to shoot them. Our biologists say it is an important method of population control! The politicians argument is that it brings tourist dollars."

"They use the same arguments here," Mitch says.

"I think any time you get a human involved in controlling a population, with the exception of neutering dogs and cats, it is fraught with disaster. Look at how well we control ourselves!" I say.

Mitch looks at me and smiles. "Do you have any children?"

"No. I never wanted to add more humans to this poor planet," I say. "I have dead-end genes that shouldn't be passed on to future generations. That's why I respect lions. I like the way the aunts are involved in raising their sister's children. It's a good system. I think baby making should be left to professionals. My mother sent me to a shrink as a child, because I used to operate on my dolls, and then euthanized them when they didn't heal properly. My stuffed animals, on the other hand, were always treated properly!"

"Sounds like you were like that little boy in *Toy Story*," Mitch laughs.

"Yeah, that was me, only I didn't blow toys up. I actually thought dolls had serious diseases that needed treating."

"We try not to add to overpopulation here too. All of the females are on contraceptives, including the lions!" Mitch laughs.

Clayton comes out of the house holding a beer. Vickers follows and lights a fire in a steel drum welded onto four legs, "Are either of you vegetarian?"

"No, one hundred percent omnivores. We eat anyone or anything that had a good life," I explain.

"Tonight we'll treat you to an old fashioned South African braai. Later we'll feed the lions," Mitch says.

We watch as a large anvil cloud forms to the west. The setting sun turns it into a bronze mass so top heavy and ponderous that it looks like it will topple out of the sky. "Do you see that?" Phil asks. "At sea that is a sight which will get your adrenaline going. Here it is just plain beautiful."

Mitch heads inside to get a bottle of South African wine. He returns with three glasses. "Have you ever seen a bush baby?" he asks.

We shake our heads. He pours the wine and then walks over to the edge of the veranda. "MONKEY-MONKEY-MONKEY!" he calls into the thick stand of gum trees behind the house, which are coming alive with twitters and tweets as the sun sets. Vickers and Clayton stand up too, looking into the dark branches of the trees overhead.

"I saw him!"

"There he is, man!"

Suddenly a tiny creature not much bigger than a tennis ball jumps from the branches onto Mitch's hat. "There you are, you little rascal." He picks the tiny bush baby off his hat and showers him with kisses.

"He has to be the cutest thing I have ever seen," I say as Mitch hands him to me. He has eyes as big as small planets and large Yoda-like ears. Among the smallest primates, bush babies are well adapted to their nocturnal life in the treed regions of Africa's savannas and forests.

"You're not alone in thinking that. This is another illegally trafficked animal, this time though, for the pet industry," Mitch says.

"It can't be too brisk of a business because I've never seen one as a patient. Either that, or they are very healthy animals. Why do you think human nature is such, that when we see something really cute we automatically want to possess it? Even right now I am getting those feelings. How old is he?"

"Five months. Kelcey and I raised him. We are giving him limited freedom now."

Monkey jumps from my hand over to Phil, and then from Phil he leaps his way back into the house. "He's pretty fast," Phil says.

Mitch's cell phone rings, he disappears into the house talking.

Soon Clayton and Vickers are showing Phil how to SMS on the cell phone.

"We SMS all the time," they tell him.

"The other day Clayton left the burner going on the stove and he SMS'd Mitch to turn it off. It saved us a fifteen minute bakkie drive," Vickers says.

I sit back sipping my wine, listening to the sounds of the bush about me. It seems slightly ironic to be so far from anywhere and yet get schooling in, what for us, is new technology. Phil and I are both in our element.

André comes out of his room wearing blue jeans and a short-sleeved shirt.

"How long have you been volunteering here?" I ask him.

"I'm on break from school in England. This is my third week."

"How do you like it?" I ask.

"It's been very interesting. Very different from what I am used to. There are aspects of living here to which I am very sympathetic, and then others I just don't comprehend," André says with a proper British accent.

"Like what?'

"The discrimination. I really respect Mitch and what he is trying to do, but sometimes it is frustrating listening to the South Africans complain about their workers."

"They are a bloody lazy lot, all of them," Clayton says listening in. "Look at the state workers along the road, half of them are asleep."

"How much does the average South African worker make a day?"

"Black or white?" Clayton asks.

"Is there a difference?" I ask.

Clayton shakes his head and goes back to showing Phil all that his cell phone can do.

Mitch comes out of the house with a worried look on his face.

"How's Kelcey making out?" Vickers asks.

"It's not going well," is all he says.

"Mitch, how much do you pay the workers here?" André asks.

"Most get between twenty and forty Rand per day. My stonemason gets 65 Rand per square meter and he can do ten square meters a day. Why?"

"André and I are trying to figure things out in South Africa," I say. "We're doing the typical American and British thing of coming in and running a county. Do you pay property taxes?"

"No, not much, income tax, yes. Things like TV usage and cell phones, those are taxed, but we don't have the services like you have in America and Great Britain. There are no fire departments. You can't rely on the police when you are in trouble."

"A TV tax?" Phil asks in disbelief. "How can that be enforced?"

"Not easily. There's a black market for that too."

"How do your workers get in here?" I wonder.

"Walking or getting a lift in a bakkie," Mitch replies.

"OK, so the average worker gets forty Rand a day, which will buy ten cans of Coca Cola. The minimum wage an American worker makes is roughly $5.00 and hour, and they can buy around 30 cans of Coca Cola per day, after the income tax is taken away."

"Don't forget the South African worker is usually supporting a family of ten," Mitch adds.

"Alright, so that means he makes enough to buy himself one can of Coke a day. I have to say that if I had to walk seventeen kilometers to work and made enough to buy one Coca Cola after the family took their share, I'd be sleeping on the job a lot, too. Maybe the people aren't lazy, they are just tired and hungry."

"Or sick," Mitch adds. "Sixty five percent are infected with AIDS. They don't understand the concept of a virus. African men think sex is a right. Having multiple partners or wives is a sign of strength. Our current president, Mbeke started out by steering people away from western treatments for AIDS. Mandela and Desmond Tutu had to educate him."

"You see," Clayton explains, "the problem is that when apartheid ended, all the blacks instantly thought they would be living like whites. I had one chappie say to me, 'in just a few weeks, man, it will be me driving your bakkie and you will be working for me.' The blacks thought everything would be automatically handed over to them. In Zimbabwe, under Mugabe it was. And now that country is in peril because the blacks have no training to farm or to produce commodities."

Suddenly a very loud siren blares over the treetops, overwhelming the evening sounds of the bush.

Mitch flies off the veranda, jumping into a small truck, with Vickers close behind. As I watch Vickers leaping over the stone parapet of the veranda wall,

I notice for the first time that he wears a handgun. Clayton brings up the rear, choosing the stairs over the action hero route. He has to jump into the back of the small pickup truck as it pulls away, as Mitch isn't waiting even for him.

André, Phil and I are left staring at one another. "What the heck is going on?" I ask.

"That alarm is for the outer perimeter fence of the lion enclosure."

"You mean a lion has escaped?" I ask with great hope.

"Possibly," André says. "But it also could mean that someone might be trying to break in. Mitch is terribly worried that his former boss is planning to nick his lions, or worse. It's probably nothing. It went off a few weeks ago. Any bush animals wandering around the outside can trip it."

A few minutes later they drive back. "I am sorry for leaving you like that. False alarm. I apologize for being on edge. This is really a very tense time for us all," Mitch says to Phil and me.

"You don't think this Nazi-man would try and kill the lions, do you?"

"I hope not. They are too valuable, but still you never know," Mitch says.

For dinner we have steak, chicken, chops and boerewors, a type of sausage, cooked South African style on the braai. "Don't you guys eat vegetables?" I tease.

"Vegetables?" Mitch asks.

"Isn't chicken a vegetable?" Vickers jokes.

"I remember eating a vegetable once," Clayton laughs.

"Tonight will be the ultimate carnivore experience," Mitch says. "Actually, in all honesty, I did make a salad. I forgot about it though."

"What do you feed the lions?" I ask.

"We have an abattoir not far from here. We use what we can. They eat every two to three days. You have to be careful about feeding beef from the slaughterhouses because it can be a source of tuberculosis for the lions."

"Do you TB test the lions periodically?" I ask.

"Yes, that is part of their health screen along with the birth control implants," Mitch says.

"Is there much FIV here?" I ask.

"Not like up north in Botswana. They are having serious problems with it."

"How old were the cubs when you started caring for them?"

"Just a few days," Mitch says sipping his wine.

"It must be neat to take care of a purring bundle of fur that could grow up into an animal that can eat you," I say.

"None of the roaring cats can purr like a house cat, even when they are very young. Lions are prolific breeders, and, because tourists will pay good money to play with the cubs, even the young are exploited. The issue is what is done with the lions once they are grown up. That's my main concern."

After dinner, Phil and I climb into the back seat of Mitch's bakkie. Several dead calves and body parts lay sprawled in the bed of the pick up.

"Keep your windows closed. The lions are hungry and get a little aggressive when they want to eat," Mitch explains.

Clayton drives while Andre sits in the seat next to him. Vickers rides in the back with the meat. We come to a large fenced area, and Mitch unfastens the

locks while we drive in. He locks this fence behind us, while we drive forward to a second tall locked gate. We drive through and are now fenced in with the lions. If nothing else, the enclosure is impressive.

Mitch walks beside the truck calling the lions by name. They come galloping up to him, rubbing their cheeks on his legs and then pounce into the back of the truck like college students at a free buffet. Despite the fact that eight lions are getting fed, they are relatively orderly about it, with only a minimal amount of growling and snarling. Mufasa the oldest male, an impressive lion with full mane, gets the proverbial lions share, a whole calf.

When all the bodies and parts have been dragged off into the darkness we drive the truck around the enclosure. The headlights shine on blissfully dilated pupils while blood stained lips crunch on bony parts. Everyone is sublimely happy.

The next day Mitch, Vickers and André take us on a hike to see a waterfall located at the edge of the ten thousand acre property. Phil keeps the overall pace slow as he stops to photograph every plant and insect along the way. I think he is actually doing it to prevent a reoccurrence of the hike from hell the weekend before.

One week earlier, we had been hiking with my sister in Drakensburg, and I was acutely awoken to the fact that shipboard life has turned me into an old woman as I could barely keep pace with her. My hip was doing something strange, too; it felt as if it was trying to subluxate, or pop out of the joint. When it happened, I fell to the ground in acute agony, unable to put any weight down on my right leg. I lay in the trail pleading with Phil and her to jump on me and pop it back in place. They would just stand there shaking their heads and sympathizing with one another for having to live with such a drama queen, neither one of them offering to put me out of my misery. It didn't help that we were followed by a South African bird that sang, "BIG-fat-cow! BIG-fat-cow," every time I fell to the ground.

I am thankful that my hip is acting fine on this hike. We arrive at a stream we have to wade across. The men all charge ahead, while I remain in the water and lazily lean up against some rocks. The water is cool while the sun is roasting hot. It is lovely and what's more, there are no mosquitoes. In fact I haven't seen one mosquito in all of South Africa, yet we were diligently taking our doxycycline as a preventive for malaria. I finally get out of the water and run downstream, totally soaked, shaking water like a cocker spaniel as my clothes and shoes make splorping sounds treading over the smooth rocks to catch up with the others, standing on the edge of the waterfall. It is impressive from our perspective as it courses through the valley eating away at the soft sandstone.

"Ok, I am 100% jealous now," I say to Mitch. "This is pretty awesome to have in your back yard. It would be even more cool if the lions could be enjoying it, too."

"I would love to have this property completely enclosed for the lions," Mitch says while munching on a stalk of grass. "But it will never happen. The locals are terrified of predatory cats. We are doing our best to educate children about living with them, but their parents have taught them that the only good lion, is a dead lion."

"It doesn't sound like Disney and *The Lion King* have infiltrated the local MacDonald's."

"Not yet," Mitch laughs. "Would you be interested in handling one of the lions?"

"Would I ever!" I say simultaneously to Phil's "No way!"

"Tomorrow morning then."

That evening we sit on the stone veranda while Vickers feeds wood into the braai. "Just so you don't think we never eat vegetables, we will have potjiekos in a traditional braii using the potjie."

"God bless you," I say to Vickers incomprehensible English. Using an oven mitt, he pulls a small cauldron on three legs out of the steel drum fire- "Potjie," he says pointing. He browns a chicken in the bottom of the cauldron and grinds spices over it, then layers cabbage, onions and more spices, finishing off with carrots at the top. "This will be finished just now."

"Ah, the South African just now," I say shaking my head. "It took me awhile to catch on to what you guys mean! On the radio, the weather gurus would always say they were coming on with the weather 'just now', and then they never did. I thought they must be a little old and doddering and had forgotten. It took us awhile to figure out that 'just now' means 'later' in South African!"

While we are waiting for dinner, Mitch fires up the generator and shows us the video of the Cook report. It is disturbing to say the least.

"Why do you suppose humans have this need to take lives for no good reason? I mean it's one thing to kill an animal if you are hungry and need to eat, or if a murderer is threatening your child. But to shoot a lion for sport?" I ask.

Mitch takes the tape out of the VCR and places it in a bookcase. "I don't know. I have seen a lot of senseless killings in my life. I led South African troops against insurgents in Angola for three years."

"I bet you saw a lot of gruesome things. It must be a balance thing, Yin and yang, or whatever. People who give back life, balanced with those who need to take it away." I look over at a wooden African mask hanging on the wall. Two big bright eyes stare at me from inside the carved right hand eye socket. "There is something behind that mask!" I say quietly, not wanting to scare whatever is hiding in the carving.

"Monkey," Mitch says. "He absorbs world events from behind those empty eye sockets."

*   *   *

The next day Phil and I follow behind Mitch to the lion enclosure. It is going to be another hot day. The sun cuts the air like a saw blade, and the cicadas provide the whir to its hot engine.

"Are you sure you want to do this?" Phil asks me.

"Yes. I don't feel scared. Cautious, but not apprehensive. I just got over my period, so I should be OK," I whisper.

"What's that got to do with anything?" Phil whispers back.

"Well, at the clinic, cats don't usually behave themselves when any one of

us women is about to have our period. It's weird but true. I can't imagine the big cats would be any different."

"You have worked with plenty of animals as a vet. You know better than anyone how animals can sense fear," Mitch calls to me over his shoulder. "We don't let just anyone do this, but I can tell you will be fine."

He unlocks the fence into the holding enclosure. "I'll get one of the males, and bring him in. Wait here." Mitch calls for a lion named Mpandi who comes slowly over to the fence.

Mitch brings the two-year-old lion over to me. He is beginning to grow a mane, and I can see so many similarities between him and Stewart, that for a moment I hold my breath.

I introduce myself and he rolls over on his back so I can scratch his belly.

"My god," I say. "They really are just big pussy cats."

Suddenly, as if to prove me very wrong, Mpandi opens his mouth as wide as it will go, and with very sharp teeth encloses my entire hip in his mouth and bites down ever so gently. Mitch quickly hits him on the nose.

"NO MPANDI!" The big lion looks at Mitch and reluctantly lets go of a potentially fun chew toy, then latches onto Mitch's leg.

"Yah, you big knuckle head," I say. "If you are going to eat my hip, please do me the favor of attacking the other side, as it is messed up anyhow!" I give him a firm pat on the chest.

I look at Mitch, but his gaze is fixed on the lion. He firmly scolds him again. He has complete control of the situation. "I'll put him back," Mitch says. "He's in a teenage mood right now. It's really too hot for the lions, anyhow."

"Not to mention the fact that their last meal was two days ago," I add.

*   *   *

That afternoon we leave the lion facility and decide to drive back to Iwalani via Swaziland, a tiny country to the north of South Africa run by a benign monarch with a passion for young wives. Our route takes us on a well-maintained highway high up into the hills, but eventually the road fades away into just a wide walking path. Blocking our passage down the single lane dirt track is a mammoth pile of dirt. We turn around and retrace our steps three times, restart the GPS and laptop twice, and scratch our heads. There is no denying it; this dirt track is R30 into Swaziland.

"Oh great," Phil moans. "Another Amy tour."

When we get back to the pile of dirt, I figure that with expertly timed pressure to the accelerator, coupled with just the right amount of externally applied human power to the back end, we might just squeeze the Dung Beetle past the dirt pile.

I can hear heavy machinery off in the distance coupled with human voices. A whole herd of children is screaming and yelling from the bushes below us and is stampeding in our direction.

"Honey," I say to Phil through the open window. "Not to get your adrenaline going, but about forty children are running in our direction with hands outstretched, hoping we will give them something. As we have nothing to give them, I suggest giving all we have- to the accelerator!"

I push, while Phil guns the Dung Beetle ahead, and we just barely squeeze the car through to the other side. I jump in and we drive off with the children still running after us. "I think there is more road construction ahead. At first I thought the dirt pile was a decoy to trap unsuspecting tourists."

"Where did all those kids come from?" Phil asks.

"Under bushes. I think people grow on trees in Africa. I have to pee."

"Do you want me to stop?"

"No way. Not if I have to piss in front of half a country."

"Well, what do you want me to do? It's not like there are any rest areas or gas stations?"

"I don't know, I'll survive. I guess."

We continue driving into the higher elevations until we reach the bulldozers and backhoes grading the road. They seem a little surprised seeing us drive by, but don't try to stop us. Off in the distance, we see logging trucks, where workers are clear cutting large stands of pine. Soon there are no other signs of civilization, just thousands of acres of mature pine, treetops swallowed by the fog which swirls about us at such a high elevation, like the breath from an ancient tree eating monster.

"OK, I am getting to the critical point. Pull over here while I jump in the bushes."

"Look overhead for leopards," Phil warns.

"Yeah right, I wish."

I walk through the pine-needled woods until I find a suitable bush. When I have finished peeing, I spy not fifty feet away from me, a man sprawled under a bush taking a nap, or at least I hope he is taking a nap. I start to run back to the car. From the corner of my eye I can see he is indeed napping, and my sudden flight has sprung him to action and he starts to give chase.

"Feel better?" Phil asks as I throw myself in the car.

"Jesus. I can't even pee in the middle of nowhere in peace. Where do all these people come from? I'm beginning to think humans really do grow on trees."

Chapter 26

Durban Disease

December 2002-January 2003
Richards Bay to Durban
South Africa

Leaving Richards Bay on a Friday, our first ever Friday departure, is fraught with autopilot problems, alternator charging problems, and anxiety over ignoring our own tenet of always obeying tradition and never going against the superstitions of the sea. On the way to Durban, Phil manages to diagnose and fix Iwalani's alternator problem, does some jiggling of the autopilot wires, and seems to cure the latter of its 'no data' error message. Despite our misgivings we make the overnight passage with no casualties. Since we are still dealing with the Agulhas Current sweeping down from the north, we are not afforded the luxury of being able to choose the day of departure. We can ride it like a river only if the winds are going in a similar direction. Along this coast we are completely at the mercy of the incomparable South African weather gurus, Fred and Alistair, and the never-ending parade of low-pressure systems spinning around the South Pole.

We arrive in Durban a week before Christmas. A few days later, we are hauled out and start to paint the bottom of the boat. "It's a little bit of a tint clash," I say stepping back to admire my work while dripping paint on my shoe. We could not get green colored bottom paint and therefore went with red, a bit different from the bulwark stripe painted a pinky maroon in Australia, and the hard dodger painted an even darker shade of rose.

"I don't know, it all kind of goes together in a way," Phil says.

A van drives up, and Fred from Peri Peri radio unfolds his large frame from the driver's side, painfully stepping out into the hot sun. "Just thought I'd pop over and see how you was making out," he says.

"Well, that's very nice of you, Fred. We're having a discussion on the artistic merits of such a mélange of maroon. What do you think?"

"She's a fine looking boat."

"How 'bout some coffee, Fred?" I ask.

"No thanks, I'm awash already. Listen, I brought over my welder. Thought maybe you could use it to repair your bowsprit railing."

"Great," Phil says. "That will be a big help. Thank you. It was a bad day in Madagascar when it broke."

"I'll say," I add. "That was the day our cat died."

"That would make anyone have a bad day," Fred says. "Speaking of pets, Eva wants to know if you would come over for Christmas Eve dinner?"

"Wow, we'd love it," we say together.

"Do you consider your wife a pet?" Phil asks.

"No, man. You'll find out when you come to our house. We've got six dogs, eight cats, and a part time tortoise we share with the neighbors. I'll phone you with the details about dinner. Say, why don't you hire one of these chappies to paint Iwalani?" he asks pointing to a man painting the bottom of a boat next to us. "You wouldn't have to pay him but a few Rand a day."

I look over at the marina worker Fred is referring to. Earlier in the day he had been grinding toxic bottom paint off a boat, singing away, with just a filthy rag wrapped around his face. Explaining that it wasn't good for him to be breathing the dust from the paint, I gave him one of my bandanas, which was only slightly better than his rag. He now has the bandana wrapped around his head; the old rag is missing.

Over the last few days I have been having sleepless nights trying to decide what is the morally correct thing to do with the inexpensive labor rates in this country. Phil vetoed my idea of sheathing the bottom in copper, so we are left with having to repaint the bottom. Should we hire someone to work on our boat at the going rate, helping them to support their family even if it is only a few dollars a day? Should we also buy them the proper protective equipment in order to ease our guilt about knowingly putting another person's health at risk to do our own toxic dirty work?

"Phil and I made a vow that we would try and do everything on this boat ourselves, so that's what we do," I explain to Fred.

After Fred leaves Phil's cell phone rings; it is the parents of a former student calling to invite us to dinner Christmas Day.

"We've never had so many invitations out in such a short time span," Phil says.

"These South Africans just haven't gotten a chance to know us. I'm sure I'll end up offending someone, somehow, somewhere."

"You're too hard on yourself," Phil says.

"I haven't told you this, but I'm getting a urinary tract infection. I'm going to be even harder to live with over the next few days."

"Oh great!"

"Don't worry. I started antibiotics; everything will be under control. It's just now that the boat is high and dry on land, living fifteen feet off the ground, and one rickety ladder trip away from the boatyard bathroom is going to be a tad difficult."

*   *   *

Our Christmas is spent with newfound friends sweating, laughing and hearing about the difficulties of living in a place where green monkeys regularly break into houses and raid refrigerators, and their larger descendants aren't averse to breaking a fellow human's neck over a cell phone or an automobile.

Between parties, we quickly finish the work on Iwalani and with the help of hot drying winds and Fred's welder, we are back in the water and ready to continue southward as soon as the weather will allow.

My bladder infection isn't getting any better, and neither is my computer, so under the guise of picking my computer up from one more service center, Phil tricks me into getting my own problems addressed at a nearby hospital, a modern glass and steel building high on a ridge looking out to sea. I am the last person to consult with MD's over my own health problems. It's not that I have anything against them; it's just that I would rather fix my own ailments. But sometimes I reach a stumbling block and have to admit to needing a second opinion, and this has become such a time. My urinalyses on the boat are all negative; it does

340

not appear I have an infection. Yet it feels like someone is taking a stiff bottle brush dipped in hot pepper spray and is merrily scraping away at the inside of my urethra. I think my screaming and shooting high into the air each time it happens is starting to get on Phil's nerves.

The prognosis for my computer is grave. The fourth and final technician says there is nothing more that can be done for it. Despondently, we carry Arnold back to the boat in his little plastic coffin while we wait for the lab tests on my own disease.

A call to Phil's cell phone from the doctor makes us return back to the hospital that afternoon, when the doctor finds out that, yes, indeed, I have been spending time in some of South Africa's streams. He refers me to a urologist and also wants me to be tested for bilharzia. There are some concerns I may have contracted the disease while indecorously availing my open orifices to the parasite while peacefully lollygagging in the stream at the lion refuge. The new test necessitates that I run up and down the stairs for fifteen minutes in order to loosen up any parasite eggs that could be holding tightly to the lining of my bladder, before I give them another urine sample. With ten flights of ultra modern steel and granite steps, I have my work cut out for me.

Phil attempts to cheer me on by positioning himself on various landings via the elevator, as I pant past him. "How are you doing?"

"Terrible. This is nothing short of torture," I gasp.

A few painful flights later, "How are you doing? Hey! The nurse said you are supposed to be really jumping hard on the steps as you run."

"The only good thing about this is that we are in South Africa."

"Why? What's so good about that?" Phil asks.

"After I collapse on this stairwell from a heart attack, I will be in the preeminent place for a heart transplant," I pant. "South Africa was where they were invented."

"Oh, come on, this isn't so bad!"

"I don't see you running along beside me!"

Finally, fifteen minutes later, the nurse hands me a plastic cup and shows me the way to the ladies room. This is a nice hospital, brand new, clean, with well-trained staff. I feel confident in their abilities. I shut the door behind me and rinse my sweating face off at the sink, before attempting to pee in the cup. When I pull my underpants down, I have the biggest shock of my life. It is an event so sinister, so vile, so Herculean in its grossness that I think I actually see every embarrassing time of my teenage years flash before my eyes, paling in comparison to this very moment. Never before has such a disgusting thing happened to me. I am just thankful that all the girls in my high school who mastered the art of humiliation using me as the victim of their refinement, are thousands of miles and hundreds of wrinkles to the west, for they would have had fair fodder indeed. As my underpants come down, an intrepid hitchhiker uses that very moment to affect his escape. An inch long cockroach falls from my underpants to the floor. I scream like a woman in a horror movie, an outstanding performance really. One worthy of at least an Academy award.

"You OK Mum?" the nurse says while knocking at the door.

I can hear Phil, too, outside the door, trying to jiggle the knob. The cockroach has scuttled away so fast and I stand so transfixed in shock that it never had a chance of getting splattered to oblivion by the stomp of my sandal.

"Honey? Are you alright?" Phil asks with concern through the door.

"Sorry about that, I'm fine now," I say in a high weak voice.

"It's a little bit painful for her to urinate," I hear Phil telling the nurse. "She usually doesn't scream that bad though."

After the specialist examines me, he writes out a prescription for another antibiotic, as well as the treatment for bilharzia. He will call us when all the tests are back. After all the tests, exams and medications are tabulated, I pass my credit card to the cashier at the hospital and wince in anticipation of the bill. The total for everything, converts to just seventeen U.S. dollars.

"Are you sure that's correct?" I ask in disbelief.

"Yes, dear, I am sorry it is so many Rand, but you had a lot of work done."

I bite my lip and hand her the credit card. At home, a nail trim on a fractious poodle would have cost more than that.

"I thought all that would have cost hundreds of dollars. We've got money to burn. What should we do to celebrate New Year's tonight?" Phil asks me when we get back to the car.

"Drink hemlock," I respond.

"Why what's wrong?"

"We have a serious problem on the boat," then I tell him about my little friend in the bathroom.

"So that's what the scream was about. You nearly gave everyone in the hospital a heart attack!"

"Including myself."

"I meant to tell you this, but on the trip down from Richards Bay I killed two at the nav station on my watch late at night. You don't actually think the cockroach was… you know, up your, you know…"

"ACK! Stop the car! I'm going to throw up. No, Jesus- I don't know! Is it possible? No way. It is physiologically <u>impossible</u>. I think. No, <u>don't</u> stop the car. We need to take serious action. Turn at the mall. We're going to a pet store for New Years!"

And so it was, we came away from Durban with our new pet for 2003, a tiny little gecko I name Martin, after one of the charming people we met at one of the Durban Christmas parties.

"He seems kind of small," I say while examining him through the plastic cage. "Not much bigger than a cockroach. Are you sure he'll be able to eat those bruisers on the boat?"

"You just wait and see," Phil says. "But, I am not sure about his name. Can't you think up something else? Maybe a better name will come to you later."

We return to the boat, and, while Phil sets up the barbeque for dinner, I decide to set Martin free inside Iwalani. I have to admit, that at times, some of my actions can be a bit peculiar, or at the least somewhat unusual, and that afternoon is certainly no different. For some reason, when I pick Martin up from his little plastic cage, I have an overwhelming desire to hug and kiss him, tickle his tiny little chin, cuff his puny little gecko ears, and count his wee little fingers. It has been almost two months since Stew died, and I am still feeling terribly pet-less.

Unfortunately, Martin does not share in this same desire, and when he sees this enormous woman with big trembling, puckering lips coming his way, he does what an self respecting lizard victim would do. He sheds his tail.

For the second time that day I give another milk curdling scream. Martin's tail flips, bloodlessly, around the galley counter like a hooked fish. In my fright, I drop poor Martin, who slowly skulks off into the shadows while I try to subdue the crazed tail. Now this is a phenomenon I know full well about. In fact, one could say I am a professional about this very survival strategy, as I get paid to explain to my clients about tail loss in lizards. Yet, I have never seen the actual event in reality, and it works above and beyond Mother Nature's and Dr. Wood's expectations.

Phil comes running to see what the problem is. "Another cockroach?" he pants down to me with bright blue eyes.

"No," I say sniffling back tears. "Look at what happened to Martin." I hold up the still twitching tail for Phil to see. "I was just trying to kiss him."

That evening I am convinced I killed poor Martin, though logically I know better. Phil too, tries to reassure me that he is fine. I am feeling guilty for taking him from his former lizard life, whatever it was. How is he ever going to find a Mrs. Martin on Iwalani?

"Cheer up," Phil says. "At least now he has a name that fits. We'll have to call him Stumpy."

"Oh, god. You're not helping," I sniffle.

"You're right. Tell you what. After seeing you sitting there working on your poor excuse of a laptop computer, with all those wires and that ridiculous external keyboard—how about if I try and fix it for you? I know I swore I would never work on Arnold because it is such a worthless piece of crap, but I can't stand seeing you looking so sad. For New Years I will try and fix your computer for you."

"How can you? He's been to six computer hospitals on three continents and everyone says it's hopeless." I know I have just spoken the magic words. To tell Phil something is impossible, or hopeless, is to invoke a challenge. I have yet to see him fail at fixing anything when presented with the two words, "It's impossible." But he and Arnold had a definitely antagonistic relationship, and he swore off ever touching him when we left home. I gratefully unplug the peripherals, which gave Arnold the nickname "Frankenputer," and hand Phil his patient. I stay up as late as I can, but head to bed faintly aware that all of Durban is celebrating the New Year without us. Fireworks, sirens and laughing humans pulse in the city that surrounds our small ship.

At two, I wake up and Phil is still not in bed. At three, he finally climbs between the sheets. "Any luck," I mumble. No answer. Not a good sign.

"We are making progress," he says eventually.

By noon the next day, Phil screeches "Eureka! I am Eenvinseebull!" and I know that he has succeeded where no one else could.

"What was wrong with him?" I ask.

"Something that has been wrong with him since the day you bought him, a defective RAM chip. I took it out, and he works fine. You no longer need the external keyboard and all those cables."

"You are a genius! Thank you," I say hugging him. "Now if we can just find

Stumpy."

*   *   *

The weather looks good for leaving over the weekend, but we have to clear out of Durban, despite the fact that our next port is still in South Africa. This necessitates spending an afternoon driving around getting clearance paperwork stamped. Fred offers to take us to all the necessary stops on Friday afternoon, and we are grateful for his assistance.

Our neighborhood in Durban. The Spanish yacht Islero is on the right.

On Saturday, Fred and Alistair announce that the weather window has become too short. Phil's satellite antenna picture looks good, and I am ready to go, but the weather gurus say to sit tight. Reluctantly we stay, and yes the winds remain favorable longer than predicted.

By the following Thursday, the weather starts to look good for another Friday departure. The ultimate crow's nest, Phil's satellite antenna, shows clear skies all around the Cape; the weather faxes all look good, and Fred from Peri Peri radio says we have a good window. All of a sudden we have three other yachties knocking on our hull for weather information: a German named Hans with too much caffeine in his system, Jacques, a happy-go-lucky Frenchman, and Isi, a cheerfully exuberant Spaniard.

All of us filed a flight plan with port control the week before. Whether we have to re-file our flight plans this week is open to dockside debate. I head into the marina office to settle our account and to ask whether we need to re-file our flight plan. The secretary phones the harbormaster and yes indeed, the flight plan is over one week old. "Things could change in one week, new crew, hull color, you name it," she says.

"No, everything is the same," I respond.

"You must realize," she says in her best look-down-the-nose voice, "that these flight plans are designed to protect you yachties. The Agulhas current is very, very dangerous. This part of the coast is very dangerous. How else are the authorities going to know what to look for if you are sinking?"

"But, there are at least five other yachts all wanting to leave. Must we all trudge around the city to re-file the flight plan?" I finally ask, trying to refrain from whining.

"That is the system," she says matter-of-factly.

I return to the nervous huddle of yachties with the bad news. "Look, this is ridiculous," Hans the German says with fury. "The marina manager told me we didn't have to refile our flight plans."

"Well the marina office just called port control and they told me we had to," I say.

"No we don't," Hans says.

"Yes, we do," I say gently.

"Augh, I hate this country. The left hand has no idea what the right hand is doing."

"It's a bit frustrating, but we need to respect South Africa's laws and the policies they are trying to institute," I say.

"What's the difference between a tourist and racist?" Hans asks me, pushing his face just inches from my nose.

"I don't know," I say politely.

"Three days," he spits.

I stare back at him unblinking.

"Augh, no one has any humor anymore. I'll see for myself about the flight plan," Hans says storming off.

Isi, Jacques and I stand on the dock waiting. "That man has too much coffee," Isi remarks as Hans nearly rips the door off the office building.

"No," Jacques counters, "too much sauerkraut."

Hans triumphantly emerges a few minutes later waving his paperwork. He manages to convince the authorities that we do not need to re-file the flight plan, and is the first to leave bucking against the headwind, his chiseled face turned to the southwesterly rain not looking back at us, while his new Asian bride huddles down below seasick and scared.

"He is a madman," Jacques says shaking his head. "I will wait for the sun at least to come out." The sun does come out, and he and his wife Genevieve leave next.

Isi, the Spanish singlehander, backs up his boat *Islero* from the slip. His propeller shaft shoots out of the stern like a torpedo and spears itself into the mud bank behind his boat. *Islero* quickly fills up with water through the shaft log. Not one to panic, even while sinking, Isi shrugs nonchalantly and yells at us to leave, he will be fine.

Glad to finally be on our way, Phil and I motor Iwalani out of the harbor, a bit apprehensive that it is a Friday. As soon as we swing the tiller south, a "NO DATA" error message appears on the autopilot compass display. As a result, the the tiller starts swinging backand forth like a metronome. Thanks to the cell phone and our friends in Durban, we order a new fluxgate compass before we are back at the dock. *Islero* has been safely towed to the boatyard and hauled out.

We install the new compass and Saturday morning motor out into Durban Harbor to adjust it. Around and around we circle to check the deviation. It is way off. The deviation on the old compass had been way off too, even as far back as Maine, but Phil opted to ignore it, saying the actual numbers on the display are irrelevant to the self-steering. Could it be that after two years this error is now biting us? The variation in the dealer set-up is also way off. Instead of 12E, or –12, the data we entered in New Caledonia, we now have a variation of 25W, or +25, quite a discrepancy. (Don't bother looking this up in the glossary: the deviation is magnetic factors within the boat, which affect a compass; the variation is magnetic anomalies outside the boat.) Could the deviation and variation together add up to such an error that on a due south heading the autopilot's brain is getting addled? I reset the variation, and Phil moves the new compass behind the bulkhead.

Avoiding tugs, container ships, cruise ships, dinghy racers, and booze cruise boats, we re-swing the compass, steering the boat in wide circles in Durban Harbor. The new compass position gives us a much smaller deviation, but it is still above what the book recommends. However, the autopilot now seems to be working fine.

So, now what to do? It is 2:30 Saturday afternoon; the next Southwester is predicted to come late Sunday night. I look at our own satellite image and see nothing but clear skies and favorable winds for at least three more days. Still, it will take us forty-eight hours to reach the next harbor, East London.

"We have to wait for the next weather window," Phil states flatly.

"But the satellite looks good," I plead.

"If you want to get a job with the South African weather service, be my guest! Just leave me at the dock."

"If we go back to Durban, I will go nuts," I respond. I look at the calendar, it is an odd numbered day, so I actually have the power to make the ultimate decision. I swing Iwalani in another circle while I make up my mind.

"You know, Amy, this is the Agulhas Current we are dealing with. We made the decision not to take any unnecessary risks," Phil says.

I guess it is the fact that Phil called me Amy and used the word Agulhas, a name that started long ago shivering my timbers when we were first preparing for this trip, that finally cracks my confidence. This particular stretch of the African coast is known to snap huge ships in half or fold up others like an accordion. The autopilot steers us around in circles with no problems. Yet, I don't want to be off this part of coast, an area where there is no place to turn for refuge should the weather go downhill with my husband saying "I told you so." I eventually turn the autopilot off and swing the heavy tiller outboard pointing Iwalani back to the marina. Of course, the wind stays favorable for three days, but I never say, "I told you so."

*   *   *

"So how was Swaziland?" Danny asks us politely trying to bring up a subject other than the touchy business about our still being in Durban. We are having dinner with Coco from our hometown and her boyfriend, Danny, at the Durban Yacht Club.

"Well, considering we were only there for four hours, long enough to drive in one end and out the other, we didn't see much, but it appears prosperous and the people seem happy and are very friendly. Everyone looked up from reading their newspapers and waved as we drove by," Phil says.

"Yeah, you don't see that here," Danny responds.

"What's been happening with you guys?" I ask.

"Still waiting for the Yamaha outboard to get fixed. I took it out of the first repair shop, as they seemed inept and it was taking too long. I'm not sure this new place is any better."

I look at Phil who is sipping a gin and tonic. Usually he launches into an oral diagnostic routine when confronted with any contrary machinery, but he remains silent.

"What's wrong with it?" I ask.

"It runs for awhile and then dies."

"Is it pumping water?" I ask looking sideways at Phil for help in this conversation.

"Yes, the impeller is fine."

"Carburetor?" I ask.

"Probably. They think it's gummed up," Danny responds.

"Do you shut the fuel off and run it dry before you store it?" I ask.

"Sometimes, but not always."

"Well, that's the extent of my carburetor knowledge," I say.

Phil remains silent. I can tell he is thinking about his sons.

"And how was the trip to the lion facility?" Coco asks.

"Great," I answer and tell her about our experiences.

"Did they do any field sustainability analyses to see if the land can support eight lions?" Coco asks.

"I don't know," I respond. "It's all rather a passionate thing. But we are talking about a chunk of land almost the size of a small country. I am sure they might need to bring in a few kudu and zebra to start, but leopards already are living there."

"Have you been taking malaria preventive?" Dan asks us.

"Just while we were north of here," I respond. "Doxycycline, nothing else. As chief medical officer I consider it a failure on my part if we get tropical diseases. I had to go to a doctor here in Durban as they thought I had bilharzia, but thank goodness I didn't. I was just suffering from Durban Disease."

"Durban Disease?" Coco asks.

"Stress," I say.

"We've had almost every disease you can get. I figure you're not really into the heart of cruising until you catch something," Danny remarks.

"Dengue was especially bad," Coco says shaking her head.

"But not as bad as getting robbed in Mozambique!" Danny exclaims.

"They came on the boat while we were on shore and took all our underwear, my shoes, socks, some food. It was horrible. You feel so violated."

"But they left the electronics, thank goodness," Danny adds.

"Have you had any trouble here in Durban?" Coco asks.

"No, we've been lucky, so far," Phil says. "Most every other cruiser we know has either been mugged or assaulted."

"It's quite a city," Danny says. "A bit depressing with the highway ramps just ending in midair, not completed.

"But, the tile mosaics in the sidewalk," Coco says whistling, "they can take your breath away, they are so intricate. Have either of you tried a 'bunny'? We see signs for bunny chow all over and are wondering what they are."

"They are loaves of white bread with the insides scooped out and filled with bland curry. Not exactly a gourmet delicacy," I respond.

Somehow I drift off, half listening to what our compatriots are saying. I am trying not to think about being stuck in Durban or about the on going e-mail battle Phil is having with his ex-wife, which I know is preoccupying his thoughts. I know the anger is resurfacing in him over the court's decision years ago to grant him half of the financial responsibility for rearing his children with little chance to interact in their upbringing.

My mother warned me years ago that a human mother, when perceiving a threat to her children, will act no different from a lioness, and Phil's ex-wife is no exception. And what about the lions? I start thinking about the eight lions to our north and hope that the South African court system will be wise enough to do the right thing for them.

Little do I know, that at that very moment, a small airplane has already landed at the rehabilitation facility's grass airfield. Armed with a court order, Mitch's former boss has the go ahead to dart and remove the lions to a small enclosure near Johannesburg. The ensuing melee results in one lion being left behind and teenage Mpandi getting darted three times with a potentially lethal dose of anesthetic. But the lion's will to live is strong, and he does not die, despite the confusion, the heat, the tears, and the overloaded airplane taking off from the compound in a violent thunderstorm.

The South African court system has decided to remove the lions from the two humans that can nurture and care for them best. It is better that they go from a pen of forty acres, to one of just two. In their new facility, they will now be free to get shuffled and absorbed into the canned hunt system. Their freedom will be gone, their future in question, and someday their heads, too, may grace the walls of a trophy-loving huntress, lifeless victims of a very unfortunate human power struggle.

Mitch and his lions

Chapter 27

Battle Plans

February 2003
East London and Mossel Bay
South Africa

Durban and the mighty Agulhas finally let go of our keel and we arrive at East London with a big push from the south setting current. At one point, Iwalani cruises southward at ten knots on just a whisper of wind. There is ample opportunity for problems to surface from either the compass or the autopilot, but they never do. As soon as we leave the harbor and finally head south, the air becomes drier and easier to breathe. In Durban, even the sun perspires. We see a black backed gull, our first in two years- a sure sign that the Atlantic is just around the corner.

We are now officially broke. The cold cream jar is empty, and what remains in our savings account has to go towards health insurance, mortgage payments and the boy's upcoming college expenses. It will all be gone by September. I budgeted seventeen thousand a year for the three years we were gone. This would have been pretty close if we had not spent so much on Stewart. We also hemorrhaged money over the last few months on things that we should have been more cautious about purchasing.

In the process of trying to get our web page uploaded, Phil helps a young couple get their new Internet café up and running. They generously pay him for his time, which gives us a small pocketful of cash. Phil finds the source of their trouble is the phone line, which they can't get replaced for weeks.

We guiltily enter a competing café to update our webpage. While I wait for Phil, a handsome man with an electric personality and equally vibrant dreadlocks strikes up a conversation from the computer next to me. "How do you like East London?" he asks me.

"We have only been here a day," I say, "but it sure beats Durban. Maybe it's the weather, but it feels less oppressive."

He asks me where we are from, and I tell him about our trip so far.

"You must be excited about almost being home," he says.

"Yes and no. For the last two years I was hopelessly homesick, always comparing everything we encountered to America. Now that home is literally just around the corner, I am getting cold feet about going back. I am worried about going home to a country that is on the brink of war. I think if Americans lived exemplar lives we would not be targeted out for terrorist acts. At home we have these people called the Jehovah's Witnesses. They drive up to your house and make you feel like you are inferior to them if you do not believe in their god, or their religion. America is doing a Jehovah's Witness thing: knocking on other country's doors, only with tanks and missiles in hand, not bibles, saying how good our system is and how everyone should be just like us."

"Don't you think democracy in America is good?" he asks.

"Yes, I do. It's just our marketing approach that's a little disturbing."

"Marketing, yes, that is the secret for everything. Isn't it? Whether you are a weaverbird, a crocodile, or a New Yorker, getting sex and a meal at the end of the day all depends on how well you sell yourself. By the way, my name is Ayanda."

"I'm Amy."

"Pleasure," he says extending the vowels. "Do you have tribal differences in America, too?"

"Centuries ago, yes, but for the most part, America is pretty united. But, I think maybe now that is changing. America is making two tribes, the Democrats and the Republicans. I never really thought about it in that way until I came to Africa. I think it was the Zulu that made me see that there are tribal differences."

"Yes, a tribe is really an extended family. The Zulu, they are true warriors. They are the only tribe in Africa to defeat the British."

"Yes, we drove through some of the battle sites. The Zulu are different. Oh brother, here I am sounding very ethnocentric."

"No, that is the way it is. Our name, our heritage, who we are, is who we were."

"So what does Ayanda mean?" I ask.

"It is Xhosan and the closest word in English is 'fecund'."

"You're probably not old enough to know if you live up to that name!"

Ayanda laughs, "No, I plan on spreading my seed through art. That's what I am doing right now. I am planning a beauty pageant here in East London to celebrate both traditional African and Western beauty."

"When is it?" I ask.

"March. You should stay and be in it."

"I thought you said it was a beauty pageant, not a dog show," I joke.

"Don't be so hard on yourself. Everyone, everything has beauty. Everywhere there is beauty. People just need to be trained sometimes to see it."

I turn to look at Phil who is typing away on the computer, completely oblivious to the conversation I am having. I lean in and whisper to Ayanda. "I've been feeling

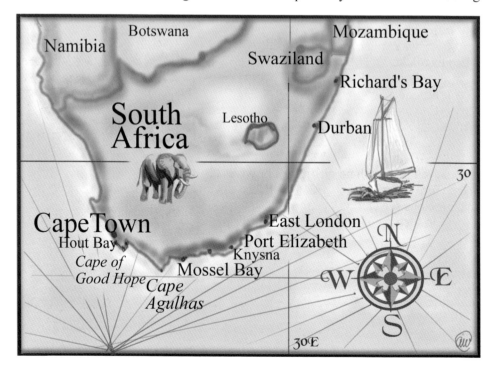

like a plant that's gone way beyond the flowering stage, and sort of getting beyond the seedpod stage too. My roots seem stuck in dry soil and I've been trying to figure out the meaning of life. Why are we here? What's the point?"

"Why are we here? Do you not know Einstein and the equation $E=MC^2$?" Ayanda asks.

I wrote my college honors thesis on General Relativity and how it may relate to biological processes; I thought I knew a little at least about Special Relativity. I shake my head no, hoping for the Xhosan explanation.

"The point of life is to keep the equation balanced. If a person is mass or "M", they must put out as much energy "E," as that person "M" uses," Ayanda explains.

"I see," I say knowing full well the answer to my next question. "And the C^2?" I ask innocently. I know full well that the speed of light is fixed and physicists assigned it as the constant "C", with a value of "1", meaning that the C^2 is cancelled out, so Mass and Energy are equal.

"The C is calories. Lots of calories in, means lots of energy out," Ayanda says.

$$* \qquad * \qquad *$$

After Phil and I leave the café, we pick up some fruits and vegetables at the local market and walk back to the boat. "Seems like you had a good time at the café," Phil jests.

"Yes, what a character. I think I met the next Nelson Mandela,"

We slip down a dirt path I saw earlier which looked like a shortcut to Iwalani. It passes under a bridge where several women are walking with bundles piled high on their heads. When they see Phil carrying plastic shopping bags, they all break into catcalls and taunts, leaning over the bridge and pointing at my poor husband. Men carrying bags is not a sight you are likely to see in South Africa.

"You can't have him!" I yell up to them. "He's all mine. He even washes the dishes and does the laundry!"

"Jesus, Honey. Keep it quiet. They may come and abduct me."

"No, we're more likely to get attacked by a man who doesn't want you setting a bad example. You know, I think that's why there are so many problems where there is polygamy. Too many men having no partners. I think these men we see sitting around are at the root of all the problems. They are bored and horney. Maybe that's why there are so many violent men in the Middle East. Too many idle men. Nature didn't intend for a ratio of eight women to one man."

"Oh, come on, think of how good that would be!" Phil kids.

"Well, maybe it would take some of the pressure off me! But what about those seven men with no girlfriends or wives?"

"Turn them all into monks or priests so they can do battle with their subconscious selves," Phil suggests.

"Or, turn them into soldiers so they can battle the rest of the world."

$$* \qquad * \qquad *$$

Still guided by Fred and Alistair, we continue our way down the eastern end of South Africa until we arrive at Mossel Bay. White sand beaches and brilliant turquoise waters surround our jetty protected marina. Phil finds a job working on

351

the marina office's computer, which gives us some quick income. We decide to settle in to this beautiful spot for a few weeks, as everything we need is in easy walking distance, including a great beach for swimming. We will do our bulk provisioning here, instead of Cape Town, and get everything ready for the Atlantic crossing and our return home.

I also decide to spend money we don't have, on a local business that sinks tourists in steel cages ten feet below the surface of the bay, for an up close encounter with great white sharks. Despite pouring gallons of chum in the water and flopping a wooden seal silhouette on the ocean's surface, the proprietors don't entice a single shark to appear, much to Phil's relief and my dismay.

The interest rates in the U.S. are at an all time low. We spend time, over the Internet, trying to refinance our house. Despite our monthly payments becoming half of what we are currently paying, the banks reject our applications because neither of us have "real" jobs. While at it, we write our house sitters and tell them to expect us home on June 6, 2003. I send off resumes in order to find a job starting in September, leaving us some time over the summer to spend with Phil's boys. We also begin the painful process of advertising Iwalani for sale.

"Are you sure we should do this?" I ask Phil.

"Yes. This has been my plan all along: build Iwalani. sail around the world, sell her, and buy a floatplane. Only now it looks like I'll have to build the float plane if I am going to be the mechanic for it," Phil responds.

I can feel tears starting to well up inside me. I am painting scenes of Iwalani at various places around the globe on the seat backs of the settees.

When we launched her, I originally painted roses, trying to turn Iwalani into a mobile cottage. I recently painted over the roses, creating an off white canvas with which to illustrate our experiences. I started with a painting of Iwalani sailing in Maine. I loved the colors of Maine when I was growing up. Dark blues and greens, yellow ochre by the truckload, raw umbers, lots of gray. But now, compared to the colors of the rest of the world, they seem so dead and lifeless. I quickly move on to the next painting: Iwalani anchored on the east side of Bora Bora. Such pinks and greens! Tuomotos blues, New Caledonia orange, Australia gold, Great Barrier Reef turquoise, all these colors fill my palette with their energy.

Where is home? Our family is back home and I miss all of them terribly, but I am not the same person as when I left. I feel like a magnet that has picked up pieces of everywhere we have been. I have grown a tough outer coat that is impervious to the blows of a tempest or the death threats of humans. I have been a visitor and a guest in so many countries. I left the comforts of my own living room, walked across the street, and sat on the neighbor's front porch while looking back at my own house. I saw the paint peeling from my shutters, places where the shingles blew off, and the crumbling foundation in the corner. It is a whole different view from that of looking out my own picture window.

I no longer feel like I can call America home. Earth is home. The kitchen is in Suwarrow, where food can be plucked off the trees or fished from the sea. The living room is the Australian bush where a person can live without books, music, media, or any other entertainment other than that provided by kookaburra, wallaby, lorikeets and magpie. And the bedroom? The erotic forests of the Marquesan hills, where sleep and lust intertwine in a continuous dance of dripping, rhythmic sensuality.

"What is wrong?" Phil asks me. "Why are you crying?"

"I am not sure about selling Iwalani. She has become much more than a boat."

"We have to," Phil states flatly. "We need the money. Think about Nathaniel. I can't continue with this lifestyle. It is too selfish. Think about Iwalani too. Do you want to see her rotting on a mooring in Maine? She was built to cross oceans."

"Exactly. Let's keep going," I suggest.

"And live on what? How do we pay the mortgage on our farm, or do you want to sell it?"

"I don't know what I want to do," I say. "I do miss growing our own food. I miss my dachshund, Polly, I should get home for her, especially since we got email that she's got cancer, too."

"Come on. Let's go for a walk," Phil says. "I'll treat you to a petit four at the bakery. Then we can walk down to the point and look for rock dassies."

I grab my backpack and follow Phil off the boat. A cruise ship is anchored out in the bay, and the tourists are being shuttled in by a launch. A group of young local school children wearing plastic frond skirts are assembled along the green carpeting winding from the dock to the open mouth of an air-conditioned bus. The school children serenade the tourists with traditional African songs, while the gray hairs limp and shuffle by, photographing it all before climbing up into the bus. "That could be us," Phil says.

"I don't think so."

We walk up the hill toward the town center using a shortcut that crosses over railroad tracks and winds through an abandoned lot. Two small children are asleep under a bush near the path.

"Those are the kids that were at the restaurant yesterday!" I say to Phil.

The day before, while we were waiting for our laundry, we had lunch at a nearby café. Two small waifs appeared under the porch railing where we were seated, asking for money. As we were the only patrons, I got up from our table and went to play the peanut game with them.

In Durban, people wanting money accosted us every twenty feet. These varied from packs of small dark colored children wearing rags, to older white couples with finer clothes and better vocabulary than Phil and I put together. "We're beggars, mum," they would tell me when I asked why they needed money. To these well off people I would say, "Bugger off!" but for the people appearing poorer than us, I asked three questions. Who is the president of South Africa? What do you get when you add two plus two? And then I would write a letter, usually a "B" and ask what it was called. If a child or group of children could answer all three questions they got a cash reward; otherwise they each ended up with a bag of peanuts as a consolation prize. While walking in Durban, I carried a backpack full of bagged peanuts. So far, no one had been able to answer all three questions, and our meager cash supplies were untouched.

When I asked the Durban street children why they weren't in school, they replied that they had no money. School fees, books and uniforms amounted to near two hundred U.S. dollars for each child. Yet, when I asked our white friends about this, they told us that schooling was free for all children in South Africa and we were only being swindled by children whose drug addicted parents were usually hiding nearby waiting to receive the money brought in by their begging offspring. I wasn't sure whom to believe.

These two small boys at the restaurant were the only beggars we saw in Mossel Bay. I knelt down so I could be at their height. The older of the two, had conjunctivitis. Both were very skinny

"We are going to play a game. You have to learn to work for money. There is no such thing as a free lunch in life," I said to them. "I am going to ask you three questions, if you get all three right I will give you ten Rand. OK?" They both slowly nodded their heads up and down, leery of what they had suddenly gotten themselves into. "Who is the president of South Africa?" I asked.

"Mandela," the larger boy said.

"Are you sure? He once was, but Mbeke is now. That is a wrong answer."

"Now we lose? I am hungry," the smaller boy said looking at the older one while tugging at his dirty T-shirt.

"Do you have parents nearby watching us?" I asked.

Unsure how to answer, they hesitated for a moment. In Durban the small children emphatically shook their heads 'No!' always saying they were on their own. These two looked at each other and then nodded "yes,' each of them looking in opposite directions. I followed their gaze beyond the pastel colored stucco buildings down both ends of the street. I couldn't see anyone. I gave both of them three bags of peanuts, just as the waiter of the restaurant came out with our lunches.

"Scat, you two," he yelled. I jumped up onto my feet, ready to run, until I realized he wasn't referring to Phil and me.

"No, it's OK," I said. "I was just having a conversation." I came back up onto the veranda and sat back at the restaurant table.

"Bloody monkeys. I am sorry if they were bothering you," he said.

"What? No, they weren't bothering us at all."

And here these two boys are again, asleep under the bushes, using the hard earth as a pillow, flies feeding on the sleep forming on the corner of the larger boy's eyes. "Look at them," I say to Phil. "These boys don't have parents. They said they did yesterday, only because they thought that was what I wanted to hear. Can't we steal them and bring them home?"

"What are you nuts? And get arrested for kidnapping?" Phil asks.

"How can we get arrested for kidnapping if they have no family?"

"You don't know that for sure."

"We should let them sleep now. But if I see them again, I am going to ask them if they want to come live with us in America."

"Oh, brother," Phil says rolling his eyes.

"No 'oh brother,' I'm serious."

"I know. That's what I am worried about."

"Let's skip the pastries. I am ready to walk down to the point to find the dassies," I say.

"They might be safer for you to adopt."

When we come to the end of the point, we walk through an empty parking lot. On the far side, steep cliffs rise like catchers mitts for the cold winds of

Antarctica. We head for the rocks along the shore, where the dassies are known to hang out. As we walk by two parked cars, a man and a woman stand up from a large stone where they had been seated.

They yell at each other in a language we don't understand but can interpret strictly from the tone, and it doesn't sound good.

Suddenly, the man swings back with all his might and strikes the woman in the face with his fist. She falls over onto the ground while he continues to beat her.

I immediately drop my backpack and begin running over to help her. I am furious and am ready to kill her assailant. Phil grabs my arms and holds me back. "God damn it!" I yell at my husband. "Let me go!"

"No!" Phil yells at me, trying to pin my arms behind my back.

"Cut it out, Phil! If I have to punch you out first, I may not be in the best shape to punch that guy's lights out. LET ME GO!"

"STOP IT, AMY! This is not your fight. This is not your country. You could kill that man. I know it. And then what? You'd be in a South African prison for what?"

I turn to look at Phil. I realize he is right. The man stops kicking and hitting the woman when he sees what is happening with Phil and me. The woman sits up and covers her face with her hands. She is sobbing; I can tell she has already forgiven the man. He sits back down next to her and puts his arm around her shoulder. A police car drives into the parking lot, one of only two we have seen in all of South Africa.

"See that? They will take care of it now," Phil says.

"You mean 'just now'. I bet they don't do a thing. Those policemen just pulled in to eat their lunch."

"Rock Dassies. That's why we walked here in the first place," Phil reminds me.

We crawl under a fence railing and out onto the rocks. A strong northeasterly wind is blowing. Crashing surf sends tall plumes of salt water into the air. One of the hotels on the point has been throwing out garbage, lettuce, cabbage, and a few watermelon slices for the dassies. I walk up close to the small furry creatures to take photographs.

"They just look like woodchucks! Mangy ones at that!" I say.

Rock "dassie" aka rock hyrax

Another couple walks down the path near us. The man is wearing a New Jersey Nets basketball uniform and looks like he might be a famous U.S. basketball player.

The woman has on a red dress with matching high-heeled shoes. They are laughing and talking with New Jersey accents. "What are these animals?" she asks the tall man.

"I dunno. Chipmunks, I guess," he responds. They pause on the path for a moment to watch the dassies, neither one venturing closer than the edge of the railing.

I want to shout out to them, *'These are called rock hyrax, or dassies, if you are South African. They are the closest relative to the African elephant. They are also related to manatees and dugong. Imagine that! These furry rodent-like things related to an elephant!'* I bite my tongue. Phil is right; sometimes it's better to stay out of people's business. I let them continue on the path content with the knowledge of having just seen their first South African chipmunks.

Phil and I walk back to town and decide to stop at the grocery store. Loaded with plastic shopping bags that cut the circulation from the tips our fingers, we trudge back to the boat hoping to find the two boys along the way. We walk back down the hill and over the railroad tracks through the shortcut, but see no sign of the children.

As we come to the ramp that leads down to the dock, Phil stands transfixed staring out to sea. "What's wrong?" I ask.

"Somebody's in trouble," he says while dropping the grocery bags on the dock.

I can see a yacht plastered with advertising decals, fast approaching the breakwater outside the small harbor. The sloop has what is left of a large genoa still flying like party streamers in the thirty knots of wind. The remains are slamming and shaking uncontrollably, driving the yacht straight for the rocks at the harbor entrance.

Phil jumps into the nearest boat, an outboard belonging to the shark diving company.

"Jump in and untie us quick. It looks like Isi. Hurry up! His roller furling is fouled!" Phil yells to me.

We motor at full speed for the Spaniard's boat *Islero*. Suddenly the outboard dies. We forgot to open the fuel shut off valve.

"What an idiot, I am!" Phil screams. "Start rowing. I'll try to get it going again."

But it is an old and temperamental outboard and no amount of coaxing, cursing or cord pulling is going to get it to run again that day. I put everything I have into the oars and cover the distance at almost the same speed *Islero* approaches the breakwater. The wind has really picked up within the last half hour, and with a ragged genoa and no mainsail, *Islero* is now an unbalanced boat and no longer capable of responding to the self-steering gear. Before Isi knows what is happening, Phil hops on board and unfastens the halyard, getting the remains of the genoa pulled down out of the track. Together they start the engine and steer the Spaniard's boat away from the breaking surf with only a few feet to spare.

"Thank you my American friends," Isi says to us at the dock. "I am awake for thirty six hours. I no longer thinking clear. I do not know why I do not take the genoa down first. It ripped this morning when the wind picked up. I was tired, so I do not care anymore."

"Well, you've got several days to rest. We will have southeasterly winds for the next few days. None of us will be leaving," Phil says.

"How would you like to come for dinner tonight," I ask. "Nothing fancy or long, just a quick meal and then you can go back and sleep?"

"I would like that very much, but I have to do my radio show tonight at nine, so not much sleep for me," Isi responds.

"Radio show?" we ask.

"Shoo, in Spain I am big deal. I do live radio talk show once a week. It can be very tiring. I need to stay sharp for it," Isi says.

"Well we'll sharpen you up, you can count on it," Phil says.

Isi arrives for spaghetti and meatballs but doesn't eat much and leaves early for his radio broadcast. He has managed, through corporate sponsors and the media, to make significant amounts of money off his trip. His boat *Islero* is plastered with advertising decals, corporate slogans and websites. He also uses the web to record his trip, but his updates are done daily. With our weekly updates, sometimes several days go by before we record our thoughts or impressions. There is nothing like tincture of time to temper an emotion. In Spanish, Isi's logs are raw, immediate, and sometimes very volatile.

A few mornings later I sit out in the cockpit drinking coffee. A tan man with golden curly hair walks along Iwalani's flank admiring the deadeyes. He is smoking a cigarette so I give him no notice.

"Hey, are you poppin' fresh?" he asks me with a South African accent.

"Excuse me?" I ask.

"Are you presentable, ready for visitors? I know it's early but I have been eyeing your boat for days. My name is Jan. I am a carpenter from Oudtshoorn. I appreciate good woodworking. Who built your boat?"

"We did," I say a bit apprehensively.

Jan throws the cigarette into the water and climbs on board. Phil comes up from down below where he has been working on the computer, to join in on Jan's rather one-sided conversation on tools. In between tool talk, we tell him about our trip and how we got to South Africa.

"I have to show you this," Jan says pulling out his wallet. He hands me a picture of a wood plane. I pass it along to Phil thinking it is slightly odd that a man would carry a picture of a woodworking tool in his wallet.

"Nice," I say.

"Do you know what that is?" he asks Phil.

"Stanley number 1."

"The man knows his tools! It's the only one missing from my collection." Jan says.

He reaches into his wallet and pulls out another photo of a block plane, this one made of exotic wood with intricate carvings decorating the handle. "I made this one myself."

"It is beautiful," I say with true admiration handing the photo to Phil. He nods at the photograph and then hands it back to Jan.

"Have you been to the Oudtshoorn?" he asks us.

"Yes, we rented a car when we first got to Mossel Bay. We went to Knyssna and hiked in the woods and went to the ostrich farms inland," I say.

"Too bad. I would like for you to come to my house for a braai. Then I can show you my tool shop," Jan says.

"I'm afraid it will have to be another time. We are leaving tomorrow. In fact, I've got a lot to do still," Phil says heading back down below.

"I'll give you my phone number in case you change your mind." Jan pauses for a moment and looks to see whether Phil is still in earshot. "How does living on a boat affect your relationship?"

"It's made us a stronger couple. I can't tell if we are stronger as individuals,

357

as we decide everything together," I respond.

"I'm not sure my wife and I could do it. We would be at each others throats continuously."

"That happens to some couples," I say laughing. "But, I'd say most people are like us. Sometimes we disagree, that is natural. It's how you handle the disagreements that is critical."

"I thought about building a boat and sailing off, but South Africa has many more requirements and regulations preventing people from doing that. You have to pass courses demonstrating sailing proficiency. It can get quite expensive. I reckon in America you have none of that?"

"There are no regulations at all. Anyone can build a boat and sail away if they want to. Lots of people do and then get into trouble requiring big sea rescues costing taxpayers lots of dollars."

"It really is interesting how our two countries evolved. The Dutch and the British settled us both around the same time. We both had native peoples unhappy about it, and yet America went so much further than we did. I'd like to know why." Jan removes his dark glasses. He is handsome in spite of the cigarettes. He looks out at the harbor, then at me with piercing blue eyes.

"I would say it is because America had much better natural resources," I say trying to ignore his stare. "We had large stands of timber for shipbuilding. Our farmland is more fertile, and with more regular rainfall our land was and is more productive. Early in our history fewer people had to farm, and more people could do things like research, or art, or teach. South Africa's land is harder to make a living off of, so you need more people to farm just in order to survive."

"It's an interesting argument, but there are some people in South Africa that think it is because you got all the good blacks in the slave trade."

"You're kidding?" I respond. "That is the most ridiculous thing I have ever heard! An equally asinine way of looking at it is that we got the stupid slaves that couldn't run fast enough, or hide well enough!"

"I'm just telling you what some South Africans think." Jan smiles while polishing the lens of his glasses. It is then that I notice he has a large wad of spinach caught between his front teeth.

"Well one thing this trip has confirmed to me is that there are stupid people everywhere!" I say trying not to look at the vegetation in his mouth.

"But, as a veterinarian, don't you think that some breeds of dogs are smarter than others?" Jan asks while watching a man walk down the dock with a German shepherd.

"Yes, but, within breeds, coat color makes no difference! Well, except with albinos. When we humans created different dog breeds, we selected genes for specific tasks or traits. If you had a kennel full of fifty mix breed dogs, some would be dumb by one persons standards and others smart. Intelligence can be a very subjective trait."

"Wouldn't you consider yourself a clever person?" Jan asks.

"Heavens no! I am the gold standard of average," I say laughing. "I was lucky in having the best childhood a person could ever have, as well as a good education. But, if I start thinking with a four-ton payload on my two cylinder engine, my brain starts arcing and sparking, and then shorts out. Phil on the other hand, he's got a brain to die for, as do both of his kids."

"Well, please try to convince him that you want to see my place," Jan says replacing his dark glasses over his eyes. "I really want to understand you Americans."

*   *   *

We leave Mossel Bay the following day, but when the winds don't change as predicted and remain on the nose, we turn around and come back. Our spot on the dock is still open, and we slip into it like a foot into a well-worn shoe.

A half hour later I hear a lot of yelling and screaming. I rush up into the cockpit just in time to watch an eighteen-foot sloop ram into the rear quarter of Iwalani. I grab hold of a fender, trying to push the vessel off, and work it into the slip next to us. The weathered captain and his boat look as if they are in dire need of a bar of soap. Bungee cords are wrapped around gas cans, water jugs, and igloo ice chests. They are used as sail ties, halyards, snubber lines and lifelines. Each time I try to grab onto what I think will be a firm line, it springs away with rubbery resistance. I have never seen so many bungee cords in a single place in my life. With help from some other cruisers on the dock, we get the boat secured with actual rope, while the old man scuttles onto the dock like an aged crab.

"THANK YOU FOR HELPING," he yells. "I HOPE I DIDN'T DO TOO MUCH DAMAGE TO YOUR BOAT."

"Just a scratch in the paint," I say to him. I am not sure how Phil will take it, as he just painted the topsides while we were waiting in Durban for good weather.

"WHAT? I CAN'T HEAR YOU," the old man yells.

"DON'T WORRY ABOUT IT," I yell back.

"MY NAME IS BOB. WHAT'S YOURS?"

I tell him, but say no more, hoping Phil will come out and rescue me from this old codger. But, like the old man in the Rime of the Ancient Mariner, he holds me with his glittering eye and I cannot escape.

"THIS IS A STOUT BOAT. WHAT DO YOU CALL THIS?" he asks pointing to Iwalani's bow. I tell him.

"SO THAT'S A BOBSTAY! I ALWAYS WONDERED WHAT THEY WERE. I READ A LOT OF PATRICK O'BRIEN. SOME OF THE NAUTICAL THINGS I WONDER ABOUT. SEE, I ORIGINALLY OPERATED A FARM IN THE U.S., BUT I COULDN'T STAND THE WAY THINGS WERE GOING THERE, SO I MOVED TO CANADA AND RAN A GENERAL STORE. I COULDN'T ESCAPE THE AMERICANS, EVEN THERE, SO I BECAME A BUSH PILOT. EVEN THAT GOT TOO HORRIBLE, SO I CAME OUT HERE, BUT I DON'T KNOW MUCH ABOUT BOATS OTHER THAN WHAT I PICK UP FROM BOOKS." If the part about airplanes doesn't bring Phil up from down below, nothing will. Everyone in Mossel Bay can hear our conversation. Sure enough, Phil pops up from down below, and I leave the two of them screeching at each other about float planes.

The next morning while we are still lounging in our fo'c'sle bunk, the old codger, a Swede and another South African stand on the dock in front of our boat. Despite two inches of wood planks between us, we are as much a part of the conversation as if we were standing with them on the dock.

"THAT GEORGE BUSH IS GOING TO BRING THE WHOLE WORLD

TO WAR," Bob yells.

"Yes, I think this could be so," the Swede answers.

"GOD DAMN AMERICANS, THEY SHOULD JUST KEEP THEIR NOSE OUT OF OTHER PEOPLE'S BUSINESS."

"How can we?" I whisper to Phil. "He's practically lying in bed with us!"

"Did you know this is an American boat?" the Swede asks tapping on Iwalani's bowsprit.

"THIS BOAT? WELL I'LL BE DARNED."

"I don't trust that guy," Phil says to me when the conversation moves down the dock.

"What guy? Farmer Bob?"

"No, he's just loud, but harmless. Your buddy, Jan."

"Jan, the tool man? Why not?"

"I don't know I just don't like the way he keeps sending you SMS's every two hours. And why does he want us to go see his tool collection so badly?"

"I think he just wants the missing Stanley block plane for his collection, and he thinks you might have it," I respond.

Phil's phone beeps inside his shorts pocket hanging on a wall hook next to our bunk, indicating another SMS. Phil retrieves the phone and reads the message. "See what I mean?" Phil holds the phone for me to read.

"ProperPhoneEtiquetteRequiresAResponse2Each SMS," Jan writes.

"Give me that!" I tap out a message and push send.

"What did you tell him?" Phil asks.

"We are busy."

Another SMS comes right back. "IDon'tThinkYouAndPhilHaveSuchAGreat Relationship IThinkYouAreScaredOfMeAndOtherMen."

I look at the peculiar text message and quickly delete it. "Hmm," I say not looking at Phil. "I'm not trusting him either. Let's hope the wind comes southeasterly tomorrow. I am ready to do battle with Cape Agulhas and face the Atlantic Ocean."

Chapter 28

To the Limit

February 2003
Cape Town, South Africa

The following day is clear with a brisk wind from the southeast. As payment for Phil's fixing their computer, the Mossel Bay Yacht Club doesn't charge us for any of the time we stayed there, including the additional days when we came back. I never see the small waifs again; our transporting and adopting them in America is not meant to be. We leave late in the morning after the other cruisers, helping everyone else get away. When it is our turn to leave, we gracelessly back out of the tight quarters and into the harbor because we are unable to maneuver Iwalani's' bow into the strong wind. We start our battle with the southernmost tip of South Africa ass first.

Outside of the harbor we turn Iwalani around and head south. When we round the point at Mossel Bay, we put all sail up and head west. The wind begins to drop off, yet the seas stay rough. Iwalani's gaff rig allows our sail to remain filled while we are in the trough of waves, and we readily pass the boats that had left hours before us. At the Cape, the sun shines and the winds are light. We turn on the engine and motor sail by penguins drifting like wooden decoys and sea lions lounging with flippers rising out of the water in greeting. A few lone albatross glide around us without a single wing beat.

By nightfall we round the bend and head for Cape Town. It is a heavily trafficked area, filled with many yachts and ships. We all jostle for position without regard to size. At one point a small ship brushes past our stern. It is on autopilot and not a soul can be seen in the bridge. Past Cape Point we are now officially in the Atlantic and point Iwalani's bow northwest, a compass heading we have not seen since Australia.

By ten p.m. the winds pick up again. I leave all sail up, ignoring a remark from Phil earlier in the day that it might be prudent to put a reef in before dark. Now I have to wake him and suffer the consequences of I-told-you-so-itis, but he never grumbles or says a word; as a result, I let him sleep in an hour later into his watch.

A little after midnight, I download EGC's from the Inmarsat, which warn of icebergs just one hundred miles south of our current position. These are calves of their large Antarctic mother, floating around in their summer pastures. I e-mail my parents our current position and head back up in the cockpit to look around for ships, and, just in case the Inmarsat is wrong, icebergs. The wind is briskly cold, I long for mittens and a wool hat, but these things are buried deep in plastic under the bunk where Phil is sleeping.

A ship quickly approaches off our port bow. The navigational light configuration indicates it is heading right for us—two white lights on top of each other flanked by green and red Christmas lights. Monitoring it for a minute on radar, I plot a trajectory. It <u>is</u> heading for us, four miles away and closing fast.

I get on the radio, broadcast our position, and try hailing them. No response. In order to steer away from them, we will have to jibe. Phil wakes up after hearing my broadcast on channel 16. "What's going on?"

"The usual," I respond. "A ship is trying to run us over. We've got too much sail up, and we need to jibe. I'll try one more time hailing the ship, but we should turn every light on, too."

The ship doesn't answer me, so Phil gives it a try. I go out on deck to prepare for the jibe. I turn the brass gooseneck companionway light on, go forward to take the peak and throat halyard off their cleat and put the coils on the cabin top, making sure they will not get fouled, when they are pulled aloft as we scandalize the main. I check the position of the ship. I still see two white lights, but they are no longer on top of each other. The green navigational light for the starboard side is no longer visible. The ship has altered course. Someone on board is doing their job. "Cancel the imminent collision threat," I yell down to Phil.

The ship whooshes by us, a couple hundred yards off our portside, racing to the Far East at about thirty knots, fully laden with containers.

I scandalize the main and head forward to uncleat the preventer. Phil comes out in the cockpit and alters our course with the autopilot. He gathers in the mainsheet, and, just as the wind grabs the sail and flings it out onto the port side, I realize I forgot to release the backstay on that side. As the big heavy sail swings around in an arc filling with twenty-five knots of wind, I see it. Too late. THWACK! The sail slams right into the backstay, like a freight train trying to pluck a harp string. It sends a shudder through Iwalani's hull and up our own spines. Nothing breaks. Nothing rips. We have now done this procedure hundreds of times yet can still make mistakes. We are lucky, or so we believe, until we look aloft and see the peak halyard wrapped around the crow's nest platform. Using a spare jib halyard, Phil frees the tangled rope, as if he is flossing a giant's teeth.

I look around at the dark heaving seas as I sit on the top of the dinghy secured to the cabin top. I breathe in an exhaust-filled sigh of relief. The ship leaves an unbreathable diesel stench in its wake. I tie the tack in as we reduce sail for the second reef. Phil helps by pulling the second outhaul. Together we tie in the reef points. "I am not going to miss this one bit!" Phil yells into the dark diesel air.

"Are you sure? You could be one of millions of Americans tucked into a warm bed, dreaming of football games, late car payments and TV dinners. And then when the alarm clock blares you awake at seven a.m., your biggest decision of the day will be which socks you're going to wear. Your biggest hardship, nursing fingers that are sore from pushing buttons on the car radio while you sit in traffic."

"Well, I don't like football, my socks are all the same color, and why would we eat TV dinners? Besides, there is no traffic where we live. And car payments?" Phil asks.

"Trust me, we'll have car payments when we get home. My biggest fear is that we will forget how awful this really is. You've got to promise me you won't forget this night," I say to Phil.

"I promise," Phil says as we go below to check our speed. "We're still going too fast. We'll be in Cape Town at three a.m."

"The wind is picking up," I add.

We get the sail down and furled on the boom just as we are hit with thirty-five knots of wind. The west coast of South Africa is not far off our starboard side. I can see the outline of the shore, thanks to the remnants of a waning moon clawing its way up from behind headless mountaintops. The treeless, buttressed, spires have been lopped off by the scouring effect of a sculpting glacier. The crew-cut sentinels look oddly militaristic as they march along the shore in a dark procession. Somewhere ahead of the soldiers stands the great headless general himself, Table Mountain, commanding all the lesser hills to remain stone still.

We arrive in Cape Town with clear sunny skies and hardly any breeze, just in time for breakfast. Table Mountain stands tall and stark, void of any cloud-covering tablecloth. The yacht club sits at the fringes of Cape Town in the industrial section, surrounded by offshore oil platforms dry-docked for repairs, tankers, and foreign container ships.

Phil's cell phone beeps. "If it's an SMS from Jan, delete it," I say.

"No, it's from Fred. Isi has missed the last few radio check-ins with Peri Peri. No one has seen or heard from him."

"Oh, god! I hope he's OK," I exclaim. "He was so tired in Mossel Bay. Those ships going around Cape Agulhas are insane. What if he was hit?"

"He's OK, I'm sure," Phil says, "but, it's always been my fear to look up in the bow of one of these container ships and see a yachts rigging dangling like jewelry." Phil SMSs Fred back that we have not yet seen Isi.

The next morning we walk to the yacht club to get our mail and find out where to check in. On the way back to Iwalani, we see Islero tied to the very end of the dock. We SMS Fred that Islero is in Cape Town. A few hours later Isi arrives at our boat. "Where have you been?" we ask in unison.

"Shoo, I took the long route. I sailed a bit further out away from the coast. I thought it would be better. It wasn't," Isi says.

"I hope there were fewer ships."

"No, there were plenny! I came by to thank you again for saving me in Mossel Bay. I would like to take you for dinner. It is the least I can do for you."

"It's not anything one yachtie wouldn't have done for another," Phil says.

"No, I insist. Please."

"OK. When and where?" I ask.

"I would like to take you to the waterfront not far from here. You will be my guest. We can go right now!"

We accept his offer and decide to walk to the Victoria and Alfred waterfront a mile down the street, checking in to customs and immigration along the way.

"Are you sure this is a safe thing to do?" Isi asks us. "I not walk very much in South Africa."

"We don't at night," Phil responds. "But there's three of us, and as long as we don't look lost, we should be fine."

"Did you hear what happened to Genevieve and Jacques?" Isi asks.

"From the French boat?" I ask.

"Shoo, they were attacked and beaten in Port Elizabeth, during the day. They were walking to the grocery store."

"Are they alright?" Phil asks.

"Yes, Genevieve has a black eye, but they were robbed of all their money."

We continue along the side of the road walking in the short brown stubble of grass because there are no sidewalks. Empty liquor bottles are scattered around.

We walk under towering overpasses which provide welcome relief from the hot sun. "At least they finished these highways," Phil remarks. "It's a little weird to be in Durban and come across a highway ending abruptly in midair."

"Shoo," Isi says. "I do not like Durban. That was where I was almost robbed."

"How come 'almost'?"

"I was with Mark, the tall Dutch single hander."

"Oh yeah, the kickboxing champion," I say.

"It was us against four of them. Mark says 'Bring it on!' They take one look at him and run off!" Isi laughs.

"Yes!" Phil adds. "We tried to hang out with the Dutch whenever possible. Just their height scared most attackers away."

"You two are pretty tall. Taller than me anyhow," Isi comments.

"But in comparison to a Dutchman we are shrimps," I say.

"Shrimps?"

"Prawns," Phil explains. "It means we are short."

"What does that make me? Fish eggs? Caviar?" Isi laughs.

We find the door to ship's immigration and are directed up a set of rickety steps to the office that handles yachts. Isi has trouble with some of his paperwork, but Phil and I politely wait in the hallway, out of earshot, once ours is complete. When he is done, we resume the walk to the tourist part of town. We come out from under the overpasses and walk along some railroad tracks. As we get nearer to town, the median between the streets is landscaped with green grass and flowering plants. Here and there, men lie asleep under bushes.

"I think we take taxi back," Isi announces as he gingerly steps over a man lying prone next to an empty glass bottle.

"Good idea," Phil says.

"What if these people are dead?" I ask Phil.

"They don't smell dead," Phil says.

"Shoo, they smell pickled," Isi says while holding his nose.

We arrive at the waterfront, and at the first bar we come to Isi picks out a table under a wide umbrella where we gratefully sit in the shade. "I must protect skin. I don't want wrinkles when I am old," he quips while cleaning his dark glasses with a napkin.

The waitress comes to take our order. "Iced tea for me," I say.

"No, Amalia," Isi says to me, "you must have stronger. This is all on me. Order what you like. The sky is the limit!"

"But it's only eleven o'clock. The sun is nowhere near the yardarm," I say looking at Phil.

"What is that?" Isi asks.

"Actually it is pretty close to the yard arm," Phil corrects me. "It is an old sailing expression from square rigger days and means drinking only after eleven."

"This is a special occasion. We are celebrating a Spanish-American alliance. If your country goes to war on Iraq we are allies. Time is no longer important," Isi says.

"I'll have a gin and tonic then," I say.

"Make that two," Phil adds.

"Philip, you must not have drink for señoritas," Isi says shaking his head. "Make it a double gin and tonic and same for me."

"What do you plan to do when you get home?" Isi asks us.

"First we are going to work on the house. Then Phil is going to build an airplane," I begin.

"Shoo. You fly?" Isi asks Phil.

"I have my private pilots license. Amy still has to get hers. The deal was, if I learned to scuba dive she would learn to fly."

"Only I never thought he would overcome his fear of putting his head underwater," I admit. "I didn't think I had anything to worry about."

"I fly, too. That is, when I not crashing," Isi says wrinkling his face with guilt.

"You've crashed an airplane?" I ask in amazement.

"Shoo, I was trying to impress my girlfriend's family. I was flying too low. I caught the wing on the TV antenna and flipped the plane right into their house. They were not impressed!" Isi laughs.

"Were you hurt?" Phil asks.

"I was in hospital for three weeks."

The waiter arrives with our drinks. "Cheers!" we say together.

"Was that the end of your girlfriend?" I ask.

"No. In fact, she came with me on this trip as far as Australia. She left me and flew to Spain. She thinks I am too crazy."

"You have to be crazy in order to sail around the world. No person in his right mind would do this!" Phil remarks.

Isi raises his glass in salute. "One hundred percent!"

We finish our drinks and order refills. "What are you going to do when you get back?" Phil asks.

Isi pauses. "First I get to Canary Island. April 15, they have big celebration for me. In Spain, I have many offers. I want to spend time with my son. Our relation was not so good when I leave. I want to spend time with my mother; she is old and it is wrong of me to leave her and sail around the world."

"Phil is anxious to get back to his sons, too," I say.

"And you, Amy, what do you do when you get home?"

"I will go back to work. But, I've been thinking about getting a horse again. At sea, there are three things I really miss: the smell of a bald eagle, feeling hot earth under my fingers in the garden, and the sound of a horse munching its grain."

"What kind of horse you get?"

"A Lipizzan."

"The Spanish horse! I had twelve. I sold them before I sail. My friend he has a book he wrote on the Spanish Riding School. It is not far from where I live, in Andalusia. You will have to come visit me there."

"You better be careful what you offer because we will do it," I say.

"¡Bueno!" Isi exclaims. "My mother will cook us paella. She is a very good cook. Since you do not like hot weather, you should come in the spring."

"Alright. We will come in the April of 2004," Phil promises.

I realize I am getting very drunk. I look over at Phil who is still drinking double gin and tonics. We have not eaten anything, and I cannot remember what round we are on.

"Now, my friends, it is time to eat," Isi announces.

Isi will not allow us to pay for our drinks. When I stand up I realize I no longer have control of my skeletal system. It is completely functioning on its own, or not, as is more nearly the case, because my legs seem to be walking off without me.

"To the limit!" Isi cries, and off we sway looking for the next restaurant and bar.

"I did not know you spoke Spanish!" Isi says to me.

"¿Que?" I respond.

"You were speaking almost fluent Spanish."

"I was?"

"Si, one hundred percent!"

"To the limit!" I cry.

As the night wears on, my Spanish improves while Isi's English deteriorates. We drink and we drink, and then we drink some more. Somewhere along the line we have a pizza. When we finally arrive back at Iwalani, it is well past midnight. Phil gets sick, which is a good thing, as neither of us are used to so much alcohol, and he has drunk twice as much as me. All I can think of, as the forward bunk spins out of control with me upon it, is the story of Phil's ex-wife, who, while in Russia without Phil, became so intoxicated with alcohol she had to be hospitalized. She nearly died; the next morning I wish I had.

We awake with two freight trains simultaneously trying to plow through the gray matter of what once was healthy brain tissue. "Oh god," I moan.

"Make that a double," Phil responds.

"Why did you let me do that?" I ask.

"Shh quiet."

"Alcohol is a legal drug?"

"Ow, quit it," Phil pleads.

"I think we found the limit," I remark.

"One hundred percent."

"What's up with Isi and shoo?" I ask. "What does "shoo" mean?"

"I was hoping you would know," Phil moans. "But right now, lets just be quiet. Okey dokey?"

"Shoo."

Isi appears at our boat around noontime. He doesn't look very well either, which is good to see, as I am worried our alcohol adventure is a common occurrence for him. We invite him on board, and I make some strong coffee with ice water chasers.

"I brought this over for you." He takes a book out of his backpack and hands it to me. "I would like for you to have it." It is the book on the Spanish Riding School that his friend wrote.

"Isi, I can't take this," I say.

"No, please. It is for you. I write in it. See?"

I thank him profusely and read the inscription. *'Para mis amigos Philip and Amy muchas gracias Isidoro Arias.'*

*   *   *

The next few days are spent doing all the things we can't do at sea: checking our e-mail and updating the webpage. I have a few job offers via e-mail and on the passage from Cape Town to St Helena, I will have to decide what I want to do with my life. Our money situation is getting dire. We are living off a credit card that I am unable to pay off in full each month.

I paint a picture of Isi's boat *Islero*; put it in a mat and give it to him. As I hand it over, I realize I have not painted a figure in the cockpit. The boat looks like it is under sail by itself.

On the day we are scheduled to depart Cape Town, a knock on the hull brings me up from down below where I had been busy checking thru-hulls and stowing things for the passage.

A tall blonde woman stands on the dock next to a man dressed completely in black. Both of them have wires coming from their ears and clipboards in their hands.

"Hi, I'm Gaynor," the woman says. "I'm a film coordinator, and we are wondering if we can use your boat in a bathing shoot."

I ask her to repeat what she just said. With her staccato South African accent and rapid speech, it sounds like she wants to put Iwalani in a bathing suit. When I finally grasp what she is asking, she mentions we will be well compensated. She says she is also trying to coordinate another launch to motor alongside and photograph Iwalani under sail with Table Mountain as the backdrop.

"I'll need to talk this over with my husband," I say. "We are actually getting ready to leave this afternoon. When would you want to do it?"

"Tomorrow morning if possible," she responds handing me her business card.

I give her our cell phone number and tell her we will get back to her. I head off searching for Phil who I find walking out of the chandlery. "I think I may have found a way to solve our money problems," he says to me.

"Oh really? Me, too. You go first," I say.

"Well, the school bus on St. Helena is broken down and needs a new axle. The parts have to arrive by ship, since there is no airport there. The ship for St. Helena just left a week ago and won't be in Cape Town for another six weeks. The school children can't go to school for almost two months."

"So you said we'd be able to take the parts."

"Sure, after I asked you first, of course."

"Will we have to pay import duty or anything like that?"

"No."

"None of the other yachts can do it?" I ask.

"Well, that's where the problem comes in."

"What problem."

"The parts are kind of big."

"I see."

"And a bit heavy. No other yacht can carry them," Phil adds.

"How big and heavy?"

"Two truck axels. They weigh a few hundred pounds."

"Sure, why not? If you think you can stow them safely. Of course we may be mobbed by angry school children when they find out Iwalani brought the end to their unexpected vacation."

"And what's your money making deal?" Phil asks.

"How would you like to get paid for having lingerie models draped on Iwalani's decks?"

I tell Phil about the proposal, and he practically chokes on his drool when I tell him we will have to delay our departure one day in order to accommodate the film crew. "And we'll get paid for this, too?"

"She mentioned something about compensation," I say.

I phone Gaynor and ask how much the compensation is. She says it will be three thousand Rand. I silently jump up and down and scribble the figure for Phil, while trying to maintain a poker face tone over the phone. At the present exchange rate, it is close to three hundred dollars. I tell her we will do it. All of a sudden we become the most popular boat at the marina as everyone is hoping for a sail on Iwalani during the photo session.

At nine a.m. the entourage shows up without the accompanying launch which was cancelled at the last minute. Along with Gaynor's assistant, the director, the producer, the cameraman and his assistant, one Swedish model, the hairdresser, and the clothespin girl, Iwalani has more people on board than ever before. Phil and Gaynor go over safety protocols, while I help hang clothes down below.

Not an unpleasant way to make money...

Each time the model changes clothes, the clothespin girl has to pinch in the fabric in back and secure it with clothespins, catalogue the outfit and coordinate it with each photo session in a notebook. She is the busiest person on board. We motor around the bay with Table Mountain in the background, while the model poses on Iwalani in different outfits. The winds are light, as she hoists the sail, lounges on the boom, looks through binoculars and pretends to wave to people. When we go through all the outfits, the model poses topless in some of the same positions.

"Where exactly are these photographs going to appear?" I ask Gaynor.

"The Greek issue of *Cosmopolitan.*

"There is a Greek issue of *Cosmo?*" I ask incredulously.

The producer turns and looks at me. Even with her dark glasses I can see anger flashing in her brown eyes. "Just because you are American, doesn't mean that everyone in the world wants to look at Americans," she snaps.

"I'm sorry," I say. "I didn't realize there are different issues."

She shakes her head and says no more.

The model comes back to the cockpit so the hairdresser can put her hair in a ponytail. I have never really been in close proximity to a model before. I can see what people mean about photogenic people. It is very hard not to stare at such a beautiful body. I always thought Barbie was the result of a doll creator's overactive imagination. This woman is proof positive that this was not the case.

"Not a bit of cellulite on that one!" Gaynor whispers to me.

"No, she probably thinks cellulite is a low cost cell phone plan," I joke.

Gaynor laughs and then starts talking about an impossible situation.

"What?" I ask her confused.

"There aren't any to be found," she says.

"What do you need?" I ask.

"I can maybe get one by Thursday."

Gaynor, one astute business woman and wired to the world.

It is then that I realize that the small armband she has strapped around her upper arm connected to a wired earpiece is a cell phone; she isn't talking to me at all. Totally embarrassed, I leave the cockpit and sit with Phil on the boomkin railing.

"You ready for the South Atlantic?" he asks me.

"Yup, I'm tired of being the stupid American," I say. "Did you know that those armbands are cellphones? Gaynor must think we are complete woodchucks."

When we arrive back at the dock, Gaynor says she has forgotten our cash, but she will be happy to take me to the bank so I can cash the check she writes.

We hop in her jeep, and she drives at race car speed to the bank. In between phone calls and talking into her armband, she tells me about her childhood spent cruising with her parents and how that influenced her current career path as a film coordinator for the yacht industry.

"You know," Gaynor says winking at me, "the going rate for a yacht charter is usually five thousand Rand." She pauses while counting the three thousand Rand into my hand. "An hour."

"I guess we are even then," I say, pocketing the cash.

"How so?" she asks.

"We would have done it for free."

*   *   *

I meet Phil at the yacht club office where we pay our bill and leave a forwarding address. As we walk back to the boat, we see Isi sitting alone at a table nursing a gin and tonic. We walk over to say goodbye.

"You look so depressed!" I say to him.

"Shoo, I ready to leave today. But the genoa is not finished. It won't be ready until tomorrow."

"Cheer up! We will all be home soon enough!" I say.

"It is just the single handing," Isi confesses. "I am one hundred percent to the limit! How did things with the model go? And you did not invite me! Me, with no girlfriend."

"Ah, when all the clothes and coolers came on board, we didn't have much room," Phil says.

"I must tell you, Amy, I love my painting. *Gracias.*"

I thought back to how uncomfortable I had felt, handing it to him, when I realized I had made *Islero* look like it was sailing itself.

"*De nada* Isi, and I love the book. Just be careful in this home stretch. Americans have a saying that bad luck comes in threes: first you had the propeller shaft fall out in Durban, then the jib blowing out in Mossel Bay; you may have one more bad thing happen to you, before all is said and done."

"Shoo! I am all set then. My girlfriend leaving me, that was number three."

"Yes. I hope you are right," I say. "Still, please be careful. Most accidents happen a few miles from your house, and now that we are in the Atlantic we are all practically home. We all need to be careful in our own back yard."

"Yes, yes, you are like a mother. Is she always like this?" Isi asks Phil.

"She does worry, but in a good way."

"Will I see you in St Helena?" Isi asks.

"We'll be there!" Phil says.

"To the limit!" Isi cries lifting his glass.

"One hundred percent!" Phil and I say together.

Chapter 29
Battle Ground

March 2003
Capetown to Brazil

We were underway again. Phil and I had been looking forward to this passage. We were in the home stretch and the majority of the cruising books written by circumnavigators barely wrote more than a paragraph about this expanse of ocean. The winds are favorable and usually blowing a steady fifteen knots. The seas are relatively calm, and a favorable north setting current pushes boats away from Africa. Major storms are very, very rare.

We sail for four days with full sail and a following current pushing us home, just as the books describe. The winds are out of the southwest so we sail on a broad reach, averaging over one hundred and sixty miles a day. Eventually the winds back to the southeast, which means rolling and the ever-present threat of an uncontrolled jibe. What the books don't mention is the southwesterly swell of several meters, putting us in washing machine mode. Opposing the steady seas from the southeast, wave after wave career into our port side. We hang on with both hands and tolerate the wavy battleground.

While listening to the radio on our second night out, I manage to hear Herb Hilgenberg giving the weather forecasts to the boats in the upper Atlantic. On our third night out I take a deep breath and decide to check into his net myself. I realize it is going to be a full time commitment, but I am curious to see if our radio can reach him in Canada; after all, we are almost at the southern tip of Africa. Phil always tells me we live in the information age and that not using every bit of knowledge available is nothing short of a crime. At eleven p.m., our time, I join the fray of Caribbean boats checking into the net.

"Southbound two, Southbound two, this is Iwalani, Iwalani, twenty seven degrees south, zero-nine degrees east…" I can hear hundreds of Portugese fishing boats in the background. I don't think Herb will be able to hear me, but he does.

"Iwalani, now that's a boat name I have not heard in at least two years. Did you say you were at seven degrees south and nine degrees east?"

"Southbound two, this is Iwalani, negative, we are at twenty-seven south, twenty-seven south, zero-nine degrees east."

I can feel the excitement in Herb's voice as he doesn't usually speak with boats this far away, and our last radio contact with him was off the Ecuadorian coast. *"Iwalani, I have very strict protocols you must adhere to, you need to say, nine degrees east, not zero-nine. Otherwise I can't be sure where you are. Besides, I don't have any weather forecasts prepared for the South African region."*

"I realize that, Herb. We are just checking in for tomorrow." I see a cockroach scuttling across the chart and smash it with the fly swatter. I thought I was prepared for the Herb hour, but I had forgotten the precision requirements for his radio check-ins. I was so proud of getting this far on a circumnavigation, and so excited to talk to him from so far away, but he quickly puts my ego in its place. I wipe up the mess the dead cockroach makes on the chart. It is very near our present position. I take a pencil and write next to the brown stain. 'What is left of my ego.'

On the seventh day out, we cross from east to west, over the Greenwich meridian. Unlike its counterpart in the Pacific, we don't lose or gain a day. The only thing I now must remember to do is write "west' instead of "east" for the longitude. I can see this as a potential precision pit to fall into on the Herb hour, as my brain had been programmed for the last two years to say "east," not "west."

The following day I wake up early, hungry for lunch, and go out on deck to find Phil. He is sitting on the cabin top staring out to sea, an unusual position even for him. "Oh, god, don't tell me you are waxing prosaic about the vast expanse of beautiful blue sea," I chide.

"No way! I was just thinking how boring this is and how I won't miss it a bit."

"Have you seen anything interesting out here?" I ask.

"A styrofoam cup and a wedge of pizza with a bite taken out of it."

"What kind of bite?"

"Definitely human," Phil replies.

"Hey look! There's the rest of the pizza."

We both stand up, lean against the bulwark and lifeline, to gaze at the pepperoni pizza, minus one slice, as it floats by, still in its cardboard box.

"It doesn't look like it tastes awful."

"Looks can be deceiving."

"We must be fairly near the ship that threw this overboard. It can't be from a yacht. No cruiser would buy a frozen pizza, much less throw it overboard uneaten," I say.

"I'm not so sure. Not everyone has me on board to make fresh pizza."

Suddenly a huge wave from the southwest knocks into Iwalani from nowhere. She rolls over heavily, almost jibing in the process, but continues on after a momentary pause.

"Great. Here we are with no harnesses on, looking at pizzas floating by. We could have been knocked overboard in any lesser boat. I didn't see that wave coming. Did you?" I ask.

"No. I was too entranced by the pizza," Phil says. "Speaking of pizza what's for lunch?"

"Smoked chicken sandwiches with sliced avocado and bean sprouts. We've got another weeks worth of vacuum packed fresh meat from Mossel Bay and that's it. Then we will need to rely on my fishing abilities or move into the canned realm."

"Speaking of fish, have you seen the tuna?" Phil asks.

"What tuna?"

"Come over here and look." I follow Phil over to the port side and look to where he points. A fourteen-inch yellow fin tuna is swimming alongside us, gobbling up flying fish as they scatter with each downward plunge of our bow.

"How long has he been there?" I ask.

"A couple days. I thought for sure you had seen it."

"No, but why haven't I caught it? That's the question." I go aft to check my pink squid lure and slowly reel it in. "We need a blue flying fish lure or maybe just a net? Or a spear. Maybe we can stab him? Where did you store the lightening rod I made you take down in Canada? That tuna sure looks like sushi to me," I say.

That evening, despite my feeble attempts at trying to kill it, the tuna swims around Iwalani in big circles. While sitting in the cockpit eating supper, Phil and I watch in amazement as the tuna leaps and flips five feet out of the water as if performing at a dolphin show.

"Woohoo," Phil yells with each stunning spectacle. The fish actually looks like it is smiling as the setting sun reflects off its glittering sides.

"What do you think is the evolutionary advantage for such behavior?"

"Maybe he is hoping we'll throw some of our supper in," I say.

"Teriyaki steak stir fry? I don't think he'll like it— too spicy."

"Maybe tuna like spicy food."

"Maybe there is a bigger fish trying to eat him," Phil suggests.

"I don't see anything," I say. "Perhaps it helps him to attack smaller fish."

"He needs a name," Phil says.

"Bill. We should call him Bill."

For the rest of the week, Bill swims alongside us. When we are out in the cockpit together, Bill does his acrobatic fish act. With each leap out of the water, Phil and I shout, "Whoohoo!" But if one of us is alone, Bill just swims along on the leeward side, never going into his leaping routine.

"I've decided not to drag the lure anymore," I tell Phil one morning after I didn't set it.

"Why not?" he asks.

"It's kind of a joke really," I say. "Besides I don't want to accidentally hook Bill. He seems too smart to be fooled by the lure intentionally, but I don't want him to get hooked on it by accident."

"By accident?" Phil asks.

"Yeah, let's say he was trying to avoid a predator or something and his fin or gills got caught up in the lure."

"The chances of that happening are about a billion to one."

"Maybe, but I don't want to hurt him."

"Hurt him? Just a few days ago you were trying to eat him."

"I can't eat him now. He's the only friend we've got out here."

That night fifty dolphins swim over to Iwalani. I hear them outside the boat as I lie up forward after supper. I think to myself, that's the end of Bill; there's no way he can survive that onslaught.

But the next morning Bill is in his usual spot swimming in the lee of Iwalani under the shadow cast by the mainsail. In fact there are two Bills; it seems he now has a much smaller friend swimming next to him. I name her Mrs. Bill. She is much more skittish and swims away each time I look over the side.

*   *   *

At midnight, fourteen days after leaving Cape Town, we are eight miles away from St. Helena. The moon is shining, and we still have fifteen knots of wind, which is unusual as most of the time the wind drops off as we approach an island mass. I tell Phil I am going down below for a half hour nap and to wake me when we get near. We will need to jibe Iwalani in order to make it around to the anchorage in the lee side of the island.

Just as I doze off and before my head becomes glued to the mattress from a constant flow of saliva escaping a moving head on a tossing bunk, I am harshly awoken by Phil pounding on the forward hatch. He rarely pounds on the hatch. I toss on a shirt, throw on my harness and run out on deck. Horizontal rain, gale force winds, and a wind generator screaming in the darkness, providing enough electricity for a small city slap me awake. Glistening in the dark and wearing only a harness, Phil's naked body stands out from the dark night as he works the forward sails. He has scandalized the main in preparation for a jibe, but there is still too much sail up. We take the mainsail down entirely as we try to regain control of the boat. "Welcome to St. Helena!" Phil yells to me.

"Where is it?" I holler back.

"That's the problem. It is somewhere off our port side. I reduced the scatter on the radar, but even with that, I've lost it. I need you to look for the island and tell me when to turn. We'll come in by jib alone."

Hoping for a break, I look through the mist and driving rain. I consider, for a second, going down below and finding my diving mask. It might be the only way to see the island in the horizontal downpour. Of all the moments to make landfall, this is the worst possible scenario at the worst possible time. Suddenly, a small gap appears as the rain, and clouds lift for a ceiling of fifty feet.

"I see it!" I yell.

"How far away?"

"A quarter of a mile at the most. It's right there, and we need to turn now; otherwise, I think we'll sail right on by."

"You think?" Phil asks.

"I'm not one hundred percent sure, but for a moment I thought I saw the end of the island."

We turn Iwalani toward where I had seen the end of a dark rock wall. The fog, rain and clouds have closed in again, and we are steering by compass alone. "Maintain this heading," I say.

"I sure hope you are right."

In the lee of the island the winds drop off, and Phil has to start the engine. A break appears in the weather, and we can see a tall wall of black stone darkly illuminated by the cloud-shrouded moon. We anchor amongst the bobbing fleet of fishing boats, protected only by the formidable height of St Helena, take hot showers, make our traditional bacon and eggs breakfast, and head to bed at two a.m. When we awake a few hours later, our country is at war with Iraq.

Landing on St Helena is not for the faint hearted. Taking the dinghy ashore is not permitted. Instead, a water taxi makes rounds to the fishing boats, ships and yachts at anchor. We hail the taxi and are brought into a concrete jetty, along with our Dutch friends from Red Oranda. Several knotted ropes dangled from a horizontal bar on shore. As the launch rises and falls from the swell, one either steps gracefully onto land, holding onto the rope like an early morning commuter alighting from a subway, or, as in our case with the lurching seas, swinging from the rope like a drunken Tarzan and landing with a graceless thud on the concrete. Sometimes the swell is too much, and no one can land. If no one lands, the island can't collect landing fees, roughly 11£ per head.

Our Dutch friends cleared in the day before but wait for us while Phil and I struggle to reach the customs office, a small wooden building packed into a narrow shelf of land at the bottom of a steep cliff. "Is it just me or is this whole island moving," I say.

"It's not just you. I've got it too. We are land sick," Phil responds.

"It gets a little better. We had it bad yesterday," Sjany says.

I trip and almost fall as the pavement buckles and rises like a heaving wave. We head into the small room and hand the officials our passports and ships papers. Phil and I lean up against the wall in order to keep from falling over.

"We will need to see proof of health insurance, otherwise the health fee is ten pounds per person per day," the official says to us.

"We have health insurance, but the paperwork is with our accountant back home. We will need to e-mail her. Is the health insurance because of the dangers of trying to stand on this moving island or is there some other health risk we need to know about?"

The customs official laughs. "Everyone gets land sick here, but there are no other risks."

We tell him about the truck parts we transported, and he makes arrangements to get them off Iwalani. We don't want to be responsible for dropping them overboard. The officials don't wave our landing fees as payment for transporting the parts as we had hoped. Instead, they tell us to get in touch with owner of the garage and arrange for a tour of the island.

Looking up Jacob's Ladder

*　　*　　*

We find the owner of the garage, Colin Williams, under a car. "Hi," I say to a pair of feet sticking out like the witch in the Wizard of Oz. "We are the Americans who brought the bus axles." The feet don't move and all is silent. "Hello?" I repeat and bend down to see if the body is still alive. Reluctantly he comes out holding a wrench. Sheepishly we ask if we can get a tour of the island as payment for shipping the parts. He nods, sets down the wrench, wipes his hands and says he will take us for a tour the following day. He doesn't seem very enthused about the prospect. Phil and I leave the garage and walk around town.

"How 'bout walking up Jacob's Ladder?" Phil asks.

"Are you crazy? I can't even stand on flat ground, let alone climb seven hundred steps up a cliff. Maybe later."

St. Helena rises from the Southern Atlantic like a three year old's version of a mud pie island. Viewed from the water, slab sided walls of brown earth slough off chunks of dirt and rock hundreds of feet to the ocean below. An occasional trickle of green vegetation high overhead gives some hint of the lush green interior as plants peek over the very top. An enormous trough cuts through the brown blob down to the water.

Jamestown, a rainbow of pastel colored buildings flows along the bottom of the "V" from the water's edge to the stark brown cliffs beyond. The Portuguese discovered the island in 1502 and, keeping the island's location secret, used it to re-supply ships bound for the Cape of Good Hope and the Orient. The British and Dutch soon discovered its whereabouts, and the three nations fought over it. The British eventually gained control and built a fort on the small area of useable shoreline, complete with a moat. Jacob's ladder, a man made staircase, leads from the ground floor of the town to the very top of the cliffs above.

We begin walking out of town but are quickly picked up by a passing truck. The driver, a Canadian, cheerfully deposits us inland near the Governor's house where we walk in to the grounds and photograph large tortoises given one hundred years ago by the Governor of the Seychelles to the governor of St. Helena. We watch as the tortoises slowly chew grass like aged old men gumming asparagus. Their longevity and the after effects of such a high fiber diet on an animal weighing several hundred pounds, make us realize that giving a tortoise as a gift, has great inheritance ramifications to the unfortunate descendants. We find a path and come upon Napoleon's empty burial tomb. Over the years many prisoners of war and toppled world leaders, including a Zulu king, were brought to St. Helena for their final resting place.

The following day Colin arrives at the waterfront for our tour. Phil climbs into the back seat while I sit in front with our quiet driver. Dark skinned, with curly brown hair and green eyes, Colin typifies what a person with lineage coming from all points of the compass would look like. Wordlessly, he drives us out of town along the same route we had been the previous day. Phil and I have many questions which we fling at him like badminton serves. Undeterred with his monosyllabic responses we question him for a half hour.

St. Helena is one of the most remote outposts on Earth. There is no airport, so mail and supplies arrive by ship from Ascension Island, seven hundred miles to the north. The single ship also serves England and Cape Town, making the stops to St. Helena rather infrequent. If it is too rough to land, the ship will continue on its way. The island is divided into four regions, each with its own elected councilor and dialect. Colin is from the south and says he has a hard time understanding people from the north, on an island four miles wide and eight miles long! The governor, appointed by the British, is given this post as a reward, usually before retirement. The other British outpost islands, Ascension and the Falklands, supposedly have too much government work, so St. Helena is the crown jewel of postings. In 2002, the British allowed Saints, as they call themselves, to have passports. This resulted in the loss of one thousand young people, who left the island in search of a higher education.

Colin takes us to the north side of the island where a wind farm was set up and then abandoned. With strong, never ceasing trade winds, it is an ideal location for generating electricity; yet, it has never produced so much as a single amp hour. The Saints were told the parts needed to get it up and running are too expensive. There is talk that the Saudi's are interested in this land for building a world class golf course and international airport. Colin is doubtful it will happen.

There used to be a veterinarian on the island, but no longer. When Colin finds out about Phil's technical expertise with wind generators and computers and the fact that I am a veterinarian, our tour guide loses his reserve and becomes a St. Helena salesman.

He drives by abandoned plantations, beautiful places with fertile valleys and unending views of brilliant blue water and sky, available for just a few thousand dollars. Flax farms, too, cover the hills, abandoned as the public's interest in flax waned. I tell him he ought to think about buying up the flax farms, as flaxseed oil is beneficial for the heart, and flax will once again be valuable.

Most of the fruits, vegetables and even eggs are imported to St. Helena, because few people farm. Colin says that the climate is changing, the island is becoming drier and fruit trees no longer produce as much fruit. To us, after two weeks at sea, with only mold, a dying South African Protea plant, bean sprouts and a withered herb garden to look at for plant life, everything seems lush and green.

He takes us to his house where his wife makes tea. She puts a pot and some cups on a small table in the living room along with some biscuits, pulls out chairs for us and then withdraws to the kitchen with Colin. "This is weird," I whisper to Phil. "Do you think we smell bad or something? Why are we in the living room and they are in the kitchen?"

We quickly drink our tea and walk into the kitchen with the empty cups and pot. Colin has already gone outside. We find him coming down a small slope behind the house carrying an enormous bunch of bananas. He places them next to the house and, while indirectly pointing to them, indicates that they are for us to take. We return to Iwalani laden with bananas and pleas for us to stay and make a go at living on the island. It is tempting for a second or two, but we have families pulling us northward.

After sharing the bananas with the other yachts in the anchorage, we raise the anchor and return to sea.

*　　*　　*

"Woohoo!" Phil screams on our third day out.

"What's so Woohoo?" I yell up to him. I am taking banana bread out of the oven. We are already halfway through a banana cream pie and have had banana smoothies for lunch, bananas for snacks, bananas flambé, and fried bananas with dipping sauces. The one bad thing about a vine of bananas, they all ripen at once resulting in a banana invasion.

"Bill! He's back with us!" Phil yells down.

"That's impossible! It's been over a week since we last saw him," I say.

"Come out and see for yourself."

I set the bread down to cool and climb up the companionway to join Phil standing on the leeward side as he looks over the bulwark. After scanning the horizon for ships, a habit each of us had gotten into when first coming out on deck, I turn my attention to the water.

"It sure looks like Bill. But then, don't all yellow fin tuna look the same?"

"But isn't it weird that he would be in the same spot?" Phil asks.

"Coincidence. It must be a good place to nail flying fish."

Just as I say that, Bill turns and looks up at us. After seeing that we are both present, he swims around the boat and leaps out of the water. "Now aren't you convinced?" Phil asks.

"How could he find us in an ocean of water?" I wonder.

"There isn't exactly an ocean of boats around here. I am sure it isn't hard. We either have a trail of smells or a symphony of squeaks that get carried through the water."

"I'm still not so sure, but we'll call him Bill anyway," I say.

Phil looks aloft, then around at various points on the boat, "searching for trouble" as he puts it: signs of chafe, or potential problems before they become trouble. "I was thinking it was weird we didn't see Isi in St. Helena."

"His new sail probably had more delays. I hope so, anyway," I reply.

"Or maybe he decided to continue on. He was worried about not getting to the Azores by April 15."

"That's probably it," I say. "But I did have some weird dreams last night."

"Sex with six men?" Phil chides.

"Oh brother? Is that all you think about? No, nothing like that. I won't bother to tell you now because you'll be disappointed," I say leaning over the bulwark to watch Bill.

"No I won't," Phil says. "Please, entertain me. There's nothing else out here besides the Bill Show."

"Well, the first dream was about Stew. He was talking to me about my grandmother. He met her. They were friends. Then he started telling me stuff about my sister, but I couldn't understand what he was saying. He wasn't speaking any language I recognized."

"Ok that's weird, dead cat talking about dead grandmother. I don't know what Freud would say. What was the other dream?"

"Equally weird. It was about Isi. I saw him sitting at a table, like when we got ready to leave South Africa. He wouldn't look at me though. I was trying to cheer him up, and I said we were looking forward to visiting him in Spain and eating his mother's paella. Isi continued to stare at the table and shook his head, 'There will be no paella,' he finally said and then started to cry. I asked him if something had happened to his mother and he said, 'No that's not it at all.' "

"Hm. It was just a dream."

"Yes, but what are dreams? Why do we have them? What's the point?"

"Well, if you studied yoga, dreams are reality," Phil says while retying one of the lines holding the Grape on deck. "Nothing of what we experience during the day is real. That's why I quit doing yoga. It was too much for me, although right now I wouldn't mind thinking that none of this is real."

"What if they are a form of communication?" I ask.

"What?"

"Dreams."

"Between what and whom?"

"Well, ever since Stew died, I've been thinking a lot about death and its tie with quantum physics. What if, when you die, the part that is your soul leaves your body and enters another quantum state, another energy level, and the only way to communicate is though sleep, when our conscious filters aren't awake to block out all this quantum chit chat?"

"You've been reading too many physics books," Phil says.

"No, not enough physics books. Actually I've been listening to the stupid radio. Now that we are close enough to get NPR, all they broadcast is stuff about the war. Have you heard any of it?"

"I'm afraid so," Phil says while grabbing the mop to clean the decks.

"How do you like the catchy Iraqi Freedom theme music?" I ask.

"It's kind of sick actually. The reporters sound like sportscasters with play-by-play announcements of The Game."

"The BBC reports seem to be entirely different from the American Armed Forces Radio," I say.

"No kidding. One reporter even said that what the Americans at home are hearing is entirely different from what the rest of the world hears."

"On the American Forces Radio I heard an infomercial about abortion and how it was the taking of human life and how it was wrong, blah, blah, blah, and then, when the ad was over, they broadcast figures on Iraqi death tolls, just like they were reporting sports scores," I say while watching my husband mop.

The Inmarsat alarm goes off. Phil and I look at one another. It is the second time in as many days that it has gone off. Yesterday it was for fog around Rio de Janeiro.

"I'll go check it," Phil says as he lashes the mop onto to the cabin top.

"Thanks," I say while I continue to watch Bill.

"Unbelievable!"

"What?" I yell down to him.

"The seas around Brazil are two meters. They consider that worthy of an emergency broadcast!" Phil yells up.

That night while on watch, I entertain myself by killing cockroaches and listening to the Iraqi game on the radio. Every ten minutes I turn off all the lights, remove my headphones and go up on deck and look around. Then I sneak back down below, grab the flyswatter, wait a few seconds, turn the lights back on, and smash cockroaches. It is a very controlled aggression, a true paramilitary operation, a completely targeted mission, but I can see Iwalani and her crew are losing the battle.

The winds stay SE at 10 knots, the seas one meter, and the barometer is steady at 1015 Mbs. We average 110 nautical miles a day with clear skies and puffy trade clouds. At night, conditions remain the same, with no lines squalls to worry about and no radio anxiety to fret over, as Herb is on vacation for a week. After a week at sea, the evening battleground with the six-legged invaders becomes more heated. Where we had been killing one or two cockroaches a night, after leaving St. Helena, we are now killing four or five an hour.

Our dinnertime conversations are highlighted with bits we hear on the radio, watching Bill do his leaps, and discussing our own nighttime forays with the antennaed infantry. On April 1st, I try to think up an April Fool's trick to play on Phil. On a boat, especially while on passage at sea, one has to be careful about the practical jokes chosen; I didn't want to do anything life threatening. I consider taking a dead cockroach and making a tiny uniform for it then placing it in the nav station while it carries a little white flag; cooking up a flying fish and pretending it is Bill, or the usual, epoxying Phil's favorite pencil to the nav station, none of which I get around to doing.

At our dinner hour, we sit out in the cockpit watching the Bill show. "Did you hear anything good on the radio?" I ask Phil.

"Just the usual. Last night it was interviews with generals, GI's, latrine diggers, truck drivers and goats walking by."

"I heard a good one with a guy reading e-mail questions. Seven hundred and fifty people wrote in and asked what GI's do when they have to go to the bathroom. The sportscaster said, 'Come on, people. Look where we are standing. Don't you own a cat?'"

Phil doesn't laugh. Sometimes it is a difficult proposition getting the neurons in his brain that respond to humor to lighten up.

The Inmarsat alarm goes off again, the third time in three days.

"Alright, alright, I'll go shut it off, I know it's my turn." I set my bowl of spicy black beans and rice down on the non-skid placemat on our "dashboard" under the hard dodger and go down below to see what the latest calamity off the Brazilian coast is. Fog, big waves, it is all becoming mundane, but we still feel compelled to check it even though it is almost like the fairy tale of crying "wolf."

I turn on the computer and wait for Windows to boot up, then click on the program for the Inmarsat in the toolbar. I wait for the yellow light to turn off in the Inmarsat box before opening the EGC's on the computer.

"What is it this time?" Phil yells down. "Let me guess, cold water off Rio, dangerous clumps of seaweed off Brazil?"

This time I don't laugh. "No, it's bad. It's our biggest fear. It says 'the Spanish yacht, Islero, is overdue for St. Helena.' Isi is missing."

Chapter 30

The Demon Within

March/April 2003
South Atlantic

Phil places his bowl next to mine and comes down below. Together we stare at the computer screen hoping we see a pop up window with the statement, "Ha, Ha, April Fool's! Gotcha!" But no such message appears.

"Maybe it's nothing serious. It could be the electronics on his boat got knocked out by lightening or something," Phil suggests.

I turn to look at him. We both know that is far-fetched, as the weather has been ideal across most of the South Atlantic for the last two weeks.

"We should turn around and go look for him," I say.

Phil pulls out the chart of the South Atlantic. "His last check in on the Spanish radio net, according to the Inmarsat, put him six hundred miles from St. Helena. He is seven days overdue. That puts his last known position about here," Phil points to an area two thousand miles away from us. "There is no way we can beat back against the trade winds in a timely fashion. It would be faster for us to sail counterclockwise in the South Atlantic, avoiding the high pressure in the middle."

"It will take us three weeks to get there. I don't think it's feasible," I say.

"Then we need to tell boats sailing to St. Helena to keep a sharp look out in case he is in a raft. Move over, I'm going to check into the Alfredo net early."

"Do you smell that?" I say letting Phil sit at the nav station.

"It's bad. I didn't want to say anything. I thought it was you."

"Thanks. I was thinking it was you. It must be the bilge again."

While Phil checks into he radio net, I lift up the aft floorboard to see if Stumpy has died and is floating on the surface of the bilge water. The floorboards are starting to swell up again. We are getting closer to the equator and the relative humidity is increasing. After using a screwdriver to twist the locking mechanism, I have to use all my strength to get the board up.

I scream when I see what is in our bilge. The image that greets me is not a single dead gecko, but infinitely worse. It could be an Indiana Jones movie. Only in this horrific scene, there aren't snakes flowing over the ribs of our boat, but thousands, maybe millions of baby cockroaches. Like a sneeze of mobile passion fruit seeds sprayed throughout the bilge, they scurry for cover from the introduction of light into their damp, dark world. I spring into action and try to crush as many as possible with my bare hands. I kill a hundred or so, but after ten seconds, most are hidden in the far dark reaches of Iwalani's most private anatomy.

I can't help it. I begin to cry. I cry for Isi and for all the people killed and soon to be killed, in a war that will have no ending. I cry for the six pounds of cat fur and bones lying at the entrance to Tulear in 243 feet of water. I cry because the floorboard is digging into my thigh and it hurts; but, I also cry because I want to see my parents, Phil's parents, Ben and Nathaniel, our siblings, my clients, our friends, everyone that is to our north living a normal life, not stuck out at sea thousands of miles from anywhere with a boat full of bugs.

"Oh my god!" Phil says lifting up one of the earpieces on his headphones. "Were those what I think?"

"I knew I was a slob, but I didn't think I was that bad," I sob. Phil removes the headphones and comes over to hold me.

"It's not your fault. I blame it on Jacques boat in Reunion."

"And not having Stew, he must have been helping with all these bugs though we didn't realize it." I cry into Phil's shoulder.

"Don't cry. We'll be home soon," he says smoothing my damp, dirty, hair.

"I'm worried about that too, going home to war. Speaking of killers, where is our resident gecko?"

"Good question. I think we need bigger guns than Stumpy. Don't we have any insect spray?" Phil asks.

"We have insecticidal chalk from China, flea spray, wasp spray and another French bug spray of unknown composition. I'll get all of them and douse the bilge." I blow my nose into some paper towels and head off in search of the chemicals. I find the spray cans and try to use them in the bilge, but the metal parts on the cans have corroded and none of them work, despite the fact that they have never been used. The flea spray is also unopened, but is in a plastic pump bottle. Three years of topical temperatures and never ending motion have turned it into a gummy congealed mess. The chalk is our only defense. I draw skull and cross bones, 'death to Ossama's helpers' and other threatening messages on all the surfaces the cockroaches will come in contact with. I close up the floorboards, go into the engine room, and write similar roach death threats.

While hanging on, trying to keep from falling into the engine, I grab hold of a beam across the ceiling. Something big moves near my fingers. I grab the flashlight in the toolbox and light up the corner overhead. It is Stumpy. I inhale sharply. He is enormous. Obviously well fed and with a short tail growing back as big as the thumb of a wrestler, he is the picture of health.

Phil meanwhile, is talking on the radio nets about Isi. We are the only yacht with Inmarsat and none of the other boats knew Islero was reported overdue.

I head out into the fading light of dusk to look out for ships and nearly have a heart attack when I see a bright, fixed, white light to the east, not far off the horizon. It is Saturn, one of only a few non-twinkling lights in the sky. I mistake it for the light on a ship. I go back down below. Phil removes his headphones.

"Someone heard that Isi had gone crazy. He wrote an e-mail to someone else in Spain, and they contacted somebody on St. Helena. Everyone thinks he committed suicide."

"That's nuts. He is just as crazy as we are," I say.

Phil looks askance at me.

"He didn't commit suicide," I add.

"Another single hander from the Netherlands is also missing. He left the day after Isi."

"Great. Has anyone checked the deck of the ships arriving at Cape Town for yacht jewelry?"

"Someone else said that there are a lot of pirates or overly friendly fishing boats on the run from Cape Town to St. Helena."

"We didn't see any. Not like south of Jakarta," I remark.

"We can find out more on the Internet when we arrive at Fernando de Norhona," Phil says turning the radio off.

"E-mail my sister to check out the last entry on Isi's web site. She can read Spanish," I suggest.

"That's a good idea. There really isn't any more we can do from here."

*   *   *

My sister e-mails us back and reports Isi's last log entry is short. He was confused and depressed, she writes.

That evening I go out on deck for my 8 p.m. watch. A black bird flies out of the darkness and lands on the boom gallows, a potentially bad omen. It is a noddy. At first, I don't like having it roosting so near the cockpit. When it is asleep, I forget it is there, but when it is awake it startles me each time it flutters its wings or makes some small movement. I shriek and then will hear a "splurp" as Iwalani's decks are painted with guano. A little while later it is joined by a second noddy who takes up residence on the opposite side of the wide board.

The following night the second noddy arrives much later. He tries to land, but is met with some serious bird yelling from the first noddy. From the tone of the fight it isn't clear if the first is yelling because the second is so late, or if it isn't going to share the roosting spot this time. The second noddy has quite a defensive tone, almost like it is making up excuses. I imagine the birds are using our navigational lights as a reference for their rendezvous. From my understanding of the argument, the second noddy saw another boat with similar lights and tried to land there, only to find out it was the wrong boat. I am definitely beginning to think we have been at sea too long.

*   *   *

In mid April, we arrive at Fernando De Norhona in another squall. We reduce sail to just the jib to slow ourselves down so we can come in at first light. I will have to jibe on my watch, which is no big deal with no mainsail up.

Once the squall passes and it becomes light, I ease us in under power, waking Phil in the process. We anchor well away from shore, and then go below for a nap.

Later that morning we see Farmer Bob's boat anchored close to shore. We take the dinghy over, hoping to trade books and, because he has no radio, tell him about Isi and find out if he saw anything unusual. As we come alongside I have second thoughts. I am worried we will catch him at a bad time so I pull away as he comes up from below.

"JUST TAKING A NAP BELOW!" he yells at us. We circle back and come alongside.

He had heard from another yacht that Islero was overdue, but hadn't seen anything unusual on the trip to Fernando. He asks us if we have any books to trade. We have read almost everything on board and are well stocked. I tell him we will come by later for trade negotiations. We go back to Iwalani to put together a book trade package. After loading the dinghy we motor back to Farmer Bob's boat and climb aboard.

He has cleared a two-foot section from his cockpit seats so Phil and I can sit together, closely. But he has neglected to wipe the seat off, so we sit down on what looks like dried blood from a fish cleaning operation of several weeks ago. He comes up from down below with the first pile of books. "I put my hearing aid on," he says, "so I won't have to shout. I don't know what you like for books so I brought up an assortment."

"Wow," I whisper to Phil, "I think I underestimated Bob. He has some great books," I say leafing through his pile.

"So many people read Romance books. I hope you don't have any," he yells up from down below.

"No worries there. I did get some from the last boat we traded with, but you know what? I am ashamed to say I threw them overboard. As desperate as we are for reading material, we couldn't even read them. I feel bad for the trees that died to print them."

"I can't find my glasses," Bob says while foraging in the tiny cramped space. His world down below is about as big as our engine room.

"What do we have to do to check in here?" I ask.

"Nothing." Bob passes up another pile of books. "There isn't anyone to clear us yachts in. I just sort of smiled and waved at the police. It's a great island really."

"Have you been to Trinidad and Tobago?" Phil asks. "We are trying to figure out where we should make landfall in the Caribbean."

"Well, Tobago is much nicer really. Quieter. There is a marina in Trinidad called um, um…oh anyway, I can't remember the name. But it is full of those fancy boats from Miami," Bob says scratching his beard.

"We call that cruiseheimers," Phil says.

"What?" Bob asks.

"Cruiseheimers, like Alzheimer's, but it only afflicts cruisers."

"Oh. That's good. I'll need to remember that. I can't remember the name of the marina, but it's awful. No, actually those places aren't bad because they keep those Miami boats all cloistered together. It's too bad for the locals though; there is no hurricane season and they can't escape those people. But I kind of get a kick out of it, because they look down so at my boat," Bob chuckles.

"Speaking of Alzheimer's," Bob continues, "I had a good one yesterday. Everything comes in threes. I went to shore to get some money changed and to mail a letter to my wife. I have four one hundred dollar U.S. bills on the boat, and I thought I'd hidden them real well, only I can't remember where I put them so I couldn't find them. I vaguely remember putting them in cornmeal—or so I thought. Well, I was so mad at myself, that when I got to shore I had forgotten the letter to my wife." Bob passes up another stack of books from down below.

"What was the third thing?" Phil asks.

"The what?"

"You said you had three things…"

"Oh, yes. Well, I can't remember now," Bob says.

"That's cruiseheimers for you," Phil exclaims.

Bob comes up from below with his glasses on and leafs through the stack of books we have brought. "You've got some pretty good books here. This one I've read," he says setting one of the physics book aside. "My son is a string theorist and has given me lots to read on the subject."

"Where are you heading from here?" Phil asks.

"Back to Panama. I am on my third circumnavigation and am ready to go part way around again. This time I'm stopping in Malaysia."

"Why Malaysia?"

"I want to die there. It's cheap and they have a pretty good view of death. I don't want to be hooked up with tubes and chemicals," he says.

"Are you sick?" I ask.

"No, just old. I'll be eighty-six next month," he replies.

"What about your children? Your wife?" I ask.

"What about them?"

"Don't you want to be with them?"

"They can come visit if they want. I'm not going to stop them," Bob says.

*   *   *

We rent a motorcycle and tour the island, snorkel on an old wreck and try to restock our larders. Not being able to read or speak Portuguese is a bit of a hindrance but not a complete roadblock. Still in need of insect spray, my childhood experience with charades at family Thanksgiving Day celebrations comes to the rescue. At a small grocery store, I ask the girl at the cash register in Franco-Spano-Englese about the availability of insecticide. She shakes her head, not comprehending this new dialect. I pantomime with my fingers something walking along the check-out counter, and then jump out of the way shrieking in horror. She nods, says, something to the bag boy in Portuguese, who disappears down an aisle. He returns with a mousetrap. I shake my head and go through the routine again, this time reaching for an imaginary can of roach killer and making a hissing sound as I spray the surface of her check out conveyor belt, then folding my arms and sighing with relief.

Like a game show contestant she jumps, nods, claps her hands and returns with a very large can of insecticide. Where it was shelved I can't be sure, but our bugs don't stand a chance as we now have in our arsenal a mix of lethal substances outlawed and unavailable in the U.S. Whether we will kill ourselves in the process, I can't be sure.

On our first night away from Fernando, Bill joins us once again. He swims about Iwalani and does his leaps with added fervor as he really seems glad to see us. While listening to NPR the next morning, I hear a short report on research someone has done recently on tuna. Unfortunately, the radio reception isn't good, and the broadcast is punctuated with crackles, static and occasional periods of silence. The reporter states that tuna can swim for eleven days straight before they must take short naps. That explains how Bill can keep up with us! Only the researcher is wrong; during his longest stretch, Bill went seventeen days without sleeping.

We hear no more about Isi. In order to expedite a search and rescue operation, the Spanish radio net operator has contacted St. Helena with worries over Isi's medical condition. The airwaves carry rumors of malaria, delusional fevers, dengue, and other tropical diseases, all untrue. A P-3 Orion aircraft is sent out and scouts the Eastern Southern Atlantic area, but his yacht Islero is not seen.

The closer to the equator we get, the hotter it becomes. The only relief from the heat is the cool nights, when we spend our time outside in the cockpit. The Southern Cross sinks in the sky, like a kite losing its wind, while the Big Dipper appears in the north. It sits to the north like a cocked dog's ear listening to conversations in the south. Eventually the whole constellation floats over the horizon, scooping up southern secrets and passing them north. My own constellations, the vacuum cleaner, the evening gown, the Tasmanian devil, disappear or become so twisted in their configuration as to be unrecognizable. We can still see Magellan's clouds in the Milky Way but with greater difficulty.

For ten days we motor and drift on a favorable current through the ITCZ as we cross the equator. Herb returns from vacation and helps us to steer for cold eddies and away from any significant convection activity. Using Phil's satellite antenna system, we are able to get a picture of where the worst of the thunderstorms are located, and bring Iwalani through the doldrums as if we are playing a computer game.

One night the protea plant I brought from South Africa begins to flower. I sit out in the cockpit as the partially full moon begins to rise over our starboard quarter. The winds drop off, and I debate about turning the engine on. We are still in a cold eddy which gives us a favorable boost to the north. With full sail up and flat seas we are ghosting along at three knots.

Clouds swirl about us like modern dancers, twirling, floating, reaching for ghostlike partners, yet cleaving a clear spot where Iwalani hangs suspended in calm water. Our sister ship, a faultless reflection from the pale moonlight, sails alongside keeping perfect pace. I look off our port side and see an illuminated circle. Unable to comprehend what I am seeing, I pause for a moment. A glowing arch rises from the water like a garden arbor, beneath it, a reflection unmarred by wind or wavelets, painted in bands of silver and gray. It is a rainbow, created by the light of the rising moon and reflected in the mirror-still ocean.

*   *   *

Two weeks at sea and twelve hundred miles from Fernado De Norhona, we now sail in water the color of dark tea. We stay three hundred miles off the Brazilian coast, yet as hard as it is to believe, the great Amazon and Orinoco rivers can actually be seen because they clearly taint the ocean a murky brown. Our stalwart tuna companion also feels the effects of this fresh water. Bill begins to drag behind Iwalani, almost as if he is trying to pull us backward, or at least get us to turn around. He seems tired and no longer does his aerial displays during our dinnertime. Soon Bill follows us no more.

"There is a tropical storm forming," Phil says to me the next morning.

"What? That's impossible. It's too early in the season. Where is it?"

"It's east of here heading in a northeasterly direction. They are calling it Ana. It's going to miss us, but it will probably hit Sjany and Chris."

"Oh, no. Red Oranda is a tough boat. I am sure they'll be fine, but what a horrible way to end a circumnavigation," I say.

"No kidding."

"The e-mail from my mother said it is snowing at home."

"Maybe we should stay for a while in Tobago."

"Well, that's something I want to talk to you about."

"What?" Phil asks.

"I have sort of altered course, a wee bit."

"I noticed the compass entry in the log was off. Now where are we going?"

"I figured that with the trade winds still out of the northeast and no sign that they are going to clock to the southeast anytime to soon, we should try and head for the easternmost part of the Caribbean. That way, when the trades do shift, we will be able to reach Antigua. I have also been reading books from Farmer Bob about the holocaust, and I was kind of getting depressed, and the best thing for counteracting depression"...

"Pain au chocolat!" Phil exclaims.

"Exactly! So we are now going to Martinique not Tobago. Patisseries, French grocery stores!"

"Whoo hoo!" Phil cries.

"You're not mad?" I ask.

"Are you crazy? French territories? Topless beautiful women!"

"Don't get your hopes up on that one, this is the Caribbean we are talking about not French Polynesia."

*　　　*　　　*

At midnight May 1st we arrive at Martinique. We had been at sea for eighteen days. On the last two days of the passage we were joined by two skipjack, which did some of the same jumps as Bill but not with the same panache.

We take the sails down, get them furled and covered with the sail covers, while Iwalani's autopilot slowly steers us in. We plan on anchoring along a beach on the outside of the channel that leads into the well-protected harbor of Marin. Neither of us wants to come into the town in the dark after a long passage.

"Come here and look at the radar, I can't figure out what I am looking at," Phil yells to me as I stand lookout in the bow. "What are those?" he asks pointing to the radar screen.

"I don't know. I've never seen anything like it"

We can make out the curve of the beach easily. It matches what we are seeing with our naked eye: many orange colored lights on shore twinkling from the swaying of palm fronds. But on radar, not far off the beach, are hundreds of dashed lines. "Are they waves? Beachcombers?"

"They aren't moving," Phil says.

I take the binoculars from Phil. "I don't see anything."

"We'll anchor out here. We are in twenty feet of water. Whatever those things are on radar, we'll stay well away from them."

The next morning I make coffee and our traditional landfall breakfast of scrambled eggs, toast and bacon, while Phil heads out on deck. "You won't believe what those dashed lines were on radar," Phil laughs.

"Buoys? Fishing nets?" I ask.

"No and no."

I head up the companionway to see for myself. Straight ahead of us are hundreds of yachts at anchor. "Duh, what else would look like that on radar? We just haven't seen so many yachts in one place. And not one of them had an anchor light up. What the hell are we doing anchored way out here?"

"I was wondering the same thing."

"We look kind of foolish anchored out in the bay."

After breakfast we move Iwalani nearer to town, anchoring amidst yet more yachts in the central harbor. We take the dinghy to shore and fill out the simple forms for clearing in. We find an Internet café and fill a floppy disc with email. After buying a bag of *pain au chocolat*, we take the dinghy out and snorkel on the reef. Returning to the boat, I make supper while Phil sits at the computer reading the e-mail out loud. This time of day is particularly empty without Stewart.

"We got e-mail from Fred. They found Islero," Phil says. I remain silent. "It was found by a fisherman off Abidjan. No one was onboard."

"Do you think Isi committed suicide?" I finally ask.

"I don't know what to think. Yes, I guess he probably did," Phil responds slowly.

"I don't. I think he fell overboard. It is easier to deal with his death if I think he voluntarily jumped. The thought of someone accidently falling off while their boat sails away, is just too horrendous to deal with."

"I've always said the easy passages are the most dangerous because you get careless, and the passage from Cape Town to St.Helena was the easiest by far," Phil says.

"He was tired and getting lazy. No different from us really. Yes, let's hope our passage home isn't too easy. I don't even want to think of either of us going overboard by accident."

To Isadoro Arias:

Blue water blues, the song of the deep.
Beholden to wind, scant profits to reap
Lost to the waves a grave in the sea,
layers of blue paint infinity.
A cage with a keel, bars of slack sheets
a tall white wing hobbled to cleats
Banquets in cans, feasts of scant sleep–
Salt soaked sun too lonesome to weep.

388

Chapter 31

Hot time with the Marts

April/May 2003
Caribbean

The Caribbean islands are as cramped as a grandmother's parlor, which is not really a bad thing. With countries and islands separated by an overnight sail, getting into trouble is harder to do than in the Pacific where landmasses and countries are separated by days, if not weeks. If a fall is imminent, a person can grab hold of the couch or an armchair. It's cozier. Clustering the islands closely together keeps large seas to a minimum. But, like a parlor full of books, sleeping cats, and knitting baskets, finding a place to settle down for the night amidst all the clutter can be equally as challenging.

We work our way up from Martinique to Isle du Saints, a quiet French port near Guadeloupe. The village of Bourge de Saints is everything people on Martinique built it up to be: pristine pastel buildings with red tile roofs, tidy gardens and quiet streets curved around a well-sheltered harbor. Most of the traffic is on motorbikes or on foot. A ferry arrives from Guadeloupe early in the day and leaves in the afternoon taking most of the tourists back where they came from. We anchor on the edge of a small yacht cluster. A hundred foot classic schooner from a bygone era, anchors shortly after us. Flying the red British yacht ensign, its varnished woodwork and gleaming brass catches everyone's attention. Shortly afterwards a ninety-foot fiberglass, motor-mega yacht anchors behind the schooner, paling in comparison.

Phil and I launch the Grape and rig the small sail. We can't resist a good opportunity to snoop. Unlike a small outboard, or even a rowboat, we can get very close to waterfront mansions or large mega yachts. We are the ultimate voyeurs. We have found ourselves sometimes in the thick of arguments, lunches, or naked sunbathing.

Phil and I have completely different agendas for our forays. Phil hopes to one day come across a sexual encounter between the staff and the bikini clad yacht owner. I hope to find the ultimate terrorist nest. Ever since I was a kid, I fancied myself as a CIA agent. Some of the best agents in history have been little old ladies, or people pretending to be crazy. With both these attributes in my possession, I am, I think, dually qualified.

I position our cameras under a towel, while Phil tacks close to the yacht. Wearing matching dark blue shirts and white shorts, the crew of the classic schooner is on the bowsprit. They have just gotten through furling the sails and are now being lectured to by a woman, presumably the captain, wearing the same uniform. "Should I try and sail under the bowsprit?" Phil whispers to me. Like the daredevil doing wheelies on a motorcycle, Phil wants to show off for the pretty captain. His most favorite pastime in small yacht sailing is to charge at an anchored boat as if we were going to pierce straight through their hull, then at the very last possible second come about with a yawn and a bored stretch.

I give him a harsh look. "No, go close, but not too close. Then let's jibe and go down the lee side, close to the hull."

On the other side of the yacht a skinny old man wearing nothing but gray swimming trunks leans over the rail looking down at us. "My word, that looks fun," he feebly yells down to us with a British accent.

"Ditto," I yell back.

"No it's not really. I would give anything to be in your husband's shoes right now."

Phil smiles and waves as we sail by. "Everyone wants to get in your pants," he mutters.

"For Pete's sake, you are too weird! He was talking about how it would be nice to be unencumbered by age and wealth. My pants have nothing to do with it!"

A woman wearing a white nurse's uniform and a large well-muscled man together assist the skinny old gent down the steps to a swimming platform hanging off the side.

"Honey, I am sorry I am not rich like that guy. I wish I could give you servants and jewelry," Phil says.

"Don't be ridiculous! Look at what you have given me!" I say. "You gave me the world! From a boat that you designed and built! I am the luckiest woman that ever lived."

"Thanks for saying that."

"Well, it's true. I wouldn't want any other life."

"You wouldn't want to be captain on that boat?" Phil asks.

"Are you nuts? Having to take orders from a shriveled old guy?"

"What about being the skinny old guy's wife?" he chides.

"Yuck, that is an unpleasant thought. Plus, I would never be able to sleep. I'd be worried, no one was standing watch."

"How 'bout I take you out to lunch?" Phil asks while pulling in the mainsheet. "It's been a long time since we ate out."

"That would be a nice treat. What's a little more credit card debt?"

At a French bistro overlooking the harbor, we order and wait for our meal to arrive. Not saying much, we look over a balcony at the mega yacht, the classic schooner, the fleet of white sloops with blue sail covers, and Iwalani. There is no question, in our eyes, which is the most beautiful boat.

Two American couples come in and sit at the table next to us.

"I only said I would come here to humor Andy," one woman says to her female friend. "Personally, I think the French people are rude."

"Well, we were forewarned," her friend replies.

Phil and I look at one another. The waitress takes their order and brings them a bottle of red wine. Artfully, the waitress pours the wine into the four glasses like a professional sommelier. Leaving the bottle on the table, she retreats back to the kitchen. The larger of the two American women grabs the bottle.

"Look at this!" she says with a voice like a rusty gate. "See how the bottle is all humped up on the bottom? They are cheating us out of wine!"

The other woman joins in the assault. "Did you notice how the waitress was holding the it? She was disguising it in a napkin so we wouldn't notice!"

I study them to see if they are joking, but they aren't. "Are you sure you want to go back home?" Phil whispers.

We stay in Isle du Saints for a few days, snorkeling, hiking and riding our bicycles, or trying to, anyways. It is hot and I have gotten so out of shape that I can barely walk my bike up the steep hills. We decide to try and make Antigua in time for Phil's birthday and to spend some time catching up with former friends of his. Nick and his wife Martha moved to Antigua years ago after Nick graduated from the Apprenticeshop where Phil had been teaching boatbuilding.

We arrive at Antigua before Phil's birthday and do the usual two stooges anchoring routine, rehearsing three failed attempts, until we are both satisfied the anchor is well set on the fourth and final act. I dive in the water with my mask, hoping to check on the anchor, but the sandy bottom is so stirred up from our repeated attempts at getting Iwalani settled that I can't see anything.

"The cell phone doesn't work here," Phil says when I come back on board.

"We'll need to do it the old fashioned way and find a phone booth."

"I've got the dinghy ready to launch."

"Let's hang out here for a little while," I suggest.

"Don't you want to meet Nick and Mart?"

"Not really."

"Why not?"

"Well, weren't they friends of yours when you were still married to number one? I am sure your ex-wife sent them the complete ten page letter about what an evil person I am, like she did to everyone else."

"You have nothing to worry about. I doubt she would have spent the money on the postage; and besides, Nick and Martha wouldn't have paid any attention to it even if she had."

"Everyone else did."

"Nick and Martha are different."

"Well, there is always Zelda," I say.

"Who is Zelda?"

"The super critical, arrogant, conceited, really obnoxious woman that lives in the back of my throat."

"Huh?'

"She always gets me in trouble blurting out dumb things. I can't be responsible for her. She makes people hate me, so I might as well stay out here and keep her company and avoid embarrassing you," I say covering my head with a towel.

"You're being ridiculous," Phil says removing the towel from my face. "You'll love Martha. She's like a shaken up soda pop bottle. Once you release the cap, look out."

Reluctantly, I follow Phil to shore late that afternoon. We sit on high stools at a round table in an open-air bar. Nick and Martha are both genuinely happy to see Phil. Nick is tan with pale blonde hair. Martha, his polar opposite, is tall with dark hair.

I don't say much, trying to keep Zelda quiet, while politely sipping a gin and tonic. Phil talks about our trip and how we are eager to get home. Phil explains what he wishes we could do to help his two boys when we get back, if it isn't too late.

Martha quickly surprises all of us by bursting into tears. "Nick and I can't have children," she cries throwing her head into her hands.

Zelda is scratching on my vocal cords, trying to tear up my throat in order to escape out of my mouth. I can hear her muffled cries beating on my uvula, *'Why on earth would you want children? There are too many people as it is, why make more? Create something constructive instead of a pile of protein and double helixes of DNA, which suck up the earth's resources like the vacuum cleaner from infinity. Or, if you need to nurture, adopt a waif with no home. Or better still, take in a stray cat.'*

"It is too bad that people breed like refrigerator mold," I blurt out. *'Uh oh'*, I think to myself, *'Zelda is unleashed.'*

Martha stops sobbing and looks at me. "Refrigerator mold?" she says sniffling.

"Humans infect the far corners of the globe like the green fuzz on last month's goulash." I am a goner. Zelda is on a roll.

"Hmm. Hadn't thought of it that way," Martha says matter-of-factly. Phil is right, like a shaken bottle of seltzer, Martha's effervescence soon froths forth, the whole baby thing, was just a cork in her bottle. From that moment on, there is no stopping the banter, the jokes, the parodies, the one-liners. The Mart, as Nick calls her, is a one-stop shop of humors.

For a few days we have a blast and forget about sailing home. I usually dread Phil's birthday because of his propensity to spend it with his head under a pillow. But with Nick and the Mart, we trample the island of Antigua, almost as bad as the native goats, chewing away on the rocky, barren, deforested hills. Phil never even sees his pillow to lay his head down, let alone hide under it.

Antigua appears to have less strife than other former British colonies we have visited. The police station has a vegetable garden out front, a sure sign that domestic problems and heads of state don't need as much attention as heads of lettuce. Older women pepper the landscape, nattily dressed in Caribbean colors with trim straw hats perched on their heads. When such a woman gets onto a bus, younger men gave up their seats to them. We can see why Nick and Mart choose to claim Antigua as home; its people are just plain nice.

"We're going to need to recuperate before the final leg home," Phil says.

"I know. The weather is still too explosive to the north, lows are firing across the U.S like baseballs from an automatic pitching machine. I'm in no rush," I say.

"What if we stop at St. Martin? It's a night sail from here, just one more dose of pain au chocolat before the trip home?"

"Sounds good to me."

"I knew you would like Martha," Phil says as we round the corner leaving ̶tigua behind.

"Like her! I love her! I could pack up all my worries and run off with her and w̶ ̶ld do art on some mountaintop. There are very few people on Earth that can put ̶ ̶th Zelda and me. Luckily though, you are one of them."

"̶ ̶'t believe you showed her our cockroach collection."

"S̶ ̶n artist. I knew she would appreciate it. You've got to hand it to the French. T̶ ̶ittle cockroach houses are fantastic."

"I cou̶ ̶sist buying them," Phil says.

"Who els̶ ̶ld design a cardboard box with sticky insides, complete with a red tile roof, windows with curtains and even a tiny little welcome mat? It doesn't make me feel sorry for the cockroaches at all."

"What's our grand tally to date?" Phil asks.

"Close to four hundred. We have two different species on board. Want to see my drawings of them?"

"No, that's O.K. I'll pass. Just so long as you don't start naming them."

*   *   *

We motor sail through the night, in light winds, to St. Martin. As we get near the island, a Dutch Coastal patrol boat circles around us while I make breakfast. I put my clothes on and raise the French courtesy flag, to show we are bypassing their half and going over to the French port. I keep the radio on and tuned to channel 16 to see if they try to hail us. They continue clinging to us like an anxious security guard at an electronics store. Finally we round the bend and enter French territory, but like a dog protecting its half of the street, the Dutch stop at an invisible line separating Holland from France.

"Where do you want to anchor?" Phil asks me.

"The only place possible," I say scanning the crowded anchorage. "Slightly ahead of that beautiful old boat."

"She is a beauty," Phil says whistling. He rarely gives any boat or woman that compliment, and he never whistles on a boat. As a sign of respect, we slowly motor Iwalani in a circle around the one hundred foot Baltic trading schooner, Irene.

"Wow," we say in unison.

"I wish we hadn't painted Iwalani's hull but left it bright."

"No thanks. That's too much varnishing for me," Phil replies.

"But there are so few wooden boats in the world. It really emphasizes the wood. They must have just finished a big refit on her. No boat can look that good all the time."

Irene looks as if she just got out of the beauty parlor. We anchor right ahead of her and row to shore to check in. "Not quite white I expected. St. Martin looks like its been Americanized," Phil says to me.

"It sort of reminds me of a giant airport terminal."

A young man walks up to us and hands us a piece of paper. "If you go to this address, you can collect a free T-shirt," he says.

"What's the catch?" Phil asks me after he has moved on to the next tourist couple.

"It's our duty to find out. Don't you think?" We find the address, a small tourist office wedged between two jewelry stores. A woman with two inch purple nails sits behind the counter. She tells us she is out of T-shirts, but if we take our passports the following day, we can get a free taxi ride over to the Dutch side of the island, and there we can win marvelous prizes and get fifty dollars in cash.

"Oh really?" I ask. "And what do we have to do in order to win marvelous prizes and get fifty dollars in cash?"

"You have to sit through a salesman's pitch for a condo."

"That can't be too hard. We need the fifty dollars," I say looking at Phil.

With great difficulty we finally find a shop selling our precious pain au chocolat and a DVD rental store. We head back to the boat for wine and shrimp cocktail. We have corned beef, boiled vegetables and a huge salad for dinner. Afterwards we retreat to the fo'c'sle, to watch a movie while we wait for the ice cream to be done.

"Now this is living!" Phil says as he props up all the pillows behind us. "Arnold Schwarzenegger, and ice cream."

"Aren't you going to miss this?" I ask.

"Maybe just a little, but certainly not the passages."

A half hour later, I hear an explosion. "What was that?" I ask.

"What?"

"I thought I heard a big bang outside."

"It was just the movie, I didn't hear anything."

Ten minutes later the ice cream machine beeps that it is ready. "I'll pause the movie," I say to Phil. He heads aft to take the machine out of the engine room.

"Oh my god!" he yells.

"What! What's the matter? Are cockroaches in the ice cream?"

"Get the buckets!" He is already up on deck. I can see an orange glow behind him. I run for the engine room and grab our sheet rock buckets. Phil grabs the buckets on deck.

The aft section of beautiful Irene is completely engulfed in flames. "We're too late," Phil says.

We watch in horror as orange flames leap into the night sky. Plumes of gray swirling smoke race downwind. At least fifty small dinghies circle Irene like frightened ducklings. Not one of us has the necessary equipment to put out the fire despite all of us floating on water. Ropes are burned from their cleated positions on pin rails. They trail in the breeze like slow burning fuses on firecrackers. As it consumes recently varnished wood and diesel, the roar of the blaze sucks sound, as well as oxygen from the windy night.

"Should we maneuver Iwalani and try to put the fire out with our wash down pump?"

"We can't get close enough. It's too hot," Phil replies.

"Couldn't we put on our scuba gear, drill holes from the bottom and sink her?" I ask.

"Sinking her now would be the only way of saving her. But it's too dangerous. Flaming chunks of debris are already hitting the water. And just how do you propose to drill the holes?"

"We can't just stand here and watch her die. We've got to do something!" I begin to cry. "The wind is keeping the flames to her stern. If we climb aboard the bow, we might be able to get inside and chop holes up forward and sink her that way."

"And if the fire gets to her fuel tanks she might explode again. It's too dangerous," Phil says. As if to emphasize the point a huge explosion erupts from the mid section. "I just hope no one is injured."

A small boat arrives with a portable pump on board. Three men work hard to get the pump started. Their silhouetted outlines look like fictional characters in an old comedy film, as they repeatedly go through fire fighting antics. The pump sputters to life. A feeble jet squirts out like a water pistol onto the aft burning section. The pump dies. They restart it and for a moment it looks as if the firefighters gain the upper hand, but then the pump stops again and the glowing core of Irene flames back to life.

The Dutch patrol boat finally arrives. We can see hundreds of arms rise in cheer but hear only the fire's fury. The Dutch have a pump on board that can deliver hundreds of gallons per minute. For a while the devil is beaten into submission, but then the burning aft mast glows red and topples into the water, and a flame erupts from a hatch in the mid-section. The fire is eating Irene from the inside.

Despite thousands of gallons of water spraying into Irene, she still doesn't sink; a grim reminder that it takes a tremendous amount of water to ultimately drown a boat. The fire breaks out of the forward deck, and the jibs flash to ashes. The French courtesy flag is oblivious to its fate. Red, white and blue cloth flap in death's light. We can feel the heat and hear the roar of the future. I can watch no more, and go down below. Sickly mesmerized, Phil stays to watch the loss of history. He finally stops, just before the main mast collapses, and silently comes to bed, praying no one is hurt.

The following morning the bowsprit hovers just above the water; its fresh paint and varnish are a reminder of the beauty that had existed one day before. The masts are gone, the keel firmly settled, and black timbers lie motionless on the sandy bottom. People slowly motor around what is left, a dark shadow in the water just below the surface. We circle Irene in the Grape, just as we had twenty-four hours previously with Iwalani. How quickly things can change.

Years earlier I learned how fragile our existence is and how quickly something can be taken from you. On Christmas night, after just graduating from Veterinary school, an arsonist burned down my house in Maine. I was visiting my parents in Massachusetts at the time and had only my dachshund, George, with me. My cats, birds, and pet chinchilla were left to die in the fire. I had recently inherited valuable antiques from my grandmother, and the insurance adjuster was coming after the New Year to appraise everything and write a policy for me. Only a metal birdcage and a pair of owl andirons were salvaged from the wreckage. Everything else was reduced to ashes. After that ordeal, I vowed never again to get attached to material objects. Of course this backfired. The opposite happened. I became an even greedier hoarder, and every object got its own name and developed its own persona.

We head to shore and try to forget about the previous night. "Let's go to the Dutch side, get our free lunch, claim our fifty dollars and collect marvelous prizes," I say.

"I am not so sure about this. There is no such thing as a free lunch."

"We're strong willed people. We won't get sucked in," I say.

"Well, the last thing I would want is a condo in St. Martin. We'll do it as long as you swear we won't spend money."

"We don't have money to spend, so how can we?" I ask.

We find a taxi that will accept our voucher for a free ride to the Dutch side. I am having a hard time adjusting to the concept of two different countries existing on such a tiny island, but the inhabitants seem to handle it well. The taxi driver takes us to a large development erupting from the beach.

I stand in line waiting for a brochure and a salesman. An hour later we are ushered into a large cafeteria where at least fifty other couples and families are

395

seated at round tables with well-dressed businessmen flitting about with bulging briefcases. The "free lunch" table has been ransacked and all that remains is a handful of crackers and a few grapes. *'We're in trouble,'* I think to myself. Neither one of us ate breakfast. When Phil gets hungry, his body tenses into a combustible cauldron of unreleasable epithets. I give him the crackers and sit down to share the grapes.

"Hey, how are you all doing? I'm Jim," our sunburned American salesman says to us. "Where are you all staying?"

"On board Iwalani," I mumble.

"Where? What? What's that?"

"Our boat," I say.

Jim's face puckers. While most people believe that anyone who owns their own boat and has the means to do a circumnavigation, must have loads of money stashed away in offshore bank accounts, Jim has obviously run into cruisers before. We have the tightest, leanest wallets on the planet. We are the modern day equivalent of yesteryear's gypsies and, in most places, are still treated as such.

"Oh. Well, then. I'll be short lived," he says as he opens his brief case. From the looks of things, he is going to be anything but.

Wordlessly, we sit through his presentation for forty-five minutes, Phil dreaming of a giant hamburger and all the trimmings and I an ice cool Coca Cola in a glass bottle. I am brought back to reality with each screaming simile and mangled malapropism tripping and tumbling out of Jim's mouth.

"So there you have it! You two can become the fantastic spirit of Parrot Bay irregardless of your ability to pay. It's low cost living with high class faculties. Now, if you care to join me, we can parusal one of the units."

We walk behind him into a two-bedroom time-share.

"Hey, It's the awesomest place on the island," Jim says. "I consider myself a gourmet. See how this kitchen space is so extraneous? And the view, out of a postcard! Can I get you to throw up caution with the wind and sign up now? All this could be yours for just a down payment of five thousand dollars due at signing. And we do take MasterCard and Visa."

"Thanks for all the time you spent, but it's really not our style," Phil says.

"What can I do to make you more appealing?" Jim asks.

I look at Jim. He really isn't a bad sort. He reminds me of a cocker spaniel, panting in front of us, big brown eyes begging for our money. Zelda is pounding on my voice box like an imprisoned freedom fighter. *'Make us more appealing? Throw up caution? That's not all we're going to throw up. What on earth are you talking about? This place has too much humanity. It's a little like a condo nest for large, two legged rodents don't you think? We only came for the fifty dollars and free lunch, so better luck with the next sucker. And if you say irregardless one more time, my mother, the queen of D&D (that's "dictum and decorum" for you born after 1982 when "dungeons and dragons" swept the world) has implanted a poor-speech recognition chip in my DNA or tried to anyways, and she will turn me into a raving lunatic, so I can whack you with a dictionary and grind you to a halt with a pencil sharpener.'*

"You have no high speed internet access," Phil finally says saving the day.

"Yes, that is a problem. Irregardless of that, won't you sign up still?"

"No thanks," I say between clenched teeth and rumblings in my stomach.

Jim ushers us back to the front office where I am handed an envelope. "Is this our fifty dollars?" I ask.

"It's a coupon for your prize," a woman says from behind the counter.

"And the fifty dollars? We were told we'd get fifty dollars for suffering through, I mean sitting through, your sales pitch. I am sure this is a coupon for a very marvelous prize, but we were promised cash too." Zelda wants her freedom.

"We're all out," the woman states flatly.

"What do you mean you're all out?"

"Fine," the woman exhales sharply. "Take this voucher to the casino and they will give you fifty dollars."

"Where is the casino?" I ask. She points down the road. "This is the hardest fifty dollars I've ever earned," I whisper to Phil when we are out of earshot.

"I hate to remind you of this fact, but you don't exactly have the fifty dollars yet."

"No kidding," I reply.

"Plus we have to pay for the taxi back to the boat."

I tell the taxi driver we have to make one stop before we can go to Marigot Bay. Reluctantly, he stops at the casino where I run in at full speed to get our money.

A minute later, I surprise both of us by emerging with cash in hand. "See," I say counting our money. "We came out ahead."

"Aren't you interested in the coupon for our marvelous prize?"

"Oh yeah, I forgot. What did we win?"

"Two night stay at a timeshare condo of our choice."

I look at the destinations we have to choose from. "Yuck."

The taxi driver drops us off at the town dock. I see a newspaper stand and buy a paper that has a photo of Irene in better days on the front page.

I work on translating the article while Phil rows back to the boat.

"No one was on board," I say struggling with the French.

"That's good."

"It seems the regular St. Martin fire boat was getting repaired. If I am reading this right, Irene is the third boat fire in a month."

"That's not good."

When we get back to Iwalani we go through our fire safety protocols. I take out my journal and design a gasoline powered pump, housed in a waterproof deck box. It can be converted into either a pump for putting out fires with seawater, or into an emergency bilge pump when the boat is sinking, at the flick of a valve. This is going to be standard equipment on our next boat.

I am already planning the next boat.

Chapter 32

Last Legs

June 2003
Western side of the North Atlantic

The following day we get Iwalani ready for our final passage. Using the handybilly, we tighten the rigging. We check all her systems, patch a small leak in the water tank, and with a green light from the weather gods, we are soon ready to go.

"Should we even bother to raise the sails?" Phil asks with a touch of reality in his sarcasm.

"I know what you mean. It seems kind of pointless. Maine seems like an afternoon sail away. This part of the Atlantic is just a puddle. This will be the first time we won't have a year's supply of food on board. Who can be bothered? It just means more stuff to offload on the other end."

I stock up in espadrille shoes, as I doubt I'll be able to buy them at home with America's anti-French sentiment over their stance in the Iraq war. Other than buying a few fresh fruits and vegetables, we don't leave much money at the St. Martin supermarkets. We will survive on our supplies of canned food at sea. I am already moving stuff out of the boat in my mind and into a quarantine set-up in the garage. I am not going to extend our cockroach battle into the home kitchen. Everything on the boat will winter over in the barn to freeze, before it gets moved inside our house.

"Are you sure you want to go home?" Phil asks.

"Yes. We have to get to Nathaniel's graduation. I have to start work. I am ready to dig in the dirt and sit by the wood stove watching snowflakes falling. "

Before we leave St. Martin, we make appointments to meet with Nathaniel's counselor following his high school graduation in upstate New York. We spend time on the Internet to make sure the protocols for entering the US haven't changed since 9/11.

"I have never seen you so relaxed about a passage," Phil says to me when we are two days out.

"What's the point in getting worked up? When I lost Stewart, I lost fear. I fear losing you, but I know that if you go before me, I will be right behind. I no longer fear death. I just want to suck up as much life as possible, before the towel gets thrown in. I know this boat can get us through anything. I have a lot left to do before I cash my chips in." I retighten the scrunchie holding my hair back. "You look tired. I figured I woke you up with my chatting on the radio. There's a front coming through tonight, not supposed to be any big deal. But a low is forming in two days and that might give us trouble."

"Did you see the tri-color mast bulb has burned out? You need to send me up to replace it," Phil says.

"No way! Even though we only have ten knots of wind, look at how the top of the mast is swinging around. If I get a rope override, you'll be swinging around like a giant lure at the end of a fishing pole. Forget it."

"And how do you propose to get through the New York shipping lanes with no light on top of the mast?" Phil asks.

"We'll use the running lights and my cockpit reading light. Ships don't pay attention to us anyways. We'll need to be the ones looking out for them."

We get conflicting opinions on where the low is going. New Orleans weather fax has it turning into a gale and passing to our north. Herb says it is not going to be a gale but to pace ourselves anyway. We don't want to get caught anywhere near the Gulf Stream with this companion, whether it is a gale or not.

"What does he mean by pace?" I ask Phil during supper.

"Slow down. He wants us to pull into Bermuda and wait."

"No way! We'll be stuck there waiting for the next weather window. Our fifty dollars will buy us a few chocolate bars and a head of lettuce. And that's it. I love Bermuda, but it is more fun when you are rich. Besides, we can go there anytime; it's just five days sail away from Maine. Let's hang around out here. I'd like to go snorkeling in the Sargasso Sea. Supposedly that's where all the little eel elvers hang out." I look about us at the small clumps of golden Sargasso weed scattered in the sea like a hasty cleaning job after a ticker tape parade. We have three to four foot seas and steady winds of fifteen knots, a snorkeling expedition might be a bit difficult.

I make shrimp Creole, and we batten down the hatches waiting for the front to pass. The jib is bagged, the staysail up and the mainsail down to the third reef. By eight p.m. we have rain and sustained winds of twenty-five knots. The wind generator puts out a fair amount of electricity but not enough to run the autopilot, radar and running lights.

"I'm turning the engine on," Phil says to me.

"What? Are you nuts?"

"Since you didn't send me up the mast to change the tricolor light bulb, we have to use the running lights. They require three times the electricity as the tricolor mast light."

"It just seems wasteful when we have so much wind," I say.

"Turn off the running lights then."

"No. Just because everyone else does- no way. It's illegal."

"Turn off the radar then," Phil says.

"Nope, it's our main defense."

"Hand steer."

"Ya right."

"There you have it. The engine stays on."

I wake up early for my four a.m. watch. Phil is huddled in the cockpit wearing his foul weather gear.

"We need to take down more sail," he yells to me. The wind generator is screaming. We are in a squall with close to forty knots of wind.

"No," I say. "Let me sail this boat for once. You sail this boat like an old lady. I have more faith in what you built than you do. She is barely healing over. Let her do what she was designed for."

Phil looks at me with weary resignation. "Fine, if you want to die so near to home."

"She was built for this stuff."

I look around at the darkness and horizontal rain. I can barely see our running lights shining fifteen feet away, how is another boat supposed to see us? *'Shit, I hope I am right,'* I think to myself.

How ironic that I am the one pacifying my husband, not the other way around. I am a different person from the one three years ago, the scared woman lying crumpled at the bottom of the companionway vomiting into plastic sandwich bags. My fears had been of the unknown. But with each successive storm, winds and seas have strengthened my foundation; fear has been washed away.

Have I become a better person? Probably not. The fire that burned inside me to accomplish a circumnavigation has been transformed into a different heat. I feel as if I have turned into a person with less tolerance and far less patience. I can no longer shrug off the trash floating by as 'Oh well, there's nothing anyone can do about it.'

I start to think about the drawing I am working on in my journal. For the past year I have spent hours redesigning our house in Maine. I want it to encompass some of the things we have learned from other parts of the world and from living on a boat. I added on a twenty-foot addition to better accommodate our plans.

I leave Phil in the cockpit and go down below, checking the radar along the way, then open up my journal to the sketch. How easy it is to make some thing bigger in order to make it work. I pick up the eraser and delete the addition. Hadn't I learned anything about living on a boat? Bigger is not always better. It requires greater thought, planning and creative energy to make something fit into a smaller space. What about the eight-foot Russian boat *Said*? It had been around the Horn, and Farmer Bob's little boat, too.

This was going to be my new challenge, reverse the easy process of getting bigger. Is this the key to life, the universe and everything?

"What the hell are you doing?" Phil yells down to me from the cockpit.

"Nothing."

"We're in a gale and you're drawing pictures?"

"I checked the radar, we're all alone. I'm working on our house plans. It's technically not my watch yet. I have ten minutes left of free time."

"The wind is starting to drop off," Phil says.

"I heard. Why don't you get some sleep?"

"I won't be able to, with the roar of the bow wave and "Amy-the-Ahab" at the helm," Phil says laughing.

"Then help me with these house plans."

*   *   *

The following day the sun comes out and the wind drops below ten knots. The Gulf Stream still lies ahead of us. Herb tells us to cross as quickly as possible as another low is forming and will hit in twenty-four hours. The day before, another yacht, sixty foot *Christine*, had been caught in the Gulf Steam and is now presumed lost at sea. At the beginning of each radio check in, a call is put out for vessels to keep an eye out for her.

Our satellite images show a series of large white commas, low-pressure systems with trailing cold fronts, strung across the United States like some stuttering writer forgot to lift his finger from the keyboard. If the low doesn't hit us, the trailing front will.

We cross the Gulf Stream at midnight on June seventh. For the first time in three years, I am wearing a turtleneck, long pants and a sweater. I am still cold.

The next low hits us just as we approach New York City at midnight. Phil and I stay on watch together to try and make heads and tails of all the ships, fishing vessels, and a fleet of outbound yachts sailing in a race for Bermuda.

"Hey, is America's buoy system still red, right return?" I ask.

"You can rest assured that "Planet" America is still the same. We haven't given an inch, literally. We'll be lucky if we can find a SIM card to fit the cell phone."

"This is insane!" I say to Phil. I am below monitoring the GPS and radar, while he stands watch in the cockpit with binoculars. "We are clear of the outbound shipping lane and are almost in the inbound lane. If we maintain our speed we should avoid the next ship coming in. He's big, almost a thousand feet long, but, there is a small target at four o'clock quickly heading for us."

"It's a fishing boat."

I succeed in reaching it on the radio and explain where we are. He isn't fishing but, like us, has every available light turned on. He brushes by our stern and honks his horn as he heads for the city. "This Homeland Security thing must be some kind of joke," I say to Phil. "We are within striking distance of downtown Manhattan and haven't seen any sign of the Coast Guard or any patrol boat whatsoever. It's not like Australia, that's for sure."

"Well, there's a bit more traffic here."

"Exactly! It's mayhem! Anyone can slip in."

*   *   *

We plan on anchoring in Mattapoisett, Massachusetts, just a stone's throw away from the Cape Cod Canal. We will make the overnight sail to Maine after another low goes by. I e-mail my sister who lives close by that we will be anchoring for the night.

While at sea, I had e-mailed my mother that we didn't want any hoopla on arrival. No parties, marching bands, ticker tape parades, or dancing poodles. As we motor in to Mattapoisett, I see a van pull up to the town dock. The headlights flash, and I know that my family is waiting for us. We anchor and listen to the horn honking on shore. I sit down below contemplating a shoe problem while Phil heads out on deck and readies the Grape for launching.

"What's taking you so long?" he yells down to me.

"I'm having a shoe crisis."

"Wear your jellies."

"It's too cold. My sneakers are fossilized, and I can't remember where my leather boat shoes are."

"You're using them as fern planters."

I put on a brand new pair of St. Martin espadrilles, find a coat for Phil smelling pungently of mildew, and an only slightly less offensive sweater for myself. When I finally get on deck, Phil is already waiting in the dinghy. I feel awkward that none of his family is included in this impromptu greeting party, but he doesn't seem to mind. I position myself in the stern next to the outboard. For all semblances we are no different from any of the other American cruising boats anchored in the harbor, except we have not set foot on New England soil in three years. Slowly I motor the Grape in. My parents, siblings, nieces and nephews are standing on the dock. When we get close, they cheer and whistle. I turn the Grape hard around, pretending we are heading back out to sea. "Only kidding!" I yell, while circling back to the dock.

The sun has already set, and purple wisps of clouds hang on the western horizon like Indian smoke signals, announcing the next frontal passage. When I stand up on the dock, I feel like I too, am floating with the clouds, looking down from above, at the happiness of my family. Everyone looks basically the same, but somehow distorted, not quite like I remember. It dawns on me that it is age that has changed everyone. I haven't seen most of my family in over three years. My parents now walk with small bent steps and obvious discomfort. I walk behind them with my younger sister. "See what you did to them?" she whispers.

"Huh?" I ask.

"They have aged from worry."

"But they looked fine when we last saw them in New Zealand. How can they age that much in a year?"

"I'd say it was the Indian Ocean."

"Did it do that to us too?" I ask. My sister doesn't answer.

We drive back to my older sister's house and have a glass of wine. "What should we do about customs?" I ask my father.

"I suppose you should call them, but I'd wait until tomorrow," he replies. My father seems especially tired. He goes to bed early, while Phil and I stay up talking to the rest of my family. At midnight my sister tells us we can borrow her car so we can drive back to Iwalani.

"Can I use your bathroom, too?" I ask while following her in. I sit on the toilet while she starts to brush her teeth.

"What are you doing?" I ask her.

"Brushing my teeth," she says through a toothpaste muffled mouth.

"But why are you running the water? Shut it off. You're wasting water!"

She gives me a dirty look. "You aren't on a boat anymore."

"No kidding. But, think of the energy you are wasting."

"What? There's plenty of water in New England," she replies.

"Maybe so. But you are wasting electricity too. The electricity comes from oil, which comes from the Middle East. More people will die to make sure our oil arrives, so…"

"What do you mean I'm wasting electricity?"

"Somewhere in the system there is an electric pump which is getting the water to your house."

She keeps brushing her teeth but doesn't shut the water off. "I can't brush my teeth without the water running."

"People in Tulear would die to have that water which is running down your sink."

"I'm not in Tulear."

*   *   *

Biding our time as the low passes, we walk around my sister's hometown and marvel at things we have not seen or smelled for three years.

"Lilacs," I say sucking in the air.

"Freshly mowed lawn," Phil adds with a deep breath.

The next day we are back on Iwalani motoring up through the Cape Cod Canal. It is quiet. A few people are jogging or riding their bikes along the paths on either side. I imagined a small marching band situated on the grassy knoll on the far end, welcoming us home to the Gulf of Maine, but there are no tubas or drums, just a barking dog and a young couple embracing on a wooden bench.

Filling his lungs with air Phil says, "Do you smell that?"

"Why do you suppose the Gulf of Maine is so different? It smells like no place else."

"Look at the chart. It's really a bowl of water. The shallow waters of Georges Bank stretch from Cape Cod to Nova Scotia, separating it from the "Ocean.""

"Thanks for that, by the way," I say.

"What?"

"Not going home over Georges Bank. I don't ever want to go there again. Talk about hearing voices! That place is full of ghosts."

"Lots of ships were lost there," Phil replies. "Don't forget we nearly ended this trip three years ago when we almost got cut in two by the fishing boat on remote control."

"I know. How ironic it would be if we were killed this close to home."

We have no problems. In fact, we never see another boat or airplane as we cross the Boston shipping lanes and pass by all the other fishing ports to the north.

Early the next morning, when we get near the Portland shipping lanes, I see a tanker idling outside the harbor waiting for its pilot to arrive. I talk to him on the radio for lack of anything better to do.

"Watch out for the psycho whale," are his parting marks.

I hang up the microphone, grab my cup of coffee and head out on deck. It is seven a.m. and I still have an hour left on my final morning watch. The winds are very light. We have all sail up and the motor on. I see a fresh breeze approaching from the southeast, ease the sheets, and turn the engine off.

The skies and ocean are a dull gray, but at least it isn't raining. I circle my hands around the coffee cup in a vain attempt to keep them warm. We are gliding along at six knots with very calm seas. Iwalani is steady, with gentle rhythmic wave sounds gurgling along her flank. Porpoise swim up front enjoying our bow wave. In every direction I can see birds: shearwater, petrel, and gannet. I watch the pilot boat, three miles away, as it comes out of Portland Harbor to transfer the pilot to the ship.

I can see something else in the water circling around the pilot boat. I pick up the binoculars. It is a whale. That was what the tanker captain was referring to! With horror, I realize a sixty-foot finback whale is leaping out of the water and coming in our direction. The whale swims straight for us at about thirty knots. It is not streamlined on the surface like a torpedo, but leaping in and out of the water, piercing it like a sewing machine. "Phil!" I scream. "Wake up."

'God damn it!' I think to myself. *'I knew it was a mistake to go with red bottom paint! This crazy animal is charging at us like an enraged bull. Some welcome home. We're done for.'*

Phil rushes out of bed wearing long underwear and a T-shirt. Hidden is the tan lean body I had dubbed the "Cinnamon Stick" while we were in the tropics. "What's the matter?"

The whale is now about fifty feet away. I lower the binoculars and grab hold of the hard dodger with both hands. "Brace yourself!" I yell to Phil who is standing next to the galley sink.

"What?" he asks. The whale leaps into the water just a few feet away from our forward quarter and then disappears. I hold on for dear life with both eyes closed, waiting for the inevitable crash. The wave reflection rocks Iwalani. Nothing else happens. I open one eye. Nothing. Then both eyes. Still nothing.

"What is going on? This better be good. I was having a great dream about the sex machine you said you would make for me. I still have a half hour before my watch," Phil says while rubbing his eyes.

"I don't know where he went," I explain.

"Who?" Phil asks.

"An enormous psychotic whale. I'd call it an angry 'rottwhaler.' "

Phil comes up on deck removes the binoculars from around my neck, and scans the horizon.

"I was having a rather pleasant morning actually," I continue, "drinking coffee and marveling at how nice the Gulf of Maine is, when this crazy whale charged at us."

"That whale?" Phil asks pointing behind us.

The whale is already a half mile away and is blowing water near a flock of seabirds. "I guess so. I feel kind of stupid now. I really thought we were done for. It looked like a freight train coming at us."

"I'll take your word for it," Phil says.

"Go back to sleep."

"I can't now."

"Alrighty then," I say. "I'll make scrambled eggs and bacon."

Phil puts on his sweater and wool watch cap and entertains me by pulling his gray sweat pants up to his chin over his sweater. His white socks and skinny legs stick out of the pants like shriveled roots. "You know, it's getting cold out here with this wind picking up. Think people will recognize us?" he asks slurring his words Elmer Fudd style.

"I'd say we've been at sea too long."

A little after noontime we arrive in Georgetown, exactly one thousand days after we left. We decide to go to the marina on the other side of the island, rather than to our house, as we aren't sure what condition Iwalani's mooring is in. We furl our sails, motor around the bend in the river, and make several failed attempts at picking up a mooring.

"Geez, you'd think we would have learned something after sailing around the world," I scream into the wind.

"May I remind you, that this was the very last spot we picked up a mooring. We have been out of practice for three years."

"Good point. I don't feel so bad."

The staff of the marina is happy to see us. I ask what we need to do about customs, but no one seems to know. They give us the keys to the courtesy car so we can drive to our house. The cold front is upon us. It is windy and cold, but the rain holds off.

We arrive at our house feeling as if we had been asleep for a long time and all our experiences over the past three years have been just a dream.

The herb garden has become very overgrown. "Look at this small tree! It's a lettuce plant!" I exclaim.

At the sound of my voice, Polly, my dachshund, comes running out of the house. Her small wiggling black body earned her the nickname "Rubber Dog" when she was younger. I start to cry as she jumps up and down from excitement. I bend down to hug her while she licks the tears streaming from my face. I lift up her lips to get an idea of the tumor that is supposedly growing in her mouth. "Oh god," I say to Phil.

"Bad?"

"Very bad. Malignant melanoma."

We walk into the empty house, Polly enthusiastically tapping along behind us. Our house sitters moved out, but they left a bed ready for us out on the porch, my favorite place to sleep in the summer. The house is well cared for and all of the rooms repainted. They left us their pug too, who is blind and deaf and would not adjust well to their new house.

I walk into the bathroom checking out what the house sitters have done, while the pug follows me in snorting on my leg. "Holy shit! Who the hell are you?" I scream.

On Iwalani, we only have a small mirror that Phil used for shaving and I used for applying mascara. Two inches square, it was all we needed. I never wanted to get the whole picture of myself. Cole slaw hair, chapped lips, sunburned and peeling skin, these were not images I wanted to see. As a result, it has been over three years since I have looked at myself in a full-length mirror. "Jesus Christ Phil!"

"What? What's the matter?" Phil says as he runs into the bathroom. "Nice wallpaper."

"Why the hell didn't you tell me I had become a fat cow? Look at this. It's disgusting!" I say turning sideways in the mirror.

"Wow! Why didn't you tell me I was going bald?" Phil says rubbing the top of his head. "This is depressing. I'm going out to try and get the truck started."

"I suppose I better call customs," I say.

"Good luck finding the phone."

I follow Phil out to the barn, Iwalani's birthplace. We open the door and turn on the fluorescent lights. My boat Petrel is propped up on stands exactly as I left her. She is in suspended animation, a boat with no sea. Tools we had left hastily strewn about have not moved and have collected little dust.

"Wow, this is the only thing which hasn't changed in three years," Phil says.

"Too bad we didn't clean it up before we left. It's a bit overwhelming."

I walk up to the loft of the barn where we stored all our belongings. I find a phone in a box marked "kitchen stuff" and walk back into the house carrying it along with a chair. Fortunately, the telephone service has not been turned off. I get the number from information and sit down. After I go through the automated hoops, giving our name, address and boat name, I am put on hold. Fifteen minutes later Phil comes into the kitchen.

"How's it going?"

"I'm on hold," I reply.

"Good thing you called from home. We don't have enough quarters for this."

"How's the truck?" I ask.

"I'm charging the battery."

"Do you think it's still good?"

"I'll find out." Phil says, walking back outside.

In the past, when I arrived home from Canada in Petrel, I made the call and customs would say, "Fine, thanks, welcome home." I expected the same sort of reception. Finally, after another fifteen minutes, a man named Inspector Furious comes on the line. I explain we have just arrived in a yacht, and I am calling for information on what we have to do.

"Where are you calling from?" Inspector Furious barks.

"Our home."

"Where is that?" he asks.

"Georgetown."

"Where is the boat?"

"At the marina."

"Where?"

"Robinhood- Georgetown," I say again.

"Where is that?"

I sigh deeply. "East of Portland, West of Boothbay, South of Bath."

"When did you arrive in Georgetown?"

"Today" I reply.

"What time today?" he barks back.

"Uh, well. I am not really sure. Probably, four hours ago."

"Do you realize that you are supposed to call customs immediately? Actually, you are supposed to call 3.5 miles out from your cell phone," the Inspector screams through the receiver.

"Uh well, I've been on hold for a half hour before you ever answered the phone. I don't have a working U.S. cell phone. We wanted to come to our house to call, since it's a toll call and we don't have any American change for a public phone," I explain.

"That's a five thousand dollar violation!"

"Not having a cell phone or not having the correct change?"

He ignores my rather pitiful attempt at joviality. "Calling customs immediately means IMMEDIATELY. Not four hours later. In four hours time you could have off loaded all sorts of drugs and guns."

Is this guy for real? "Funny, you don't sound Australian. I thought we came back to America." At this point I am still under the heady fragrance of being home.

"Ma'am. You don't go home, then call customs," he says.

"OK, well, maybe people from away don't, but we are American citizens. We haven't been home in three years, and I haven't seen family and friends, pets, or our house. I guess I got a little sidetracked."

"Who's the master of the vessel?"

"What day is it?" I ask.

"The twelfth"

"Well, that would be my husband. We alternate days."

"Where's your husband?"

"Outside, trying to get our truck started," I say.

"You are not supposed to be off the boat. The master of the vessel is supposed to call. That's another five thousand dollar violation."

I am in such disbelief that I fail to notice the sweat trickling down my back. All I can think of is the Cuban cigar I have stashed away in my underwear drawer on Iwalani.

"How can you do this?" I cry. "We haven't even been home five hours and already we are in debt! A smuggler or terrorist wouldn't even bother calling you!" Zelda wants to scream, *'Hi, customs this is Osama just calling to let you know I'm comfortably anchored and ready to blow up you American infidels.'* But I overpower her voice "You've got to be kidding me! Why should we, who are honest law abiding citizens, pay a ten thousand dollar fine? We don't have that kind of money! This is outrageous!" I am sort of shrieking at this point.

"Well, actually, since you failed to be inspected, that's another five thousand dollars. Customs is going to fine you fifteen thousand dollars and your boat is now impounded."

I must confess I start to lose track of the conversation. My head is whirling. I wait for someone to come on the line and say, "Smile you 're on Candid Camera!" Maybe this is all a joke that my family has arranged? Maybe this is an American reality TV show we have only heard about.

"The information we have says the United States still has no official ports of entry for yachts, as hard as I find that to believe, and…"

"It is your duty to check the website before you enter the U.S."

"We did, while we were in St. Martin. It said…"

"Oh! St. Martin was your last port of entry? Why didn't you say so? As an official U.S. territory, clearance from the Virgin Islands is the same as the continental U.S.," he says with a hint of relief.

"But, St. Martin isn't part of the Virgin Islands," I say meekly.

"Where is St. Martin?"

"In the Caribbean."

"But it's not part of the U.S. Virgin Islands?"

"It wasn't as of two weeks ago," I reply.

"Oh. Then it still stands. Customs is fining you fifteen thousand dollars and your boat is impounded."

"Is there anyone else I am supposed to call?" I ask.

"Have you called the agricultural inspector?"

"No, I thought calling customs was the first thing I should do."

"Well, yes, but it wasn't now, was it?"

I hang up the phone and begin to cry. Welcome home! Homeland Security. What a joke! A nutty finback whale is the only thing we saw securing the American coastline. Phil walks into the kitchen and starts to wash his hands. My back is facing him so he can't see the state I am in.

"How's the truck?" I say trying to stifle my tears.

"It started right up. Nearly gave me a heart attack. What's the matter?"

"I am in really big trouble. In fact, I think I am probably going to jail. You might be next. Actually, it might give me a chance to catch up on sleep."

"What are talking about?" Phil asks. I tell Phil the whole story. "What will happen if they find out we stopped in Massachusetts first?"

"Can you say Firing Squad?" I ask.

"You didn't say anything about stopping in Mattapoisett did you?"

"I suppose I would have, but they never asked. So, no I didn't."

I next call the agricultural inspector who is very nice. "Do you have any meat or eggs on board?" he asks.

"No, we ate all the fresh food the first week out," I reply.

"Did you bring any plants from St. Martin?"

"No." I say with complete honesty. He never does ask about the plants and seeds from Australia, South Africa and all ports in between.

I tell him about the difficulty I had with customs. "What can I do? We don't have that kind of money. I hope they take credit cards."

He gives me the name of the person in charge and suggests I call him. I call the number and speak with the Portland Office.

"What can I do to make this go away?" I whine. "Why aren't all yachts entering the U.S. treated like ships and made to go to ports of entry? It wouldn't be hard, that's what we had to do in every other country. This Homeland security thing is a joke. Anyone can come into just about anywhere in Maine undetected. We are penalized fifteen thousand dollars because we tried to do the right thing!"

"It is a problem," he commiserates. "Maine is the soft underbelly of the U.S. Hopefully that will change. I understand about you being upset. Write a letter explaining what happened, and I'll try and take care of it."

The phone rings as soon as I hang up. It is my mother.

"I wasn't sure if your old phone number still worked, but I needed to call, as you are the doc in the family" she says. "When we got home from Massachusetts your father began to act very strangely. I found him sitting on the living room rug admiring the stitching."

"What?"

"Then I went into his bedroom and found hundreds of pills on the floor."

"Had he overdosed on medication?"

"No. In fact, I don't think he's been taking it correctly. He can't see well, and it looks like he was being rather arbitrary in what pills he actually was taking. He was so excited about you coming home."

"Where is he now?"

"At the hospital. They are running tests."

"Do you want me to come to Vermont?"

"No, that's alright. Your sister is coming up. You've probably got your hands full."

"That's an understatement." I tell her about the fine from U.S. customs.

"What are you going to do?" she asks.

"I don't know, Ma, but there's no way we'll pay that fine. Let me know what the doctors find out with Dad."

Chapter 33

Change is in the Air

June 2003- March 2004
Maine, U.S.A.

The doctors in Vermont can find nothing wrong with my father. He recovers and makes jokes about his recent infatuation with the living room rug. He has no explanation for it, but remembers the whole thing fully, down to the last thready detail.

Phil and I drive out to upstate New York for Nathaniel's graduation and a session with Nathaniel's psychiatrist. Virtually broke, we bring our Australian tent and decide to stay at a campground in a nearby state park. It is a cheap motel without walls. While skunks sniff around our feet, we become all too familiar with slamming car doors, arguing couples and American country western music.

You know you've beem away too long when...
outta my way
Hey! That's mine!
....mice move into your under-wear drawer
...you need a chainsaw to mow your lawn
WOW! Cool...
BOOKS
SKI CLOTHES ART KITCHEN
...moving stuff out of storage, feels like stealing from a store
ouch
...you forget where the light switches are
...you need a GPS to get to your in-laws
I thought you said go north?

"I thought In-a-god-dada-vida was the longest song in existence," I whisper to Phil, but this is ridiculous."

"Don't you know what they say about country and western? If you play it backwards you get your dog back, your wife back."

"Yeah, yeah, I've heard it all before. That's the oldest joke around. You don't actually want your job back, your dog back, your ex-wife back?"

"No. But I wouldn't mind getting my sons back."

"I'll never forget the look on your face when you saw Ben," I say.

"Ben became a man in the three years we were gone."

"Now what's he doing?" I ask.

"Who?"

"Our neighbor to the left. He's stopped yelling at his wife for forgetting the extension cord. Now he's banging his coolers."

"It's probably a skunk. Don't worry about it," Phil says.

"I suppose you're right. But this living in "rip stop nylon" suburbia is hard to adjust to. I can't believe people do this for recreation and find it relaxing. Am I a snob or what?"

"We both are." Phil sits up and shines the flashlight out the tent.

"Hard to believe that just over a year ago we were camping in the Australian bush. Remember the time we were almost killed by the red bellied blacksnake?"

"How could I forget? I thought we were goners for sure," Phil says.

"Me too, especially when it reared up and flagged its head like a cobra. We were hundreds of miles from the nearest town; we would have been dead if he had bitten us. I have never seen you so nervous, checking the zipper on the tent all night long."

"That snake did not act like any snake I have ever seen. Usually they are scared of people. Don't forget we were the biggest, warmest things around. I was convinced it was going to find a way into our sleeping bag."

"What are you checking for now?" I ask.

"Nothing. It's just a raccoon."

"You should be very proud of Nathaniel today. Despite all the crap he had to live with between his mother and us, graduating with high honors is no small feat."

Nathaniel at his high school graduation; Ben is behind to the left

"I am proud. You should be proud too. Especially the part about how if you need a cat dissected he was your man. I am sure you have influenced him too. I could never have survived that ceremony, standing on a big stage while your strengths were described. I would have run away," Phil says.

"I'm sure he wanted to," I pull the sleeping bag up to my chin, "but the meeting with the psychiatrist, we all should have run away. What a complete waste of time that was!"

"There are some things in life that will never change, my ex-wife is one of them."

I run through the imagery of the afternoon session wishing I could have rewritten the script. We had met with the counselor and the psychiatrist in charge of Nathaniel's case. The six of us sat in a circle, with our backs to the windows, in a room that overlooked a small orchard of fruit trees just past their bloom. A dollhouse crouched on a table in the corner; a small child's chair backed up to an adult desk. A stuffed rabbit sat in the small seat, ears flopped forward, chin down, staring at the floor with black button eyes. As decoration for the upcoming Fourth of July, a tiny American flag had been placed in its lap. Limp, lifeless stuffed paws hid under the red, white and blue cloth. The walls were decorated with children's drawings of houses perched on triangular hills. Yellow sun. Red flowers. Green grass.

Nathaniel sat in a chair next to his mother, his long brown hair tied back with a frail rubber band. He had on a faded black sweatshirt, black t-shirt and black jeans. His white hands held on to each other for support; folded in his lap, as fragile and translucent as snowflakes, they trembled slightly. His pale face was turned down like the stuffed rabbit in the chair. His eyes stared silently at the floor.

Dr. Klein sat cross-legged in the largest chair, holding Nathaniel's file in his lap like a scepter. "Well folks. I am glad you all made it." He opened the file and casually glanced at the first page. "We need to work out a few kinks with Nathaniel's progress. Phil, we'll start with you. How do you see your son?"

Phil stretched his long legs out and stared at his youngest son. "Nathaniel is one of the smartest people I know, but he has lost all his self-confidence. I see a boy who, in kindergarten, decided to do a project on Bernoulli's law of aerodynamics for the school science fair. He carved Styrofoam, making a wing shape and a block shape, then with a fan, he demonstrated lift. Even the teachers were amazed, but he didn't win an award because kindergarteners weren't part of the judging." Phil cleared his throat. "Next, I see him frustrated in school because his friends could not understand the misconceptions of a land yacht propelled by a fan mounted on its deck. He was chastised and ridiculed despite being right. I think he has turned inward, in order to avoid confrontations from those who are not as smart as he and to avoid being hurt. Most recently I see him in Australia, standing for the first time on a surf board!"

Dr. Klein turned to Phil's ex-wife. "Your turn."

"I think Phil, for once, is right. Nathaniel is very intelligent."

"And what do you think brought him to his most recent troubles?"

"When his father left him."

"Phil did not leave Nathaniel!" Zelda blurted out. I was no longer in control. Phil and I were at the mercy of my back throat driver. "You were the one, who, against the court order, moved from Maine to New York and then left the boys to move to god-knows-where!"

"Amy!" Dr Klein snapped, "I was not talking to you!"

"I am sorry," I said. "I won't say another word."

"As I was going to say," Phil's ex-wife adjusted her position on her chair and glared at me, "before being interrupted, Nathaniel suffered because of this most recent junket of Phil and his new wife on their trip around the world. I was left to raise these boys on my own with no support."

"How can you call living four hours away from the boys "raising"?" Phil asked her. "We just found out, from Nathaniel's guidance counselor that you moved away three <u>years</u> ago! The boys raised themselves, with no help from either of us."

"I came home on weekends, which is more than you did!"

"You did not pay child support?" Dr. Klein asked Phil.

"Yes, I did."

"And did you receive payments on time?" he asked Phil's ex-wife.

"Yes, but that's not the point. The fact of the matter is that the boy's father left them to sail around the world. He has no idea what it has been like here in America. What we went through after 9/11." She bent her head and started crying.

The rest of us became very silent. I stared at the rabbit, still slumped in his little chair with his limp ears bent down, the flag hiding its belly.

"When was the divorce?" Dr Klein gently asked Phil.

"Do you mean when was it started or when did it end?"

"I take it, it was a rather drawn out affair."

"It made World War II look like a water balloon fight," Zelda blurted out. Phil's ex-wife glared at me, the tears stopped. Nathaniel continued to stare at the floor.

"I filed for divorce ten years ago," Phil said. "I really don't see what any of this has to do with helping Nathaniel. The past is over. We all made mistakes, each one of us. We need to move forward."

"You can't just waltz back in town as if nothing happened and pretend to be a good father," Phil's ex snapped. "I jolly well won't allow it. I made enormous sacrifices for these boys. Do you think I wanted to abandon them when I moved three hours away? I was forced to because of losing my job. It's not right that you think I am a terrible mother after all I have done for them."

"I am not here to judge you," Phil said softly. "I am here to save our son."

There was silence in the room. The big black bear of depression, lurking in the shadow under the desk, finally had someone poke a stick at his nose.

"Can't you see how hard it must have been for her?" Dr. Klein asked.

"He has no idea," Phil's ex-wife sputtered. "He's been gallivanting about to all points of the compass. It would be nice if I could get an apology, but that will never be forthcoming."

I looked at Nathaniel with agony. I had always longed to give him a hug, to tell him I loved him, but fear of Phil's ex-wife prevented me from giving either of his boy's physical attention. I was always been fearful I would be arrested for child molestation. Nathaniel shifted his weight in the chair but continued to look at the floor. His mother continued to sob.

"There, there, now, everything will be okay," Dr. Klein handed her another box of tissues.

"I just want an apology," she sniffled.

"Phil? Do you think you can apologize to your ex-wife?"

Phil, like Nathaniel, stared at the floor.

"Phil?" Dr. Klein prodded.

"This is not relevant to my son's problems. We are wasting your time on a conflict that has never been resolved and never will be. This is not the way to help Nathaniel."

"Can't you just say you're sorry to your ex-wife?"

The air hung thick in the room. How do people end conflict? Especially when one has been wronged by another, each believing they are the victim and not the aggressor? Do you fight aggression with aggression? Do you take the high road? Or do you jump in the sand box and throw sand? Someone must give in if there is going to be peace. Are divorces any different from countries at war?

Phil turned his gaze upward and met Nathaniel's eyes. "I'm sorry," he whispered.

Dr. Klein tapped a pencil on his shoe. "She can't hear you," he said impatiently.

Phil continued to look at Nathaniel and repeated his apology.

"There now! Thanks. Moving along then. Nathaniel, are you having trouble with your medication?" Dr. Klein asked.

Nathaniel shook his head, and that was the end of the afternoon session.

The door slams on the camper next to us.

"Jesus, Louise, you didn't turn the valve off."

"I thought you did."

"No, I asked you to."

"Well I didn't hear you."

"Do you think your ex-wife is right, and our leaving to sail around the world caused Nathaniel's depression? I ask Phil.

"I'd say it didn't help. Her moving to New York against the court order also didn't help. Her moving three hours away from the boys was probably the crowning blow."

"Do you wish we had never left?"

"No! We had the money, we had our health, and it was the time to go. I only wish the boys had told me what was really going on before we left. I would have made them come with us, had I known what was really going on."

"Didn't you tell me when Stewart died that there is a reason for everything? The boys were meant to stay here on their own and go through 9/11 while we were a world away. Things always happen for a reason," I say pulling my sleeping bag up to my chin. "It might take a long time to find the reason, but it's there somewhere."

This man, quite possibly, spent too much time at sea...

*   *   *

We talk Nathaniel into coming back with us to Maine for the summer. I miss having Iwalani's ultimate crow's nest, so Phil convinces him to make us a satellite antenna for the house. We now receive our own satellite images in our living room. Interpreting New England weather becomes far more challenging than the weather at sea.

In preparation for selling Iwalani, we paint, varnish and polish and continue to remove three years of accumulated "highly prized artifacts" into the barn. We have many bites on her, but people still seem unsure about their futures. No one is willing to tip their life upside down, give it a shake, and pour it into a forty-two foot space.

"I think we are going to have a hard time selling Iwalani," I say to Phil while we load the dinghy with yet one more crate of junk for storage in the barn. "All of America acts like it's been sucker punched. No one wants to go anywhere. What the heck is this stuff?" I run my finger along the top of Iwalani's bulwark rail, like I am doing a white glove test. A fine black powder coats her surfaces and makes my index finger black. Some of it has run off in rivulets, leaving gray streaks which have dried like squirrel tails. Anchored far from industry, Iwalani is coated with the grime and filth from power plants a thousand miles away. This is nothing more than the after effects of rain.

"This is far worse than I remember. Do people just think this is the way it is everywhere else? This industrial grime could be getting in our food and water supply. It must coat every vegetable grown outside and every blade of grass consumed by a cow. It can't be good to eat. Most of my animals have died of cancer.

I was taught that animals are sentinels for the environment and human disease. Look at poor Polly with malignant melanoma in her mouth. I don't think sunlight is to blame for that." I have subjected our little dachshund to three surgeries to remove the cancer in her mouth, but it keeps growing back.

"Isn't there anything else you can do for her?" Phil asks taking a bag of books from me. "She is such a great little dog and waited three years for us to get home. I'd hate to lose her now."

"Animal Medical Center in New York is using an experimental vaccine for malignant melanoma in conjunction with radiation. The vets are hopeful it can really extend a dog's life, though they aren't optimistic for a cure. It would be expensive."

"It would also be worth a try. Isn't that what credit cards were invented for?"

"Do you realize you are the only man in existence who would make such sacrifices for a dog?" I ask handing down the last bag of books.

"Isn't that why you married me?"

Before we know it, the goldenrod is in bloom, and the sun starts heading south. Nathaniel goes back to New York for one year to attend community college. He is quiet but cheerful.

My father has a more serious episode of losing touch with reality. We transport him by ambulance to Boston where the doctors discover he is having several mini-strokes in his brain. While he is in the hospital, my mother takes charge of paying their bills. She comes across a large cell phone bill with frequent calls to one number in particular. My mother dials the number. On the other end of the line is a woman whom my father has been secretly seeing for over a quarter of a century.

With over fifty years of marriage behind them, my parents separate. My siblings and I, with our gray hairs and our own families, begin to feel first hand what it is like to be caught between feuding parents. This is not the life I had been dreaming about at sea.

I write my letter to U.S. customs and hear nothing back. I assume no news is good news and resist calling them on the telephone.

After Polly spends one week at Tufts undergoing radiation therapy in her mouth, we take her every two weeks to New York City for her experimental cancer treatment. We get up at three thirty in the morning, fight the city traffic so we can arrive at eleven for her appointment, then wander around New York for a few hours. When Polly is finished we drive back home, and fall into bed sometimes at two in the morning. It makes for a very long day. Throughout it all, she continues to wag her tail and convinces us we are doing the right thing. At this point having a little black wagging tail seems more important than having money, a brand new vehicle, or a united family.

*   *   *

Christmas Eve arrives, and Phil and I take our daily walk to the end of the road to get our mail. It is a little past four p.m. and for a brief moment the sun shines through a visor-like slit between purple clouds piling up thick on the horizon. The marsh and trees are bathed in an orange light as heavy as syrup, while the still waters of the marsh glow turquoise. Within one minute the sun disappears and all is cold and gray.

As we walk over the causeway that bisects the salt marsh, we see one of the orphaned great horned owls I raised and released ten years ago, sitting on a bare oak branch.

"I would have given anything to do this while at sea," Phil says.

"I know. Despite the Georgetown mosquitoes, this is still a great place to live, especially for someone with a short attention span like me. Every minute is different."

"People in the rest of the world thought we were nuts when we told them our high point of the day was walking to get the mail."

"I used to hate changes in life, but now I realize how important change is. Do you miss spending weeks at sea with nothing to look at but blue sky, blue water and black nights?"

"No way. Shoot me if I ever say I do."

When we get to the mailbox, it is already starting to snow. I reach in and pull out our mail. Layered amongst the assorted Christmas cards we received from all points of the globe, is a letter from U.S. customs.

· "Uh oh. I don't think this is a Christmas card from Uncle Sam. Are you ready to find out if you'll be spending 2004 visiting me in jail?" I ask.

"Is the envelope thick or thin?" Small flakes of snow flutter around the breath escaping from Phil's mouth.

"Thin. Why? Would thicker be worse? Would that include the questionnaire on your choice of prison attire?" I ask.

"I think international orange is your only choice."

"You can't get black and white stripes anymore?"

"Where have you been? That went out years ago," Phil laughs.

Slowly I open the envelope. Our fifteen thousand dollar fine has been reduced to one hundred and fifty dollars and the case is closed.

"Yippee!" I cry and dance a little jig while the snowflakes swirl about my feet like party streamers.

*   *   *

Over the winter, we keep Iwalani in the water at the marina. This is the best method of storing a wooden boat, rather than hauling it and letting it dry out on land. I defy any of her tropical bugs to survive New England's frigid weather. Our gecko Stumpy is never found and is presumed drowned at sea somewhere in the Atlantic. Polly's cancer slows down, but it does not go into remission.

In March of 2004, we get e-mail from a young couple seriously interested in buying Iwalani. They want to sail her to far away places and have the hope and freshness of youth and a black lab to act as official boat dog. They are eager, optimistic, and not much older than Phil's sons. They promise us Iwalani's name will remain the same. Because of our superstition about bad luck befalling a ship whose name has been changed, we accept their offer, which is quite a bit lower than our asking price.

We move Iwalani to the mooring in front of our house while the sale goes through and new owners bring their own gear on board. Phil and I make plans to go away for the weekend, I do not want to see Iwalani sail away without us.

On the day before the papers are passed, we make one last trip out to her to remove our one remaining possession.

In Mauritius I had bought a two inch bronze figurine of a tabby cat paddling a small boat. Hand made and exquisite even down to the tiniest of details—little bronze whiskers and microscopic claws clasping the paddle, it is more like a piece of intricate jewelry than a tourist trinket. It is the only reminder we have of Stewart, and we had affixed it to the radio, making sure the cat's little boat was always heading forward.

Iwalani lies anxiously on the mooring. With a three knot current on our river, her deep keel fights the water while her topsides lean with the wind. Often times, wind against the tide makes for interesting anchoring or mooring on the Back River. Like a skittish horse at the end of a line, Iwalani swings away as we row near.

"I think she's pissed at us," I say to Phil.

He rows deftly alongside while I climb aboard. She has been stripped of all reminders of our three years on her. Bare boned, she is once again like an empty book, waiting to be filled with new chapters, new experiences, and new countries.

"Are you sure you're ready to go through with this?" I ask Phil as he climbs on board.

"Yes. I have my apprehensions, but Iwalani was built to cross oceans, not rot on a mooring."

I head down below and take the little cat off the radio while Phil stays on deck checking over the rigging one last time. Everywhere I look I see something Phil and I made together, singly, or with the help of friends—the settees, the cushions, the floorboards, varnished mast, table, doors, drawers. Everything. Iwalani had risen from just a notion in our minds to a fantastic creature that could transport us to strange worlds and unimagined lands.

"Thank you, Stew," I say aloud while looking about for one last time. "But especially, thank you, Iwalani."

I hold the tiny figurine in my hand for a moment before slipping it into my pocket. I pause near the sink. What is that? I catch a faint whiff of something tropical. I turn to see where it is coming from. Lying in the soap dish, like a miniature dugout canoe, is a small sliver of Tahitian soap. I pick the soft brown remnant up and hold it close to my nose. Closing my eyes, coconuts, frangipani, and far away sunshine enter my nostrils.

I hear the rhythmic ticking of the ship's clock. The chimes begin ringing. Five, six, seven, the eighth bell fades. It is the end of our watch. Tears begin to roll down my cheeks as I realize, "We did it."

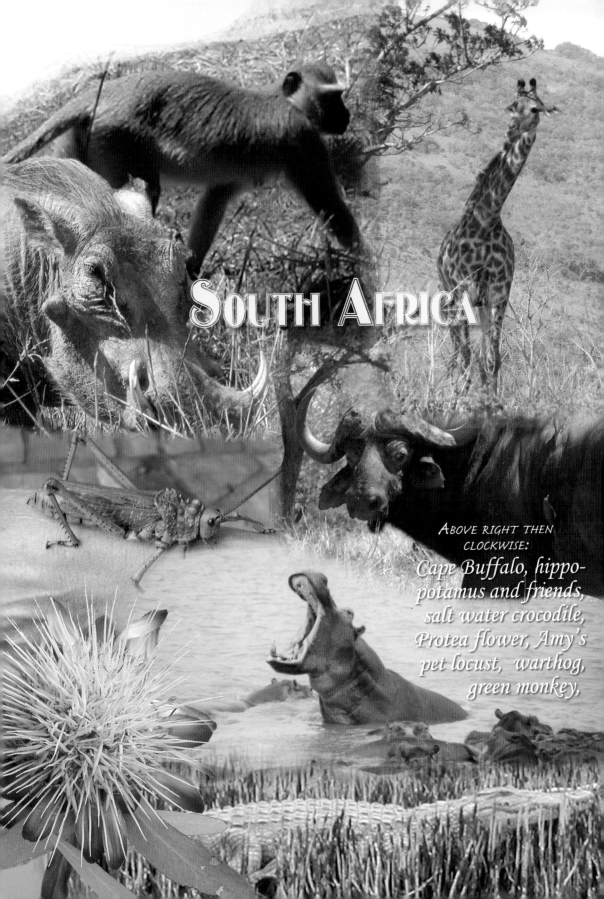

SOUTH AFRICA

ABOVE RIGHT THEN CLOCKWISE:
Cape Buffalo, hippopotamus and friends, salt water crocodile, Protea flower, Amy's pet locust, warthog, green monkey,

SOME PRETTY COOL CATS

THE SOUTH AFRICAN CLASS OF 2003

a few of the eighty cruisers going under South Africa in 2003

*Clockwise from above:
Phil hiking in Drakensburg,
Garden at Kirstenboch near
Capetown, white rhino, impala
and zebra*